Negotiating Place and Space Through Digital Literacies

Research and Practice

edited by

Damiana G. Pyles
Appalachian State University

Ryan M. Rish
University at Buffalo (SUNY)

Julie Warner
Independent Researcher

IAP
INFORMATION AGE PUBLISHING, INC.
Charlotte, NC • www.infoagepub.com

Library of Congress Cataloging-in-Publication Data

CIP record for this book is available from the Library of Congress
http://www.loc.gov

ISBNs: 978-1-64113-483-5 (Paperback)

978-1-64113-484-2 (Hardcover)

978-1-64113-485-9 (ebook)

Printed in the United States of America

CONTENTS

PART II: DIGITAL LITERACIES FROM WITHIN

PART III: TRACING LITERACIES ACROSS TIME AND SPACE

FOREWORD

THE SPATIAL TURN IN LITERACY THEORY

Kathy A. Mills

A spatial turn has sparked a revolution in approaches to educational research since the early 21st century. This follows the rise of notable spatial thinkers across a wide range of disciplines, such as cultural and physical geography, economics, anthropology, media and communication studies, international relations, and many others, throughout the late 20th century (Soja, 2004). Spatial research does not simply invoke the use of à la mode terms and spatial metaphors, such as those that circulate on Twitter and in academic discourse—of networks, rhizomes, maps, and transcultural borders. Rather, the spatial turn is a groundswell of research that begins with the fundamental realization that all space is socially produced—in other words, it arises from purposeful social practices (Lefebvre, 1991; Mills, 2010; Mills & Comber, 2015; Soja, 1980). Therefore, it could be reasoned that space is not merely a reflection of society—it is society (Castells, 1983). The meanings and organization of space are outcomes of social experience, and the social relations of production are both space contingent and space forming, as a dialectic or recursive relationship (Mills, 2010; Soja, 1989). Framed within such a perspective, this highly original collection theorizes the ways in which space is conceptualized and operationalized in digital research to see literacy and space differently.

Negotiating Place and Space Through Digital Literacies: Research and Practice, pp. ix–xiii

Each chapter in the book contributes to an emergent, vibrant, and transformative rethinking of digital literacy practices and research, and toward radically different forms of thinking about social space. As Soja (2004, p. x) argues, "something remarkable happens when literacies and spatialities are conjoined in a process of mutual construction, a dialectic if you will. For literacy scholars and educators, the traditional confines of the classroom explode with new possibilities of interpretation." Some of these include expanded worlds of cultural hybridities, identity formations, new formations of critical consciousness, political positionings, and layers of geographical scale, from the local to global, and back again. Amidst the rapid transformation of networked digital media environments, the information explosion, and the digital data deluge (Mills, 2017), the spatializing of literacy research is a field replete with new opportunities to incorporate the study of virtual spaces, online communities, different mobilities, and cyborg bodies, of complex geospatial and agentive spaces of contemporary literacy practices. The authors of *Negotiating Place and Space Through Digital Literacies* have recognized these transformative potentials in bringing original research together in a unique and future-orientated monograph.

A consistent and powerful theme undergirding the studies is a distinctive critical and "spatial justice" (Soja, 2010) stance on digital literacies that seeks to reveal, rather than render obsolete, the inequitable geospatial distribution of digital literacy practices, such as for those in rural and remote regions of the world, or those with nondominant identities. These are still the blackspots of both physical and social geographies, and the blackspots in current thinking about literacy research. This critical stance is tied to a knowledge of the politics and power relations of social space and digital literacies, whether economic, political, social, cultural, geographical. or gendered, that are caught up in its stratification (Mills & Comber, 2015). It is a necessary basis for interpreting the sometimes in/visible and complex geopolitics and contestation of the private and public spaces of digital communication, and geographies of digital marginalization and exclusion.

The authors explode our understandings of the ways in the which digital media is caught up in the imagined or real social identities that traverse urban, rural, suburban and exurban spaces, and online and offline worlds, presenting agentive research of digital literacies from multiple of identities or subjectivities to disrupt notions of "metronormativity" (Herring, 2010). This work cuts across the politics of difference, including intersections of race, class, gender, sexuality, ability, and language, geography, and nation-state, and the entwining of cultural practices with digital media across time and space.

An outstanding feature of many chapters in the collection is a willingness to challenge existing notions of digital literacies and their associated spatial assumptions, such as disrupting in-school and out-of-school spatial binaries (see Bruce, Sullivan, Barrett, & Gonzalez, this volume), urban-centrism in digital literacy research, and overly celebratory views of digital literacies. For example, one study demonstrates how clusters of literacy practices that were initially performed face-to-face by the authors in tangible work carrels, and later when they worked in geographically diverse, online "virtual carrels," were often very analogous (Buchholz et al., this volume). A central realization is that virtual and physical spaces constitute interrelated social practices that are connected via multiple channels, involving relationality, multiplicities, and the movement of people, artefacts, ideas, and emotions within a community.

The book provides accounts of digital practices that rupture the English centrism of online spaces, such as the chapter by Song and Cho, who found that teens used the resources of Korean and English for different purposes depending on cultural and linguistic features in the online spaces. The volume challenges deficit views of social loafing in online spaces—the tendency to reduce individual effort in a group (see Neal & Vicars, this volume). It offsets deficit views of rurality and digital practices (see Connors & Daugherty, this volume; and Bruce et al., this volume), and theorizes both the new mobilities and "im/mobilities"—the emotionally paralysing or uncomfortable effects of literacy practices—without valorizing digital technologies (see Rust, this volume).

The book follows a spatial turn in digital literacies research, offering a contemporary and edgy reterritorializing of digital practices that obliterates homogenization. It achieves this by repositioning accounts that are typically marginalized, while acknowledging that places are shaped by oppressive institutional and social forces. Edward Soja, the noted American urban geographer and social theorist, would approve, because *Negotiating Place and Space Through Digital Literacies* speaks to his central proposition that critical social theory needs to take space seriously if it is to make sense of society (Soja, 1996). Each account in the book contributes to a digital literacies landscape that connects practices and places as lived, multiple, intersecting, fluid, and contested; interlinked yet interdependent; social and political, and located in power geometries (Hubbard & Kitchin, 2011).

The book makes a compelling case for the profound importance of spatiality in research of digital practices and intersecting relations of spatial power. A vivid example of this is an account of Indigenous activism of the Kiowa people near Carnegie, Oklahoma (see Woodward, this volume). The Kiowa established a social activist Facebook site to save Longhorn Mountain (SLM)—a place of cultural, historical and spiritual significance—from destruction by a mining company. Here, we see evidence of the contestation and power geometries that arise through shifts in the spatial organization of capitalist relations. The SLM Facebook page became an online space for Kiowas, residents, and supports of the SLM movement to build alliances across space-time. In this way, globalized forms of digital practices through social media spaces performed an integral role in the fight to preserve the sacred spatial organization of place and relations, and to resist capitalistic claims to spatial power (Massey, 1991).

The intersecting relations of power in digital literacy spaces are recurring in other chapters of the book. For example, Saunders and Salazar narrate the messy politics of adolescents' social media uses that entangle students, schools, and the public in the wilderness of online spaces, breaking down the spatial boundaries between school and public arenas. Similarly, highlighting the contested nature of digital practices and power, Thomas-Reid posits a "queering" of trolling texts online. This unique work highlights the pedagogical potentials of queering the offensive comments that are socially and spatially "in the margins" of online texts to reconfigure spaces, while pointing to evidence that humans are in fact, different people in online spaces than when interacting face-to-face. Jurich's chapter could be read as a response to both online studies (i.e., Sauders & Salazar, this volume; Thomas-Reid, this volume), sharing an original model for mediating dialogue in online affinity spaces, where even participants with a shared passion in an online community frequently encounter contested and "off-topic" viewpoints. Each of these studies illustrates the interstitial spaces of online interaction that can function as symbolic meeting places of both homogeneity and difference, conflict and mediation, identity politics and authentic community. Power geometries are also creatively uncovered in Sikkema and colleagues' research of art-based curricula that involved creating and wearing headdresses, literal masks, and digital posters to aesthetically negotiate and challenge identity politics and cultural representation as change agents.

Space and literacy practices are consistently seen to be enmeshed and mutually constitutive. For example, Abas traced signs and objects, such as portraiture and art installations in public places, and then followed the online reposting of photographs of those portraits, mapping the interactional spaces and audiences entangled with their tangible and digital circulation. Narrating a journey of a digital street performance from a taxi, Jackson's innovative research foregrounds the remaking of the urban working-class city of Hull, a place which was socially and theatrically produced, negotiated, lived, remembered, and enacted. In Opmeer and colleagues' research of digital heritage practices using 3D geospatial modelling in an ecomusuem, identities, places, and practices are seen as inextricably linked. Abram and Rowsell trace tacit modalities—the meanings that are felt or implied without being stated, including sentimentality and emotions that one connects to artefacts, whether a tangible object or a memory. Such explorations push back against the fixity of space, while pointing to the ever-evolving nature of meanings as they are perceived, experienced, remembered, and reexperienced tacitly across time and space.

In sum, the vibrant contributions to this new work forges new ground in current conceptions of digital literacy practices. Together, these studies are united by three central propositions in Massey's (2005) volume, "For Space," in which space is seen as constituted in interactions and interrelations, as spheres of coexisting heterogeneity and plurality, and perhaps most outstandingly in this volume, as always being remade.

REFERENCES

Castells, M. (1983). The city and the grassroots: A cross-cultural theory of urban social movements. Berkeley, CA: University of California Press.

Herring, S. (2010). *Another country: Queer anti-urbanism*. New York, NY: New University Press.

Hubbard, P., & Kitchin, R. (2011). *Key thinkers on space and place* (2nd ed.). London, England: SAGE.

Lefebvre, H. (1991). *The production of space* (D. Nicholson-Smith, Trans.). London, England: Blackwell.

Massey, D. (1991). A global sense of place. *Marxism Today, June*, 24–29.

Massey, D. B. (2005). *For space*. London, England: SAGE.

Mills, K. A. (2010). Filming in progress: New spaces for multimodal designing. *Linguistics and Education, 21*(1), 14–28.

Mills, K. A. (2017). What are the threats and potentials of big data for qualitative research? *Qualitative Research, Online first*, 1–13. doi:10.1177/1468794117743465

Mills, K. A., & Comber, B. (2015). Socio-spatial approaches to literacy studies: Rethinking the social constitution and politics of space. In K. Pahl & J. Rowsell (Eds.), *Handbook of literacy studies* (pp. 91–103). London, England: Routledge.

Soja, E. (1996). *Thirdspace: Journeys to los angeles and other real-and-imagined places*. Oxford, England: Basil Blackwell.

Soja, E. W. (1980). The socio-spatial dialectic. *Annals of the Association of America Geographers, 70*(2), 207–225.

Soja, E. W. (1989). *Postmodern geographies: The reassertion of space in critical social theory*. Oxford, England: Verso.

Soja, E. W. (2004). Preface. In K. M. Leander & M. Sheehey (Eds.), *Spatialising literacy research and practice* (pp. ix–xv). New York, NY: Peter Lang.

Soja, E. W. (2010). *Seeking spatial justice*. Minneapolis, MN: University of Minnesota Press.

PREFACE

Damiana Pyles, Ryan Rish, and Julie Warner

Imagine the folded, paper map you might pick up at the entrance to a large amusement park, or the giant store directory map mounted behind glass on one side of those large standalone three-sided advertising structures in the middle of a mall. Those maps probably include arrows or stars or dots with large text declaring, "You are here." But if you look away from those maps, you may not be able to figure out where you are at all. Wherever the map says "here" often does not represent your position in the world. And even when the mapped representation accurately identifies where you are, it hardly accounts for the smell of the food vendor a few feet away, or the sound of children playing close by, or the piece of gum you just stepped in, or your feelings of anxiety or joy or relaxation. Even though the map presumptuously proclaims, "You are here," the way you experience your "hereness" may not on the map at all—or barely there. Your hereness is likely complex, nuanced, multidimensional, historical, and fluid. How are you regarded in this place? When were you last here? What's different around you? What do you see around you that is not represented on the map at all? Did you once kiss a teenage crush in a spot a few feet away? Are you frustrated that you can't find, on the map, the one store you came to shop at? Who was "here" before there was a mall? The map has something to say about your hereness in the world and the things around you, but you quickly realize so much is missing from the map's representation.

Negotiating Place and Space Through Digital Literacies: Research and Practice, pp. xv–xxxii

As early-career researchers who have worked in southern regions and/or rural communities in the United States we initially came together years ago as a research and writing group in reaction to what we recognized as a lack of representation of southern and rural places in digital literacies research, which started with a single tweet and moved forward from there (see Figure 1).

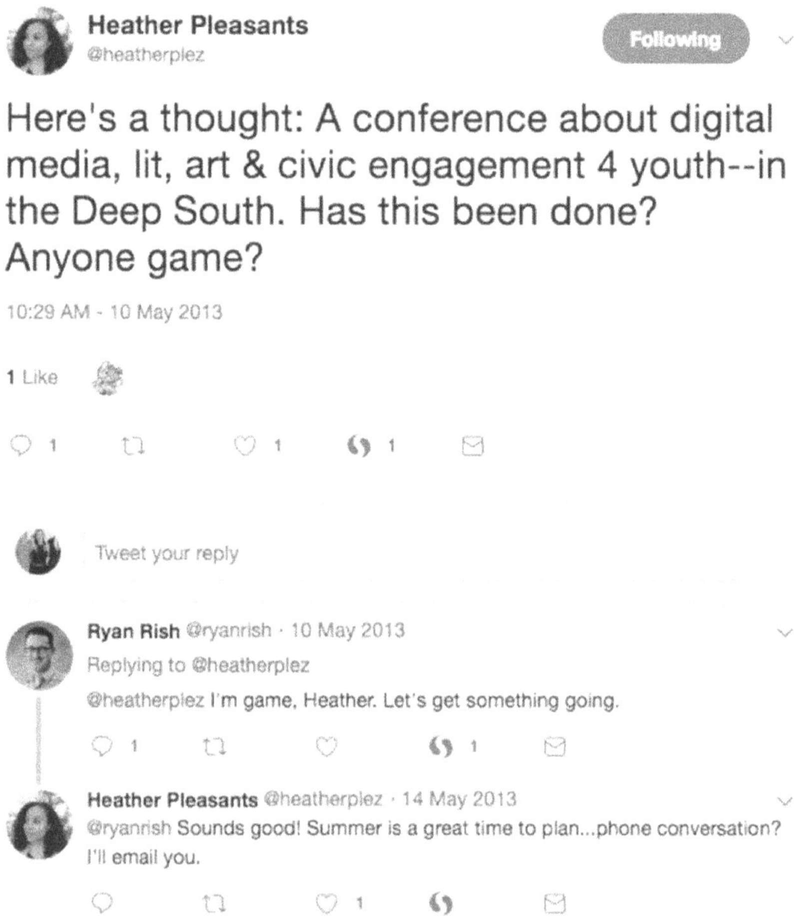

Figure 1. The Tweet that Sparked Southern Places Digital Spaces.

Along with a handful of other scholars,[1] we formed the Southern Places Digital Spaces collaborative and met over the course of a few years each month both online and offline, and we shared what with learned with others, often in online spaces. Although we came together initially because of our shared experience of doing digital literacies research in the U.S. South, our collective critical engagement with place-based and spatial theories in education research has broadened our focus. Rather than examining representation of the U.S. South exclusively, we came to consider the issue of representation of places and spaces more expansively (Literacy Research Association, 2014) (see Figure 2).

LRA Research to Practice · Episode 13

Figure 2. Southern Places Digital Spaces on LRA Research to Practice.

Through discussions rooted in readings on place-based and spatial theories, we sought to critically consider what kind of social spaces and which geographic places were and were not represented in the literacies research and what shaped those convergences and gaps.

What our explorations taught us were that digital literacies research has, for the most part, centered on urban places, spaces, and voices. In addition, we noted that in social and spatial imaginaries (Appadurai, 1996) we encountered in conversations and in the articles and books in our field, the U.S. South was often constructed as a monolith; yet, in actuality, notions of what the U.S. South is/is not, was/will be are continually contested, negotiated, reified, and renegotiated across large landscapes (Lewis Ellison, Noguerón-Liu, & Solomon, 2016). By considering the heterogeneity of the U.S. South across intersections of differences, including but not limited to race, class, gender, sexuality, ability, and language, we were beginning to see through our reading and discussions that studies of digital literacies had great potential for informing how the investigations of other regions within and outside of the U.S. could be conducted with regard to social, spatial, and historical considerations. And, as our own mobilities for work and life changes took us to different regions, we came to recognize a need to understand the intersections between geographic places, social spaces, and the ways that people navigate their relationship to those places through their use of digital technologies and locative media. In doing so, we sought to follow the lead of researchers in literacy studies who have considered how space is produced and experienced (mediated by analog and digital means) as people engage in literacies practices (Green & Corbett, 2013; Leander & Sheehy, 2004; Leander, Phillips, & Taylor, 2010; Mills & Comber, 2013).

With this volume, we widen our scope and bring together the work of global colleagues who conduct research into how people take up digital technologies as they teach, learn, and move across diverse physical and digital landscapes. This book represents an exploration with national and international scholars about how the field of literacy research could (re) conceptualize both geographic places and digital spaces, and the extent to which particular spaces and places are represented and considered integral to the way humans live, work, and play within an increasingly digitally-mediated world.

Digital Literacies, Place, and Space

Digital literacy practices have often been celebrated as means of transcending the constraints of the physical world through the production of new social spaces (Avila & Zacher Pandya, 2013; Pleasants & Salter, 2014). Indeed, in our own work, we have seen youth use digital tools and practices to create new spaces that went beyond the immediate boundaries of the physical spaces of their lives to explore their identities and connect with others (Gibbons, 2010, 2014; Rish & Cun, 2018; Rish, Cun, Gloss, & Pamuk, 2018; Warner, 2016, 2017). Gibbons (Pyles) (2010, 2012, 2014), in a study of youth filmmakers in rural and urban nonprofits, she worked to conceptualize rural media literacy and considered youth media production as a way of representing self, place, and social space in ways that respected their communities and fostered new senses of identities. She found that youth explored the potential of digital literacy practices and available tools to share their stories across time and space with different iterations of their own work refined and shared with others in their community and online in social spaces. Rish and his colleagues (2018) have examined how student inquiry can be supported by the use of mobile devices and the collection of locative data and media. Warner (2016, 2017) described the practices of youth composing with mobile phones and found that they moved not only with but also through new media. She looked at the ways identity markers, ideas, and relationships created new spaces as youth traveled with/through their mobile phones across physical or geographical boundaries.

However, we, like many other digital literacies researchers, have been wary in our work of taking on an overly-propitious view of technology as a panacea that can or will deliver resources to under-resourced places and marginalized peoples or render physical and material realities irrelevant (e.g., Warschauer, 2006; Wilder & Dressman, 2006). We have seen first-hand the way that, for example, challenges associated with geography, such as how rugged terrain or dense forested land can constitute infrastructural constraints to bringing broadband Internet to some schools and towns. To deny the importance of the material world to digital inequities would be disingenuous at best and, at worst, perpetuate disparities between resourced and under-resourced places by obscuring or ignoring those disparities (Watkins, 2018). To us, providing equitable access to resources for digital literacies and learning and working within spatial and historical complexities are issues of spatial justice (Soja, 2010).

In this volume we take a deep dive into investigations into the social, cultural, historical, and political aspects of literacies. We consider how the sociohistorical, sociocultural, and sociopolitical are enacted in/through landscapes that traverse urban, rural, and suburban/exurban, with emphasis placed on the ways digital technologies participate in the creation of identities and do work within social, digital, and material worlds. In particular, as we conceptualized this volume, we sought chapters that explored agentive work in digital literacies from a variety of perspectives that disrupted "metronormativity" (Herring, 2010) or urban centrism. We wanted to focus on how learning and teaching is fostered in often under-explored spaces where people worked for authentic engagement with their communities and with surrounding communities. Looking across/through intersections of difference (including, but not limited to race, class, gender, sexuality, ability, and language) and places, these studies of digital literacies have potential for informing how investigations of place, space, and mobilities within and across national and transnational contexts can be conducted in regard to the throwntogetherness of people, spaces/places, and texts (Massey, 2005). That is to say, these studies investigate various dimensions of the challenges, possibilities, inequities, and relationships inherent to negotiating space and place vis-à-vis digital literacies.

Part I: Reconsidering Digital Literacies From the Edges

Part I of this volume, Reconsidering Digital Literacies From the Edges, includes chapters with perspectives on how digital literacies intersect with learning and meaning making within and across various spaces with a special emphasis on the interactions between people, often familiar from school settings or from engagement in social spaces, and between people and digital texts. Some of these chapters focus on how people's interactions with one another and with texts foster learning, or in some case, include enough space for what appears to be a distancing from the learning interactions. Others focus on how people's interactions with texts are impacted by their own social and/or linguistic positionality, and the inherent complexities those bring. And, some chapters in this section explore what happens when people interact with one another in online spaces in ways that are both contradictory and uplifting. All of these chapters attempt to engage in the question of digital literacy from the edges as each chapter in Part I builds on and challenges current theoretical constructs around digital literacies, such as affinity space, social presence, multimodality, and monolingualism, by shedding light on the ways that people come to literacies from a new angle or from a different identity marker to help us understand the need to continually adjust the ways we consider and make meaning within and across spaces.

The social sciences over the past 50 years have seen several "turns" or foci in new directions that highlight different dimensions of literacy practices. While literacies researchers have, in part, adopted a spatial lens as a means of addressing the inequitable distribution of material resources, connections, and other capital (Mills & Comber, 2013), the "spatial turn" was a reaction to the digital turn's focus on the ways digital media challenged dominant conceptions of space as a container (Mills, 2010). Before the digital turn and spatial turns, literacy practices were often dichotomized into "in school" and "out-of-school" literacies, thus foregrounding physical space; this bifurcation of literacies as, in the case of "out of school" literacies, at-home, unsanctioned, nonacademic, and informal was contrasted with at-school literacies that are sanctioned, academic, and formal literacy practices. This spatial bifurcation was problematic because the divided conception of how literacy practices are framed, by definition, causes us to see them as fragmented; whereas, in reality, they are more fluid, with continuity (and surprising discontinuities) between what occurs across spaces. A bifurcated view results in a kind of a myopia where observers fail to acknowledge school-like practices at home or home-like practices at school (Hull & Schultz, 2001, 2002) amid the flows of modern life (Appadurai, 1996). The spatial turn engendered a more panoramic view of digital literacy practice.

Within this more panoramic view of literacies, some of the chapters in this section highlight how youth resist and respond to constraints imposed by particular spaces. In "Translanguage as a (Meta)cognitive Tool for Navigating and Learning in the Online Environment," Song and Cho challenge the common perception of English language centrism in online spaces of learning as they reveal the complex ways two Korean teens in the U.S. engaged in translanguaging. They found that the teens used the resources of both of their languages for different purposes depending on the cultural and linguistic features in the online spaces where they interacted. This finding is in keeping with other studies that show how people are blending online spaces to better navigate and express transnational identities (Christiansen, 2017). In much the same way, some digital literacies research has focused on how youth construct multimodal texts as a way to connect with other people and things, such as music, media, and so forth, in their places (Burn & Parker [Needs reference], 2003; Domingo, 2011). Sikkema and his coauthors' chapter, "Digital Media Explorations: How Space and Identity Become Sources of Learning" situates this conversation of resistance and response within an urban context as the chapter explores how teachers set up inclusive learning environments using digital tools and material products to help teens explore their own identities and positionalities in their Chicago neighborhoods.

Other chapters delve into the power dynamics at play in how people (re)use, communicate with, and/or foster identities with and through media in online spaces (Christiansen, 2017; Leander, Phillips, & Taylor, 2010). In "Social Loafing and Participatory Learning in a Networked Space," Neals and Vicar widen the scope of what is considered social interaction in online learning as they put a posthuman lens on digital participatory learning. Rather than viewing social loafing (the idea that people do less work when they are working in groups than alone) as a detriment to online learning, Neals and Vicar found that social loafing actually offered a new way to learn online and enrich students' experiences and connections to one another. Jurich's "Mediating Dialogue in Public Affinity Spaces," also challenges previously held notions of social interactions and meaning making within affinity spaces as primarily driven by a shared passion by demonstrating how disagreements and conflicts are negotiated in online affinity spaces for bass guitar players. In "Queering Text: Literacies Surrounding Cyber Trolling," Thomas-Reid considers the significance of what he calls "trolling artifacts" in online spaces designed for social justice teaching. Through the lens of queer theory, he suggests that these artifacts can be used for interrogation and enriching collective understandings of people's responses to social justice dialogue. In "trolling for truth" in negotiated, and often troubled, online spaces, Thomas-Reid's piece asserts a new kind of queered pedagogy that creates hope for more inclusive and truthful learning.

In this section, we hope to shed light on how "social space is not a static background against which activity develops, but rather space is both produced and productive" (de Haan & Leander, 2011, p. 320). These chapters call into question how different relationships in different spaces complicate ideas around agency and identity in both school and nonschool settings bringing the edges of space more to the center.

Part II: Digital Literacies From Within

Part II, Digital Literacies from Within, explicitly asks how digital literacies are fostered or contested in particular places given the spatial turn. We have come to understand space and place as relational constructs. Our considerations of social space that is constructed among people who are copresent and/or virtually remote include the significance of the materiality of a place and its history for what actions were taken therein and by whom. The people constructing the social space matter in relationship to each other, but they also matter in relationship to that particular place. For example, Finney (2014) documents how the legacies of Jim Crow, slavery, and racial violence have shaped cultural understandings of natural places and who should have access to them. People of color creating the social space of a conversation in a U.S. national park are doing so in relationship to a place in which they were historically excluded in a shared understanding of who should visit national parks. Likewise, places as built environments are designed for particular purposes with particular people and social relationships in mind. These purposes often do not only come from individuals or groups with special interests, but they may also come as part of larger government-sponsored agendas to separate people in systemic ways that are written into policies and laws and reinforced through the practices of people. Historically in the United States, this has taken the shape of state-sponsored segregation (Rothstein, 2017), which has created a legacy and entrenched practices of designing places based on preferences for particular classes and races of people. For example, in cities and suburbs across the U.S. basketball hoop removal from parks has been used to prevent the gathering of young men of color (Armborst, D'Oca, & Theodore, 2017). This is a very intentional reshaping of the material conditions of the place to thwart particular people from creating a particular social space (e.g., pickup basketball game). These two parks use examples that demonstrate the relationships between space and place. With national parks example, the access to the natural place has been defined in part by the aggregate of social spaces shared there by particular people over time. With city and suburban parks example, the places have been intentionally re-designed to discourage the sharing of particular social spaces by particular types of people.

However, we do not consider these constructs of space and place to be deterministic of the actions and meaning that is taken therein. We understand space as a "practiced place" (de Certeau, 1984), but not irrespective of the history and ideologies that gave shape to that particular place. Conversely, we understand place not only as "an order of distributed relationships, location, and fixity" (Talburt, 2000, p. 19), but also as sites where the social imaginary and acts of resistance can reinvent and transform through the social spaces that are shared there (Kinloch, 2010). Pressed further for a more precise definition of space and place, we respond by holding the two constructs in tension with one another in considerations of how the history and materiality of a place is significant when determining the "so what" of work involving digital media and literacies. We attempt in this volume to bring to the fore examples of how examining the relationships between space and place help us to understand digital literacies and their significance to the people involved. In these chapters, place is foregrounded or central to the argument. The chapters in this section interrogate the relationship between place and digital literacies across less studied settings.

Some of these chapters widen the lens on digital literacies in place(s) by exploring rurality, which has been a blind spot in the research on digital literacies. While literacy researchers have carried out robust research in the area of digital literacy practice over the past two decades, most of this research has focused on the engagement of people in urban contexts (e.g., Black, 2009; Chandler-Olcott & Mahar, 2003; Davis, 2010; Guzzetti & Gamboa, 2005; Hull & Nelson, 2005; Mackey & McClay, 2008). While this scholarship on urban areas doesn't discount rurality per se, a fuller understanding of "rural literacies" (Donehower, Hogg, & Schnell, 2007, 2011), in comparison, there is still much to be known about how rurality intersects with and/or constrains/fosters literacies in ways that are different than in other types of places (Green & Corbett, 2013), especially in terms of digital literacies (Pyles, 2016). In "Full of Sound and Fury," in their study of a professional development institute called Writing with Video, Bruce and his coauthors demonstrate the relationship between student digital composing processes and issues of identity within space by showing how both real and imagined aspects of space(s) are leveraged by participants. The work in this chapter illustrates the ways in which issues of space and place complicate the notion of "the field" and situatedness (Baron, 2008; Buckingham, 2008; Ito Okabe, & Matsuda, 2005; Ling, 2004; Livingstone, 2008; Mazzarella, 2005; Stornaiuolo, Smith, & Phillips, 2009) while avoiding a deficit perspective of rurality. Instead, the authors show the ways that the students used the "available resources of their ruralities" as they created video projects. In "Leveraging Digital Literacies to Critique Narratives about Southern Spaces and Places," Connors and Daugherty examine how digital media can be used to present opportunities for producing and disseminating counterstories (Delgado, 1989) about people and places in the southern United States. The digital videos the preservice teachers were asked to produce brought together the oral histories and the emerging teachers' own analytical perspectives on the people, places, and literacies of the Arkansas Ozark region. These chapters offer a rich picture of digital media and people from rural communities. These chapters further our argument that the digital divide binary, often applied to discussion of education in rural places, is, in essence, a deficit approach, but by refusing a deficit perspective, such studies offer insight into rich and meaningful uses of technologies by people in particular places.

Researchers have also attended to the conceived nature of space (Lefebvre, 1991; Soja, 1989), and technology integration has been explored as a means of addressing the educational needs of particular places. When it comes to rural places, in particular, researchers have approached technological tools and digital texts as a means of countering the lack of literacy resources and geographic isolation of some rural places (e.g., Howley, Wood, & Hough, 2011; Larson & Murray, 2008; Mitra, Dangwal, & Thadani, 2008). This research also foregrounds agency for the people living in those places. Woodward's "Indigenous Activism in the Digital Sphere: A Transrhetorical Analysis of the 'Save the Longhorn Mountain,' " applies a view of a social media site as a transrhetorical means toward preserving a geo-sacred site from mining. Woodward's study of Indigenous activism in the digital sphere demonstrates a digital literacy of social action dependent upon alliance building and reveals the need to further explore the ways in which digital literacies are influenced and created through social action. Woodward challenges us to consider how digital platforms contribute to change in the physical realm.

Other chapters explore how place as the central focus can lead to newer ways of utilizing digital media to re-see and re-conceptualize the place and/or its people. In "Innovative Technologies in Support of Local Heritage Management," Opmeer and his coauthors examine how GIS and 3D modeling facilitate people in a local community to create and share not only the history of the region in an ecomuseum but also their own relationships to the history and that area through the mapping and mobile apps that they created together in workshops. In this way, the local residents are marking their place in history as well as in their actual geographic area in ways that transcend both. Jackson's "From the Screen to the Streets: A Digital Performance Project to Remember and Reimagine Hull's Sense of Place," too, highlights the ways in which literacies travel across places and spaces. Through a series of interactive performance journeys traveling through a city entitled *Now | Then* (as one reviewer noted, a literal trip down memory lane) that evoked and explored relationships to the city of Hull in the United Kingdom over time. Translating digital media into performance becomes for Jackson a means for "establish[ing] heritage from below, and transcend[ing] grand narratives, so that individual stories and narratives can become contributors to a city's sense of place." Jackson maps the ways place is constructed centrifugally through human lives and memory, speaking back to hegemonic stories of place imposed from without through centripetal force.

The chapters in this section explore agency and space in new ways. The contributors demonstrate that people use literacy practices to reconfigure and conceptualize space in ways that are both concrete as well as conceived. These pieces call into question notions of agency defined simply as *the power to act* by highlighting the real ways that spaces both digital and conceived catalyze impacts in the physical world.

Part III: Tracing Digital Literacies Across Time and Space

In this last section, Part III, Tracing Digital Literacies Across Time and Space, the chapters offer some models for the use of digital literacies within lived experiences to promote social good within the "throwntogetherness" (Massey, 2005) of communities. In some ways, with the inclusion of these chapters, we are asserting a new digital politics that harkens back to Massey's recognition that we need a way of being together as people (and things) that:

> pays attention to the fact that entities and identities (be they places, or political constituencies, or mountains) are collectively produced through practices which form relations; and it is on those practices and relations that politics must be focused.... [W]hat this means in turn is that the politics itself might require a different geography: one which reflects the geography of those relations. (p. 148)

This call by critical geographers, such as Massey, has been taken up in these chapters by attempting to de-center digital literacies in pedagogy, collaboration, language, and community in different ways. By exploring how a variety of groups have used digital practices within their work for social change, we encourage others to imagine possibilities for engaged digital literacies within their own spaces and places. Despite a rich body of scholarship on space and digital literacies, questions about the role of the material world when one takes on a spatial perspective persist.

To grapple with the role of the physical world from a spatial orientation, many researchers have acknowledged the material as just one part of the "field of relations" or nexus of practice (Olwig & Hastrup,1997). In this view, space is not thought of as a container or "simply a static background 'upon' which human activity is played out" (Leander & McKim, 2003, p. 212); instead, one may think of space as an intersection, a never-ending expanse of connections, which includes (but is not limited to) the material/physical aspects of space. Yet, spatially-focused research has also acknowledged that space is, in part, conceived or imagined (Lefebvre, 1991; Soja, 1989). For instance, we know people use literacy practices, digital or analog, to "be part of the story," to claim a space, construct an identity, or take a social position (Moje, 2000). In this way, some literacy researchers have theorized space as similar to agency, as in the space people create for themselves to participate (De Hann & Leander, 2011; Moje, 2000; O'Brien, 1998, 2003; O'Brien, Springs, & Stith, 2001).

Mobile digital literacy practices in particular inspire a need to reconsider how we conceptualize space and agency. Mobile interfaces, and in particular GPS-enabled, locative media, affect how people think about and experience space (Farman, 2011). Taking this idea further, Farman (2011) posits that space is always "constructed simultaneously with our sense of embodiment" (p. 18). In much the same way, Wargo (2015) examined how one youth participant used digital mobile applications to mediate affective experience, and in doing so presents a laminated view of the material and digital as embodied experience, challenging us to reconsider the role of the material in relation to the digital with regard to mobile technologies. Mobile technologies allow us to bring the digital into the everyday spaces of our lives and thus reconfigure space.

The authors in this section also present challenges to long-standing theoretical constructs through their critique of static notions of multimodality by asking how time and space play a role in understanding subjective, sensory-based meaning making. In their chapter, "Immateriality Redux: Tacit Modalities and Personal Meaning Across Timescales," Abrams and Rowsell consider the tacit nature of modalities beyond typical considerations of affordances and constraints to consider how meaning making with artifacts changes over time and across space, foregrounding the significance of affect in meaning making. Artifactual meaning making is presented as ever evolving. Abas, in her chapter, "Repatriating Desaparacidos Across Time and Space," examined the ways that signs created by an artist-activist traveled from their physical origin, an art installation, to many nodes on a network through their posting to digital media. By focusing on place as linguistic landscape (centering upon linguistic texts, often markers and signs, in public spaces) they saw the way that language and space are enmeshed. In this way, the many spaces touched by the signs were shown to be inextricable and fluid. Abas shows us that flow can be a characteristic of space that can be leveraged for teaching and learning. In "Virtual Carrels," Buchholz and her co-authors shift from communicating in face-to-face carrels in their graduate studies to a range of online and offline spaces, such as Google Hangouts, Google Drive, and SMS/texts, in their first academic jobs. They find that the way they communicate creates a range of opportunities for personal and professional development as they navigate tricky political situations in their new jobs. These chapters represent an intriguing addition to the research on literacy and globalization, diasporas, and transnational communication (Brouwer, 2006; Lam, 2000, 2004, 2006, 2009; Skop & Adams, 2009), illuminating the ways people engage across a multitude of boundaries and borders. Such views of space are salient now, as the online adds a new layer to (or new nodes within) social space for literacy researchers to consider.

In this section, the chapters also work through some of the contestations that happen when people, places, and things are "thrown-together." By including these chapters, we are attempting to move away from prior assumptions that digital literacies will level the educational playing ground for students in underresourced places and spaces toward a more nuanced understanding that digital literacies are operating within existing power structures in communities but when one can see the "diffractions" (Barad, 2007) of the literacies, new understandings can emerge. For instance, in this last section, in particular, we are interested in exploring transliteracies, specifically how "..materials, persons, practices, and texts are dynamically configured across varied temporalities and spaces (Stornaiuolo, Smith, & Phillips, 2017, p. 70), including how people interact with *things* with similar complexities in power relationships. For instance, Rust's chapter, (Im)mobilizing Literacies," explicitly uses Storniaiuolo, Smith, and Phillips (2017) concept of immobilities to discuss how young people in different schools created digital media that was shared with other students both digitally and in a face-to-face workshop. Through examining the phases of the project, Rust found that some children experienced insecurity due to age and race when creating and responding to the youth media created, and those immobilities were present in different ways even when they were in a face-to-face workshop. The focus on immobilities provides a counter-narrative to an idea that media production helps all children equally, suggested by the proliferation of 1–1 tablet programs, connectivity, or coding initiatives in the early 2000s.

Living, Being, Learning Together Through Digital Literacies

Although these views of space predate "networked society" (Castells, 1996), digital literacies research has necessitated a re-theorization of space. The purpose of this volume is to consider through a variety of scholarly inquiries from global contexts how researchers and practitioners conceptualize and operationalize space and place in digital literacy research specifically. In our own respective inquiries into matters of space and place in digital literacy and in reading across the works submitted for inclusion in this volume, what we have recognized is that places are made up of elements that Massey (2005) calls *throwntogetherness* [author's italics] in which "places pose in particular form the question of our living together" (p. 151), and we would contend, of our learning together as well. "Place, in other words, does—as many argue—change us, not through some visceral belonging (some barely changing rootedness, as so many would have it) but through the practising of place, the negotiation of intersecting trajectories; place as an arena where negotiation is forced upon us" (Massey, 2005, p. 154). Therefore, in this volume, we consider how space/place, identities, and the role of digital literacies create opportunities for individuals and communities to negotiate living, being, and learning together in ways that have been unexplored or underexplored.

Conducting research on digital literacies practices always entails the risk of focusing too much on the tools that mediate literacy practices—at looking at the world from the angle of the tool at the expense of the world and its people around it. We have found that a focus on place and space is one means toward avoiding such reductionist views of digital literacy practices. Looking across the contributions in these pages one thing is clear: understanding the world around us and our place in it is a shared human endeavor. We view the chapters in this collection as significant contributions to our emergent understandings.

NOTE

1. Heather Pleasants, Lindy Johnson, Sean Connors, Darren Crovitz

REFERENCES

Armborst, T., D'Oca, D., & Theodore, G. (2017). *The arsenal of exclusion and inclusion.* Bacelona, Spain: Actar.

Appadurai, A. (1996). *Modernity at large: Cultural dimensions of globalization.* Minneapolis, MN: University of Minnesota Press.

Avila, J., & Zacher Pandya, J. (Eds.). (2012). *Critical digital literacies as social praxis: Intersections and challenges.* New York, NY: Peter Lang.

Barad, K. (2007). *Meeting the universe halfway: Quantum physics and the entanglement of matter and meaning.* Durham, NC & London, England: Duke University Press.

Baron, N. (2008). *Always on: Language in an online and mobile world.* New York, NY: Oxford University Press.

Black, R. W. (2009). Online fan fiction, global identities, and imagination. *Research in the Teaching of English, 43,* 397–425.

Buckingham, D. (Ed.). (2008). *Youth, identity, and digital media.* Cambridge, MA: MIT Press.

Brouwer, L. (2006). Giving voice to Dutch Moroccan girls on the Internet. *Global Media Journal,* 5(9). Retrieved from http://dare.ubvu.vu.nl/bitstream/handle/1871/25786/194682.pdf

Castells, M. (1996). *The rise of the network society: The information age: Economy, society, and culture* (Vol. I). Oxford, England: Blackwell.

Chandler-Olcott, K., & Mahar, D. (2003). "Tech-savviness" meets multiliteracies: Exploring adolescent girls' technology-mediated literacy practices. *Reading Research Quarterly, 38,* 356–385.

Christiansen, M .S. (2017). Creating a unique transnational place: Deterritorialized discourse and the blending of time and space in online social media. *Written Communication, 34*(2), 135–164.

Davis, K. (2010). Coming of age online: The developmental underpinnings of girls' blogs. *Journal of Adolescent Research, 25,* 145–171.

de Certeau, M. (1984). *The practice of everyday life.* Berkeley, CA: University of California Press.

De Hann, M., & Leander, K. (2011). The construction of ethnic boundaries in classroom interaction through social space. *Culture & Psychology, 17*(3), 319–338.

Delgado, R. (1989). Storytelling for oppositionists and others: A plea for narrative. *Michigan Law Review, 87*(8), 2411–2441.

Domingo, M. (2011). Analyzing layering in textual design: a multimodal approach for examining cultural, linguistic, and social migrations in digital video. *International Journal of Social Research Methodology, 14*(3), 219–230. doi:10.1080/13645579.2011.563619

Donehower, K., Hogg, C., & Schell, E.E. (2012). *Reclaiming the rural: Essays on literacy, rhetoric, and pedagogy.* Carbondale, IL: Southern Illinois University Press.

Donehower, K., Hogg, C., & Schell, E. E. (2007). *Rural literacies.* Carbondale, IL: Southern Illinois University Press.

Farman, J. (2011). *Mobile interface theory: Embodied space and locative media.* New York, NY: Routledge.

Finney, C. (2014). *Black faces, white spaces: Reimagining the relationship of African Americans to the great outdoors.* Chapel Hill, NC: University of North Carolina Press.

Gibbons, D. (2010). Tracing the paths of moving artifacts in youth media production. *English Teaching: Practice and Critique, 9*(1), 8–21.

Gibbons, D. (2012). Developing an ethics of youth media production using media literacy, identity, & modality. *Journal of Media Literacy Education, 4*(3), 256–265.

Gibbons, D. (2014). Rural places meet media literacy: Representing truth and self in rural social space. *Journal on Images and Culture, 6.*

Green, B., & Corbett, J. (2013). *Rethinking rural literacies: Transnational perspectives.* New York, NY: Palgrave MacMillan.

Guzzetti, B., & Gamboa, M. (2005). Online journaling: The informal writings of two adolescent girls. *Research in the Teaching of English, 40,* 168–206.

Herring, S. (2010). *Another country: Queer Anti-Urbanism.* New York, NY: New York University.

Howley, A., Wood, L., & Hough, B. (2011). Rural elementary school teachers' technology integration. *Journal of Research in Rural Education, 26*(9), 1–13.

Hull, G., & Nelson, M. (2005). Locating the semiotic power of multimodality. *Written Communication, 22,* 224–261.

Hull, G., & Schultz, K. (2001). Literacy and learning out of school: A review of theory and research. *Review of Educational Research, 71,* 575–611.

Hull, G., & Schultz, K. (Eds.). (2002). *School's out! Bridging out-of-school literacies with classroom practice.* New York, NY: Teachers College Press.

Ito, M., Okabe, D., & Matsuda, M. (Eds.). (2005). *Personal, portable, pedestrian: Mobile phones in Japanese life*. Cambridge, MA: MIT Press.

Kinloch, V. (2010). *Harlem on our minds: Place, race, and the literacies of urban youth*. New York, NY: Teachers College Press.

Lam, W. S. E. (2000). Second language literacy and the design of the self: A case study of a teenager writing on the Internet. *TESOL Quarterly*, *34*, 457–482.

Lam, W. S. E. (2004). Second language socialization in a bilingual chat room: Global and local considerations. *Language, Learning and Technology*, *8*(3), 44–65.

Lam, W. S. E. (2006). Culture and learning in the context of globalization: Research directions. *Review of Research in Education*, *30*, 213–237.

Lam, W. S. E. (2009). Multiliteracies on instant messaging in negotiating local, translocal, and transnational affiliations: A case of an adolescent immigrant. *Reading Research Quarterly*, *44*, 377–397.

Larson, R. C., & Murray, E. (2008). Open educational resources for blended learning in high schools: Overcoming impediments in developing countries. *Journal of Asynchronous Learning Networks*, *12*(1), 85–103.

Leander, K., & McKim, K. K. (2003). Tracing the everyday "sitings" of adolescents on the Internet: A strategic adaptation of ethnography across online and offline spaces. *Education, Communication & Information*, *3*, 211–240.

Leander, K., & Sheehy, M. (Eds.). (2004). *Spatializing literacy research and practice*. New York, NY: Peter Lang.

Leander, K. M., Phillips, N. C., & Taylor, K. H. (2010). The changing social spaces of learning: Mapping new mobilities. *Review of Research in Education*, *34*(1), 329–394.

Lefebvre, H. (1991). *Critique of everyday life* (Vol. 2). New York, NY: Verso.

Lewis Ellison, T., Nogueròn-Liu, S., & Solomon, M. (2016). Co-constructing place, space, and race: African American and Latinx participants and researchers' representations of digital literacy research in the South. *Journal of Literacy and Technology*, *17*(3), 62–99.

Ling, R. (2004). *The mobile connection: The cell phone's impact on society*. San Francisco, CA: Morgan Kaufman.

Literacy Research Association. (2014, Nov. 12). LRA Research to Practice—Episode 13. Retrieved from https://youtu.be/lr5ykG3AnPE

Livingstone, S. (2008). Taking risky opportunities in youthful content creation: Teenagers' use of social networking sites for intimacy, privacy and self-expression. *New Media & Society*, *10*, 393–411.

Mackey, M., & McClay, J. K. (2008). Pirates and poachers: Fan fiction and the conventions of reading and writing. *English in Education*, *42*(2), 131–147.

Massey, D. (2005). *For space*. London, England: SAGE.

Mazzarella, S. (2005). *Girl wide web: Girls, the internet, and the negotiation of identity*. New York, NY: Peter Lang.

Mills, K. A. (2010). A review of the "digital turn" in the new literacy studies. *Review of Educational Research*, *80*(2), 246–271.

Mills, K. A. (2015). *Literacy theories for the digital age: Social, critical, multimodal, spatial, material and sensory lenses*. Bristol, England: Multilingual Matters.

Mills, K. A., & Comber, B. (2013). Space, place and power: The spatial turn in literacy research. In K. Hall, T. Cremin, B. Comber, & L. Moll (Eds.),

International Handbook of Research in Children's Literacy, Learning and Culture (pp. 1–26). London, England: Wiley-Blackwell.

Mitra, S., Dangwal, R., & Thadani, L. (2008). Effects of remoteness on the quality of education: A case study from north Indian schools. *Australasian Journal of Educational Technology*, *24*(2), 168–180.

Moje, E. (2000). To be part of the story: The literacy practices of gangsta adolescents. *Teachers College Record*, 102, 652–690.

Moje, E. (2004). Powerful spaces: Tracing the out-of-school literacy spaces of Latino/a youth. In K. Leander & M. Sheehy (Eds.), *Spatializing literacy research and practice*. New York, NY: Peter Lang.

O'Brien, D. G. (1998). Multiple literacies in a high school program for "at-risk" adolescents. In D. E. Alvermann, K. A. Hinchman, D. W. Moore, S. F. Phelps, & D. R. Waff (Eds.), *Reconceptualizing the literacies in adolescents' lives* (pp. 27–49). Mahwah, NJ: Erlbaum.

O'Brien, D. G. (2003). Juxtaposing traditional and intermedial literacies to redefine the competence of struggling adolescents. *Reading Online*, *6*(7). Retrieved from http://www.readingonline.org/newliteracies/lit_index.asp?HREF=obrien2/

O'Brien, D., Springs, R., & Stith, D. (2001). Engaging at-risk high school students: Literacy learning in a high school literacy lab. *Constructions of literacy: Studies of Teaching and Learning in and Out of Secondary Schools*, 97–116.

Olwig, K. F., & Hastrup, K. (Eds.). (1997). *Siting culture: The shifting anthropological object*. London, England: Psychology Press.

Pleasants, H. M., & Salter, D. E. (Eds.). (2014). *Community-based multiliteracies and digital media projects: Questioning assumptions and exploring realities*. New York, NY: Peter Lang.

Pyles, D. G. (2016). Rural media literacy: Youth documentary videomaking as a rural literacy practice. *Journal of Research in Rural Education, 31*(7), 1–15.

Rish, R.M., & Cun, A. (2018). Co-navigating mobilized student inquiry across multiple contexts. *Proceedings of the International Conference on the Learning Sciences*. London, England.

Rish, R. M., Cun, A., Gloss, A., & Pamuk, M. (2018). Mobile asset mapping as community inquiry. In S. Arafeh, D. Herro, R. Ling, & C. Holden (Eds.), *Mobile learning: Perspectives on practice and policy* (pp. 119–141). Charlotte, NC: Information Age Publishing.

San Pedro, T. J. (2015). Silence as Shields: Agency and Resistances among Native American Students in the Urban Southwest. *Research in the Teaching of English, 50*(2), 132–153.

Rothstein, R. (2017). *The color of law: A forgotten history of how our government segregated America*. New York, NY: Liverlight.

Siegel, M., & Panofsky, C. P. (2009). Designs for multimodality in literacy studies: Explorations in analysis. In K. M. Leander, D. W. Rowe, D. K. Dickinson, M. K. Hundley, R. T. Jimenez, & V. J. Risko (Eds.), *58th Yearbook of the National Reading Conference* 5 (pp. 99–111). Oak Creek, WI: NRC.

Skop, E., & Adams, P. C. (2009). Creating and inhabiting virtual places: Indian immigrants in cyberspace. *National Identities, 11,* 127–147.

Soja, E. W. (1989). Postmodern geographies: The reassertion of space in critical social theory. New York, NY: Verso.

Soja, E. W. (2010). *Seeking spatial justice.* Minneapolis, MN: University of Minnesota Press.

Stornaiuolo, A., Smith, A., & Phillips, N. C. (2017). Developing a transliteracies framework for a connected world. *Journal of Literacy Research, 49*(1), 68–91.

Talburt, S. (2000). *Subject to identity: Knowledge, sexuality, and academic practices in higher education.* Albany, NY: State University of New York Press.

Wargo, J. (2015). Spatial stories with nomadic narrators: Affect, Snapchat, and feeling embodiment in youth mobile composing. *Journal of Language and Literacy Education, 11*(1), 47–64.

Warner, J. (2016). Adolescents' dialogic composing with mobile phones. *Journal of Literacy Research, 48*(2), 164–191.

Warner, J. (2017). *Adolescents' new literacies with and through mobile phones.* New York, NY: Peter Lang.

Warschauer, M. (2006). *Laptops and literacy: Learning in the wireless classroom.* New York, NY: Teachers College Press.

Watkins, S. G. (2018). *The digital edge: How Black and Latino youth navigate digital inequality.* New York, NY: New York University Press.

Wilder, P., & Dressman, M. (2006). New literacies, enduring challenges? The influence of capital on adolescent readers' Internet practices. *Reconceptualizing the Literacies In Adolescents' Lives, 2,* 205–229.

PART I

RECONSIDERING DIGITAL LITERACIES FROM THE EDGES

CHAPTER 1

DIGITAL MEDIA EXPLORATIONS

How Space and Identity Become Sources of Learning

Scott Sikkema
Chicago Arts Partnerships in Education

Louanne Smolin
LIS Curriculum Research

Joseph Spilberg and Mark Diaz
Chicago Arts Partnerships in Education

Erin A. Preston
External Research Consultant,
Chicago Arts Partnerships in Education

Classrooms are contested spaces. Compliance measures, educator professional development focused on alignment with mandates, punitive oversight systems, and notions of universal curriculum potentially threaten to remove the individuality and identity of classrooms (Darling-Hammond,

Negotiating Place and Space Through Digital Literacies: Research and Practice, pp. 3–20

2013; Kohn, 2011; Ravitch, 2010). Digital literacies offer a process for teachers and students to unpack this context, to reshape it, and in the process, redefine their identities as learners. Digital literacies move beyond adding technology into the mix of learning activities. Rather, they offer a collaborative process for learners to investigate and redefine their worlds both in and outside of the classroom. Our work is drawn from digital media arts partnerships between Chicago Arts Partnerships in Education (CAPE) and urban, public school classroom teachers in both professional development and classroom settings. The potential to shift perceptions of school space led CAPE collaborators to pedagogies that examined space, including alternate community spaces, and identity as site for art making.

The purpose of this chapter is to examine the digital literacy practices within our arts integrated school curriculum, affording opportunities for arts teachers and students to transform their learning spaces and reconceptualize their identities as learners. Specifically, we ask: How can the possibilities of digital media accelerate or deepen student and teacher exploration and production of space and identity? How can digital media, expressed through artmaking, be used as material to reproduce or perform space and identity through the act of making?

This chapter includes three sections. We begin by discussing the digital literacy foundations that ground our arts integration partnerships. We, then, explore digital media as artistic material. Finally, through curricular cases, we examine how arts teachers and students investigated space and identity through arts integrated curriculum.

THEORETICAL FOUNDATIONS OF DIGITAL LITERACY PRACTICE

As teachers and students engage in digital literacies, they activate processes that necessitate their engagement in multiple modalities where "the textual is also related to the visual, the audio, the spatial, the behavioral, and so on" (The New London Group, 1996, p. 64). The New London Group (1996) redefined literacy, shifting the field from a focus on text based literacy to multiple "literacies" that recognize there are "multiple ways of communicating and making meaning" (Leander & Boldt, 2012, p. 23). These multiliteracies are "complemented by, or replaced by, other ways of crossing time and distance, such as recordings and transmissions of oral, visual, audio, gestural and other patterns of meaning" (Kalantzis & Cope, 2012, p. 2). This redefinition raises two important implications for learning: (1) meaning is shaped by multiple modes of representation and (2) the contextual boundaries in which we experience these modes become expanded as well. In other words, students encounter multiple forms of literacies in multiple contexts.

Although these ideas have shaped the field of new literacies, over the years, critique has been voiced. For example, Leander and Boldt (2012) raised concerns about how the work of the New London Group (1996) has been taken up in research and practice. In particular, they see as problematic the notion of "youth literacy practices as purposeful rational design" which involves a "domestication that subtracts movement, indeterminacy, and emergent potential from the picture" (p. 24). Their critique sought to reconceptualize learners' literacy engagement as "the moment-by-moment unfolding or emergence" of experience (p. 25). CAPE's arts integration methodologies are, in fact, more reflective of emergent practices rather than structured design, and have shaped the ways in which digital media has been explored in our partner classrooms.

Additionally, we have often found in the urban educational settings in which we work, classrooms are becoming "non-places" disconnected from anything relational or historical, and so also unconcerned with any sense of individual or collective identity (Augé, 1995). In this context space is not used and individuality is not valued. Therefore, identity is not considered to be material or product with which to work. However, in our work we seek to reclaim these spaces through an expansion of classroom literacies, including digital literacies.

Digital literacies inclusive of space and identity bring multiple variables into play. First, *students' experiences* contribute to multiliteracies. This has instructional implications because "in bringing space and place into the frame of literacy studies we see a subtle shift—a rebalancing of the semiotic with the materiality of lived, embodied, and situated experience" (Mills & Comber, 2013, p. 412). Therefore, students' experiences become a part of the curriculum. Sheehy (as cited in Mills & Comber, 2013) discusses this dimension of curriculum as a permeable territory, defining it as "in between spaces." These in between spaces consist of: The difficult interactional negotiations that can occur when teachers attempt to shift from reproducing literacies that are disembodied from the materiality of students' lives—worksheets, tests, and typical school knowledge—to focus on the meaningful events, objects, literacy practices, and knowledge inherent in students' own lives (Mills & Comber, 2013, p. 414). As students' lifeworlds, including the spaces surrounding students' interactions in their classrooms, homes, peer relationships, and digital explorations, are factored into the literacy curriculum, their voice and generative creativity become valuable resources for learning, expanding curricular options and, therefore, their potential for meaning making.

Second, within a digital literacy framework, *space is situated within a social context*. Multimodal interactions are embedded in social spaces, and, therefore, the space becomes defined through relationships. As Massey (2005) describes, space is built through the

> [p]ractices of engagement and the power-geometries of relations, of the structuring of space (both through enclosure and through flow) through such relations, and through an understanding of those relations as differentially (and unequally) empowering in their effects. Such practices do not so much measure space as create it, the "distances" they engender may be ones of physical force, of political (dis)alignment, of imagination. (p. 100)

In CAPE's digital media partnerships, teachers and students create space by examining the relations of power between and among them and by exploring how those relations move within defined spaces, such as the classroom. This relational conception of space can transform teaching and learning. As Leander and Boldt (2012) described, "when social space is reimagined as activity or process rather than as dimension … freedom, dislocation, and surprise characterize our sense of the social" (p. 39). Using digital literacy practices and the multimodalities they encompass, classrooms can develop into participatory learning cultures. In this process, space and relationships are created anew. The normative power relationships between teachers and students becomes disrupted. The learning environment becomes inclusive of "a more heteroglossic authentic interaction—a new area of negotiation and representation, where official and unofficial, formal and informal spaces become permeable and create potential for new kinds of learning" (Mills & Comber, 2013, p. 413). This counters oppressive classroom structures and situates learning in a context where students have voice, expertise, and agentive power (Mills & Comber, 2013).

Finally, digital literacies encompassing of space foster possibilities for *identities to become dynamic and fluid*. As teachers and students form new space and relationships, they develop new understandings of their identities. Massey's (2005) view of space as relational leads to the continual negotiation of relations and differences, a process never totally settled. Identities shift between individual and collaborator as teachers and students explore digital media, and these negotiations are "productive of political, and personal, identity" (p. 182). This description is counter to the normative classroom culture that typically contains formal roles, limited opportunities for collaboration, and a narrow to nonexistent audience. A classroom that embraces participatory culture can be transformed by its liberatory qualities, including dialogic practices and a flattening of authority and expertise (Mills & Comber, 2013).

Digital Media as Artistic Material

The framework described above contextualizes digital literacies in social spaces and created by each individual's experiences, dynamic identities, and relationships (Leander & Boldt, 2012). This has implications for digital arts practices. Massey (2005) described space as being composed of the interrelations of our practices, and, as such, space is never finished being constructed by those of us interacting within the space. Thus, to examine, deconstruct, and reconstruct space is to do the same via ourselves and our identities. When students experiment with technology as material, then digital space affords them an environment where "forms of expression and bodies (content) are more or less in constant movement between stasis and change" (Leander & Boldt, 2012, p. 39). In manipulating digital material, students and teachers directly experience simultaneity and disconnections from the new, and they are always in the flux of determining new relations (Massey, 2005). As a result, students can use digital media as artistic material to examine and construct space and identity.

Moreover, when students use digital media as material, what they construct embodies their thinking which can then be used to experiment with evolving understandings of space (Papert, 1990). In this way, digital media gives materiality and physicality to one's mental model (Papert, 1990). Students can use digital media to better understand technology by "seeing the process" in material and "also see representation of the process as it plays out" (Resnick & Rosenbaum, 2013, p. 174). For example, when editing digital video footage, students can immediately see the effects of editing decisions on their film in playback. When combined with a participatory culture where students learn with and through technology, they are afforded the opportunity to see the relational processes of creating space. When creating digital products, such as digital videos, students can take on various roles with each other including screenwriter, director, actor, and editor. Students can examine and (re)create the structures of relations or power in their classroom, their school, their neighborhood, or their community. Creating digital space is a way for students to disrupt normative power structures and restore emergent potential for relations. In this process, a student's relationship to both technology and space can transform into one more individualized and transparent (Turkle & Papert, 1990). Technology and space can become material to think with in order to gain command of expression and communication (Massey 2005; Turkle & Papert, 1990).

Digital space impacts how students develop identity. Boyd (2008) described digital environments as spaces where students experiment with and perform their identity, taking on identities, such as community members, tinkerers, and experts (Ito et al., 2009). When students make choices about how to perform identity and create forms of expression in digital spaces, it is a nonlinear practice emerging from interrelations and multiliteracies (Leander & Boldt, 2012). The interplay between the virtual and physical impacts a student's sense of body and identity due to "a constant 'reproduction' of the self without the body" (Paul, 2015, p. 165).

This fluctuation of presence and identity across digital spaces prompts students and teachers to rethink the precepts of identity, body, and space, and enables the potential to form new statements of identity in spaces, whether digital, physical, or a combination (boyd, 2008; Ito et al., 2009; Palfrey & Gasser, 2008; Wilson, 2017). By embracing the ways digital space has changed how and where students develop their identities and engage in literacy practices, teachers can activate the liminal qualities between a classroom and digital spaces where norms, roles, and identities can be renegotiated.

If transforming spaces can play a role in transforming identities, and if digital media can become artistic material rather than merely a tool, how can the possibilities of digital media accelerate or deepen student and teacher exploration and production of space and identity? How can digital media, expressed through artmaking, be used as material to reproduce or perform space and identity through the act of making? The cases below provide examples in which we explore how CAPE's arts teachers and students transformed their learning spaces and how this transformation helped them reconceptualize their identities as learners.

CURRICULAR CASES

CAPE's partnerships utilize a conceptual approach to art and art making, generating opportunities for exploring site or location, as a way into space and identity (Kwon, 1997). In this conceptual approach CAPE's teacher artists, student artists and viewers utilize technology as artistic material, collaboratively constructing cultural and sociopolitical inquiries in multiple spaces within and surrounding schools and enabling these spaces to transform the identities of all the collaborators. In the curricular examples that follow, we examine this digital literacy framework, describing how space and identity are transformed when digital media is conceived of as material through which students and teachers learn.

Connectivity and Collaboration: Curricular Example 1

In CAPE's professional development for teachers, we reconceive how technology is used and understood. To achieve this, we engage teachers in experiences that help them see and use digital technology as a material in-and-of-itself rather than using it simply as a tool to create known end products, such as self-portraits or movies. During the *connectivity and collaboration* workshop, teachers explored the physicality of digital devices versus learning basic operations, enabling them to find new ways to manipulate digital media. Teachers were shown examples by contemporary artists where digital devices not only captured something about a space, they were set up in the space itself to redefine the experiencing of that space. This way of thinking about devices as a literal, physical part of the art was a new way of thinking for our teacher participants. They were tasked to utilize digital devices in small groups to create a new understanding of their identity as a group in relation to the space they were in. They investigated group dynamics, stories, and the workshop space itself. They performed for video or captured sounds or images of the space and shared with each other the array of media they created. They then examined each media file to identify patterns and ideas that emerged from the footage. After settling on a connective theme, they reworked or created new media files to execute the final project.

One group realized a common current running through their thoughts and feelings were reactions to the 2016 election. They created individual voice recordings of their reactions and set these recordings on each of their devices to an appropriated video of a campfire. They arranged their devices with the voice recorded campfire videos around the workshop space for their colleagues to encounter.

Figure 1.1. Campfire.

This group's creation, installation, and encounter reflects Massey's (2005) notion that space is a "sphere of dynamic simultaneity, constantly disconnected by new arrivals, constantly waiting to be determined (and therefore always undetermined) by the construction of new relations" (p. 107). As one teacher stated:

> I learned a lot about the value of collaboration as well because I never would have thought about that alone. Although I had parts in coming up with that idea. We do a giant fireplace on the stage during our winter dance, and I was like, "Oh, yeah. So everyone brings something to the table." And so we got thrown into it over and over again. (CAPE, 2018a)

The teachers created this new, "campfire" space through extended negotiations with each other as to their differences and relations, a negotiating process that was as much digital as it was verbal. This process created new spaces, generating a "political, and personal, identity" (Massey, 2005, p. 182). As the above teacher stated:

> Just the idea that we were using technology in a way I had never thought of using it before.... And everyone that day, everyone did really interesting pieces of, iPads inside of iPads.... [The facilitator] also just left that really open for us. You're pulling from every experience of your life.... Everyone used it in such different ways. (CAPE, 2018a)

This teacher aptly describes how exposure to her peers' ideas not only opened her up to new ways of thinking, but also helped her to dig deeper to mine her own experiences. In this professional development example, and all of those above, teachers were given permission to build on their basic understanding of technology by directly connecting with aesthetic concerns in the arts integrated lessons they teach, strengthening their knowledge of both aesthetic and technological realms. For example, they created both sculpture and aural composition through installation of iPads as artistic material and digital recording processes. As Qvortrup (2003) described, "the artwork object to be observed by the audience is not just the resulting image or projection" but a "complex system of material interferences and of textual interreferences" (p. 251). In Figure 1.1, iPads were used as sculptural material and communication medium, going beyond their normative use as personal information device. Together teachers created an intertextual experience for their audiences, an experience that invited them to make meaning of the multiple modes of expression present in the installation. In this way, the creators of the art and the audience could acknowledge and process their thinking and emotions about the election.

Other groups investigated interferences and interreferences. For example, one such group experimented with the space around them, as depicted in Figure 1.2 and explained below.

Figure 1.2. Space reproduced.

Figure 1.2 displays still shots from this group's video. The video is composed of multiple iPad devices simultaneously playing back slow tracking shots from multiple perspectives of the expanse of the space. As digital artists, this group of teachers moved away from creating a discrete art object. Rather, the "digital technologies offer multiple possibilities for an enhanced cinematic representation in installations, a continuation of the spatialization of the images in a physical environment" (Paul, 2015, p. 96). Their installation created a hybrid form that disrupted a linear narrative in which participants are presented with a single projection on a wall with the support of a picture plane. Participants reconceptualized the narrative flow by moving through the space to view the multiple channels. In creating this installation, the teacher-artists chose to *emphasize experience* by assembling multiple objects and digitized spaces. This led them to raise different questions than they might have considered if emphasizing art as object. Can the digital technology transform how an audience might interact and participate with the art? How might the audience see and experience the space they are in when they are immersed in every angle of it at once? Using questions such as these to guide their installation, teachers created an experience for participants to examine their relationship with space.

In the *connectivity and collaboration* case, teachers developed an understanding of how devices themselves occupy space, how they can be arranged to activate a location, and how they then can enhance the meaning of an artistic experience. Their experiments in technological approaches forefronted communication, collaboration, and the materiality of the technology itself. In contrast to artworks as objects, these examples of digital art challenged viewers to see digital media as material. In the process, teachers re-imagined their space of learning as well as creating a space for exploring their relationships as co-creators of conceptual art.

Me Behind the Mask: Curricular Example 2

This curriculum was implemented in an alternative urban high school that provides students with academic, behavioral, and truancy challenges a second chance to complete a high school diploma. World Literature and Journalism teacher Avery G. partnered with teaching artist Charles J., an interdisciplinary digital/visual artist. Avery and Charles wanted students to consider what characterized a social problem while also working through design and engineering problem solving methods. Students studied world cultures through an inquiry: What are ethnocentric views, and what is the appropriate way to learn respectfully about another culture? The learners were also interested in analyzing through a study of media, identity politics, and cultural reproduction, how identities, including their own, are visualized and performed. Considering their own alternative high school as a culture and identity as well as a particular and unique space, they analyzed how their own culture and identities are stereotyped and what they themselves want to project about their culture and identity.

The medium for this examination became masks. Students researched how cultures around the world created masks and headgear that had social value and represented aspects of their culture. They created their own headdresses and wrote text or messages that carried a personal meaning for them. The messages they incorporated functioned as life mottos or rules to live by. For example, one student wrote: "Being humble is not being weak." Upon close inspection, the shapes of the headpieces made of crisscrossed rods are visually connected to the text. A young woman wears a shoe shape construction which bears the phrase "Take a walk in my shoes." In the below image, a young man is adorned by something that appears to cage his head and holds up a sign stating "Mind your own business" (see Figure 1.3). Figure 1.3 is provocative in its portrayal of a body encaged. It sparks our engagement, prompting us to learn more by participating in a thoughtful dialogue with the artist. We might think about cages and where we actually see them. Perhaps we think about where they

Figure 1.3. Mind your own business.

exist but are unseen? How does our knowledge that this image appears in a school impact the meaning we might make? Is this student-artist making a statement about classrooms as cages? Is he communicating with and admonishing those who have opinions about classrooms and students? In this example the student is not only thinking about how material can convey ideas, but also how it can provoke questions.

In the final iteration of this project, students photographed each other adorned with their structural headdress and holding up their bold text and created digitized posters. They discussed where their posters might go up in the school, wanting to create "democratic public spaces … operating with a sense of spatiality which keeps always under scrutiny the play of social relations which construct them" (Massey, 2005, p. 153). This was realized as the students debated who they wanted to encounter the posters, and thus what kinds of dialogue and ideas they hoped the posters would prompt. This debate was particularly appropriate to the space of this alternative school, which occupies a floor within a much larger, multistory building. There is little outside this building to identify it as a school or educational setting. Additionally, the school itself has a number of spaces typically closed off from any general public. Considering all these factors, it was critically important to the students to choose places where the posters could spark debate from their peers and raise consciousness with school visitors. As such, social space, digital media and shared dialogue came together, creating a participatory culture that altered "the focus of literacy from individual expression to community involvement" (Jenkins, Clinton, Ravi, Robinson, & Weigel, 2009, p. 6). As the social space of the school was made a site for inquiry, the nature of the dialogue became transformed. The ratio of teacher and student talk was rebalanced, student voice became amplified, and their engagement with their original inquiry intensified.

The network of who the students communicated with and learned from went beyond the classroom teacher. Through this engagement of others, students confronted "what is typically unmentionable in an institutional setting" (Mills & Comber, 2013, p. 414), such as who they are as students, how stereotyped expectations of students of color exist in school settings, and what the potential is for nontraditional students to achieve. As the classroom teacher stated: "The projects were received very well and the posters created quite a buzz around school, which was a special experience for the student artists" (CAPE, 2018b). These transformations enabled the students to re-form their identities as actors within their schools, becoming agents of change, creating spaces for their reflection and generating new potential for their learning.

In the *Me Behind the Mask* curriculum, technology afforded students the ability to produce physical products and redefine school spaces, crafting opportunities for naming and challenging the hegemony of school spaces. Their use of mediated imagery went beyond their own individual identities to a broader sociocultural context, challenging the culture of school space. Their process highlighted how technology informs understandings of identity, and specifically, how identities become stereotyped, enculturated, and reproduced. They effectively pulled back the curtain that renders unseen the normative learning practices dominating classrooms.

Anger Pets: Curricular Example 3

Teacher Kindra H. is an art teacher at an urban elementary school. She, teaching artist Adrianne S, and a seventh grade class of students examined the use of social media in history and its role in personal contexts for a curriculum project, called *Anger Pets*. Students began their inquiry by analyzing how print media depicted people's struggles and mass protests during the Civil Rights Movement. They then investigated the present-day manifestation of civil rights within the Black Lives Matter movements, examining how young activists used social media to express their concerns about racial issues in the United States. These engagements deepened students' knowledge of how technology shapes information.

Using "anger" as a big idea, students investigated expressions of anger through this historical lens and made connections to their personal experiences with anger. Identity thus became a part of the curriculum, as students examined their own identities through the anchor of anger. They fabricated "anger pets"—sculptural embodiments of anger—out of various materials, including clay and fabric. Students then created videos and animations incorporating these figures. They thought about the causes, effects, and consequences of anger as they grappled with how to create sculptures that could "perform" their chosen emotional attributes. Students' conceptions of anger became expanded in the process.

As the unit progressed, opportunities to utilize the videos presented themselves, and the use of digital technology became materials that students shaped in order to communicate their messages. These technologies included cell phone videos, stop motion animation, and audio recordings. Students used this digital media to further explore how anger is depicted and shared in digital spaces, both personally and in a sociocultural context. The use of phones for video recording was convenient, but it is also the same technology used to document police brutality as a criminal justice tool as part of the Black Lives Matter movement. This connection was an important learning tool; it enabled students to interrogate the sociocultural implications of how anger, violence, and activism are depicted in digital spaces.

Kindra remarked on the relationship between technology and identity. As Kindra stated, digital media explorations enabled her students to "personify their anger, look at it objectively, and appraise how it impacts them" (CAPE, 2018c). As such, they had an opportunity to examine an aspect of their identity typically not addressed within academic curriculum. To concretize anger, students experimented with ways to make the attributes of their anger pets visible through technology explorations, and, as Kindra stated, making "choices in camera angles and movement, sound and some special effects that they invented" (CAPE, 2018c). She maintained that "using the technology allowed students to separate themselves from their own anger (something very personal), and view it objectively" (CAPE, 2018c). As such, "self-reflection and analysis were both possible because of the use of technology" (CAPE, 2018c). Further, digital media enabled the students to see from themselves to the other in their classroom. They gained new understandings of the commonality of anger, forging what Massey (2005) calls a "grounded connectedness" (p. 188). In Figure 1.4, an anger pet is surrounded by student reflections of different attributes of anger characteristics such as "anger is a lonely place." With this installation, they remade their classroom space by establishing a new collective identity, or connectedness, within it using media itself to express identities, emotions, and connectedness.

Kindra expanded curriculum to encompass the potential of their digital literacies for learning. For example, the particular uses of media in this

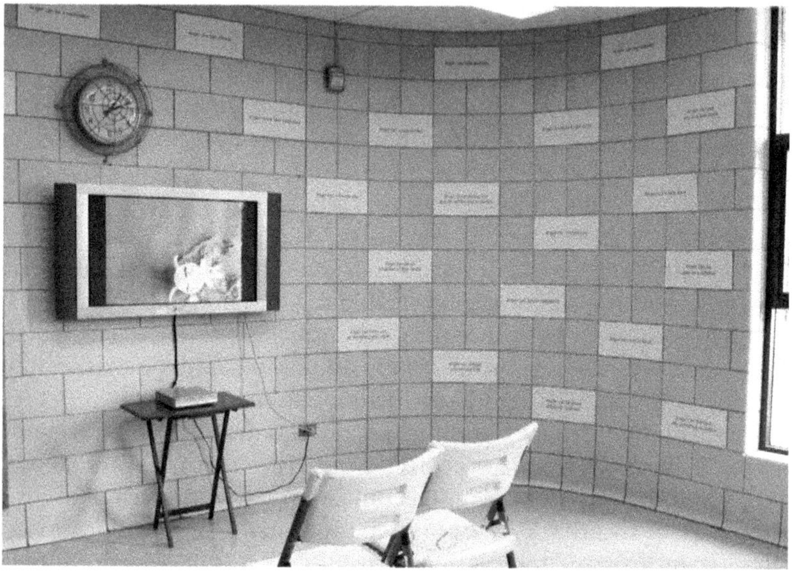

Figure 1.4. Anger pets installation.

unit connected students' life experiences and digital communication with historical research. As Kindra stated:

> The concept of anger with middle schoolers is strongly expressed on social media today. Cell phones play an important role in their lives. Using the cell phone's video camera was the natural choice. We took the same tool that is often used as their "weapon of destruction" and used it as a tool of expression. Students walked in with a great deal of prior knowledge in terms of the subject as well as the vehicle. This allowed them to concentrate on how they would express their ideas rather than learning the nuts-and-bolts of a new art medium. (CAPE, 2018c)

Counter to Leander and Boldt's (2012) contention that "design leaves out movement and surprise" (p. 43), Kindra's curriculum design enabled students to investigate and experiment with anger in multiple modalities. In this process, students were able to play with their expression, understanding, and representation of anger which resulted in "emergent combinations that [took] flight into something anew" (p. 43). Students had authorial control to visualize and give voice to their anger based on their individual conceptualizations and technological choices. By extending students' exploration of anger through digital media, representations became visceral and, when combined with the sculptural forms, called into question whose anger is valued and what anger must look like in order to be valued. Connecting this back to the sociocultural context, digital media allowed students to materialize something ephemeral, like an emotion, into an artifact which could then be examined to better understand identity.

Digital media flattened the normative hierarchy between students and teachers, adults and schoolchildren. As Kindra stated: "Because of the technology aspect, my students and I did quite a bit of role reversal, making them the teacher and me the student" (CAPE, 2018c). This enabled students to have a greater voice throughout the entire process, and because of that Kindra's students learned that "taking the lead is a responsibility and that there is a seriousness that has to be maintained in order to take the reins and direct what your artwork will say and how it will speak" (CAPE, 2018c). Her students rose to the occasion. This project expanded Kindra's instructional repertoire and her identity as a teacher, artist, and learner. She stated in her written reflections that she became "more flexible and willing to change, and release control" (CAPE, 2018c).

CONCLUSIONS

The above curricular cases examined how CAPE's arts teachers and students investigated space and identity through media arts integrated curriculum. We began by asking the following two questions: How can the possibilities of digital media accelerate or deepen student and teacher exploration and production of space and identity? How can digital media, expressed through artmaking, be used as material to reproduce or perform space and identity through the act of making? CAPE's teachers and students cocreated curriculum that diverged from the linearity of instruction, conceiving of digital technology as material to produce space and identity and creating opportunities for all to better understand the world and themselves. Through their agentive work, they conceived of space as dynamic, social, and permeable. In the *connectivity and collaboration* professional development workshop, teachers used technology to redefine the experiencing of space and incorporating the personal and political into their identities as co-creators. In *Me Behind the Mask,* students challenged the status quo concerning what constitutes a school space by elevating their voices within that space and becoming agents of change. In the *Anger Pets* curriculum, students' digital media use enabled them to examine anger personally and in a wider sociocultural and historical context.

An aesthetic pedagogy changed the emphasis of the type of materials and practices used for instruction including how to rethink the use of digital media. Rather than acquiring content knowledge through traditional literacies, such as written texts, students engaged with academic content using digital media as material. For example, in the *Me Behind the Mask* unit students examined world cultures through paper tubing, digitized posters, and the participation of their school community. As middle school students created *Anger Pets* and discussed their interpretations on films they made, they learned about the impact of media in historic and contemporary contexts. In both projects, technology was intrinsic to the artistic practice of production, and it enabled a process for students to delve into the complexity of academic concepts, such as understanding civil rights, posing problems, and to conveying their ideas.

Key to understanding technology as a material is the emphasis on manipulating and reassembling existing information or forms to achieve hybrid forms. iPads moved beyond a simple tool to become installations that enabled audiences to rethink the space around them. Digital images build upon what spaces, such as lunchrooms and hallways, are typically used for, redefining them so that they become sites of dialogic inquiry. In the curricular examples described above, a disruption in thinking and doing occurred around digital media that immersed teachers and students in remaking space, producing and reproducing identities. Students engaged with big ideas, such as conceptualizing how space creates norms of behavior and how they can disrupt such norms, thinking in new ways about who they are in school, and in turn, understanding how school has shaped their identities as learners. Through this process, their identities as agents of change, generative learners and active communicators grew.

As learners experimented with technology as material, their relationship with technology became a personal one shaped by their individuality, including their interests, aesthetics, and approaches to knowledge construction (Papert, 1990). Using digital media as material, multiple and personal approaches to meaning making were made possible, and thus the learners described above had the potential to create an "epistemological pluralism" (Turkle & Papert, 1990) in their learning spaces. As a result, normative classroom strategies for thinking and learning were expanded from one of "logic and planning" (Resnick & Rosenbaum, 2013, p. 167) to include personal and exploratory approaches to knowledge construction.

Learning spaces were rethought. The novel spaces exemplified in this chapter probed new understandings of individual, collective, and social identities through investigations and enactment of the materiality of digital media and space. Hallways, cafeterias, streets and community centers became materials to disrupt and reshape. CAPE students, teachers, and artists experienced and articulated their interrelatedness in working with digital material, and such interrelatedness was inherently spatial, reflecting the concept that sociability implies and requires spatiality (Massey, 2005). In experiencing and creating with the digital as material, learners saw and forged new identities, thus making new spaces for identities to interrelate.

Student voice was elevated and they became active agents of sociocultural debate. They took up the responsibility of making their own decisions while creating their own artistic products. They mined their own experiences, thoughts, and perspectives to drive their creations.

Through their participation in CAPE's arts integration professional development programs, teachers explored theoretical ideas about literacy and digital media, making these ideas more accessible within the realities of their instructional contexts. For these teachers and their students, digital media became an effective part of space reproduction, transformation, and identity formation because of its use as a material. This provided a context in which teachers and students could interrogate and push beyond the constraints of school spaces, countering hegemonic school based practices. This disturbance of the normative curriculum engendered by digital media encouraged teachers to diverge from the linearity of instruction and enabled students to experiment, shape, and convey their deeper understandings of the world. As such, they both teachers and students stepped out of their respective normative roles, collaboratively questioning and re-imagining learning in classrooms, contesting and reclaiming their shared spaces.

REFERENCES

Augé, M. (1995). *Non-places: An introduction to supermodernity*. (J. Howe, Trans.). New York, NY: Verso.

boyd, d. (2008). Why youth (heart) social network sites: The role of networked publics in teenage social life. In D. Buckingham (Ed.), *Youth, identity, and digital media* (pp. 119–142). The John D. and Catherine T. MacArthur Foundation Reports on Digital Media and Learning. Cambridge, MA: The MIT Press.

Chicago Arts Partnerships in Education (CAPE). (2018a). *Project ATLAS (year 3 teacher interview)* [transcription data file]. Chicago, IL: Author.

Chicago Arts Partnerships in Education (CAPE). (2018b). *Artist/researcher partnerships* [digital portfolio documentation]. Retrieved from http://at.bulb.re/pYu

Chicago Arts Partnerships in Education (CAPE). (2018c). *Project ATLAS (year 2 performance measure)* [digital portfolio documentation]. Retrieved from http://at.bulb.re/pYt

Darling-Hammond, L. (2013). *Getting teacher evaluation right: What really matters for effectiveness and improvement*. New York, NY: Teachers College Press.

Ito, M., Horst, H., Bittanti, M., boyd, d., Herr-Stephenson, B., Lange, P. G., … Robinson, L. (2009). Living and learning with new media: Summary of findings from the digital youth project. *The John D. and Catherine T. MacArthur Foundation Reports on Digital Media and Learning*. Cambridge, MA: The MIT Press.

Jenkins, H. (with Purushotma, R., Weigel, M., Clinton, K., & Robison, A. J.). (2009). Confronting the challenges of participatory culture: Media education for the 21st century. *The John D. and Catherine T. MacArthur Foundation Reports on Digital Media and Learning*. Cambridge, MA: MIT Press.

Kalantzis, M., & Cope, B. (2012). *Literacies*. New York, NY: Cambridge University Press.

Kohn, A. (2011). *Feel-bad education: And other contrarian essays on children and schooling*. Boston, MA: Beacon Press.

Kwon, M. (1997, October). One place after another: Notes on site specificity., *80*(Spring), 85–110.

Leander, K., & Boldt, G. (2012). Rereading "a pedagogy of multiliteracies": Bodies, texts, and emergence. *Journal of Literacy Research*, *45*(1), 22–46.

Massey, D. (2005). *For Space*. London, England: SAGE.

Mills, K. A., & Comber, B. (2013). Space, place and power: The spatial turn in literacy research. In K. Hall, T. Cremin, B. Comber, & L. Moll (Eds.), *International handbook of research in children's literacy, learning and culture* (pp. 412–423). London, England: Wiley Blackwell. Retrieved from https://doi.org/10.1002/9781118323342.ch30

New London Group. (1996). A pedagogy of multiliteracies: Designing social futures. *Harvard Educational Review*, *66*(1), 60–93.

Palfrey, J., & Gasser, U. (2008). *Born digital*. New York, NY: Basic Books.

Papert, S. (1990). A *critique of technocentrism in thinking about the school of the future* (circulated title: *M.I.T. Media Lab Epistemology and Learning Memo No. 2*). Media Lab, School of Architecture + Planning, Massachusetts Institute of Technology, Cambridge, Massachusetts. Retrieved from http://papert.org/articles/ACritiqueofTechnocentrism.html

Paul, C. (2015). *Digital art* (3rd ed.). New York, NY: Thames and Hudson.

Qvortrup, L. (2003). Digital poetics: The poetical potentials of projection and interaction. In G. Liestol, A. Morrison, & T. Rasmussen (Eds.), *Digital Media revisited: Theoretical and conceptual innovations in digital domains* (pp. 240–261). Cambridge, MA: MIT Press.

Ravitch, D. (2010). *The death and life of the great American school system: How testing and choice are undermining education*. New York, NY: Basic Books.

Resnick, M., & Rosenbaum, E. (2013). Designing for Tinkerability. In M. Honey & D. Kanter (Eds.), *Design, make, play: Growing the next generation of STEM Innovators* (pp. 163–181). New York, NY: Routledge.

Turkle, S., & Papert, S. (1990). Epistemological Pluralism and the Revaluation of the Concrete. *SIGNS: Journal of Women in Culture and Society*, *16*(1), 128–157.

Wilson, N. (2017). Sociotechnical and pedagogical barriers to technology integration. In M. Grassetti & S. Brookby (Eds.), *Advancing next generation teacher education through digital tools and applications* (pp. 19–36). Hershey, PA: IGI Global.

CHAPTER 2

MEDIATING DIALOGUE IN PUBLIC ONLINE AFFINITY SPACES

Chuck Jurich
University of North Carolina, Wilmington

Outside of our safe and comfortable Web 3.0 ideological bubbles, contemporary online discourse is increasingly marked by anti-social and uncivil commenting practices (Cheng, Bernstein, Danescu-Niculescu-Mizil, & Leskovec, 2017; Coe, Kenski, & Rains, 2014). Reagle (2015) describes "comment" as a kind of genre marked by short, asynchronous, and reactive communication, and while online comments can function to inform and improve, they are regularly used to manipulate, alienate, and shape readers and participants. Online discussion forums are open venues for "trolls," "haters," and "cyberbullies" who provoke, flame, intimidate, and victimize fellow commenters, often to regulate spaces (Phillips, 2015). From subtle jabs to the abhorrent invasion of privacy of "doxing" (or publicly documenting someone's contact, financial, and/or health information), online spaces can feel unwelcoming and unsafe.

Readers with any passing experiences with online commentary can attest to comments' general lack of intelligence, contention, and cruelty. The idea of authentic and sincere interaction amongst strangers online, in the year

Negotiating Place and Space Through Digital Literacies: Research and Practice, pp. 21–40

2018, may seem laughably naive, yet, these spaces exist. One such space is Talkbass (http://talkbass.com), a heavily trafficked public online discussion forum and virtual affinity space for people who play, or have an interest in, the bass guitar or upright bass musical instruments. Despite the massive size, heavy participation, and long history of the space (270,000 registered members and over one million discussion threads), the negative practices mentioned above are virtually nonexistent on Talkbass and helpfulness and civility are normalized behaviors.

This chapter investigates how people from diverse and distant locations, with wide ranging backgrounds, experiences, and world-views, engage with and learn from one another within online interactions in a coconstructed online affinity space. The purpose of this study is to examine and describe how discussion and interaction on Talkbass works with the belief that these insights can be used to improve dialogue and discussion in other contexts. I consider online discussion forums as virtual shared spaces for the potential negotiation, development, and mediation of human interactions through asynchronous dialogue.

Talkbass as an Affinity Space

Affinity spaces are physical, virtual, or hybrid spaces of shared passion, organized around a common interest or activity where the user generated content and interactional organizations reflexively shape each other (Gee, 2004). Affinity spaces offer multiple paths of participation, opportunities to engage with and learn with others, and a complex web of interest-driven interaction (Lammers, Curwood, & Magnifico, 2012). Affinity spaces are accessed via a "portal" such as the Talkbass website but also through common search engines which attract and invite new participants. Focusing on the space itself (content, signs, organization, portals) versus the community and "belongingness" of its individual members, Gee (2004) describes affinity spaces as having 11 specific characteristics but cautions that an affinity space is not an all-or-nothing concept, rather, the more the space has these characteristics, the closer it is to being a "paradigmatic affinity space" (p. 77). Using these criteria, Talkbass is a well-defined affinity space (see Table 2.1) with a clear common endeavor, multiple routes to participate and garner status, and the acceptance of a variety and range of knowledge.

The Off Topic Subforum of Talkbass and Authentic Dialogue

In an online affinity space, Gee (2004) argues that variables such as race, class, gender, sexuality, ability, and education level, while not eliminated, are backgrounded to a common or shared interest. Online affinity spaces

Table 2.1.
Characteristics of Affinity Spaces (Gee, 2004) and Talkbass.com as an Affinity Space

#	Characteristics of Affinity Spaces (Gee, 2004)	Talkbass as an Affinity Space
1	Common endeavor is primary, not race, class, gender, or disability	The "bass" is the common endeavor and all other member demographics are secondary to the shared interest.
2	Newbies, masters, and everyone else share common space	Experience, skill, real world fame (some members are notable musicians) are not requirements to participate.
3	Some portals are strong generators	On the web, top searches on information concerning the bass frequently lead to Talkbass.com.
4	Content organization is transformed by interactional organization	Members give feedback to and request features from gear manufacturers, particularly "boutique" builders who cater to players "geeking out" (Ito et al., 2010).
5	Both intensive and extensive knowledge are encouraged	Members help each other design and buy their bass "rigs" and encourage the modification of instruments, amplifiers, speaker cabinets, and more.
6	Both individual and distributed knowledge are encouraged	Members teach and learn how to be better bass players via discussion on technique, equipment, professionalism, band management, and more.
7	Dispersed knowledge is encouraged	Members discuss and link to topics that are outside the scope of the bass, particularly true for the Off Topic sub-forum addressed in this study.
8	Tacit knowledge is encouraged and honored	The most common inquiries in the space are questions based on tacit knowledge and real world experience: "Has anyone tried ____?"
9	There are many different forms and routes to participation	Participation takes place in a variety of ways including reading (views are counted), "liking" posts, starting a thread, contributing a post, and moderating a subforum.
10	There are lots of different routes to status	Status comes in many forms including being a moderator, "Supporting Member," or super-user, starting a popular thread, accumulating "likes" and "points," contributing highly specialized knowledge, and more.
11	Leadership is porous and leaders are resources	Overt leaders include paid staff and moderators. Some superusers have earned leadership roles and can influence member behaviors and interactions. All members can report posts for moderation.

are unique in that they provide opportunity for individuals who may not share the connections typically associated with one another to gather and share common ground (Black, 2007). While the bass is the endeavor that initially brings participants together on Talkbass, there is also an active "Off Topic" subforum where the same members congregate to discuss anything and everything *except* playing the bass. After receiving good advice on what bass or amplifier to buy, appreciative participants return to the site inquiring about nonbass related subjects such as their career, relationships, health concerns, or how to deal with road rage, deadbeat landlords, grief/death, and countless other personal topics. Much like an "edge city" (Garreau, 1991), a growing satellite city that would not exist without the larger and more established central city, the Off Topic subforum has become its own destination for many members. Off Topic is a unique space to study in that the one interest that brought participants together is relegated but the social connections from the larger affinity space still links members. As a result, Off Topic discussions are diverse and unpredictable, like putting all motorcycle enthusiasts together to discuss their relationships with their parents, and this diversity provides opportunities for rich dialogue.

The term *dialogue* is used to describe an act of creation by people who authentically want to understand one another and solve problems (Freire, 1970). The Freirian concept of *authentic dialogue* is about unveiling the limit-situations and the obstacles that come with revealing the truth itself. When discussing topics and problems, what are the obstacles (limits) that create these problems and what are the actions (limit-acts) that might help solve them? I approach the study from a critical perspective of new literacies where online affinity spaces such as Talkbass have the potential to foster authentic dialogue between participants who have conflicting and contrasting value systems and world views. In many ways, online affinity spaces behave as "culture circles" where posters ask questions and generate themes of inquiry and the resulting discussions are attempts of the participants to make sense of their lives and the world by "reading the word" and "naming the world" in their posts and comments (Freire, 1970). Applying this framework to Talkbass, authentic dialogue may or may not occur in the discussions; however, disagreements and differing viewpoints are excellent starting points for potential dialogue.

The research question guiding the study was: what are the characteristics of dialogue in online affinity spaces when the discussion and subjects move away from the focal shared interest and what does this dialogue tell us about the spaces in which it occurs? Through studying the language of the comments, I looked to describe and map out threads and posts to better understand how discussions develop and how disagreements and conflict is negotiated. In this chapter, I first describe the research site and share the methods used in the study. Next, I outline the structure and attributes of Talkbass discussions using examples from recent threads. I conclude by detailing the characteristics of this affinity space that make it different from other online forums and identify five specific actions participants in any forum can do to help mediate and move discussions towards authentic dialogue.

METHODS

Site and Participants

Celebrating its 20th year in January of 2018, Talkbass (http://talkbass.com) has over 20 million public posts logged. There are over 80 subforums available for members that target various aspects of bass playing such as "Technique," "Strings," "Effects," and many more. The site of the research is the Off Topic subforum which is the third most popular subforum (2.4 million posts) behind "Basses" (5.1 million) and "Amps and Cabs" (2.8 million). All discussion threads are public and open for anyone in the world to read. (Note: Readers can view all the threads mentioned in this chapter and follow along with the data presented.) Membership is required in order to post however anyone can browse, read, and search the forums. There are vast numbers of "lurkers," members and nonmembers, who only read threads as well as highly visible "super-users" with thousands of authored posts. Any member can be reprimanded and/or banned from making posts for breaking forum rules. Membership is free but "Supporting Members" and "Gold Supporting Members" pay an annual membership fee and have additional benefits, most notably the ability to buy and sell musical equipment/gear on the site and an advertisement-free spatial environment.

Data Collection

Data for the study comes from the publicly available Off Topic discussion subforum (found at http://www.talkbass.com/forums/off-topic-bg.34/). Over a 4-month period, I read and sorted the most recent Off Topic threads (n = 680) searching for "data-rich" discussions for close post-by-post analysis. Specifically, I looked for threads that had: (1) an original post with an identifiable question or generative theme posed, (2) a focus on social or political issues where participants had differing perspectives, experiences, and/or opinions, (3) at least 40 posts in the thread at the time of analysis (evidence of engagement), and (4) evidence of multiple voices and many participants within a thread (not just 3–4 people contributing all the posts in a thread). At the time of this writing 22 of the 680 threads met this criteria; within these 22 threads, approximately 1,800 posts were collected for analysis.

Data Analysis

Data was analyzed using the method of *categorical aggregation,* or the sorting and rendering of information into large clusters of ideas and providing details that supported the themes (Creswell, 2007). Specific strategies used were reading posts and assigning codes to them, reducing related codes to themes and categories, writing analytical memos, relating categories to one another, and relating categories to the theoretical framework. I used a *process coding* scheme, focusing on the actions and interactions of participants in response to situations or problems (Saldaña, 2009). I chose this scheme because interactions between posters were often done with an objective or goal in mind (e.g. "complimenting," "clarifying," or "telling their story") or dealing with a problem or issue (e.g. "disagreeing"). For example, in the thread "How do you deal with road rage?" (MJ5150, 2017), the member Funkhead posted a comment and mentions another member, @OP>>. (Note: all "screen names" mentioned in this chapter are real however they are likely pseudonyms.)

> **Funkhead:** I am a trucker and I have to constantly remind myself of all that is at stake. I don't want to ruin my career or risk hurting someone. @ OP>> Thanks for posting this. I really needed a reminder after this week. (MJ5150, 2017, post 32)

Funkhead's post was coded as "agreeing" (with the preceding comment) and "appreciating" for thanking the member @OP>>. Process codes exclusively take on the form of gerunds (verbs used as nouns) and can suggest or capture the processes taking place in the data.

THE STRUCTURE OF ONLINE DISCUSSION SPACES

Threads and posts on Talkbass have consistent and identifiable structures and characteristics. Threads begin with an original post where the "Original Poster" (OP) poses a question or a generative theme for discussion. For example, Ironbar started the Off Topic thread: "Advice needed: Seriously considering divorce." In the first lines of the initial or "original post" he writes:

> **IronBar:** I ask this question here because with the exception of BassCliff, I've never met any of you in person, and this forum provides a modicum of anonymity. For reasons I won't dwell on, I'm seriously considering divorce from my spouse. (Ironbar, 2017, post 1)

The theme of divorce is introduced and the question of what the poster should do is presented. Sometimes the question/theme is in the thread title itself such as in the thread "Anyone here have any stories/advice about immigration abroad?" (anavar, 2017).

After the start of the thread, there are three main categories of posts that follow: (1) *My Two Cents*, brief monologues where posters share their thoughts and ideas, (2) *Contention to Moderation,* posts which center on winning the debate and being "right," and (3) *Community to Mediation,* posts which focus on social relationships and discovering the object of knowledge of the topic. Figure 2.1 outlines the structure of online discussion spaces on Talkbass and shows the relationships between the original post and the three main categories of posts in a thread. After the original post, early comments that follow are typically *My Two Cents* posts but as participants start to respond to each other and not just the OP, discussions fracture and grow in many dialectic directions at once. Threads simultaneously turn to contentious disagreements that can lead to interventions by the Talkbass staff moderators (described in the *Contention to Moderation* section*) and* evolve into community building spaces leading to mediated dialogue (described in the *Community to Mediation* section). While the model appears linear, the actual processes and interactions in a discussion thread are dynamic and multiple.

My Two Cents Posts

In *My Two Cents* posts, participants share their stance, thoughts, and opinions on the question or generative theme introduced in the Original Post. The name originates from the casual, opinionated, and often flippant feel to the posts. They are ubiquitous, easily representing over half of all posts studied. While they can appear at any time, *My Two Cents* posts are particularly prevalent early in threads. A typical *My Two Cents* post is *Think/Splaining* which has the general structure of "I think (blank) because (blank)." In response to the OP, geegeedemocracy, in the thread "Going to lunch with my ex," Chicory Blue, *Think/Splained*:

> **Chicory Blue:** Trying to hold together a relationship that's in the process of falling apart is just delaying the inevitable and hurting yourself more in the process.... If there's any hope for you at all, it isn't here and now, not

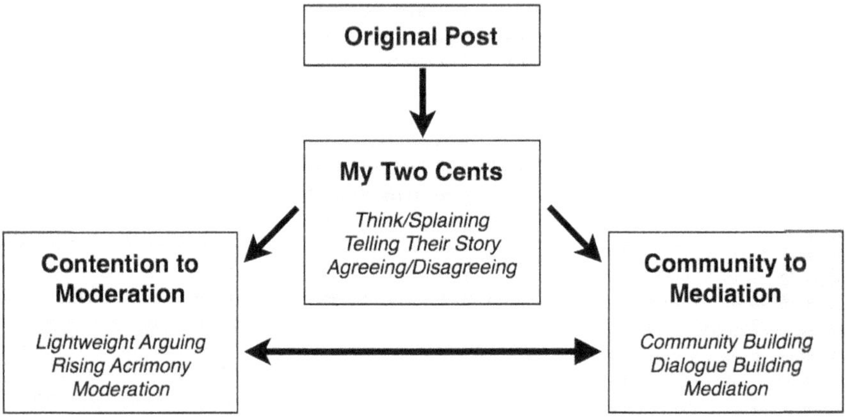

Figure 2.1. The structure and relationships between post categories on Talkbass.

> while everything is still in flux and volatile. Be brave, let it go, and find your peace elsewhere. (geegeedemocracy, 2017, post 9)

Chicory Blue states what he/she thinks, "let it go" for now, but also explains why, (because) "everything is still in flux and volatile." The post is thoughtful and his/her explanation is evident however many posters emphasize the "I think" portion but are light on the "because." For example, Joedog responded to the OP: "Go into it w/an open mind, but don't expect much. Best of luck!" (geegeedemocracy, 2017, post 21). The post is casual and supportive but does not explain why the OP should not expect much from the lunch meeting.

Some posters use narrative structure to express their stance or opinion. *Telling Their Story* posts highlight a similarity or connection between the OP's situation with their own. Stories are engaging, personal, and compelling but they also function as a rhetorical device to organize an argument. For example, member Funky Ghost shared his story about trying to get back together with his ex:

> **Funky Ghost:** I am currently dating my ex wife.... We have talked about all the reasons why we came to an end and were completely honest about it all. We accepted our parts in it (an important step to have a real shot at a reboot imo) and we have cautiously been working our way back to a full relationship. I made it clear, yesterday in fact, of my intention to win her heart back. It was received well Take it slow, talk and be honest with yourself and her about your reasons for being there. (geegeedemocracy, 2017, post 23)

Through his story, Funky Ghost shared his stance on the topic and his explanation is embedded in the narrative itself suggesting that if he and his ex can make it work, maybe it can also work for the OP. He advises, "take it slow, talk and be honest with yourself and her."

Another common variety of *My Two Cents* category is *Agreeing/Disagreeing* posts. Here, participants post in an affirmative or negative response to the question or generative theme of the OP or posts that come before them. The posts tend to be accompanied by a quote or reference to what they are agreeing/disagreeing with. In the thread "Man, are we really this sensitive? Do we need to be offended THIS badly?" the OP, two fingers, does not so much ask a question as much as *Think/Splains* on a topic and then asks who agrees with him. The subject of the thread is a Dove soap TV commercial where a Black woman takes off her shirt to reveal a Caucasian woman underneath. The OP became aware of the commercial when he saw many posts on Facebook that were critical of the ad, commenting on its racist undertones because it visually suggests that soap cleans the Black woman and transforms her into a Caucasian. After viewing the commercial, two fingers vehemently *Think/Splained* in a lengthy initial post that he did not think it was racist at all and inquired who agreed or disagreed. Mayatch disagreed:

> **Mayatch:** It's an ad for soap; it shows a black woman turning into a white woman. I don't think it should require huge logical leaps to see how that could offend someone. Did you see the pictures in the linked article of old soap ads literally showing scrubbing the black off people? (two fingers, 2017, post 56)

The tone of posts matters. In general, "agreeing" feels affirming and "disagreeing" feels more like a slight; however, variations of *Agreeing/Disagreeing* can often flip the tone of the post. Further, "agreeing *but*" may be perceived as picky and argumentative and "disagreeing *but*" can feel open-minded and compromising. For example, bholder who was the first to reply in the thread, agreed with the OP two fingers but in a variation ("agreeing but") commenting: "I'm not terribly offended, personally, but I think it was an incredibly stupid move and understand those who are offended." (two fingers, 2017, post 2).

Alone, *My Two Cents* posts read like a series of monologues, and considered alone are not dialogic in the sense that the comments are only in relation to the Original Post. However, *My Two Cents* posts serve as important raw discussion materials needed when moving towards potential dialogue later in the thread. While expressed opinions and lived experiences are important to the ones sharing, Freire and Macedo (1995) argue that stories are only useful to authentic dialogues if they can be connected to the larger issues that they frame. Lived experiences are good points of departure but participants have to universalize them. The exchanging of stories turn dialogue into conversation overly focused on the individual and removed from the "object of knowledge" while universalized posts are arguably the most convincing.

Contention to Moderation Posts

After sharing their initial "two cents" comments, participants in *Contention to Moderation* posts start to respond to each other's comments and not just the OP. These posts focus on the debate between thread posters, from "contention" (when two posters express that they disagree with one another) to "moderation" (when the rules of the virtual affinity space are enforced or threatened to be enforced). Talkbass has 10 rules that guide member interaction including "respect your fellow members" and strict moderation of culturally insensitive remarks and trolling (Talkbass, 2018). The Off Topic subforum has additional rules with a heavy emphasis on the restriction of discussions concerning religion and politics:

> Religious/political discussions are challenging enough to moderate when people are face-to-face.... In an impersonal, anonymous medium such as this, such threads tend to require constant moderation, create enemies out of prior friends, and generate more hate and anger than anything else.... If you want to discuss religion on TalkBass, the limited-access Lounge Lobby forum is available for such discussion (Supporting Membership required). (john turner, 2007, post 6).

The moderators recognize the limitations of the medium and the potential for contention with these topics. Off Topic moderators often remind participants of forum rules and adapt rules to current events. For example, gun advocacy/gun control is now a banned topic. The moderator Robert R. Tyler explained: "Much like politics, these threads tend to only breed contention amongst the membership even if the initial intention of a thread was good" (Brian R. Tyler, 2016, post 1). Violators of any forum rules face warnings, suspensions, and possible banishment.

Even with nonforbidden topics, contention and disagreement still occurs. I describe contentious posts as *Lightweight Arguing*. Here participants keep to the topic but dig in their heels and try to convince the other side that their proof is suspect, thinking is flawed, or experiences are irrelevant. The primary goal is to win the argument. The thread "Is Billy Joel disgusting for having a kid at age 68?" is an insightful example of how *Lightweight Arguing* can develop. After a series of *My Two Cents* posts, two camps formed. Arguing against Billy Joel having kids at age 68, blue4 wrote: "There's enough data out there to suggest that very old parents have a higher risk of having autistic children so myself I would never do it, regardless of the womans age. !" (GK Growl, 2017, post 46). Jazz Ad rebutted:

> **Jazz Ad:** First it's only the mother's age. Then it increases for younger moms too. Finally, the risk goes from .5 to 2%. Which basically means you have no control over it. It isn't a sound enough reason to orient a personal choice. (Gk Growl, 2017, post 63)

Typically, debate would continue however blue4 did something unusual in *Lightweight Arguing* and acknowledged the point. Referencing Jazz Ad, blue4 wrote: "There's enough for me. That's sound enough. I didn't criticize him in my post, just stating I wouldn't do it myself." (GK Growl, 2017, post 73). The comment from blue4 that the evidence was "sound enough," was a courteous concession, though blue4 did reiterate in the end "I wouldn't do it myself." However, this exchange represents only one small strand in a complex rope of interactions from multiple members on the topic. Jumping in and agreeing with Jazz Ad's earlier post, Buldog-5151bass sarcastically added "How DARE you start arguing facts here. : D" (GK Growl, 2017, post 75). This comment provoked blue4 to rebut and reiterate: "A quick Google search shows that the 'facts' are far from settled. As I stated before, there's enough there regarding not just autism but other mental health issues to give me pause." (GK Growl, 2017, post 76). This exchange shows how, even if two participants can come to an understanding on an issue, the dynamic and multiple nature of online forums keeps the interaction on edge. There is a bit of uneasiness involved in *Lightweight Arguing* and while it typically ends in a "tie," where both sides make their point but no one changes their mind, there is always the threat that it may escalate. While tolerated, *Lightweight Arguing* does not help build positive relationships leading to community.

Escalating beyond *Lightweight Arguing* are posts that dispense with the care of civil debating and moves towards antisocial and negative behaviors. I call these posts *Rising Acrimony* in order to highlight the "bitterness" that is central to the comments and they include posting practices such as dismissing, judging, jabbing, sarcasming, name calling, and more. In the thread concerning the Dove soap advertisement, Pbassmanca viewed the commercial and agreed with the OP: "Whats the problem? To me this is just smug idiots looking under every rock to find something racist" (two fingers, 2017, post 148). Here, he/she calls anyone who disagrees with them a "smug idiot" and dismisses the issue/topic outright. Sarcasm in particular is used to silence, dismiss, belittle, or negate another posters response. In response to the Billy Joel question, Gravedigger Dav wrote

"Trouble finding something that offends you this morning?" (GK Growl, 2017, post 39), effectively dismissing the OP. Practiced under the guise of humor, sarcasm divides and polarizes. As I will elaborate in the next section, humor is essential to developing positive social relationships in Talkbass, but sarcasm creates two groups: those who agree with the quip and those who are stung by it. *Rising Acrimony* such as name calling and sarcasming is regularly reported and watched closely by moderators because it leads to division, something Talkbass moderators take great measures to avoid.

Moderation

Off Topic has four moderators who participate in discussions and enforce the general rules of Talkbass as well as the specific rules of the Off Topic subforum. The two biggest areas of concern on Off Topic are politics and "divisiveness." When the threads dip into forbidden topics (e.g., guns and gun control, politicians) or specific posts are deemed in violation of rules, moderators privately contact the poster and issue warnings and consequences using a point system similar to the one used for driver's licenses (soulgeezer, 2007). While moderation takes place mainly in the background and is rarely addressed openly, the status of suspended or banned members shows up in all of their prior posts which remain even if they are banned. Anyone can report a post for being in violation of forum rules as all posts have a "Report" button at the bottom of the post. Although there are only four moderators in Off-Topic, every member is essentially an apparatus of the site's moderation team (Althusser, 1971).

Nearly all references to moderation that I observed in the threads studied were self-imposed. For example, in the thread "Anyone here have any stories/advice about immigration abroad?" the poster MJ5150 hinted that the United States was not necessarily the ideal country it is typically depicted. When asked by another member to elaborate with some details (*Lightweight Arguing*), MJ5150 responded by naming four or five issues but stopped him/herself short saying "There are others, but it will quickly become argumentative and divisive it I were to go into details." (anavar, 2017, post 37). Later on, in the same thread, member Oddly agreed and added to MJ5150's sentiment but limited his/her comments writing: "And that's all I'm gonna say because expanding on that will get this thread closed and me banned" (anavar, 2017, post 39). Self-silencing is common and highlight how hegemony (Gramsci, 1971) works in Talkbass; the four moderators do not control the behaviors of the posters as much as the members controlling themselves via self-censorship and reporting. The situation is dialectic; a top-down *and* grassroots power dynamic. When challenging topics are introduced, such as the Dove soap advertisement, both self-moderation and site-moderation come into play. Commenting on the tenuous civility, the OP, two fingers, wrote: "Hey we are almost 8 pages into a civil conversation about this! Yay us! (:hyper:)" (two fingers, 2017, post 139). Ultimately, the moderators decided to shut down the thread as it was deemed "divisive" and "too political" to continue. Moderator Chris Fitzgerald explained:

> **Chris Fitzgerald:** Interesting discussion. Unfortunately, the issues of race relations, racial sensitivity, race baiting, and racial "dog whistles" have become embedded in the national consciousness as a political football at this time.... After some mod discussion, the consensus seems to be that the subject of "is this racist or are people too sensitive to racial issues these days" is inherently political in today's current divisive climate; to imply that something appears racist is easily construed as taking a side, as is denying that something is racially charged. Personally, I find this sad, but have to admit that these are the times we live in. For this reason, this topic is considered too political for TB because it is too likely to divide. (two fingers, 2017, post 177)

The Talkbass users' fear of divisiveness prevent discussions to linger too long in contention because the well-being of the affinity space is more important that the individual members' right to debate. While the moderators' decision can be viewed as silencing perspectives and voices, the moderators argue it is to protect the community as a whole. The strategy of the moderators is to restrict certain subjects, but perhaps it is not topics that are divisive but how participants discuss with one another that divides.

Community to Mediation Posts

Community to Mediation posts build positive, playful, and meaningful interactions between posters and lead towards the mediation of dialogue. Community building in Talkbass is accomplished through persistent attention to the spatial mood as well as the contributions and well-being of other members. In the thread "How we react to death," the OP, OldDog52 (2017), shared a story about how he did not cry when his parents died, nor when 58 people were killed in the Las Vegas shootings, but he did cry when the musician Tom Petty passed away recently. He felt guilty about it. After 20 posts of sincere and personal discussion, the OP wrote "Thanks everyone for the thoughtful comments." *Community Building* posts show appreciation, sympathy, empathy, support, and more. Joking in particular was one of the most common types of *Community Building*. No matter how dire the topic, participants joked frequently, and members showed appreciation for the humor.

In the thread "Advice needed: Seriously considering divorce," member Catcauphonic joked that the OP should consider the timing when scheduling the sit-down talk with his wife: "I'd move that ultimatum date up till the week before Christmas ... gives you enough time to get her some gifts if she accepts. Otherwise, you get yourself something nice ;). I kid, I kid." (Ironbar, 2017, post 35). Even the serious acts of rule enforcement come with humor and positivity: "Transgressions will result in a thwack from the Modstick. You don't want that, do you?" (john turner, 2007, post 5). Joking was done to lighten the mood, to provide a break from intensity, but also to keep participants engaged and reading. Unlike sarcasming, which functions to divide, joking is for everyone and thus helps build community.

Dialogue Building posts address and focus on the object of knowledge in the question or generative theme. These posts involve making connections, speculating, observing, contextualizing, and universalizing ideas from specific stories to larger themes. Before the Dove soap ad thread was shut down by the moderators, member mellowinman focused on the complexities of the object of knowledge in his story:

> **mellowinman:** Let me offer some attempted wisdom. I have been dating interracially for quite some time now, and one thing I've learned is that I'm about 1/2 as smart as I always thought I was. So when people of other ethnicities talk to me, I really try to listen and understand, and let go of my preconceived notions. I was raised in the 60s white suburbs, and I harbor all kinds of dumb stereotypes, and false assumptions. I caution the women I date that I may be an absolute idiot at times, and ask that they be understanding, and help me to learn.... Before we make an assumption about anything, it's a good idea to try and look at it from the other person's point of view. I would rather be a bit silly, and oversensitive towards others than just blatantly disregard anyone's feelings. (two fingers, 2017, post 51)

mellowinman's post starts by *Telling Their Story* ("I have been dating interracially ...") and then later *Think/Splains* his stance on the topic when he writes (I think that) "before we make an assumption about anything, it's a good idea to try and look at it from the other person's point of view." What makes this post different than a *My Two Cents* post is how he helps build dialogue by positioning himself as someone who, though he doesn't intend to, has made and will continue to make "dumb stereotypes" and "false assumptions" concerning race. He has learned that he is "half as smart as I always thought I was" and if you listen to his "wisdom," you'll be smarter than him. It highlights the object of knowledge of the thread and suggests that understanding race is complicated so we should "really try to listen and understand." The post helps pose new questions: Can I be a good person and also say and do things that are perceived as racist?

Mediation posts were the most rare of all the subcategories of posts however they are some of the most important kinds of posts on the site. *Mediation* posts attempt to identify the "limit-situation" of the object of knowledge. Freire (1970) describes limit-situations as obstacles to ones' liberation with dialogue as the primary tool to reveal and overcome these limits. Limit-situations are not closed borders where possibilities end, but instead, exposed borders where possibilities begin. For example, in the thread "How do you deal with road rage?" (MJ5150, 2017) posters responded with their tactics but ultimately the topic developed into a debate between two world views, "the world is full of idiots who happen to be driving" versus "the world is full of good people who happen to make errors while driving" but this observation was never shared overtly in the thread. It takes an unusual participant to read all the posts, synthesize what has been written, identify the themes in the thread, and then summarize the findings for all the other participants. It is rare but exactly what is needed to push a typical *My Two Cents* discussion into mediated dialogue. Participants did come close. After many anecdotes of road rage committed and averted, ToneMonkey commented: "I'm starting to appreciate that certain threads here at TB are excellent training for the discipline of just walking away, ignoring the people, and breathing deeply." (MJ5150, 2017, post 73). ToneMonkey shows appreciation (*Community Building*) but also makes a key act in mediation which is to summarize contributions to the thread. Responding to a poster complaining about bicyclists on roadways, member slobake refocused the thread to the object of knowledge and began to connect this post with the larger limit-situation.

> **slobake:** Anyone can see insane/jerky people using all sorts of transportation. If there is an us vs them it is regular folks who are just trying to get to work and or home and morons who think the roads were built for them alone. What form of transportation they are using is not the problem but attitude is. (MJ5150, 2017, post 91)

The post draws attention to the idea that it is not cars or bicycles that are the problem (limit) but the attitude of drivers who believe the road space is theirs alone. Finding the limit-situation is a challenging act requiring effort, attention, and mediation. While rare, it is certainly doable, especially when posters know that it is even a possibility.

WHY IS TALKBASS SO ... NICE?

While I was able to describe posts and see definite patterns and characteristics within threads, I began to wonder why discussion on Talkbass stay civil and do not devolve in ways I have observed in other forums and comments sections of websites. There are similarities between the members (English speaking, mainly Western, generally males) but differences that matter (region, age, socioeconomic status, political leanings, and affiliations) are regularly revealed in discussions, yet, there is consistent civility. I posed the question "Why is Talkbass so nice?" to members and many responses pointed towards the role of enforced moderation on the site but a second factor that emerged was the focus on positivity and community in the affinity space. hrodbert696 wrote:

> **hrodbert696:** I think the thing about stricter moderation is that it not only cuts back the weeds but also helps make more room for positive growth to flourish. The mods can't make the positivity happen, that's to the credit of a lot of great TBers who share their experiences and insights generously here.... So for a healthy community you need both - people willing to contribute as positive members of the community, and some enforcers to allow the positive stuff room to breathe so it doesn't get choked out. (SLIV, 2018, post 31)

The poster asserts that the "mods can't make the positivity happen." So while moderation is really important, it only "makes room" for members to do the work of contributing community building, and dialoging. He/she credits the Talkbass community's positivity and generosity. Highlighting the sharing culture of Talkbass, PWRL wrote:

> **PWRL:** I think it's partly the rules, but I think there's more to it. For one thing, this site is a tremendous knowledge base for all things bass-related. If you treat others well, people will be more likely to share knowledge with you, but if you're a jerk and you turn everybody off, you're likely to get ignored (SLIV, 2018, post 8)

The Off Topic subforum is an active space of the larger affinity space of Talkbass as a whole. This "tremendous knowledge base" is a highly desirable resource for everyone with an interest in the bass. Members give and receive and if you're a "jerk" you will not receive any help which is the central reason for participants to join the space in the first place. For many members sharing and giving through pleasant interactions are a satisfaction in itself. As member D M C wrote, "TalkBass, come for the bass info, stay for the joy of the membership" (SLIV, 2018, post 53).

Thus, on Talkbass, two conditions are present that help members learn and grow together: (1) active moderation and (2) supportive, positive interactions. Still, a strong "police" presence and "nice neighbors" do not inherently make a community and neither moderation nor courteousness can create dialogue where diverse people can learn from one another. Dialogue requires the skills and motivation to listen, appreciate, synthesize, connect, and mediate. I observed that threads with strong dialogue all had one or more key posts with certain characteristics. These are specific actions that posters can do to help move discussions towards mediated dialogue. The first two actions help build community, the second two help build dialogue, and the last one, mediating dialogue, is the most challenging but the ultimate goal.

- ***Demonstrating listening.*** Participating in threads is important but responding to specific posters builds community. Referencing, quoting, and acknowledging other posters demonstrates listening. Even a simple "I agree" with some elaboration (or clicking the "Like" button) makes posters feel like their contributions matter.
- ***Showing appreciation.*** One of the most simple ways to build community is to show appreciation for those who took the time to post thoughtful and reflective comments. "Thank you" or "I appreciate" go a long way towards supporting participants who oftentimes make themselves vulnerable in posts.
- ***Synthesizing.*** Synthesizing, summarizing, and looking for patterns in threads is a way of moving from personal opinions to identifying the object of knowledge.
- ***Making connections.*** Making connections and adding new contexts helps move individual stories to universalized themes. While anecdotes can be powerful, taking people's personal stories and generalizing them gives new life and potency to these anecdotes.
- ***Mediating dialogue.*** Through mediated dialogue, thread participants learn to identify and name the limit-situations, or the obstacles/limits that create the problems in their lives that they wish to solve. Once uncovered, the "limit-acts" of the generative theme can be addressed, explored, and acted upon to overcome the limit-situation.

CREATING CONDITIONS AND SPACES FOR DIALOGUE

I believe the data presented here shows that affinity spaces like Talkbass have the structure, stability, affordances, and diverse leadership to help participants mediate human interactions and better understand one another. I do not want to overstate the volume and magnitude of *authentic dialogue* (Freire, 1970) that occurs in discussions on Talkbass but the conditions for potential dialogue are well developed in the space. At its dialogic best, the Talkbass Off Topic subforum functions as a "third space" community (Gutierrez, Rymes, & Larson, 1995) that sits between the first "official script" of bass knowledge distribution and the second "counterscript" of trolling and flaming (which is actively squashed by moderation.) In these third space discussions, many participants experience meaningful moments, when they entered looking for specific information or casual company but instead found themselves learning something new about the human condition or perhaps themselves. The affinity space brings people from far-away places together, positive interactions gives them important and meaningful experiences, but it is perhaps the community that develops, via third space discussion, that keeps them coming back.

As Gee (2004) defines them, most online discussion boards and comment sections lack a clearly articulated shared interest and are not well-defined affinity spaces. Without this "official script" of the space, counterscripts such as flaming and trolling can run rampant. In order to reign these practices in, the trend of popular news websites such as USAtoday.com and chicagotribune.com is to remove anonymous commenting with the hope that "real world" identities and the lack of anonymity would discourage transgressive practices and create greater accountability and more civil discourse (Shanahan, 2013). Despite these changes, *Lightweight Arguing* and *Rising Acrimony* are still normative behaviors on these sites. ESPN.com converted to Facebook-linked commenting in 2013 but quietly removed *all* comments from their site in July of 2018, even choosing not to archive comments from past content. ESPN isn't the first major site to eliminate comments altogether. *Popular Science* shut down its comments section in 2013 after expressing concern that comments could not only trigger flame wars, but change people's interpretation of the articles themselves (LaBarre, 2013). On these sites, the counterscript has overwhelmed the official script of the actual articles and content. The two factors that appear to matter the most in creating dialogic conditions in the Talkbass affinity space, moderation and community building, are rarely if ever present.

Writing in the late 1960s, and predating electronic communications as we know them, Freire's ideas on dialogue are very much applicable to contemporary online discourse and particularly to affinity spaces such as Talkbass. Freire (1970) argues that dialogue is not achieved when one person, expressing their opinion "deposits" ideas into another. It is not a simple exchange of ideas to be "consumed" by the posters as they read each other's anecdotes and stories. Dialogue is about discovering and acting upon the obstacles that come when new truths are revealed. For authentic dialogue to grow, participants must join willingly, participate if it matters to them, generate their own topics, and contribute what they are comfortable in contributing. Affinity spaces like Talkbass bring diverse people together to discuss their shared endeavor, but in the act of learning together via dialog, a shared social space is cultivated. This is evident in the popular Off Topic subforum where online identities develop, evolve, and change alongside parallel real world identities. For many members, this is a comfortable, engaging, and safe *place*, and places change us, even if they are digital.

REFERENCES

Althusser, L. (Ed.). (1971). Ideology and ideological state apparatuses. In *Lenin and philosophy and other essays*. New York, NY: Monthly Review Press.

Anavar. (2017, November 21). Anyone here have any stories/advice about immigration abroad? [Electronic message board]. Retrieved from https://www.talkbass.com/threads/anyone-here-have-any-stories-advice-about-immigration-abroad.1314086/.

Black, R. (2007). Digital design: English language learners and reader reviews in online fiction. In M. Knobel & C. Lankshear (Eds.), *A new literacies sampler* (pp. 115–136). New York, NY: Peter Lang.

Cheng, J., Bernstein, M., Danescu-Niculescu-Mizil, C., & Leskovec, J. (2017). Anyone can become a troll: Causes of trolling behavior in online discussions. *CSCW : Proceedings of the Conference on Computer-Supported Cooperative Work. Conference on Computer-Supported Cooperative Work, 2017*, 1217–1230.

Coe, K., Kenski, K., & Rains, S. A. (2014). Online and uncivil? Patterns and determinants of incivility in newspaper website comments. *Journal of Communication, 64*(4), 658–679.

Creswell, J. W. (2007). *Qualitative inquiry and research design: Choosing among five approaches* (2nd ed.). Thousand Oaks, CA: SAGE.

Freire, P. (1970). *Pedagogy of the oppressed*. New York, NY: Heinemann.

Freire, P., & Macedo, D. (1995). A dialogue: Culture, language, and race. *Harvard Educational Review, 63*(3), 377–402.

Garreau, J. (1991). *Edge city: Life on the new frontier.* New York, NY: Anchor Books.

Gee, J. P. (2004). *Situated language and learning: A critique of traditional schooling*. New York, NY: Routledge.

Geegeedemocracy. (2017, August 30). Going to lunch with my ex. [Electronic message board]. Retrieved from https://www.talkbass.com/threads/going-to-lunch-with-my-ex.1301411/

GK Growl. (2017, October 24). Is Billy Joel becoming a father again at 68 disgusting? [Electronic message board]. Retrieved from https://www.talkbass.com/threads/is-billy-joel-becoming-a-father-again-at-68-disgusting.1309478/

Gramsci, A. (1971). *Selections from the prison notebooks*. New York, NY: International Publishers.

Gutierrez, K., Rymes, B., & Larson, J. (1995). Script, counterscript, and underlife in the classroom: James Brown versus *Brown v. Board of Education*. *Harvard Educational Review, 65*(3), 445–471.

Ironbar (2017, November 26). Advice needed: Seriously considering divorce [Electronic message board]. Retrieved from https://www.talkbass.com/threads/advice-needed-seriously-considering-divorce.1314777/

Ito, M., Baumer, S., Bittanti, M., boyd, d., Cody, R., Herr-Stephenson, B., ... Tripp, L. (2010). *Hanging out, messing around, and geeking out: Kids living and learning with new media*. Cambridge, MA: MIT Press.

john turner. (2007, April 20). Off topic forum rules: Read before you post. [Electronic message board]. Retrieved from https://www.talkbass.com/threads/off-topic-forum-rules-read-before-you-post.952126/

LaBarre, S. (2013, September 24). Why we're shutting off our comments. *Popular Science*. Retrieved from https://www.popsci.com/science/article/2013-09/why-were-shutting-our-comments

Lammers, J. C., Curwood, J. S., & Magnifico, A. M. (2012). Towards an affinity space methodology: Considerations for literacy research. *English Teaching: Practice and Critique, 11*(2), 44–58.

MJ5150 (2017, November 18). How do you deal with road rage? [Electronic message board]. Retrieved from https://www.talkbass.com/threads/how-do-you-deal-with-road-rage.1313514/

OldDog52 (2017, October 3). How we react to death [Electronic message board]. Retrieved from https://www.talkbass.com/threads/how-we-react-to-death.1306342/

Phillips, W. (2015). *This is why we can't have nice things*. Cambridge, MA: MIT Press.

Reagle, J. (2015). *Reading the comments: Likers, haters, and manipulators at the bottom of the web.* Boston, MA: MIT Press.

Saldaña, J. (2009). *The coding manual for qualitative researchers.* Thousand Oakes, CA: SAGE.

Shanahan, M. (2013, July 16). More news organizations try civilizing online comments with the help of social media. *Poynter*. Retrieved from https://www.poynter.org/news/more-news-organizations-try-civilizing-online-comments-help-social-media/

Soulgeezer. (2007, February 13). Can someone explain "infractions" and "points"? [Electronic message board]. Retrieved from https://www.talkbass.com/threads/can-someone-explain-infractions-and-points.309494/

SLIV. (2018, January 6). Why is Talkbass so... nice? [Electronic message board]. Retrieved from https://www.talkbass.com/threads/why-is-talkbass-so-nice.1321436/

Talkbass. (2018). Terms of service and rules. [Electronic message board]. Retrieved from https://www.talkbass.com/help/terms

two fingers. (2017, October 9). Man, are we really this sensitive? Do we need to be offended THIS badly? [Electronic message board]. Retrieved from https://www.talkbass.com/threads/man-are-we-really-this-sensitive-do-we-need-to-be-offended-this-badly.1307120/

Tyler, B. R. (2016, August 15). Gun and gun control threads are no longer permitted here. [Electronic message board]. Retrieved from https://www.talkbass.com/threads/gun-and-gun-control-threads-are-no-longer-permitted-here.1238665/

CHAPTER 3

QUEERING TEXT

Literacies Surrounding Cyber Trolling

Matthew Thomas-Reid
Appalachian State University

If at its basic level literacy is concerned with the ability to read and write *text*, our present digitized reality requires us to stretch our collective imaginations to understand the word *text* in this new virtual context. What constitutes text, and who makes these decisions? When teachers using digitized versions of 30-year-old textbooks are still warning students to stay away from Wikipedia, it seems clear that the same antiquated processes by which we have vetted text to be suitable for educational purposes are often being employed in digital contexts, and that these processes could do with a good queering. In general terms, I mean to suggest here that a queer methodology can potentially reorient perspectives to destabilize tacit assumptions about a given topic. A queer methodology allows a consumer of contemporary digital texts in a higher education context the opportunity to construct a more robust set of meanings by considering

---

This chapter is based in part on a paper presented by the author at the Philosophy Education Society (PES) 2017 conference entitled "Trolling Toward the Human, Cyber Artifacts, Social Justice, and Queering of intercorporeality."

Negotiating Place and Space Through Digital Literacies:
Research and Practice, pp. 41–57

not only the body of an online text, but perhaps also the comments that troll underneath. Rhetorically, both "queer" and "troll" take on multiple meanings, and I to some extent 'play' with these meanings throughout this chapter. Methodologically, I begin with a theoretical framework for reconsidering how trolling comments might be understood as the articulation of oppressive opinions that are denied within normative public discourse. I then conclude by grounding the theory in a more concrete scenario of a discussion board about privilege used on a college campus. This chapter ought not be thought of as a set of instructional methods, rather an exploration of how, as university educators, we might reorient our relationship with particular types of online texts.

Beyond the slur that you might have heard during your school playground days, the word queer in an academic context has a more nuanced meaning, though it does manage to retain its irreverent disruptive quality, even as it is reclaimed and appropriated by the academy. Adam Greteman (2014) parses out the term succinctly through its versatility as multiple parts of speech:

> queer we realize here at the outset is a slippery term operating as a noun used to define people's identity (e.g., LGBT) and an adjective to modify theory. It might even come to operate as a verb that "makes strange" or queers something. (p. 420)

It is really in action, in this verb form, that queer has power, both as the action of queering text and also as the verb of doing queer work, the praxis and pedagogy of teaching queerly. Deborah Britzman (1995) points this out by suggesting that while many might "think the term queer as a noun or an identity, ... the queer and the theory in queer theory signify actions, not actors. It can be thought of as a verb, or as a citational relation that signifies more than the signifier" (p. 153).

In this way, when I talk about queering *text*, it does not necessarily imply gender or sexuality related textual content in the text; rather I use a queer methodology to disrupt the very idea of what text is and can be. Text might, in a postmodern sense, have a wide possible range of meanings, from Mark Lamont Hill's (2009) use of hip hop music as text to Kate Kedley's (2004) suggestion that teachers' bodies themselves might be read as text. Queer theory is well positioned as a lens through which to disrupt understandings of text in a digital era as queer because queer theory cannot be constrained into a single fixed definition and explication of method. Queer theory requires an understanding that normative, or dominant, culture is not fixed, and therefore the approaches to challenging these dominant structures also cannot remain fixed. Deborah Britzman (1995), "refuses to secure queer theory to a fixed content, to a set of guidelines" (p. 155).

Instead Britzman is attempting to "articulate a thought of a method rather than a pronouncement of content," to bring to pedagogical spaces consideration of what Edelman terms "unstable differential relations" (p. 155).

When reading an article online how often do you to scroll to the bottom and read the comments? As a consumer of these texts, it is almost a compulsion for me at this point to scroll down and see the trolls at work; somehow reading the candid, often angry comments contextualizes something for me, allowing a glimpse into a world outside of my sphere of influence. If we accept, as Nicola McClung (2017) writes, that "all texts are ideological, and all readers (and writers) are complicit in upholding or confronting the injustices reinforced in print," then why should we ignore the confrontations that play out in the spaces right below the text (p. 403)? There is something queer about these texts, these cyber artifacts that lurk just below the surface:

> I may provisionally call queer a text ... that not only works against narrativity, the generic pressure of all narrative toward closure and the fulfillment of meaning, but also pointedly disrupts the referentiality of language and the referentiality of images, what Pier Paolo Pasolini, speaking of cinema, called "the language of reality." (de Lauretis, 2011, p. 244)

Academic discourse has rules, and when you read the comments section under online articles there is a subversion of the rules, or what de Lauretis (2011) called the language of reality. There is something else queer in the comments of online trolls, and this is their ability to break the rules in reference to the taboo language of sex, although generally in oppressive and offensive ways. There is something queer in this action: "an antisocial politics of queer theory" (p. 254). de Lauretis goes on to suggest that the antisocial aspect in queer theory is beyond "political contestation, opposition, or antagonism," it is the inclusion of the overtly gendered and sexual. You do not have to go far in any comments section to see this highly sexualized language, often designed to emasculate their political enemies, as in the example of calling liberals "butthurt" or "Progressive Snowflake effeminate male cucks" (Neff, 2016, comments). Butthurt, a clear allusion to anal sex, and cuck, a term used to describe a man who lets other men have sex with his wife, are commonly used antiliberal epithet in online comments. Imagine a space where a person would hurl that type of insult at another—it certainly does not resemble the discourse in the academy or the digital spaces that the academy attempts to create. Returning to de Lauretis (2011), we might think of these comment sections as queer because they are "the space of a transit, a displacement, a passage and transformation, not a referential but a figural space (p. 246). I envision cyber trolling as a powerful contextual reference point for academic ideas;

in this space below the official text, one can examine often complex and important social responses to academic ideas. In short, the educator can see the often ugly truths about how ideas are being received by particular cross sections of the public.

Can the university educator ignore these spaces or texts held in them? Might anything be gleaned from these texts beyond the understanding that some people are just mean? What might it mean to teach with these digital artifacts created by cyber trolls? Employing another queer methodological technique, I come from a place of personal queer identity and draw on queer traditional practices like trolling to make sense of this online trolling phenomenon. Rich lessons can be gleaned from queer histories. Online spaces have proven replete with opportunities both for queers to troll their marginalized desires as well as queer consumers of cyberspace to witness hateful trolling by those who feel empowered in anonymous spaces (Adkins, 1998, p. 446) (Herring, Job-Sluder, Scheckler, & Barab, 2002, p. 371). How might texts gleaned from these spaces, which we might think of as *trolling artifacts,* be viewed as texts to be critically analyzed and from which new literacies might be developed? This critical analysis relates to Friesen's (2008) words that "when compared to their counterparts in the 'real' world, virtual artifacts manifest a pliability, brilliance, discontinuity, and disposability that can have educational value" (p. 111). Might we develop a literacy utilizing trolling artifacts to enrich learning experiences, and what lessons might pedagogues take from the phenomenon of cyber trolling in both of these contexts?

Using a phenomenological methodology and queer theoretical framework I seek to posit a queer approach to cyber trolling with a view to realizing its pedagogical potential in higher education classrooms. To clarify this purpose, suggesting value or potential in the examining of cyber artifacts does need to be approached with caution. Racism, sexism, homophobia, and transphobia abound in the realm of these comments, and any attempt to validate a perspective of hate is always problematic. The value of these trolls, as I suggest throughout this chapter, is often in their ability to elucidate the tacit beliefs that some consumers of texts might have and to more fully interrogate these trolls as a straw person as opposed to direct confrontation with students, and to address potentially problematic reception of the official text.

I juxtapose two specific usages of the word troll, contrasting the queer usage "wander[ing] around looking for sex" (Atkins, 1998, p. 446) with the online parlance of flaming and harassing hate speech (Herring et al., 2002). Trolling then becomes a linguistic bridge linking the queer experience of trolling for sex with the contemporary usage of troll, where online users fill discussion boards and chat rooms with offensive content that would likely not be used in civil face to face discourse (Herring et al., 2002,

p. 372). If we think of trolling in its simplest form as *to bring to the surface that which is hidden*, we might posit a shift from online technologies being used solely for students to demonstrate understanding toward trolling that which students might keep hidden both about themselves and others. In other words, to peek into the often dark and problematic ways that our students at the collegiate level interpret texts but may never share in class.

First, I explore how the phenomenon of trolling developed from queer nonnormative experiences intent on connection and how this notion of trolling evolved into modern day Internet parlance intent on disconnection. Next, I consider how we troll past normative spaces into hidden worlds created in response to the normative confines of dialogue in social justice classroom spaces. Finally, I suggest that these trolling responses to social justice topics might actually be used as "cyber artifacts," or texts (in a postmodern sense) to be critically interrogated within university classrooms, enriching collective understanding of human responses to social justice dialogue. Ultimately, I believe that using queer traditions, we might refigure trolling responses to social justice topics to push at the hidden desires for connection, however contentious, embedded in their meanderings. In short, how might the queer experience of trolling inform pedagogies?

A Queer Journey: An Alternate History of the Troll

My first lesson about flirting came with a warning: "stop looking at me like that faggot, or you will get a fist to the face." I suppose I must have stared a little too long at my middle school crush, and I learned a valuable lesson from the experience: I must keep this side of myself hidden from view. This was the mid-90s, and for the most part queer adolescence was about keeping a low profile. The year I went off to college, Matthew Shepard was beaten and left for dead on a Wyoming fencepost; that year I learned that the cost of inciting "gay panic" in straight guys could be death. I learned to be subtle in my advances; I learned to observe others and see their interest, while at the same time learning how to convey mine without drawing too much attention to myself. In short, I learned how to troll, in a very different sense of the word than we often consider today. No, this is not a memoir of a gay man cruising for sex, rather an exploration of a queer subjectivity, a history of how a community learned to keep certain "fragments of human capacities," hidden from view (Williams, 1995, p. 84). What lessons, if any, might the teacher take from the tradition of queer trolling? Considering this alternative meaning of trolling, I agree with Ernesto Martinez's suggestion that the educator might "think from … an understanding of identity and experience as useful resources for the acquisition of better, more accurate knowledge" (Martinez, 2012, p. 6).

When facilitating discussion in my classrooms I have, recently, began to think of myself as trolling my students. Lest you all begin harboring thoughts of calling my dean to warn her of a predator on campus, let me be clear about what I mean here: Fearing that students will simply parrot that which they see as "politically correct," I long to troll their thoughts, their feelings, their visceral understandings of the kinds of issues that arise from dialogue surrounding social justice in the classroom. Thinking from personal queer identity and experience is salient to my concern about dialogue in social justice classroom spaces insofar as there might be a limitation to what we can learn about each other, as "I will never know how you see red and you will never know how I see it. But this separation of consciousness is recognized only after a failure of communication" (Merleau-Ponty, 1964, p. 17). Because, you see, I consume the texts available in social media, I visit blog sites, I read the kinds of comments that students make about "liberal indoctrinating professors," and I look out over my classes and wonder, "just what are they thinking?"

With a queer mindset, I accept this limitation and seek acquisition of knowledge differently: *trolling* for these human fragments. I argue these trolling artifacts might actually be able to inform instruction. As an example, after reading numerous trolling artifacts that used 'human nature' as an argument against social justice education, I now actually teach a lesson interrogating the very notion of human nature. Drawing on both the phenomenological language of above referenced Maurice Merleau-Ponty (1964) and the queer methodological approaches of Britzman, Ahmed, and Butler, we can enrich classroom conversations around social justice by legitimizing the use of what I will refer to as cyber-trolling artifacts as a *straw person* entry point for interrogating social justice ideas in academic discourse. As a follow-up, we can develop means by which we might manage to troll student understanding much as the youthful version of me trolled to find out if that cute guy in the corner liked me.

Queer history is steeped in a tradition of both hiding fragments of human identity and developing techniques for trolling these fragments, therefore becoming a framework with which to uncover deeper human understanding. While a more detailed exploration of my multiple usages of queer and troll will unfold later in the chapter it is useful to understand that the term "trolling" has deeply queer roots, and can be traced to the ostensibly dead gay language known as *British Polari*, meaning to "wander around looking for sex" (Atkins, 1998, p. 446). As an artifact of gay history, trolling manifests itself beyond gay language codes into the gay hanky codes of the United States in the 20th century and even into hookup applications used commonly today.

Imagine in a cafe there is a businessman in an expensive suit at another table. Perhaps you are able to read his performance in terms of race, class, gender, mannerisms, and so forth. Imagine further that you have an application on your smartphone called Grindr, which allows users in close proximity to see their hidden queer desires. Imagine the surprise when the man pops up on your Grindr app with a profile that reads: *leather daddy ISO hookup*. Outside queer culture, this description seems baffling: you would need to know that *ISO* means in search of, and that *leather daddy* means an older dominant man. Consider the implications of trolling for fragments of humanity in this queered illustration: we are limited in our understanding of another's *meaning making* because we keep fragments of our identity in other worlds, often in cyber space, hidden from view. We phenomenologically structure our own realities in this way, as Norm Friesen (2008) writes, "the life world that the computer presents has its own, manifold, experiential times and spaces" (p. 111).

A queer perspective illustrates how virtual spaces harbor particular manifestations of identity that do not fit in normative discursive spaces. It should be made clear at this point that while historically marginalized communities have trolled to express aspects of self, modern cyber trolls are often manifestations of normative perspectives lashing out against a perceived loss of power. With this said, I invite you to join me in *trolling* these hidden worlds in order to enrich our encounters with others in the public world. If something of our identity and understanding is hidden in private spaces, then it is worthwhile to examine evidences of these private spaces that we might enrich our public dialogue around social justice.

Queers, Trolls, and the Intercorporeal

I use trolling as a linguistic bridge linking the queer experience of trolling for sex with the contemporary usage of the word where online users troll discussion boards and chat rooms with offensive content that would likely not be used in civil face to face discourse (Herring et al., 2002, 372). Imagine a person alone in their self-structured surrounding where a screen allows them perceived freedom to express themselves without regard for conventions of normative, or indeed even civil, discourse. Lacking in this scenario is a connection with others, which I identity as intercorporeality. Marjorie O'loughlin defines intercorporeality in *Embodiment and Education* as a "carnal bond between human subjects, indicating that embodied subjects are connected in their belonging to a common world" (Friesen, 2008, p. 94). Rather than suggesting a common bond is present in online spaces, I argue the lack of intercorporeality in the act of Internet trolling is what makes these thoughts salient—they are the result of private thought devoid of an encounter with the corporeal *other*.

Maurice Merleau-Ponty (1968) suggests in *The Visible and the Invisible* that intercorporeality outlines two connected spheres, the sphere of physical living and the sphere of empathy (Friesen, 2008, p. 94). Withdrawing from empathy of others in order to express often malicious and normatively inappropriate comments mirrors the tradition of trolling for queer sexual encounters insofar as they are both, at least in perception, rejected by a normative society that does not want to deal with the fact of their existence. My approach of connecting these ideas is queer because queer theory often utilizes "techniques to make sense of and remark upon what it dismisses or cannot bear to know" (Britzman, 1995, p. 154). When one reads a particularly inflammatory trolling comment online, a sort of queer moment occurs, "when the world no longer seems the right way up ... [and] the effect is "wonky" (Ahmed, 2006, pp. 561–562).

Perhaps you have read a comment in a discussion forum and thought to yourself "who could possibly write such a thing, let alone actually believe it?" Indeed, in an online post about a "privilege board" installed on my university campus, a commenter suggested that "The white male students need to start wearing masks and doing a little push back" (Hutchison, 2016, comments section). Rather than dismissing this type of comment as disingenuous or sociopathic, refer back to the example of the businessman on Grindr and consider that both of these examples illustrate a very real piece of human identity that is not apparent in public spaces governed by normative rules of discourse.

With this juxtaposition of public and private identity in mind I posit a novel approach: this kind of discourse might provide a glimpse into the private self-structured surroundings that exist just below the surface of normative discourse. These online artifacts might serve as fragments of how some tacitly react to issues of social justice. There might be, to use the words of Marc Lamont Hill (2009), a "realness" in these fragments, if so there might also be pedagogical application. Realness does not imply that these ideas are legitimate, but might allow the teacher an inroad into interrogating problematic perspectives. Well-chosen comments, therefore, might be usable texts within class discussions of social justice themes, and further these artifacts of online trolling might be used to troll classroom spaces to probe more deeply into what our students might really be thinking about critical perspectives in race, class, gender and sexuality. Ultimately, pedagogical use of trolling comments might actually serve to create learning experiences that disrupt students' current understandings of social justice.

These fragments, or trolling artifacts are important precisely because although intercorporeality in a classroom allows for empathy, there is the potential that face to face dialogue can be disingenuous. It is this classic "I will say one thing and think another" which makes trolling artifacts potentially useful. Outside of the empathetic intercorporeal sphere, individuals will more often share what they really think, particularly when these thoughts are toxic and hurtful. Specifically, some students might simply decline to speak about topics of race or gender in front of the perceived other. From an exploration of the interconnectedness of queering and trolling, I hope to glean from the carnage of online trolling that cyber artifacts can become queer incursions that provide powerful pedagogical interruptions in intercorporeal classroom spaces.

Obvious Troll Is Obvious: Queer Trolls to Cyber Trolls

In 1950s England, one might well stroll through a park and hear a man say to another: "charper that butch omme ajax; if we flutter our ogle riahs he might just troll over;" the Polari-English translation being: check out that the straight acting "man nearby; and if we fluttered our eyelashes, he might just wander over" (McCullagh, 2011). If nobody understands the exchange, the two men can continue to speak openly about their queerness without fear of recourse from authorities. Sarah Ahmed (2006) suggests the need to develop a private space for queer dialogue is because "the queer subject within straight culture hence deviates and is made socially present as a deviant" (p. 554). In this way queer spaces develop under the radar of intercorporeality because our physical actions and words can belie actual thoughts in public encounters (Merleau-Ponty, 1964, p. 114).

Two salient features emerge: first, we cannot know what another is thinking, and second, because we cannot know this, we use information from the body to fill in the narrative about the interaction (Merleau-Ponty, 1964, p. 114). Referring back to the Polari encounter above we see a clear limitation: the gestures and words used are coded in precisely such a way as to obfuscate understanding. We would have to familiarize ourselves with the language of trolling in order to enrich our meaning making of the encounter. Trolling for sex in queer communities, then, often relied on false intercorporeal impressions to hide their intentions from a disapproving world. Referring back to the fictional example of the business man and Grindr, in his dress and bearing he uses signifiers of heteronormativity to hide his actions, while trolling in a distinct world just under the surface of the normative world. It is as if a queer discursive space develops in the cracks of a constructed world that denies this voice, and the apparent shared corporeal reality is in juxtaposition with a new shared reality of the psyche manifesting itself in spaces of coded language, behaviors, and of course, online spaces. To develop meaning as an outside observer would require exploration in order to crack this code.

Recontextualizing this concept in the normative space of contemporary discourse, in a society claiming to embrace norms of respectful dialogue, queer thoughts and actions might be framed differently. Imagine when a student is confronted with what they perceive as *politically correct* culture in the public sphere and thus retreats to the cyber world to express their thinking. Bracketing out for a moment the overtones of *politically correct*, at play here is a new normativity that regulates public discourse to the point that individuals who dissent feel uncomfortable sharing their thoughts and feelings publically. This phenomenon leads to the development of discursive spaces that mirror that of the queer experience, but in this instance, the trolling is not for sex, rather for the articulation of an oppressive opinion that is denied to them within normative public discourse. In this sense, we can easily see how

> online discussion forums provide a new arena for the enactment of power inequities such as those motivated by sexism, racism, and heterosexism. The relative anonymity of the Internet releases some of the inhibitions of a civil society, resulting in flaming, harassment, and hate speech online. (Herring et al., 2002, p. 371)

Now, contextualize online spaces as queer or perhaps as producing queer incursions into straight spaces, much in the same way historical queer trolling has done for decades. Though clearly the queer community is responding to oppressive heteronormativity and the online trolling community is responding to a *perceived* suppression of their privileged hate speech, the end result is the same— a retreat into online spaces to articulate their position. Precisely for this reason both examples might be thought of as "queer." The double meaning of queer here might seem at first confusing until queer is understood as both a noun or state of being in terms of identity, as well as an adjective describing phenomenon of making blurry that which was once clear. As Deborah Britzman (1995) points out,

> Queer Theory does not depend on the identity of the theorist ... rather ... Queer Theory anticipates the precariousness of the signified: the limits within its conventions and rules, and the ways in which these various conventions and rules incite subversive performances, citations, and inconveniences. (p. 153)

Returning to our cyberspace troll, we note that their performance in public [read normative] spaces might have a particular signification, but the signification might not provide a full picture of what the individual really thinks.

Returning to intercorporeality with these above examples in mind, a queer disconnect forms. Merleau-Ponty (1964) suggests that consciousness is observable through our comportment in the world, and it is in "the manner in which the other deals with the world, that I will be able to discover [their] consciousness" (p. 117). Merleau-Ponty is suggesting that an intercorporeal encounter with the other is predicated on my ability to empathize with the body of the other-to see a smile and understand it because I smile when I am happy (p. 117). The potential fallacy here is that I can discover consciousness through conduct; if the history of gay trolling tells us anything, aspects of consciousness are often obfuscated from view in normative spaces where these aspects are deemed inappropriate or unappreciated. So, to posit, in the words of Susan Herring (2002), "internet trolling as a manifestation of a much broader phenomenon whereby individuals take pleasure in disrupting the social order out of anger, perversity or contempt" might not necessarily always be true (p. 382).

Internet trolling might then be a phenomenon of hiding aspects of consciousness because these aspects are not acceptable in public spaces, with very good reason, of course. Confronted with an intercorporeal encounter with the other, I might not give voice to what I am truly thinking, and this manifests itself in the only outlet that I have available for my aggression: online spaces. Herring (2002) goes on to suggest an important idea that will drive my further inquiry: "It would be interesting to compare online disruption with disruptive behavior in face-to-face groups in playgrounds, classes, meetings, support groups, and social events" (p. 371). Now rather than a correlation there is in fact a disconnect between online activity and face to face encounters in public spaces, or in Merleau-Ponty's (1964) language, a disconnect between the "perceptual fields that can be given in his experience … and his relations with his human and social surroundings" (p. 108). Applying this disconnect to pedagogy, I now turn to specific examples of trolling on my own university campus to more clearly illustrate the disconnect between personal perception and social relationships.

Troll in Campus: The Political Becomes Personal

Conversations about power and privilege are common at mine and many other institutions of higher education across the country in recent years. While occasionally in my classes I encounter what Merleau-Ponty (1964) calls "psychological rigidity," or the inability to see beyond a clearly delineated sense of black and white truth, generally there is a sense of mutual respect or at least civility (p. 101). The reason for general civility in face to face interactions might connect to intercorporeality, or transferring the intimate experience of one's own body to that of an "other" (p. 115). I can see a flushed face, hear shaking in a voice, and generally sense angry muscles tensing in someone that I am talking to; in this sensory experience, I connect these significations to my own body, and therefore develop a sense of empathy— if not empathy to ideas, then at least empathy to individuals manifesting in surface politeness.

And yet when attending to cyberspace there are at least some students (maybe even my own, though it is precisely my lack of knowing that becomes problematic) who have rather angry and dissenting opinions that they are willing to articulate in very aggressive ways. After a group of student leaders put up a *privilege board* in a residence hall the campus of the university where I teach, the event was reported to the conservative website www.campusreform.com, and an article was written berating the board. The article points out significant social media reaction to this privilege board, citing comments from students such as "if you can express your political opinions without being called racist, sexist, bigot, etc. you have liberal privilege" (Hutchison, 2016, comments). Further, the comments under the article teemed with angry posts, some claiming to be authored by university students, and some not. One comment declares "white Christian males … founded and made this country great," while another commenter suggests that it is their "privilege to work 40 hours a week to pay for [the university's] girly men" (Hutchison, 2016, comments). Note again the queer connection to gender and implicit sexuality in the last comment.

Why does the vitriol of anonymous Internet trolls matter? Queer phenomenologist Sarah Ahmed (2006) provides language to put these comments into context by suggesting that we consider our orientation to phenomena (p. 545). In an academic context, if I want to consider how students are engaging with issues of social justice I likely draw on a rather narrow set of evidences, including classroom dialogue and student assessment and reflection. Because of the limitations of these evidences, I really cannot know if these very students are retreating into the cyber world and articulating very different points of view. Reorienting our thinking, imagine taking seriously online comments as "moments of disorientation, which involve not only 'the intellectual' experience of disorder, but the vital experience of giddiness and nausea, which is the awareness of our own contingency and the horror with which it fills us" (Ahmed, 2006, p. 544).

Perhaps we are so quick to dismiss online trolling because it does horrify, and with good reason. With comments calling universities a "four-year rape apology seminar" and professors "lesbianic femenists" (sic), it is easy to first react with anger and then almost instant dismissal, and yet what happens when the trolling hits closer to home, and makes the transition from cyberspace space to physical space (Neff, 2016, comments)? Shortly after the privilege board scenario, a group of students literally trolled the streets, using chalk to post messages over the walls and walkways of the campus with slogans like "white privilege is a lie" (Cole, 2016, comments). When a group of students reacted against the "chalkings," wiping them away, people once again took to social media to troll the situation with comments like "I'm actually concerned with how butthurt (sic) these students are getting" (Cole, 2016, comments). Specifically I am referencing comments made on the forum itself, but similar comments were peppered throughout facebook and other social media with hashtags including #liberalprivilege, and those on the other side of the issue including #racismatappalachian.

In civil public discourse we do not refer to people being genuinely offended as *butthurt*, but this speaks to the sense that online spaces provide the opportunity to say cruel things without having to see the faces of the targets of the cruelty. When uttering a cruel remark to the face of another person I can see signifiers including flushed faces, teary eyes, physical recoiling, and aggressive posturing begin to arise. These signifiers become together a totality of expressions presented to me, and as I decode them "I witness, I project, so to speak, what I myself feel of my own body ... I transfer to the other the intimate experience I have of my own body (Merleau-Ponty, 1964, p. 115). While certainly not everyone will decode and project in the same ways, these projections of bodily understanding can prevent us from saying the hurtful things that we might feel in face to face public encounters, and instead retreat to the anonymity of the Internet perhaps not so that the "other" does not see them, but that they do not have to see the "other."

Troll as the Straw Person: Implications for Classroom Spaces

Consider the normative space the exists in a university classroom: there are norms of civil discourse, and particularly when faced with critical conversations of social justice centering on race, class, gender, and sexuality, "artful facilitation is imperative in order to effectively manage the content, conflict, and emotions that invariably arise in any meaningful classroom engagements" (Bettez, 2008, p. 280). This facilitation of dialogue allows for interruptions and encounters with difference, but as noted, there might be a limitation to what we can genuinely learn about each other in face to face discourse. Cyber-trolling artifacts might serve to provide an important secondary facet to the understanding of a person's consciousness: the part kept hidden in normative spaces. If, as some of the trolling comments are to be believed, students might feel "intimidated by liberal professors," the cyber world might provide examples of how some students' consciousness's respond to divisive issues of social justice without students having to disclose in discussion (Hutchison, 2016, comments). Given the intercorporeal space of the physical classroom, imagine being able to critically interrogate a controversial or dissenting opinion without a student having to risk a sense of safety by voicing this opinion; further consider the opportunity for self-reflection and interrupted thinking without the student fearing judgement (Friesen, 2008, p. 95). One fascinating product of this queering of the conversation is that the trolling artifact begins to mediate the conversation in such a way that students who might actually agree with the troll are able to witness, and even participate in, a relatively safe critical engagement with the idea. I have had multiple students reflect after classes that they secretly agreed with the troll at first, but through the process were actually able to see the alternative in a more positive light, and in some cases these student experienced a complete reversal of their previous opinions, all happening completely out of view of their fellow classmates. The troll becomes the "straw person" here because the class can interrogate this unembodied artifact as opposed to interrogating each other.

Returning now to the lens of intercorporeality, we can more clearly see a radical disconnect between what a student says in class versus their articulation of thought in cyber spaces. Through the lens of intercorporeality it becomes clear that we are bound by space and place in terms of both meaning making and expression of thought: "the specificities of place and all environments have body-subjects who are at different times, in differing cultures, related to them" (O'Loughlin, 1997, p. 27). As the body subject relates to space and place differently as these variables move, we might begin to think for the constitution of consciousness variable based on space and place, or that in fact we ARE different people in front of a screen than face to face: Judith Butler (1990) writes "the body is not a 'being,' but a variable boundary, a surface whose permeability is politically regulated" (p. 239). Further, Butler notes "there is no 'I' who stands behind discourse and executes its volition or will through discourse," meaning in this context that in a social justice classroom conversation, the intercorporeal moment might constitute a consciousness different from that of the same person sitting in front of a screen with only their thoughts and the surroundings of their room to constitute their consciousness (p. 18).

Might there be value to interacting with the kinds of ideas that students would not utter in class? At this point it should be made clear that I am not suggesting a professor stalk the Facebook feeds of their students, quite the contrary. An anonymous representation of tacit student thinking can be presented through simply setting up trolling comments as a "straw person" for continued interrogation, and in Norm Friesen's (2008) words, "when compared to their counterparts in the 'real' world, virtual artifacts manifest a pliability, brilliance, discontinuity, and disposability that can have educational value" (p. 111). It is this disposability that makes a trolling comment useful —students are not required to interrogate personalized values, rather ideas that some might have encountered. In reading student reflections after such lessons, I have observed on multiple occasions students admit to having shared perspectives with the cyber trolls, and that the lesson and subsequent discussion allowed them to reconsider these perspectives. Whether ideas confronting ideas like "I don't see color" or "women are just naturally different," reading cyber artifacts can be useful in bringing these ideas to the surface to critically interrogate.

Rich understanding might be attained by challenging the hateful online trolling as text to be critically considered, extending "beyond its physical limitations through its engagement with other figurative bodies, such as the 'body' of the text ... an 'enlarged' view of all human being" (Friesen, 2008, p. 95). Here we might think about the background of online spaces, or what students think when they are not paying attention to the public or foreground: inhabiting the familiar makes things into backgrounds for action ... the background is a "dimly apprehended depth or fringe of indeterminate reality" (Ahmed, 2006, p. 549).

I have also taken to actively trolling my students through using anonymous tools to collect responses. I literally call these sessions "trolling for the truth." The danger here, of course, is to allow the voices of oppression a platform to further marginalize vulnerable groups. Here is where the before mentioned artful facilitation of dialogue becomes important: unpacking student comments together with both empathy and judgement is the responsibility of the artful facilitator of discussion. The addition of judgement here is critical, as the educator must be able to critically trouble the waters of student opinion, and interrogating anonymous comments together can develop real movement toward critical social consciousness. This is difficult work, as trolling in order to open up dialogical spaces can be volatile, and can easily lead to destabilization of traditional structures of power in the classroom. It is for this reason that the goal of this chapter, as stated earlier, is not to provide a systematic guide for the pedagogical use of cyber artifacts, rather to reorient the dialogue around what types of text might be considered usable within the context of classroom spaces. Deeper considerations of pedagogical practice is absolutely necessary and will inform further inquiry on this topic. But approaching this topic queerly also means having the courage to leave application more open ended.

I would like to believe optimistically that the phenomenon of intercorporeality creates spaces of empathy, and that the social justice pedagogue might embrace queer cyber artifacts, not as pieces of truth, rather as texts that might be seen as authentic fragments of humanity to be used to move toward developing greater empathy in social justice classroom spaces. However, the sea change in victim politics in this country has left social justice discourse in this country in a queerer state than it has been in recent years, a state that I cannot gloss over with a happy ending— the stakes are just too high. With the dominant culture pushing back at the suppression of their oppressive speech, sanitizing classroom discourse ironically plays right into the narrative that is being created.

The dominant culture in this country has embraced what Lauren Berlant (2006) might refer to as a *cruel optimism* (p. 20). In this cruel optimism, those with power have repositioned themselves as the powerless, and have, however erroneously, taken on the mantle of the oppressed. With this in mind, those with historical privilege have developed a strange kinship with the historically marginalized queer; they have embraced the identity of Troll as a false sense of voice, a simpatico that allows them to project themselves into cyberspace with a sense of liberation, a cruel optimism that they are fighting against forces of oppression.

This "condition of projected possibility" in fact "creates a fake moment of intersubjectivity" (Berlant, 2006, p. 22). In Berlant's (2006) words, those historically with power have developed a "rhetorical animation that permits subjects to suspend themselves in the optimism of a potential occupation of the same psychic space of others" (p. 22). With this in mind, the project seems now to require the pedagogue to find new kinds of texts in order to "troll," that we might displace this cruel optimism, to reclaim queer for the marginal, for the wonky, for the skewed, for the misfits ... in short, those who claim to be opposed to the queer ought to be confronted with the cyber evidences of their own misguided attempt at queering.

The power in this confrontation is that trolls like staying in the shadows. There is an interesting occurrence when you take a thing like a troll out of its habitat. Like a fish out of water, it does not survive very well. The sort of visceral vitriol that happens in online spaces tends to cool a great deal when faced with real people in real world spaces. For this reason the use of the troll to mediate conversation does not become an extension of cyberspace; it does become tempered with intercorporeality, and this seems to be where there is real value behind this approach: by bringing the troll into the intercorporeal light of day, they will turn to stone.

REFERENCES

Atkins, D. (1998). Skinny, 'White' chicks and hung, buff boys: Queer sex spaces and their disconnects. In D. Atkins (Ed.), *Looking queer: Body image and identity in lesbian, bisexual, gay, and transgender communities* (pp. 439–454). Binghamton, NY: Haworth Press.

Ahmed, S. (2006). Orientations: Toward a queer phenomenology. *GLQ: A Journal of Lesbian and Gay Studies, 12*(4), 543–574.

Berlant, L. (2006) Cruel optimism. *Differences, 17*(3), 20–36.

Bettez, S. (2008) Social justice activist teaching in the university classroom. In J. Diem (Ed.), *Unsettling beliefs: Teaching theory to teachers* (pp. 297–300). Charlotte, NC: Information Age.

Britzman, D. (1995). Is there a queer pedagogy? Or, stop reading straight. *Educational Theory, 45*(2), 151–165.

Butler, J. (1990). *Gender trouble: Feminism and the subversion of identity*. New York, NY: Routledge.

Cole, M. R. (2016). Appalachian state students of color become target of harassment after racist chalkings on campus. *Fresh U*. Retrieved from https://www.freshu.io/mia-renee- cole/appalachian-state-students-of-color-target-of-harassment-after-chalkings

de Lauretis, T. (2011). Queer texts, bad habits, and the issue of a future. *GLQ: A Journal of Lesbian & Gay Studies, 17*(2–3), 243–263.

Friesen, N. (2008). *The place of the classroom and the space of the screen: Relational pedagogy and Internet technology*. New York, NY: Peter Lang.

Greteman, A. J., & Wojcikiewicz, S. K. (2014). The problems with the future: Educational futurism and the figural child. *Journal of Philosophy of Education, 48*(4), 559–573.

Herring, S., Job-Sluder, K., Scheckler, R., & Barab, S. (2002). Searching for safety online: Managing "trolling" in a feminist forum. *The Information Society, 18*, 371–384.

Hill, M. L. (2009). *Beats, rhymes, and classroom life: Hip-hop pedagogy and the politics of identity*. New York, NY: Teacher College Press.

Hutchison, S. (2016). 'Priveldge board' gets prominent placement at App State. *Campus Reform*. Retrieved from https://www.campusreform.org/?ID=8022

Kedley, K. (2015). Queering the teacher as a text in the English language arts classroom: Beyond books, identity work and teacher preparation. *Sex Education, 15*(4), 364–377.

Martínez, E. (2012). *On making sense: Queer race narratives of intelligibility*. Stanford, CA: Stanford University Press.

McClung, N. (2017). Learning to queer text: Epiphanies from a family critical literacy practice. *The Reading Teacher, 71*(4), 401–410.

McCullagh, J. (2011). Polari, a secret gay language born of homophobia. *PositiveLite*. Retrieved from http://www.positivelite.com/component/zoo/item/polari-a-secret-gay-language-born-of-homophobia

Merleau-Ponty, M. (1964). *The primacy of perception and other essays on phenomenological psychology, the philosophy of art, history and politics*. Evanston, IL: Northwestern University Press.

Merleau-Ponty, M. (1968). *The visible and the invisible* (Alphonso Lingis, Trans.), Evanston, IL: Northwestern University Press.

Neff, B. (2016). Video: Students erase pro-trump chalk, threaten to run creators off campus, *The Daily Caller News Foundation*. Retrieved from http://dailycaller.com/2016/09/15/video-students-erase-pro-trump-chalk-threaten-to-run-creators-off-campus/

O'Loughlin, M. (1997). Corporeal subjectivities: Merleau-Ponty, education and the postmodern subject. *Educational Philosophy and Theory, 29*(1), 20–30.

Williams, B. (1995). *Making sense of humanity: And other philosophical papers 1982–1993*. New York, NY: Cambridge University Press.

CHAPTER 4

LIFTING THE VEIL

Social Loafing and Participatory Learning in a Networked Space

Greg Neal and Mark Vicars
Victoria University

INTRODUCTION

Participation in digital networks is an ever-expanding social phenomenon that has brought together a constellation of previously unimagined communicative practices. Social network sites such as LinkedIn, My Space, Facebook, Twitter, and Snapchat are all high traffic social sites worldwide in which many young people "socially loaf" or "hang out" on-line. "Social loafing," defined as "the tendency to reduce one's efforts when working collectively" (Karau & Williams, 1993, p. 683) is associated with individual production where responsibility within a group, is diffused. However, narratives from students who participated in a global collaboration project have suggested how asynchronous opportunities allowed participants to peruse content at their leisure, read widely in a nonlinear style, access information in their own place and space and determine when/if they wanted to contribute online.

Negotiating Place and Space Through Digital Literacies: Research and Practice, pp. 59–76

Bijker and Law (1992) have noted how "Technologies ... are subject to contingencies" (p. 8) and Hutchby (2001) suggests "When people interact through, around or with technologies, it is necessary for them to find ways of managing the constraints on their possibilities for action that emerge from those artefacts' affordances" (p. 450).

"Hanging-out" online as Gee (2008) has identified, invariably involves the "other stuff" of language, namely: "social relations, cultural models, power and politics, perspectives on experience, values and attitudes, as well as things and places in the world" (p. 1) that encapsulate the "new ethos" (Lankshear & Knobel, 2006) of new literacies. If, as we are suggesting in this chapter, social loafing draws on the "other stuff" in maintaining an online identity then it could be argued how "Being [online] in every sense is entangled, connected, indefinite, impersonal, shifting into different multiplicities and assemblages" (St Pierre, 2013, p. 653). Paradoxically not being visibly present formed constructive learning opportunities for students who had not worked in this kind of distributed online environment before. While social loafing might not fit within constructing conventional understandings of deep learning, it does in the context of the project provide an understanding for how content information, despite periodic lack of connection, was exchanged and interrogated across spatial and temporal divides.

Davies (2012) has noted the need to be aware of how contemporary literacy behaviors involve "all kinds of social 'stuff'" (p. 20) that surrounds texts, and she argues for an acknowledgment of how these have generated multiple textual affordances (Gibson, 1979) that "do not exist apart from the social practices in which they are embedded and in which they are acquired" (Lankshear & Knobel, 2006, p. 13). As digital technologies increasingly transform and multiply opportunities for literacy practices, both within and beyond educational domains, the epistemological and ontological 'new' situates literacy is an ever-emerging assemblage of meanings, practices, technologies and contexts. Luke (2003) has noted how "texts of the new technologies have mutated into complex hybrid systems that have made new demands on reading and writing, viewing, social exchange, and communication" (p. 401). As an articulation of the "new," social loafing is an under documented phenomenon that we suggest is an effect of digital, distributed, asynchronous online communication.

The production and consumption of texts online is increasingly becoming an open-ended joint construction: a "we" space. A space in which learning involves intra-action of social environment and identities across time, place and multimodal affordances (Keene & Zimmerman, 1997). Becoming ontologically and epistemologically re/attuned to the principle of the "We-hermeneutic" is one that Sepie (2017) suggests draws on an understanding of self that is derived from "our awareness of the fundamental human relationships that we have within the broader ecologies within which we are embedded" (p. 2).

While there continues the "race to the top" for students to achieve social and academic objectives, there are fewer opportunities for students to linger in their learning and occupy a different kind of literacy practice. The social and cultural expectations of literacy in a schooling context demand a prescribed compliance: literate behaviors look and sound in a very particular way (Gee & Gee, 1990). However, as readers and writers are enacting identities in textual practice(s) and relationships, the learning of and about literacy is always in constant evolution: "new literacies have emerged ... embodied in new social practices—[in] new ways of participating as a citizen in public spaces, and even perhaps new forms of identity and personality" (Cope & Kalantzis, 2009, p. 167). It therefore becomes pedagogically generative to think about how literacy is becoming socially embedded in larger life practices and discourses (The New London Group, 1996) and to incorporate into formal learning those activities that extend across a range of texts and communicative practices.

Students' reading and writing behaviors generate complex and crucial pedagogical questions on a daily basis. One of the many challenges is to understand how the changing cultural landscape impacts on how on-line reading and writing behaviors are being resituated. Scholarship has drawn attention to the salience of resisting and refuting the paradigm that literacy is only learned within the narrow margins of an established architecture of pedagogic orthodoxy (Snyder, 2008). Roberts (2005) has called for an interrogation of pedagogical approaches that correspond to the social practices of the 21st century learner and, in this chapter, we endeavor to respond to the challenge of making sense of "networked interconnectedness, through globalized and local, virtual and material social fields" (Luke & Carrington, 2002, p. 231). We have sought to understand how "social loafing" online within a global learning network could have a productive pedagogical impact for individual students participating in professional and personalized teacher education dialogue. We endeavor to provide an account of how teacher education students' social loafing, defined as: "the tendency to reduce one's efforts when working collectively" (Karau & Williams, 1993, p. 683) can be thought of as a natural occurring phenomenon of intra-activity and of deep learning in digital domains. Intra-activity as opposed to interactivity signals an ontological shift towards a post human thinking about cultural practices in which "The interest in 'more than human ontologies' lies in understanding the intra-actions or agentic-in-between-ness of humans and non-humans in producing knowledge(s), relationship(s) and reality(ies)" (Kuby, 2017, p. 878). We recognize the problems that accompany any endeavor to untangle the complexity of intra-activity in digital domains. Drawing upon the "social stuff" extracted from out of everyday habits and ways of being between human and nonhumans, we situate social loafing as an affordance within the entangled spaces of contemporary digital communicative practice (Barad, 2007). In this chapter, we have endeavored to think with:

> "More than human ontologies" [as] a perspective that can widen, deepen our understandings of education and provoke new thinking about mainstream accounts of humans interacting with each other and intra-acting with the material world. Posthumanist perspectives in education, specifically literacy, have potential to offer theoretical, methodological, and pedagogical possibilities. (Kuby, 2017, p. 878)

And, in doing so, we pay attention to practices of engagement and relationality as a pedagogical assemblage to provoke new thinking about learning in digital domains. The network spaces that were drawn upon by the participants in the study included online multimedia platforms such as; Facebook group, online blogs, Google docs, Voice thread, and Wikis.

HERE, THERE, AND EVERYWHERE: KNOWLEDGE-BUILDING ACROSS DIGITAL PLATFORMS

In 2012 a global collaboration project was established between teacher education candidates from a University in Victoria, Australia and a University in West Virginia, United States. The Australian university is one of 39 public universities in Australia and is a dual-sector university (students can pathway from vocational education to higher education). There are over 40,000 enrolled higher education, vocational or training students. It is situated in Melbourne's western metropolitan region, a largely urban society, growing fast in size and population and very culturally diverse. In comparison, the U.S. university, also a public university, is regarded as a liberal arts institution, situated in a semirural location with an undergraduate enrolment of approximately 2,000 students.

The goal of the project was to change teacher educational instructional practices from where learners are often passive recipients of information to become more actively involved in the construction of new knowledge. To compare and contrast their current understanding of global education, the project situated learners in shared knowledge-building communities across two very culturally different tertiary educational settings.

The global collaboration was conceived by teacher educators from the two institutions, with participating teacher candidates undertaking similar units of study from their respective degrees. The teacher candidates were required to achieve similar learning intentions from the collaborative examination of the similarities and differences of each nation's education systems. Using a variety of digital resources to exchange, discuss, and cocontribute to shared knowledge-building, the integrated use of specific online applications, as well as those from social media forums, were employed to contextually engage the students in 21st century digital literacies.

The project, in the mutual creation of a shared virtual space was intentionally designed to situate local and international partners in collegial dialogue that foregrounded cultural interpretations of given topics. The participants were asked to explore and compare two diverse school systems and discuss the realities of each other's global context utilizing a range of online digital resources. The information that was exchanged was collectively gathered, shared and coproduced validating knowledge as a social construction and a mutual process of reacculturation (Thompson, 2004). A pedagogic intention for the participants promoted the use of new digital resources in authentic ways to enable the transfer of newfound skills into their own teaching practices.

However, it was quite apparent that some of the participants were at varying stages of competency with digital literacies and the inclusion of digital technologies further challenged them to operate functionally in an online environment. This was especially apparent when participants were required to communicate across cultures with international partners. While some participants reported the online applications as challenging, they also reported it as an opportunity to "have-a-go," For example, the predetermined digital resources (e.g., Skype, VoiceThread, Google Drive) were deliberately selected after ascertaining the prior knowledge of teacher candidates and their identified digital literacies at the beginning of the semester.

Following this determination, the teacher candidates had to utilise and evaluate online resources they may not have previously experienced. Encountering the use of digital resources in an authentic way in an online space, generated opportunities to focus on the learning processes as distinct from the learning of content. As such, teacher candidates initially challenged by the digital platform often reported positive reactions toward the integration of unfamiliar digital resources and were appreciative of the chance to gain in proficiency and confidence.

This chapter presents evidence collected during 2014, a year when four cohorts of students (approximately 40–50 each semester) from the two universities were linked together to participate in the study for a duration of 4–6 weeks. Two cohorts from both universities were selected from the identified units of study from their respective degree programs within each semester. Once initial contact had been made, the teacher candidates were organized by the lecturer's random allocation into teams of four that comprised two local and two international partners (some groups may have had three or five participants depending on available numbers from each university). The participants were provided with learning goals, weekly topics, and specific digital resources, both synchronous and asynchronous to be used as a minimum ongoing contact source. The students were required to exchange and share information, present current local literature and research evidence, and add personal anecdotes to uncover "truths" between the two education systems. They were asked to add to the factual content vignettes taken from their life stories and include subjective opinions, that in discussion with their overseas partners, could be further questioned, analyzed, and evaluated. The following structure was provided to the participants to frame and sequentially structure the online communication:

- In week 1, teacher candidates were required to discover and explain the different school systems, funding arrangements, university requirements, and the perceived value of teachers in society. The information was to be exchanged by creating a shared online space such as a social media platform, for example, Facebook, to co-create with group members.
- In week 2, students linked up using an online forum, for example, Skype, Facetime, to speak with their overseas partners and exchange information about issues confronting education in the respective countries.
- In week 3, students used a multimedia program (e.g., VoiceThread, or a blog or a wiki) to exchange information about the culture and society and the ways teachers adopted strategies to accommodate 21st century learners.
- In week 4, students concentrated on assessment practices and how they impacted teaching and learning. The students used Google Drive to cocreate a shared account of the main facets of assessment happening in schools.
- In the weeks following the initial period after exchanging information, local group members were required to collate and construct an end-product of findings to inform others of their new knowledge and report on the inclusion of digital resources into their online space.

STUDY METHODS AND THE COLLECTION OF DATA

In 2014, 90 students out of a cohort of 183 completed an online survey at the start of their respective semesters and 69 students completed the same online survey at the end of their semester. This data enabled a comparison between pre- and post-responses after having participated in this project as well as other unit of study focused exercises in order to conform to and address their respective unit of study's intended learning outcomes.

All associated unit of study participants were invited to an online interview after the conclusion of semester assessments. Participants were able to asynchronously respond and send their notes directly to the researcher or via online forums, including social network sites (private). The online response was guided by the following evaluation questions:

1. What do you think you have gained from the collaboration for your own learning?
2. What teaching and learning strategies have you gained for your own classroom practice?
3. Were there any issues you encountered that caused you problems in communicating with someone from overseas?
4. What would you like to see changed as a result of your participation in this collaboration?

The use of online data collection methods allowed the participants to respond at their convenience within a given time frame. The survey instruments had been assessed by the research team as being relatively easy to use; they were accessible and safe and encouraged the use of any technology resource, including mobile devices. There continues to be some uncertainties about the efficacy of how technology resources are specifically used to collect data (Beddall-Hill, Jabbar & Al Shehri, 2011). Meho (2006) and Curasi (2001) have reported that the quality of data gained through online research, for example, e-mail, blogs, can be a viable alternative to face-to-face and telephone interviewing.

From the initial evaluation questions, a joint decision was made by the research team to follow up with participants by e-mails and blogs and obtain first-hand accounts of their involvement in the participatory networks. Open-ended invitations were e-mailed to all 90 teacher candidates seeking their feedback on their experiences and, in particular, what would they change in the project. The purpose of the follow up data collection was to try and better understand any perceived relationship between social loafing from their individual practice and the impact within their allocated group. The data did not clearly specify time moments of private study where students may have chosen to "loaf" while working in their own online space. Collated responses from the initial data alerted the researchers to some of the virtual pedagogy challenges (participating in collaborative learning tasks in online web-based platforms) that individuals experienced as they participated in their group's work commitments.

CONTEXTUALIZING THE GLOBAL COLLABORATION

The teacher candidates reported that the selection of local group members was unproblematic. However, the challenge of working in preselected groups was to ensure they self-managed to benefit all online members as an effective way to operate. The group allocation had been determined by the university lecturers prior to the commencement of the project, and the teacher candidates were placed with local randomly preselected partners as well as preselected group members between the two countries to eliminate possible preformed friendship groups. This approach of having two local and two international teacher candidates was considered by the lecturers at the time as the preferred learning model. This sort of online group connection was designed to challenge individuals to be cooperative and collaborative—skills associated with deep learning (Fullan, 2013).

It was reported across groups from both universities that the participants had concerns that the corresponding overseas students allocated to their groups were often perceived as not meeting the demands and expectations of the local group. Team productivity and performance were viewed as inequitable in terms of workload as highlighted by one teacher candidate[1] below:

> Our experience was very frustrating due to the lack of effort on the part of our partners in (country). We made significant contribution from our end—and received the equivalent of about 30 mins work from each of them. This was disappointing as the assignment seemed to have potential to be rewarding. (Jessica e-mail June 2014)

A disconnect between reluctant group members has been noted an ongoing issue in collaborative endeavors (Davies, 2009) and to overcome any perceived disconnect, the University lecturers deliberately organized the teacher candidates to engage with real time, synchronous forms of communication early in the project. The rationale for the early inclusion of week 2's face-to-face contact was in response to the likes of Worchel and colleagues' (1998) identified need to understand and appreciate the social identity of their partners. The intentions to have all partners build a relationship and to encourage comradery among the group were confirmed by the participants as a positive step and helped to lessen the blame game when the task was undertaken:

> Skyping with our group members allowed me to put a face to someone's name, experiences and opinions. By talking to them, I was able to create a better mental image of these people, understanding better their points of view, stopping me from being judgemental or confused. (Amber e-mail Dec. 2014)

However, there was clear evidence to suggest that a portion of the groups encountered some sort of communication problem or resource challenge as part of the overall online connection. There were a large number of individuals who found the online experience frustrating particularly caused by the large time difference between the two countries (14 hours). The time difference often required asynchronous responses which for many young people, is a very different way of operating in their world of instant gratification (Boyd & Onofry, 2013):

> The time differences were difficult as when I had set time aside to get things done they were not available and then their responses would arrive at times when I didn't really have time to spend on that specific component. (Liam e-mail Oct. 2014)

Some individuals thought the delayed online process was a personal imposition as expressed by a teacher candidate in a survey response: *The human aspect of considering time-zones, workloads, other peoples' commitments can be irritating* (Hamish online survey, 2014). And, the experience for the student below highlights personal frustration when there is a reliance on international group members to complete the required tasks and for those participants who did not fully justify their commitment:

> It did feel a little artificial because there was a sense of just getting it done. For example, on the blog, there would be one response from us and one from them, but then nothing. So the opportunity to go deeper into an issue did not happen. (Ken e-mail, Oct. 2104)

In order to assist and overcome connections between group members, the lecturers became the conduit between the two countries: participants would e-mail their respective lecturer who would then email or Skype their overseas colleague in order to address any perceived communication concerns. This was seen as a very effective "push" to have things happen and also enabled the number of contact issues that required their intervention to be quantified. In 2014 there were only 9 interventions required by the teacher educators out of 46 groups overall. This indicated most groups enabled their own group connection and ongoing contact quite readily. It was apparent that many individuals in the different groups were willing to accept the challenges of communicating in a virtual space and were able to reflect on the experience in a positive way:

> There are general issues with virtual collaboration— lack of visibility of participation, lack of accountability etc. but I think these are things that people experience in business every day so they form constructive new learning for students who have not worked in this kind of distributed

> environment before. Challenge is good—as often we find we become more creative in the face of difficulty. (Jade e-mail, Oct. 2014)

For some of the participants, online exchanges were clearly valued and identified as more relevant to them as digital learners and in this context it became important to collect the personal narratives of participants to further examine social loafing as a virtual "socio-cultural practice and process" (Leander & Sheehy, 2004, p. 1). The conceptualization of social loafing from the participants narratives that were considered salient features were: (1) engaging in online virtual spaces which afforded a pedagogic potential, (2) for online participation in collaborative learning to be distributed across geographical and temporal domains, (3) for participants to have agency when operating within their own communities of practice, (4) for participants to deepen knowledge through self directed learning (5) for the emergence of distributed learning to develop in what had been previously been utilized as recreational spaces.

GOING ONLINE AND HOOKING-UP; "SOCIAL LOAFING" A PEDAGOGY IN VIRTUAL PRACTICE

The pedagogic intention underpinning the project was for the participants to learn how to use the digital resources in authentic ways to enable the transfer of newfound skills into their own teaching practices. Neal (2007) has noted, individual teachers who encourage 21st century teaching-learning with digital technologies can scaffold the learning process by encouraging students to apply different thinking strategies to achieve social and academic objectives with an informed criticality that is *less* concerned with "getting the right answer" but is *more* concerned with "getting inside" competing claims, and showing an understanding of how different arguments are constructed. We recognize the *problematic* and *contestable* character of *knowledge claims*, including:

- the presence of underlying values and assumptions (including those embodied in competing paradigms, discourses, rationalities and ethical principles);
- recognition that "meanings" can be conveyed through communicative devices other than formally reasoned argument, for example, via sound and visual images, by use of rhetoric;
- the significance of knowledge communities and cultures, and of claims-makers' interests and allegiances; and
- the associations between knowledge and power.

This prompted our thinking of the ways in which technology has harnessed readerly and writerly behaviors that are connected to "hanging- out" online. The potential of the digital world to throw together people across spaces/ places and texts potentially to form communities of practice, with shared interests and participation has enabled learning to be an online, anytime, anywhere endeavor.

However, within formal education domains an individual's contribution and participation in a group's shared learning process is encountered as a perennial pedagogic problem. Piezon and Ferree, (2007) quantativley surveyed 227 undergraduate and graduate students enrolled in an on line course and employed the concept of "social loafing" to describe the actions of individual students engaging in behavior that lessens the quality of learning for themselves and their group members. Existing research regarding the existence of the social loafing phenomenon in the online learning environments is sparse. One of the few known research investigations that has identified social loafing in technology-supported groups was undertaken by Alnuaimi, Robert, and Maruping (2010) who used an experimental design to test the hypothesis of how individuals worked when placed in groups and reported that team size and dispersion were the two main factors that contributed to a deficit model of social loafing. Piezon and Ferree (2007) also found that distance learning issues such as geographical separation, a lack of visual cues and time zones differences can exacerbate social loafing when students work in online environments. However, both these studies position social loafing as a deficit practice. With the development of global shared knowledge-building communities, where students become active constructors of collective knowledge (Scardamalia & Bereiter, 1999), it is timely to reconsider and re/position social loafing as a productive pedagogy within networked social ethnoscapes of digital learning. The narratives from the students suggests how social loafing was effective in ways that it established consistent task related communication between team members and....

One of the very first social psychologists to investigate social learning in groups prior to the introduction of digital technologies was Latane (1981). His social impact theory stated that individual group members' behaviors change when they join a group and the impact is greater if the group is separated by physical and/or psychological distance. One of the most significant ways to lessen the effect of problems such as this was to build healthy relationships among group members and understand and appreciate the social identity of each other (Worchel, Rothgerber, Day, Hart, & Butemeyer, 1998).

Another challenge clearly evident in digital participatory networks is temporal and spatial separation. Reconsidering how the epistemic landscape around technology has radically altered and how communicative practices are being redefined, Moore-Gilbert (1997) refer to the "imperative to reconsider [pedagogic] positions that once seemed self-evident and normal" (p. 98). Participation in digital networks involves re/negotiating intricate discursive relations with others in which

> fundamental frameworks of knowing, being and acting are challenged ... [As] Our frameworks for understanding the world, ourselves, our actions, our values and our relationships with each other proliferate. Those frameworks cut across each other, overlap with each other, are in tension with each other and may be incommensurable with each other. (Barnett 1998, p. 59)

The narratives from the participants show how the intentions of the project, that aimed to encourage students to experience opportunities to personalize the learning by sharing first-hand accounts and engage in relationship building, were initially challenged by social loafing in online teamwork.

LIFTING THE VEIL

The particular challenge of forming online groups from different countries was in how individual behaviors, attitudes, and cultural influences materialized in the shared virtual spaces.

> There were a number of challenges for me, particularly being partnered with someone I don't know well and was not forthcoming when trying to arrange things. (Carly e-mail, Oct. 2014)

> There was a lack of investment in each other's learning because we didn't really know each other. (Peter e-mail, Oct. 2014)

The glocal (global and local) disconnect of learning in a virtual space for some participants was initially of a technical nature:

> I did not gain any new skills from the process. I stuck to what I was good at (research/answering questions/going off on tangents) and let the other group members pick up the technological requirements (setting up Skype and blog). (Michelle e-mail, Oct. 2014)

This aspect led to a breakdown in participation in some groups particularly when individual students had to contribute to collective responsibility for shared knowledge-building. The challenges of virtual collaboration emerged in a deficit understanding of online synchronous presence: of a perceived lack of visibility, of participation and accountability. However, according to Edwards and Wilson (2004) virtual social presence can assist educators to begin to think differently about social loafing and learning. Engagement with learning and knowledge building was constructed in a "space [that] was increasingly entangled with ongoing situations of breakdown, surprise, bewilderment, or wonder" (Alvesson & Karreman, 2011, p. 722). As one participant noted:

> I found the collaboration to be a "co-operation" rather than a collaboration. We allocated "jobs" and just got through it. At some points, communication dropped off (for various reasons) and certain group members had to chase others. (Trevor e-mail, June 2014)

Despite a decentralization of decision-making some participants took a key role in directing their own learning and in facing the challenges of a virtual collaboration. From the narratives there is support for the view that while social disconnect existed in some of the groups social loafing in a virtual space may in fact be a useful addition to an individual's deep learning. Evidence from the participants indicated how:

> Researching and learning about stuff for my assignment is just one case where I have had a positive experience with ICT in terms of my learning. Although not always easy, the ease of access it enabled me to peer review texts (through Google Scholar), videos where I could see theories or classroom activities in action (via YouTube) and resources collated by other teachers (via Pinterest for example) enabled me to contribute to the group assignment and research in a manner and at times which worked for me. It offered me great flexibility and choice. (Felix online survey, 2014)

> The asynchronous technologies allow for anytime, anywhere contributions and access yet their lack of social presence lead to confusion and rework for the team. Asynchronous technologies are good when working across significant time differences, when you want to give the respondent time to collate information or consider their response or for simple one-to-one threads. But negatives include message threads being lost or people starting new emails or replying to inappropriate ones. (Monica e-mail, June 2014)

Mitigating the deficit understanding of social loafing was made possible when the technology offered sufficient time and space for all individuals in the group to participate and respond dialogically. Murris (2016) suggests how "thoughts … are created in the relational and dynamic process of interaction offering a philosophical justification for interactive, dialogical and democratic pedagogies" (Murris, 2016). An asset understanding of social loafing is how digital domains can maintain engagement and mitigate against the constraints of immediacy and contextual framing as some of the participant's comments have indicated:

> The online access to conversations provided us with an impression of how the students feel about their home towns, the education system they learn in and also their future roles as teachers that you cannot get from static research. In this case, the rich information exchanged, and therefore new knowledge constructed, could not be authentically learned any other way. (Joanne blog, April 2014)

> Sharing personal stories was much more meaningful, it enabled me to relate to the information provided on a deeper level, relating their own experiences to mine. (Kaye e-mail, Oct. 2014)

> I think that accessing real life experiences and having personal exposure to the Australian education system made the information much more relevant to me as I could directly relate or compare to my own experiences of our system. (Gary e-mail, Oct. 2014)

Barad (2007) suggests how increasingly meaning is being produced "in relation to the particular apparatus used" (p. 120) and Murris (2016, p. 6) directs thinking about the being "in" the space "between" the person as embodied organism and the material world [to think through how] space relations between all material organisms act upon each other. If as we suggest social loafing is inseparable from "public displays of connection" (Donath & Boyd, 2004) then what it means to learn with and in digital networks is one in which social loafing is connected to the process of becoming a learner. It draws on as one of the participants noted technology:

> to make social connections at the outset to replace the face-to-face contact we are unable to have. For me the human factors are much more important than the technology in this day and age. What are harder to identify and apply are the extensions [of technology] to our interpersonal skills, to make our intentions visible to the other persons through the technology. (Emily Oct., 2014)

REASSEMBLING UNDERSTANDING

Social loafing, when read against the epistemic space and place of formal learning is in many ways antithetical to dominant educational discourses and practices that are rooted in industrial models of teaching and learning, structured in and through paradigmatic and pedagogic orthodoxies. The tension for educators working with and in digital domains are increasingly connected to what Egan (2002) has suggested are postmodern characteristics of digital literacy in learning. These being how

> fundamental frameworks of knowing, being and acting are challenged. Our frameworks for understanding the world, ourselves, our actions, our values and our relationships with each other proliferate. Those frameworks cut across each other, overlap with each other, are in tension with each other and may be incommensurable with each other. (Barnett, 1998, p. 59)

Social loafing provides a window to understanding what it means to learn with and in digital networks. Vicars (2013, p. 132) suggests how embodied practices in which "students perform individual and collective literacies within complex social worlds should be pedagogical knowledge" and Barad (2007) has urged an understanding of how reading and writing on line has become "horizontal, rhizomatic [in] nature, [in] its virtuality and mutability, its diffraction and reassemblages" (p. 26).

> Social loafing in asynchronous environments as one of the participants commented ... allowed me to work independently and conduct the weekly questions and organise the session according to my own schedule. (Marcelle online survey, 2014)

Moving beyond a deficit understanding of social loafing requires acknowledgement of how dominant discourses and practices can become manipulated and in doing so

> afford individuals and collective groups opportunities to experiment with literacy practices that are informal, situated and which operate through horizontal processes and mutual collaboration. (Hickey-Moody & Haworth, 2009 p. 83)

Thinking from the participants' narratives that referenced how the asynchronous technologies allowed for anytime, anywhere contributions (Cogburn & Levinson, 2002), we started to think through spatial, temporal and material interactions of social loafing and the pedagogical implications. Limited synchronous contributions to the group work were initially read as being problematic due to periodic lack of connection. The ways in which information was being accessed, exchanged and new knowledge was being constructed was not immediately visible or recognizable to us, however, the participants' comments indicate they did not share our instructional concerns:

> I have used ICT for learning from watching recorded videos. It was positive as I could learn at my own convenience from my preferred place and time. (Eliza online survey, 2014)

> In the ICT environment I tend to become more self-directed and do a better job at taking learning into my own hands. (Chantal online survey, 2014)

> I would have gained more from completing the collaboration individually and then participating in a group reflection (I quite enjoyed that part). Perhaps I'm not a great team player. I prefer working alone. (Ligia online survey, 2014)

The narratives from the students suggests how social loafing was most effective in ways that it established consistent task related communication between team members. While it might not fit within constructing conventional understandings of deep learning, it does pedagogically point towards how students navigated the thrown togetherness of the project as readers and writers. This increasingly occurred in a digital "space [in which their habits and practices as readers and writers] was [situated out of] an entangled state of 'social' and 'natural', 'material' and 'discursive' negotiations" (Jackson & Mazzei, 2012, p. 269). It is therefore worth considering how as educators we respond to social loafing and interpret it as a practice that is concomitant with 'new' ways of learning within a 24/7 digital literacy landscape.

NOTE

1. Pseudonyms are used for all inserted quotes from the voices of the teacher candidates

REFERENCES

Alnuaimi, O. A., Robert, L. P., & Maruping, L. M. (2010). Team size, dispersion, and social loafing in technology-supported teams: A perspective on the theory of moral disengagement. *Journal of Management Information Systems, 27,* 203–230.

Alvesson, M., & Karreman, D. (2011). *Qualitative research and theory development: mystery as method.* London, England: SAGE.

Barad, K. (2007). *Meeting the universe halfway: Quantam physics and the enlightenment of matter and meaning.* Durham, NC: Duke University Press.

Barnett, R. (1998). Supercomplexity and the University. *Social Epistemology, 12*(1), 43–50.

Beddall-Hill, N. L., Jabbar, A., & Al Shehri, S. (2011). Social mobile devices as tools for qualitative research in education: iPhones and iPads in ethnography, interviewing, and design-based research. *Journal of the Research Center of Educational Technology*, 7(1), 67–89.

Bijker, W. E., & Law, J. (1992). General introduction. In W. E. Bijker & J. Law (Eds.), *Shaping technology/building society*. Cambridge, MA: MIT Press.

Boyd, P. O., & Onofry, R. M. (2013). *Finding lost marbles: Remembering the '50s in River City*. Bloomington, IN: AuthorHouse.

Cogburn, D. L., & Levinson N. S. (2002). Understanding distributed collaborative learning between the United States and South Africa. In *Networked learning in a global environment: Challenges and solutions for virtual education* (pp. 144–159). Berlin, Germany: ICSC Academic Press.

Cope, B., & Kalantzis, M. (2009). "Multiliteracies": New literacies, new learning. *Pedagogies: An International Journal, 4*(3), 164–195. Retrieved from http://newlearningonline.com/~newlearn/wp-content/blogs.dir/35/files/2009/03/M-litsPaper13Apr08.pdf

Curasi, C. (2001). A critical exploration of face-to-face interviewing vs. Computer-mediated interviewing. *Journal of the Market Research Society, 43*(4), 361–376.

Davies, W. M. (2009). Groupwork as a form of assessment: common problems and recommended solutions. *Higher Education, 58,* 563–584.

Davies, J. (2012) Facework on Facebook as a new literacy practice. *Computers and Education, 59,* 19–29.

Donath, J., & Boyd, D. (2004). Public displays of connection. *BT Technology Journal, 22*(4), 71–82.

Egan, K. (2002). *Getting it wrong from the beginning: Our progressivist inheritance from Herbert Spencer, John Dewey, and Jean Piaget.* New Haven, CT: Yale University Press.

Edwards, A., & Wilson, J. (2004). *Implementing virtual teams: A guide to organizational and human factors.* Burlington, VT: Gower.

Fullan, M. (2013). Great to excellent: Launching the next stage of Ontario's education agenda. Retrieved from www.edu.gov.onca/eng/document/reports/fullan.html

Gee, J. P. (2008). *Social linguistics and literacies: Ideologies in discourses.* London, England: Falmer Press.

Gee, J., & Gee. P. (1990). *Social linguistics and literacies: Ideology in discourses*. London, England: Falmer Press.

Gibson, J. J (1979). *The ecological approach to perception*. Boston, MA: Houghton Mifflin.

Hickey-Moody, A., & Haworth, R. (2009). Affective literacies. In D. Masny & D. Cole (Eds.), *Multiple literacies theory*. Rotterdam, the Netherlands: Sense.

Hutchby.I (2001). Technology, texts and affordances. *Sociology, 35*(2),441–456.

Karau, S. J., & Williams, K. D. (1993). Social Loafing: A meta-analytic review and theoretical integration. *Journal of Personality and Social Psychology, 65,* 681–706.

Keene, E., & Zimmerman, S. (1997). *Mosaic of thought.* Portsmouth, NH: Heinemann.

Kuby, C. R. (2017). Why a paradigm shift of 'more than human ontologies' is needed: Putting to work poststructural and posthuman theories in writers' studio. *International Journal of Qualitative studies in Education, 30*(9), 877–896.

Lankshear, C., & Knobel, M. (2006). *New literacies: Everyday practices and classroom learning.* New York, NY: Peter Lang.

Latane, B. (1981). The psychology of social impact. *American Psychologist, 36,* 343–356.

Leander, K., & Sheehy, M. (2004). *Spatializing literacy research and practice.* New York, NY: Peter Lang.

Luke, A., & Carrington, V. (2002). Globalisation, literacy, curriculum practice. In R. Fisher, M. Lewis, & G. Brooks (Eds.), *Language and literacy in action.* London, England: Routledge/Falmer

Luke. C. (2003) Pedagogy, connectivity, multimodality, and interdisciplinarity. *Reading Research Quarterly, 38*(3) 397–403.

Moore-Gilbert, B. (1997). *Postcolonial theory: Contexts, practices, politics.* London, England: Verso.

Meho, L. I. (2006). E-mail interviewing in qualitative research: A methodological discussion. *Journal of the American Society for Information Science & Technology, 57,* 1284–1295.

Murris. K. (2016). *The posthuman child.* New York, NY: Routledge.

Neal, G. (2007). Thinking and learning with information and communication technology (ICT): Student voices. *International Journal of Technology, Knowledge and Society, 3*(1), 83–91.

New London Group. (1996). A pedagogy of multiliteracies: Designing social futures. *Harvard Educational Review, 66*(1), 60–93.

Piezon, S. L., & Ferree, W. D. (2007). Perceptions of social loafing in online learning groups. Retrieved from https://www.researchgate.net/publication/267548237_Perceptions_of_Social_Loafing_in_Online_Learning_Groups/download

Roberts, T. (2005). *Computer-supported collaborative learning in higher-education.* Hershey, PA: Ideas Group.

Scardamalia, M., & Bereiter, C. (1999). Schools as knowledge building organisations. In D. Keating & C. Hertzman (Eds.), *Developmental health and the wealth of nations: Social, biological and educational dynamics* (pp. 274–289). New York, NY: The Guildford Press.

Sepie, A. (2017). More than stories, more than myths: Animal/human/nature(s) in traditional ecological worldviews. *Humanities, 6*(78), 2–31.

Synder, I. (2008). *The literacy wars.* Crows Nest, Australia: Allen & Unwin.

St Pierre, E. (2013). The posts continue becoming. *International Journal of Qualitative Studies in Education, 26,* 646–657.

Thompson, J. (2004). *Cooperative learning in computer-supported classes.* Melbourne, Australia: University of Melbourne.

Vicars, M. (2013). Literacy: Books? Who needs books anyway? It is not kewl. In T. Mckenna, M. Cacciatollo, & M. Vicars (Eds.), *Engaging the disengaged.* Cambridge, England: Cambridge University Press.

Worchel, S., Rothgerber, H., & Day, E. A., Hart, D., & Butemeyer, J. C. (1998) Social identity and individual productivity within groups. *British Journal of Social Psychology, 37,* 389–413.

CHAPTER 5

TRANSLANGUAGING AS A (META)COGNITIVE TOOL FOR NAVIGATING AND LEARNING IN THE MULTILINGUAL ONLINE ENVIRONMENT

Kwangok Song
University of Kansas

Byeong-Young Cho
University of Pittsburgh

In this chapter, we challenge the common perception of English centrism in the online world, acknowledging the increasingly diverse situations of digital literacy practices in a today's multilingual environment (Barton & Lee, 2013; Lee, 2017). Our critique of such linguistic status-quo is motivated by the idea of multilingual online users' complex translanguaging practices. Informed by resource approaches to the pedagogy of language and literacy, we view translanguaging as a metacognitive tool that is useful and valuable to learners in a multilingual online setting. To describe the nature of translanguaging situated in online reading, we use bilingual

Negotiating Place and Space Through Digital Literacies: Research and Practice, pp. 77–94

students' think-aloud data from our empirical study of adolescent bilingual learners' use of comprehension strategies and translanguaging strategies in online reading. The verbal excerpts represent how the learners use their two languages as they identify and learn from multilingual texts online. We close the chapter with a discussion of scientific and pedagogical implications for translanguaging as a tool for learning and relevant literacy practices on the multilingual digital media environment.

MULTILINGUAL INTERNET AND HYBRIDIZED DIGITAL LITERACY PRACTICES

Language use on the Internet has become increasingly dynamic and diverse over the last few decades. As of 2017, approximately 75% of Internet participation is carried out in languages other than English, although English as *lingua franca* remains the most common language of the Internet (Internet World Stat, 2018). Examining languages used on the Internet across 12 years, Pimienta, Prado, and Blanco (2009) reported that the Internet usage increased significantly in the countries where English is not the dominant language during the period of their study, suggesting that the Internet activities and online texts have become more linguistically diverse. Thus, the portrait of English-dominating literacy practices in the online environment has been revised to include the assemblage of multiple languages, texts, and codes (Danet & Herring, 2007). Whereas monolingual users may rely on websites written mostly in their native languages, multilingual individuals with experiences in other languages, in one way or another, are likely to traverse linguistic borders in the Internet environment. Not only do they search for information from multilingual sources, but they also engage in online communities using more than one language. The users from different linguistic and cultural backgrounds negotiate differences in their ways of communicating by using their multiple linguistic repertoires and identity representations (Barton & Lee, 2013).

Such dramatic changes in the language usage in communication and textual representations contribute to shifting and problematizing the common perception of English dominance on the Internet. From the perspective of Bakhtin's (1982) heteroglossia, the Internet can be considered to be a hybrid space in which multiple languages, texts, and modalities co-contribute to newly imagined choices and opportunities. On the Internet, language choice matters as one participates in gathering information, building knowledge, and exchanging perspectives. Barton and Lee (2013) noted, "[L]anguage choice is tied in closely with the perceived affordances and action possibilities of the medium. How a site is used is not predetermined but is based on different purposes for different communicative situations" (p. 59). The availability of multilingual information spaces (e.g., personal, commercial, and public websites, communities, and networks) and the language functions of digital tools (e.g., multilanguage information searching, automated translation) on the Internet provide multilingual individuals with a multitude of opportunities to explore information resources in different languages. Flexible uses of such knowledge and skills are crucial as users navigate the multilingual text environment of the Internet to identify, analyze, and make sense of a wide range of information toward achieving their individual and social goals.

Students who have literacy experiences in two or more languages may take advantage of the multilingual Internet by communicating in both languages across physical and virtual borders in the online space (Lam, 2014). Research has documented how bilingual adolescents explore the online spaces by making the most of their repertoires of linguistic and cultural knowledge and strategies. For example, code-switching and transliteration can allow bilingual adolescents to participate actively and confidently in online chatting with other people who use either language or both. These participants share similar linguistic backgrounds, experiences, and resources within the social, epistemic, and emotional space in which they feel free to apply and navigate their knowledge about their two languages (Lam, 2004; Vandekerckhove & Nobels, 2010; Yi, 2009). Bilingual adolescents' language choice is both mediated and constrained by several sociocultural aspects, such as textual languages available on the online space, their interpersonal relationships with other users on the Internet, and genres and medium with which they present themselves (Androutsopoulos, 2015). Language choice in online communication allows bilinguals to enact social roles, negotiate their positions in social structures, and claim their linguistic and ethnic affinity in transnational contexts (Lam, 2014). However, very few studies have examined how bilingual adolescents accessed and utilized multilingual resources on the Internet by activating their knowledge of two languages. To add to the current literature on multilingual learners' use of their two languages to navigate multilingual resources, this chapter reports the findings from a study that examined how Korean emergent bilingual students navigated multilingual online resources by using their skills and strategies in using both of their two languages.

READING AS FOUNDATION FOR LEARNING AND COMMUNICATION IN THE MULTILINGUAL INTERNET

Reading in the Internet context is an integral part of digital literacy practices. Online reading requires specific strategies due to the multiplicity and complexity of the online context. These strategies enable users to search and identify necessary information and synthesize information across different sources while navigating multiple online texts. Furthermore, the Internet users need to make critical decisions to evaluate, explore, select, and read online sources (Leu et al., 2015). Adolescents possessing these skills and strategies can manage their thoughts and actions to search, evaluate, and identify credible information (Coiro, 2011; Coiro & Dobler, 2007).

Culminating research has paid attention to adult English-as-a-second-language (ESL) readers' strategy use in online reading (e.g., Anderson, 2003; Chun, 2001; Huang, Chern, & Lin, 2009; Park & Kim, 2011; Park, Yang, & Hsieh, 2014). These studies indicate that advanced adult ESL readers use not only comprehension strategies similar to those used in reading printed texts but also additional strategies to explore hyperlinked online texts in their second language. However, how biliterate learners can search for and read texts in different languages on the multilingual Internet has rarely been considered in this line of literature. Because online reading is situated in the multilingual text environment of the Internet, bilingual readers are likely to use their knowledge and skills in both languages to access and obtain information in different languages. More research could provide an understanding of bilingual adolescents' use of multilingual sources on the Internet. Building on the previous studies on ESL/EFL students' use of comprehension strategies in an online reading task, the current study aimed to demonstrate how bilingual learners utilize their linguistic resources to comprehend online texts.

TRANSLANGUAGING FOR MEANING MAKING IN READING

Digital literacy practices are multilingual by nature, and translanguaging is central to the multilingual individuals' digital literacies (Lee, 2017). The idea of translanguaging explicates multilingual individuals' transformative and flexible use of their linguistic knowledge and resources for meaning-making in literacy practices across different modalities (e.g., listening, speaking, reading, writing) in their social interactions (García & Li, 2014). Translanguaging encompasses not only shuttling between named languages as in code-switching but also translation and other bilingual abilities (McSwan, 2017). Although translanguaging often explains bilinguals' use of their linguistic repertoire in social interaction, it can also be a metacognitive tool for multilingual individuals to negotiate and create meaning and to evaluate their cognitive processes. In fact, García and Li (2014) indicated that translanguaging is "a meaning-making social and cognitive activity that works in-between conventional meaning-making practices and disciplines and goes beyond them" (p. 40).

With Vygotsky's (1934/1986) idea of language as a mediational tool for cognitive processes, Swain (2006) argues, "[L]anguaging serves as a vehicle through which thinking is articulated and transformed into an artifactual form" (p. 97). Influenced by Swain's notion of languaging, Li (2018) noted that translanguaging helps multilingual learners "gain knowledge, to make sense, to articulate one's thought and to communicate about using language" (p. 1224). Bilingual learners' linguistic repertoires for cognitive processes facilitate their learning in a classroom context in which the socially dominant language is the instructional language. Therefore, the idea of translanguaging reconsiders the role of L1 in bilingual learners' learning and cognitive development in a classroom context (Li, 2018). Multilingual learners can use translanguaging to construct meaning, mediate their use of one language, activate their funds of knowledge, compare meanings across different languages, and monitor their meaning-making processes (Canagarajah, 2013; Martin-Beltrán, 2014).

By using a think-aloud approach, researchers attempted to examine how bilingual readers accessed their two languages during a reading task. Although bilinguals think beyond the boundaries of named languages as Li (2018) indicated, identifying language choice during think-alouds in this line of literature seems to demonstrate how dynamically and flexibly bilinguals use linguistic knowledge and resources in their reading processes. Bilingual readers traverse between their two languages not only to extract, construct, and negotiate meaning but also to evaluate and monitor their comprehension processes when reading in their second language (Kwon & Schallert, 2016; Upton & Thompson, 2001). Translating, using cognates, and using bilingual resources, such as bilingual dictionaries, are identified as reading comprehension strategies that bilingual readers use to clarify, refine, and negotiate meaning across their two languages (García & Godina, 2017; Jiménez, Gacía, & Pearson, 1996). Regardless of their L2 reading proficiency, bilingual readers' use of their two languages during reading represents their strategic decision making on when and how to select a language to facilitate comprehension and monitor their reading processes (Kwon & Schallert, 2016; Seng & Hashim, 2006).

In sum, research has proven that bilingual learners' use of their two languages is integral to their meaning-making from texts. However, most existing studies focused on bilingual learners' use of their two languages only in printed-text reading contexts; very few studies examined the online context that may allow bilingual learners options to read texts of their choice in their both languages. Thus, building on the idea of translanguaging, this study adds to the previous studies by examining adolescent bilingual readers' use of translanguaging for learning from multilingual online texts.

EMERGING BILINGUAL ADOLESCENTS' TRANSLANGUAGING IN ONLINE INQUIRY

Here, we discuss how emerging bilingual adolescents accessed and used their two languages in the online context. Drawing from a more extensive study, we focused on two Korean bilingual adolescents in this chapter: Ho-Youg (All names are pseudonyms), a sixth-grade boy, and Yoonah, an eighth-grade girl. They were invited to participate in our lager study about bilingual learners' use of their two languages in online reading as we looked for emergent bilingual adolescents who had had previous schooling experience in their home country and had spent only up to 3 years in the United States. Both had lived in the United States with their families for approximately two years. They had first learned English as a foreign language when they were in third grade as part of South Korean elementary school curriculum. Ho-Youg had about four years of schooling experience in Korea; whereas, Yoonah had 6 years. Both of them regularly read both in Korean and English. English was the primary language for academic reading; whereas, Korean was for pleasure reading. They had a positive view of themselves as readers in both languages despite their preference for Korean. Their reading ability in Korean was around their grade levels; whereas, their English reading proficiency was slightly lower than their actual grade level. Ho-Youg and Yoonah admitted that they used the Internet almost everyday not only to search for information for school work but also to access social media both in English and Korean and to use online bilingual dictionaries whenever necessary for their understanding of unfamiliar English words.

In examining the metacognitive aspects of Ho-Youg's and Yoonah's translanguaging processes, a think-aloud approach was used in this study. Ho-Youg and Yoonah were asked to select a topic of interest and learn about the topic by using the online resources. To assess their content learning from the online inquiry, the focal participants were also asked to write in English what they had known about the topics before the online inquiry and to write what they learned about their topics after the online inquiry. The language choice for writing tasks was intended to emulate an academic writing task in the United States. The following sections delineate how similarly and/or differently Ho-Youg and Yoonah used translanguaging during the online inquiry. As we explain these two bilingual adolescents' translanguaging as part of their (meta)cognitive processes, differentiating their two named languages is necessary to show how Ho-Youg and Yoonah flexibly used translanguaging for their learning from online sources.

HO-YOUG: TRANSLANGUAGING FOR CONFIRMING AND REFINING INFORMATION

Ho-Youg chose Zika virus as his topic for the inquiry because he learned from the news about the spread of Zika virus. During the online inquiry, Ho-Youg used his skills in both Korean and English and purposefully chose a textual language for his learning on the multilingual Internet. His choice of textual language was somewhat linear. He first examined the information about Zika virus on the Korean version of Wikipedia and then moved to the English edition of Wikipedia to learn further about the topic and to confirm what he had learned from the Korean edition. Thus, he tried to cross-check the information he read in one language by rereading the same information in the other language. In the following excerpt, Ho-Youg acknowledged that he looked up information in both languages when necessary (Please note that the words underlined in translation indicate the ones that the participants code-switched to English while speaking in Korean.).

> 제가 usually 하게는 먼저 영어로 search를 해요. 왜냐하면은, (집에 있는 컴퓨터 키보드에) 한국말 그게 없고, 그래서 영어가 편해서 그렇게 하는데, 그 다음에, 한국 사이트에서도 한 번 봐 봐야 겠다 그러면, command한 다음에 한 글자씩 찾아서 다 쓰고 찾아 보죠.
>
> [I usually search in English first because there are no Korean letters (on the computer keyboard at home), so (searching in) English is convenient. That is why I do so. And then, if I think I need to look up (the information) on a Korean site, I press the command key and look for each (Korean) letter to type (a search term) to look up.]

During the online inquiry for this study, however, the computer offered to him had the bilingual keyboards with letters in both Korean and English. Ho-Youg decided to take advantage of the linguistic affordances of the tool to visit the Korean edition first. Reading the same information both in Korean and in English seemed to enable Ho-Youg to clarify what he learned, enhancing his comprehension. His choice of textual codes during the online inquiry reflected his knowledge about the Wikipedia as a translingual website that provides content in different languages.

Ho-Youg also used both Korean and English to comprehend texts written in either language, and each language has a different role in his think-alouds. His language choice for his think-alouds during the online task suggested that he used Korean to make sense of the content regardless of the language of a text. He intermittently used English words directly from the text without translation to facilitate the flow of his thinking. Some of those words were commonly used in his life; whereas, others were likely to be used only through transliteration when used in Korean. By selecting the Korean language as his primary tool for thinking, Ho-Youg also engaged in translating the information that he read in English into Korean. He was actively paraphrasing and summarizing what has been written in English into Korean. His translation as demonstrated in his think-alouds was not the literal or word-to-word translation. Instead, he selectively chose information from the texts he was reading in English and synthesized multiple pieces of information together. The following excerpt shows how Ho-Youg used his two languages strategically to summarize what he learned from the text.

> 처음에 여기에서 Zika forest of Uganda에서 나왔다니까 우간다에서 먼저 이렇게 발견됐다는 것을 볼 수가 있고, 댕기나 황열 바이러스 아니면 일본 뇌수막염, 그런거 바이러스와 related 되어 있고 댕기열이랑 거의 똑같고, 이렇게 mild symptoms 그런거 있고 …
>
> [First, here, because it says that it (Zika virus) was originated from <u>the Zika forest of Uganda</u>, I can see it was first discovered in Uganda. And it is <u>related</u> to dengue fever, or yellow fever, or Japanese encephalitis. It is almost similar to dengue fever, and it has <u>mild symptoms</u> like that.]

In the excerpt above, Ho-Youg's translated summary demonstrates several aspects of his translanguaging for cognitive purposes. First, his direct use of English words (e.g., "forest," "related," "mild symptoms") without translation seems to suggest that he might have internalized those words that were frequently used. Thus, such direct use of English words from the text did not hinder the flow of his thinking. Second, although the original text had more detailed information about how Zika virus spread, his summary focused only on where it came from and what other diseases are similar to Zika. By using translanguaging, Ho-Youg selected the information that was important to him and synthesized the information pieces coherently. Third, his translation seemed to benefit from his reviewing of the Korean edition. The names of diseases such as *Dengue* and *yellow fever* might be challenging for Ho-Youg to translate because these words were specialized terms and were not used commonly in his everyday life or at school. Yet, in this excerpt, he successfully recognized these words in English and was able to make connections to the terms in Korean.

Ho-Youg's inference to *Japanese encephalitis* as a relevant disease was interesting because of the lack of the target word in both of the texts that he read. The English entry states, "Zika virus is a mosquito-borne flavivirus closely related to the dengue and yellow fever viruses (Wikipedia, n.d.)" Likewise, The Korean edition of the Wikipedia entry on Zika virus suggests: "보통 가벼운 증상으로 뎅기열과 유사하다 [Usually, the light symptoms are similar to those of Dengue]" (위키백과, n.d.). As shown in these excerpts from the entries from two different language versions, however, there was no mention of Japanese encephalitis [일본뇌염] in either entry. His connection to Japanese encephalitis shows that he might have activated his prior-knowledge to make an inference by using a context clue in the text (e.g., the fact that Zika virus is transmitted via mosquitos) and his cultural knowledge and experiences with Japanese encephalitis vaccination encouraged by Korean Center for Disease Control especially for elementary students. In fact, the Korean word, "뇌수막염" that Ho-Youg chose for *encephalitis* means meningitis, and the correct word in Korean for *encephalitis* is 뇌염. Due to the shared syllables (뇌 and 염) in these two Korean words (뇌수막염 and 뇌염) and his insufficient knowledge about these diseases, his confusion of these specialized terms was understandable. Although his connection was not entirely accurate, it is still notable that Ho-Young was able to activate his cultural and linguistic knowledge to make an inference to try to get a better understanding of the symptoms as he was translanguaging. Overall, translanguaging allowed Ho-Youg to attend to the necessary information selectively, to create a coherent summary of what he read, and to activate his prior knowledge to make an inference.

Additionally, Ho-Youg used translanguaging to regulate and appraise his reading processes during the online inquiry to facilitate his learning. Ho-Youg monitored his understanding during reading, his use of two languages during the inquiry, and his choice of expressions in his think-alouds when reading on a website written in English. The following excerpt is an example of how Ho-Youg used translanguaging for a metacognitive purpose while he was reading about the significant consequence of the infection of Zika virus.

> Zika virus 하면, 이거 소두증? 그런거 같아요. 이렇게 (He points to one photo on the page.) 뇌가 작아진다거나 아니면, 이거 뭐랄까나? bone이 없다는거? Smallness of head, 이게 microcephaly 가 이렇게 작게 된 것 같아요.. 소두증.. [<u>Zika virus</u> seems to be related to small, smallness of head? I think it is. Like this. A brain gets smaller or how can I say this? No <u>bone</u>? I think that is. <u>Smallness of head</u>. This, microcephaly, it seems to become small like this. Smallness of Head."

In the excerpt above, Ho-Youg reviewed why Zika virus was particularly dangerous by reviewing the images of microcephaly. His self-questioning about the term ("소두증 [microcephaly]?") and his paraphrasing ("bone 이 없다는거 [no bone]?") demonstrates that he was monitoring his understanding of what microcephaly involved. Furthermore, his use of metalinguistic question (e.g., "이거 뭐랄까나 [How can I say this?]") shows that he might have been considering different ways to express the symptom of microcephaly. Such monitoring of his language use demonstrated that he tried to search the most appropriate expressions or words to refine his understanding of the original texts. Furthermore, re-reading of "smallness of head" in English and re-translating it into Korean ("이렇게 작게 된 것 같아요 [it seems to become small like this]") indicates that he monitored and confirmed his interpretation of what microcephaly is. Throughout this process, as shown in the excerpt, he was traversing two languages across different modes (e.g., reading a text and reviewing images) to reconfirm and refine his understanding of the term microcephaly.

YOONAH: TRANSLANGUAGING FOR MONITORING PLANS AND PROCESSES

Yoonah chose Ebola virus as her topic for the online inquiry because she thought that she might have heard that Ebola virus had spread in South Korea. However, by searching information on the Korean portal site, she soon found out that Ebola virus had not yet been found in South Korea. Like Ho-Youg, Yoonah's textual code-switching was dynamic in that she went back and forth between websites written in English and in Korean several times during her online inquiry. Figure 5.1 shows how Yoonah navigated websites written in Korean and English and how she used two languages to search information about the topic.

To learn about Ebola virus, she first searched how Ebola virus impacted South Korea on Google by using a search term in English. After she found out that no search results were about what she had expected, she accessed the most popular Korean portal site, Naver (www.naver.com). Because this site provides services in Korean, she chose the Korean language to search information about Ebola virus [에볼라 바이러스] by changing the keyboard setting. Her choice of a website seems to reflect her knowledge and experiences that a portal site developed in Korea could provide more comprehensive search results reflecting the relevance of the topic to the Korean context. From the search results, she first chose the link to 네이버 백과사전 [Naver Encyclopedia] to read the entry about Ebola virus. After she skimmed the entry quickly, she went to back to the search results to click the link to another service called 네이버 지식iN [Naver Intellectuals]. This service embedded in the focal portal site allows the Internet users to ask and answer questions. She chose the question about the transmission of Ebola virus. After her initial searches on the Korean portal site, she went to Google again to continue her search in English. Throughout her inquiry process, she revisited the Korean portal site to complement her understanding of what she read in English. Through textual code-switching, Yoonah was able to verify the information across different sites in different languages.

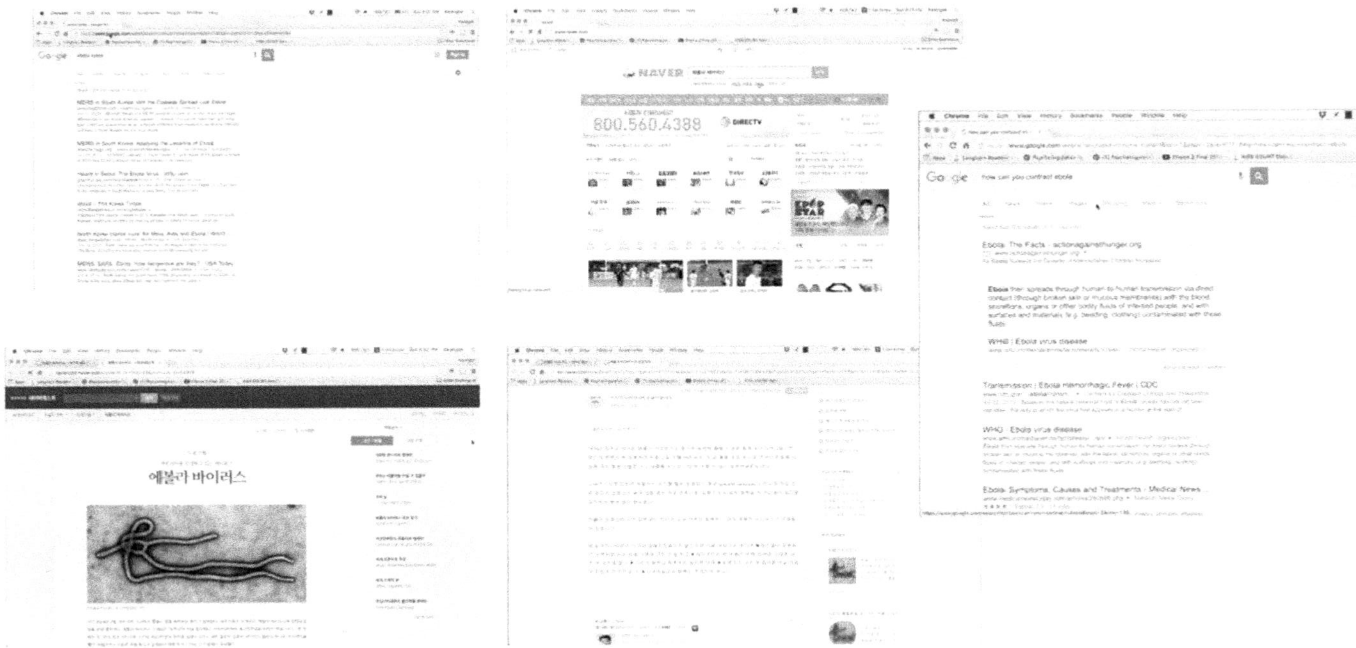

Figure 5.1. Yoonah's textual code-switching during her navigation of different sites.

Yoonah also used both of her languages to understand the content throughout her inquiry process to make sense of what she read. Her ways of translanguaging changed depending on different steps of her processes. During the initial examination of the information about Ebola virus, Yoonah's language choice in her think-alouds generally matched with the language of the text that she read. In other words, she chose Korean in her think-alouds when reading in Korean and English for reading in English. The following two excerpts show how Yoonah switched her primary language for her think-alouds while engaging in reading. The screenshots of the pages that Yoonah was reading are shown on the left side and her verbal reports on the right (see Figures 5.2 and 5.3).

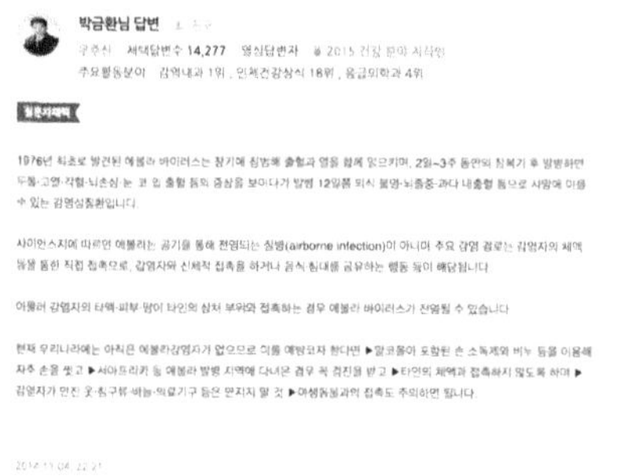

Figure 5.2. A screenshot of the Korean website (박금환, 2014) that Yoonah was reading.

So they find, they find Ebola virus at first in 1976, and the virus, umm, 2일에서 3주동안 몸에 있다가 병이나면은, 머리가 아프고, 이제 열나고 그 다음에 눈이랑 코랑 입에서 피가 나는 병.. [(the virus) can stay in the body for 2 days to 3 weeks. When symptoms start, there is a headache, fever, and bleeding in the eyes, nose, and mouth.]

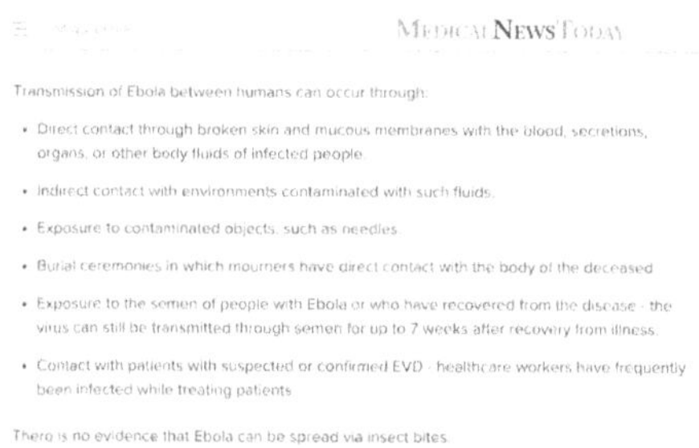

MEDICAL NEWS TODAY

Transmission of Ebola between humans can occur through:

- Direct contact through broken skin and mucous membranes with the blood, secretions, organs, or other body fluids of infected people.
- Indirect contact with environments contaminated with such fluids.
- Exposure to contaminated objects, such as needles.
- Burial ceremonies in which mourners have direct contact with the body of the deceased.
- Exposure to the semen of people with Ebola or who have recovered from the disease - the virus can still be transmitted through semen for up to 7 weeks after recovery from illness.
- Contact with patients with suspected or confirmed EVD - healthcare workers have frequently been infected while treating patients.

There is no evidence that Ebola can be spread via insect bites.

Figure 5.3. A screenshot of the English website (Nichols, 2017) that Yoonah was reading.

So, you can, you can get … get the virus from the dead body like who has died from Ebola, and, and the blood.

And, the like, umm, needles, and then you can get infected by the animals when they meet. And, it's different like from, umm, normal flus because you cannot get through the air and water, food, and mosquitos, but animals.

As shown in these excerpts, it seems that she relied on the language of the text to frame her thought processes and construct her understanding of the symptoms and transmission of Ebola virus. The content of Yoonah's verbal reports when reading demonstrated that she engaged heavily in summarizing, paraphrasing, and inferring. Although her verbal reports hardly showed how she applied metacognitive strategies to monitor and assess her comprehension processes, her hesitation, pauses, and repeating during think-alouds suggested that Yoonah might continuously monitor and assess her comprehension. Adopting the language of the text as the primary language of bilingual readers' think-alouds was also noted in Kwon and Schallert's (2016) study with advanced bilingual graduate students who strategically chose the textual language to facilitate their analysis of texts.

Interestingly, in the first excerpt, Yoonah initially chose English as her primary language for her verbal reports. Soon, she switched to Korean in her verbal reports. Her code-switching in the middle of her think-alouds seemed to be facilitated by the textual language of the website. On the one hand, it might have been possible that translating from Korean to English was cognitively challenging for Yoonah as shown in her hesitation. On the other hand, it can be viewed as a strategic language choice because Yoonah might have felt that constructing meaning by using the textual language was more effective than using translation because she was able to borrow expressions and specialized terms from the texts. Traversing her two languages across different texts and in her verbal reports seems not to obscure her comprehension of what she read, but it was her intentional and deliberate choice to take advantage of the linguistic resources available in the texts for learning.

Although Yoonah preferred English to answer interview questions and chose English as her major language for her think-alouds for her learning from online texts, it was notable that Yoonah relied primarily on Korean when reviewing the information again for her post-task writing. Her verbal reports revealed that she employed metacognitive strategies to appraise, plan, and regulate her processes as shown in the following excerpts. These excerpts came from different stages of her reviewing processes, and the texts she read during this time were in English.

> 제가 쓰고 싶은 거는 Ebola virus 가 어떻게 음.. 많은 South Africa 에 있는 사람들이 죽었는지에 대해...
>
> [What I want to write about is how <u>Ebola virus</u>, umm, ... many people in <u>South Africa</u> came to die] (Then, she opens Google on the screen and types "what is Ebola" in the search box. After the search results appear on the screen, she starts reviewing each of them).

> 잘은 모르겠는데, 그 두 살 아이가 죽었는데, West Africa에서 죽었는데, 그게 Ebola 라는 거는, 그러니까 그 아이가 죽고서, 인제 더 커져서 바이러스가 활동하는게 커져서, 그래서, 어 그래서 이렇게 퍼진 것 같은데
>
> [I'm not sure, not sure, but a two-year-old child died, died in <u>West Africa</u>, that was (due to) <u>Ebola</u>,, which means the child died and then it (the Ebola virus) became more active, the activity of the virus became active, so it seems to come to spread around] (After she took notes of the information about a 2-year-old's death, she went back to the Wikipedia to confirm the information.)

The first excerpt shows how Yoonah planned out what she wanted to write about first, and her planning eventually guided her to carry out an additional search to review the information about how Ebola virus outbreak started in South Africa. The second excerpt demonstrates that Yoonah assessed her understanding about the first outbreak of Ebola virus by expressing uncertainty while reviewing the text written in English: "잘은 모르겠는데 [I'm *not sure*], 퍼진것 같은데 [it *seems to* spread around]." Her uncertainty showed that she monitored her comprehension of what she read, and it further led her to searching for additional information to confirm what she had found was valid. Furthermore, she confirmed and clarified her understanding by repeatedly rephrasing the information about the cause of the Ebola virus diffusion written in English through translation into Korean as shown in: "which means the child died and then it (the Ebola virus) became more active, the activity of the virus became active, so it seems to spread around." In the above examples, translanguaging facilitated her application of metacognitive strategies to monitor her inquiry processes, make and revise a plan, and assess her comprehension.

TRANSLANGUAGING PRACTICES AND ONLINE INQUIRY ON THE MULTILINGUAL INTERNET FOR BILINGUAL LEARNERS

In this chapter, we highlighted two focal Korean-English bilingual adolescents' translanguaging during the online inquiry. The focal bilingual learners were able to traverse between their two languages as they searched for and learned from multiple online texts written in both languages. They also demonstrated their ability to access and utilize multilingual resources as they were given a choice of using their linguistic resources to explore the multilingual Internet. The focal bilingual learners' translanguaging operated both at cognitive and metacognitive levels. Translanguaging, as represented in the focal bilingual learners' think-alouds, suggested that they activated their linguistic repertoire and to make sense of texts (e.g., García & Godina, 2017; Upton & Lee-Thompson, 2001). They drew on their knowledge and experiences with the multilingual Internet while activating their skills in both languages and deliberately pursuing information written in both languages to cross-check different multilingual websites and to make inferences.

Translanguaging is also critical for the participants' application of metacognitive strategies as it facilitates their decision making and planning during reading. Through translanguaging, they monitored their understanding of what they had read and refined their plans to determine what to read in which language. Additionally, the focal adolescent bilingual readers' textual language choice to access multilingual online resources as shown in the findings may have been their purposeful decision to reexamine and reconfirm the information written in two different languages by making the most of their knowledge about the translinguality of information in a particular online space. Such metacognitive use of both languages was to monitor their processes to gain knowledge about the topic and to refine their understanding constructed from reading. Therefore, translanguaging during online inquiry may have the metacognitive nature as it involves explicit and implicit decision making across two different languages to facilitate learning processes (Li, 2018; Swain, 2006; Vygostky, 1986). Decision making with languages during the online inquiry could also suggest that the focal emerging bilingual adolescents had agency in using translanguaging to clarify and refine meaning, to make inferences, and to select and synthesize necessary information.

As shown in this study, bilingual learners may already possess such skills and strategies to take advantage of the affordances of the multilingual Internet to explore, evaluate, and select information written in different languages on the online space (Lee, 2017; Lam, 2014). However, it is imperative that such knowledge and abilities that bilingual learners have developed in an out-of-school context could be further cultivated in a classroom context in which English is the only medium of the instruction. Although the scope of this study was limited, the findings suggest a few pedagogical implications for educators who seek ways to support bilingual learners. It is critical for teachers to acknowledge emergent bilingual learners have agency in using their skills and strategies to explore multilingual resources for their learning. Therefore, translanguaging should be recognized as integral to multilingual learners' cognitive and metacognitive processes when they learn from texts because it facilitates bilingual learners' engagement with texts written in different languages (Li, 2018; McSwan, 2017). Teachers could also encourage bilingual learners to use translanguaging for their content learning in their second language. In supporting bilingual students' learning, therefore, an online inquiry as an instructional approach could be built on the understanding that the Internet as a translingual space in which information could be represented in different languages and that bilingual learners are active participants on the multilingual Internet. Through online inquiry activities that allow bilingual learners to access multilingual resources, bilingual learners with extensive out-of-school experiences with the Internet may be able to leverage knowledge and strategies to navigate resources in different languages to facilitate and strengthen their learning. Therefore, literacy instruction designed to support adolescents' digital literacy skills should provide bilingual learners with authentic opportunities to navigate, compare, contrast, and evaluate resources written in different languages for their learning on the Internet.

CONCLUDING REMARKS

The multilingual Internet offers affordances that bilingual learners can undertake as they search for and learn from online resources, and such affordances can be further activated by users' skills and strategies to use (Barton & Lee, 2013). Furthermore, multilingual users' agentive engagement in digital practices is critical because their intention and willingness to explore multilingual resources on the Internet and to utilize their linguistic knowledge can make the most of what the Internet offers. In some ways, the multilingual Internet can transcend the constraints that monolingual-oriented classroom practices unintentionally impose on bilingual learners. With additional and unrecognized linguistic resources and strategic knowledge excavated from their cross-linguistic experiences in out-of-school contexts, bilingual learners may benefit from exploring and navigating multilingual online resources with a purpose to learn. Ultimately, constructing knowledge and making meaning from texts can take place beyond named languages. Although this study provides an exploratory understanding of adolescent bilingual learners' use of translanguaging during an online inquiry, further research is necessary to investigate sophisticated ways of using translanguaging when searching for information and learning in the online context. Additionally, it is imperative to examine how translanguaging can be implemented in a classroom context to support emergent bilingual students' learning with the multilingual Internet.

REFERENCES

박금환 (2014, Nov. 4). 에볼라바이러스 감염 증상화 전염경로에 대해서. *Naver 지식 iN*. Retrieved from https://kin.naver.com/index.nhn.

위키백과. (n. d.) 지카 바이러스. Retrieved from Korean Wikipedia: https://ko.wikipedia.org/wiki/%EC%A7%80%EC%B9%B4%EB%B0%94%EC%9D%B4%EB%9F%AC%EC%8A%A4

Anderson, N. J. (2003). Scrolling, clicking, and reading English: Online reading strategies in a *second*/foreign language. *The Reading Matrix, 3*, 1–33.

Androutsopoulos, J. (2015). Networked multilingualism: Some language practices on Facebook and their implication. *International Journal of Bilingualism, 19*(2), 185–205.

Bakhtin, M. (1982). *The dialogic imagination: Four essays*. Austin, TX: The University of Texas Press.

Barton, D., & Lee, C. (2013). *Language online: Investigating digital texts and practices*. New York, NY: Routledge.

Canagarajah, A. S. (2013). Negotiating translingual literacy: An enactment. *Research in the Teaching of English, 48*(1), 40–67.

Chun, D. (2001). L2 reading on the web: Strategies for accessing information in hypermedia. *Computer Assisted Language Learning, 14*(5), 367–403.

Coiro, J. (2011). Predicting reading comprehension on the Internet: Contributions of offline skills, online reading skills, and prior knowledge. *Journal of Literacy Research, 43*(4), 352–392.

Coiro, J., & Dobler, E. (2007). Exploring the online reading comprehension strategies used by sixth-grade skilled readers to search for and locate information on the Internet. *Reading Research Quarterly, 42*(2), 214–257.

Danet, B., & Herring, S. C. (2007). Introduction: Welcome to the multilingual Internet. In B. Danet & S. C. Herring (Eds.), *The multilingual Internet: Language, culture, and communication online* (pp. 1–39). New York, NY: Oxford University Press.

García, G. E., & Godina, H. (2017). A window into bilingual reading: The bilingual reading practices of fourth-grade, Mexican American children who are emergent bilinguals. *Journal of Literacy Research, 49*(2), 273–301.

García, O., & Li, W. (2014). *Translanguaging: Language, bilingualism and education*. New York, NY: Palgrave.

Huang, H.-C., Chern, C.-I., & Lin, C.-C. (2009). EFL learners' use of online reading strategies and comprehension of texts: An exploratory study. *Computers & Education, 52*(1), 13–26.

Internet World Stats. (2018). *Internet world users by languages: Top 10 languages*. Retrieved from Internet World Stats: https://www.internetworldstats.com/stats7.htm

Jiménez, R., García, G. E., & Pearson, P. D. (1996). The reading strategies of bilingual Latina/o students who are successful English readers: Opportunities and obstacles. *Reading Research Quarterly, 31*, 90–112.

Kwon, H. J., & Schallert, D. L. (2016). Understanding translanguaging practices through a biliteracy continua framework: Adult biliterates reading academic texts in their two languages. *Bilingual Research Journal, 39*(2), 138–151. doi: 10.1080/15235882.2016.1167139

Lam., W. S. E. (2004). Second language socialization in a bilingual chat room: Global and local considerations. *Language, Learning & Technology, 8*(3), 44–65.

Lam, W. S. E. (2014). Literacy and capital in immigrant youths' online network across countries. *Learning, Media and Technology*. doi:10.1080/17439884.2014.942665

Lee, C. (2017). *Multilingualism online*. New York, NY: Routledge.

Leu, D. J., Forzani, E., Rhoads, C., Maykel, C., Kennedy, C., & Timbrell, N. (2015). The new literacies of online research comprehension: Rethinking the reading achivement gap. *Reading Research Quarterly, 50*(1), 37–59.

Li. W. (2018). Translanguaging as a practical theory of language. *Applied Linguistics, 39*(1), 9–30.

Martin-Beltrán, M. (2014). "What do you want to say?" How adolescents use translanguaging to expand learning opportunities. *International Multilingual Research Journal, 8,* 208–230.

McSwan, J. (2017). Multilingual perspective on translanguaging. *American Educational Research Journal, 54*(1), 167–201.

Nichols, H. (2017, May 23). *Ebola: What you need to know.* Retrieved from https://www.medicalnewstoday.com/

Park, H.-R., & Kim, D. (2011). Reading-strategy use by English as a second language learners in online reading tasks. *Computers & Education, 57*(3), 2156–2166.

Park, J., Yang, J., & Hsieh, Y. C. (2014). University level second language readers' online reading and comprehension strategies. *Language Learning & Technology, 18*(3), 148–172.

Pimienta, D., Prado, D., & Blanco, Á. (2009). *Twelve years of measuring linguistic diversity in the Internet: Balance and perspectives.* The Information Society Division, Communication and Information Sector (Ed.). Paris, France: UNESCO.

Seng, G. H., & Hashim, F. (2006). Use of L1 in L2 reading comprehension among tertiary ESL learners. *Reading in a Foreign Language, 18*(1), 29–54.

Swain, M. (2006). Languaging, agency and collaboration in advanced language proficiency. In H. Byrnes (Ed.), *Advanced language learning: The contribution of Halliday and Vygotsky* (pp. 95–108). London, England and New York, NY: Continuum.

Upton, T. A., & Lee-Thompson, L.-C. (2001). The role of the first language in second language reading. *SSLA, 23,* 469–495.

Vandekerckhove, R., & Nobles, J. (2010) Code eclecticism: Linguistic variation and code alternation in the chat language of Flemish teenagers. *Journal of Sociolinguistics, 14*(5), 657–677.

Vygotsky, L. S. (1986). *Thought and language* (A. Kozulin, Ed.). Boston, MA: The Massachusetts Institute of Technology Press. (Original work published, 1934).

Wikipedia (n.d.). *Zika virus.* Retrieved from Wikipedia: https://en.wikipedia.org/wiki/Zika_virus

Yi, Y. (2009). Adolescent literacy and identity construction among 1.5 Generation students from a transnational perspective. *Journal of Asian Pacific Communication, 19*(1), 100–129.

PART II

DIGITAL LITERACIES FROM WITHIN

CHAPTER 6

FULL OF SOUND AND FURY

Rural Students' Use of Digital Literacies in Exploring Space, Place, and Identity

David L. Bruce
University at Buffalo

Sunshine R. Sullivan
Houghton College

Nichole M. Barrett
University at Buffalo

Charles H. Gonzalez
Alabama A+M University

INTRODUCTION

On a Wednesday evening in mid-June, we gathered with other people from across the region in a school auditorium. Attending were teachers, administrators, and parents, all who chose to take a break from the tyranny of the state exam season to support the crowd of students—all dressed in

Negotiating Place and Space Through Digital Literacies: Research and Practice, pp. 97–116

formal attire—whose video productions had been nominated to represent their individual districts in a first ever, regional student film festival. The foyer had tables of food and drink while ushers passed out programs with voting ballots containing the names of the students and the projects they had created. The 31 student entries had been divided among three viewing flights with a brief intermission between segments. During those breaks, classic movie scenes and montages filled the auditorium screen while attendees ranked their favorites from each division. After all films had been screened, judges tallied the votes. The top winners from each flight were invited to the front of the auditorium and asked to share a few insights about their projects. Finally, an emcee read the names of the audience's choice award and presented them with a trophy.

That evening was the culmination of a year-long effort of a group of teachers from rural contexts who had attended a regional professional development institute called Writing with Video (WWV). In this institute, the teachers formed a community of practice (Wenger, 1998; Wenger, McDermott, & Snyder, 2002) around the use of digital tools. Participation in communities of practice refers to "being active participants in the *practices* of social communities and constructing *identities* in relation to these communities" (Wenger, 1998, p. 4, original emphasis). Wells (1999) adds, "learning is an integral aspect of participation in practices that have some other object in view" (p. 123). In addition to learning how to compose with digital video (DV), they also planned and developed curricular applications of these tools for their shared classroom use.

This chapter situates the ways in which their students used the available resources of their multimodal tools and ruralities as they composed their video projects. We work to illustrate how their students used both spaces and places that were part of their individual and collective ruralities to explicitly complete academic assignments, while tacitly exploring their identities.

REVIEW OF LITERATURE

Our work is informed by issues surrounding space and spatial literacies, rurality, and multimodal literacies, specifically the use of DV as a meaning making tool. In this section, each will be addressed in turn. Theobald (1997) posits that place-conscious pedagogy can occur when we are engaged in educational experiences that lead to *intradependence* between us and our local and broader spaces. Brooks (2003) adds that it is the "[focus] on the necessary relations-cultural, natural, agricultural—that shape a given place and its human communities" (p. 6).

As people move in and out of life experiences, they also move within and across boundaries and spaces that are lived (Lefebvre, 1974/1991). These spaces are inextricably linked to mental and material "biographies and geo-histories" (Soja, 2010, p. 18). Therefore, spatiality can be understood as the result of interactions with historically situated, socially constructed geographies that have impacts—both positive and negative, enchanting or limiting—on the way that individuals conceptualize their surroundings and their role within space. A space becomes a place when we take time to see it, listen in it, or recognize it as a part of our life, our process. Space transforms when a connection is developed (intentionally or tacitly) over time as a result of varied purpose and levels of intentionality and reflection. It is when we take a moment to spend time in spaces, to recognize and embrace them with purpose, that they become an important part of our histories and identities, and influential in the meaning making process. If, as Soja (2010) argues, time and space are both socially constructed through lived experience and shaped by existing circumstance, then understanding how rural students draw on their surroundings as a part of their meaning making processes can be explored by looking at the ways that they negotiate the boundaries between spaces and places.

Both real and imagined places have consequences on learning and affect how individuals reflect upon and negotiate their identities and roles across boundaries. Rural spaces and places are constructed through experience, and although more than half of the students who attend public school in the United States do so in rural spaces, educational research emphasizes the experiences of urban and suburban students (Green, 2013; Schafft, 2016; Tieken & San Antonio, 2016). Current research addressing rural education positions rural students in direct opposition to their urban peers, neglecting to take into consideration realities of rural life (Donehower, Hogg, & Schell, 2007, 2012; Eckert & Alsup, 2004), and the learning and teaching that occurs outside of classroom boundaries (Gruenewald, 2003). Instead, narratives of rurality and rural education construct a deficit view of what it means to occupy spaces and places outside of urban boundaries. These views perpetuate an escape narrative that encourages students to seek out a more urban narrative in favor of their existing impoverished one (Eckert & Alsup, 2014) and strengthen "metro-centric" attitudes towards literacy and learning (Green, 2013). Hodges (2004) also argues that not all rural communities are the same. Each community has its own stories, its own history, and its students will each have their own experiences all connected and defined by their individual rurality. Leveraging a community's resources (e.g., landmarks, museums, local library, landscape), histories, and stories can be a way for students to take ownership over their rural spaces and the affordances they offer.

What is missing from research in rural education is an emphasis on how students draw upon rural spaces and places as they negotiate both their identities and literacy practices. Looking at how students incorporate their rural spaces and experiences as a part of their literacy practices—even implicitly—is one way that we can begin to understand the approaches students use to work to define and redefine themselves in terms of their surroundings, as well as how they negotiate local and global definitions of rurality. Since the research in this chapter occurs within rural spaces, it draws attention to the need for emphasis on the individual stories of rural students and all of their spaces and places.

Drawing on sociocultural views of literacy (e.g., Gee, 1992), educational research exploring the impact of space on student learning and identity has often focused on drawing connections between students' literacy practices in schooled and non-schooled spaces (e.g., Hull & Shultz, 2002; Moje, 2004; Schultz, 2002; Skerrett & Bomer, 2011) as well as the impact that family and community have on students' literacy practices (e.g., Heath, 1983; Moje et al., 2004; Pahl & Kelly, 2005; Street, 1984). There is also a growing body of research that advocates for spatial (e.g., Barton, Hamilton, & Ivanic, 2000; Mills & Comber, 2015) and place-conscious (e.g., Brooke, 2003; Comber, 2015; Mills & Comber, 2013; Somerville, 2013; Theobald, 1997) approaches to literacy and literacy instruction as a way to incorporate the impact that space can have upon student learning and identity development.

Research addressing the positive impact of students' multimodal (e.g., Albers & Sanders, 2010; Cope & Kalantzis, 2000; Miller & McVee, 2013; Ranker, 2008; Siegel, 2006) and digital (e.g., Curwood, Magnifico, & Lammers, 2013; Lankshear & Knobel, 2006; Tavares, 2015; Vasudevan, 2010) literacy practices has gained momentum. However, this research tends to highlight the use of multimodal and digital literacies in relationship to academic gains and/or metrics (e.g., Abrams, 2009; Beach, 2012; Miller, Knips, & Goss, 2013), rather than explore the impact that digital and multimodal literacy practices have upon students' meaning making processes.

As approaches to teaching and learning shift as a result of technological advances, there is need to explore the affordances of DV composition in relationship to space and place. Manovich (2001) notes that digital and new media, as opposed to traditional media and movie making, "is characterized by variability" and "typically gives rise to many different versions" (p. 56). He draws attention to the impact that digital technologies have on an author's interaction with and across modalities. More specifically he notes that, "In the process of interaction the user can choose which elements to display or which paths to follow, thus generating a unique work" (p. 66). While research drawing attention to the value of students' digital compositions as multimodal (e.g., Bruce, 2008; Chandler-Olcott & Lewis, 2010; Doerr-Stevens, 2015; Smith, 2017) and mobile (e.g., Ehret & Hollett, 2014; Wargo, 2015; Warner, 2016) has grown, these studies mostly occur in urban or suburban spaces (e.g., Chisholm & Olinger, 2017; Vasudevan, Shultz, & Bateman, 2010). In the studies where students used DV in rural spaces, researchers found that their compositions were impacted by their settings, with students often highlighting personal connections to the community spaces within their rural settings (Pyles, 2016; Wake, 2012). This study, then, illustrates how students used DV for academic purposes while exploring the spaces, places, and experiences of their rural landscapes.

METHODOLOGY

Context

The data in this chapter are part of a larger study where higher education faculty provided professional development and examined how professional learning communities (PLC) enroot when teachers from across a primarily rural region engaged in digital literacies together.

During the summer of 2016, WWV offered a weeklong summer institute focusing on digital literacies in the classroom. ELA and history teachers from a rural region were invited to participate. Twelve teachers from six school districts participated in developing their own digital literacy competencies and making plans to integrate 21st century literacies in their curriculum. Throughout the following academic year, we met for day-long fall and spring reunions where teachers continued the work they began in the summer as well as shared their teaching and student work within their learning community. In between the reunions, they remained connected with one another through online forums and e-mail threads, sharing ideas and student work samples. Throughout our first year's work together as a community of practice—in our reunions and online forums—the teachers continued collaborating on incorporating the digital literacies in their classrooms. A culminating celebration of both their growth as educators and their students as composers of video occurred in a public venue through a year-end film festival that the teachers collaboratively designed, promoted, and hosted. The videos analyzed for this research were premiered at this film festival.

Participants

Brendan Heaney. Brendan was one of our participating teachers and his school hosted the film festival. He taught an elective film class as well as a World Literature course. In one of his units for the latter, he had students create a video in response to one of the several Shakespeare texts they had read and viewed. Specifically, he gave an open set of directions to the students: interpret your choice of a theme, passage, scene, or play by Shakespeare using DV as your compositional means.

Alicia & Jess. These two students were in Brendan's class and chose to create a video around MacBeth's "Tomorrow and tomorrow and tomorrow" soliloquy (Act V, scene v). Jess was a senior and Alicia was a junior. While they worked collaboratively throughout the project, Alicia originated the concept for their video, and guided much of the content. Jess, having expertise with camerawork and editing, did the majority of the production work. Together, they attended to the content through compositional moves to present a shared vision for the project. Alicia said they wanted to show "the soliloquy though a modern lens and highlight that it's still relevant now and people are still struggling with the same things." We selected their project for analysis because it was textually rich in both production quality and interpretation of the source text.

Data Collection and Analysis

Teacher and student interviews. We conducted two formal interviews with each participating teacher. The first interview occurred near the end of the weeklong summer institute and teachers were asked to share about their learning experiences with digital literacies. The second interview took place during the summer following the academic year. Teachers were asked to share about their curricular use of and student learning through digital literacies. Additionally, the two focal students were interviewed the following academic year. One of the students had graduated high school and gone to college, and the other was now a senior in high school. They were asked about their composition processes and to reflect on what they had discovered through making the DV class project. They also viewed the finished video and were asked retrospective analysis questions about their work.

All teacher and student interviews were listened to in their entirety. While listening, researchers made analytic memos (Strauss & Corbin, 1990). The interviews were transcribed and entered into NVivo qualitative software analysis program. Two researchers looked for thematic connections among the interviews, creating initial coding through open nodes and then coalesced the emergent threads into tree nodes. Where there was congruency in content, these nodes were used to inform the video content analysis.

Teacher artifacts. We collected two types of artifacts from the participating teachers. The first came from their multimodal composition work within the institute, and included conceptual planning, final digital projects, and reflections on their process and product. The second type of artifact was comprised of curricular planning, lessons, and/or projects the teachers planned to enact with their students. Artifacts related to the curricular work that led to student work being entered into the film festival were reviewed for contextual material regarding the student videos.

Online community. We used Schoology as our learning management platform. We posted discussion threads on various topics to which teachers responded. The format was largely dictated by the teachers and became a virtual space for curricular examples, reunion planning and reflections, and a forum for numerous aspects of the film festival.

Video content analysis. There were a total of 31 student videos from five school districts submitted to the film festival. Of these, we completed content analysis of 15 videos, namely, those that used the affordances, spaces, and places of their rural contexts. Specifically we examined the topic/theme, class and assignment, use of indoor spaces and outdoor spaces as well as general production observations. Additionally, we conducted a detailed shot analysis on Jess and Alicia's video, Tomorrow and Tomorrow.

Two researchers concurrently viewed, analyzed, and coded each shot of Tomorrow and Tomorrow. The 3:10 minute video had 73 shots in total, which were analyzed for location, camera angle, visual information, ambient audio, voice-over, music, and special effects.

FINDINGS

In academic assignments, students' assignments and audience are often limited within the four walls of the classroom and the curbs of the school property. While they may use the Internet for virtual explorations, their space within academic boundaries is often within the school confines. Through these video assignments, our teachers' students were given the chance to venture outside of those academic spaces. While some students kept their productions within the school—some by assignment, necessity, time constraints, and so forth—others ventured beyond those borderlines and traversed in and through their community landscapes.

For their literature class assignment of responding to a selection from Shakespeare using DV, Alicia and Jess selected MacBeth's soliloquy, *Tomorrow and tomorrow and tomorrow*. In thinking about making Shakespeare relevant to today, Alicia said,

> I immediately thought about that soliloquy and wanted to capture the idea of somebody struggling with suicidal thoughts and what would be going through their mind rights as they were deciding, when they were on the brink of deciding between life and death.

The audio component of their video had Alicia's voice—halting and pausing throughout the delivery—quoting the text while a haunting instrumental served as background music. The visuals showed her in alternately disheveled and polished appearances, inhabiting spaces around the community, her expressions ranging from contemplative, angry, and weary, to desperate. The penultimate image of the video showed her standing at a waterfall's edge. The final shot was a black screen, the ending left intentionally ambiguous.

In making their video, Alicia and Jess used both spaces and places in their community in two main ways. First, they moved intentionally in and through their landscape, exploring and highlighting a number of community spaces and places. Secondly, through their use of production processes—using camera and editing techniques—they elevated commonplace events in their lives.

Moving in and Through the Community

In making their video, Jess and Alicia operated in and through the landscape of their rural community. Specifically, they used various affordances of their camera as a means of exploration, attending to lighting and time of day, and pushing boundaries of access to capture unique perspectives and vantage points in their production. In their interviews, they indicated that the camera became a source of empowerment—through investigation and exploration—while also using the lens' affordances to compose in purposeful ways. They filmed in nine distinct locations for their production: a waterfall, field, church, gas station, home, grocery store, abandoned house, woods, and trail entrance. However, in each of those settings, their use of space was not limited to one perspective within that location. Instead, they often explored the setting—using the affordances of the camera to see, frame, and record their surroundings. While filming in Alicia's house, for example, they used different places such as her kitchen, living room, and bedroom. In a similar manner, they used their camera to explore each filming location through numerous spaces and places in and around the setting.

One specific way Jess and Alicia moved through and richly explored their selected settings was through their positioning of the camera. This happened in the first scene (shots 1–3) where the central character is introduced in a grocery store. They placed the camera at the floor level so that the audience sees the floor, the feet and legs of the faceless shopper, and the wheels and lower parts of the cart within the shot. This type of exploration is also seen in their footage inside Jess's church. The low level shots (36 39) frame Alicia kneeling along the altar. The camera was situated at the floor level, making the images within the camera's frame—the rail, the altar, and the stained glass window—appear heightened. That sequence—keeping the same scene framing—also showed Alicia sitting with her back against the altar, legs outstretched on the floor. Each of those framing techniques highlighted for the viewer an usual perspective not normally accessible to a shopper or parishioner. Throughout this project, Alicia and Jess were empowered with their teacher's challenge, time, and Jess's camera to tour through their rural community spaces. With their compositional tools, time, and purpose, Jess and Alicia noticed, sought, captured, and edited details of their ruralities that helped them communicate the relevance of Shakespeare's soliloquy to their lives and their peers' lives.

The lighting of the time of day was important to the way in which Jess and Alicia emphasized spaces. In reflecting on the final video, they discussed the importance of the golden hour—first and last light of the day, ideal for photography—in their work as they explored the outdoor landscapes of their community. Tess said, "We had to plan things out because I really wanted to do golden hour so everything looked with the sun, really beautiful." This is most clearly seen and felt in the field setting. A number of shots (15 of the 71) happened within this general setting, in and around an open field. However, they used the golden hour to literally highlight this space, guiding the viewers' ability to see and become aware of this part of their community that reflected different parts of the text's focal soliloquy. Using the golden hour, both the large and the small of the field is accented. The large is felt with the long shot scenes with Alicia walking through the vast space of the open land. The minutia of the surroundings are highlighted through shifting the focus on extreme close ups: the dead blossoms on last year's weed stalks, the emerging buds on twig limbs, and the insects backlit against the light of the setting sun are offerings that were gathered from and for their community. Clearly, their attention to the use of lighting to feature available spaces emphasized elements of their community that might not be seen or felt without the sophisticated use of a camera lens.

The freedom to select and use locations outside of the classroom for their academic project also made room for Alicia and Jess to push their boundaries in ways they may not have otherwise done. Alicia shared that portraying some of the scenes on camera were uncomfortable for her. For example, one of the locales they selected for their video was at an abandoned house. Both had never been there before. In talking about their experience filming there, Alicia said, "I was scared about everything. I was like, I can't believe I'm doing this because I'm the least rebellious person ever." According to Alicia, they are both perceived as "good students" and "rule followers." They would not have considered visiting the abandoned house as part of their normal routines. However, using their camera for this project gave them license to trespass the boundaries of their normal community spaces.

In looking across the larger set of student videos, stretching their identity and community boundaries while moving in and through their lived spaces and places were not unique to Alicia's and Jess's experience. Many of the videos detailed close and expanded perspectives of their rural contexts. In the video "Untitled," the students captured the setting for their story by traversing across fields, through woods and into an abandoned hunting cabin. Another student showed a number of pastoral scenes—including shots of a large pond with ducks— in his rap video, *I Don't Do Poetry*. In the video *Dystopian Asylum,* two students videotaped their entire project by trespassing into a condemned building. Through framing various perspectives and highlighting different angles, the students took exploratory license with their videos as they framed the familiar and unfamiliar spaces in their rural communities, transforming some of their community spaces into places. We contend that these portrayals and representations go beyond students simply 'showing their surroundings.' Rather, the teachers' flexible and responsive mediation supported the students' choices and ability to visually represent the features of their rural experiences, moving away from performative academics to reinforce Theobald's (1997) notion of place-conscious pedagogy.

Elevating the Ordinary

As our teachers' students used the affordances of video composition to move in and through their community landscapes, they heightened the importance of the mundane in their community spaces. Stephen, one of the teachers in our WWV community of practice, developed what he called an *elevation project*. This assignment had students highlight, draw attention to, or elevate an everyday item, event, or routine. While Alicia and Jess were not in Stephen's class or necessarily familiar with the assignment parameters, their project drew attention to and elevated the ordinary elements portrayed in their video. The girls used three specific editing techniques—use of repetition, rapid jump cut edits, and juxtaposing images—to heighten audience attention of the ordinary.

One way they demonstrated elevation was a repetitive series of routine events. Setting their initial footage at a grocery store, a gas station, and a kitchen sink, each of these scenes follow a pattern. At those settings a specific action is repeated in edits 4–16.

Setting	Repeated motion (three times)
Grocery store	opening freezer door, removing item
Gas station	selecting fuel grade, removing nozzle from pump
Kitchen sink	setting dish in sink, lifting dish soap, turning on water

At the different settings, each take was filmed from the same perspective—with Alicia wearing a different outfit for each shot—and then edited together with the voice-over of the opening lines of the text, "tomorrow and tomorrow and tomorrow." The effect of the visual repetition was both to parallel the language and to create a sense of an ordinary event happening the same way repeatedly throughout life. Olivia said, "I was thinking about the idea of life rushing by and the repetitiveness of it that the soliloquy is trying to convey." Even though they are showing the same things happening again and again, the effect elevates the mundane, the routine, by highlighting to the viewer to see, hear, and become aware of something. The girls intentionally used this repetition to make the audience aware how Shakespeare's soliloquy might be relevant to today's tomorrow and tomorrow.

Alicia and Jess used other editing moves that elevated the everyday, specifically their implementation of rapid jump cuts to interrupt the visuals of the scene. For example, in shots 41–44, Alicia is framed within the trailhead exiting a wooded trail system. In this sequence, she looked directly at the camera while standing next to a sign that said DO NOT ENTER. The entire segment lasted approximately 5½ seconds. However, instead of this being a single shot, it was edited into 4 separate scenes, the longer ones interrupted with edits lasting a fraction of a second. Regarding that editing technique, Alicia said, "Obviously the jumpiness of that editing just kind of looked cool ... we liked that part." The effect of having these jump cuts—no transitions to ease switch between images—jars the visual continuity, thus creating a narrative disruptive sense of *pay attention and look closely!* What would be a "normal" shot—albeit beautifully framed—now startles the viewer awake to consider with more care what is being communicated. They used this jump cut editing technique 11 different times throughout their video.

Juxtaposing images was a third editing technique that Alicia and Jess used to elevate the ordinary in their community. By placing dissimilar images next to one another, they drew attention to the similarities and differences among the settings they chose to include and share from their community.

In the most striking instance of juxtaposition, Alicia was framed standing near the edge of a church balcony rail. Jess edited that image, placing it aside a similarly framed shot of Alicia standing on a ledge overlooking a waterfall. They not only framed the images in a parallel fashion, they also kept the continuity of Alicia's movements. For example, at one point, while in the balcony, she looked upward, tilting her face toward the ceiling, as if she were in prayer. As she looked down, the downward movement of her head continued into the next shot of her standing by the waterfall. The parallel images continued with her taking a deep breath, beginning her inhale on the church balcony and then concluding the intake breath at the waterfall's edge. The effect of this not only highlighted the literal setting, it also figuratively emphasized the inner turmoil the character was dealing with. In doing so, the planned sequence leaves the audience with a sense of ambiguity. Alicia said,

> You're not really sure, has she given up hope completely? You're just a little bit unsure. Has she given up on God? Did she find answers? That was supposed to be a little bit ambiguous, but the head placement was intentional.

While this paralleled movement through the two different settings was planned, Alicia and Jess revised their plan through the editing process. In talking about the balcony and waterfall, Jess said,

> We knew we wanted that back and forth because they're kind of like opposites ... they were going to be in different parts of the film. And, at the end we knew we wanted the same shot, we knew we wanted the same shot of her on the church balcony and at the falls, we just didn't know that we were going to put them back to back and like switch them. And, that happened accidentally when I put all the footage into iMovie and it ended up like that and we were like, "Wait, that's really cool. That's what we want."

Originally conceptualized as occurring in different sections of their narrative, they decided to sequence these settings together, creating Alicia's fluid movements across both settings. Their final version called attention to these moments of breathing and choosing that are part of life, elevating the ordinary of their lived spaces and places.

DISCUSSION AND IMPLICATIONS

Before considering some of the implications of this study, we had to return to the issue of identities and ruralities, specifically considering why the rural context mattered. Could researchers find similar findings in urban and suburban settings as well?

In the interview with Jess and Alicia, they never specifically addressed how the rurality of their context affected their identity. However, they did discuss one significant component of their rural community, namely faith and faith-based institutions and the tensions felt in and about these spaces and places. Olivia said,

> We both grew up in church and faith was a big part of our lives and is a big part of our lives. And, I think that we wanted to show that it's not always a comforting thing, even for somebody that grew up in the church, religion isn't always something that you run to when you're sad. Sometimes it's very frustrating and I think that because that part is very personal to us. If we were struggling with something, I think both of us have experienced people from our churches being like, "Pray more" and then maybe we wanted to throw a Bible.

Their video, replete with religious settings and imagery, visualized their verbal affirmation and irritation with church-related issues.

Implicitly expressing their lived ruralities was not limited to Alicia and Jess. Throughout the larger data set of videos, students never explicitly addressed the context of issues surrounding rurality head on. There were no overt signs, statements, or claims to rural identity such as "country life" or "country boy/girl" throughout any of the videos. However, elements of rural life flow through their work, images, and themes.

One such element throughout a number of the videos dealt with an awareness of openness and opportunities for solitude in their surrounding landscape. A number of videos contained images of open fields, farmland and rolling hillsides. Likewise, wooded settings were featured as framing or boundary devices or, conversely, spaces to enter and explore. In highlighting the geographic features of the area, the students implicitly demonstrated the context of their rural experience. Thus, rurality as an expression of identity issues—at least with these students—was never foregrounded but was a constant background in their rural landscapes. While the case could be made that students in urban or suburban spaces would include their surroundings as part of their work, we contend that the rural settings portrayed in these videos were more than mere locations—these spaces and places were deeply embedded into their identities, backgrounds against and within which these students lived, composed, and shared their lives. While students in urban and suburban backgrounds would look and sound necessarily different, bringing these rural backgrounds to the foreground of educational research alongside the urban and suburban spaces and places pushes back against the scant representation in the literature. Additionally, while there was limited explicit talk of rurality, the way that students represented their lived experience demonstrated an implicit awareness.

In the following section, we propose three other implications to this research. First, these student explorations into community spaces would never have occurred without the teachers providing flexible time, resources, and mediation. Secondly, through their work on these projects, students earned a measure of status within the larger community. Finally, these projects were examples of liminal spaces and experiences.

Teachers Mediated Exploration Within and Beyond Classroom Spaces

The students' explorations of their community landscapes were only captured and shared within the school walls because they were given the challenge and freedom to do so for academic purposes. Of the 31 videos that teachers from our WWV cohort submitted for the film festival, all projects had been assigned as academic projects. The assignments varied in nature and included video adaptations of academic assignments, such as personal essays, vocabulary definitions, literary themes, poetry interpretations, short stories, rhetorical analysis, book reviews, and a research thesis.

These varied assignments in which students located opportunities to explore parts of their identity is important to note because a commonplace justification for not using digital literacies in the classroom is that the curriculum does not allow it. These teachers, through the community of practice in our WWV work, identified ways in which curricular objectives and mandates could be met through various DV projects that also invited students to capture, share, and celebrate their lived spaces and places together.

The importance of the teachers' craft in creating these multimodal curricular assignments is paramount: without teachers mediating the content and process of these assignments—originated in classroom settings—the students would not have had the opportunity for academic inquiry to explore their spaces and places within and around the community.

Students Gained Notoriety Through Their Videos

An unexpected outcome of the film festival was how students gained a reputation through their productions. This first happened locally in their classrooms and schools when teachers engaged their classes in viewings and discussion. The regional film festival brought an entirely new level of fame which persisted into the following academic year. One of the many examples of these shifting identities occurred after the viewing of Alec's video, *Dystopian Asylum*. In his school, Alec was perceived as an academic outsider. His teacher recounted the story of showing Alec's video in class and how positively his peers reacted to it, eventually selecting his video as one that would be submitted to the festival. Alec arrived at the film festival without his production partner and chose a seat by himself in the front of the auditorium. During the intermission that followed the session in which Alec's video was shown, he had numerous people talking with him about various aspects of his composition. His video was selected as one of the finalists and he became a defacto celebrity at the festival. Alec and other students found new identities—in his case, a highly visible creator with notable narrative and production chops—through the public viewing and sharing of their projects.

The teachers all agreed to use the festival submissions as content and/or production exemplars in their classes the following year. As videos were shown broadly throughout different districts across the region, the students who produced or starred in the videos earned a reputation for creativity, production skills, and/or artistic credibility. In the WWV discussion boards and reunion gatherings, teachers shared stories of their students mentioning the specific titles and authors of videos produced by students from other districts. As of this writing, another film festival is being planned to culminate the end of the current academic year. The teachers report stories of current students working on their projects, using the content and production quality of last year's submissions as a benchmark for their work. In talking about this phenomenon, the teachers have discussed how no academic assignment they have worked on has been taken up by so many of their students and with so much enthusiasm. This happened, in no small part, because the DV compositions have put students at the front and center of the authorship and audience.

Liminal Spaces and Experiences

A final implication of this research involves the *liminality* by which the students composed the videos. Originally coined in sociology to describe transitional aspects of rites of passage (van Gennep, 1909), liminality refers to what Turner (1967) calls the "betwixt and between" (p. 93). We contend that in making the videos, the places and processes were liminal in terms of space and experience.

In terms of space, "liminality can relate to specific places, thresholds ... areas or zones" (Thomassen, 2009, p. 16). The process of students creating these DV projects for academic assignments had these elements to it. DV has often been presented as either an in-school literacy (e.g., Bruce, 2008; Cercone, 2017; Doerr-Stevens, 2016) or as an out of school literacy (e.g., Halverson, 2010; Hull, 2006). However, in making these projects, students often crossed the in/out of school thresholds, not occurring wholly in one or the other. Rather, they could be framed in terms of what Szakolczai (2009) refers to as "the 'in-between' ... a temporary situation betwixt two structured orders" (p. 151). While the projects were technically contained within a curricular unit, the projects had their assignment and assessment origins within the confines of the classroom. However, nearly all of the videos submitted for the festival were completed outside of the physical and temporal confines of the actual class. Namely, it was the *process* of making the video that had transitional elements. Brainstorming may have begun in the clustered desks of the classroom, but the composition process spilled out to continue into hallways, lunchrooms, bus and car rides, homes, chatrooms and phone calls, and extended community spaces. Thus, these projects occurred in the transitional spaces of academic and personal identities.

Liminality also can refer to shared experiences which leave "a common imprint, rendering possible the existence of a group of humans as a community" (Szakolczai, 2009 p. 151). While the latter refers to the binding power of transitional rites and ceremonies, we argue that there was a liminality of experience surrounding these videos. The shared aspect of the videos began in the classrooms where all of the teachers had their students publicly view the finished projects with their classmates. The public audience continued at the film festival where students, teachers, administrators, and parents from all over the region came to view the projects. Aspects of film festival rituals were followed—specifically, formal nominations of submissions, programs and promotional posters, formal attire, refreshments, and award ceremony—in viewing and celebrating these completed projects. Teachers reported that on the returning bus rides to the respective home schools and in subsequent classes following the festival, there were numerous comments and conversations detailing the experience of the festival as well as looking forward to and planning for next year's event. The festival became a sedimented experience, *a common* imprint, for those involved. In the process of spaces and places becoming liminal, the movements created passages for students to share, shape, and evolve in their identities.

CONCLUSION

In many ways, the film festival was both a conclusion and a beginning. It was a culmination of a yearlong effort by a group of committed teachers to highlight and celebrate student work in a communal and public setting. While the film festival lasted only a few hours, the space and experience of that event shaped new curricular preparation, lesson instruction, and student planning for the current academic year. Teachers have been planning for this year's festival, adding more opportunities for student work to be highlighted. There are competitions for the festival posters, programs, and movie trailer style promotional videos. Many students began the year with a goal of having their work submitted to the festival.

The film festival also germinated the research in this chapter. It was only when our research team watched the collective work of the students whose rural geographic boundaries span across an enormous region of our state, that we first saw the students' use of space and place across and within their rural landscapes. We had seen the individual submissions but it was the effect of seeing the totality of the projects—the variety and expanse of their lived spaces—that took us by surprise. Our festival afterglow conversations darted between individual submissions and memorable images within the videos. However, we kept returning to the unique backgrounds of their rural landscapes, imposing facets of its grand visage through the many videos. And we only saw it because the students, in an academic assignment, captured those spaces through their camera lenses, arranged the landscapes with their editing programs, and shared their discoveries and compositions publicly.

REFERENCES

Abrams, S. S. (2009). A gaming frame of mind: Digital contexts and academic implications. *Educational Media International, 46*(4), 335–347.

Albers, P., & Sanders, J. (Eds.). (2010). *Literacies, the arts, and multimodality.* Urbana, IL: National Council of Teachers of English.

Barton, D., Hamilton, M., & Ivanič, R. (Eds.). (2000). *Situated literacies: Reading and writing in context.* New York, NY: Routledge.

Beach, R. (2012). Constructing digital learning commons in the literacy classroom. *Journal of Adolescent & Adult Literacy, 55*(5), 448–451.

Brooke, R. E. (2003). Introduction: Place-conscious education, rural schools, and the Nebraska writing project's rural voices, country schools team. In R. E. Brooke (Ed.) *Rural voices: Place-conscious education and the teaching of writing* (pp. 1–19). New York, NY: Teachers College Press.

Bruce, D. L. (2008a). Visualizing literacy: Building bridges with media. *Reading & Writing Quarterly, 24*(3), 264–282.

Byas, T. & Cercone, A. (2016). HIPs with technology: A peer mentoring journey. *The International Conference on E-Education, E-Business, E-Management, and E-Learning (IC4E) Jakarta, Indonesia–Conference Proceedings.* World Research Library Online.

Cercone, J. (2017). Standing at the crossroads: Content creation in the 21st-Century classroom. *The English Journal, 106*(3), 25–31.

Chandler-Olcott, K., & Lewis, E. (2010). "I think they're being wired differently": Secondary teachers' cultural models of adolescents and their online literacies.

In D. E. Alvermann (Ed.), *Adolescents' online literacies* (pp. 163–182). New York, NY: Peter Lang.

Chisholm, J. S., & Olinger, A. R. (2017). "She's definitely the artist one": How learner identities mediate multimodal composing. *Research in the Teaching of English, 52*(2), 122–155.

Comber, B. (2015). *Literacy, place, and pedagogies of possibility*. New York, NY: Routledge. *Communication, 12*(1), 27–53.

Cope, B., & Kalantzis, M. (Eds.). (2000). *Multiliteracies: Literacy learning and the design of social futures*. New York, NY: Routledge.

Curwood, J. S., Magnifico, A. M., & Lammers, J. C. (2013). Writing in the wild: Writers' motivation in fan-based affinity spaces. *Journal of Adolescent & Adult Literacy, 56*(8), 677–685.

Doerr-Stevens, C. (2015). "That's not something I was, I am, or am ever going to be": Multimodal self-assertion in digital video production. *E-Learning and Digital Media, 12*(2), 164–182.

Donehower, K., Hogg, C., & Schell, E. E. (2007). *Rural literacies*. Carbondale, IL: SIU Press.

Donehower, K., Hogg, C., & Schell, E. E. (2012). Constructing rural literacies: Moving beyond the rhetorics of lack, lag, and the rosy past. In K. Donehower, C. Hogg, & E. E. Schell (Eds.), *Rural literacies* (pp. 1–36). Carbondale, IN: Southern Illinois University Press.

Eckert, L. S., & Alsup, J. (2014). Literacy teaching and learning in rural communities: Problematizing stereotypes, challenging myths. In L. S. Eckert & J. Alsup (Eds.), *Literacy teaching and learning in rural communities: Problematizing stereotypes, challenging myths* (pp. 1–10). New York, NY: Routledge.

Ehret, C., & Hollett, T. (2014). Embodied composition in real virtualities: Adolescents' literacy practices and felt experiences moving with digital, mobile devices in school. *Research in the Teaching of English*, 428–452.

Friesem, E. (2014). A story of conflict and collaboration: Media literacy, video production and disadvantaged youth. *Journal of Media Literacy Education, 6*(1), 44–55.

Gee, J. P. (1992). *The social mind: Language, ideology, and social practice*. New York, NY; JF Bergin & Garvey.

Green, B. (2013). Literacy, rurality, education: A partial mapping. In B. Green & M. Corbett (Eds.), *Rethinking rural literacies: Transnational perspectives* (pp. 17–33). New York, NY: Palgrave Macmillan.

Gruenewald, D. A. (2003). The best of both worlds: A critical pedagogy of place. *Educational Researcher, 32*(4), 3–12.

Halverson, E. R. (2010). Film as identity exploration: A multimodal analysis of youth-produced films. *Teachers College Record, 112*(9), 2352–2378.

Heath, S. B. (1983). *Ways with words: Language, life and work in communities and classrooms*. New York, NY: Cambridge University Press

Hodges, V. P. (2004). Using a sense of place to teach at-risk rural students. *English Journal, 93*(6), 27.

Hull, G. A., & Schultz, K. (Eds.). (2002). *School's out: Bridging out-of-school literacies with classroom practice*. New York, NY; Teachers College Press.

Lankshear, C., & Knobel, M. (2006). Digital literacy and digital literacies: policy, pedagogy and research considerations for education. *Nordic Journal of digital literacy*, *1*, 12–24.

Lefebvre, H. (1991) *The production of space*. (D. Nicholson-Smith, Trans.). Cambridge, MA: Blackwell. (Original published in 1974)

Manovich, L. (2001). *The language of new media*. Cambridge, MA: MIT Press.

Miller, S. M., Knips, M. A., & Goss, S. (2013). Changing the game of literature with authentic assessment: The promise of multimodal composing. *English Journal*, 88–94.

Miller, S. M., & McVee, M. B. (2013). Multimodal composing: The essential 21st century literacy. In S. M. Miller & M. B. McVee (Eds.), *Multimodal composing in classrooms: Learning and teaching for the digital world* (pp. 1–12). New York, NY: Routledge.

Mills, K. A., & Comber, B. (2013). Space, place, and power: The spatial turn in literacy research. In K. Hall, T. Cremin, B. Comber, & L. C. Moll (Eds.), *International handbook of research on children's literacy, learning, and culture* (pp. 412–423). Malden, MA: John Wiley & Sons.

Mills, K. A., & Comber, B. (2015). Rethinking the social constitution and politics of space. In J. Rowsell & K. Pahl (Eds.) *The Routledge handbook of literacy studies* (pp. 91–103). New York, NY: Routledge.

Moje, E. B. (2004). Powerful spaces: Tracing the out-of-school literacy spaces of Latino/a youth. In K. Leander & M. Sheehy (Eds.), *Spatializing literacy research and practice* (pp. 15–38). New York, NY: Peter Lang.

Moje, E. B., Ciechanowski, K. M., Kramer, K., Ellis, L., Carrillo, R., & Collazo, T. (2004). Working toward third space in content area literacy: An examination of everyday funds of knowledge and discourse. *Reading Research Quarterly*, *39*(1), 38–70.

Pahl, K., & Kelly, S. (2005). Family literacy as a third space between home and school: Some case studies of practice. *Literacy*, *39*(2), 91–96.

Pyles, D. G. (2016). Rural media literacy: Youth documentary videomaking as a rural literacy practice. *Journal of Research in Rural Education, 31*(7), 1–15.

Ranker, J. (2008). Composing across multiple media: A case study of digital video production in a fifth grade classroom. *Written Communication*, *25*(2), 196–234.

Schafft, K. A. (2016). Rural education as rural development: Understanding the rural school–community well-being linkage in a 21st-century policy context. *Peabody Journal of Education*, *91*(2), 137–154.

Schultz, K. (2002). "Looking across space and time:" Reconceptualizing literacy learning in and out of school". *Research in the Teaching of English*, *36*(3), 356–390.

Siegel, M. (2006). Rereading the signs: Multimodal transformations in the field of literacy education. *Language Arts*, *84*(1), 65–77.

Skerrett, A., & Bomer, R. (2011). Borderzones in adolescents' literacy practices: Connecting out-of-school literacies to the reading curriculum. *Urban Education*, *46*(6), 1256–1279.

Smith, B. E. (2017). Composing across modes: A comparative analysis of adolescents' multimodal composing processes. *Learning, Media and Technology*, *42*(3), 259–278.

Somerville, M. (2013). Place, storylines and the social practices of literacy. *Literacy, 47*(1), 10–16.

Soja, E. W. (2010). *Seeking spatial justice.* Minneapolis, MN: University of Minnesota Press.

Strauss, A., & Corbin, J. M. (1990). Basics of qualitative research: Grounded theory procedures and techniques. Thousand Oaks, CA: SAGE

Street, B. V. (1984). *Literacy in theory and practice.* New York, NY: Cambridge University Press.

Szakolczai, A. (2009). Liminality and experience: Structuring transitory situations and transformative events. *International Political Anthropology, 2*(1), 141–172.

Tavares, M. (2015). Digital poetics and remix culture: From the artisanal image to the immaterial image. In E. Navas, O. Gallagher, & x. burrough (Eds.), *The Routledge companion to remix studies* (pp. 192–203). New York, NY: Routledge.

Theobald, P. (1997). *Teaching the commons: Place, pride, and the renewal of community.* Boulder, CO: Westview.

Thomassen, B. (2009). The uses and meanings of liminality. *International Political Anthropology, 2*(1), 5–27.

Tieken, M. C., & San Antonio, D. M. (2016). Rural aspirations, rural futures: From "problem" to possibility. *Peabody Journal of Education, 91*(2), 131–136.

Turner, V. W. (1967). Betwixt and between: The liminal period in rites de passage. In *The forest of symbols.* New York, NY: Cornell University Press.

van Gennep, A. (1960). The rites of passage (Monika B. Vizedom & Gabrielle L. Caffee, Trans.). Chicago, IL: University of Chicago Press.

Vasudevan, L. (2010). Education remix: New media, literacies, and the emerging digital geographies. *Digital Culture & Education, 2*(1), 62–82.

Vasudevan, L., Schultz, K., & Bateman, J. (2010). Rethinking composing in a digital age: Authoring literate identities through multimodal storytelling. *Written Communication, 27*(4), 442–468.

Wake, D. G. (2012). Exploring rural contexts with digital storytelling. *The Rural Educator, 33*(3), 23–36.

Wargo, J. M. (2015). Spatial stories with nomadic narrators: Affect, snapchat, and feeling embodiment in youth mobile composing. *Journal of Language and Literacy Education, 11*(1), 47–64.

Warner, J. (2016). Adolescents' dialogic composing with mobile phones. *Journal of Literacy Research, 48*(2), 164–191.

Wells, G. (1999). The zone of proximal development and its implications for learning and teaching. In *Dialogic inquiry: Towards a sociocultural practice and theory of education* (pp. 313–334). New York, NY: Cambridge University Press.

Wenger, E. (1998). *Communities of practice: learning, meaning, and identity.* New York, NY: Cambridge University Press.

Wenger, E., McDermott, R., & Snyder, W. M. (2002). *Cultivating communities of practice: A guide to managing knowledge.* Boston, MA: Harvard Business School Press.

CHAPTER 7

COMPLICATING PROBLEMATIC NARRATIVES ABOUT SOUTHERN PEOPLE AND PLACES THROUGH COUNTERSTORYTELLING

Sean P. Connors and Erin Daugherty
University of Arkansas

INTRODUCTION

In a popular TED Talk, author Chimamanda Adichie (2009) cautions against the dangers of a single story, a term that she uses to refer to stories that portray a population of people "as one thing, as only one thing, over and over again." As researchers who work at a large university that is located in the South, and more specifically, in the Arkansas Ozark Mountain region, we are aware of a single story that imagines people in this part of the United States as intolerant, backward-looking, and somewhat less well educated than people in other regions of the country. It is possible to understand the iconic figure of the hillbilly, a stereotype that is reproduced in popular culture texts such as the film *Winter's Bone* (Granik, 2010), the

Negotiating Place and Space Through Digital Literacies: Research and Practice, pp. 117–136

book *Hillbilly Elegy: A Memoir of a Family and Culture in Crisis* (Vance, 2016), and the Netflix series *Ozark*, as an embodiment of this single story. While we do not deny that the history of the South, and of the Arkansas Ozark region, includes a troubling legacy of bigotry, fundamentalism, and anti-intellectualism, our experiences as people who live and work in this part of the country allow us to recognize this narrative as grossly incomplete. In our work as educators, we have found that many of the college undergraduates we teach, particularly those who grew up in Southern contexts, are cognizant of (and bothered by) this same single story. As critical educators, we consequently endeavor to create opportunities for students to use digital technologies in the service of producing and disseminating counterstories (Delgado, 1989) about Southern people and places.

One way we seek to accomplish this is through our implementation of the Literacy in Ozark Lives research study, a community inquiry initiative that involves a collaborative partnership between the university where we work and a regional history museum, and which asks preservice English teachers in an introductory literacy studies course to become researchers of literacy in their local contexts. Specifically, the project tasks preservice teachers with collecting oral history interviews from people in the Arkansas Ozark region for the purpose of answering the research question: *What is the relationship between the place where someone lives and the value and purpose of literacy?* Additional research questions include: *What role do literacy sponsors play in the lives of people,* and *how do economic and political systems shape people's literacy?* Having analyzed the data they collect, the preservice teachers produce short digital videos in which they use the oral histories they collected to answer the aforementioned questions. In answering these questions, they are also tasked with using their data to complicate single stories (Adichie, 2009) about people, places, and literacy in the Arkansas Ozark region. To disseminate their findings, the preservice teachers screen their videos for a public audience at the Shiloh Museum of Ozark History, a nonprofit regional museum that is dedicated to documenting and preserving Ozark culture and history. Additionally, to share their work with a larger audience, the preservice teachers embed their videos on an interactive Google Map of the Arkansas Ozark region, which we in turn publish on the course website.

In this chapter, we examine the Literacy in Ozark Lives project for the purpose of demonstrating how it invites preservice teachers to reflect on the relationship between literacy and place, and how, by extension, it challenges them to contest single stories (Adichie, 2009) about people, places, and literacy in the South. To begin, we construct our conceptual framework, drawing on the work of scholars who have discussed the social and political dimensions of place and who theorize it as a site of contested meanings. Next, we introduce the concept of placemaking (McCann, 2002; Sánchez, 2011), a term that is traditionally understood to refer to the work of people who are involved in constructing the built environment of a place. Approaching the concept of placemaking from a critical perspective, however, we argue that it also constitutes a sociopolitical activity wherein people actively "affirm, interrogate, and construct knowledge about place" (Sánchez, 2011, p. 333). As we will argue, telling counterstories (Delgado, 1989) that challenge single stories (Adichie, 2009) about a place and the people who live there is also a form of placemaking. Having established our conceptual framework, we next offer a close reading of a digital video that one preservice teacher, Jordan (first name used with permission), produced for the Literacy in Ozark Lives research study. In doing so, we examine not only how she came to understand the relationship between literacy and place, but also how completing the project challenged her initial perceptions of the working-class community where she conducted her research. Set in the Ozark Mountains, this particular community has a reputation for racial intolerance, an unfortunate legacy that persists to the present day due to the presence of White supremacist groups in the area. Viewed from this perspective, the community appears to reproduce a single story (Adichie, 2009) that equates Southern people and places with racism. As Jordan learned, however, there are also people in the community who are invested in working for change. This understanding led Jordan to argue that "place should not be seen as one stereotyped story, but as an assemblage of thousands of equally important stories," an observation that we suggest approximates Massey's (2005) theorization of place as a product of intersecting stories that come into contact as people attempt to navigate their "throwntogetherness" (p. 141). To conclude our chapter, we address the implications of our work for educators. In doing so, we argue that when teachers tap into the knowledge that is available in their local communities, and when they create opportunities for students to produce and share counterstories (Delgado, 1989) about people and places they come to know, they lay a foundation for rich learning and identity work.

CONCEPTUAL FRAMEWORK

Place as Socially and Politically Constructed

In recent years, literacy researchers have theorized the relationship between power, literacy, and place (see, e.g., Comber, 2015; Green & Corbett, 2013; Leander & Sheehy, 2004). In doing so, they have expressed an interest in understanding place as something more than a built environment or coordinates on a map; instead, they argue that place is characterized by a social, as well as a material, dimension. Massey (2005), for example, theorizes place as the product of human relations, arguing that it is always under construction, and hence always undetermined (p. 7); within this purview, people from different backgrounds and with different life trajectories are understood to contribute to the production of place as they go about their everyday lives and navigate their "throwntogetherness" (p. 141). Important to our argument, Massey explicitly links stories to place when she conceptualizes "space as a simultaneity-of-stories so far" (p. 9). If this is the case, she argues, "then *places* are collections of those stories, articulations within the wider power-geometries of space" (p. 130, emphasis added). Like Massey, McDowell (1997) also establishes a relationship between story and place when he argues "places are both concrete and symbolic. They are literally and metaphorically made up: of buildings, field systems, roads and railways as well as of myths and legends, statues and ceremonies that link people to a place" (p. 2). In the context of these arguments, coming to "know" a place is understood to involve more than developing a sense of familiarity with its built environment. Rather, as Massey argues, it also entails "joining up with, somehow linking into, the collection of interwoven stories of which that place is made" (p. 119). In the context of our argument, we suggest that contributing one's own stories to this larger tapestry is also important.

If place is socially constructed, it also has a political dimension. Mills and Comber (2013), for example, argue that places are organized in ways that "constrain and enable social practices in the interests of maintaining and reproducing established hierarchies" (p. 417). Likewise, Green (2012) observes that because places are realized in social space as much as they are physical space, they are not "positioned equally, or distributed on a level plane, or playing field. Some places are more important socially, and also culturally and economically, than others; they may be bigger, or more prestigious, or powerful, and so on" (p. 379). Green's comments call attention to the fact that places do not exist in isolation; rather, they gain meaning as a result of their position relative to other places. As one example, the South, as a social construct, might be said to take on certain meanings when it is juxtaposed with other regions of the United States. For example, compared to the Northeast, the South may be imagined as both a site of conservatism and evangelicalism, as well as a place of rich tradition. In this way, the region serves as a canvas on which the nation projects both its faults (i.e., racism) and its desires (i.e., national pride) (Duck, 2006). Green's (2012) comments also call attention to the role power plays in constructing place, so that some places—for example, urban centers—are afforded more cultural prestige than others—say, rural areas. Nevertheless, as Mitchell (2000) argues, the possibility for "contestations over meanings, over borders and boundaries, over the ways we make sense of our worlds and the ways we live our lives" (p. 159)—in short, the practicing of cultural politics—enables people who are seemingly without power to contest and resist oppressive narratives about place.

Counterstorytelling as a Form of "Placemaking"

"To say that something is socially constructed," writes Cresswell (2004), "is to say that it is within human power to change it" (p. 30). So too, Mills and Comber (2013) argue that if places are socially produced, they "can [also] be contested, reimagined, and remade" (p. 412). In this chapter, we draw on the concept of placemaking, which is traditionally found in literature that pertains to the work of architects, developers, and others who contribute to the built environment of a place, but which some scholars suggest also encompasses people's interrogating "relationships between power and the production of place" (Sánchez, 2011, p. 333). Reminiscent of Massey's (2005) theorizing place as a product of people's negotiating their "throwntogetherness" (p. 141), Sánchez's (2011) discussion of placemaking is based on his conceptualizing place as "a site of conflict as various constituents struggle over its meaning and identity and wrestle over tensions of transformation and preservation" (p. 333). Moving placemaking outside the realm of professionals, Sánchez (2011) argues that it is "something we *all* do as we affirm, interrogate, and construct knowledge about place" (p. 333). In this chapter, we understand the sharing of stories and counterstories (Delgado, 1989) about place as a form of placemaking.

As educators, we are interested in understanding how teachers can engage students in placemaking by creating opportunities for them to produce and share counterstories, a type of story that, according to Delgado and Stefancic (1995), aspires "to cast doubt on the validity of accepted premises or myths, especially ones held by the majority" (p. 144). Like other kinds of stories, "counterstories can open new windows onto reality, showing us that there are possibilities for life other than the ones we live" (Delgado, 1989, p. 2414). In doing so, "[t]hey invite the reader [or viewer] to suspend judgment, listen for their point or message, and then decide what measure of truth they contain" (p. 2415).

Our understanding of counterstorytelling as a form of placemaking is foundational to our work with the Literacy in Ozark Lives research project, a community inquiry initiative that positions preservice teachers as researchers responsible for collecting, and curating, other people's stories about literacy. The project also invites students to practice counterstorytelling by using the stories they collect to complicate single stories (Adichie, 2009) about people, places, and literacy in the Arkansas Ozark region. To accomplish these tasks, we ask the preservice teachers to demonstrate their learning by producing digital videos, which we later embed in a Google Map and publish online. Our decision to ask students to produce digital videos, and hence to gain experience working with different digital tools, is motivated by several factors. First, in the context of the literacy studies course we teach, our study of literacy is framed by various sociocultural perspectives (Perry, 2012) influenced by Vygotsky's (1978) work, with the result that we acknowledge literacy as a social practice and understand people as practicing multiple literacies. Our understanding of literacy is also informed by scholarship on multimodality and social semiotics (e.g., Kress & Van Leeuwen, 2001; New London Group, 1997; Van Leeuwen, 2005), so that we understand people as communicating through a range of modes, one of which is print. In the context of the course, we consequently aspire to create opportunities for students to gain experience with different forms of composing, and hence with different literacies, one of which is digital literacy.

At the same time, we also understand digital videos as a potentially potent form of storytelling. Delgado (1989) argues that counterstories appeal to an audience's emotions, and as such, have the potential to "quicken and engage conscience" and "stir imagination in ways in which more conventional discourse cannot" (p. 2415). We suggest that this effect is heightened in the case of digital videos, which appeal to multiple senses simultaneously by commingling still images, video footage, and music with spoken narration. In the two iterations of the Literacy in Ozark Lives research project to date, it has not been uncommon for people whose lives have served as the focus of students' videos to express emotion upon viewing them. On a final note, the ability to publish student work online in a digital format permits us to disseminate it more widely, and hence to create a more authentic audience for student writers.

In the next section, we introduce the Literacy in Ozark Lives research project in more detail, and present the methodology preservice teachers employ to conduct their individual research studies. Having done so, we offer a close reading of a digital video that one preservice teacher produced for the purpose of examining how she came to conceptualize the relationship between literacy and place, and how she used her video to respond to a single story about the community in which she conducted her research.

THE LITERACY IN OZARK LIVES RESEARCH PROJECT

Influenced by scholarship on critical pedagogy and place-conscious pedagogy (Comber, 2015), the Literacy in Ozark Lives research project is a whole class, IRB-approved research study that asks preservice teachers taking an introductory literacy studies course to become researchers of literacy in their local communities. The design of the project is influenced by Bruce's (2014) community inquiry cycle (see Figure 7.2). The project begins with preservice teachers *asking* a series of research questions, the central one being: *What is the relationship between the place where someone lives and the value and purpose of literacy?* An additional subset of research questions includes: *What role do literacy sponsors play in the lives of people?* And, *how do economic and political systems shape people's literacy?* As discussed above, throughout the course, the preservice teachers' study of literacy is framed by different sociocultural perspectives (Perry, 2012), specifically the New Literacy Studies, which theorizes literacy as a social practice (e.g., Street, 1984), and scholarship on multimodality and social semiotics (e.g., Kress & Van Leeuwen, 2001; New London Group, 1997; Van Leeuwen, 2005), which argues that the ability to communicate effectively in the 21st century necessitates using multiple modes of representation, one of which is print. As a result, within the context of the Literacy in Ozark Lives research project, literacy is defined broadly, and understood to include new literacies (e.g., blogging; game playing; social media; etc.) as well as old literacy (reading and writing print).

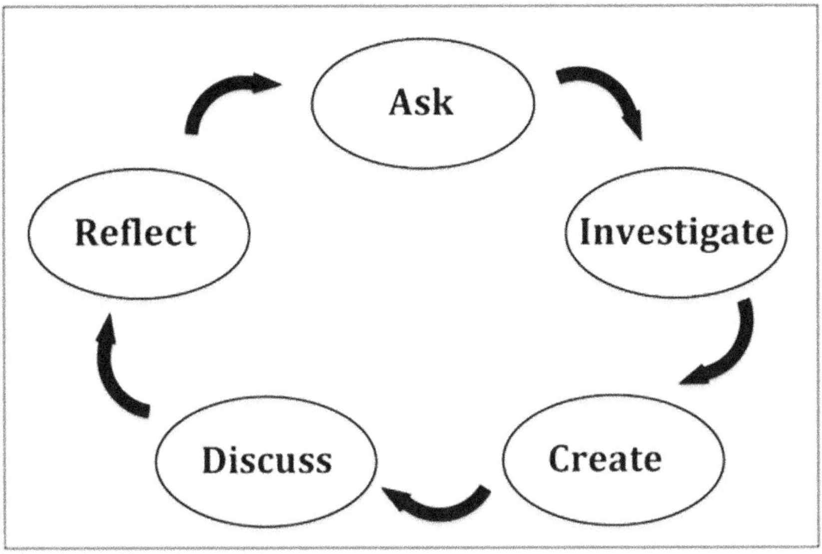

Figure 7.1. The community inquiry cycle.

To *investigate* the aforementioned research questions, the preservice teachers are assigned to collect oral histories about literacy from residents of different counties in the Arkansas Ozark region, an area that spans the northern portion of the state. To recruit participants for the study, we have partnered with the Shiloh Museum of Ozark History, a non-profit regional museum that is dedicated to documenting and preserving the culture and history of the Arkansas Ozarks. Susan Young, the museum's outreach coordinator, has proven to be a valuable asset, as she conducts oral history research in her work at the museum, and is able to tap into its extensive network to identify people who are willing to share their literacy narratives with our students. In spring 2017, the most recent iteration of the project, and the one that serves as the basis for our discussion, we interviewed a total of 20 people. This included college students and senior citizens; college-educated professionals and people from working class backgrounds; and people who traced their roots in the Arkansas Ozarks through several generations and others who had relocated to the area from elsewhere in the United States. The latter group included immigrants whose families had traveled to the region in search of work. The participant pool was also characterized by racial and ethnic diversity, as it included people who identified as European American, African American, and Latino/a. This layering of diversity was intentional: we hoped to help the preservice teachers with whom we worked complicate a single story (Adichie, 2009) that regards people in the Arkansas Ozarks as predominantly White and working class.

Prior to their collecting data for the study, Susan Young visited our class and talked with the preservice teachers about the work involved in conducting oral history research. Specifically, she offered them advice on how to prepare for an interview, how to introduce questions designed to put an interviewee at ease, how to ask follow-up questions to probe points of interest in greater depth, and how to prompt less gregarious informants to share stories and anecdotes. Susan also talked with the students about the ethics of conducting oral history research, and the importance of respecting an interviewee's right not to share information. Having reviewed the interview protocol we created for the study, we set aside time in class for the preservice teachers to pilot it by interviewing each other for practice. Finally, we assigned each of them an interviewee and shared that person's contact information with them. Interviews for the research study took place in a range of settings, including public libraries, coffee shops, an adult English language learning class, and (in a few instances) people's homes. In cases where the ability to conduct interviews entailed traveling long distances, we traveled together in a university van. The interview protocol we used for the research study consisted of 29 questions that examined the following territories: people's memories of literacy in their childhood homes and at school; the ends toward which they put literacy in their work lives; and the ends toward which they put literacy in their personal lives. The interviews were audio-recorded and, on average, lasted approximately one hour. Having collected their data, the preservice teachers transcribed their interviews in their entirety using an agreed upon set of conventions that were established in class. Both the audio-recordings and the transcripts of their interviews were later archived at the Shiloh Museum of Ozark History.

Having transcribed their interviews, the preservice teachers next analyzed their data using structural coding, a process that involved their applying a "conceptual phrase representing a topic of inquiry to a segment of data that relates to a specific question used to frame [an] interview" (Saldaña, 2013, p. 66). Prior to releasing them to code their data independently, we first practiced coding a transcript of an interview that one of us (the lead author) had conducted. To begin, we drew on the research questions that guided the study to establish sensitizing concepts (Charmaz, 2006) we could apply to the data during the initial phase of coding. These included: "literacy," "literacy sponsors," "economic systems," "political systems," "value," "purpose," and "place." As we applied these codes to the data, we developed additional codes that were structured around them. By searching for relationships between codes and placing them into categories, the preservice teachers eventually identified recurring themes, which represented their findings.

To present their findings, the preservice teachers *created* digital videos in which they used the oral histories they collected to answer the research questions that guided the study. In doing so, they identified literacy sponsors (Brandt, 2001), local as well as distant, who appeared to have supported or constrained their interviewees' literacy, and economic or political conditions that impacted their literacy. Additionally, the preservice teachers used their data as the basis for a counterstory (Delgado, 1989) about literacy, people, and places in the Arkansas Ozark region. Prior to producing their videos, the preservice teachers brought their scripts to class and exchanged them with at least three other people during a peer response/editing activity. As they responded to each other's work, they *discussed* their interpretations of their data and the strengths and limitations of their scripts, which promoted *reflection*. They also offered recommendations about how their scripts could be improved. In some cases, this led them to identify additional questions they wanted to ask their interviewees, resulting in their conducting follow-up interviews via e-mail or telephone. Discussion was an integral part of their experience presenting their work at the Shiloh Museum as well. The latter event took the form of a gallery walk, at which time guests moved between computer stations in order to watch the preservice teachers' videos. Throughout the evening, the preservice teachers fielded questions from guests, which prompted still further *reflection*. Finally, to conclude the project, we embedded their videos in an interactive Google Map of the Arkansas Ozark region, which we published on the class website.

To illustrate the learning that occurs when educators position students as researchers of literacy in their local communities, we next offer a close reading of one student's video. While we try to account for the text's multimodal design in our discussion, we encourage readers to view the video online at http://bit.ly/2CTM1Y6.

"LITERACY'S WAY FORWARD"

At the time she completed the Literacy in Ozark Lives research project, Jordan was a junior in college. Bright, self-motivated, and articulate, she aspired to teach secondary English, and she took the introductory literacy studies course we have described to satisfy a prerequisite for admission to the graduate teacher education program at the university she attended. Having grown up in a community that abuts an urban area in the central part of the state, Jordan's familiarity with the Arkansas Ozark region was largely limited to the area where she attended school. Asked in an interview that occurred prior to her completing the project whether she was familiar with stereotypes about people in the Arkansas Ozark region, she, like the majority of her classmates, suggested that people are perceived as "less well educated" and "a little backwards." Significantly, she also shared her belief that people in other parts of the United States were likely to describe people from the state of Arkansas in a similar way.

For the Literacy in Ozark Lives research project, Jordan was assigned to interview John Henderson, a resident of Harrison, Arkansas. A small, predominantly White working-class community with a population of just over 13,000, Harrison is located approximately 76 miles northeast of the university Jordan attended. Beginning with a pair of race riots in 1905 and 1909, and extending through the present day, the city has historically been saddled with a reputation for intolerance. A 2017 article in *Intelligence Report,* a publication of the Southern Poverty Law Center, identified hate groups that are known to operate in the area that surrounds Harrison, and in recent years, the placement of billboards alongside public roadways that have promoted White supremacist ideology has drawn unwanted attention to the community and sparked protests. While she had not previously traveled to this part of the state, Jordan was familiar with Harrison's reputation for racial intolerance. In the same interview referred to above, she volunteered that she had heard the city was "the headquarters of the KKK or something." In this way, the city of Harrison appears to reproduce a single story (Adichie, 2009) about prejudice and intolerance in the South. This is not the entirety of Harrison's story, however.

Chimamanda Adichie (2009) argues, "The problem with stereotypes is not that they are untrue, but that they are incomplete. They make one story become the only story." So too, in the case of Harrison, some local residents are working to change the city's negative image. An article in a 2014 issue of the Southern Poverty Law Center's *Intelligence Report*, for example, described how some city leaders and residents had created a Community Task Force on Race Relations to "counter the city's racist reputation and create a more racially welcoming present and future." In the same article, the Task Force's mission is described as follows: "Reconciling the past. Recognizing the present. Reaching for the future." In 2016, the Task Force received the Dream Keeper Award, which is "presented by the state's Martin Luther King, Jr. Commission for notable efforts to improve race relations, particularly among young people" (Schulte, 2017). Interestingly, although she was unacquainted with either the Task Force or its mission, Jordan's conversation with Henderson, who teaches social studies at a local middle school in Harrison, led her to view him as a person who was also committed to working for the betterment of his community.

Jordan's digital video, which is entitled "Literacy's Way Forward," is approximately seven minutes long and combines still images, video footage, and background music with spoken narration to share Henderson's literacy narrative and consider what it potentially suggests about the nature of the relationship between literacy and place. This relationship is at the center of Jordan's concern, a fact she communicates in the video's opening moments. As footage of a rotating earth as viewed from space gives way to footage of a cityscape, she narrates, "To understand an individual's value of literacy in relation to their place, we must first look at place differently." Suggesting that "place is much more than coordinates on a map," she goes on to argue that it is "socially constructed by sponsors who influence literacy's value, and the economic and political forces that shape its path." As a camera pans an Ozark waterfall, Jordan links her discussion of literacy and place to the concept of the single story (Adichie, 2009). In doing so, she shares a definition of place that strikes us as approximating Massey's (2005) theorization of place as a "simultaneity of stories so far" (p. 9), though we assume that she was unfamiliar with the latter's work. Specifically, Jordan explains, "For the people who call the Ozark region home, they understand all too well how place should not be seen as one stereotyped story, but as an assemblage of thousands of equally important stories."

Having established this point, Jordan introduces the subject of her video, John Henderson, a middle-aged, White male who lives and teaches in Harrison, Arkansas. Born in Phoenix, Arizona in 1957, Henderson grew up in what appears to have been a literacy-rich environment. In his interview with Jordan, he recalled "grandparents who wrote letters and read detective magazines; a grandfather who loved history and read old westerns; his mother, who enjoyed reading; and a sister who wrote letters to pen pals across the world." In addition to modeling different literacy practices, these people also sponsored Henderson's literacy by providing him with access to different resources, such as "books, comics to trade with friends, records, and board games." Henderson recalled a grandmother who gifted him a book about Kennedy's assassination for Christmas one year, sparking his love of nonfiction. Later, when he attended school, he encountered other literacy sponsors, including a friend with whom he competed to see who could read the most biographies. As Brandt (2001) explains, literacy sponsors can constrain as well as support a person's literacy, and this was the case for Henderson, who explained that the library at a school he attended was unable to purchase new books due to limited resources. As a result, once he had finished reading the school's collection of biographies, he was forced to "move on to books he was less interested in," resulting in his reading less often. An encounter with a fifth-grade teacher who belonged to a local chapter of the John Birch Society, a conservative group that gained influence in the 1960s, also appears to have influenced Henderson's attitude toward school. As an image of a child with a teardrop falling from his eye appears on screen, Jordan explains that this particular teacher often shared his political views in class, and once even insisted that a young Henderson attend a Birch Society chapter meeting. This experience tainted Henderson's view of school, and it was not until the following year, when he worked with a teacher who encouraged student confidence, that his interest in school returned.

In her video, Jordan suggests that self-confidence and self-sufficiency were qualities that Henderson's parents valued in the home, and which he later embraced in his life. Henderson recalled his father embarking on a business venture that involved his building a roller skating rink that he owned and operated as a small business. In the absence of any formal training, his father "read books on construction and secured financing in tandem with a few clever tricks." John appears to have acquired his father's business acumen, as he recalled having used his weekly allowance to purchase comic books (a literacy resource he valued) one at a time to avoid meeting the minimum amount required to pay a sales tax. Later, as an adult, Henderson embarked on his own business ventures. As a picture of a video game console gives way to an image of an arcade, Jordan explains that Henderson "dropped out of college to launch a successful video game venture." Later, after arcades grew in popularity, he tried his hand at real estate; still later, he dabbled in trading commodities. Each of these experiences resulted in Henderson acquiring new literacies, thereby expanding his repertoire of literacy practices.

The influence of these collective experiences was felt years later when Henderson followed his parents to Harrison, Arkansas, where they purchased a farm. Having learned that he was unable to work on the farm due to severe allergies, Henderson's interest in history, which he had cultivated reading biographies and nonfiction as a child, led him to develop an interest in teaching. In the absence of a 4-year college that offered a teacher licensure program, and exemplifying the same spirit of self-sufficiency his father had modeled, Henderson completed an online bachelor's degree. Later, he took advantage of a nontraditional teacher licensure program that the state department of education had created to fill teaching positions in high-need schools. Eventually, Henderson was hired to teach social studies at the lone middle school in Harrison, where he spearheaded the development of an EAST (Environmental and Spatial Technology) program. Guided by tenets of progressive education, the EAST initiative is a project-based, service-learning program that aims to provide elementary and secondary students with opportunities to use advanced technologies in the service of addressing authentic problems in their local communities. Henderson's involvement with the EAST program presumably helped him to expand his repertoire of literacies still further. Likewise, as Jordan explains, literacy practices he had cultivated outside of school—for example, reading on an e-reader and consuming digital content on websites such as Audible—began to influence his work in the classroom, as he reported searching for content "that might impact his students, making something he enjoys have a larger purpose." In this way, as Jordan suggests, Henderson has become a sponsor of other people's literacy.

So what did Jordan learn about the relationship between literacy and place as a result of interviewing Henderson? In the final segment of her video, she turns to this question, suggesting that the time and place where a person lives can set the terms and conditions for his or her literacy. As a child growing up in the 1960s, for example, Henderson's literacy practices revolved largely around print, and included his reading nonfiction, biographies, and comic books. Granted, he also recalled playing board games, listening to music, and watching television, but new media were still in their nascent years when he was a child. Years later, after technological advancements made possible the production of video games and other kinds of digital texts, and as Henderson gained experience using technology in the context of the EAST program he had helped develop, his literacy repertoire expanded to include digital literacies, as evidenced by his learning to use devices such as computers, software, and e-readers, and his consuming digital content such as audiobooks and podcasts in his life outside of school.

In Henderson's story, one sees how literacy sponsors (Brandt, 2001) in his local community both supported and constrained his literacy. He credited a book that was given to him by a grandmother with sparking his life-long love of nonfiction, an interest that was further cemented when he participated in friendly reading competitions with a classmate at school.

At home, his father modeled literacy as a form of self-directed learning, reading and writing in order to learn how to build a roller skating rink and run his own small business. Later, Henderson exemplified a similar spirit of self-sufficiency, learning new literacies as he ran his own small business, dabbled in real estate, and traded commodities before finally finding work as a middle school social studies teacher. In this way, as Jordan explains, Henderson's literacy narrative suggests that a person's literacy is "the product of the many interactions that occur over the span of their lifetime." An aspiring educator herself, Jordan's interview with Henderson prompted her to consider how what she had learned from interviewing him might one day inform her own interactions with students. She concluded: "Understanding the effect that place has on a student's literacy, teachers should transform their approach working with students, as each is unique, coming from different places that are actively shaping their literacy."

Jordan was especially impressed with Henderson's contributions to his school's EAST program, which provided students with opportunities to learn different technologies in the service of addressing problems in their local community. Indeed, she came to understand Henderson's work as a form of activism, arguing toward the end of her video: "Every individual can identify improvements to be made in their community and make a difference. John's story proves this by his advocacy despite pushback to implement the EAST program, which focuses on how technology can solve problems in the community." As someone interested in teaching, Jordan's experience interviewing Henderson helped her to appreciate the value of "encouraging students to recognize the impact that their own story has, and how it can shape the place in which they live." Despite preconceptions she had held about the community of Harrison prior to traveling there to interview Henderson, Jordan brought her video to a close by offering a counterstory about this Ozark community. Returning to the same footage of a rotating earth that opened her video, thereby signaling that her argument has come full circle, she revisits her understanding of place as a compilation of stories. "Due to the misplaced stigma that plagues the city, upon hearing Harrison, Arkansas one may not think of education as a priority," Jordan states. "But Harrison, Arkansas is not one story. It is John's story, and thousands of other stories, each bringing rich literacies to form the place they call home."

Asked in an interview that occurred not long after the course had ended why she had chosen not to name the "stigma" she alluded to at the conclusion of her video as racism, Jordan explained that she was hesitant to do so due to her concern that it would reinforce the very stereotype she had sought to complicate in her video. In her opinion, associating Harrison with a single story (Adichie, 2009) of racism in a video she knew would be seen by a larger audience risked perpetuating a deficit view of the community that already plagued it. Moreover, she suggested that to do so would be to overlook the efforts of more progressive-minded people in the community who, like Henderson, were invested in bettering their community. Having paused to collect her thoughts, and without any prompting, Jordan offered the following rationale for her decision to title her video in the way she did:

> That's actually kind of why I named my video *Literacy's Way Forward*, because [Mr. Henderson's] so forward thinking and he is all about the future and teaching students that are learning literacy now to learn to create a better future.... So yeah, I guess just being presented with someone who didn't think that way, who saw the potential, who understands that stigma but who is looking toward the future and finding a way to change it, that's what I wanted to focus on.

We would have preferred that Jordan explicitly name the problem she sought to critique in her video as racism. At the same time, in retrospect, we also appreciate that the nature of the assignment placed her in a difficult position: knowing that she was expected to share her video with a public audience that potentially included residents of the community where she had conducted her oral history research, we suspect that Jordan may have been hesitant to take a strong political stance. We regard this as a limitation on our part as instructors, however, as we could (and should) have done more to support her as she sought to navigate the situation in which she found herself. At a minimum, we could have encouraged Jordan to articulate her vision for her video similar to the way she did in the excerpt above, as this would have allowed her to name the problem of racism while still celebrating the people in the community of Harrison who are committed to addressing it. Nevertheless, we also argue that in electing to understand the city of Harrison as a collection of diverse, sometimes conflicting, stories that come into contact as its residents navigate their "throwntogetherness" (Massey, 2005), Jordan is in the process of developing a more nuanced, more complex understanding of this Ozark community.

IMPLICATIONS FOR EDUCATORS

Having discussed stereotypes of the Australian Outback that are commonly found in popular culture texts, and which they suggest have come to dominate Australian consciousness, Reid et al. (2010) argue that "these are representations. They are not *necessarily* 'truth,' and they are most certainly not the whole truth" (p. 267, emphasis in original). The same can be said of single stories (Adichie, 2009) about people, places, and literacy in the U.S. South. When educators design instruction that invites students to use digital technologies in the service of telling counterstories about their communities, a practice that we have argued constitutes a form of placemaking (Sánchez, 2011), they encourage students to understand themselves as agentive people capable of responding to narratives they recognize as problematic. This work is especially generative for beginning teachers, who may end up teaching in communities that do not resemble the communities where they grew up. In talking with preservice teachers who grew up in urban or suburban contexts, for example, we have noted a tendency for some of them to reproduce a single story (Adichie, 2009) that regards rural communities in deficit terms—that is, as places of lack or want. The opportunity to talk with people from rural communities, and to hear their stories, may help preservice teachers to appreciate the resources and assets that are available to people in those communities. In the same way, talking with people from urban neighborhoods whose schools are deemed "underperforming" may foster preservice teachers' appreciation for the rich literacies that people embrace in their lives.

Encouraging preservice teachers to talk with other people about their literacy practices may also support their moving beyond understanding literacy as a set of autonomous skills. As they develop a sense of appreciation for the many literacies that people employ in their everyday lives, and the different purposes toward which they put them, their understanding of literacy may come to resemble Street's (1984) ideological model, which acknowledges that literacy, far from a mere technical skill-set, is instead embedded in social practices that shape how people use, understand, and value it. From this perspective, literacy "is always contested, both its meanings and its practices, hence particular versions of it are always 'ideological,' they are always rooted in a particular world-view and a desire for that view of literacy to dominate and to marginalise others" (Street, 2006, p. 2). Students intuitively seemed to grasp this point as a result of their having completed the Literacy in Ozark Lives research project. As one student remarked during an interview that occurred at the project's conclusion: "We always say that literacy is the same for everybody, but it's not. It's not just reading and writing; it's how people use reading and writing, their purposes for it and the forms of communication that we use." Other students observed that when schools privilege a narrow range of contexts and purposes for using literacy, and when they limit their definition of literacy to print, they risk marginalizing the diverse practices and purposes that students acquire for using different literacies as they participate in the daily routines of their home and local communities.

Positioning preservice teachers as researchers of literacy in their local communities may also facilitate important identity work. Literacy theorists have argued that learners "try on" new identities as they experiment with new Discourses, a process that involves their "learning how to act and talk so as to take on a particular role that others will recognize" (Gee, 1989,

p. 18). In the case of the Literacy in Ozark Lives research project, preservice teachers experimented with performing the role of researcher as they practiced using an interview protocol, transcribed and coded data, and drafted conceptual memos. Moreover, at the project's conclusion, they presented their work to an audience at the Shiloh Museum of Ozark History, at which time they fielded questions about their research and their videos. Each of these experiences contributed to their gaining insight into what it means to read, write, and talk like a researcher. We also argue that these experiences support Comber's (2015) assertion that students stand to "build a positive sense of their academic identities as they engage with and inquire into the everyday world" (pp. 66–67).

Burke and Greene (2015) argue that young people "learn best when they personally connect to and engage with a given subject like place" (p. 390). Indeed, we have found that positioning students as researchers of their local communities elicits a high level of engagement. As they came to see themselves as curators of other people's stories, a point we emphasized in class, a number of the preservice teachers we worked with expressed feeling a sense of personal responsibility for those stories. In class meetings and post-project interviews, the vast majority of the preservice teachers we spoke with recalled having experienced a desire to honor the stories their interviewees had shared with them. This was due in no small part to their knowledge that the people they interviewed would see their videos, either by accessing the interactive Google Map we created or by attending the public exhibition of their work. In this sense, the opportunity to share their work with an authentic audience, a distinct affordance of digital composing, appeared to change how the preservice teachers approached their schoolwork. As one student explained,

> There's a sense of pride that you get from this project. I'm writing an essay later tonight for this test, and like I'm just getting it done so that I can get to summer break, but that's not what [the Literacy in Ozark Lives] project was, 'cause I know the data I'm analyzing is going to the [Shiloh] museum and I know that my video is going to be seen by the person I interviewed.

Finally, and arguably most importantly, we propose that students benefit when they are given opportunities to share stories and counterstories about people and places they have come to know. According to Ohler (2013), "[Stories] make order out of what would otherwise be the ongoing chaos of life and help each of us create a sense of personal identity in relation to our communities and the world in which we live" (p. 9). In transposing the oral histories they collected into digital stories, the preservice teachers had no alternative but to impose a narrative structure on them. This necessitated their engaging in the kinds of higher-order thinking processes that Robin (2008) suggests digital storytelling encourages, including "synthesizing, analyzing, evaluating, and presenting information" (p. 225). In addition to analyzing the oral histories they collected, the preservice teachers also had to make difficult decisions about which aspects of a person's story were worth sharing in their videos, and which were less relevant in light of their purpose, an undertaking that involves both synthesis and evaluation. While much of this work occurred independently, they were also asked to share drafts of their scripts for their videos with classmates, who critiqued the extent to which they had satisfactorily used the data they collected to persuasively address the specified research questions.

Massey (2005) writes, "There can be no assumption of pre-given coherence, or of community or collective identity. Rather the throwntogetherness of place demands negotiation" (p. 141). At a time when our society is caught in the grips of extreme ideological polarization, and when single stories (Adichie, 2009) about groups of people are carelessly bandied about by politicians and media pundits, our ongoing work with the Literacy in Ozark Lives research project is suggestive of the value involved in creating opportunities for preservice teachers to navigate their "throwntogetherness" (Massey, 2005) in relation to others. In doing so, they may come to appreciate the communities where they teach as constellations of diverse, yet equally important, stories, all of which are worth knowing and sharing.

REFERENCES

Adichie, C. (2009). *The danger of a single story*. Retrieved from http://www.ted.com/talks/chimamanda_adichie_the_danger_of_a_single_story.html

Brandt, D. (2001). *Literacy in American lives*. New York, NY: Cambridge University Press.

Bruce, B. C. (2014). Community inquiry. In B. C. Bruce, A. P. Bishop, & N. R. Budhathoki (Eds.), *Youth community inquiry: New media for community and personal growth* (pp. 1–13). New York, NY: Peter Lang.

Burke, K., & Greene, S. (2015). Participatory action research, youth voices and civic engagement. *Language Arts, 92*(6), 387–400.

Charmaz, K. (2006). *Constructing grounded theory: A practical guide through qualitative analysis*. Thousand Oaks, CA: SAGE.

Comber, B. (2015). *Literacy, place, and pedagogies of possibility*. New York, NY: Routledge.

Cresswell, T. (2004). *Place: A short introduction*. Malden, MA: Blackwell.

Delgado, R. (1989). Storytelling for oppositionists and others: A plea for narrative. *Michigan Law Review, 87*(8), 2411–2441.

Delgado, R., & Stefancic, J. (1995). *Critical race theory: The cutting edge* (2nd ed.). Philadelphia, PA: Temple University Press.

Duck, L. A. (2006). *The nation's region: Southern modernism, segregation, and U.S. nationalism*. Athens, GA: The University of Georgia Press.

Gee, J. P. (1989). What is literacy? *Journal of Education, 171*(1), 18–25.

Granik, D. (Director). (2010). *Winter's bone* [Motion Picture]. USA: Anonymous Content & Winter's Bone Productions.

Green, B. (2012). Literacy, place and the digital world. *Language and Education, 26*(4), 377–382.

Green, B., & Corbett, M. (Eds). (2013). *Rethinking rural literacies: Transnational perspectives.* New York, NY: Palgrave Macmillan.

Kress, G., & Van Leeuwen, T. (2001). *Multimodal discourse: The modes and media of contemporary communication*. London, England: Arnold.

Leander, K. M., & Sheehy, M. (Eds.). (2004). *Spatializing literacy research and practice*. New York, NY: Peter Lang.

Massey, D. (2005). *For space.* London, England: SAGE.

McCann, E. J. (2002). The cultural politics of local economic development: Meaning-making, place-making, and the urban policy process. *Geoforum, 33*, 385–398.

McDowell, L. (1997). Introduction: Rethinking place. In L. McDowell (Ed.), *Undoing place?: A geographical reader* (pp. 2–12). London, England: Arnold.

Mills, K. A. & Comber, B. (2013). Space, place and power: The spatial turn in literacy research. In K. Hall, T. Cremin, B. Comber, & L. Moll (Eds.), *International handbook of research in children's literacy, learning and culture* (pp. 412–423). London, England: Wiley-Blackwell.

Mitchell, D. (2000). *Cultural geography: A critical introduction*. Malden, MA: Blackwell.

New London Group. (1997). A pedagogy of multiliteracies: Designing social futures. *Harvard Educational Review, 66*(1), 60–92.

Ohler, J. B. (2013). *Digital storytelling in the classroom: New media pathways to literacy, learning, and creativity* (2nd ed.). Thousand Oaks, CA: Corwin.

Perry, K. (2012). What is literacy? A critical overview of sociocultural perspectives. *Journal of Language & Literacy Education, 8*(1), 50–71.

Reid, J., Green, B., Cooper, M., Hastings, W., Lock, G., & White, S. (2010). Regenerating rural social space? Teacher education for rural-regional sustainability. *Australian Journal of Education, 54*(3), 262–276.

Robin, B. R. (2008). Digital storytelling: A powerful tool for the 21st century classroom. *Theory Into Practice, 47*, 220–228.

Sánchez, L. (2011). Building on young children's cultural histories through placemaking in the classroom. *Contemporary Issues in Early Childhood, 12*(4), 332–342.

Saldaña, J. (2013). *The coding manual for qualitative researchers* (2nd ed.) Thousand Oaks, CA: SAGE.

Schulte, B. (2017). The alt-right of the Ozarks. *Slate.* Retrieved from http://www.slate.com/articles/news_and_politics/politics/2017/04/what_harrison_arkansas_fight_with_the_kkk_says_about_the_alt_right.html

Southern Poverty Law Center. (2014). Ghosts of Harrison. *Intelligence Report.* Retrieved from https://www.splcenter.org/fighting-hate/intelligence-report/2014/ghosts-harrison

Southern Poverty Law Center. (2017). Active hate groups. *Intelligence Report.* Retrieved from https://www.splcenter.org/fighting-hate/intelligence-report/2017/active-hate-groups-2016

Street, B. V. (1984). *Literacy in theory and practice*. Cambridge, England: Cambridge University Press.

Street, B. V. (2006). Autonomous and ideological models of literacy: Approaches from New Literacy Studies. *Media Anthropology Network*. Retrieved from http://www.philbu.net/media-anthropology/street_newliteracy.pdf

Vance, J. D. (2016). *Hillbilly elegy: A memoir of a family and culture in crisis*. New York, NY: HarperCollins.

Van Leeuwen, T. (2005). *Introducing social semiotics*. London, England: Routledge.

Vygotsky, L. S. (1978). *Mind in society: The development of higher psychological processes*. Cambridge, MA: Harvard University Press.

CHAPTER 8

INDIGENOUS ACTIVISM IN THE DIGITAL SPHERE

A Transrhetorical Analysis of the "Save Longhorn Mountain" Facebook Page

Jordan Paige Woodward
University of Oklahoma

Longhorn Mountain is a sacred site to the Kiowa people. Located near Carnegie, Oklahoma this mountain is visited by Kiowas for spiritual and cultural practices; it is also the only place Kiowas say they can harvest the unique flat leaf cedar that is used ceremonially for protection, healing, and praying. Flat leaf cedar is believed by Kiowas to be a gift from God. In 2013, this geosacred tribal site was threatened after Stewart Stone, a rock crushing company based in Cushing, Oklahoma, stated intentions to mine the western side of the mountain for gravel. As mining the mountain would destroy a site of spiritual and cultural significance to Kiowas, contribute to the destruction of natural landscapes in the area, and potentially lead to negative health ramifications for residents of the area, Kiowas began a movement to save the mountain. This movement has been predominantly carried out through the use of various digital media platforms, one of

Negotiating Place and Space Through Digital Literacies: Research and Practice, pp. 137–153

which is the Save Longhorn Mountain (SLM) facebook. The SLM facebook is a transrhetorical site where Kiowas employ rhetorical strategies, such as appeals to the intersections of geosacrality to cultural identity and cross-cultural alliance building, to protect Longhorn Mountain.

Longhorn is geosacred in that Kiowa, along with Comanche, Kiowa-Apache, and other Plains tribes visit the mountain for vision quests, in times of death and illness, to collect cedar, to fast, and to pray (Ofana 2013). William C. Meadows (2008) describes a geosacred place in *Kiowa Ethnogeography* as a geographical formation or landscape which holds religious or spiritual significance to a people. In geosacred spaces, the land and religious/spiritual connection to it are intertwined. The landscape provides a sanctuary for religious practice while, simultaneously, belief and ritual practices elevate the physical geography into a sacred space. Phil "Joe Fish" Dupoint, a tribal historian at the Kiowa Tribal Museum, stated in an interview with *State Impact OK* (2013), "The old people used to come here [to Longhorn Mountain], and they used to pray. God guided the Kiowas here. This particular mountain here, God gave it to them. And what grows here, God gave it to them." Dupoint's interview describes both the embodied and metaphysical connection Kiowas have to Longhorn. Not only is the cedar seen as a divine gift from God, but Kiowas also physically use their bodies to go to the mountain to collect the cedar, which is then given back as offering in prayer and ceremony. This cyclicality blurs the distinction between the physical and the spiritual. Dupoint's interview was shared on the SLM facebook and illustrates Kiowa rhetorics of geosacrality regarding Longhorn.

Longhorn's geosacrality is the central argument employed on the SLM facebook to protect the mountain from mining, around which other arguments relating to environment, historical preservation, and health circle. As the argument of Longhorn's geosacrality is conveyed via social media, it occurs across physical and digital spaces as well as across time. From this, I argue the SLM facebook is a transrhetorical site in which there is a "movement of meaning across space and time" and "where meaning encounters meaning, concepts change, and rhetorics adapt for multiple audiences" (Jackson, 2016, pp. 9–10). Rachel Jackson (2016) explains that she uses *transrhetorical* in her dissertation, *Red State Reclaimed: The Transrhetorical Recovery of Resistance in Oklahoma*" to characterize the movement of rhetorics themselves, often by individuals acting as rhetorical agents, across multiple location categories—historical, spatial, temporal, cultural, local, regional, national, global, as well as across disciplines" (p. 11). The SLM facebook then, is a site through which Kiowa rhetorical practices from various locations and times travel through and interact with other rhetorics and rhetorical agents.

Jackson (2016) outlines three primary ways transrhetorical sites, and specifically Kiowa transrhetorical sites, function: (1) Kiowa transrhetorical sites and Kiowa rhetorical strategies "work across time. They bridge current Kiowa cultural activist practices with historic practices.... This positions present-day activists as part of a rhetorical continuance of cultural resistance" (p. 177); (2) "they move cultural literacy" from inside a small Kiowa space, "to the Kiowa community more broadly, then beyond to non-Kiowa spaces" (p. 178); and, (3) "Their strategies exemplify cultural and rhetorical adaptations that subvert suppressive rhetorical tactics" (p. 178). It is from within this framework that I ground my rhetorical analysis of SLM facebook, as well as how I understand it to operate as a transrhetorical site by satisfying the above three criteria. Expanding Jackson's framework into the digital realm further complicates the notions of time, space, and subversive rhetorical tactics, as well as understandings of digital literacy as alliance building.

Looked at cohesively, as well as in their disparate parts, the status updates, comment threads, and shared articles on the SLM facebook travel transrhetorically: across time, as movements of cultural literacy from Kiowa to non-Kiowa and non-Native allies, and as subversive rhetorical tactics to (an) oppressive force(s). These interactions occur across time, meaning that communications are not limited to a synchronic moment, but rather move, develop, and evolve diachronically. This distinction between synchronicity and diachronicity only exists in physical spaces. However, in digital spaces, through transrhetoricity (or the movement of rhetorics across time and multiple locations), the distinction between synchronicity and diachronicity blurs. For example, a status update on the SLM facebook can be made in real time, then a week later a person in a different physical location can read and respond to the update (i.e., diachronically). Further, a third person can read the status update and comment as if both happened synchronically, and also comment (diachronically). The convergence of sync/diachronic time in a digital space exemplifies Jackson's point of transrhetorical sites as "movement(s) of meaning" through time (Jackson, 2016, p. 19).

The second indication of a transrhetorical site, and in this case a Kiowa transrhetorical site, is that the site moves cultural literacy from a hyper-localized Kiowa space to a general audience space. The SLM facebook is a repository for various elements of Kiowa cultural literacy, ranging from religious to historical, accessible to both Kiowa and non-Kiowa alike. For example, numerous news articles as well as status updates are shared via the SLM facebook that contain insights and interviews from those within the Kiowa community (such as Dupoint) and information about Kiowa cultural and religious traditions (such as visiting Longhorn to collect flat leaf cedar to be used in prayer and ceremony). The expression of Kiowa cultural literacy directly correlates with the third indication of a transrhetorical site as it "exemplif[ies] cultural and rhetorical adaptations that subvert suppressive rhetorical tactics" (Jackson, 2016, p. 178). The SLM facebook appeals to the emotion and logic of diverse audiences in order to build alliances against the mining of Longhorn. The mining of the mountain can be seen as a suppressive tactic as it would directly impact (and oppress/eliminate) various expression of Kiowa cultural and religious practice. One status update published on July 17, 2013 writes that Longhorn Mountain "has been leased to Stewart Stone ... a rock crushing company that intends to strip mine the Kiowa tribe's sacred mountain, turning it into gravel that would be used to pay our highways. The loss of the mountain would be an act of cultural genocide perpetrated against the Kiowa people." Likening the mining of the mountain to an act of cultural genocide emphasizes the intensity of efforts to protect Longhorn. The SLM facebook thus is a cultural and rhetorical adaption to share efforts of resistance with a broader audience.

The ability to communicate with others in a sync/diachronically convergent way that moves Kiowa cultural literacy to non-Kiowa spaces as an act to subvert suppressive forces (i.e., attempts to mine a Kiowa sacred site) through social media platforms also represents a digital literacy of action and alliance building. Martin (2006) defines digital literacy in "Literacies for the Digital Age" (2006) as,

> the awareness, attitude and ability of individuals to appropriately use digital tools and facilities to identify, access, manage, integrate, evaluate, analyze and synthesize digital resources, construct new knowledge, create media expressions, and communicate with others, in the context of specific life situations, in order to enable constructive social action; and to reflect upon this process. (p. 19)

The SLM page expresses Martin's definition of digital literacy in several ways. For example, the page shares digital resources related to the protection of Longhorn, such as news articles, blog posts, posts from personal or group pages about the topic or other causes related to Indigenous efforts to protect land and culture, numbers and addresses of local and national representatives whom supporters of the SLM should contact regarding Longhorn, and a petition to protect Longhorn (which received 2,122 signatures). The compilation of these shared resources enables the constructive social action of followers of the SLM page, as it provides avenues to become more informed about the issue at hand and to take action (such as contacting representatives and signing petitions).

Within the page, dialogue occurs with native and nonnative participants and makes appeals to concerns of Kiowa cultural preservation and spiritual expression, as well as environmental and historical conservation and public health (i.e., constructive social action). Contributors are physically located in different places and also share information from and to other digital platforms, including other facebook pages, videos, and blogs, which demonstrates a literacy of digital social networks, especially as the page is used to build alliances and ultimately protect Kiowa sacred space. Moreover, the participants' ability to read/write sync/diachronically is evidence of a transrhetorical digital literacy.

Using transrhetorical inquiry, this chapter traces (in brief) the cosmological and historical connections Kiowa have to Longhorn Mountain, the events that lead to the attempts to mine the mountain, and analyzes select posts from the SLM facebook. The analysis explores how the SLM Facebook page not only functions as a transrhetorical site where meaning moves across space, time, and audiences but also how the site is sophisticated in its ability to enable a digital literacy of social engagement through cross-cultural alliance building centered around geosacred space. Participants on the site are simultaneously working towards preservation of the physical, the spiritual, the cultural, and the historical through the digital. Exploring the ways in which multiple locations (digital and physical; Longhorn Mountain and the homes/places of work, and so forth, from which the SLM participants contribute to the page) are entwined and influence one another hints at the simultaneously subtle and complex ways that cultural and digital literacies are utilized for place-based social action.

COSMOLOGICAL AND HISTORICAL CONNECTIONS TO LONGHORN MOUNTAIN

The Kiowa's origin story and migration to Oklahoma beginning in the 1700s illustrate what Elizabeth Maynor (2014) refers to as the Kiowas's "living relationship" to the land in her master's thesis *Native American Cultural Identity and Land Access: The Kiowa Tribe and Longhorn Mountain*. The Kiowas' living relationship to land was impacted by treaties such as the Medicine Lodge Treaty of 1867, the Dawes Act of 1887, and eventually the change in ownership of Longhorn Mountain from Kiowas to non-Native owners (pp. 6–7, 19). These events simultaneously contextualize the current movement to maintain the geosacrality of Longhorn (as the transfer of Longhorn to non-Native landowners made possible the efforts to exploit the mountain for capitalistic enterprises) and highlight the spiritual, historical, and cultural importance of the mountain.

N. Scott Momaday's (1969) telling of the Kiowa origin story illustrates the primordial connection Kiowas have with the land. Momaday writes,

> You know, everything had to begin, and this is how it was: the Kiowas came one by one into the world through a hollow log.... They looked around and

> saw the world. It made them glad to see so many things. They called themselves *Kwuda*, "coming out."

The conception of coming out into the world, through an element of the earth, speaks to the Kiowas' living relationship to the land. The land is intrinsically tied to Kiowa origins of themselves as a people, and that tie is woven into contemporary Kiowas' reverence for and protection of Longhorn Mountain.

This living relationship to land, and specifically to Longhorn, is a longstanding one. Prior to their migration to the southern plains into what is now "present-day western Oklahoma, Kansas, southeastern Colorado, and the Texas panhandle between 1790 and 1830" the Kiowa inhabited the Black Hills area of South Dakota and western Montana (Meadows, 2008, p. 18). A status update on the SLM facebook from September 29, 2013 references the Kiowa's historical relationship Longhorn Mountain, writing, "The Kiowa have been going to Longhorn since the 1700s. Generations of Kiowa medicine men have gone to Longhorn to pray, conduct vision quests, and gather medicine." Meadows contends "that despite migration and changes of residence, the Kiowa maintain a distinct sense of homeland, now centered on dispersed allotted communities in southwestern Oklahoma and the surrounding southern plains" (Meadows, 2008, p. 4). The Kiowa's sense of homeland, their living relationship to land maintained through rituals and stories is dependent upon as well as contributes to the geosacrality of Longhorn Mountain and the sacred cedar that grows there. This sense of homeland and living relationship are the what SLM facebook group was created to protect.

Stewart Stone's stated intentions to mine Longhorn Mountain in 2013 has direct connections to the Medicine Lodge Treaty of 1867 signed by the Kiowa, Comanche, and Apache. The Medicine Lodge Treaty of 1867 placed Longhorn Mountain "within reservation boundaries," and therefore it legally belonged to the Kiowa (Maynor, 2014, p. 6). However, with the Dawes Act of 1887, the land originally included in the Medicine Lodge Treaty "was split into allotments, dividing the landscape among tribal members and selling surplus land to non-Natives.... Due to financial reasons the tribal members who held the Longhorn Mountain allotments, including the Longhorn family, either sold or lost the land" (Meadows, 2008, p. 7). As mentioned previously, currently five non-Native families own Longhorn Mountain and some of the surrounding land. In the early 2000s the non-Native land owners leased their land to Stewart Stone, which lead to plans to mine Longhorn. Thus, Kiowa have had to employ rhetorical strategies to stake their historical, social, cultural, and religious relationships to the land. The Kiowa relationship to the land, and specifically to Longhorn, is nourished and replenished through ritualistic interactions with the mountain, prayers, and activism to protect it. The relationship is corporeal, metaphysical, ongoing—the relationship is living.

The geosacrality of Longhorn Mountain to Kiowa also grows out of various practices and rituals which take place at or because of the mountain. In Meadows's (2008) description of geosacred places to Kiowa, he explains,

> Another geosacred site that has remained particularly important to contemporary Kiowa is Long Horn Mountain, southwest of Mountain View, in Kiowa County, Oklahoma. Because the cedars on this mountain are said to be sweeter than any other in the area, this mountain has become a preferred site for gathering cedar sprigs to dry and use for cedaring ceremonies—prayers and blessings using burning cedar as incense. Cedar incense is commonly used in cleansing and blessing a new home, as a blessing after nightmares, ghost encounters, or funerals, in Peyote and naming ceremonies, prior to a marriage, by dance societies prior to ceremonials, or just for receiving a blessing.... Many Kiowa go to great effort to gather their cedar from this mountain, and a host of offerings, including feathers, tobacco bundles, cloth strips, coins, food, and other items, have been placed on the mountain (p. 93)

The flat leaf cedar has its own unique scent and is believed to hold sacred qualities. Dupoint stated in an interview with KGOU, which was shared on the SLM facebook, in June 2013 that he has smelled cedar across the United States and Canada, "But Longhorn just has its own unique scent, no other place in the world can you get it but here." In the interview Dupoint also explained "they've tried to transplant it but it just doesn't seem to take or grow." Dupoint believes God is the only one who could know why this cedar was given to the Kiowas.

A status update from September 29, 2013 on the SLM facebook elaborates on the importance of the cedar to Kiowa way of life, stating,

> The loss of the mountain would be devastating to Kiowa culture and spirituality as Longhorn Mountain cedar is used in all aspects of Kiowa life.... It also plays a prominent role in Kiowa Native American Church services and all night prayer gathers. Traditional Kiowa households also have it on hand to attend to their daily needs, as they have done for generations.

The September 29th status illustrates the transrhetorical importance of the cedar by describing its connection to various rituals and how the cedar's significance spans generations. This status illustrates transrhetoricity in the ways the past practices with cedar have been carried into the present (meanings from the past encounter meanings from the present). This generational Kiowa cultural literacy regarding the importance of Longhorn cedar to their ways of life is shared on the SLM facebook, with Kiowa and non-Native audiences to resist the mining of the mountain. Thus, the knowledges embedded within the Longhorn cedar are directly threatened by Stewart Stone's plan, as mining the mountain would at the very least endanger, and the worst eradicate, the unique flat-leaf cedar which grows (only) there. The destruction of a historical, cultural, and spiritual component of Kiowa identity and way of life will occur if Longhorn is mined.

ATTEMPTS TO MINE LONGHORN MOUNTAIN

As previously mentioned, Stewart Stone obtained a lease in the early 2000s from the non-Native landowners of the western side of Longhorn Mountain (Maynor, 2008, p. 7). Attempts to protect Longhorn Mountain began in 2013 after Stewart Stone stated plans to mine the western side of the mountain for gravel. As the sacred cedar used ceremonially by Kiowas grows on the eastern side of the mountain, fears arose that the mining would hinder the growth of the cedar, and thus Kiowa tribal traditions. Kiowas, along with other residents of Carnegie, Oklahoma also expressed concerns that the gravel mining would cause impediments to their health "caused by the dust and air pollution from the rock crushing as well as the damage caused to their home due to the dynamite" (Kline, 2013). While health impediments due to mining is a concern both Natives and non-Natives can recognize, bridging an understanding of Kiowa reverence for the geosacrality of Longhorn can prove more challenging for non-Kiowa.

Non-Kiowa and many non-Native communities do not root their ideas of the sacred within the earth. For instance, some evangelical Christian groups understand rooting ideas of the sacred within the earth as blasphemous to God as this would prioritize the creation and not the Creator, which is significant in this particular ideological framework. Meadows (2008) describes the division between Anglo-American and Native conceptions of land by stating, "Outsiders often have difficulty in viewing physical landscapes in the ways the Native Americans do: as physical forms bearing traces of their ancestors, and as form intertwined with the concepts of the past, origins, language, oral history, personal conduct, and spiritual morals and direction" (p. 32). Vine Deloria (1973) also writes in *God is Red* of the contrasting perceptions of land from a Christian worldview compared to an Indigenous one. Deloria writes,

> Tribal religions do not have the massive institutions which Christianity requires to perpetuate itself.... The religious ceremonies of the tribal religions ... [often] take place in sacred locations where the people can be in contact with the spiritual powers who have always guided the tribe. (pp. 220–221)

An August 1, 2013 status on the SLM facebook (described in more detail in the following section) articulates the differences in understandings of sacred spaces for Native and non-Native communities (specifically between Kiowa and Christians). The status appeals to similarities between the faith practices in order to build alliances between these practices. In this way, "meaning encounters meaning" so that concepts are able to change. In other words, *meaning* as Kiowa understandings of sacred space encounters the *meaning* of Christian sacred space, so that concepts of what can be included within a sacred space can change/expand for non-Native audiences. Kiowa cultural literacy is thus shared in such a way as to build alliances. It is important to not romanticize the relationship Native peoples have and continue to have to land, yet understanding the spiritual, cultural, and historical importance of geosacred sites is essential to the protection of the land and to furthering movements such as the SLM.

To mine the mountain for gravel therefore not only hinders generational tribal traditions, but also threatens a core piece of Kiowa identity and way of life for those who currently interact with the mountain as well as for future generations of Kiowa. As Kiowas do not have legal ownership of the western side of the mountain, they had little other recourse against the threat of mining the mountain than to use their voices to bring awareness to and build alliances around the issue, which they did through the SLM facebook.

TRANSRHETORICAL ANALYSIS

The social media platform utilized by SLM functions as an interconnection of rhetorical networks. Jackson (2016) argues that to engage in transrhetorical inquiry is to "look for *networks* of rhetorical locations rather than one, and defines *one location in terms of many*" (emphasis added p. 10). Thus, although the SLM page exists (or can be viewed) as one location, it is embedded within digital social networks of information sharing (personal facebook pages), engaging in asynchronous dialogue (comment threads and status updates), and referencing events which occurred in the past or have the potential to occur in the future (i.e. the historical connections Kiowa have to Longhorn Mountain and the present/future plans to mine it by Steward Stone Rock Crushing Company) or in different places at the same or different time.

The SLM facebook is a digital space connected to the physical place of users through dialogic engagement (in comment threads, status updates, and even silent readers of the page), which integrates and references digital and physical spaces outside of the SLM facebook (most visibly, Longhorn). Additionally, through status updates the SLM facebook shares articles from blogs, news outlets, YouTube, or from other digital or physical networks that either reference Longhorn Mountain directly or are related to other Indigenous movements and issues relating to land. For instance, in 2015, SLM posted about pollution of the Animas River, which runs through Navajo land, protests to protect Sacred Oak Flat from mining, and in 2016, several posts were made about the Dakota Access Pipeline and Standing Rock. Commenters share information from other locations within the digital sphere, discuss their physical (and sometimes spiritual) place, and/or their relationship to the physical space of Longhorn Mountain. From these interactions, the SLM facebook is a nexus where we can see the convergence of "networks of rhetorical locations," which is apparent within the SLM facebook as conversations and statements are both archived and ongoing (i.e., convergent in sync/diachronic time) (Jackson 2016, p. 9). Thus, Kiowa cultural literacies held within a particular post or update can evolve across time or space (i.e., other peoples' facebook pages and/or other digital platforms). Jackson (2016) describes this meeting of temporal and physical/digital as when the "time axis and space axis—intersect" (p. 19). The evolution of meaning across time and space enables participants or readers of the site from various backgrounds, locations, and/or cultural contexts to not only learn about the SLM but also engage in or renew discussions that have happened in the past (i.e., contribute to the site diachronically).

A status update posted September 29, 2013, at the height of the site's activity, particularly illustrates the complex rhetorical engagement within this transrhetorical site, as it moves through the movement of three points outlined by Jackson (2016), while also emphasizing a digital literacy of alliance building through appealing to history, emotion, and health. This status update powerfully describes the connection the Kiowa people of Oklahoma have to Longhorn Mountain through examples ranging from spiritual practice, religious mythology, historical and cultural events associated with Longhorn, and transgenerational interaction. The status update also appeals to the physical health of the community and animals that would be at risk if Stewart Stone were to mine the mountain. The September 29th status is lengthy, detailed, and eloquent in its description of the importance of the mountain to the Kiowa and those living near the area. An excerpt from status emphasizing the historical, cultural, and religious importance of Longhorn (2013) states:

> The Kiowa say God led them to Longhorn Mountain and to use its cedar.... The loss of the mountain would be devastating to Kiowa culture and spirituality as Longhorn Mountain cedar is used in all aspects of Kiowa life.... All Kiowa societies, such as the Black Leggings Warrior Society, Ohoma Lodge, and Gourd Dance Societies utilize the smoke of the cedar in their ceremonies. It also plays a prominent role in Kiowa Native Ameri-

> can Church services and all night prayer gatherings. Traditional Kiowa households also have it on hand to attend to their daily needs as they have for generations.... The Kiowa have been going to Longhorn since the 1700's. Generations of Kiowa medicine men have gone to Longhorn to pray, conduct vision quests, and gather medicine. Some without heirs to their healing powers are said to have also left their spiritual "medicine" to the mountain.

Within this excerpt, the status makes rhetorical appeals to a diverse audience, Native and non-Native alike, who may prioritize different issues. It does so by sharing Kiowa cultural literacy of historical and religious connections of Kiowa to Longhorn, such as that God led Kiowa to Longhorn, that Kiowa have been visiting Longhorn since the 1700s, and that "generations of medicine men have gone to Longhorn to pray, conduct vision quests, and gather medicine," even stating that some of the medicine is left to Longhorn itself. Jackson describes that transrhetorical sites can be seen in "relationships occurring between multiple sites of meaning-making, particularly where they link locations and meaning across difference" (p. 11). These appeals expressed in the status demonstrate the ways the meaning of the geosacrality (the physical intersecting with the sacred) of Longhorn to Kiowa of the past continues to make meaning for present-day Kiowa in similar and different ways, "this positions present-day activists as part of a rhetorical continuance of cultural resistance" (p. 177). Thus the one physical location of Longhorn then comes to symbolize two temporal locations (past and present) where meaning is constructed for Kiowa ways of life. Alongside temporal difference, the September 29th status also links meaning across difference in that this status, and the very existence of the SLM facebook itself, convey that other communities may have different conceptions (or no conceptions at all) regarding the geosacrality, historical, and cultural importance of Longhorn. Linking meaning across difference in this status has the intended effect of both educating diverse audiences and building alliances with them in order to stand against the mining of Longhorn. The September 29th status also references the preservation of historical sites, such as caves bearing pictographs or petroglyphs, as well as the environmental and health implications mining could have on the surrounding area and communities. This excerpt expresses:

> The local farmers around the mountain, many of which have lived there for generations since the early 1900's, do not want the rock crushing to begin either as they fear for their livestock's health as limestone dust adversely affects grass and wears down cattle's teeth. The farmers also fear the negative health effects that breathing the dust will have upon them and their children and grandchildren.... The use of explosives on the mountain would also likely destroy a chambered cave with important historical value.

> The cave is said to have either ancient Kiowa pictographs or petroglyphs on its walls and said to be the place of a unique practice among the Kiowa where men would lure eagles to the cave entrance by placing meat there and then hiding in the cave would grab the eagle by its feet when it landed to get the meat. Thereupon they would pluck a couple tail feathers or so as they needed before releasing them.

This excerpt of the September 29th status frames the issue of mining prismatically through the lenses of agriculture, public health, and cultural and historical preservation. This prismatic framing illuminates components of the issue to mine Longhorn in such a way that appeals to various stakeholders—those who may support maintaining the geosacrality of Longhorn to those whose primary interest is in support of public health. Highlighting the numerous impacts mining could have on different communities demonstrates the intention to build alliances with diverse followers of the page. Jackson, when expressing movements across transrhetorical sites, contends, "Ideas, issues, and events engage multiple groups and locations in the collective construction of meaning. Rhetorics, both as messages and the vehicle for messages, necessarily change as a result of these transactions, yielding generative and cumulative adaptations, co-optations, and applications" (p. 12). The framing of this status excerpt reveals that, by outlining the range of ways mining Longhorn would negatively impact not only Kiowa culture but also non-Natives who live nearby, a variety of ideas and issues were chosen to engage multiple audiences in the cause to stop mining. To a Kiowa-only audience, some of these issues would not be expressed in the same way because of a general consensus of Longhorn's importance. Instead, the construction of a public facebook page, alongside status updates such as this one, convey that multiple audiences are meant to be reached. This underscores a digital literacy employed for efforts of action and alliance building.

The September 29th status itself constitutes a rich site of rhetorical strategies to build alliances cross-culturally. The comment thread also contributes to particular representations of the transrhetorical nature of the site. This particular post was shared 47 times, thus expanding the reach of the information to different digital spaces and communities. Additionally, the comment thread demonstrates the sync/diachronic aspects of the way time functions in this transrhetorical place. For instance, SLM facebook posted the status on September 29th and then commented on the post the same day, asking followers to "Please help us save Longhorn Mountain" (Longhorn Mountain, 2013). A follower of the page commented almost a year later on July 7, 2014 with a link to an environmental forum. In these ways, the comment thread allows for meaning to travel across space and time through connecting multiple networks, such as personal facebook accounts, documentaries, blogs, forums, and other digital spaces in such a way that complicates notions of what it means to participate in dialogue that converges sync/diachronic time.

A later status update from August 1, 2013 also engages in alliance building and displays how "rhetorics adapt for multiple audiences" (Jackson, 2016), specifically with non-Native communities and members of major religious groups. By drawing parallels between other religious traditions' sacred spaces and Longhorn Mountain, the August 1st update encourages non-Native followers or readers of the status to make connections to spaces of cultural and religious importance in their own traditions and/or communities. The status states:

> It may be difficult for non-Native to understand that Native Americans did not build churches, but had sacred places in nature where they went to pray and seek the presence of God.
>
> Christians, Jews, Muslims, Hindus and Buddhists all over the world have sacred places that they have been making pilgrimage to for thousands of years. The Kiowa, Kiowa-Apache, and Comanche have been making pilgrimages to Longhorn Mountain to pray, fast and seek the guidance of the creator for centuries. (August 1, 2013)

The status concludes with a blog post titled "The Importance of Protecting the Kiowa Tribe's Longhorn Mountain and Other Sacred Native American Sites" aims to develop a place of shared understanding through communicating cross-culturally with non-Native religious audiences (Oofana 2013). Oofana (2013) makes the Kiowa veneration of Longhorn Mountain relatable to Christians by drawing similarities between the ways Christians feel about sacred spaces, such as churches, to how Kiowa feel about Longhorn. In other words, the status describes the geosacrality of Longhorn Mountain in such a way that allows various audiences to empathize with the cause. The comment thread on the August 1st status illustrate that the post is effective in its goal to build alliances through cross-cultural engagement.

The first commenter in the comment thread, posting 6 days after the initial post, seemingly positions themself as non-Native by stating, "We as Americans have never did much for the tribes other than try to wipe them off the face of the earth.... We could always build a human chain around this mountain and lay our lives down to help the Indians for a change." The commenter expresses the importance they see in protecting Longhorn, especially in light of the historical colonial forces of oppression and violence against Native people and communities. The commenter also connects their spiritual practice of prayer to efforts to protect the geosacrality of Longhorn by expressing, "I pray good sense and respect win out and this hallowed ground remains untouched." This comment shows a built alliance between a non-Native follower of the page and the SLM movement.

The September 29th and August 1st statuses and comment threads reveal the site as a nexus between multiple networks of relationships and meaning-making, which occurs in a bringing together of past and present times and locations in order to share Kiowa cultural literacy to resist destructive intentions of a geosacred space—in this way they demonstrate the site's transrhetoricity. Transrhetorical sites are ideal locations for alliance building cross-culturally, as well as cross-temporally and cross-spatially, to occur.

Thus the status, shared blog post, and comment thread are dialogic—they begin from multiple origins in terms of physical, temporal, and digital spaces, and therefore depend on and enable social action. In other words, the creation of the SLM facebook depended on social action to create a platform to disperse information regarding the issue facing the Kiowa, and simultaneously the page enables *further* social action through alliance building *because of* the creation of the SLM facebook. Thinking of social media platforms, such as the SLM facebook, as spaces where digital literacies of social action take place independent of a coincidence of place or time opens up new ways of exploring how alliances can be built cross-culturally for a shared goal.

CONCLUSION: A "REVOLUTION OF RELATEDNESS"

The efforts to protect Longhorn's geosacrality are not over. On December 5, 2016 the SLM facebook posted the following status:

> Rock crusher Larry Stewart of Stewart Stone is attempting again to destroy Longhorn Mountain by having it mined for gravel. The Obama Administration has been instrumental in protecting sacred Native American sites, public lands and places of historical significance.. bama remains in office until January 20th. Please call the White House at 202-456-1414 or click on the link below for the White House's contact page and leave a message asking the president to protect Longhorn Mountain by declaring it a Native American sacred site.

The status was shared 19 times. Considering the SLM facebook was most active in 2013, with the most shared post was shared 47 times (September 29, 2013), the amount this call to action was shared is impressive. The amount of times it was shared also highlights that alliances to the SLM are still active and are attempting to build a wider circle of alliances through introducing the information in the status to a personal facebook page. Presently, Longhorn Mountain still remains protected from mining efforts.

In *Back to the Blanket* Wieser (2017) "calls for a revolution of relatedness that we must achieve to save the earth and humanity from environmental destruction" (p. 34). By building alliances transrhetorically, the SLM facebook answers Weiser's call and joins the revolution of relatedness in order to protect a site of cultural, spiritual, and historical significance to the Kiowa. Viewing the SLM facebook as a case study of Indigenous activism in the digital sphere that impacts physical space and reality by enacting a digital literacy of social action contingent upon alliance building reveals the need to further explore the ways in which digital literacies are influenced and created through social action.

The efforts to protect the geosacrality of Longhorn are transrhetorical—they move from the past to the present, from physical space to digital and back to physical again; they share Kiowa cultural literacy, build alliances, and do so in such a way as to subvert oppression forces of mining interests. The digital literacies of action and alliance building enable and are supported by the transrhetoricity of the SLM facebook. It is thus essential to consider how digital platforms contribute to change in the physical realm, and how digital platforms cultivate the digital that take place and grow within them.

In *MixedBlood Messages: Literature, Film, Family, Place* Louis Owens (1998) states,

> The future of that wilderness and, of course, the future of all life depends upon whose stories we listen to: the stories that tell us we are bound in a timeless and inextricable relationship with the earth which gives us life and sustains us, or the stories that tell us the earth is a resource to be exploited until it is used up. (p. 211)

The SLM facebook is a site that share stories of Kiowa culture and ways of life, and also reveals the power in building alliances cross-culturally. Owen's poignant note that "the future of all life depends on whose stories we listen to" is continually relevant—the SLM facebook, and other Indigenous led social media campaigns, provides opportunity for us to listen to those stories that tell us "we are bound in a timeless and inextricable relationship with the earth." The SLM facebook illustrates how meaning-making is woven through, but not limited to, constructs of time and space, and how meaning evolves, who contributes to meaning's making, and who listens.

NOTES

1. For more on cross-cultural alliance building, see Angela Haas's (2008) dissertation, *A Rhetoric of Alliance: What American Indians Can Tell Us About Digital and Visual Rhetoric*.

2. Maynor's (2014) thesis documents interviews with members of the Kiowa community in Oklahoma about their connections to Longhorn Mountain. Her thesis is the only other academic documentation I have found of the attempts to mine Longhorn Mountain and its impact on the Kiowa community in Oklahoma.
3. For more information on the Medicine Lodge Treaty of 1867, see "Medicine Lodge Treaty of 1867" entry in *Oklahoma Encyclopedia of History and Culture* (Rand, n.d.).
4. For more information regarding the Dawes Act of 1887, see "Dawes Commission" entry in *Oklahoma Encyclopedia of History and Culture* (Carter, n.d.).
5. For further reading on the Kiowa's sense of homeland, see Steven M. Schnell's "The Kiowa Homeland in Oklahoma" (2000).
6. For additional information regarding government interference with Kiowa land, look for information regarding the court case Lone *Wolf v. Hitchcock* and the Jerome Commission in *Lone Wolf vs. Hitchcock: Treaty Rights and Indian Law at the End of the Nineteenth Century* (Clark, 1999).

REFERENCES

Carter, K. (n.d.). Dawes Commission. *The Encyclopedia of Oklahoma History and Culture*. Retrieved from www.okhistory.org

Clark, B. (1994). *Lone Wolf v. Hitchcock: Treaty rights and Indian law at the end of the nineteenth century*. Lincoln, NE: University of Nebraska Press.

Haas, A. (2008). *A rhetoric of alliance: What American Indians can tell us about digital and visual rhetoric*. (Doctoral dissertation). Michigan State University, East Lansing, Michigan.

Jackson, R. (2016). *Red State reclaimed: The transrhetorical recovery of resistance in Oklahoma* (Doctoral dissertation). University of Oklahoma, Norman, Oklahoma.

Kline, C. (2013). Longhorn Mountain: Sacred places and cultural genocide. *Intercontinental Cry: A Publication of the Center for World Indigenous Studies*. Retrieved from intercontinentalcry.org/longhorn-mountain-sacred-places-and-cultural-genocide/

Longhorn Mountain. (2013). *Documentary* [Video File]. Retrieved from https://www.youtube.com/watch?v=NzXTGNrkV5g

Martin A. (2006). Literacies for the digital age. In A. Martin & D. Madigan (Eds.), *Digital Literacies for Learning*. London, England: Facet.

Maynor, E. (2014). *Native American cultural identity and land access: The Kiowa Tribe and Longhorn Mountain* (MA Thesis). University of Oklahoma, Norman, Oklahoma.

Meadows, W. C. (2008). *Kiowa ethnogeography*. University of Texas Press, Austin, Texas.

Momaday, N. S., & Momaday, A. (1969). *The way to Rainy Mountain*. University of New Mexico Press, Albuquerque, New Mexico.

Oofana, B. (2013 June 17). The historical and spiritual significance of Longhorn Mountain. *Ben Oofana's Blog*. Retrieved from benoofana.wordpress.

com/2013/06/17/the-historical-and-spiritual-significance-of-longhorn-mountain/

Oofana, B. (2013, August 1). The importance of protecting the Kiowa Tribe's Longhorn Mountain and other sacred Native American Sites. Retrieved from http://benoofana.com/the-importance-of-protecting-the-kiowa-tribes-longhorn-mountain-and-other-sacred-native-american-sites/

Owens, L. (1998). *Mixedblood messages: Literature, film, family, place*. Norman, OK: University of Oklahoma Press.

Rand, J. T. (n.d.). Medicine Lodge Treaty. *The Encyclopedia of Oklahoma History and Culture*. Retrieved from www.okhistory.org

Save Longhorn Mountain |Facebook. (n.d.) *Save Longhorn Mountain | Facebook*, www.facebook.com/SaveLonghornMountain/?fref=ts.

Schnell, S. M. (2000). The Kiowa Homeland in Oklahoma. *Geographical Review, 90*(2), 155–176.

Deloria, V. (1973). *God is red*. New York, NY: Grosset & Dunlap.

Weiser, K. (2017). *Back to the blanket: Recovered rhetorics and lived literacies in American Indian Studies*. Norman, OK: University of Oklahoma Press.

CHAPTER 9

FROM THE SCREENS TO THE STREETS

Translating Digital Engagement Into Performance Practice to Facilitate Multiple Contributions to Placemaking

Wayne Steven Jackson
The Arden School of Theatre, UCEN Manchester

INTRODUCTION

In 2017, Hull became the UK City of Culture, the second city to be awarded the title since it was established in 2009. The focus throughout the year, and throughout the years leading up to it, was on the potential effect that the UK City of Culture status could have upon the people of Hull. However, the decision making, curation, and promotion of the yearlong event was controlled, framed, and only made possible, by the government initiative, which, as an institution in itself, positions the program of cultural regeneration as hegemonically influenced. Furthermore, while a large number of projects aimed to involve inhabitants of Hull, there were limited

Negotiating Place and Space Through Digital Literacies: Research and Practice, pp. 155–176

opportunities for those who, while still identifying the city as home, no longer resided there.

Throughout this chapter I present how a translation of digital engagement into performance practice can be utilized to reach, include, and activate multiple individual contributions to placemaking. To do so, I acknowledge, and exploit, my own connections to the city; I was born and raised in Hull but moved away in 2001. My performance work has always been influenced by my attachment to home and, during 2017, I returned to Hull to present *Now | Then*, a series of performance journeys. My practice investigated how individual experiences of the city, after being uploaded to my website, could be theatrically interpreted. I purposefully located *Now | Then* amidst the cultural celebrations of 2017 but, importantly, outside of the UK City of Culture framework. I did not receive funding from the UK City of Culture program, and while the performance did feature on the event's official website, additional support, such as the production of a promotional video, was only initiated once *Now | Then* had already gained media interest and attention.

Gertner and Kotler (2004, p. 50) suggest that a "place's image is defined [...] as the sum of beliefs, ideas and impressions that people have of that place." Throughout this chapter, I position place as a multifaceted projection, constructed from numerous acknowledged, accepted, and amalgamated individual attachments, including those of people who are no longer residents. As such, my research explores how the multiple relationships with Hull that were exposed through *Now | Then* support and evoke individual attachments to the city. Furthermore, I present strategies with which I translated my project's collected individual experiences out of digital engagement and into performance, from the screens to the streets, as examples of how performance can support multiple renegotiations of place.

DEFINING HULL AS A PLACE

I situate my research within the English city of Kingston upon Hull, or Hull as I refer to it throughout this chapter, at a time of its transition into becoming the UK City of Culture 2017. However, while my research is specific to Hull, it is also representative of other urban areas undergoing cultural regeneration; in any process of regeneration, there is an objective for the identity of place to be transformed. Places are ultimately unfixed, experienced, and constructed through practice; "[w]hat begins as undifferentiated space becomes place as we get to know it better and endow it with value" (Tuan, 1977, p. 6). Thus, the transformation of place is heavily reliant on the actions and interactions of its occupants (Cresswell, 2009).

Hull is a working class city, in the north east of England, located at the end of the M62 motorway, atop of the River Humber. Covering an area of 28 square miles, the city has a population of over 260,000 people, and a gross disposable household income that is 6000 pounds less than the national average. Hull is a city undergoing change: cosmetically, economically, and culturally. In 2016, the city reportedly spent 25 million pounds resurfacing its streets, in 2015 it won Siemens's 160 billion pound contract to manufacture wind energy turbines, and, in 2017, it experienced a shift in terms of cultural engagement. The UK City of Culture interim report produced by University of Hull's Culture, Place and Policy Institute (2017) highlights that only 36% of Hull residents engaged in cultural activity during the first three months of 2013. In the same three months of 2017, at the start of the UK City of Culture year, cultural engagement in the city had risen to 90%. However, where the city is situated, its contents, buildings, and its engagement with cultural activities, do not alone make Hull, Hull.

Agnew (1987) suggests that place is constructed and understood through a combination of three elements. Its location, the measurable and literal point in space, and its locale, the place's urban makeup, provide objective definition. However, the third element is much more subjective; it is a definition made from the more nebulous meanings associated with a place, "the feelings and emotions a place evokes" (Cresswell, 2009, p. 1): its sense of place. It is here that the essence of a city is negotiated, both individually and collectively, through how the city is felt and experienced, where "cities' identities are socially produced through the ways we act in them" (Harvie, 2009, p. 47). There is a clear differentiation between a communal understanding of Hull that stands alone from personal relationships to the city and an understanding of Hull that includes emotional connection, where there is an "insistence on the centrality of human consciousness and experience" (Cresswell, 2009, p. 7). Cresswell (2009) further suggests, home is "the location where meanings and attachments are most intense," an extension of the element of place construction Agnew defines as sense of place. The location and locale of Hull are literal and concrete, shared and validated by numerous different people. However, as Etchells (2009, p. xii) explains in relation to performance, a city "is used at the same time by many people, sectors, factions, groups whose interests do not by any mean coincide," and as such, sense of place can be understood as being constructed through an innumerable amount of personal relationships and experiences. Michalski (2009, p. 101) states that a "city becomes fluid, and landmarks and people write themselves upon us. This text, written by the streets has many authors," and thus, the city is a patchwork, created from multiple attachments, memories, and experiences.

As with all constructions of place, Hull, the resulting combination of location, locale, and sense of place, is always in flux. Hull's locale has experienced a number of alterations in recent years, as has its location due to shifting parameters of what is and is not included within its boundaries. As such, and similar to the multiplicity of sense of place, Hull's location and locale can be understood as unfixed entities. Alongside the cosmetic, economic, and cultural changes, Hull has undergone a number of conceptual transformations involving its name, logo, and marketing straplines. There has been a desire to amend, change, and mould Hull as a place contextualized by its history; it "suffered severe deindustrialisation from the 1980s with the loss of its shipbuilding and fishing industries [and as a consequence became] blighted by its drab reputation [and] poor external image" (Julier, 2005, p. 883). For Hull, renegotiations of place focused on the external image of the city, in attempts to unburden itself as England's "Number One Crap Town" (Jordison & Kiernan, 2005).

Methods of reconstructing place, from collective acts of erecting buildings and assigning names, to individual acts of personal experience and memory, parallel the relationship between Agnew's location, locale, and sense of place. Thus, those factors that affect the transformation and definition of a city as place are constant, unrelenting, and subjective. Consequently, as Harvie (2009, p. 6) suggests, cities "are better understood as urban process because they are constantly changing." Goal-Holmes (2012, p. 205) states that the qualities of sense of place give shape to a fixed place that is "only temporarily established, necessitating a continuous state of negotiation and renegotiation," and is thus in constant fluctuation. Furthermore, the multiple individual emotional and experiential connections involved in sense of place leads Parkerson and Saunders (2005, p. 242) to suggest that there is an "elusiveness of any single city image." If in flux, a city, as place, can be renegotiated at any point. By reexperiencing the city through an exposition of subjective connections, individuals contribute to a continual process of placemaking.

Proshansky, Fabian, and Kaminoff (1983) coined the term place attachment in order to articulate the effect that place has upon an individual's sense of self: the emotional, experiential, and subjective connections to place. Furthermore, Morgan (2010, p. 11) highlights humanistic approaches to place theory that "explore the deeper significance of place to human existence and the subjective, emotional quality of people's relationship to places." The similarities between place attachment and Agnew's sense of place create ambiguity and confusion within place theory; place attachment and sense of place are often used synonymously (Jorgensen & Stedman, 2001; Lewicka, 2008). However, Scannell and Gifford (2010, p. 1) offer a distinction between the two, defining place attachment as the meaningful bond an individual has with sense of place. In this reciprocal relationship, I understand place attachment as an individual's abstraction of sense of place, and sense of place as the coalescence of multiple individual place attachments. Sense of place, in this understanding, is formed through majority; it is a representation shared and accepted by a number of individuals. Place attachment, in turn, is an individual's interpretation of, and response to, sense of place, which intrinsically involves a reaction to representation. Place attachment, in this understanding, asks why sense of place has been constructed in that way, and, ultimately, signifies whether an individual accepts or rejects it. As such, the relationship between place attachment and sense of place, through action and response, provides individuals with an opportunity to determine how they understand their city.

PERFORMANCE, CULTURE, AND PLACEMAKING

Millard (2015, p. 4) acknowledges culture as having the "transformational power" to renegotiate, specifically, external impressions of a city. Culture in this way has been utilized successfully in a number of projects for UK cities, such as the European Capital of Culture, which saw Liverpool and Glasgow benefit cosmetically and economically as a result of regeneration. In both of these cases, the renovation of locale played a major part in the cities becoming venues for the practicing of culture and, thus, the renegotiation of place. Similarly, impressions of Hull were undoubtedly affected by a cosmetic restoration that supported the city's cultural regeneration. As well as the repaving of streets, derelict buildings were replaced, water features were introduced in the squares, new street signs were erected, and greenery was planted. However, the cosmetic changes that framed the presentation of cultural events were at times in contrast to existing place attachments, especially those of individuals who did not experience the city's improvements directly. As a consequence, a tension grew between the city's representations from the past and in the present. Humber Street, for example, in contrast to its location as the city's old fruit market with a locale of factories and warehouses, was regenerated for 2017 to house café bars and restaurants, art galleries, and reclamation shops. The renewed facade and atmosphere breathed life into the street's old buildings; live music, street theater, and outdoor socializing became features of its identity.

Hull, as place and home, was confounded by the methods of regeneration that the city employed in order to become a venue for its tenure as UK City of Culture 2017. The winning bid aimed to bring the city "out of the shadows," promising that the UK City of Culture accolade would help shed its external image as a declining and deprived port city. Garcia (2005, p. 844) highlights that the UK government in 2004 was "supportive of the use of culture as a tool for regeneration, with the Department of Culture, Media and Sport (DCMS) framing it as one of its key objectives." In the

Hull 2017 strategic business plan, Green (2015, p. 9) states that the overall objective of the UK City of Culture year was to "position the city as a cultural powerhouse as strong as any other in the north and across the UK." The focus, through utilizing culture as a tool with which to grow capital and boost economy, was "to maximise the benefits and economic impact of Hull's year as U.K. City of Culture and recent private sector investments in the city" (Hull 2017 Strategic Business Plan, 2015, p. 41). In preparation for 2017, a hive of activity took place in Hull that had not been experienced or witnessed before, as though the title bestowed upon the city had given justification and reason to unveil new work and explore new ideas. What began to emerge was a new narrative for the city, established and reinforced through the programming of cultural events, the regeneration of the streets and squares, and the creation of performance.

In their exploration of the effects of social and cultural practices, Dollimore and Sinfield (1988, p. ix) articulate cultural materialism as "inseparable from the conditions of their productions and reception in history." In this way, I suggest, that which constituted Hull as a venue for the yearlong UK City of Culture program also affected individual place attachment. However, the regeneration of the city's locale cannot so easily be isolated as contradictory to understandings of Hull as home; Humber Street has become a popular, reputable, and accepted area of the city. The representations of Hull's past and the present do not necessarily establish a binary opposition; they instead become a continuum of renegotiation. In 2017, the city of Hull became a venue of cultural regeneration that contributed to place attachment in the present *and* a venue of individual experience and history that contributed to place attachment from the past. Undoubtedly, the program of cultural regeneration positively impacted the city in terms of its economy and external image. Support for the regeneration can be seen in the overwhelming response from its inhabitants and local businesses; more than 2,800 events took place across the city that reached an audience of over 5.3 million. Indeed, University of Hull's preliminary outcomes evaluation (University of Hull Culture, Place and Policy Institute, 2018) highlights that three in four residents were proud to live in Hull and that almost half of the population of the United Kingdom and suggests that 2017 had positively changed the perception of the city for almost half of the population of the United Kingdom. However, while there were numerous new and exciting commissions for the yearlong celebrations, the UK City of Culture program not only predominantly engaged those who still inhabited the city, it also promoted a single, albeit new and more positive, narrative of rejuvenation. As such, I question the degree to which this renegotiation of sense of place was conducive to a heterogeneous process of placemaking that aims to include all residents.

Programs of cultural regeneration, such as the UK City of Culture scheme, have the potential to galvanise individual contributions to sense of place. In line with the aims of regeneration that Richards and Wilson (2004, p. 1993) describe, Hull was able to make use of the "particular valuable form of cultural currency, [that of] an image-enhancement tool." The Hull 2017 Strategic Business Plan (2015, p. 14) explicitly outlines this objective, focusing on the transformative nature of culture and clearly states that, for Hull, there would be change. The instillation of pride and community through placemaking is an important cultural practice when renegotiating place attachment. However, sense of place can often be stabilized through hegemonic influence and political power. When a single narrative is promoted through cultural regeneration, that interpretation of the past can become the projected and accepted version of events, regardless of how the city is experientially felt. University of Hull's (2018, p. 214) impact report reflects on the future of the UK City of Culture, stating, "[a]ttention needs to be paid to achieving the right balance of commissioning local and external artistic partners." As such, I highlight a need for performance makers to contribute to cultural regeneration by promoting multiplicity so that processes of placemaking are inclusive of place attachments from a wide range of individuals that identify the city as home.

As Hull underwent a cultural regeneration, I identify a limited number of projects in its yearlong program that challenged the city's renovated narrative. The program instead presented and celebrated Hull's shared history through the frame of, and adherence to, the UK City of Culture's key objectives and thus resulted in a stabilized sense of place. While the UK City of Culture generated a number of positive outcomes, such as a restored sense of pride, a boosted economy, and an increase in cultural engagement, its program supported minimal deviations to, or renegotiations of, the promoted single narrative. In this way, I suggest, culture was utilized as a tool with which to control placemaking as opposed to supporting a renegotiation, and indeed a remembrance, of the city outside of the parameters set, presented, and performed by the hegemonically influenced cultural regeneration.

THE IMPORTANCE OF MULTIPLE NARRATIVES

During the process of placemaking, a stabilized sense of place that concretizes, and constantly reaffirms, a promoted narrative offers little room for the multiplicity of individual place attachments. Instead, reconstructions of place are limited by a frame that is dictated and governed by hegemonic control. Throughout the remainder of this chapter, I present how a translation of digital engagement into performance practice can challenge and destabilize single narratives. In this way, I suggest, multiple place attachments that intrinsically invite varying interpretations of, and connections to, a city should be favored and celebrated.

Robertson (2008) suggests that individual experiences, in contributing to place attachment, can oppose a sense of place manufactured from positions of power. He describes this process as heritage from below. The essence of heritage from below manifests within any proposition that residents take ownership of the contributions to, and interpretations of, sense of place. Here, the power of placemaking is relinquished from any promoted single narrative and relocated within multiple individual narratives. Current research suggests that, unlike in more prominent public spaces where place is constructed through hegemonically controlled social signifiers, ordinary and mundane spaces can elevate individuals to become the producers, curators, and makers of place (Atkinson, 2008). These ordinary and mundane spaces are not typically labelled as sites of cultural significance; they are the derelict buildings, the graffitied walls, and the tenfoots.[1]

Performance opens up potential for change and, as Harvie (2009, p. 7) states, can become more than a reflection of a city by becoming a "*part of* urban process, producing urban experience and thereby producing the city itself" (original emphasis). Thus, I highlight the potential to practically explore performance as heritage from below through utilizing Cresswell's (2014, p. 16) assertion that "[m]ost places have stories [...] that become hidden or silenced only to abruptly re-emerge as new constellations of place appear." I question how, through an engagement with individual experiences of Hull that are not influenced by a promoted single narrative, multiple place attachments can be represented, redefined, and reconstructed.

MY PLACE ATTACHMENT

I pause here to reflect upon my own relationship to Hull, as a researcher, as a performer, and as a nonresident. I acknowledge and appreciate the numerous occasions throughout the course of my life where my home has informed not only my life decisions and my work, but also my identity. A city, as home, harbors the most strongly felt and practiced subjective reconstructions of sense of place, where personal attachments are supported by continued relationships with the city. Hull is maintained as home by its inhabitants through a range of activities that, while including an engagement with the city's location and locale, are ultimately governed by sense of place and the individual experiences of autobiography.

However, I no longer live in Hull. I am not a resident of the city. Jackson (1995, p. 122) articulates home as "a relationship, a tension," whereby an individual's subjective understanding of the place in which they reside is connected to past experiences. This suggests that not only is home underpinned by personal history, but with it there is also "a notion of what is chosen—the open horizons of a person's life" (p. 122). Jackson's depiction of home allows for individual accounts and interpretations of place to be understood as something other than the literal location and locale of habitation. In this way, place attachment becomes more about an individual relationship to, and experience of, a city than a literal choice of residence. While I have un-chosen Hull, deselected my literal connection to its location and locale, I still understand the city as home. My relationship to Hull is now informed by return visits, interactions with family and friends who reside there, and digital engagements with websites and social media. Online, and through digital means, I am able to remotely contribute to the process of placemaking, and thus maintain my own connection and attachment to the city. As a consequence, when developing *Now | Then*, I utilized digital media as a tool with which to engage and include individuals that were outside of the city in Hull's cultural regeneration and in the renegotiation of sense of place.

RESEARCH METHODS AND METHODOLOGY

I identify as Hullian.[2] As a consequence, my research was unequivocally affected by my relationship to Hull as well as my experience of performance making; the theatrical strategies that I engaged with in my research, and my analysis of the ways in which other people viewed my home city, were influenced by my place attachment. Thus, through an ethnographic framework, my first-hand knowledge and experiences of Hull allowed me to not only effectively communicate with the participants, but, as Lahlon, Bellu, and Boesen-Mariani (2015, p. 217) suggest, to "share to some degree their own 'emic' perspective (in the participant's own terms)." The position this created, and the acceptance that the information and data collected is subjectively interpreted, is pertinent to exploring multiple attachments as opposed to a single narrative; my research was conducted from within the heterogeneous social group I was investigating. Therefore, my research benefits from a position of knowledge, whereby my own experiences provide a context for not only the examination and analysis of practice, but also the presentation of the performance outcome as heritage from below.

I began the process of creating *Now | Then* with an online memory collection[3] designed to gather and present individual anecdotes, stories, and personal narratives of Hull. The call for participants had only one criterion for initial self-selection: the participants should identify as being from Hull. This criterion was purposefully ambiguous, allowing for the research project to explore individual relationships to Hull that were not defined through borders or boundaries. Participants were directed to the website via an online social media campaign and a flyer campaign at the city's museums, libraries, and galleries. Furthermore, to avoid the website targeting specific demographics, and to allow for inclusivity, I also hosted a live launch at Hull History Centre on January 16, 2016, where I met with the public and uploaded, live, their experiences of Hull directly onto the website. Between December 2015 and April 2017, 104 experiences of Hull were uploaded to the website from 70 participants. The website included an interactive map of the city (see Figure 9.1) and its surrounding area where participants were able to share their experiences of Hull by locating them at the specific site, street, or building at which they occurred. The digital map provided participants with the opportunity to reflect on their city in isolation to its immediate and literal environment; the city needed to be imagined as opposed to witnessed. The contributions could be viewed, shared, discussed, and extended upon by visitors, strangers, and fellow Hullians. For me, the website became a digital interpretation of the American Political Scientist Benedict Anderson's (1983) imagined community. In his influential exploration of nationalism, Anderson theorized the perception of attachment to place, suggesting that the conception of belonging creates strong connections between people that have not even met.

Figure 9.1. The map of memories.

The second stage of my research involved the extraction and analysis of the experiences submitted to the website and their translation into performance. I examined and collated the contributions based on the content, location, themes and issues, and my interpretation of the projected place attachment. Once I had established any commonality between the varying experiences of the city, I categorized the text in order to represent a number of time periods. Ultimately, the experiences I utilized as part of the performance text were selected because of their resonance to my autobiographical memories. This process allowed me, as curator, not only to examine the relationships between the texts, but also to consider the participants' experiences in relation to my place attachment. My adaptation of the text created a disjointed structure that would facilitate multiple contributions to placemaking, without overly editing the participants' contributions and thus distorting their meaning. I delivered the translated text as experiences from one single person, shifting the narratives from first person into second person. My intention was to present the fragmented stories of Hull's past in such a way that invited and instigated the audience to adopt, adapt, or develop, them in relation to their own place attachments.

My translation of digital engagement into performance led to a performance outcome that explored the renegotiation of individual attachments to the city. It focused on the reconstruction, even recreation, of experiences that were widely unknown, as opposed to those already established, accepted, and validated through a stabilized sense of place. My aim was to establish performance as a means of supporting reengagements with Hull, unrestricted by, and unlimited to, any existing or promoted single narrative. Furthermore, the series of performances were also a method of data collection; the audience were invited to answer questions concerning their individual relationship to Hull after they had experienced the performance. I use these responses, as well as my autoethnographic observations and experiences of the project, to inform the subsequent analysis and to draw my conclusions.

STAGE ONE: THE WEBSITE

The contributions to the website ranged in content, length, and style, some were short and succinct bite-sized narratives, others were more descriptive, proffering subjective detail and texture. Each submission to the website offered a unique insight into experiences that the participants felt inclined to digitally share. As such, the online map became a tapestry of fragmented and unconnected stories that, as Calvin Innes (2016) states in his article for Hull Daily Mail, together formed a "deeply personal montage of what Hull looks like to the people who live [there]." There were general stories about street parties, pastimes, and schools, and more specific stories about blades of grass, shop monkeys, and the sound of clogs. The value and relevance of each memory submission was specific to the individual contributor but participants were also able to contribute to other people's experiences by adding comments to the uploaded stories. The website served to map Hull in a digital space through individual experiences, memories, and attachments, and, as a consequence, I understand it not only as an act of placemaking, but also as an act of heritage from below. This digital marking of the city was an opportunity to destabilize sense of place. Importantly, participants who no longer resided in Hull could exercise their own attachments to the city at their leisure, in their absence, by reflecting on the location, locale, and sense of place of their home.

DIGITAL MEDIA IN PERFORMANCE

Before I discuss the ways in which I translated the digital engagement with personal experiences into performance, it is important to expose the effect that developments in digital media have had on theatrical practice. As well as challenging and adapting personal and social engagement through the way in which the fleeting moments of everyday life can be stabilized by photographs, video, and the many varying applications on mobile phones, the possibilities that arise from the inclusion of digital media in performance are constantly increasing. Oddey (2007, p. 43) suggests that these developments have established a "techno-culture, which is about immateriality, the digital and disembodied virtuality, where anyone can make their own computerised Photoshop work of art in an instant." Consequently, subjective interpretations of the world become not only documentation and preservation, but also reconstruction. Digital media frames the content of the experienced past as well as the way in which those past experiences are reengaged with.

The use of digital media within performance, that can be located under the umbrella term intermediality,[4] enhances the unstable nature of performance when the spectator forges a subjective interpretation of the interconnected mediums, actively selecting those moments understood as important. The consequences of this kind of spectatorship support the suggestion by Chapple and Kattenbelt (2014, p. 12) that intermediality becomes "a process of transformation [...] a re-perception of the whole, which is re-constructed through performance." A theatrical use of digital media has the potential to have an impact upon perception by highlighting the disparity that occurs when live and technological materials become symbiotic within the performance's present. The acknowledged and accepted incongruence between the live and the mediatized image becomes the basis upon which Woycicki (2014, p. 39) argues that intermedial techniques and strategies can stimulate "the audience to become more active in the process of meaning-making." Here, performance can embody processes involved in digital literacy in order to support an audience to find and evaluate information that has been interpreted through and from technological practices.

STAGE TWO: THE PRACTICAL OUTCOME

My translation of digital engagement resulted in a series of performances that took place in a taxi (see Figure 9.2) for up to five people at a time, as it journeyed through the streets of Hull. The series of intimate performance journeys, which started and finished at 'oss Wash[5] on Victoria Pier, were open to the general public and so contribution to the website was not a prerequisite. While audiences were driven around the city by my dad, I delivered text, created from the multiple engagements with my website, from the front passenger seat. The performances were accompanied by a soundtrack that blended music, narration, and conversation. Between April and June 2017, the *Now | Then* journey was made 104 times, up to eight times a day, and each time with a new audience, varied routes, and a new backdrop provided by the changing scene of the city. The literal journey through Hull experienced by the audience was echoed in a strand of the narrative, which followed a little boy as he walked through a city that he could not place, among buildings that felt unfamiliar. As the performance progressed, the stories and experiences of others aided his ability to ultimately remember, and reconnect to, home. The story derived from a personal exploration of my own connection to Hull as it underwent its transition to become the UK City of Culture. The little boy was not only the boy of my childhood, lost in an unknown city, he was also the boy of my adulthood, lost within, and yet removed from, a changing city.

Now | Then aimed to directly influence, support, and affect renegotiations of place attachment and it was important to expose and utilize the project's digital roots. Furthermore, the use of intermediality highlighted the duel nature of translation; not only were individual experiences translated through digital engagement with the website, they were also translated through digital engagement with the performance. *Now | Then* was underscored by a soundtrack specifically written for the project that structured the journey and consisted of text, interpreted from the website, and music, written by a composer familiar with the medium of film.[6] A literal conversation was established between the performer past and the performer present; the two mediums of live and prerecorded performance interacted

Figure 9.2. Inside the Taxi.

and, on occasion, shared lines. This dialogue intrinsically created a tension between experience and imagination. Information, stories, and experiences were not simply accepted; previous understandings of the city were juxtaposed or refuted so that any promoted single narrative was questioned in relation to each audience member's individual place attachment.

During the performance, the audience were tasked with completing a card, attached to a feather on a string, with "a word or phrase that describes what the city means to [them], something that makes the city [theirs]." They were invited to tie their contribution to a tree in the city center (see Figure 9.3). Sholette (1997, p. 17) states that "[m]etaphors of urban decay, rebirth and incubation suggest that the process of "constructing nature" has its corollary in the act of naturalizing culture." In this way, Hull's cultural regeneration was not only connected to the concept of natural life cycles, but, through the marking of the city, individual place attachments were being made visible. While the contributions were new, unconnected to the website in terms of content, by utilizing feathers, which were the icons of the original online contributions, digital engagements were being remembered. The task offered a moment for individual reflection in and among the narrative of the little boy and the multiple strands of stories and experiences. HC, a member of the audience, stated that the process of her own contribution "had quite an impact on [her] realising [her] sense of belonging and connection to Hull." These markers, remnants of place attachments that were individually mapped onto the city, together created a visual representation of an alternative sense of place. Collectively, the 361 feathers became signifiers of a heterogeneous process of placemaking. Hull was marked by stories and experiences of the city that included contributions that were not only from those inside of the city, but that were also influenced and informed by the digital contributions of those outside of the city.

Figure 9.3. The feathers and cards left at Queen's Gardens.

APPLICATION AND ANALYSIS

Hull's tenure as UK City of Culture can be understood as a means of making and practicing place. The yearlong cultural event was a framework that supported the renegotiation of sense of place, providing the possibility for Hull to rewrite its external perception, to regenerate itself, and to instil within its residents a sense of pride. However, the framework through which sense of place was renegotiated was hegemonically influenced. The consensus within current research suggests that processes of identity construction, reconstruction, and preservation originate from the authority of political power (Harvey, 2008). Thus, the renegotiation of sense of place is often a tool with which to exercise and influence a city's representation. McLean's (2008) exploration of museums identifies how preservation can be used to promote and amend the reconstruction of place, and thus directly impact upon individual place attachment. An application of this model to a city undergoing cultural regeneration highlights the curatorial role of the political power who, by reconstructing the locale of the city, not only controls *what* is remembered, but also *how* it is performed. In this instance, place is practiced through a frame dictated and enforced by hegemony that projects and promotes a single narrative desired by the political power (Graham & Howard, 2008).

Hull's established and enforced narrative, its external image of economic growth, prosperity, and entrepreneurship promoted as a result of being awarded the title of UK City of Culture 2017, was in contrast to the existing sense of place. As a historically working class city, firmly rooted in the fishing industry, Hull's image is one of poverty and struggle. Agnew's identification of a symbiotic relationship between location, locale, and sense of place in his definition of placemaking suggests that any significant, dramatic, and immediate change to one of the three components could result in the city's identity becoming fractured and manufactured. The possibility, then, is that a hegemonically directed cultural regeneration, commanded to specifically renavigate placemaking, while positive and celebratory, comes in isolation to, and sometimes in spite of, individual place attachments. In these circumstances, those who identify the city as home, particularly those not residing there, become isolated from renegotiations of sense of place and, left outside of the process of placemaking, are in danger of losing their sense of belonging.

My translation of digital engagement into performance during *Now | Then* did not just serve to document individual experiences; it also provided an opportunity to reflect upon place attachment. If place is constructed through an amalgamation of multiple narratives, my digital map, which was collaborative and multidirectional, explicitly offered the opportunity to renegotiate place outside of any promoted single narrative. Furthermore, when I questioned my audience about their experience of *Now | Then*, their responses referenced individual interpretations of not only Hull's changes, but also the ways in which they affected how the city was perceived externally. However, the majority of responses were concerned with how the city was felt on an individual and subjective level. AP discussed how she "reconnected with [her] happy time and sense of belonging [she] had there [and] also felt at peace about where [her] life is at," DK highlighted that "the new confidence [he] felt around Hull [...] was further reinforced by the journey." and EW stated that *Now | Then* "reminded [her] how [the] city is embedded within [her]." Furthermore, those audience members that were not originally from Hull reflected on how the performance exposed their connection to the city. While YO acknowledged that her relationship with the city was still being established, she stated that the performance journey made her "feel more connected, [she was] part of what Hull has always done—made people want to stay once they arrive."

The task of completing the cards on the feathers was inescapably subjective and so any attempt to quantitatively analyze the contributions is redundant; the comments were all incredibly and wonderfully different. However, after coding the responses into Agnew's (1987) categories of location, locale, and sense of place, the responses highlight a clear predilection. After experiencing *Now|Then,* audiences were overwhelming more inclined to reflect on, interpret, and document Hull in relation to sense of place and place attachment (see Figure 9.4). The reflections of place attachment proffered through this task, while varied and unique to each audience member, had reoccurring themes. From the 167 memory cards collected, 24% referenced people, friends, and family, 29% used adjectives to describe the city, of which 44% referenced the notion of home. The contributions were wholly personal, the word "I" was used 13 times, and represented the city through an array of positive interpretations, of hope and new opportunities; of the 20% that referenced emotions, 34% used the term pride. 21% of responses were extremely specific, referencing subjective details such as "hidden secrets," "mushrooms on toast," and "Little Iris and the Iguanas," which out of context do not mean anything except to the individuals who wrote them. These subjective responses are characterised by one individual who stated that Hull was their city of "belonging and knowing who I am."

As a consequence of the structural and intermedial devices I utilized, my translation of digital engagement into performance established a subjective framework through which to explore place attachment. In her book, *theatre & the city*, Jen Harvie (2009, p. 49) discusses the use of performance in urban settings to challenge hegemonic oppression. She highlights Baudelaire's term flaneur, "who confounds dominant uses of the city by casually strolling through it, making his own pathways through it, and so his own *version* of it through his manner of performing it" (original emphasis). Locating *Now|Then* both outside (the screens) and inside (the streets) of Hull was integral to the project's ability to position its audience as flaneurs. As the audience travelled through Hull, both literally and digitally, they were tasked with exploring the city outside of their regular experience and, specifically, reconnecting their own individual relationship to it. As such, no single narrative or interpretation of Hull took precedence. Thus, the contributed experiences I collated as part of *Now|Then* suggest that my audience were not only able to engage with place attachment but were also able to interpret it within a renegotiation of sense of place. Through translating the personal experience of digital engagement from a website into performance, *Now|Then* supported reengagements with Hull, unchained to the promoted single narrative of the program of cultural regeneration, as individual and unique representations of the city.

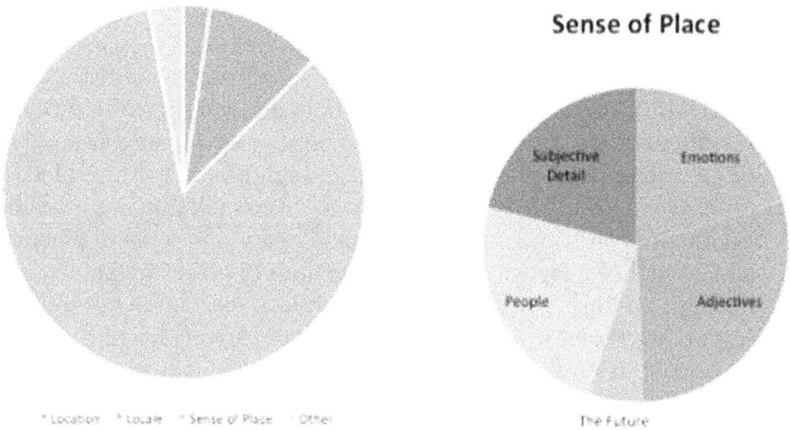

Figure 9.4. The categorized contributions.

CONCLUSION

Now|Then marked the city of Hull through its transition from the screens to the streets. The initial stage of the project asked those who identified as being from Hull to digitally mark the city with their own experiences. The resulting online map documents the ways in which Hull was interpreted and remembered in the build up to 2017 and connects the city to the 104 experiences that were submitted. In the second stage of the project, by utilizing the city as the backdrop to performance, specifically governed by the website's contributions, multiple individual experiences were created that replicated the subjectivity of digital submission. Throughout the project, the 70 participants who submitted memories and the 361 audience members who experienced *Now|Then* were encouraged and supported to resee their city in multiple ways that were unique to individual place attachment. The participants moved through the city, confronted numerous strands of personal narratives, and left traces of place attachments both online and in the streets.

I present the strategies I engaged with in order to translate digital engagement into performance as tools with which to establish heritage from below. This practice, I suggest, transcends the stabilization of sense of place so that individual stories and experiences can become contributing factors in the process of placemaking. Furthermore, *Now|Then* supported the representation, redefinition, and reconstruction of individual place attachment even for those who no longer resided in the city. When place is presented as unfixed, and when the process of reconstruction is embraced, promoted single narratives can lose their dominance to multiple, varying, and subjective experiences. Thus, translating digital engagement into performance supports the multiplicity and idiosyncrasy of individual place attachment. Any definitive position that cements place through location, locale, and sense of place can be challenged through interchangeable and adaptable representations that are open to renegotiation, adaptation, and development.

In its 2018 impact report, University of Hull highlighted that 8 in 10 audience members said that the UK City of Culture provided them with a different experience of the city, and that this "suggests that the programme was successful in exploring and promoting new narratives and ways of seeing the city" (2018, p. 123). However, only 51% of Hull's residents said that they were likely or very likely to continue to attend cultural activities after 2017. The report highlights that this "is perhaps lower than might have been hoped for [which] gives a note of caution on the extent to which audience levels [...] can be sustained in future years" (p. 85). Furthermore, the impact report highlights that less than 35% of the city's inhabitants felt represented by the cultural activities. One resident is referenced as stating "this was a year of events that was used in and done to the people of Hull rather than done with them" (p. 83). This position was mirrored in my audience's reflections of Hull's year as UK City of Culture. When I questioned HC about how the performance journey affected her relationship to the city, she discussed the ways in which the 2017 program of cultural events had left her "feeling at times alienated from the place [...] as it hadn't always reflected [her] experience of coming [...] and choosing Hull as home." In contrast, she stated that her experience of *Now | Then* was "really moving and unusual and intense [...] connecting me to Hull [...] and even if 'I'm not from round here' that I belong here too."

A city is both existing, and continually redeveloping, made up of multiple individual place attachments and, through human interaction, its "space is turned into place. Your place" (Cresswell, 2014, p. 7). When ordinary and mundane sites are promoted through the translation of digital engagement into performance, the power of placemaking is situated outside of hegemonic influence, creating an opportunity "to celebrate and memorialize *from within* the lives and thoughts of those otherwise hidden from history" (original emphasis) (Robertson, 2008, p. 147). It is my conclusion, therefore, that the stabilization of sense of place, through the promotion of single narratives during programs of cultural regeneration, can be rebalanced through a translation of digital engagement into performance. As such, performance making strategies that promote multiple narratives can be utilized in order to create transformative work that facilitates and engages contributions from a wide range of individuals that identify as being from a city in the renegotiation of placemaking, even those that no longer reside there.

NOTES

1. Tenfoots, specific to Hull, refer to the 10-foot wide passageway located behind, typically terraced, houses.
2. Some people prefer to use the term Hullensian to describe those who identify as being from Hull, but I have only ever used Hullian.
3. To view the online map, the participants' contributions, and the visitors' comments, please visit www.waynestevenjackson.co.uk
4. For a detailed exploration of this term and its practices, see Chapple and Kattenbelt's (2014) *Intermediality in Theatre and Performance.*
5. 'oss Wash is Hull slang for "Horse Wash." an area on Victoria Pier, Nelson Street, where workers at the Fruit Market would cool and clean their horses in the River Humber.
6. Christopher Benstead, a fellow Hullian, received an OSCAR and BAFTA for his work on *Gravity* and, when he created the soundtrack for *Now | Then,* had recently finished working on the score for Disney's live action remake of *Beauty and the Beast.*

REFERENCES

Anderson, B. (1983) *Imagined communities.* London, England: Verso

Atkinson, D. (2008). The heritage of mundane places. In B. Graham & P. Howard (Eds.), *The Ashgate Research Companion to Heritage and Identity* (pp. 381–396). Surrey, England: Ashgate,

Agnew, J. A. (1987) *Place and politics: The geographical mediation of state and society.* Boston, MA: Allen and Unwin.

Chapple, F., & Kattenbelt, C. (2014). Key Issues in intermediality in theatre and performance. In F. Chapple & C. Kattenbelt (Eds.), *Intermediality in theatre and performance* (pp. 11–25). Amsterdam, the Netherlands: International Federation for Theatre Research.

Cresswell, T. (2009) *Place.* London, England: Royal Holloway

Cresswell, T. (2014). Place. In R. Lee, N. Castree, R. Kitchin, V. Lawson, A. Paasi, C. Philo, S. Radcliffe, S. M. Roberts, & C. W. J. Withers (Eds.), *The SAGE handbook of human geography* (pp. 4–21). London, England: SAGE.

Dollimore, J., & Sinfield, A. (1988). Foreword: Cultural materialism. In G. Holderness (Ed.), *The Shakepeare myth.* Manchester, England: Manchester University Press

Etchells, T. (2009). Foreword. In J. Harvie (Ed.), *Theatre & the city.* London, England: Palgrave Macmillan.

Garcia, B. (2005). Deconstructing the city of culture: the long-term cultural legacies of Glasgow 1990. *Urban Studies, 42*(5–6), 841–868.

Gertner, D., & Kotler, P. (2004). How can a place create a negative image? *Place Branding, 2,* 43–52.

Goal-Holmes, P. (2012). (Re)calling 'home.' *Crossings: Journal of Migration & Culture, 3*(2), 201–212.

Graham, B., & Howard, P. (2008). Heritage and identity. In B. Graham & P. Howard (Eds.), *The Ashgate research companion to heritage and identity* (pp. 1–18). Surrey, England: Ashgate.

Green, M. (2015). *Hull UK City of Culture 2017 Strategic Business Plan, p. 9.* Hull, UK: University of Hull. Retrieved from https://cmis.hullcc.gov.uk/cmis/Portals/0/HULL2017_STRATEGICBUSINESSPLAN_1518.pdf

Harvey, D., C. (2008). The history of heritage. In B. Graham & P. Howard (Eds.), *The Ashgate Research Companion to Heritage and Identity* (pp. 19–36). Surrey, England: Ashgate.

Harvie, J. (2009). *Theatre & the city*. London, England: Palgrave Macmillan.

Hull UK City of Culture 2017 Strategic Business Plan. (2015). Hull, UK: University of Hull. https://cmis.hullcc.gov.uk/cmis/Portals/0/HULL2017_STRATEGICBUSINESSPLAN_1518.pdf

Innes, C. (2016, April 9). Calvin on culture. *The Hull Daily Mail.*

Jackson, M. (1995). *At home in the world.* London, England: Duke University Press.

Jordison, S., & Kiernan, D. (2003). *Crap towns: The 50 Worst Places to Live in the UK.* London, England: Pan Macmillan

Jorgensen, B., S., & Stedman, R. C. (2001). Sense of place as an attitude. *Journal of Environmental Psychology, 21,* 233–248.

Julier, G. (2005). Urban designscapes and the production of aesthetic consent. *Urban Studies, 42*(5), 869–887.

Lahlon, S., Le Bellu, S., & Boesen-Mariani, S. (2015). Subjective evidence based ethnography: Method and applications. *Integrative Psychological & Behavioural Science, 49,* 216–238.

Lewicka, M. (2008). Place attachment, place identity, and place memory. *Journal of Environmental Psychology, 28,* 209–231.

McLean, F. (2008). Museums and the representation of identity. In B. Graham & P. Howard (Eds.), *The Ashgate research companion to heritage and identity* (pp. 283–298). Surrey, England: Ashgate.

Michalski, D. (2009). Cities memory voices collage. In R. Candida Smith (Ed.), *Text & image: Art and the performance of memory.* London, England: Transaction.

Millard, R. (2015). *Hull UK City of Culture 2017 Strategic Business Plan, p. 4.* Hull, UK: University of Hull. https://cmis.hullcc.gov.uk/cmis/Portals/0/HULL2017_STRATEGICBUSINESSPLAN_1518.pdf

Morgan, P. (2010). Towards a developmental theory of place attachment. *Journal of Environmental Psychology, 30,* 11–22.

Oddey, A. (2007). *Re-framing the theatrical: Interdisciplinary landscapes for performance.* Hampshire, England: Palgrave Macmillan

Parkerson, B., & Saunders, J. (2005). City branding. *Place Branding, 1,* 242–264.

Proshansky, H. M., Fabian, A. K., & Kaminoff, R. (1983). Place identity: Physical world socialisation of the self. *Journal of Environmental Psychology, 3,* 57–83.

Richards, G., & Wilson, J. (2004). The impact of cultural events on city image. *Urban Studies, 41*(10), 1931–1951.

Robertson, I. J. M. (2008). Heritage from below: Class, social protest and resistance. In B. Graham & P. Howard (Eds.), *The Ashgate research companion to heritage and identity* (pp. 143–158). Surrey, England: Ashgate,

Scannell, L., & Gifford, R. (2010). Defining place attachment. *Journal of Environmental Psychology, 30,* 1–10.

Sholette, G. (1997). Nature as an icon of urban resistance: Artists, gentrification and New York City's Lower East Side, 1979–1984. *Afterimage.* Retrieved from https://www.questia.com/library/journal/1G1-20236308/nature-as-an-icon-of-urban-resistance-artists-gentrification

Tuan, Y. (1977) *Space and place: The perspective of experience.* Minnesota, MN: University of Minnesota Press.

University of Hull Culture, Place and Policy Institute. (2017). *City of Culture interim impact findings.* Hull, UK: University of Hull. Retrieved from https://www.hull.ac.uk/work-with-us/more/media-centre/news/2017/city-of-culture-impact-findings.aspx

University of Hull Culture, Place and Policy Institute. (2018). *Cultural transformations: The Impacts of Hull UK City of Culture 2017.* Hull, UK: University of Hull. Retrieved from http://impact.hull.ac.uk/

Woycicki, P. (2014) *Post-cinematic theatre and performance.* Basingstoke, England: Palgrave Macmillan.

CHAPTER 10

GEOSPATIAL TECHNOLOGIES IN SUPPORT OF COMMUNITY ENHANCEMENT AND CREATING INCLUSIVE HISTORICAL NARRATIVES

Investigating the Affordances of Collaborative Mapping Software, Location-Based Applications and 3D Reconstructions to Facilitate Place-Based Digital Literacies for the Ecomuseo Della Via Appia in Latiano, Italy

Mark Opmeer, Gert-Jan Burgers, Rosanne Bruinsma, Ron Janssen, Christian Napolitano, and Ilaria Ricci
Vrije Universiteit, Amsterdam

INTRODUCTION

Technology plays an important role in enhancing the discussion on the role of cultural heritage in society. Currently, it is widely recognized that digital

Negotiating Place and Space Through Digital Literacies: Research and Practice, pp. 177–195

applications can be important tools to connect people with shared ideas and interests, to facilitate place-based storytelling, and to foster the debate on the preservation and conservation of heritage resources (Charitonos, Blake, Scanlon, & Jones, 2012; Han, Shih, Rosson, & Carroll, 2014; Sommerville, 2007). Although scholars embrace the potential of digital applications for heritage-oriented organizations, the affordances of these innovative tools for facilitating digital literacies on people's emotional connection with historical objects and events remain comparatively underexplored.

This contribution aims to provide interesting insights on the added value of digital technology for representing a sense of place and belonging within local communities. In particular, we look at how collaborative mapping software, location-based applications, and 3D reconstructions can be successfully employed as workshop instruments to facilitate digital literacies that negotiate place-based narratives and identities in the *Ecomuseum della Via Appia (EVA)* in Latiano, Italy. We argue that these geospatial technologies are powerful facilitators for creating digital literacies that reflect the community's awareness of history and identity and involving local communities in decision-making activities on local heritage management. Our findings are based on activities and stakeholder meetings that were organized by EVA in close collaboration with the *Spatial Information Laboratory* (*SPINlab*) of *VU University Amsterdam* in southern Italy in 2016 and 2017.

This chapter is divided into four sections. Part One aims to explain the ecomuseum philosophy and its current role in developing place-based narratives on local heritage and identity. The second and third part of this chapter describe how the technology-enhanced workshops facilitated digital literacy practices and mediate inclusive place-based associations and fostered feelings of shared heritage ownership and belonging. Finally, the conclusion of this chapter provides an overview of lessons learned to support professionals in different fields of study in successfully employing the discussed technologies for creating digital literacies that represent local voices and identities in an ecomuseum context.

RESEARCH BACKGROUND: ECOMUSEUMS AND THE ECOMUSEO DELLA VIA APPIA

Ecomuseo della Via Appia

The *Ecomuseo della Via Appia (EVA)* is a recent initiative of citizens of the Italian municipalities of Latiano and Mesagne (Brindisi, Italy), implemented in collaboration with *VU University Amsterdam* and the *Soprintendenza archeologia belle arti e paesaggio di Brindisi, Lecce e Taranto*. The installation of the ecomuseum is deeply linked to the gradual reshaping of the cultural landscape between the municipalities of Mesagne and Latiano, and, in particular, to the exploration and valorization of the archaeological site of Muro Tenente. The ruins of this 124 acre site represent more than 3,000 years of local history and include monumental fortifications, cemeteries, and sacred buildings, all buried under extensive vineyards, olive groves, and uncultivated fields. Since the 1970s, they have progressively been unearthed by teams of the regional heritage board, the *Soprintendenza ai Beni Archeologici della Puglia* (now *Soprintendenza archeologia belle arti e paesaggio di Brindisi, Lecce e Taranto)*, and *VU University Amsterdam* (excavations *in concessione* of the Italian Ministry of Culture, *MIBACT*) (Alberda, Burgers, Burgers, Karel, & Yntema, 1999; Burgers, 1998; Burgers & Napolitano, 2010; Burgers & Yntema, 1999). Both institutions have also put much energy into the valorization of the site, in collaboration with the municipalities of Mesagne and Latiano, local interest groups, and the *Università del Salento*. Together, they also proposed the creation of an archaeological landscape park in the area, called the Parco Archeologico di Muro Tenente. Ecomuseum EVA aims to coordinate public activities to foster increased local understanding and awareness of the cultural significance of Latiano's intangible and tangible heritage.

The Role of Place in the Ecomuseum Philosophy

Ecomuseums are not buildings that simply house collections; but rather, they refer to a specific living environment and its inhabitants (e.g., villages, urban neighborhoods, or industrial peripheries). They are important catalysts for promoting continuous discussion on place, heritage, and local identity (Bowers, 2016; Davis, 2011). To this end, a bottom-up approach in the decision-making process was employed in order to create a shared ownership and a sense of awareness of the value of local heritage. Because all involved stakeholder groups had the chance to be heard, a forum for public interaction was created where thoughts, feelings, and interests about the sense of the ecomuseum's place could be expressed more freely. Ecomuseums also commonly aim to strengthen community bonds by engaging communities in the management of their 'own' heritage, thus strengthening links between the present and the past. Indeed, one of the key objectives of the ecomuseum philosophy is to democratize the collective historical memory and to foster a sense of shared heritage ownership and belonging in the local community (Bowers, 2016). Organizing local stakeholder workshops where community members can share previously untold place-based experiences and stories with each other is one of the strategies that ecomuseums employ to ignite intellectual and emotional connections with a region's tangible and intangible heritage (Borrelli & Davis, 2012). These workshops are, for ecomuseum practices, highly rewarding, since it is assumed that the people local to a place offer a better, more in-depth understanding of the locality's heritage features (Davis, 2009). With the local input that were generated during public participatory sessions, multilayered, digital narratives were shared that capture the tone of place and articulate personal feelings on place identity and belonging (Onciul, Stefano, & Hawke, 2017).

The concept of place plays a crucial role in the ecomuseum philosophy. Ecomuseums are considered to be signifiers of a place as they try to connect (local) memories, meanings and events with specific locations. Ecomuseum philosophy promotes the idea that places should be experienced instead of described. The identity of a place can only be understood when one looks beyond its physical appearance and tries to achieve an integral understanding of its social and emotional attributes (Buttimer & Seamon, 1980). As such, place refers not only toward a specific physical reality, but also to a collective sense of belonging as well as personal concepts of identity (Smith, 2015). At EVA, geo-based tools were employed in the summer of 2016 to facilitate these types of digital literacies to negotiate the community's collective image of place.

METHODOLOGY: FOSTERING PLACE-BASED NARRATIVES WITH GEOSPATIAL TECHNOLOGY

Geospatial technology (also known as geo-based or spatial-oriented technology) can be used to support collaborative processes. Typically, geospatial tools combine different methods, such as simulation models, spatial multicriteria analysis, visualization, and optimization. User-friendly interfaces allow multiple users to provide input and to generate real-time output to support negotiated (spatial) decisions (Eikelboom & Janssen, 2015; Geertman & Stillwell, 2009; Janssen & Diaz, 2017). By providing an interactive environment as a common interface, geo-based technology acts as a medium for synthesis to promote exchange among scientists and decision makers, and it can engage stakeholders in developing digital literacies around place-based experiences (Nassauer, 2015; Cunsolo Willox, Harper, & Edge, 2013).

Also for community-led heritage projects, such as ecomuseums, geospatial tools promise to be effective facilitators for developing digital literacies as they are able to amplify the voices of various local stakeholders, including marginalized ones, to help make informed decisions on defining the territory of intangible heritage and historical landmarks (Leanza, Porto, Sapienza, and Cascone, 2016). Moreover, geospatial technology support storytelling about place-based memories and connections. For example, Springett (2015) demonstrated how involving stakeholders in creating maps can contribute to inclusive and democratic representations of time and space, which has the potential to establish multivocal understandings among residents of their community's geographical history.

In this chapter, we postulate that collaborative mapping software, location-based technology ("apps"), and 3D reconstructions are three geo-based tools for facilitating digital tools for reflecting on a community's collective experience. During the last two decades, these resources are leveraged to share cultural and ecological dimensions of one's home, or home-place, with the ecomuseum community and the potential tourist audiences (Kuroczynski, 2017). Accordingly, they provide engaging ways to integrate user-generated content, and to negotiate these materials with visitors and the local community in a dynamic and visually appealing manner.

In the following section we demonstrate how collaborative mapping software, location-based applications, and 3D reconstructions facilitated digital literacies that represent place-based narratives and identities during the EVA ecomuseum workshops with local stakeholders in Latiano.

PROCEDURE: THE WORKSHOPS

Two workshops were conducted at the Palazzo Imperiali in the city center of Latiano on July 18, 2016. About 30 people were involved, representing the various groups in society who had an interest in cultural heritage. This included people from social and agricultural cooperatives, the local tourist board, various associations, city government, the library, several societies, the local music and historic associations, and the local museum.

The objectives of the first workshop with the collaborative mapping software were: (1) to increase the awareness of tangible and intangible heritage of Latiano; (2) to complement and correct the available heritage data; and (3) to design a heritage walking trail and a heritage cycling trail. The first workshop started with an introduction to the various types of heritage. This could be elements, such as churches, but also traditions, such as processions and festas, as well as regional food specialities and local musical traditions. People were asked to comment to the maps presented and make additions were appropriate. The workshop room was decorated with posters with high quality 3D reconstructions of disappeared or transformed historical landmarks in the ecomuseum's territory. These reconstructions were created by professional designers in close collaboration with the local stakeholders. As such, they reflect the community's opinion on which tangible heritage sites collectively tell the historical development of Latiano and its surroundings. For this reason, we argue that 3D reconstructions are digital literacies that negotiate place-based narratives and identities in an innovative, geospatial way.

In the next round of the first workshop, this information was used to design two heritage trails: a walking trail within the city and a cycling trail around the city. Participants interacted with the collaborative mapping application *Phoenix,* a software package designed to support visualization (http://www.geodan.com/products/phoenix/), loaded on a Lenovo Horizon touchscreen device (27"). To draw on the map, a participant first had to select the drawing tool and a color, after which they could use their finger to draw the line.

Figure 10.1. Participants at work with the Lenovo Horizon touchscreen.

The aim of the second workshop was to assess the content quality of the heritage itineraries with a mobile tourist application in the field. The trails are designed to facilitate digital literacies in which place-based narratives and identities were reflected, and during the testing field trip the local stakeholders had the opportunity to see whether the app appropriately told the story of the people of the place.

Two types of a heritage trails were designed in the next round of the workshop: a walking trail within the city and a cycling trail in the region around the city. A content management system for creating mobile tourist apps (IZI.Travel) was used to process the heritage itineraries to mobile devices, such as a smartphones or tablets. IZI.Travel allowed all members of the project team to cocreate and moderate the itineraries simultaneously, without requiring any technical experience in developing software for smart devices. It is also a free service, which enables cultural institutions with tight budgets, such as ecomuseums (us included), to enhance their visitor experience with a location-based, digital heritage storytelling application. Last but not least, the IZI.Travel platform has proven to be highly stable and reliable, which is an aspect that should not be underestimated when employing mobile technology for (ecomuseum) workshop purposes.

During the location-based application workshop, the same people attended who had participated in the previous workshop. Because we were not primarily interested in the cognitive beliefs of tourists (e.g. perceived usefulness) and the itinerary's effect on the appreciation and understanding of the cultural landscape, we focused deliberately on the affordances of mobile technology for facilitating digital literacies that reflected place-based identities and narratives of the local residents.

The participants were divided into a hiking and a cycling group. The hiking group evaluated the urban tour, and the cycling group assessed the rural trail. The duration of both tours was approximately two hours. At the end of the testing session, the participants gathered in the workshop room of the Palazzo Imperiali for an evaluation session on how they had experienced location-based technology as a digital tool to mediate their personal feelings and their connections with the ecomuseum's cultural landscape. In the following, our impressions of using collaborative mapping software, location-based technology, and 3D reconstructions for facilitating digital literacies are discussed.

FINDINGS: GEOSPATIAL TECHNOLOGY IN SUPPORT OF DIGITAL LITERACIES ON CREATING PLACE-BASED IDENTITIES

From the 1970s–2000s, ecomuseums were conceived from an essentialist perspective as relatively closed sociospatial entities. They were established especially in rural communities because of their perceived social stability, traditionalism, and shared, homogeneous history and heritage. However, ecomuseums, as other new museologies, are now increasingly adopting more pluralist and constructivist attitudes towards heritage management. The latter approach is also key to the *Ecomuseo della Via Appia*, with its aim of giving a voice to the multiple stakeholder groups interested in the cultural heritage of the Brindisi district, from civil society institutions to individual citizens and local entrepreneurs. Ultimately, the main aim of the ecomuseum is local dialogue: to open continuous discussions between different views about landscape, history, and heritage, and to foster feelings of shared heritage ownership and belonging among the people of a particular place.

To facilitate such a dialogue, we have experimented with the geospatial tools discussed in this chapter. Inspired by the work of Cunsolo Willox et al. (2013) on digital storytelling with indigenous communities, the outcomes of our investigations have been organized according to Smith's (1999) categorization of indigenous community projects. These communal endeavors are created by indigenous researchers or social scientists and aim to preserve native cultures and languages by fostering the people's self-awareness of their own identity and history. As such, they have similar objectives as EVA, which makes Smith's list with activities suitable to organize our project's findings but from a community building point of view. These categories are: storytelling, creating, sharing, remembering, connecting, representing, networking and intervening. By organizing the workshop outcomes according to Smith's framework, we were able to examine how the geospatial-enhanced workshops evoked specific storytelling actions and responses and facilitated digital literacies that negotiated the community's place-based narratives and identities.

Storytelling and Creating

Storytelling is a highly powerful and creative activity allowing for eco-museums to explore and develop place-based narratives. It enables the articulation of local landscape experiences, the negotiation of multiple perspectives on the community's history, and the transfer of local wisdom to the following generation (Smith, 1999). Throughout the workshops the participants were very keen to share their stories and to express their sense of connection to their "home place" with other stakeholders. Place-based associations and memories were digitally stored and processed into the collaborative mapping software. This software served as a common frame for discussion and linked the stories of the participants to specific locations. Each contribution triggered additional contributions. This way the stories cascade over the map. As the map was also projected on the wall everybody could see what was happening.

The collaborative mapping software consists of a user-friendly interface. The mapping application is shown in Figure 10.1. The interface shows the list of available map layers on the left, the drawing tool at the top right and the symbol tool on the right. The tool included a library of icons representing different types of heritage. Participants could draw on the map and add icons and text.

A total of 25 map layers were included in the library on the left of the screen. This included festivities, archaeology, historical monuments, music festivals, food festivals, chapels, olive groves, a messaria, traditional industry, local producers, historical monuments, theaters, museums, special restaurants, churches, squares, gardens and parks. The map layers could be opened and closed using the eyes icon in the layer tool. Participants were able to add comments, symbols and drawings to the map. The map layers served as input for the design of the heritage trails in the next step.

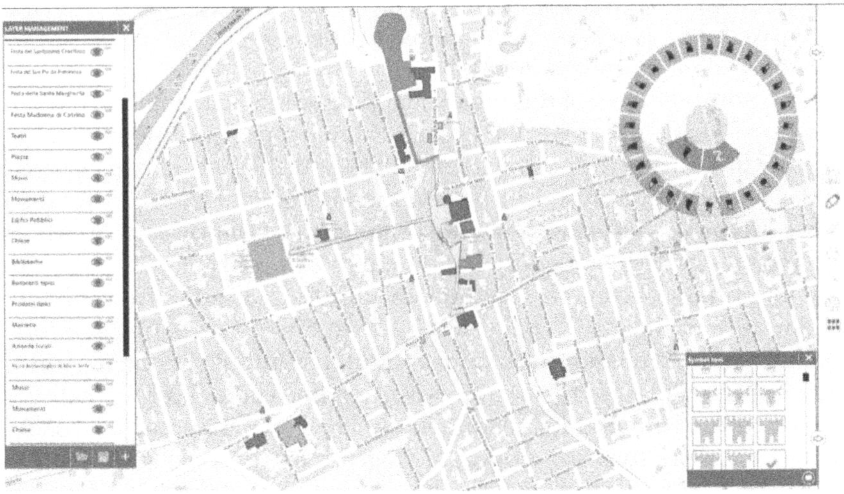

Figure 10.2. Interface of the collaborative mapping application *Phoenix*.

Throughout the workshop, a multilayered map with historical, ecological and personal layers was created, which included a multivocal and non-linear spatial representation of the ecomuseums' landscape. This spatial digital literacy can be seen on Figure 10.1: the various drawn shapes and colors highlight the place-based narratives and memories people had when approaching these historical landmarks. For instance, the blue rectangles represented stories that were connected to political or military buildings, such as the Palazzo Imperiali, and the pink and purple shapes reflected the people's associations with monasteries, churches, and other religious buildings. Accordingly, the workshop with the mapping software acted as a rich digital literacy practice that negotiates a local sense of place, identity and belonging.

The cocreated, multilayered map encouraged dialogue between people around different kinds of topics and complex issues. For example, some participants became emotional when discussing the position in Latiano's history and communal identity of newcomers who had arrived in the 1970s. Moreover, the mapping software contributed to the community building process as it stimulated the negotiation about the ecomuseum's strategy and the identification of tangible and intangible heritage that represents the region's collective identity. During the workshop, the community was given the opportunity to discuss and select the elements that better represented the community of Latiano, from the most important landscape and natural elements to tangible heritage to religious celebrations. As one of the participants explained, building collective conservation values and discussing opportunities to revitalize traditional crafts and events "was a real pleasure. It was fun and exciting to meet different people from Latiano and to highlight places on the map that tell the story of the region's past" (personal communication, 2016).

Using the outcomes of this digital mapping sessions, a tangible community map of Latiano was created by an artist that represents the area's local identity and distinctiveness. The artist showed the participants various updates on his drawings, which were then critiqued. The final product is the *Mappa di Comunità del Paesaggio of Latiano* (Figure 10.2) in which the region's collective identity is presented as two pages of a book. We see, for example, references to the local cuisine and to the typical house architecture of the area. The artwork also interweaves examples of folklore, geography, religious artefacts and the natural environment, which makes this multilayered map a multivocal representation of the cultural identity of Latiano and its surroundings. These experiences with collaborative mapping software support Springett's (2015) conclusion that the co-creation of deep maps sparks debate about the documentation and portrayal of people and places (Springett, 2015). As such, we argue—in line with Smith (1999)—that the collaborative mapping software is a strong facilitator of digital literacies; it fosters self-awareness of collective place-based identities in local societies and creates a tangible expression of a community's sense of place.

Sharing, Remembering, and Connecting

The second part of the collaborative mapping workshop was aimed at developing a richly layered narrative that represents the shared and personal histories of Latiano's community. By remembering moments from the collective fabric, incorporating the shared memories and place-based associations within a larger storytelling theme on Latiano's past, and connecting these oral representations to iconic heritage sites within the ecomuseum's territory on the digital map, an inclusive place-based narrative was created that hopefully strengthens local and visitor's awareness of the cultural significance of the tangible and intangible heritage within the ecomuseum's territory. This act of remembering and creating multivocal narratives helps to bring the community's history into the present moment (Cunsolo Willox et al., 2013).

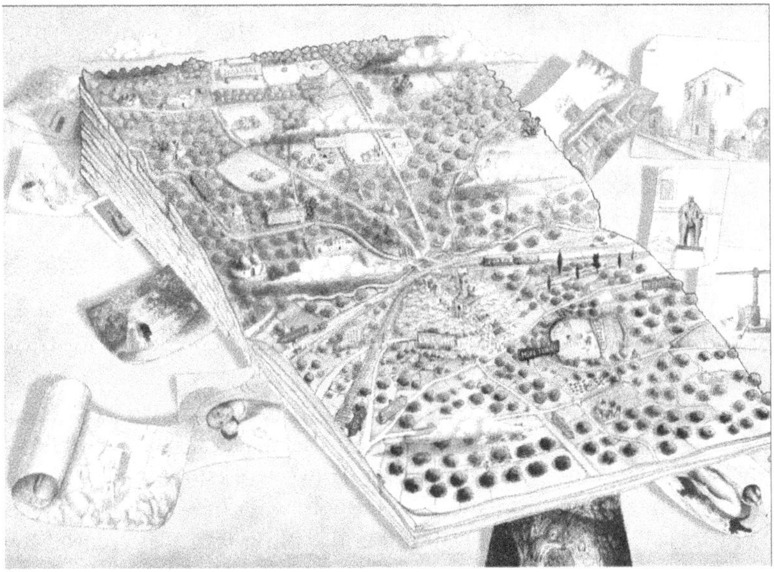

Figure 10.3 Mappa di Comitá del Paesaggio of Latiano (Copyright Vincenzo Camassa).

Smith (1999) explains that remembering is not only meant to focus on positive historical events, but that this activity is also an invitation to talk about specific painful moments in the region's history. In order to prevent the construction of an idealized past narrative that only tells one side of the story, the historical place-based narrative should contain a healthy balance between beloved and painful historical events. For this reason, stories about living conditions during World War II and the impact of mafia violence on the inhabitant's daily life in the second part of the twentieth century—to name a few—were also included in the overall storytelling framework of Latiano's past. Sharing personal memories about these traumatic experiences sparked emotional discussion about the role of the participant's ancestors during these episodes, which resulted in an increased mutual understanding of each other's opinions and perspectives. As one of the workshop participants commented: "storytelling is a great way to gain a better understanding of each other's place-based connections. This activity contributes to the community wellbeing as it brings people together and it strengthens personal relationships in the group" (Surlago, personal communication, July 22, 2016.).

The collaborative mapping software supported the storytelling activities, especially when the group members were invited to assign weights to specific stories and the interrelated tangible heritage sites on the digital map. Accordingly, the Lenovo touch screen with the Phoenix software mediated the community's sense of place and belonging through a digital map with a combined set of iconic landmarks. Moreover, identifying key narratives that represent the city's past contributed to an emotional process in which the participants linked themselves with family and ancestors, the geographical environment, and with the region's inhabitants. To this end, the collaborative mapping workshop acted as a digital literacy practice to enhance a community building activity, and in the words of Smith (1999), to establish good relations between the people of the place and their surroundings.

Representing

The main objective of the third part of the mapping workshop was to create tourist itineraries that negotiated the place-based narratives and identities—as developed in the previous two workshop phases—toward tourists or other community members. By drawing lines between the identified historical landmarks, a walking and cycling tour was created by the workshop participants on the touch-screen device. During the second workshop on the next day, the content of these itineraries were critically evaluated in the field by the workshop participants.

Figure 10.4. Drawing a walking and cycling tour in *Phoenix*.

Developing participant-created tourist itineraries with collaborative mapping software can be fruitfully extended with location-based technology. When integrating the outdoor trails in a mobile application, the local stakeholders have the ability to represent the region's local identity and distinctiveness via a smartphone or tablet device. It allows visitors and other community members to learn about people in other places (Cunsolo Willox et al., 2013). Developing a mobile tourist application becomes then a powerful digital literacy practice through which historical narratives and place-based experiences can be virtually shared with other people—both locals and tourists.

Using location-based technology for creating mobile apps also allows ecomuseum practitioners to mediate the place-based narratives in a multimodal and interactive way. Compared to traditional interpretive materials, such as printed booklets and information sheets, location-based tools for smartphones or tablet devices have the ability to enrich the tour with high quality images, audio and video, and to link these texts and media to the coordinates of a specific point of interests. Because the IZI.Travel platform is a user-friendly service that does not require advanced technical experience, the ecomuseum community can create a mobile tourist application without the need for hiring a professional, often costly, engineer for the technical development of the app.

During the evaluation session, most participants found it highly rewarding to see the outcomes of the first workshop brought together in a professional and intuitive mobile tourist application. Although some mistakes were identified during the testing process (mostly typos), the fact that a small group of volunteers were able to develop a final draft version of a tourist "app" that offers authentic place-based narratives, in a dynamic and multimodal way, was experienced as a rewarding and fruitful activity, capturing local knowledge and sharing this with tourists and other community members. One stakeholder commented that the ability to view context-specific locational information during a landmark visit helped him to critically study the different layers of the cultural landscape and the heritage objects that are located within this environment: "Normally I only looked at one or two specific [landscape] points … but because I know more now about the history, I see more details and I feel personal connections with them" (Personal communication, 2016). Other stakeholders praised the ability to cocreate and adjust the tours to their own insights, and mediate their senses of place and identities through a location-based application.

To this end, the mobile application facilitated the negotiation of digital place-based literacies. The cocreation of a location-based tourist application is a digital literacy practice that encourages people to make new connections with new or existing places and establishes (in)direct connections between places and local identity. We therefore conclude that telling stories with location-based applications allows local communities to represent themselves in an authentic, multimodal, and interactive way, which turns these tools into powerful facilitators of digital literacies that express place-based narratives and identities.

Networking and Intervening

The collaborative mapping and mobile tour-workshops were organized by EVA as social events where local people could foster relationships and share place-based thoughts and feelings. According to Smith (1999), sharing is a form of oral history. Social gatherings are fora that enable communities to disseminate local knowledge and to keep everyone informed about important events and issues (Smith, 1999). But as demonstrated previously in this chapter, sharing memories or stories with geospatial technology is also a fruitful way to negotiate digital place-based literacies and to allow people to rediscover their roots and local identity. Therefore, we argue that ecomuseum workshops are not only storytelling events but are also networking facilitators that provide community members the opportunity to build local movements for protecting and conserving their tangible and intangible heritage.

The ecomuseum movement tries to make local people aware of the intrinsic value of their history and to train them to be agentive ambassadors that help to preserve the landscape's cultural treasures. From this perspective, ecomuseums can be considered as intervention projects that aim to convince policy makers to sustainably develop significant heritage sites and to preserve them for future generations. For EVA this is a major challenge, as most tangible pieces of history from the Classical period are still being excavated. In order to provide a better understanding and appreciation of Latiano's heritage, 3D reconstructions were made to visually inform policymakers, community members, and visitors about the region's historical significance.

Although these reconstructions were designed by professionals, the ecomuseum participants were highly involved in the iterative development process. For example, the initial version of the 3D reconstruction of the imperial palace's internal courtyard was seen from a helicopter perspective and did not include any atmospheric lighting or natural details (Figure 10.5). The same goes for the 3D reconstruction of the Holy Church from the medieval period (Figure 10.6): the first version provided a rather schematic impression of the building. After some discussion with the participants of the ecomuseum, it was agreed upon to add more scenic details to both reconstructions as they remember and experience these sites as highly lively places with their own voice and soul. By choosing a different camera perspective and adding natural atmospheric lighting and environmental details (e.g. trees, grass), these 3D images gave a far more successful impression of the community's sense of place. On the basis of these observations, we concluded that making 3D reconstructions of historical landmarks facilitated a digital literacy through which the community's place-based memories and associations were negotiated.

Figure 10.5. Latiano, Palazzo Imperiali: 3D reconstruction of the internal courtyard.

Figure 10.6. Latiano: 3D reconstruction of the Chiesa Matrice between the 13th and 15th centuries.

During the workshops, the 3D reconstructions were printed on posters with historical representations of Latiano's heritage showcased in the meeting area. We observed that the participants felt encouraged to share their personal stories and memories after viewing the high resolution images. These images functioned as an effective vehicle for engaging the inhabitants of Latiano in bottom-up discussions on the conservation and preservation of their own shared heritage. Because the workshop participants were highly impressed by the historical significance of their region, the 3D reconstructions also sparked fruitful dialogues on their own history and its relationship with a shared cultural identity. They encouraged the participants to actively (re)discover the secrets of Latiano's historical and cultural assets, and fostered a growing understanding and appreciation of the town's history and its heritage features. Second, because the selection of historical landmarks for the 3D reconstructions were chosen by and iteratively developed with local stakeholders, they represented the community's view of the buildings that played a significant role in the historical development of the region. The collection of reconstructed objects explains indirectly which landmarks symbolize Latiano's distinct identity according to the local inhabitants, and as such, can be regarded as artifacts of digital literacies that represent place-based experiences and associations in an innovative way.

CONCLUSION

An important goal of the ecomuseum is to foster the democratization of collective heritage through the involvement and ownership of the community (Davis, 2004, 2008). In this chapter, we aimed to share our findings regarding the use of geospatial technology to co-create inclusive narratives on Latiano's local sense of place and belonging in the context of the *Ecomuseum della Via Appia (EVA)*. In particular, we assessed the affordances of collaborative mapping software, location-based applications, and 3D reconstructions for facilitating digital literacies that negotiated the stakeholder's place-base narratives and identities in an innovative way. The discussions during the workshops provided valuable insights on the added value of employing these tools for mediating local identity and place-based associations.

The geospatial-enhanced workshops were experienced as rewarding digital literacy practices for creating place-based literacies and for representing the community's sense of place and belonging. Participants felt invited to share both positive and traumatic memories and to discuss local particularities with each other. In line with Smith (1999) and Cunsolo Willox et al. (2013), we observed that collaborative mapping software supported storytelling, sharing, creating, remembering, and connecting activities during the first workshop. Secondly, location-based technology allowed the stakeholders to represent their local identity and cocreated place-based literacies towards a broad audience. Last, the public development of the 3D reconstructions of the ecomuseum's heritage sites reflected the community's view of the buildings that played a significant role in the historical development of Latiano and its surroundings. It helped to make local people aware of the intrinsic value of their history and stimulated them to become proactive ambassadors for preserving the landscape's cultural heritage.

On the basis of the findings of this ecomuseum project, we conclude that geo-based technologies are strong facilitators of digital literacies that can negotiate a community's sense of place and belonging. The collaborative mapping software in combination with the 3D reconstructions on display proved to be valuable for facilitating the storytelling process and for connecting personal narratives with historically significant points of interest. Combining fragments of personal stories and knowledge into a richly layered and inclusive narrative on the history of Latiano was broadly considered as fun, challenging, and rewarding. Because all participants had the chance to be heard, a pleasant and democratic atmosphere of interaction was created during the development and evaluation sessions.

Furthermore, the extensive development and testing process of the mobile tourist application gave the participants the opportunity to represent their local identity and distinctiveness on 21st century devices, such as smartphones and tablets, to a wider audience. Because all participants were allowed to share their stories and personal documents during the workshop and because these materials were carefully selected and implemented in an inclusive narrative, the mobile tourist application expressed not only the dominant, but also the personal, histories of Latiano's community. These findings support our assumption that the cocreation and evaluation of a digital community map, mobile tourist application, and 3D reconstructions can be a fruitful digital literacy practices for negotiating place-based narratives and identities for community members and others.

ACKNOWLEDGMENTS

The authors would like to thank the staff members of EVA for helping us to conduct this research, in particular to Fabiana Dirella, Barbara Spigola, Arturo Clavica, Margherita De Matteis. We would also like to thank Heleen Duinker for preparing the touchtable software for the workshop. For the 3D reconstructiosn we would like to thank IMPACT Coop. and Massimiliano Passarelli for *ITLab CNR IBAM-Lecce*. Furthermore, we thank the

Soprintendente Maria Piccarreta at *Soprintendenza archeologia belle arti e paesaggio per le province di Brindisi, Lecce e Taranto*, the architect Francesco Baratti, the *ProLoco Latiano*, the *Biblioteca Civica "G. De Nitto"* of Latiano, the *Università del Salento* and the municipalities of Latiano and Mesagne for assisting in this project. Lastly, we express our gratitude to the reviewers and editors for providing constructive feedback for improvement.

REFERENCES

Alberda, K. van, Burgers, G. J., Burgers, H., Karel, D., & Yntema, D. (1999). *Muro Tenente. Centro messapico nel territorio di Mesagne, a cura di A. Nitti,* Mesagne, Italy: Mandria.

Baratti, F., (2012). *Ecomusei, paesaggi e comunità. Esperienze, progetti e ricerche nel,* Salento, Italy: Sogein.

Bender, B. (1992). Theorising landscapes, and the prehistoric landscapes of Stonehenge. *Man (N.S.), 27*(4), 735–755. doi:10.2307/2804172

Boiano, S., Bowen, J. P., & Gaia, G. (2012). Usability, design and content issues of mobile apps for cultural heritage promotion: The Malta culture guide experience. In S. Dunn, J. Bowen, & K. Ng (Eds.), *E London 2012 Conference Proceedings, Electronic Workshops in Computing (eWiC)* (pp. 66–73). London, England: British Computer Society.

Borrelli, N., & Davis, P. (2012). How culture shapes nature: Reflections on ecomuseum practices. *Nature and Culture, 7*(1). doi:doi.org/10.3167/nc.2012.070103

Bowers, J. (2016). Developing sustainable tourism through ecomuseology: a case study in the Rupununi region of Guyana. *Journal of Sustainable Tourism, 24*(5), 758–782. doi:10.1080/09669582.2015.1085867

Burgers, G.-J. (1998). *Constructing Messapian landscapes: Settlement dynamics, social organization and culture contact in the margins of Graeco-Roman Italy*, Amsterdam, The Netherlands: Gieben.

Burgers, G.-J., & Yntema, D. G. (1999). The settlement of Muro Tenente. Third Interim report. *Bulletin Antieke Beschaving, 74*(2), 111–132.

Burgers, G.-J., & Napolitano, C. (2010). L'insediamento messapico di Muro Tenente. Scavi e ricerche 1998–2009, Mesagne, Italy. In A. Buttimer & D. Seamon (2015). *The human experience of space and place*. Abingdon, England: Routledge.

Buttimer, A., & Seamon, D. (1980). The human experience of space and place. London, England: Routledge. https://doi-org.proxy006.nclive.org/10.4324/9781315684192

Charitonos, K., Blake, C., Scanlon, E., & Jones, A., (2012). Museum learning via social and mobile technologies: (How) can online interactions enhance the visitor experience? *British Journal of Educational Technology, 43*(5), 802–819. doi:10.1111/j.1467-8535.2012.01360.x

Cunsolo Willox, A., Harper, S. L., & Edge, V. L. (2013). Storytelling in a digital age: Digital storytelling as an emerging narrative method for preserving and promoting indigenous oral wisdom. *Qualitative Research, 13*(2), 127–147. doi:10.1177/1468794112446105

Davis, P. (2004). Ecomuseums and the democratization of cultural tourism. T*ourism, Culture & Communication, 5,* 45–58.

Davis, P. (2008). New Museologies and the Ecomuseum. In B. Grahamand & P. Howard (Eds.), *The Ashgate Research Reader in Heritage and Identity* (pp. 397–414) Hampshire, England: Alderhot.

Davis, P. (2009). Ecomuseums and the representation of place, *Rivista Geografica Italiana, 15*(3), 483–503.

Davis, P. (2011). *Ecomuseums: A sense of place* (2nd ed.). London: Continuum International.

Eikelboom T., & Janssen R. (2015). Comparison of geodesign tools to communicatc stakcholdcr valucs. *Group Decision and Negotiation, 24*(6), 1065–1087. doi:10.1007/s10726-015-9429-7

Geertman, S., J. Stillwell, & Charles, H. (2009). Planning support systems best practice and new methods. *GeoJournal Library, 95,* 490.

Han, K., Shih, P. C., Rosson, M. B., & Carroll, J. M. (2014). Enhancing community awareness of and participation in local heritage with a mobile application. *CSCW 2014-Mobile Apps for Enhancing Connectedness* (pp. 1144–1155). New York, NY: ACM Press. doi:10.1145/2531602.2531640

Janssen, R., & Dias, E. (2017). A pictorial approach to geodesign: A case study for the Lower Zambezi valley. *Landscape and urban planning, 164*(3), 144-148. doi:10.1016/j.landurbplan.2017.03.014

Kuroczynski, P. (2017). Virtual research environment for digital 3D reconstructions—Standards, thresholds and prospects. *Studies in Digital Heritage, 1*(2), 456. doi:doi.org/10.14434/sdh.v1i2.23330

Leanza, P., Porto, S., Sapienza, V., & Cascone, S., (2016). A heritage interpretation-based itinerary to enhance tourist use of traditional rural buildings. *Sustainability 8*(2), 47–66. doi:doi.org/10.3390/su8010047

Nassauer, J. I. (2015). Visualization verisimilitude and civic participation. *Landscape and urban planning, 142*(3), 170–272. doi:doi.org/10.1016/j.landurbplan.2015.07.013

Onciul, B., Stefano, M. L., & Hawke, S. (2017). *Engaging heritage, engaging communities.* Woodbridge:, England: Boydell Press.

Sommerville, M. (2007). Place literacies: Significance of space to teaching. *Australian Journal of Language and Literacy, 30*(2), 149–165.

Smith, J. (2015). Anticipating deep mapping: Tracing the spatial practice of Tim Robinson. *Humanities, 4*(3), 283–303. doi:10.3390/h4030283

Smith, P. L. T. (1999). *Decolonizing methodologies: Research and indigenous peoples.* London, England: Zed Books.

Springett, S. (2015). Going deeper or flatter: Connecting deep mapping, flat ontologies and the democratizing of knowledge. *Humanities, 4*(4), 623–636. doi:10.3390/h4040623

PART III

TRACING LITERACIES ACROSS TIME AND SPACE

CHAPTER 11

IMMOBILIZING LITERACIES

Collisions of Difference During the Digital Dialogue Project

Julie E. Rust
Millsaps College

Many in the literacy education research community have been buoyed by the potentials inherent in digital meaning-making opportunities, particularly those that breed collaboration across contexts (e.g., Bruce, 2009; Curwood & Cowell, 2011). However, not all projects that connect participants across divergent political, educational, and religious spheres result in productive dialogue across difference (Mayblin, Valentine, & Andersson, 2016). In this chapter, I explore the resonances of the Digital Dialogue project, a semester-long journey that invited five very different classrooms to share digital compositions virtually in small, heterogeneous groups and then to meet face-to-face for embodied performances of key lines from those compositions. This "throwntogetherness" (Massey, 2005) of students across difference illuminates the wide range of immobilities that can surface when youth from different contexts and age groups are asked to compose multimodally for imagined audiences, watch virtually and comment on

Negotiating Place and Space Through Digital Literacies: Research and Practice, pp. 199–218

each other's digital compositions, and then meet face-to-face to collaboratively construct an embodied skit that mashes up their individual stories.

TRANSLITERACIES AND IMMOBILITY

This chapter pays special attention to the ways the "entangled we" (Ehret, Hollett, & Jocius, 2016, p. 374) brought together during a series of literacy events (from page to screen to bodies) simultaneously creates and breaks down boundaries across difference as human agents experience a myriad of affect-laden (im)mobilities. In this section, I explore the way that transliteracies as a framework foregrounds the degree to which socially-constructed literacy practices across spaces are sometimes inhibited in their mobility.

The framework of transliteracy initially denoted communication across a range of platforms, tools, and media (Liu, 2005; Thomas et al., 2007). In this chapter, I take up Stornaiuolo, Smith, and Phillip's (2017) critical (re) imagining of transliteracies. In their expanded conceptualization, transliteracies perspectives not only aid in tracing the way that meaning-making travels across a range of contexts; but also, they have the capacity to illuminate "how people and things are mobilized and *paralyzed* [emphasis added], facilitated and *restricted* [emphasis added], in different measure and in relation to institutions and systems with long histories" (p. 72). Stornaiuolo et al.'s (2017) transliteracies framework introduces Leonard's (2013) paradox of mobility as one of its central tenants. The paradox of mobility highlights the irony that, while literacy practices are becoming more and more mobile, not all meaning-makers experience the same degree of fluid mobility and uptake from outside audiences. While the paradox of mobility emerged as namely a framework for thinking about traveling multilingual practices, this chapter takes up the concept much more broadly to make sense of how participants affectively experienced meaning-making across a range of platforms, spaces, times, and imagined audiences. Mobility as a construct is utilized in this chapter not merely to focus on "the movement of people, things, modes, and ideas" but instead to more closely pay attention to the circulation of power, emotion, boundaries, and hierarchies that inhibits or invites this movement (Smith & Wargo, 2017, p. 41). In this chapter, I conceptualize *immobilizing literacies* as socially-situated meaning-making that provokes lived experiences that are characterized as constraining, disorienting, lacking, misunderstood, and/or silencing. While those of us who research literacies have been quick to embrace the mobilities inherent in making meaning, we have had a tendency to pay less attention to the sometimes immobilizing nature of meaning-making (Leonard, 2013). The extent to which humans experience immobility in any given moment is a deeply affective experience that is rooted in the agency, power, and connection that is felt in that socially-constructed space. By paying attention to moments when participants describe feeling *less* mobile as they practice space with others during school sanctioned literacy events, this chapter works to apply the abstract paradox of mobility to applied experiences of youth participating in designed pedagogical interactions. In the sections below, I operationalize immobilizing literacies as sociomaterially constructed, affect-laden, and often inequitable.

Immobility as Sociomaterially Constructed

This chapter takes on immobility as a construct that is sociomaterially produced. Just as space features the "throwntogetherness of human and nonhuman" (Massey, 2005, p. 160), the immobilizing, restricted experience of that space is made up of an entangled constellation of materials, platforms, emotions, and relationships. The introduction of different tools, materials, platforms, and places for meaning-making (e.g., a classroom, a virtual platform, a stage performance) invariably shifts the experience of a moment-in-time to be more or less mobilizing. Adding the digital into spatial assemblages necessarily compels "different socialities," "encounters," "performances," and "enactments" (Thompson, 2016, p. 487).

Massey (2005) similarly reminds us that space is "always under construction ... never finished, never closed ... a simultaneity of stories-so-far" (p. 9). It naturally follows, then, that space is not a monolithic construct but is one that is continually evolving, experienced differently by socially-contextualized individuals in any given slice of time. For example, at the very same moment that one person feels a sense of *mobilizing* significance and agency after posting their digital story on a virtual platform for an audience, another might experience an *immobilizing* sense of discomfort at the amount of personal details shared as they view the very same story in the same space.

A sociomaterial understanding of immobilizing literacies highlights the seamless flow across channels that makes up constellation of everyday literacy practices. I argue, as many before me (e.g., Buck, 2012; Hollett, Phillips, & Leander, 2017; Leander & McKim, 2003), that the digital doesn't exist in a category distinct from physical realities. The two blur together as youth walk from class to class with their iPhone in hand, laughing with their friends while hitting "like" on an Instagram post. Dovchin and Pennycook (2017) remind us that all spaces "in which ...young adults interact are complexly conjoined, with meanings, resources, and identities crossing over from one space to the other" (p. 220).

It is the overarching social purpose, then, that brings the spatial, human, temporal, and material into the realm of meaningfulness. When literacies are experienced as a mobile practice, meaning successfully lands in the proper destination with the intended result. But when literacies are experienced as immobilizing, a much bumpier journey ensues. A sociomaterial view of immobility highlights that this lack of movement is not simply a result of a human agency but arises from an entanglement of humans, emotions, social situations, materials, spaces, and technologies. Broadly conceived in this way, examining "who and what moves, how, why, and under what conditions" (Stornaiuolo et al., 2017, p. 70) aids in making sense of the ways that people make meaning in social contexts with a range of materials, more or less inhibited by micro- and macroconditions.

Immobility as Affect-Laden

Affect, emotion, and the body are indeed central tools for making sense of the entangled assemblage of materials, people, time, space, and technologies that engage in world-making (Ehret & Hollett, 2013; Stornaiuolo et al., 2016). In order to highlight the dance between perceived hierarchies and emotional response, I operationalize mobility as in-the-moment, affective experiences of freedom, agency, joy, confidence, and/or potential to push past previously assumed boundaries. Immobility, in contrast, is operationalized as producing a lived experience that feels more paralyzing or uncomfortable, thus reifying already-existing boundaries or creating new blockades that prevent movement. This emotional mapping of immobility is resonant with Smith, Stornaiuolo, and Phillips's (2018) application of transliteracies when they sought to uncover the ways in which classroom engagement caused students to "feel uncomfortable or comforted, silent or vocal, powerful or powerless" (p. 25). Smith et al. conclude that "students' affective responses were integral to the literacy event, not peripheral or inconsequential" (p. 25). This chapter similarly takes up emotion as central in meaning-making.

Of course, just because an emotion is negative does not mean that students are immobilized by that negative emotion. In fact, oftentimes emotions that are perceived as negative can have mobilizing effects, such as anger or resistance pushing youth to more critically examine a text toward social justice (e.g., Lewis & Tierney, 2013). When anger or sadness result in action or movement, I conceptualize them as mobilizing. When the same emotions result in paralysis and/or deterioration of agency, I conceptualize them as immobilizing. Affect can be characterized, then, not so much by whether it makes an individual feel good or bad, but by what is produced by its presence.

Immobility as Inequity

Perhaps most importantly, I characterize immobility in literacy practice as often highlighting inequities. Whereas mobilizing literacy practices result in boundary-crossing and fluid movement across difference and toward equity, immobilizing literacy experiences are fraught with blockades at every turn. The contemporary understanding of transliteracies crucially adds emphasis on the critical work that is necessary in, not merely celebrating the many literacies that emerge in our diverse landscape, but also noticing the ways in which some groups, media, objects, and individuals experience varying levels of freedom and agency in their production of space (Smith, Stornaiuolo, & Phillips, 2018).

Central to this understanding is the fact that human bodies engaged in this production of meaning and space are not neutral; rather, they carry a diverse set of signifiers (e.g., race, gender, age, dis/ability) that are "consequentially read and produced in everyday human interactions that involve feeling, sensing, touching, and moving" (Hollett, Phillips, & Leander, 2017, p. 149). These heterogeneous agents collide in classrooms to evoke what Pratt (1999) calls a "contact zone," a space marked by difference and inequity rather than sameness and untroubled community. Spaces are not, as Massey puts it, "unproblematically open to all" (p. 153).

Clearly the paradox of mobility has eye-opening implications for issues of equity, access, and justice among youth in traditionally disenfranchised communities. Because it attends to what does and doesn't gain traction for movement, a transliteracies framework "has the potential to orient researchers to everyday, and often systematic, practices of exclusion and marginalization that move with/alongside/against youth and communities" (Stornaiuolo et al., 2017, p. 18). By tracing immobilizing moments that emerged from literacy engagements from page to screen to body among a diverse range of participants, I seek to untangle how one particular collaborative project had the dual capacity to (dis)empower youth. In this particular chapter, I delve into moments that were experienced as confining or restraining rather than agentive. Such a focus is especially valuable because of the need for an honest look at the wide spectrum of ramifications of the pedagogical situations we create.

METHODS

Context and Participants

This study is a small piece of a larger codesigned teacher-researcher partnership, the Digital Dialogue Project, which included 81 participants

(75 students, 5 teachers, and 1 administrator) across a diverse range of schools in a metro area in the Deep South. (See Table 11.1 for a specific description of contexts represented.) Ranging in age (3rd–12th grade), class subject (technology, social studies, English), and school context (rural public, urban public, charter, private), each teacher/class was deliberately invited (via purposive sampling) to help make up a representative slice of the varied communities in the local radius. Teachers interested in joining the project met multiple times throughout the spring semester of 2016 to share information about their schools, discuss their varied goals for their participation, pass along materials and approaches for scaffolding students' digital compositions, create a timeline for the virtual sharing of the compositions, and collaboratively plan the culminating face-to-face field trip.

Table 11.1.
Digital Dialogue Participants

SCHOOL	TYPE/ LOCATION	CLASS	DEMOGRAPHICS
St. Francis Episcopal School	Independent School (2 campuses: Suburban and urban)	3rd Grade Technology 6th Grade Technology	*71.5% White; 13.5% Black; 8.1% Asian; 6.1% Multiracial *Yearly tuition: $17,130
Scholar Prep Charter	Charter School: Urban	5th Grade History	*>95% Black; <5% White, Hispanic *>95% Free/Reduced Lunch
Clark High School	Public School: Rural	8th Grade English	*79% White; 21% Black; .3% Hispanic *52% Free/Reduced Lunch
Smith High School	Public School: Urban	12th Grade AP English	*97% Black; 2%White; 1% Hispanic *100% Free/Reduced Lunch

The Digital Dialogue Project

All participants engaged in three phases of the Digital Dialogue Project, which I logistically directed in partnership with teacher participants:

> *Phase 1: Digital Story Composition*—During this phase, teachers from all five schools designed a prompt and series of scaffolding activities that integrated their own curricular goals (e.g., students

will gain experience comparing/contrasting historical events to current events) with student creation of a multimodal product of some kind (e.g., a podcast or iMovie). For most, this phase took place in the regular classroom during regular class time.

Phase 2: Virtual Sharing, Viewing, and Commenting—Once all digital stories were created, students uploaded them to Voicethread (an online platform that enables multimodal sharing and commenting), and heterogeneous groups of four to five students (typically representing one student from each school and grade) were formed. Students were then instructed to view their group members' compositions and then comment (via text, audio, or video) in a substantive way.

Phase 3: Face-to-Face Collaborative Performative Experience—At the culmination of the viewing/commenting phase, groups met each other face-to-face during a field trip to the college. During the two hours together, students engaged in warm up theater games and were asked to create a skit or poem weaving together key lines from all of the digital stories represented in their group. The event ended with pizza and a vote on "the best" skit in various categories.

Analysis

Analysis initially involved an iterative Critical Discourse Analysis process (Gee, 2014). I first transcribed and emergently coded online comments that took place in each small group's virtual sharing of digital compositions. I then coded reflective interviews accumulated from the 75 student participants after all three phases were over. The initial iterative coding process included marking focal moments in gathered transcripts as "border" or "bridge" to indicate whether students indicated feeling closer to or more distanced from the members of their group from different schools.

At this stage I began to feel limited by the perceived cut-and-dry dichotomy between border and bridge, and I began to do a bit more "thinking with theory" (Jackson & Mazzei, 2012), particularly the ideas outlined above around the paradox of mobility. Thus, I began to be less attuned to borders/bridges and more aware of the various levels of mobility that participants experienced through each of the three phases of the project: from multimodal composition to virtual viewing/commenting to collaborative embodied production. While there were many reported instances of high mobility in youths' literacy practices across the Digital Dialogue Project, this chapter highlights the unanticipated tensions and limitations that participants reported in their interviews. The central question of this chapter thus evolved to become: How did immobility manifest across all three phases of the Digital Dialogue Project?

FINDINGS

In the sections below I trace each of the three phases of the Digital Dialogue Project (described above) with special attention to the ways that participants experienced *immobility* in their meaning-making, which often surfaced as a sense of paralysis or heightened self-consciousness. Findings are organized chronologically in order to juxtapose the different immobilities that emerged for participants as they moved from composing their own digital story in their individual classrooms (Phase 1), to virtually sharing their multimodal production and watching/commenting on their group members' digital stories online (Phase 2), to creating a collaborative dramatic performance with their group members when meeting face-to-face at a culminating field trip (Phase 3). Each subsection begins with a description of the space produced in each phase and then moves to share representative cases of student interview data that point to one foregrounded theme of immobility that surfaced in the data during that phase.

Phase 1 (Multimodal Composing): Imagined Audience as Immobilizing

As they embarked on multimodal design, students were introduced to the fact that they were composing, not just for a grade in the class or for their familiar peers, but for a larger project that would put them in a group of four to five students they had never met who represented five very different schools and age levels in the metro area. While this imagined audience was experienced at times as motivating (which I conceptualize in this chapter as mobilizing), other times participants described moments in which the anticipation of how the unknown others in their small group would react to their posted digital stories stymied their creative process. In this section, I explore the diverse ways that youth in the process of composing their multimodal pieces evoked the notion of *imagined audience* as impeding their design process.

Oftentimes, creating the opportunity for an authentic audience for student writing, outside of just the teacher or their direct classmates, is hailed as a key way for ELA teachers to enhance engagement and relevance for their young writers (Duke, Purcell-Gates, Hall, & Tower, 2006; Kixmiller, 2004). While many interviewed did express a sense of excitement for composing for a diverse youth they had never met, a surprising number described a heightened sense of self-consciousness. For example, a sixth grader who attended St. Francis reported that he'd have preferred to do a paper instead of the podcast because

> writing a paper you can just type down whatever you're thinking and you don't have to talk out loud. But actually making an audio file, you have to talk, which I don't like doing a lot [...] I feel really embarrassed. I've done some stuff with my brother when he has a Youtube account, and when I just watch the video, I sound so dumb. (Personal communication, April 29, 2016)

Note that he transfers his out-of-school experiences making Youtube videos with his brother to inform his affective response to this school-required assignment, thus revealing the interplay between these often dichotomized spaces. His sense of immobility (embarrassment) is closely tied to the multimodality that a digital product affords. He feels safe writing a paper, but sharing an audio file of his voice elicits a sense of heightened vulnerability. This, then, hints at the sociomaterial assemblage (Latour, 2005) contributing to his sense of hesitancy: the audial affordances of the technology are entangled with the social nature of the assignment, thus resulting in an almost paralyzing situation.

While the young man above traced his embarrassment to the sound of his voice, a fifth grader from Scholar Prep described the imagined audience listening to her piece as paralyzing:

> You know how you [feel] standing in front of a crowd doing some type of speech? It felt like I was doing that and [...] it felt like there was a lot of people around me even though there wasn't, it was just y'all. So I decided to- I spoke low. (Personal communication, May 2, 2016)

For this fifth grader, it is less the sound of her voice and more the anticipated crowd of listeners that served as an immobilizing agent, one that caused her to speak so quietly that her words in the video are nearly undecipherable. Newkirk (2017) writes about the original meaning of the word embarrassment as "barrier ... obstacle ... an impediment that might used in a fortification ... barricade" (p. 15). Without a doubt, metaphors, such as barrier, obstacle, and barricade directly elicit immobilizing lived experiences. In both quotes, voice is linked to a sense of embarrassment. Interestingly, the student above likens the experience of making a digital video to the face-to-face experience of giving a speech to a crowd. Immobilization, then, is quite viscerally socially produced through her imagined sense of audience. In addition, note the repetition of the phrase "it felt like." Clearly the affective experience of self-consciousness triggered by the imagined audience of "a lot of people" who were strangers listening to her digital composition inhibited her.

A high school senior in the project felt immobilized, not by embarrassment elicited by imagined audiences, but by a sense of duty to sanitize his message for younger students. Below he describes the way he felt limited in the content he could share with the third through eighth graders in the project:

> So I cut out so much material [...] because like in this class I'm the most behaved [...] and even that's not saying much. In other classes they know how I work [...] Just to put it bluntly, I'm a very vulgar guy, that's how I present myself [...] the way I am really is influenced by the hardness [...] I would wake up where I'm from [...] by hearing somebody, just domestic violence in my neighbors. [Having to make a digital story with] all rainbows and unicorns ... that was weird. (Personal communication, April 29, 2016)

It seems that this young man's sense of disjuncture between his range of experiences and the range of experiences he deemed appropriate for his younger group members (namely "all rainbows and unicorns") triggered self-censorship practices that he felt de-authenticated his story in some ways. Rather than motivating him to go deeper, his imagined audience of younger peers compelled him to water down his truth into something he viewed as more palatable for an audience who did not share his background. This duty to create what he viewed as a more appropriate, but inferior, and less truthful final product reveals the way that this particular multiaged pedagogical situation appear to have immobilized him. This student clearly had internalized the message that his truth, his community, is not deemed acceptable for popular consumption; here immobility as inequity is made manifest.

Phase 2 (Virtual Viewing/Commenting): Unfamiliarity as Immobilizing

In the second phase of the Digital Dialogue Project, participants uploaded their digital compositions to VoiceThread, and they were broken up into small groups of five, generally composed of one student per school. One group, for example, featured five stories: a podcast about school uniforms uploaded by a sixth grader, a "my favorite place" story with voice-over by a third grader, a digital composition connecting civil rights for African Americans with civil rights for Muslims including images and voice-over uploaded by a fifth grader, an artistic rendering of *Lord of the Flies* with a voiced-over artist's statement by an eighth grader, and a personal digital story created with iMovie uploaded by a 12th grader. Each participant was asked to view the other four compositions and then to add a substantive comment. Phase 2, then, consisted of: (1) watching multimodal compositions authored by people from different schools; (2) commenting on the videos watched; (3) reading comments that others posted about one's own composition. During this virtual feedback phase, youth reported feeling immobilized by both unfamiliarity with their diverse small group peers and the experiences/content of the digital stories these peers produced.

Many students reported difficulty with coming up with how to respond to the digital stories uploaded to their group on VoiceThread due to the lack of a previously established face-to-face relationship with the other members of their heterogeneous virtual groups of four to five students. For example, an eighth grade student from Clark High School described hesitancy to post anything critical about the stories produced by younger students he did not know in his group:

> I could give a fair deal if they were my classmates, however they were not. Plus it is impolite to give fair to strict criticism to those I did not even know or first met. Not only is that a formula to make enemies but is also a classless way to make a bad first impression on another individual. (Personal communication, May 16, 2016)

By clearly articulating his culturally-embedded norms of interaction, this young man reveals real discomfort with the charge to engage in honest virtual dialogue with the strangers in his group; critiquing the digital stories of youth he does not know as "impolite" and "a classless way to make a bad first impression." Most fascinating here is his assertion that had he been commenting on his classmates' stories, he could have given them "a fair deal," or more honest and substantive critique and feedback. If immobility is sociomaterially constructed, it naturally follows that a lack of shared social history among group members destabilized the entangled Voicethread-human-digital story-emotion-filled space. In other words, just because a virtual platform affords social interaction through a host of multimodal commenting features does not mean they will be taken up fully. Before delving into these interviews, the classroom teachers and I had assumed that students' often short, surface-level affirmations about their group members' digital compositions were a result of their lack of interest in posting responses on Voicethread. Instead it appears that students were being far from careless—they were deliberately leaving superficial yet positive feedback to avoid hurt feelings and to mirror the lack of depth of relationship and familiarity they had with their group members. More in-depth, specific critique was effectively immobilized because of the social forces acting on the rhetorical situation.

In addition to a hesitancy to go deep in their comments because of their unfamiliarity with their group members, several fifth graders at Scholar

Prep Charter articulated a struggle with responding to very personal details that the seniors integrated into their personal narrative iMovies. For example, a fifth grader from Scholar Prep reported his shocked reaction to his group's twelfth grader's story about her sister having a skin condition: "She was really open with it, and I was like, 'You don't even know who those people are, and you're being really open!' " (Personal communication, May 2, 2016). This particular story featured graphic images of the family member's skin alongside affect-filled narrative about the way this condition impacted everyone's lives, and it is likely that the immobility the fifth grader experienced in commenting after viewing is a direct result of the especially emotionally moving nature of the multimodal composition. While surprise at peers' vulnerability is not by itself immobilizing, it can have the impact of creating a sense of discomfort with the mandate to leave thoughtful comments on such personal stories when shared by a stranger.

Another fifth grader from Scholar Prep explained the strange space created when viewing and commenting on a multimodal story that seemed to confide so much in her, a complete stranger:

> The hardest part about it was finding something to say because this girl she was talking about a really lot of personal stuff, like her mom got divorced. I guess I think she said her dad had died or something. I did not know what to say. I just said, "That's a lot of personal information [...] Maybe you should talk about something a little less personal, but otherwise it's all good." (Personal communication, May 2, 2016)

It appears that the fifth grader above was experiencing some degree of immobility in attempting to interact with this digital story because her own lack of established relationship with the senior composing the video clashes in uncomfortable ways with the vulnerability exposed by the digital piece. The disconnect that the fifth graders described illuminates the dance of affect and social affiliations in literacy enactments. It appears that when social connections are in place, affective responses to vulnerability are experienced as safe and mobilizing. However, without those secure relationships established, these moving digital stories felt risky, as though the seniors producing them were leaving themselves open for attack from outside strangers. The fifth graders were left uncomfortable and, in a sense, unable to virtually respond.

Another reason the student quoted above may have felt uncomfortable was her lack of experience with the personal content shared (e.g., divorce, a parent dying). Given the range of age groups and digital story material, it is perhaps unsurprising that when asked about this phase of the project, the younger students involved in the project experienced a range of immobilizing moments related to how well they did and did not relate to their group members' digital stories as they viewed them virtually. In contrast to the younger students in the project, the high school seniors experienced a much higher degree of mobility as they viewed and commented on the younger peers' digital compositions. One senior from Smith High School listed her connection to each of the digital stories she viewed from her group:

> So for the first girl, she was I believe in Middle School, and she did *Lord of the Flies*. It took me back to when I read the book, and I was like, "OK, I can connect. I can relate. I was there." For the guy, he did a piece on Muslims, and when I watched his I was like, "You're woke." I was like, "You understand." And he was so young; he was like nine! And then I had another girl who did like an interview on school uniforms. Which again, I wore school uniforms, and I could relate. Like, man, I hated it, I could understand [her] pain. And for the last girl, she was really, really, really young and she did it about her best friend's house. And so I liked it because she was so innocent, and I was just like, "Where did the days go?" (Personal communication, April 29, 2016)

Note that, for this (and many) of the seniors, the ability to access group members' digital stories directly correlated with the ability to connect the content of the story to their own past and present experiences. This time-traveling capacity to view text and think "OK, I can connect, I can relate, I was there" is perhaps at the heart of mobility. When youth can activate prior experiences/identities to connect with texts produced by others, they are more equipped to leverage shared affinities to network into new relationships. This, then, enables them to more freely traverse across borders of difference. The senior quoted above is able to remember reading the same novel as the eighth grader, is able to access critical perspectives about oppressed groups that the fifth grader is digging into, and is able to dig deep into her own frustration when she had to wear uniforms for school. In addition, positive emotion colors her recounting of the stories her group members created. She feels sentimental about the novel; she feels amazed and inspired by how "woke" the fifth grader is; she feels deep empathy with the sentiment of the uniform podcast; she feels nostalgia in relation to the third grader's story ("where did the days go?"). In addition, many of her points of connection with the stories revolved around issues of equity (e.g., uniforms are unfair; Muslims are mistreated). Age, affect, and experience, then, served as enhancers of mobility toward equity in this virtual sharing space.

Phase 3 (Face-to-Face Collaboration): Difference as Immobilizing

In the final phase of the Digital Dialogue Project, students moved from screen to face-to-face communication and embodied performance at a culminating meet up at the college. Chairs were set up in small groups of five so that once students arrived they had to break away from their friends and familiar classmates to sit with the members of their virtual groups. After a series of warm-up theater games, the 17 groups of 3–5 participants were assigned their mission for the day: to create a collaborative performance that mashed up a key line from each of the virtual stories represented. The energy of the room was visceral as groups moved around, practiced tableaus, typed scripts for skits, or prepared a snake poem. Each group bravely took the stage to share their quickly-composed creative enactment, and the meet-up concluded with a whole-group reflection on how things went, a vote for the "best of" the performances, a pizza party, and a final announcement of the winners of the day.

For the organizers and helpers in the event, the day felt like a victory. The majority of students interviewed described joyful surprise at the mobility they experienced through the traversing of perceived borderlands at the culminating field trip. Many were amazed how nice they older students were. Others commented that the White children did not make fun of them as they feared. They certainly revealed the fact that, within the 2-hour span of time they spent together physically, students navigated boundaries and difference with a good deal of mobility, much more mobility than they had experienced than when they had viewed each other's videos and commented virtually. But even in the energetic space, there were immobilities being experienced above and beneath the experience related to difference in age, race, and class.

Age, much like in the virtual phase of the project, was experienced as immobilizing by younger students during the face-to-face field trip phase. One third grade girl from St. Francis confessed that during the bus ride conversation on the way to the college they "were starting to go overboard and were talking about all the bad things that could happen" (Personal communication, April 21, 2016) due to their status as the youngest members of each group. Interestingly, the sociomaterial space provoked by the field trip, a large room on a college campus featuring face-to-face collaboration and embodied performance, provoked a particularly unsettling affective impact.

In other words, while age-induced confusion or discomfort merely inhibited the ability of third graders to comment on the virtual platform during Phase 2, age-related immobility during Phase 3 *felt* scarier. One fifth grader from Scholar Prep described a sense of fear when he walked into the room and saw two group members that looked to him like adults: "I thought they would be mean [...] I thought they might be talking about [...] stuff like Facebook, Instagram" (Personal communication, May 2, 2016). It is especially interesting that he links his sense of distance from his older group members to their usage of social media platforms, digital tools that mobilize teenagers to move freely across virtual networks but are experienced as immobilizing by those who cannot yet access them. In both cases, the younger participants experienced immobility in their anticipation of injustice; the third graders were "talking about the bad things that could happen" and the fifth grader feared "they would be mean" simply because of the uneven circulation of power related to age.

In post-interviews, nearly all the young people described being surprised by how kind the older students ended up being, despite the anxiety that preceded the event. But despite the overarching narrative of overcoming age-related boundaries, students occasionally described the process of actually creating the collaborative performance as still impacted by asymmetrical power relations. One third grader from St. Francis recalled her unwillingness to share her dissatisfaction with the skit idea the senior proposed: "We are so young, and they're all so old ...I decided it was a good [skit idea] and [to] just go along with it" (Personal communication, April 21, 2016). She effectively felt silenced by the social situation, unable to contribute and collaborate. It is clear that the younger participants almost exclusively faced immobility in relation to their age and expected expertise, while the seniors enjoyed almost unlimited power in shaping the direction of the group skits.

While the sense of self-consciousness and age difference followed across all three phases of the project, differences around categories of race and class came up far more in reflective interviews about this particular face-to-face phase of the project. For example, one fifth grader from Scholar Prep explained: "Not to be racist or anything but they had like there was three white people and only two black people so I only got nervous [...] and I thought the other three white kids would be talking about my color" (Personal communication, May 2, 2016). The nervousness and heightened sense of self-consciousness this young man described worked to immobilize his participation in the initial warm up theater games at the start of the field trip; his typical confident and energetic demeanor was replaced with a much more sober and subdued one. Another fifth grader from the same school articulated his field trip fear that "some people would be like talking to you because you're another race" (Personal communication, May 2, 2016). It was clear by his tone that "talking to you" referred to, not informal banter, but language used to insult, put down, or disempower minority groups. It is heartening that after the event both youth shared that their group members were, in fact, kind. But the fact remains that youth of color reported a greater degree of anxiety as they walked into the physical social space of the final field trip. These affective experiences of nervousness were heightened by the social space produced by the face-to-face collaborative encounter.

While eighth grade students from the predominantly White rural school did not mention race, they did mention class multiple times in their reflection. One eighth grader from Clark High School wrote of her imagination of his group members before meeting them:

> I hadn't really heard of any of the schools that we participated with beforehand, but I did know that they weren't from far out in the country like we are. The only preconceptions that I had about these students were that they probably aren't a lot like us and were raised around different things, for instance nice cars and big houses instead of tractors and cattle farms. (Personal communication, May 16, 2016)

Note the sociomaterial composition of this immobilizing distinction between private school kids ("nice cars and big houses") from the familiar kids at her school ("tractors and cattle farm.") Materials, such as cars and tractors, places, such as big houses and farms, and even animals like cattle lurk large in her social boundary mapping between the self and other. Socioeconomic class is a clear immobilizing agent here, but just as strong is the participant's status as representing the only rural school in the project. It is no coincidence that another eighth grader from Clark reflected that he assumed students from the private school (St. Francis) would "be very clever in a rude way" (Personal communication, May 16, 2016). While this fear did not materialize as true at the field trip, it is accurate that some youth from the rural school walked into the physical space with particular inferior self-positionings in mind. Inequities around class and negative stereotypes about "rural kids," both likely informed by past experiences, are at the center of these immobilizations.

SIGNIFICANCE

Using a transliteracies framework to examine the Digital Dialogue Project highlights traveling literacy practices (from page to screen to body) in socially constructed online and physical spaces. But most poignantly, analyzing with an eye toward the paradox of mobility reveals that not all youth experience the same levels of free-flowing fluidity in all meaning-making situations, even when we design communicative opportunities with the best of intentions. It is essential that we as teacher educators and researchers pay attention to various socially-constructed immobilizing forces if we are committed to preparing young people to dialogue across difference (Burbules & Rice, 1991). As Stornaiuolo et al. (2017) point out, we can no longer afford to pay exclusive attention to triumphs, to "the opportunities and possibilities afforded by people's mobile literacy practices, particularly across digital spaces" (p. 70). We must, instead, turn our eyes to something a bit less sanguine, but equally real: "the contingency, instability, and emergence of mobile literacy practices that simultaneously open some opportunities and foreclose others" (p. 70).

In all phases of the Digital Dialogue Project, participants experienced a range immobilities. The findings in Phase 1 above point to the instability youth face when curating and designing multimodal products for an imagined audience. While creating authentic opportunities for youth to produce multimodal products for audiences beyond their immediate classroom can be an incredibly powerful pedagogical practice, the entanglement of audio-image-words-others can also produce a design space that is experienced as intimidating for some and creatively stifling for others. Both lived realities (the sense of self-consciousness when recording your voice and the impulse to water down your message for a younger audience) can be experienced as immobilizing.

Analysis of Phase 2 (sharing their creations online and commenting on peers' stories they have not yet met) revealed similar immobilizations around accessing and commenting upon the stories made by these unfamiliar others. Students from third grade to eighth grade especially faced immobilizing difficulty in first accessing multimodal content produced by others that was personal and then determining how/if to substantively respond in their virtual comments. For third graders attempting to make sense of an eighth grader's painting of a dead pig from *Lord of the Flies* or an iMovie, this second phase resulted in frustration, miscomprehension, and, for some, refusal to even view or comment on peers' videos. Even when digital stories were accessed and understood, various youth expressed concern with the appropriate level of honesty/vulnerability to share online with strangers they had not yet met. In contrast, most senior participants experienced mobility in both accessing and responding to their group members' produced stories.

Because Phase 3 involved a face-to-face field trip, it elicited a myriad of immobilities around differences in race, age, and class. It is likely that it was the open-ended, spontaneous, face-to-face space of the field trip that made visible these tensions. While the virtual space of Phase 2 enabled teachers to monitor each comment made by students viewing stories in the comfort of their familiar classroom, the sociomaterially produced space in Phase 3 initiated by the entanglement of bodies and collaborative emergent theater activities at the field trip was far less stable, far less predictable. Younger students, students of color, and students from the rural school experienced anxiety on the way to the field trip since, after all, it is much easier to subversively undermine others in an emergent, noisy, collaborative face-to-face space. Before this third phase interviews indicated that many youth involved were still fairly distanced from their group members, informed by a set of assumptions about who they were and were not. However, after the field trip, nearly all youth interviewed described a movement toward increasing mobility across borders. In sum, analysis reveals that pushing young people to virtually view and comment on each other's very divergent digital compositions before they met face to face resulted in a mixed bag of connection, confusion, and surface-level engagement. However, the final face-to-face, collaborative performance phase was vital in (re)shaping students' perceptions of the other members of their groups.

Across all three phases, it became clear that different spaces were produced through the interaction of youth, platforms, materials, time, and emotion. Emotion in particular played a leading role in signifying mapping lived experiences of (im)mobility. Embarrassment, self-consciousness, and nervousness lurked large throughout, and it was clear that particular groups (the younger students, students of color, students from rural areas) were disproportionately impacted by these very real immobilities. Teachers/researchers who design virtual-embodied collaborations across race, class, and other categories of difference must work to design more just interactions that don't unfairly load labor on our students of color, those with dis/ability, or those that come from homes of lower-socio-economic origins (Hollett et al., 2017). Having reflective conversations with youth who have engaged in collaborations across difference after the fact is essential in making visible the ways in which our literacy enactments can work to enhance, rather than inhibit the mobility of others.

Literacies are on the move, and youth engaged in meaning-making are inevitably swimming in a milieu of socio-relationally-produced emotions, identities, and flows that are more or less impeded by inequities, embarrassments, and missed opportunities. We as teachers and educators who appreciate the potential in collaborating across difference and communicating across spaces, times, and platforms must have our eyes wide open to this truth as we seek to make the way clear for youth to curate representations of self and then practice space with a range of others.

ACKNOWLEDGMENTS

I am indebted to Dr. Christy Wessell-Powell, who thought/presented with me during the genesis of this analysis, as well as Dr. Lenny Sanchez, who generously gave his time in reading and providing feedback on an earlier draft.

REFERENCES

Bruce, D. (2009). Writing with visual images: Examining the video composition processes of high school students. *Research in the Teaching of English*, *34*(4), 426–450.

Buck, A. (2012). Examining digital literacy practices on social network sites. *Research in the Teaching of English*, *47*(1), 9–38.

Burbules, N., & Rice, S. (1991). Dialogue across differences: Continuing the conversation. *Harvard Educational Review, 61*(4), 393–417.

Curwood, J., & Cowell, L. H. (2011). iPoetry: Creating space for new literacies in the English curriculum. *Journal of Adolescent & Adult Literacy, 55*(2), 110–120.

Dovchin, S., & Pennycook, A. (2017). Digital metroliteracies. In K. A. Mills, A. Stornaiuolo, A. Smith, & J. Z. Pandya (Eds.), *Handbook of writing, literacies, and education in digital cultures* (pp. 211–222). New York, NY: Routledge.

Duke, N. K., Purcell-Gates, V., Hall, L. A., & Tower, C. (2006). Authentic literacy activities for developing comprehension and writing. *The Reading Teacher, 60*(4), 344–355.

Ehret, C., Hollett, T., & Jocius, R. (2016). The matter of new media making: An intra-action analysis of adolescents making a digital book trailer. *Journal of Literacy Research, 48*(3), 346–377.

Ehret, C., & Hollett, T. (2013). (Re)placing school: Middle school students' countermobilities while composing with iPods. *Journal of Adolescent & Adult Literacy, 57*(2), 110–119.

Gee, J. P. (2014). *An introduction to discourse analysis: Theory and method*. New York, NY: Routledge.

Hollett, T., Phillips, N., & Leander, K. (2017). Digital geographies. In K. A. Mills, A. Stornaiuolo, A. Smith, & J. Z. Pandya (Eds.), *Handbook of writing, literacies, and education in digital cultures* (pp. 148–160). New York, NY: Routledge.

Jackson, A. Y., & Mazzei, L. A. (2012). *Thinking with theory in qualitative research: Viewing data across multiple perspectives*. New York, NY: Routledge.

Kixmiller, L. A. (2004). Standards without sacrifice: The case for authentic writing. *English Journal, 94*(1), 29–33.

Latour, B. (2005). *Reassembling the social: An introduction to actor-network-theory*. New York, NY: Oxford University Press.

Leander, K. M., & McKim, K. K. (2003). Tracing the everyday sitings' of adolescents on the Internet: A strategic adaptation of ethnography across online and offline spaces. *Education, communication & information, 3*(2), 211–240.

Leonard, R. L. (2013). Traveling literacies: Multilingual writing on the move. *Research in the Teaching of English, 48*(1), 13–39.

Lewis, C., & Tierney, J. D. (2013). Mobilizing emotion in an urban classroom: Producing identities and transforming signs in a race-related discussion. *Linguistics and Education, 24*(3), 289–304. doi:10.1016/j.linged.2013.03.003

Massey, D. (2005). *For space*. Thousand Oaks, CA: SAGE.

Mayblin, L., Valentine, G., & Andersson, J. (2016). In the contact zone: engineering meaningful encounters across difference through an interfaith project. *The Geographical Journal, 182*(2), 213–222.

Newkirk, T. (2017). *Embarrassment: And the emotional underlife of learning*. Portsmouth, NH: Heinneman.

Pratt, M. L. (1999). Arts of the contact zone. In D. Bartholmae & A. Petrosky (Eds.), *Ways of reading* (5th ed, pp. 582–596). New York, NY: Bedford/St. Martin's Press.

Smith, A., & Wargo, J. (2017). Experiencing electracy: Digital writing and the emerging communicative landscapes of youth composing selves. In K. A.

Mills, A. Stornaiuolo, Smith, & J. Z. Pandya (Eds.), *Handbook of writing, literacies, and education in digital cultures* (pp. 37–49). New York, NY: Routledge.

Smith, A., Stornaiuolo, A., & Phillips, N. C. (2018). Multiplicities in motion: A turn to transliteracies. *Theory Into Practice*, *57*(1), 20–28.

Stornaiuolo, A., Smith, A., & Phillips, N. C. (2017). Developing a transliteracies framework for a connected world. *Journal of Literacy Research*, *49*(1), 68–91.

Thomas, S., Joseph, C., Laccetti, J., Mason, B., Mills, S., Perril, S., & Pullinger, K. (2007). Transliteracy: crossing divides. *First Monday*, *12*(12).

Thompson, T. L. (2016). Digital doings: curating work–learning practices and ecologies. *Learning, Media and Technology*, *41*(3), 480–500.

CHAPTER 12

ADOLESCENTS IN THE WILD

Critiquing and Arguing Back Through Mediated Social Spaces

Jane M. Saunders
Texas State University

INTRODUCTION

In the current rapid-response networked environment in which we find ourselves, it is difficult to remember a time prior to the onset of social media like Facebook, Twitter, and Instagram, and their primacy over what is left of our free time. The gratification and at times *fixation* with receiving positive responses to postings is evident through even a cursory engagement with social media, one's twitter feed, or viewing the evening's news. In its more negative enactment, we might find a political Twitter spat replete with pithy clapback that goes viral through exponential retweeting. The movie *Ingrid Goes West* (Spicer, 2017) portrays a darker side of social media through its protagonist's cross-country pursuit of an Instagram "influencer" and viral fame. Within the space of social media, literacy educators are called to help students understand and engage with the multiheaded

Negotiating Place and Space Through Digital Literacies: Research and Practice, pp. 219–239

hydra that is the result of a burgeoning cast of social networking sites (SNS) in addition to their other responsibilities.

Recent research suggests that new media show potential for "achieving a more equitable society through increased social participation" (Burnett & Merchant, 2011, p. 41). Scholars call for examples of how students use Web 2.0 tools in and out of schools (Greenhow, Robelia, & Hughes, 2009) and how these tools might leverage greater civic participation in our larger culture (Jenkins, Clinton, Purushotma, Robison, & Weigel, 2006). This call is complicated, however, by school settings that limit students' engagement with the world outside of the classroom either via written restrictions and browser blockers, or the intense focus on standards, scripted curricula, and regimes of testing inside the classroom.

This chapter begins with an innocuous school event—a school presentation by a member of the local community—that burgeons into a public debate about forsaking one's education in pursuit of one's passions and the role that social media play in disseminating competing public messages about schooling, following a dream, and making a difference in the world. I then examine how a group of students draw on social media and public spaces to critique the event, and the ugly and public responses they received in return. Drawing on multiple media sources and conversations to tease out the story behind the story, I provide recommendations for teachers considering entering the "wilds" of mediated online spaces but who may be worrying about the potential fallout from this type of engagement.

A REVIEW OF CRITICAL MEDIA LITERACY

In 2012, the International Reading Association's (now ILA) report on Adolescent Literacy made recommendations for reading and writing instruction that supported adolescents' coming of age in the 21st century. Among these was a request for educators and schools to draw on a variety of print and digital texts; to assist students in connecting with texts and each other orally; and, to help students "use literacy in the pursuit of civic engagement" (International Literacy Association, 2012, p. 10). Likewise, in its 2013 position statement regarding 21st Century Literacies, the National Council of Teachers of English (NCTE) affirmed the importance of helping students to create, critique, analyze, and evaluate multimedia texts (National Council of Teachers of English, 2013). Critical media literacy as it is defined by Alvermann, Moon, and Hagood (1999) includes: the use of print and nonprint materials to construct knowledge of the world; employs the creation of communities of readers who are active and exercise agency; is representative of cultural practice; and can be related to power and popular culture. Enacting a critical media approach, according to Kellner and Share (2005), can be complicated because

> it is not a pedagogy in the traditional sense, with firmly established principles, a canon of texts, and tried-and-true teaching procedures. It requires a democratic pedagogy which involves teachers sharing power with students as they join together in the process of unveiling myths and challenging hegemony. (p. 373)

Indeed, it is often in these power-sharing situations where students begin to understand that information is "never neutral and always mediated by sociocultural, political, and historical contexts of when, where, why, and by whom they were created" (Gainer, 2013, p. 18).

Students today are immersed in a media-rich world that requires a sophisticated set of tools to unpack what is supported by fact, versus infected by misinformation (Burnett & Merchant, 2011; Lewandowsky, Ecker , Seifert, Schwarz, & Cook, 2012). And, it is only by "demystifying media messages through critical inquiry" (Kellner & Share, 2005) that students can develop the tools needed to engage effectively and participate in our larger, socially mediated and connected culture. Jenkins et al. (2006) noted that teachers play an important role "in helping students acquire the skills they need to become full participants in our society" (p. 4). However, there are few roadmaps available for teachers in this new role. Garcia, Seglem, and Share (2013) asked teacher education students to rebrand common everyday products like yogurt or create podcasts that retold a nursery rhyme from a different perspective as a means of modeling what critical media literacy might look like in practice. In doing so, they affirmed critical media literacy as a space to deepen "literacy education to critically analyze relationships between media and audiences, information, and power" (p. 111), while reminding educators of the importance of media production itself, "as it empowers students to create their own messages that can challenge media texts and narratives" (p. 111).

Similarly, Garcia, Mirra, Morrell, Martinez, and Scorza (2015) offered high school students the opportunity to create counterstories to hegemonic norms by asking them to critique the movie *Waiting for Superman* (2010), read and respond to the writings of Antonio Gramsci via social media, and create and curate digital shorts as a means to renegotiate social and power relationships. These examples offer models for teachers interested in helping students hone their tools as critical creators and consumers of text and in developing agency in both in-school and out-of-school literacy practices. And certainly, research related to the role that social media can play in democratizing the spread of information and misinformation is growing in number (e.g., Mihailidis & Viotty, 2017). In spite of these, however, there are few studies that describe students engaging in real-world conversations while navigating the shark-infested waters of public response through social media present in the literature. This chapter offers up just such an example.

METHODS AND DATA

Envisioned as a qualitative case study, the work described here sought understanding about how students draw on in-school learning to engage in both in and out-of-school response and critique through written interactions with teachers, students, and the public at large. It was part of a larger study investigating the critical media literacy practices of high school journalism teacher Isabelle Salazar, her students, and *The Maroon*, the print/online newsmagazine (also publicly available) she oversaw. Those featured in this chapter are not masked by pseudonyms as the bulk of data described are publicly available via the Internet, making it is impossible to mask participants. And, while this research was approved by my university's institutional review board and the participating school district, because of the public nature of the events described in this chapter, I included only the students who were adults at the time of this research (over age 18) and who gave additional written assent (beyond their parent's initial consent for the larger project) to include their work for the purposes of research.

Among the data gathered for this study are in-class observations of Ms. Salazar's class for the documentation of the interaction styles, pedagogical choices, and curricular decisions she employed in helping students critically engage with print, video, and visual media. I kept careful notes of what students were writing and the aesthetic choices they made to strengthen each other's work. Interviews with students and Ms. Salazar, occurring in March 2015 with follow up conversations in April served to clarify students' impressions of their work in the class and reaction to the events described in this chapter. Data were collected from January to May 2015 and subsequently analyzed inductively using guidelines delineated by Huberman and Miles (1983). Triangulation of multiple data sources, such as observations, news articles from *The Maroon*, and so forth, was built into data collection and analysis for the purposes of achieving trustworthiness. Data fall into two categories, providing both an insider/outsider's view to the portrayed events.

In examining data, several of Creswell's (1998) notions of validity and quality were kept in mind. Trustworthiness and triangulation were accomplished through the use of multiple data-collection methods, sources, and perspectives; peer review and debriefing; member checking; and rich, thick descriptions that allow readers to enter the research (pp. 201–203).

Analysis of this data is also informed by Kincheloe's (2005) description of the "interpretive bricolage" (p. 335). This method of interpretation locates the researcher—or bricoleur—inside social spaces "where different perspectives offered by people located in diverse locations" allow for multidimensional interpretations of events "in relation to larger social, cultural, political, economic, psychological, and educational structures" that intersect while conducting research. In addition to multiple perspectives, Kincheloe describes the task of the bricoleur "to move into the domain of complexity ... uncovering the invisible artifacts of power and culture" and to use "the tools at hand" (p. 324) in order to explore and explain the complexity and lived experiences of those studied.

Given that the events described here happened quickly, across technological platforms and social spaces, it is difficult to draw on the sanctioned models of written research (research question, review of literature, methodology, and the like) to tell this story. This is also in keeping with employing bricolage as a method, which privileges understanding and the presentation of multiple viewpoints over restrictive research norms. To expedite understanding, I organized the described events sequentially, drawing on students' experiences, their critique and the critique of others, and the way these unfolded publicly. This allowed me to present students as agentive members of social media spaces and to accurately capture the events described in this chapter. The overarching question guiding this work was:

- What critical media literacy practices does Ms. Salazar's employ that support students' identity development and participation in public, civic, and community life?

RESULTS AND DESCRIPTION OF EVENTS

Isabelle Salazar has spent the past decade as a teacher in a large urban school district in the Southwestern United States. Having started her career as a high school English and English language learner teacher, she transitioned to a journalism position when one became available in her district. Upon entering into this position, Ms. Salazar noticed the absence of cultural or linguistic diversity among her advanced journalism students. Because the students responsible for writing and disseminating information through the school newsmagazine, *The Maroon*, hailed largely from the white middle/upper class population of the school, she began informally developing and recruiting students of color enrolled in her entry level journalism I courses. After several years, the demographics of her publications team more closely reflected those of the larger school population, including editors on the leadership team of *The Maroon*. This helped Ms.

Salazar realize the goal of reporting news and human interest stories from a multiplicity of perspectives—both in terms of who covered the news and the stories themselves.

In early conversations with me, Ms. Salazar acknowledged, "I'm always telling students how important their writing is … how important it is to get personal stories out." After a story on depression was pitched at an editor's meeting I attended in January 2015, a student complained, "None of those kids want to talk to me about that." Ms. Salazar responded, "That is such a misconception. Everyone wants to tell their story. But, once it's out, keep in mind you never know where it goes." She reminded students that their news magazine, *The Maroon*, was not just read by the school community; alumni from the school, community members, and professionals regularly commented on student-produced stories. Because the publication comes out both in print and online, the readership has grown exponentially over the past several years. An advocate of teaching skills that prepare students for college and beyond, Ms. Salazar has come to understand that her teaching practice has an impact she did not anticipate when moving into her journalism position. Little could she imagine its reach.

The Assembly

The first week of the spring semester in 2015, students were called to a school-wide assembly. This was not uncommon, as speakers regularly gave pep talks for the following purposes: to rev students up about extra-curricular opportunities, to help prepare students for college applications, and to disseminate information about a particular program or activity. Student and *Maroon* editor Ellie Breed remembered, "Everyone in the building was required to be there. And there wasn't really any information at all. We didn't know what we were walking into. Didn't know what to expect." What the school community encountered was a presentation by local entrepreneur and businessman Kash Shaikh, who spoke of the importance of students identifying and going after their dreams and passions. Kash Shaikh's message drew on a TEDxUWMilwaukee talk he gave (Shaikh, 2014), where he "Called everyone out" (including himself) for being all talk and not following through on their passions. In both speeches—the TEDx talk and at Austin High School—Kash Shaikh wove sensational phrases like "Having no balls," "Calling bullshit," and current business-speak like the "Sharing economy" and "Going all-in" to relay his message.

He told the story of becoming disillusioned with his work and taking an idea he had been harboring—to create a "motivational movement" and platform that allowed people to "do what they love" while "make a living at it." This movement was called #besomebody, and it relied on a blog, app, and the Internet to disseminate its goals for participation in the burgeoning sharing community and to match folks who had similar passions to one another.

Kash Shaikh's (2014) message to the students mirrored Campbell's (1949) "hero's journey" in *The Hero with a Thousand Faces*, a schema useful for mapping plot in stories and novels that many high school students and teachers find familiar. Kash Shaikh placed himself in the role of the hero; in this case, disenchanted with his work as a marketing guru in major companies like Proctor and Gamble and GoPro, he was called to make a change. After finding encouragement from others and developing a plan of action, he created a web blog that evolved into a business, complete with an app that matched "passionaries" (folks with a skill or talent) with those who had an interest in learning about that passion. For example, a person who had expertise in teaching yoga might offer one-on-one classes to a novice hoping to develop a yoga practice. Kash Shaikh's talk used metaphors delineating his journey:

- **the cave**—where the flame of an idea was discovered;
- **the cliff**—where you had to let go of what you were doing to explore what you *really* wanted to do. His suggestion: throw yourself off that metaphorical cliff;
- **the path**—this involved sacrifice, a struggle, and suffering. Then hopefully, success.
- **the bridge**—this was the final path toward realizing your dream—no turning back. Kash Shaikh urged listeners to set fire to the wooden bridge behind them— "No turning back, and No Plan B. If you have a Plan B you will never execute Plan A."

He called students up to the stage to state their passions publicly, to end the event. Although there were those who initially questioned parts of the message, *The Maroon* student reporters Rowan Pruitt and Daniel Wallach acknowledged some attendees who were "positively affected by what he had to say." Upon returning to Ms. Salazar's class, students discussed their impressions of the assembly and considered coverage of it in an upcoming edition of *The Maroon*. This is where the story began to change. What most would view as a typical event in the life of a school—a motivational speaker offered a message of inspiration, students received the message positively or otherwise, and then the community went back to the business of teaching and learning—incited a social media storm extending long past the day of the assembly.

The Critique

In their call for a new view of literacy—one that reflects the growing diversity of learners in schools and the variety of texts with which students engage—the New London Group (1996) envisioned a notably different literacy pedagogy than what students were experiencing in schools. They wrote,

> If it were possible to define generally the mission of education, it could be said that its fundamental purpose is to ensure that all students benefit from learning in ways that allow them to participate fully in public, community, and economic life. (p. 60)

Currently, opportunities for this kind of participation are limited in schools, for reasons as varied as concerns over testing and curricular coverage as an absence of authentic events that necessitate a public response in the first place. Additionally, given the rapid-fire response we are all subjected to after making our voices heard through public spaces (like posting to social media, commenting on web stories, or creating a cogent editorial), teachers may worry over the fallout that could result from such voices rising up. In terms of critiquing Kash Shaikh's presentation, this concern was warranted.

After returning to their classrooms, Ms. Salazar's students discussed writing a story for *The Maroon* about the #besomebody presentation and began conducting background research into the speaker and his organization. After digging into Kash Shaikh and his company, students discovered that the #besomebody app was little more than a matching service that took a 20% cut from all services matched through its interface. They learned the company had received a million dollars in start-up funds to get it online, and to spread its message through the beating heart of the social media system. Students began questioning the central message of the "movement" that the speaker presented at the assembly. They saw the message as somewhat disingenuous given that this was less a movement and more a profit-making endeavor, with Kash Shaikh seeding future customers through his talks at high schools across the country. The conversation evolved into a critique coalescing around three fronts:

- Bro culture—the language Kash Shaikh used at the assembly and the physical nature of his interactions, including fist-bumping, high-fiving, and using "bro" as a familiar;
- Disingenuousness of the message—while the assembly focused on Kash Shaikh's journey from marketing guru to #besomebody startup founder, it omitted the reality that he was selling a service. The students were also critical of the implicit message of his pre-

sentation, suggesting that students—many of whom relied on free and reduced lunches and would need aid to attend college—did not need an education to make a success of their lives;
- Branding over substance—the #besomebody "movement" relied on heavy marketing in person and online, with the potentially dangerous message that followers should let go of fallback plans and focus solely on their passions to realize success.

In addition to conversations in the journalism classroom, visual media arts students from the school—who oversaw its own media channel KHAS (pronounced "chaos")—decided to create a parody of the presentation. Media students regularly uploaded their work to a YouTube channel to make it visible for public consumption; when they finished their lampoon (KHAS, 2015), they tweeted it out to #besomebody, starting a dialogue on Twitter between the journalism and visual media arts students.

Ms. Salazar's students decided that, rather than devoting a full spread to the assembly, they would include an editorial about the presentation instead. *The Maroon* staff writer Sean Saldana penned the piece which appeared in print January 23, 2015 and online February 16, 2015. Unaware that Mr. Gillion, one of the school's teachers, had attempted to post a letter to Kash Shaikh's #besomebody blog (it was not viewable publically on their site until February, 2015), Sean's critique drew on some of the same themes discussed by Gillion. Among these was Kash Shaikh's message of giving everything up for passion and being willing to suffer and struggle in order to realize one's dream seemed unrealistic to students who are not "in the same boat" as he was with a college degree, financial backing, and years of highly competitive corporate experience.

Sean wrote, "For every Kash Shaikh, there are hundreds and hundreds of minimum wage retail workers who couldn't find a sustainable way to practice their passions." Sean acknowledged that while the message of #beseomebody was "moving to anybody who is hesitant to take a nonconventional career path," it was problematic to spread to impressionable high school students who were still forming their identities related to the future, college, and in work. Finally, he critiqued the intent of the presentation, which on the surface appeared as a message of motivation, but in the end was really a pitch for students to explore and spread word of an app, a money-making endeavor. He continued:

> … sure #besomebody has a feel-good message meant to inspire the youth, but at its heart, #besomebody is a company. Companies have a mission to make money, as much money as possible. And there's just something inherently wrong about a company coming to a public school, wasting government resources … to half advertise to people who have no choice

about whether or not they want to hear. The whole thing is just kinda gross. (Saldana, 2015)

Absent the power and reach of social media, Sean's editorial would likely have been read by his immediate community and quickly forgotten as the next big event came to light. But after one of the KHAS media team tweeted from their school media account, "Shout-out to our friends over at *The Maroon*" along with a photograph of the editorial to Kash Shaikh and #besomebody, the story of the speaking event, the critique, and the fallout from the critique spread quickly through both traditional and social media.

The Backlash

Just as we have experienced through current political and news events, Twitter users often strike before thinking through how their message might be received. Kash Shaikh responded quickly through Twitter. He posted his thoughts under the heading "You Have No Idea What PASSION Means," along with links to an extended blog essay that rippled through both the school community and the Twitter-sphere (see Figure 12.1).

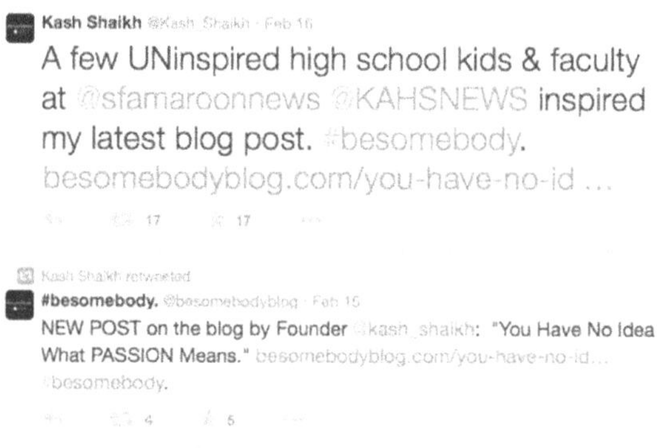

Figure 12.1. Kash Shaikh's tweet, February 16, 2015.

Due to the interconnectedness of social media, Kash Shaikh's lengthy post made its way via a variety of hosts—Twitter, Facebook, the #besomebody app blog—and this served two purposes. One, the blog post allowed Kash Shaikh to speak directly to the editorial and to the parody that critiqued his presentation; two, the post served as an additional tool for branding the #besomebody movement. Kash Shaikh was, after all, a marketing expert. The response began with attacks on his critics as "fear-driven, weak-minded" people who did not understand the role passion played in shaping one's success and included a lengthy explication of the author's understanding of the word passion. Included in this was his belief that passion required: discipline ("the toughest path" requiring "unwavering commitment"); pain ("you have to be willing to take as many punches as you give"); and senselessness ("being blind to criticism ... walking forward without an ounce of doubt"). Employing profanity, business-speak, and an extended discussion of how following one's passions can involve suffering and going against the grain, the post ended with a call to action.

The implication for Sean and *The Maroon* team was they could not possibly be passionate and simultaneously disagree with the messaging presented by the #besomebody author. Through this public posting, Kash Shaikh also reached out to Sean directly, calling Sean's editorial "completely off base" before cataloging all of his accomplishments. He then moved on to what he characterized as "tough love," where he criticized public schools and suggested the need for a new system that did not rely on college degrees to alleviate the growing financial aid debt crisis. This was particularly ill-conceived, given that many of Ms. Salazar's students were relying on their success in public schools to leverage future opportunities. And, unlike Kash Shaikh, who spoke of cashing in a 401K in order to help finance his #besomebody movement, they were not in the position to consider taking on the kind of risks his presentation proposed. In the students' estimation, Kash Shaikh had already earned a college degree and could then discount it; they understood that he was speaking from a position of power that was no doubt available because of that very college degree he then discounted in his direct response to Sean (see Figure 12.2).

The students tuned into various social media channels as this story and its response moved across platforms. What they discovered was a concerted effort by supporters of #besomebody to push back against *The Maroon* editorial through blog posts and tweeted responses, which were then responded to in kind. Teacher Mr. Gillion, seizing this opportunity to repost the letter he had written in January, took issue with Kash Shaikh and his supporters' critique of teachers and the school community, as well as the inappropriate and sexist tone of Kash Shaikh's presentation to the school (see Figure 12.3). Kash Shaikh responded with a defense of his company and reiteration that those who critiqued his presentation were full of "negative energy" reflective of a flawed educational system. He also pitched the notion that Mr. Gillion sign on as a "Passionary" to teach Spanish through the #besomebody app (see Figure 12.4).

In support of Kash Shaikh, commenter Michael Maldonado wrote a lengthy response to Mr. Gillion about his passion for fitness and the lack of support he experienced from his high school teachers in drawing on this as a potential profession. He ended with the rejoinder that schools

Kash

February 16, 2015 at [illegible] pm #

Hey Sean – I am sure you had good intentions in your article. A couple of your teachers questioned my credibility in sharing "my message" of following your passion. I think i'm pretty credible, but you'll have to do your own research and decide on your own. But in the same way, I, of course, can and do question your credibility in your article. Who are you to tell people to not SOLELY and ONLY reach for the stars? And more importantly, how did you get that in your head? I thought your article was completely off base, any I originally referenced it above because a student brought it to my attention.I was shocked to learn that a student wrote that (a few of your classmates told me it was written by a teacher, so that was my bad for being misinformed). When I heard it was a student today, I nearly fell out of my chair.

You're right that I have a good "fall back" plan if needed. I made great grades in school, founded 3 organizations at UT, created the largest single day of community service in the state of Texas, and worked 12 years at two amazing companies. The whole time though, I had the same BS pounded into my head. The same "be reasonable" message that you dangerously wrote to your fellow students. So it took me until I was 30 years old to pursue my passion. I wasted a lot of time… Yes, because of that, I can get a job doing something else if I want Sean, but I don't to! Everyday I'm hit up to do consulting projects for big brands for compensation that ranges from $200-1000/hour. I take ZERO of those opportunities. Instead I use my time to talk to people, speak for free at schools like yours (and, for the first time, in this instance, I witnessed some misguided classmates of yours post racist

Figure 12.2. Response to Sean from #besomebody blog, March 5, 2015.

Kevin Gillion

February 16, 2015 at 4:43 pm #

I am an Austin High School teacher who wrote a letter directly to you via your 'contact us' option, but I never received a response. It is odd that you posted negative statements about my school just when the jokes about you had died down around here. Maybe you are thirsty, as they say. Regardless, I am posting my letter to you here in the spirit of fairness. We are all working very hard here, and you run the risk of appearing the Goliath to our David if you continue to argue with high school students. Please leave us alone. The following was written the evening after I witnessed your 'passion.'

January 5, 2015

Dear Young Motivational Speaker 'Bro' Who Gave My Students Questionable Advice,

All students and faculty at my school were required to attend your presentation this morning, and I am writing to take issue with a couple of the comments you made. Your use of the term 'balls' as a metaphor for courage was inappropriate and sexist, and your depiction of suffering and struggle as traveling in an RV or living in a studio apartment was ridiculous and offensive.

On the matter of balls, did you toss the term around to convey to us that you are somehow edgy, and, as a result, authoritative or trustworthy? If so, I recommend that you revise your strategy by providing data that support your recommendations. You can curse like a Tarantino script, but my students will not benefit from your message if it lacks tangible proof or meaning. Secondly, and more importantly, by invoking 'balls' as a metaphor for courage, you are telling my female students that there is an anatomical requirement for bravery that they lack. It is a worthless cliché both because a truer analogy is that those that possess ovaries have been

Figure 12.3. Kevin Gillion's letter in response to #besomebody presentation, March 5, 2015 (underlined passages enhanced by author).

cause I believe in what we're doing, and I know we're helping people. Our business model for our platform is based on people making money doing what they love. We get 20%, they get 80% of any money they generate on our platform. This is all incremental income for our Passionaries. I know your passion is Spanish, but do some googling of the "sharing economy" or #besomebody and you will learn a lot more. You could be great Passionary for Spanish, for example. And our platform could help provide you with supplemental income that could help those years without a raise. The educational system is flawed, and we are providing a new platform for people to teach and learn.

It's a bummer that you are appear to be one of the people I refer to in the blog post above – negative and insistent on finding the bad in things instead of unearthing and embracing the good. You and some of your colleagues/students spent a lot of time producing and sharing negative energy. Why? Was it helpful to you? I hope so. It did help me, as I wrote above. Tactically, it helped me remember that though I was told to come "share my Ted Talk" at your school (I only spoke 20 mins), that next time I will look to share the broader/original talks from the past that speak more to the universal nature of passion, vs my metaphoric journey. That was a good lesson.

I was blessed to spend two years in some of the poorest neighborhoods in the world, helping people. My career at Procter & Gamble was focused on Cause-related efforts, including providing clothes to families after disasters, or providing food to people living on the streets. These are the people who taught me that there is no correlation between money and happiness. These are the people that reminded me the relative-nature of 'suffering.' My resume may not

Figure 12.4. Kash Shaikh's response to Kevin Gillian, captured from #besomebody blog, March 5, 2015 (underlined passages enhanced by author).

purposefully squelch students' dreams and the #besomebody hashtag, which students came to conclude suggested a relationship. Indeed, students later discovered that almost all of the positive posts about #besomebody were written by "passionaries" who had a financial stake in the success of the business since they were among the instructors. Although silent up to this point, Sean—author of the original editorial—rejoined the conversation, offering a far more balanced perspective of life past high school to Mel, another #besomebody supporter. He offered his bona fides, "Peep my insta if you don't believe me: amnohate" and reminded Mel of the importance of "reaching for the stars" while still having a reasonable plan back here on earth.

While these blog conversations, tweets, and responses were hitting their mark through social media spaces, a local education journalist noticed a parallel conversation taking place on Reddit. Reddit user space_manatee (2015) discussed the assembly at the school, Saldana's *Maroon* editorial, and the blog rebuttal posted to the #besomebody site. In contrast to the comments to Kash Shaikh's "Uninspired" blog which reflected a shared commitment to his message, the Reddit community not only agreed with the students' critique of Kash Shaikh, they also acknowledged the "Bro" demographic targeted by the #besomebody community (see Figure 12.5).

Figure 12.5. Tweet representing the bro culture of #besomebody, captured from Twitter, March 5, 2015.

Honest_arbiter compared #besomebody's message to the "Emperor's New Clothes," reminding the community in that case "the innocence of youth uncovered the scam on the Emperor" much like what was happening here as well. Redditer "spiritofdunkey," a senior at the school at the time, thanked the community for noticing "this little incident that went down" and discussed a blog response (since taken down) from Kash Shaikh noting "how uninspiring our teachers were and how they taught us to not follow our passions," which s/he disagreed with completely (see Figure 12.6).

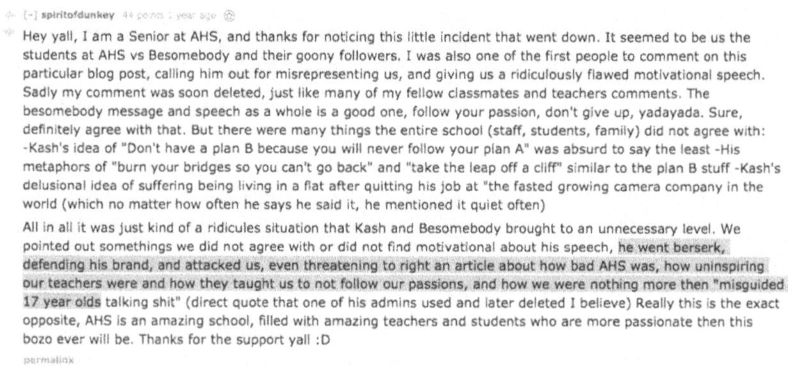

[–] spiritofdunkey

Hey yall, I am a Senior at AHS, and thanks for noticing this little incident that went down. It seemed to be us the students at AHS vs Besomebody and their goony followers. I was also one of the first people to comment on this particular blog post, calling him out for misrepresenting us, and giving us a ridiculously flawed motivational speech. Sadly my comment was soon deleted, just like many of my fellow classmates and teachers comments. The besomebody message and speech as a whole is a good one, follow your passion, don't give up, yadayada. Sure, definitely agree with that. But there were many things the entire school (staff, students, family) did not agree with: -Kash's idea of "Don't have a plan B because you will never follow your plan A" was absurd to say the least -His metaphors of "burn your bridges so you can't go back" and "take the leap off a cliff" similar to the plan B stuff -Kash's delusional idea of suffering being living in a flat after quitting his job at "the fasted growing camera company in the world (which no matter how often he says he said it, he mentioned it quiet often)

All in all it was just kind of a ridicules situation that Kash and Besomebody brought to an unnecessary level. We pointed out somethings we did not agree with or did not find motivational about his speech, he went berserk, defending his brand, and attacked us, even threatening to right an article about how bad AHS was, how uninspiring our teachers were and how they taught us to not follow our passions, and how we were nothing more then "misguided 17 year olds talking shit" (direct quote that one of his admins used and later deleted I believe) Really this is the exact opposite, AHS is an amazing school, filled with amazing teachers and students who are more passionate then this bozo ever will be. Thanks for the support yall :D

permalink

Figure 12.6. Reddit conversation captured on March 9, 2016.

A highly upvoted comment (author unknown) suggested that the school was fulfilling its job of preparing students to listen and read critically (see Figure 12.7).

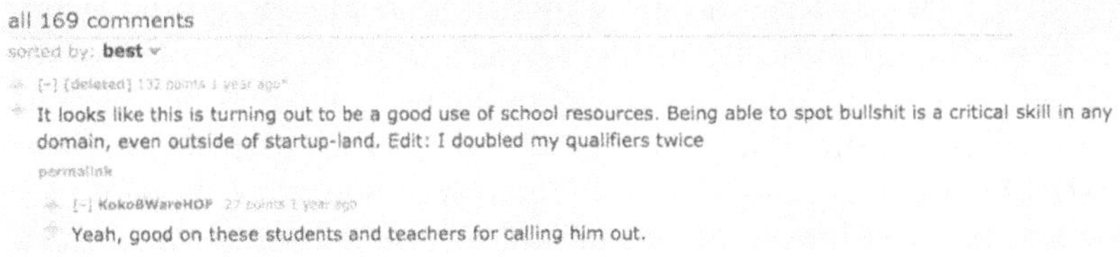

Figure 12.7. Reddit conversation captured on March 9, 2016.

As a result of these conversations Kate McGee, a journalist for the local NPR Station KUT did some detective work, tracking down the #besomebody founder, as well as several students who sat through the presentation. She described the back and forth that transpired through Twitter, Facebook, and the #besomebody blog, offering a balanced account of events. Kash Shaikh conceded to McGee (2015), "I probably got into the debate too quickly and that's some things [sic] I would do differently, probably not get into the back and forth too much. But the one thing we won't do is change our message." Several other publications, like *Texas Monthly* (Solomon, 2015), *BBC News* (Trending, 2015), and the *PBS Newshour* (Segal, 2015) followed suit offering additional perspectives and commentary. Responses to the *PBS* piece posted online supported the students' perspective, with commenter Nimh Frisby acknowledging that while Kash Shaikh's speech "may have been great in starting a discussion amongst the students," it was not "realistically achievable." Frisby noted, "They really did put thought into what he was saying and were paying attention. I give credit for that to their parents and teachers." Miamisid, another commenter on the *PBS* site, concluded

> Feeding students pabulum as if it were a universal truth is an age old tradition. It is good to hear that the students recognized it for what it is. Taking a leap of faith without a backup plan is a luxury most cannot afford. Kudos to the students.

By mid-March, Ms. Salazar asked her students to stop engaging through social media and to turn their attention to other projects. Interestingly enough, several of *The Maroon* editors and Ms. Salazar had secured press passes to attend the multimedia portion of the South by Southwest (SXSW) conference. There, they ran across the #besomebody founder and several of his employees at a marketing booth decorated with graffiti intended to mimic tagging, with loud music pulsating through their space. Folks from the company were high-fiving others walking through the exhibit hall and drawing lottery tickets for an experiential give-away: a motor-cross driving lesson would go to a lucky winner who downloaded the app that day.

According to Ms. Salazar, she and student editors Ellie Breed and Daniel Wallach had the opportunity to meet briefly with Kash Shaikh to talk through what had transpired between #besomebody and their school community. Skaikh told them that while he found the video parody produced by the KHAS students funny, "the opinion piece really hurt him. He felt that we had attacked him ... personally" (I. Salazar, personal communication, March 13, 2005). Ellie Breed suggested,

> I don't think he realized how big his audience was when he tweeted that blog at us. He didn't realize the following we had—the support from the student body that we had. He thought it would be a dialogue between him and our publication and his organization. But then all of the students that were behind us started getting in on it—against him.

This point drove home to students that words have power and they matter—even when the critique is coming from students with less education and experience. Daniel Wallach proposed that the reason Kash Shaikh reacted so negatively to the students' critique was because "he can't really untangle his personal life and what he's doing on the app now." The criticism felt personal. Ellie agreed saying,

> he made [the presentation] a really personal thing. And I think when it's presented to you like that you are less likely to question it if it looks like it's this grassroots 'my story' kind of thing" as opposed to a business trying to sell you an idea. Several students felt that Kash Shaikh had actually enjoyed the opportunity to spar with the school and *The Maroon* publicly as it brought more attention to #besomebody, driving internet traffic and potential users of the app which would filter into the company's bottom line. They speculated he likely "didn't even mind the negative press. Attention was attention and if it brought more clicks to his website, that generated more traffic and advertising dollars.

Student journalist Ana Szachacz viewed the #besomebody assembly as an easy opportunity to build on students' frustration with having "been told to do this stuff so much" [e.g., do well in school, go to college so you can get a job] that they were an easy target for his message of "don't do mainstream stuff. Come and have more fun." That sounded great on the surface, but Ms. Salazar's students saw a college education as necessary for achieving these long-term goals. In the end, the take-away from the experience reflected the hope of most literacy educators: students saw their work as contributing to a larger dialogue as it made its way through a complex and media-saturated world. Their ideas mattered. Ana noted, "we definitely did learn what not to do—we owe it to the person who did the work (as Sean had) to actually read what they say and critically think about it … otherwise, they put it out there for nothing." Reflecting on this Ms. Salazar revealed,

> You know, I don't know how many times in education the things that we are teaching actually get to be applied and authentic. So the things I've been telling my students over the past four years—how important their writing is and how important their voice is. How important to focus on social justice and equity and all those things. I've had students and they haven't had this moment. So I wonder how many teachers really get to have that authentic application. That's what's been the neatest thing.

DISCUSSION

The landscape of public schools is complicated by a host of factors that make researching there difficult when events like those described here surface in public, though social media, web pages, news articles and the like. Kincheloe (2005) explains that "the task of the bricoleur is to attack [the] complexity, uncovering the invisible artifacts of power and culture and documenting the nature of their influence" (p. 324) on scholarly endeavors. Among the data collected for this project were over 200 screen grabs of tweets, blogs with their resulting comments, web pages, photo images, interviews with individual and small groups of students, e-mail correspondence, artifacts of teaching, video, and news articles. In attempting to make sense of these artifacts, I first drew on interviews with the students and with Ms. Salazar; these framed my impressions of Kash Shaikh and what he was promoting at the school. I then investigated #besomebody's web and app presence, confirming students' belief that the company privileged brand over substance, and promoted problematic notions of aspirations versus education through business-speak, persuasive devises, bandwagon presentation skills. This analysis supports the findings that Ms. Salazar's work with students developed them in their ability to read media critically and in terms of acting as agentive participants in the world outside of school.

CONNECTIONS TO THE RESEARCH

In terms of how to support students' "authentic applications," when engaging through Reddit or the twitter-sphere, there is a limited body of research from which to draw. For one thing, social media is continuously morphing into something new and is disseminated widely—with tentacles extending beyond an original posting. And in spite of the Internet and social media's potential for creating spaces for first person accounts, and the inclusion of marginalized voices, it is important to help students gauge the credibility of those who write, blog, post, and tweet. It is impossible to anticipate when something will go viral through the Internet or social media. When this happens to a school community, its draws in a host of complicating issues, like determining how far to let students go in their engagement, reminding them they represent something bigger than themselves when posting, and helping them see the permanence of Internet posts and the consequences that might bring. Jenkins et al. (2006) have explored some of the challenges of a participatory culture in an increasingly connected world, acknowledging that students' "writing is much more open to the public and can have more far-reaching consequences." They go on, "The ethical implications of these emerging practices are fuzzy and ill-defined. Young people are discovering that information they put online to share with their friends can bring unwelcome attention from strangers" (p 17). This was certainly the case with *The Maroon* students, but the experience also provided a valuable learning experience for all involved, particularly as students grappled with the tenets of constructing a sound argument.

In today's world of Facebook and Twitter shaming, anonymous postings to blogs, and a less than civil discourse, it is tricky helping students determine when to put down the mantle and move on to the next thing. That is certainly what Ms. Salazar worried about with her students, eventually asking them to write a reflection on their interactions with Kash Shaikh and the #besomebody community. Student responses varied from questioning his motives, to wondering how Kash Shaikh gained entry into the school in the first place. Calling attention to a "fragile ego," student journalist Lauren Marigold expressed surprise that Kash Shaikh had not received criticism from other school presentations, and worry that he locked down the commenting feature of his blog to limit dissenting voices. Writing a letter as his response, Sonny Stephens discussed #besomebody's favored treatment of "certain passions over others," many of which he saw as hobbies rather than career opportunities. He acknowledged the "amazing school that you attack and denigrate so viciously (has) allowed me to follow my passion" and develop the skills and knowledge to gain entry into a prestigious college. Senior Des Magness conveyed frustration that Shaikh employed "name-calling toward those who critiqued #besomebody," explaining ad hominem arguments diminish the message.

CONCLUSION

In the 3 years since the assembly, the #besomebody brand has changed significantly. After facing a backlash in the Central Texas community, their founder moved the company up to Boston. Media reports (Gallaga, 2016; O'Brien, 2017) indicate that after appearing on the television show Shark

Tank and not receiving the support of any of the investors, #besomebody shuttered its business, morphing into a company that matches employees to jobs and offering life coaching and training. Kash Shaikh deleted the original webpage in early 2017 where the blog, marketing materials, linked tweets, and responses to Ms. Salazar's students lived. Having scrubbed those interactions from the Internet, one has to access the Way Back Time Machine [available at http://archive.org/web/] in order to view earlier iterations of the company, its web presence, and blog. This is a reminder of the ephemeral nature of online spaces and a telling lesson for Ms. Salazar's journalism students who have also moved on to college or work, replete with an entirely new list of responsibilities and learning to undergo.

This chapter suggests that helping students "read the world" and critically examine media is invaluable to navigating their lived experiences—both in person and online. The events explored here happened organically, and students at times adopted pseudonyms (as was the case of the Reddit responders) allowing them to enact their identities more honestly and with greater agency. What is clear from talking with the students in the spring of 2015: they wanted their voices heard, particularly after feeling attacked by Kash Shaikh and his passionary squad. By drawing on their roles as student journalists and enlisting the perspectives of others, students gained efficacy in engaging in literate activities in both familiar and less familiar spaces. These negotiations of public discourse and disagreement taught students about the importance of maintaining their cool in public, given that they were representing not just their school, but their newsmagazine and each other. They were supported by faculty and their local community, which no doubt helped students in balancing multiple identities—that of teenager, writer, editor, critic, and human. In talking with Rowan, who helped edit the newsmagazine and met in person with Kash Shaikh, she acknowledged that the back and forth between students, the public, and #besomebody community was beneficial to Shaikh's company. At South by Southwest he told her, "We have record breaking downloads because of y'all." Rowan told me, "he definitely overplayed things because of the effect it could have" in leveraging more traffic to his app, his webpage, and blog. Because of this, students worried that their critique was more beneficial to #besomebody than a glowing review.

In their discussion about the "spreadable spectacle" of today's media, Mihailidis and Viotty (2017) discuss the notion that teaching students to "question, critique and inquire about the credibility of media" (p. 450) is no guarantee that they will be able to ascertain what is sourced and truthful over what is specious and untrustworthy. The spread of disinformation from human to human, after all, can carry the sheen of reliability once it has passed through large numbers of newsfeeds without critique, particularly as people rely on each other as sources of information more than the mainstream press. We carry an expectation that students today are digitally savvy, yet as Morrell (2012) notes, "for all of their digital expertise, there is still a great deal that [youth] have to learn about how to process the information that they are inundated with via these new portals of information" (p. 301). As we continue to explore the varied literacy practices that our students, schools, and communities engage in, we must help find ways to help students read and respond to their world across platforms and spaces, uncovering truth and calling out fabrication, exaggeration, and other verbal manipulation. It is only through this that students can develop power and agency in their lives as readers, writers, doers, and thinkers.

REFERENCES

Alvermann, D., Moon, J. S., & Hagood, M. C. (1999). *Popular culture in the classroom: Teaching and researching critical media literacy*. Neward, DE, & Chicago, IL: International Reading Association and National Reading Conference.

Burnett, C., & Merchant, G. (2011). Is there a space for critical literacy in the context of social media? *English teaching: Practice and critique, 10*(1), 41–57.

Campbell, J. (1949). *The hero with a thousand faces*. Princeton, NJ: Princeton University Press.

Chilcott, L. (Producer), & Guggenheim, D. (Director). (2010). *Waiting for Superman* [Motion Picture]. United States: Electric Kinney Films.

Creswell, J. (1998). *Qualitative inquiry and research design*. Thousand Oaks, CA: SAGE.

Gainer, J. (2013). 21st-century mentor texts: Developing critical literacies in the information age. *Journal of adolescent and adult literacy, 57*(1), 16–19.

Gallaga, O. (2016). #besomebody, which launched in Austin, brutally turned into chum on 'Shark Tank' Retrieved from http://www.512tech.com/technology/besomebody-which-launched-austin-brutally-turned-into-chum-shark-tank/TC2YxeScUaQTZcK8N7ebsL/

Garcia, A., Seglem, R., & Share, J. (2013). Transforming teaching and learning through critical media literacy pedagogy. *LEARNing Landscapes, 6*(2), 109–124.

Garcia, A., Mirra, N., Morrell, E., Martinez, A., & Scorza, D. A. (2015). The council of youth research: Critical literacy and civic agency in the digital age. *Reading & Writing Quarterly, 31*(2), 151–167.

Greenhow, C., Robelia, B., & Hughes, J. (2009). Learning, teaching, and scholarship in a digital age: Web 2.0 and classroom research: What path should we take now? *Educational Researcher, 38*(4), 246–259.

Huberman, A. M., & Miles, M. B. (1983). Drawing valid meaning from qualitative data: Some techniquest of data reduction and display. *Quality and Quantity, 17*, 281–339.

International Literacy Association. (2012). *Adolescent literacy* (Position statement, Rev. 2012 ed). Newark, DE: Author.

Jenkins, H., Clinton, K., Purushotma, R., Robison, A., & Weigel, M. (2006). *Confronting the challenges of participatory culture: Media education for the 21st century*. Chicago, IL: MacArthur Foundation.

Kellner, D., & Share, J. (2005). Toward critical media literacy: Core concepts, debates, organizations, and policy. *Discourse: studies in the cultural politics of education, 26*(3), 369–386.

KHAS. (2015, January 9). #bekahs. #besomebody [Video]. Retrieved from https://www.youtube.com/watch?v=DUDhJ-KiGLg&t=34

Kincheloe, J. (2005). On to the next level: Continuing the conceptualization of the bricolage. *Qualitative Inquiry, 11*(3), 323–350.

Lewandowsky, S., Ecker, U. K. H., Seifert, C. M., Schwarz, N., & Cook, J. (2012). Misinformation and its correction: Continued influence and successful debiasing. *Psychological Science in the Public Interest, 13*(3), 106–131.

McGee, K. (2015). #besomebody speaker draws controversy at austin high school. *KUT News*. Retrieved from http://www.kut.org/ website: http://kut.org/post/besomebody-speaker-draws-controversy-austin-high-school

Mihailidis, P., & Viotty, S. (2017). Spreadable spectacle in digital culture: Civic expression, fake news, and the role of media literacies in "post-fact" society. *American Behavioral Scientist, 61*(4), 441–454.

Morrell, E. (2012). 21st-century literacies, critical media, pedagogies, and language arts *The Reading Teacher, 66*(4), 300–302.

National Council of Teachers of English (NCTE). (2013). 21st Century Literacies, Curriculum, Instruction, Literacy (Position statement, Rev. 2013 ed.). Urbana, IL: Author.

New London Group. (1996). A pedagogy of multiliteracies: Designing social futures. *Harvard Educational Review, 66*(1), 60–92.

O'Brien, K. (2017). Boston startup Besomebody, once featured on 'Shark Tank,' shuts down app Retrieved from https://www.bizjournals.com/boston/news/2017/01/07/after-sinking-on-shark-tank-boston-startup.html

Saldana, S. (2015, February 16). #Besomebody. [Commentary]. Retrieved from http://sfamaroon.org/593/opinion/besomebody/

Segal, C. (2015). High school kids call out motivational speaker's #besomebody message. *PBS Newshour*. Retrieved from http://www.pbs.org/newshour/rundown/high-school-kids-call-motivational-speakers-besomebody-message/

Shaikh, K. (2014, December 18). Video. Going ALL IN on your passion. Retrieved from https://www.youtube.com/watch?v=hf3_BJ7Lk8Q

Solomon, D. (2015). Austin tech bros from #besomebody are losing the fight they picked against local high school students. *Texas Monthly*. Retrieved from http://www.texasmonthly.com/website: http://www.texasmonthly.com/the-daily-post/austin-tech-bros-from-besomebody-are-losing-the-fight-they-picked-against-local-high-school-students/

space_manatee. (2015). #besomebody founder attacks austin HS students and staff online. [Message board]. Retrieved from https://www.reddit.com/r/Austin/comments/2xd8bt/besomebody_founder_attacks_austin_hs_students_and/

Spicer, M. (Writer). (2017). *Ingrid goes west* [Motion Picture]. In J. Goldman, A. Plaza, T. White, T. White, A. Mirels, & R. Mirels (Producers). United States: Neon.

Trending, B. (2015). Pep talk #besomebody backfires at texas school. *BBC News*. Retrieved from http://www.bbc.com/news/blogs-trending-31754918

CHAPTER 13

IMMATERIALITY REDUX

Tacit Modalities and Meaning Across Timescales

Sandra Schamroth Abrams
St. John's University in New York

Jennifer Rowsell
Brock University

> *Just now, as I was opening a jar of salsa, I was reminded of my Nana (because just how many jars did we have to open for her, it was a lot) and the feeling that memory brought me was so sweet and happy. For a moment I was standing in the kitchen at the cottage teasing Nana about her wimpy hands and there were two 'toasted cheese' on the stove and an epic game of Rummikub on the table. I will try to hold on to that feeling as long as I can.* —Rebecca
>
> *I love those fleeting moments when it all comes back so clearly.* —Allison

Rebecca's[1] Facebook post and Allison's response call attention to the ways in which human senses play an affective role in meaning making. The simple twisting of a jar's metal cap can spur memory-based feelings associated with images of arthritic "wimpy hands," food on the stove, and intense ("epic") game play under way. All of these images cohere to represent a situated

Negotiating Place and Space Through Digital Literacies: Research and Practice, pp. 241–258

point in time, which, as Allison noted, only surface for "fleeting moments." What happens, however, when a new context, such as an illness, changes the feelings related to the artifact at hand? How can we contextualize and explain how modalities contribute to evolving, affective stances? And how do time and space play a role in understanding such subjective, sensory-based meaning making? How do culture, religion, and social class play a role within this interconnected picture? These and other questions make us wonder how tacit, embodied sensations interact with familiar texts, objects and visuals.

The field of literacy studies has moved beyond representational interpretations with a sole focus on design (Leander & Boldt, 2013; Lewis & Tierney, 2013). To greater explore *meaning making as experiencing*, this chapter introduces the nonrepresentational theory of tacit modalities as a heuristic to better understand how emotions, memories, feelings, sensations, and thoughts play a role in evolving meaning making. This is especially relevant in light of the multimodal production and consumption culture supported by digital spaces and resources.

THEORETICAL PERSPECTIVES

Multimodalities

Inherent in its name, multimodality is the understanding that meaning making occurs through the confluence of modes. The positioning of one's body, the texture and color of a fabric, the way light casts shadows, the musty smell of old books, and so on, all impact one's perception and meaning making. Just as literacy cannot be understood as an "'autonomous' variable, somehow divorced from social and ideological contexts that give it meaning" (Street, 1999, p. 55), so, too, meaning making cannot be reduced to one modality separated from its context. Kress (2010) addressed such complexity when he explained how modes can work harmoniously to convey meaning through "orchestration," which involves "assembling/organizing/designing a plurality of signs in different modes into a particular configuration to form a coherent arrangement," resulting in "ensembles," or the product of such orchestration (p. 162). In other words, multimodality involves the process of modes working in concert to produce an overall effect or meaning; typically, such meaning making is highly nuanced, socially situated and individualized in nature.

When we consider multimodal meaning making, as well as and thoughts and memories of modalities (e.g., smells, sounds, sights, textures), we acknowledge that multimodal literacies also include the connection among "story, memory, images, and experiences" (Vasudevan, 2006, p. 254).

Returning to Rebecca's recollection of her Nana's hands, therefore, we contend that memories are inherently multimodal in nature. The image of the jar, Nana's arthritic hands and the Rummikub tiles, the feeling of resistance from the salsa jar cap, the smell and/or sounds related to the toasted cheese on the stove, all suggest that multimodalities evoke emotions, feelings, and embodiment that are part of the meaning making experienced through such *tacit modalities*. Memories often include sensory-based, multimodal residues (e.g., the scent of a perfume, the sound of a particular song, the image of arthritic hands), and the related sensations are tacit—they are perceived even if they are difficult to identify and/or articulate. Tacit modalities, we argue, are important to meaning making because they bridge experiences across timescales. In what follows, we develop the concept of tacit modalities in relation to affect and timescales.

Tacit Modalities

Tacit modalities include that which is felt and sensed, and by noting emotions and feelings, we are referring to sensations registered within the body and mind, such as, joy, fear, and anxiety (Massumi, 2002). At times, these emotions may be difficult to pinpoint but, nonetheless, are acknowledged and/or believed; often they are articulated through endearing terms, such as "smells like home" or "tastes just like my mother's cooking," or jarring recollections, such as a tone that "sounds just like my ex-boyfriend," or images of recent school shootings that emerge and "make me fearful as I walk down the hall." Tacit modalities also enable readers or listeners to connect with information. Rebecca's account hints at her sentimentality, but we, as readers, cannot sense exactly what she feels. *We interpret it through our own sensed experiences*. Regardless of the subtle or overt nature of tacit modalities, they play a role in the way we construct and reconstruct meaning because tacit modalities facilitate the vivid recollection of moments passed, bringing the past into the present, even if briefly, and sometimes chaining us to a past in ways that can feel traumatic, exhausting, and painful.

What makes tacit modalities so powerful is that they involve embodiment, which represents bodily reactions to instances, spaces, and places and how bodies engage with senses (Enriquez, Johnson, Kontovourki, & Mallozzi, 2015). For instance, entering a room and having felt memories from its smell, design, or visuals on the wall may conjure sensations tied to a past moment. This became clear to Sandra, an author of this chapter, when she struggled to make sense of a traumatic event. In this chapter, Sandra describes the sensation of felt memories when she talks about revisiting her family home when her father was gravely ill. Furthermore, we suggest that these multimodal tacit memories produce an undercurrent of meaning making that may surface in new or extended feelings, interpretations, and actions. As such, an artifact that spurs the memory may have material and immaterial markers, but there are shifts in meaning making that may also complicate and disrupt the way the artifact evokes meaning. The concept of tacit modalities helps to explain why such complication and disruption occur.

Research of artifacts includes an examination of their materiality (something that is tangible, such as a journal) and immateriality (something that is intangible, such as a memory) (Burnett, 2011; Burnett, Merchant, Pahl, & Rowsell, 2014). Pahl and Rowsell (2011) called attention to the ways artifacts, or "objects and their meanings in everyday life" are inherently tied to "the situated nature of texts in places and communities" (p. 130) thereby underscoring the nuanced, culturally embedded meaning that artifacts represent and evoke. Returning to Rebecca's recollection, we can see that her handling of the obstinate lid was a material artifact that also had an immateriality. Had the salsa jar opened easily, it is possible Rebecca might not have recollected her experience with her Nana. However, it was through the struggle with the lid that Rebecca immediately thought of her Nana's hands and the grilled cheese cooking on the stove. Essentially, the immaterial can become materialized through action and intention, which also can occur in and across digital and nondigital spaces (Burnett & Bailey, 2014). We extend this discussion by examining how tacit modalities can take shape in different ways depending on the associated contexts, experiences, and memories. To do so, we first look more closely at mitigating factors—affect, crystallization, and timescales—to offer additional clarity of how tacit modalities transcend temporal-spatial bounds and offer another layer of understanding to multimodal meaning making.

Affect

Though affect has been part of the human experience, it continues to gain attention in education research, especially in relation to literacy. More specifically, Leander and Boldt (2013) addressed how practices are not simply about products and destinations, but are processes imbued with felt experiences and emotion. They perceived

> literacy activity as not projected toward some textual end point, but as living its life in the ongoing present, forming relations and connections across signs, objects, and bodies in often unexpected ways. Such activity is saturated with affect and emotion; it creates and is fed by an ongoing series of affective intensities that are different from the rational control of meanings and forms. (p. 26)

Meaning that stems from tacit modalities can be rational, controlled, and expected or irrational, uncontrolled, and unexpected; affect creates a mind-body connection that is intersensory and can be visceral in nature. The fact is that tacit modalities are related to a "series of affective intensities" that can be ever-evolving even if they are provoked or prompted by the interaction with a particular artifact. For example, Sandra's father encountered near-death experiences, and his hospital stay marked a turning point in his health. When Sandra views pictures of her father from even 5 years ago, she is confronted by the sadness she feels knowing that her father has changed, by the gratefulness she feels knowing that he is still alive, and by the guilt she feels because sadness continues to permeate her thoughts. These tensions are stirred by affective intensities and prompted by interactions with various material and immaterial artifacts. To this day, Sandra cannot listen to David Bowie's *Space Oddity*, a song she listened while negotiating interstate traffic and rushing to see her father before his life-changing surgery; the music triggers a similar psychosomatic response she felt during that drive, underscoring the connection of memory to sensory to body. Even writing about this moment creates affective intensities that Sandra struggles to manage.

Crystallization

Drawing upon this interpretation of literacy as intertextual and intersensory meaning making, we also look to the philosophical discussion of crystallization to emphasize the perception-sensory connection. Perception is hard to grasp; it is slippery, ephemeral and also linked in with synaesthetic responses to artifacts. That is, there are lived memories within artifacts (e.g., the salsa jar for Rebecca, the David Bowie song for Sandra) that resurrect thoughts, feelings, emplaced sensations, and then there are materialities (e.g., colors, textures) that can trigger other sensory responses that could be somatic, sonic, olfactory, or visual. Just as the synaesthetic cross of senses is part and parcel of tacit modalities, so too are the anticipated and unanticipated sensations and memories that the tacit modalities evoke. In other words, felt and remembered experiences create additional tacit modalities that inform the ever-evolving meaning making experiences.

In their narrative about their travels, Laurel Richardson and Ernest Lockridge (2004) explored perception and representations of meaning through sociological and narrative lenses. They discussed memories as "moorings" that guide behavior (p. 123), and the authors recalled Richardson's (2000) qualitative analytical stance of "crystallization," or the understanding *that positioning impacts perception*. More specifically, they contended that "Crystals are prisms, which reflect externalities and refract within themselves, creating different colors, patterns, arrays, casting off in different directions. What we see depends on our angle of vision" (Richardson & Lockridge, 2004, p. 240). The crystal prism and the various refractions of light are metaphors for opportunities to create and recreate, as well as interpret and reinterpret, information, and at the heart of it all is context-based, nuanced meaning making.

In essence, Richardson's image of the crystal helps to underscore the complicated nature of meaning making. What we see is not all that is present. Interpretation is impacted by

> an infinite variety of shapes, substances, transmutations, multidimensionalities, and angles of approach. Crystals grow, change, and are altered, but they are not amorphous ... there is no single truth.... Crystallization provides us with a deepened, complex, and thoroughly partial understanding of the topic. (Richardson & St. Pierre, 2005, p. 963)

In other words, the crystal represents the potential changes and dynamic understandings that stem from tacit modalities and (im)material experiences. Artifacts may be created and consumed at specific points in time, but they are not static entities bereft of emotional connection. For example, photos of Sandra's father once "moored" (Richardson & Lockridge, 2004) her to fond memories, and now the conflation of the material and immaterial trigger mixed emotions. The physical artifact (the photo) has not changed, but it is not static because of the felt experience. Once again, this sense of emotional connection can be a conscious or subconscious response driven by human instincts to colors, textures, and so forth, with tacit modalities concretizing and complicating meaning making.

Furthermore, synaesthesia helps to underscore the dynamic nature and the "constant transition, translation and transduction between modes" (Kress, 1997, p. 37). As stated above, synaesthesia can work off of or in concert with transduction when meaning making moves from one mode to another, such as from speech to writing to image to film (Kress, 2010). Synaesthesia adds texture to memories and is an inherent component of tacit modalities. Engagements with artifacts such as, the Rebecca's jar in the opening, work on similar principles where reactions can lead to meaning making acts that can move from one texture and color to dimensionality. The jar cap is not simply a round metal object; the physical feel of it and the act of twisting (and the activation of related muscles) conjure memories that then bring about other feelings and remembered scents, scenes, and sensories. These, in turn, complicate temporal-spatial boundaries, as a person and an artifact may be physically located in one space, but the feelings can transport one back in time or create new meanings related to the artifact; there are shifts in liminal planes. Lemke's (2000) discussion of timescales helps to situate and clarify the complexity of experiencing and re-experiencing in different spatial-temporal contexts.

Timescales

Lemke's (2000) discussion of timescales helps our thinking by addressing how artifacts may mistakenly be understood as objects indicative of a particular time and place: "*Things*, or *organisms*, or *persons*, or *institutions*, as usually defined, are not dynamical notions: they are ordinarily defined in terms of their stable and persistent, or invariant, properties. They are not about dynamics, not about change and doing, but about being what they are" (p. 275, emphasis in original). However, when taking into account "dynamical theory," attention turns to "what's going on, what's participating and how, and how one going-on is interdependent with another" (p. 275), and Lemke suggests that material objects created or experienced in one timescale can be reexperienced in similar or different ways in another context. For Rebecca, the salsa jar and related tacit modalities figuratively transport her back in time; for Sandra, the *Space Odyssey* song elicits lived memories and psychosomatic responses; for Allison, such memories are but "fleeting moments," that anchor her to a past. The artifacts have a different meaning to different people and connect people to the past in different ways. What is more, artifacts that may have had seemingly static meaning may suddenly change, and this is where tacit modalities offers additional dimensionality to understandings of meaning making as both situated *and* protean. As these examples suggest (and as Lemke contended), moments of experience can be revisited through heterochrony, the phenomenon in which "longer-term processes and shorter-term events [are] linked by a material object that functions in both cases semiotically as well as materially" (Lemke, 2000, p. 281). In other words, meaning making is contextual, embodied, and interactional across timescales, calling attention to various trajectories of learning that inform overall meaning making.

MODE OF INQUIRY

To document and chart tacit modalities, we adopt a method of inquiry that combines the work of Lemke (2000) with Kress (2010) and Richardson (2000) to juxtapose and analyze different multimodal texts that we have collected and to engage in a collective case study of tacit modalities. More specifically, we consider Lemke's point that "every process, action, social practice or activity occurs on some timescale (in complex cases on more than one timescale)" (2000, p. 275). Keeping his discussion of dynamical theory in mind, we aim to describe "what's going on, what's participating and how one going-on is interdependent with another" (Lemke, 2000, p. 275). We ask these questions to examine (a) how material objects are experienced and reexperienced in similar and different ways and on various liminal planes; (b) where one is (e.g., the context and space) when one engages in sensory-based reactions (e.g., memories evoked by smells, sounds, images); and (c) where, how, and in what way the responses figuratively transport one to another dimension. When engaging in such descriptive work, we explore how multimodalities and synaesthetic responses are part of the re-experienced moments and how crystallization and ever-changing understandings help to offer perspectives of positionality, recreations of truth, embodied responses to memory, and spatial-temporal tensions; these perspectives are not mutually exclusive, and, therefore, are not used to categorize our findings. Instead, in this chapter, we feature multimodal texts alongside the producer/meaning maker's stories to extrapolate felt reactions and tacit modalities displayed during meaning making and materialized within the product itself.

Data represented in the paper derive from separate but related research of undergraduate and graduate education students' examinations of artifacts. Our personal experiences offer additional insight into tacit modalities. We mined data from previous research coupled with interviews with various people about objects that they value and objects that tell a story (Pahl & Rowsell, 2010). To analyze the data, we drew on affect theory (Ehret, 2018; Massumi, 2007) to examine how emotions and feelings are registered on the body as participants talked through their object/artifact; we then drew upon Lemke's notion of timescales to connect temporal relations with material engagements and associations that participants had with their objects. Finally, engaging in a collective case study (Yin, 2014), we identified similarities and differences across the cases and developed a greater understanding of how tacit modalities inform situated learning. Inductive data analysis supported the examination of overlapping and contrasting interpretations and the use of expert knowledge to discuss the emerging phenomena in relation to extant research (Yin, 2014).

TACIT MODALITIES

In this section, we present findings from our own research studies to elucidate aspects of tacit modalities. As such, each heading represents a category of tacit modalities and its corresponding concepts.

Entangled Timescales and Tacit Modalities: Ted and His Staged Photo

As a part of Jennifer's methods class, she teaches artifactual and visual methods and asks students to bring in photos and artifacts that they value.

Ted, a 24-year-old Asian Canadian university student, was particularly keen on this activity and promptly brought in a selfie of his family. The photo (see Figure 13.1) is of his Mom, Dad, and Ted at the Toronto airport en route to New York, where his mom would run the New York City Marathon. The photograph evokes many emotions for Ted, but mostly happiness because they had not gone on a family trip for some time and they seldom took photographs of big family events. As well, it is an uncharacteristic photo of both of his Mom and Dad. Ted's Mom typically does not like photos of herself and according to Ted, "my Dad, he has a very goofy personality which does not come out as much in this photo." When he describes the photo, Ted becomes noticeably animated saying,

> This is a very staged photo, but I mean it is a happy photo, and I believe we were all generally happy, but umm it is more of a performance aspect I guess, like that smile I can replicate, like that is my picture smile, because my mom, uhh like I had bad photos for school, like in grade school, and she was like you really need to get like a better, a good smile (both laughing), like you are doing a really cheeky thing, a closed grin thing, you need like an actual smile. Umm so I developed that smile, and then my dad is being very polite.

Within the photo there is the timescale of Ted's school photos when he could not get his "picture smile" right for a long time and then finally got it. Thinking about Lemke's (2000) timescales, the material world has many scales (e.g., space, time, matter), and Ted's reflections harken back to a younger age when he felt awkward during school photos and developed a staged self for more formal shots. He has this same smile in this affect-filled photo. What also arises in this photo is the notion of the performative, Hallmark card family photo wherein people visualize themselves in a particular way to speak to tropes. This kind of visual narrative carries tacit modalities with longer timescales both enacted and experienced.

In addition, speaking to the concept of timescales, Ted reflected on his dad's unusually relaxed smile and his mom's exuberant look, noting, "it was a moment and that is why I keep it." The act of taking the photograph and the resultant image sediments a memory for the family and crystallizes roles within the family. When asked if the photo carries feelings, Ted observed:

> Yeah I think photos are just inherently, like just snapshots, they are visuals, but umm it is more so what the person looking at the photo, umm what emotions they feel when looking at it, due to their past experiences and what visual cues I guess umm bring to mind when they look at a photo.

Looking at and thinking about a photograph ushers in past experiences as longer timescales embedded within photos, as well as visual tropes that exude specific emotions (e.g., joy), but also projected emotions, such as "look at us, we are a happy family."

Figure 13.1. Ted's airport selfie.

Unpacked and Repacked Tacit Modalities: Beyond Chained Elephants

At the end of the interview, Ted referred to a large Richard Avedon photograph (see https://bit.ly/1qV6gme) in Jennifer's office of a woman in a long black gown with two elephants on either side of her. When we discussed photographs, Ted said,

> I also think like if I look at this elephant photo, umm like I can uhhh sympathize with those elephants because they are like chained, so that must not feel good. I mean if I was reading a book about like a bad circus, mistreatment to animals, that feels no good, but I think that is very base level emotion.

Jennifer responded that she admires the woman's elegant black dress and that Jennifer loves the photo because it was in her father's office. In this moment, tacit modalities are entangled within an object, another photo, that signals Jennifer's connections with her father, but also the style of photographs that he loved—carrying her back in time to sitting in his office looking at the very same photo.

During their interview conversation, there is an entanglement emerging again of Ted's selfie with Jennifer's framed Richard Avedon photograph.

Referring to it as a point of contrast, Ted points to the Avedon image as illustrating how it makes him feel sympathetic to the elephant and perhaps angry about the elephants being tethered to chains; nonetheless the photograph is reminiscent of a bygone age with its homage to Audrey Hepburn's classic style in paradoxical juxtaposition with chained elephants. As yet another dimension of the entangled timescale, Jennifer recounts the story behind the Avedon photograph as a treasured artifact from her Dad's office at work and how it makes her feel (calm, usually) when she looks at it and thinks about it. Jennifer thereby refers to the tacit modalities at play as she sits in her office contemplating her Dad's picture and their shared qualities, such as a passion for their work, their love of photography.

Nonetheless, emotions about the Avedon photograph shifted in the interview to sadness—missing her Dad—or even when Ted talks about the cruelty of chaining elephants, Jennifer sees the photo in an entirely different light. In this instance, just as crystals offer various perspectives, materialities coalesce and Ted and Jennifer see the image in a different way after sharing their initial thoughts and telling artifactual stories. This highlights the mercurial, unpredictable character of tacit modalities, which can trigger one emotion in one instance followed by a polar opposite emotion in the next moment. Tacit modalities not only evoke expected meaning (e.g., Jennifer feeling calm), but also are essential for the shifts in meaning making that come rather unexpectedly due to contextual factors, such as new situations, turns in conversations, and interactions with modes. Staged photos, such as selfies, and even images that have been part of daily routines can carry with them loaded meanings that continue to be unpacked and perhaps repacked through each interaction. Sandra describes this motif in the next category when she recalls how her family home registered on her body when she witnessed her father's postsurgery illness and how something that previously was a source of contentment and comfort suddenly fractured and became an object of fright and pain.

Fractured Tacit Modalities: Paradigm Shifts

The introductory vignette of Rebecca's encounter suggests that, through the act of opening a jar of salsa, Rebecca sensed the warmth of family represented in food, play, and time spent together. Memories and artifacts, however, do not remain static, as we see through Jennifer and Ted's interaction. Sometimes changes to liminal planes—shifts of a small or seismic nature—can fracture or even rupture existing directionalities and relationships, resulting in new paradigms that carry with them weighted (or weightless) meanings, affect, and interpretations. Take, for instance, the reflective memos written during a time when Sandra's father experienced a traumatic surgery followed by a series of health issues, and she temporarily returned to her childhood home to help care for him:

> Today is the first day I think I took a breath. Yesterday was hellish; my dad had a fever of 105, and we could not stabilize his vitals. It.Was.Frightening. Today, thank heavens, my father is better. Though they still cannot locate the infection, the cocktail of antibiotics is working, and I'll drink to that (along the cocktail theme). My dad is not ready to leave the CCU [Critical Care Unit], but there's hope in sight.
>
> My dad had a pulmonary embolism and, thus, has had trouble breathing and getting enough oxygen. Things seem to be a bit more under control (knock wood), but there are other repercussions to the treatment and let's just say that I just want to get my dad back ... I pray that he will be back to himself—cognitively and with physical improvements—and with as little pain and few issues as possible. I used to like roller coasters, and now I understand the beauty of slow, controlled rides like The Small World.
>
> My dad had to be transported via ambulance (if that gives you an idea of the state he is in), and I helped my mom prepare the house to accommodate my father's needs.... We spent the majority of the time getting things set up here and am now fully versed in the specialist language of medical supplies.... With everything going on, I also have started to rethink affect, the body, data, and energies that simply cannot be named, but rather best described.... My dad is not really the dad I once had—there is a new normal—and yet I still see him/hear him/think of him as he was ... until I see him. Then there's a new person, hopefully temporarily. Who is that man? How did [this] transformation take place so quickly? And, if we ever get back to "normal," it will be a different normal, rife with the literal, emotional, and figurative scarring.

During this traumatic family experience, the pain and fear Sandra felt began to influence the way she viewed her home, and the artifacts that once were associated with joy became symbols of emotional torment. Her perception of her father as a "new person"—someone unrecognizable ("Who is that man?")—created sensations that could not "be named, but rather best described." Further complicating the matter were the emotion and sensory-based tensions between how Sandra remembered her father and the way she encountered him in person; the latter included sights, sounds, and smells related to medical supplies, illness, and physicalities unknown (e.g., atrophied muscles; reddened skin; medical tubes emerging from the arm, the nose; eyes with empty gazes).

The convergence of various modalities—the synaesthetic effect of the artifacts in her childhood home and the introduction of new sounds, sights, smells, and felt experiences—created continuous shifts in perceived understandings and sensations, while concretizing a "new normal" that included "literal, emotional, and figurative scarring." Tacit modalities entangled with fractured memories disrupted Sandra's underlying paradigm for home. Her father's deterioration belied representations of strength; the sounds of medical equipment and the stagnant air signaled illness, not growth; and the artifacts of bygone moments emphasized a reversal in roles: Sandra was now the caregiver. Although memories of childhood in that very house still existed, the timescale was fractured and memories soon became tainted by visceral, affective responses. The sounds of childhood joy became muted. Tacit, embodied modalities signaled permutations in meaning and experiential shifts in seemingly non-linear ways. These examples underscore the complex role of tacit modalities in meaning making, especially because these modalities include that which may be difficult to label or define.

Material and Immaterial Dualities Within Tacit Modalities: Genevieve and Her Journal

Genevieve is a 20-year-old undergraduate Hispanic-American Education student who has been journaling "since [she] was a little girl," but has a particular connection to her most recent journal because of its symbolization of freedom and hope. When engaged in a discussion of artifacts and learning, Genevieve explained,

> The first time I wrote in this journal was on my first plane ride to New York on August 5th, 2015. When I look at it I feel a sense of home ... I remember my darkest entry, and that day, and how hopeless and lost I felt moving out of my mom's house when I loved her so much but knew it wasn't a safe place anymore.

Genevieve struggled with the concept of "home," and dualities in meaning supported the material and immaterial entanglements and crystallizing views of what it means to be home and feel safe.

Through the journal, Genevieve's immaterial thoughts and feelings became materialized, and perhaps it is for that reason that she became fearful about "losing it [the journal] I lose things and don't really have anything tangible from childhood, so I feel sort of scared holding it sometimes (like what if I drop it in the subway and the train comes and my life is just rat food now!!)." So perhaps I feel more safe when I just see it laying on my bed or whatever." Because of tacit modalities, the sensory meets the embodied ("what if I drop it in the subway and the train comes and my life is just rat food now!!). To Genevieve, losing the journal would be like losing her identity, and tacit modalities support the material-immaterial duality that enables Genevieve to literally and figuratively hold on to memories.

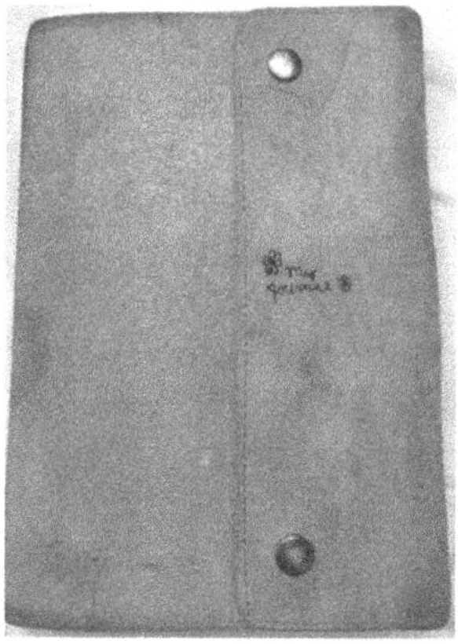

Figure 13.2. Genevieve's journal.

Furthermore, Genevieve seems to feel "moored" to and by her journal, an artifact that she has had for over ten years. She affectionately describes it as she considers how it represents her experiences with it:

> I love the material of the cover of my journal. When you open up the little flap to go inside the journal, you can see it's a lot more vibrant red on the inside. This shows how long I've had it and how it became so faded over the years.

The journal's physical attributes represent longer timescales while its internal links (e.g., the written memories) to other timescales enable Genevieve to move in and out of felt spaces.

Shifting Timescales: Teresa and Her Birds

Above we see how tacit modalities are entwined with identity practices, such as journal writing, as well as complicated timescales that Genevieve traverses when she writes in her journal, when she holds her journal, and when she thinks about her journal. Tacit modalities also highlight identity practices through shifting timescales, something that the story of Teresa helps to exemplify.

Teresa's fascination with birds and photographing birds helps to solidly exemplify visuals that have shifted with time and life changes. Built on her commitment to the work of Richard Shusterman (2008) and somoaesthetics (e.g., the body and its experiences as a sensory and aesthetic entity), Teresa developed a habit of taking photographs as a philosophical and embodied practice. "Somoaesthetics" is an intense look at the body and its function in developing our knowledge and construction of the world. Teresa's doctoral work examines how photography can be an act of consciousness, of actually thinking about the process of making images as a daily, philosophical practice. The lens, therefore, becomes an apt metaphor, capturing the philosophical, the ontological, and the physical, and being behind a camera lens crystallizes how Teresa understands the world in varied ways.

Our interview focused on birds and her lifelong fascination with birds. She talks about birds as messengers and as souls of the earth. She talks about the Janus-faced nature of vultures who are beautiful when they soar, but unattractive when you see them up close. Teresa grew up in Dallas, Texas and talks about growing up with vultures who were in plentiful supply on the "sides of roads, eating." The importance of the triptych in Figure 13.3 is that it reminds Teresa of the importance of her work: "These photographs have literally changed my life in that I can show visually what my work is comprised of … words fail to convey the concept of 'conscious photographing' as well as the pairing of these three photos." Although Teresa grew up around vultures, it was only a few years ago when she was sitting on the deck at her brother's house in Athens, Texas when she saw the Turkey vultures (Figure 13.3) dancing on the roof. What struck her was the dance that they were engaged in at that very moment. Observing the dance from afar gave Teresa a calmness that stuck, and looking at the photographs even now reminds her of that epiphany.

Since then, Teresa has taken so many photos of birds at different angles and in different postures. Teresa talked far more than other participants about the feeling and affect that she experiences when she takes the photographs as opposed to looking at photographs. Such documentation not only sediments Teresa's identity as a photographer and birdwatcher, but also offers symbolic representations of her academic journey: "the meaning of these photos has increased and become the "solid" proof (to me) that my ideas of photographing, along with the literature have validity. My project is my legacy." In this way, there is a timescale that extends beyond herself; just as photography materializes her philosophies and beliefs, it also creates immaterial, boundless extensions of her values. There are shifts in timescales that enhance Teresa's relationship with photos of birds, especially as these photos are embedded into her everyday and serve as a strong signifier of her identity.

LOOKING FORWARD

A scent. A song. A taste. A texture. An image. These and other modalities individually or in concert with others can trigger an affective response typically associated with memories or physical (dis)comfort, and tacit

Figure 13.3. Teresa's birds.

modalities complicate our notions of place, space and time. Given the communicationally complex texts that students encounter on a minute-by-minute basis, literacy policy and practice need a far more robust and nuanced approach to addressing the orientation and presentation of meaning making.

The concept of tacit modalities supports the exploration of the felt, the sensed, and the imagined, enabling one to experience a mooring to a particular time and space, and yet engage in a reinvention of time, space, and self. Genevieve's journal offered her entree to a space that she could call home during a time she did not have one. Rebecca used Facebook to document her recollection of her Nana's hands, receiving affirmation and creating opportunities for crystallization. Jennifer and Ted found entangled modalities and affective responses prompted by an image that had layers of meaning beyond its physical appearance. We contend that the concept of tacit modalities offers educators and education researchers opportunities to rethink meaning making in light of contextualized, embodied, and interactional aspects that illuminate various trajectories of experience; in essence, the learner can be making meaning on multiple, but distinct planes, something that takes much more time and space to unpack than conventional education spaces and practices support.

Put together with the context of in-school and out-of-school meaning making, the discussion of tacit modalities underscores the ever-evolving nature of meaning. We consider the implications of nondigital and digital artifacts and the tacit modalities that are entangled across timescales. For instance, what does the finger-paint picture mean to the child and the parent today? Tomorrow? In 10 years from now? What happens when a child's work or photo is circulated via social media? How might digital resources and spaces create or mutate tacit modalities, ultimately sedimenting or distorting identities? Relatedly, what and how might digital enhancements and remix, or even the sharing and resharing of material and immaterial artifacts, offer new crystallizations and create alternate timescales rife with permutations and even fractures of meaning?

As we look forward and consider the discussion of tacit modalities and meaning making in and beyond the classroom, we contend that tacit modalities might help to reframe an understanding of progress and formative learning; tacit modalities elicit felt and embodied experiences, which, as the vignettes suggest, can have opposing, fracturing, or reaffirming effects. If progress and formative learning were considered with a holistic view of where, when and how learners make meaning along the way, then perhaps these learning residues will reveal the depth and complexity of each person's ever-changing journey. Furthermore, we suggest that a focus on tacit modalities might help educators, education researchers, and students become more keenly aware of negotiations of place, space, and reimagined meaning, especially as digital and nondigital practices have multiple "truths" and include multiple trajectories moored in one space and crystallizing other dimensions.

NOTE

1. With the exception of author names, all names are pseudonyms.

REFERENCES

Burnett, C. (2011). The (im)materiality of educational space: interactions between material, connected and textual dimensions of networked technology use in schools. *E-Learning and Digital Media, 8*(3), 214–227.

Burnett, C., & Bailey, C. (2014). Conceptualising collaboration in hybrid sites: Playing Minecraft together and apart in a primary classroom. In C. Burnett, J. Davies, G. Merchant, & J. Rowsell (Eds.), *New literacies around the globe: Policy and pedagogy* (pp. 50–72). Abingdon, Oxon: Routledge.

Burnett, C., Merchant, G. H., Pahl, K., & Rowsell, J. (2014). The (im)materiality of literacy: the significance of subjectivity to new literacies research, *Discourse: Studies in the Cultural Politics of Education, 35*(1), 90–103. doi:10.1080/01596306.2012.739469

Bowie, D. (1969). Space Oddity. [Recorded by David Bowie]. On *David Bowie.* [Single]. London, England: Trident Studios.

Ehret, C. (2018). Propositions from affect theory for feeling literacy through the event. In D. Alvermann, N. Unrau, & R. Ruddell (Eds.), *Theoretical models and processes of reading* (7th ed.). Newark, DE: International Literacy Association.

Enriquez, G., Johnson, E., Kontovourki, S., & Mallozzi, C. A. (Eds.). (2015). *Literacies, learning, and the body: Putting theory and research into pedagogical practice*. New York, NY: Routledge.

Jenkins, H. (2006). *Convergence culture: Where old and new media collide*. New York, NY: New York University Press.

Kress, G., & Van Leeuwen, T. (2001). *Multimodal discourse: The modes and media of contemporary communication.* London, England: Arnold.

Kuhn, A. (1995). *Family secrets: Acts of memory and imagination*. London, England: Verso.

Leander, K., & Boldt, G. (2013). Rereading "A pedagogy of multiliteracies": Bodies, texts, and emergence. *Journal of Literacy Research, 45*(1), 22–46.

Lemke, J. L. (2000). Across the scales of time: Artifacts, activities, and meanings in ecosocial systems. *Mind, Culture, and Activity, 7*(4), 273–290.

Lewis, C., & Tierney, J. D. (2013). Mobilizing emotion in an urban classroom: Producing identities and transforming signs in a race-related discussion. *Linguistics and Education, 23,* 289–304.

Massumi, B. (2002). *Parables for the virtual: Movement, affect, sensation*. Durham, NC: Duke University Press.

Pahl, K., & Rowsell, J. (2011). Artifactual critical literacies: A new perspective for literacy education. *Berkeley Review of Education, 2*(2), 129–151.

Richardson, L. (2000). Writing: A method of inquiry. In N. K. Denzin & Y. S. Lincoln (Eds.), *Handbook of qualitative research* (2nd ed., pp. 923–948). Thousand Oaks, CA: SAGE.

Richardson, L., & Lockridge, E. (2004). *Travels with Ernest: Crossing the literary/sociological divide.* Walnut Creek, CA: AltaMira Press.

Richardson, L. & St. Pierre, E.A. (2005). Writing: A method of inquiry. In N. K. Denzin & Y. S. Lincoln (Eds.), *The Sage handbook of qualitative research* (3rd ed., pp. 959–978). Thousand Oaks, CA: SAGE.

Shusterman, R. (2008). *Body consciousness: A philosophy of mindfulness and somaesthetics.* Cambridge, MA: Cambridge University Press.

Street, B. V. (1999). Literacy and social change: The significance of social context in the development of literacy programmes. In D. A. Wagner (Ed.), *Future of literacy in a changing world* (pp. 55–72). Cresskill, NJ: Hampton Press.

Vasudevan, L. (2006). Looking for angles: Knowing adolescents by engaging with their multimodal literacy. *Journal of Adolescent & Adult Literacy, 50*(4), 252–256.

Yin, R. K. (2014). *Case study research: Design and methods 4th edition.* Thousand Oaks, CA: SAGE.

CHAPTER 14

REPATRIATING *DESAPARACIDOS* ACROSS SPACES

Suriati Abas
Indiana University, Bloomington

INTRODUCTION

Earlier studies in the field of linguistic landscape relied on Landry and Bourhis's (1997) definition of linguistic landscape (LL), which is limited to languages in public spaces within a given physical, geographical boundary. The shortcoming of this perspective is that it ignores the reality of space as dynamic, fluid, and mobile. However, an increasing number of studies have expanded the terrain of Laundry-Bourhis's seminal work to examine non-fixed or transient signs (e.g., Abas & Damico, 2018; Hanauer, 2015). Although Troyer (2012) and Chun (2014) had, earlier on, studied physical-digital spaces, both took on an etic perspective in their interpretations of publicly accessible languages. Thus, I aim to fill in the gap by "giving voices" (Silverman, 2014) to these signs. Building on the works of literacy scholars who found that there is a natural transcendence when users treated digital spaces as a continuity to the physical (e.g., Buck, 2012; Leander & Aplin, 2014), my study delved into two areas: the LL created

Negotiating Place and Space Through Digital Literacies: Research and Practice, pp. 259–274

by an American sign-creator named Ben Clark (pseudonym) who resides in Argentina, and the effect of his digital literacy practices leveraging the affordances of technology.

In using LL, I refer to signs that took the form of portraits used in physical spaces, photographed, posted onto digital spaces, and/or resemiotized across spaces. Given that each of these portraits are historically situated, I argue that their circulations across spaces function as teaching and learning tools for raising awareness of the autocracy of the past and present social situations in Argentina. The notion of teaching and learning is viewed from the perspective of Paulo Freire's (1970) critical pedagogy which involves making connections with broader exploitative social, political and structural contexts, to enable social change.

Drawing upon hybrid frameworks of nexus analysis (Scollon & Scollon, 2004), critical pedagogy (Freire, 1970), and Kress and van Leeuwen's (1996) concept of *interactional systems*, the following questions were addressed: (a) How does an American sign-creator attempt to teach people about the Argentine community that he lived with, through the construction of LL? (b) In what ways do particular digital literacy practices that the sign-creator employed challenge monolithic notions of space, his own identities and those of the Argentines?

HYBRID FRAMEWORKS: NEXUS ANALYSIS, CRITICAL PEDAGOGY AND INTERACTIONAL SYSTEMS

I employed hybrid frameworks as the LL data that I collected was shaped by the affordances of technology, moving across physical-digital spaces. Scollon and Scollon (2004) defined nexus analysis as "the mapping of the semiotic cycles of people, objects, and discourses" (p. x). In nexus analysis, the *sites of engagement* occur at the intersections of three elements: *historical body, discourses in place,* and *interaction order*.

Historical body is the background information. For instance, the portraits of *desaparacidos* (the disappeared) that Ben painted were meant to remember victims of Argentina's final military dictatorship (1976–1983), a period where an estimated 30,000 people were forcibly disappeared. The second element, *discourses in place,* which I referred to as *materials in place*, are images and/or texts found at two *sites of engagement*: the physical spaces of Buenos Aires and the digital space that Ben constructed. The last element, *interaction order*, considers social engagements initiated by the sign-creator on sign-viewers and vice versa. In Ben's daily activities, these elements interact with one another to form a *nexus of practice.*

To understand how *nexus of practice* functions as tools for teaching and learning, I refer to Freirean ideas of critical pedagogy. Briefly described as a pedagogical philosophy that challenges the "banking" model of education (a metaphor for a traditional transmission-oriented method of education), critical pedagogy promotes the exploration of real-world problems through reflection, dialogue, and problem-posing. Since the sign-creator's work centered on portraits of *desaparacidos* (the disappeared), Kress and van Leeuwen's (1996) concept of *interactional systems* afforded a means for unpacking how the portraits engaged with viewers. In this system, visual cues such as the direction of the *gaze* (or positioning of a character's eyes) which either conveys a *demand* (when a character is looking directly at viewers) or *offer* (when a character is looking away from viewers), have an impact on the viewer's meaning-making process (Kress & van Leeuwen, 1996).

METHODOLOGY: FOLLOWING THE OBJECTS

I applied the methodological approach of "following the objects" (Lash & Lury, 2007) to track repeated movements of "objects" and their transitions across spaces (see Figure 14.1). The process of data collection comprised two phases which, included the following:

Phase I

While I was in Buenos Aires, I wrote observational fieldnotes, collected photographic data, and conducted interviews with 100 participants on the streets to find out what was going on in the city, which was filled with images and/or texts specific to the 40th commemoration of The Day of Memory, Truth, and Justice. Ben was one of the participants who contributed to the cultivation of LL on that day. The multicolored portraits which he painted and carried down the streets were unique as all other signs of *desaparacidos* (the disappeared) came in somber black and white.

Phase II

Upon returning to the United States, I interviewed Ben several times via Skype. Through his Facebook posts, I discovered multiple online manifestations of the portraits that he had painted. They were produced and reproduced across sites and locales. In following the trajectory of these "objects," I traced their production within and across *nexus of practice*, circulation and mediation. To put this in terms of Scollon and Scollon's (2004) *nexus of practice*, the movements of "objects" can be summarized as in Figure 14.1.

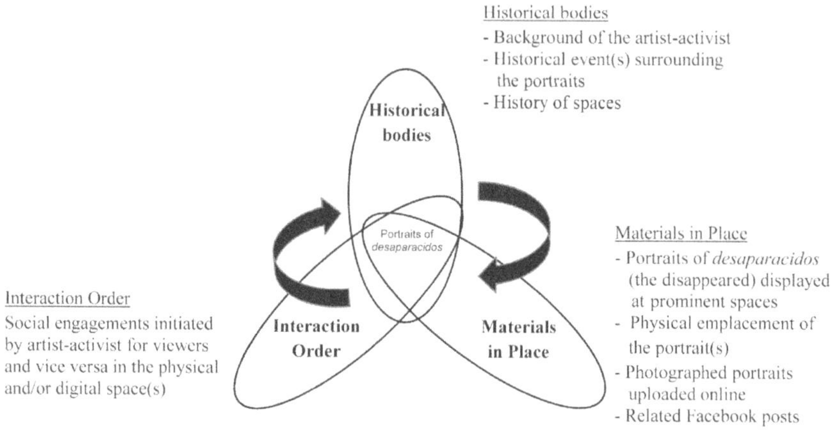

Figure 14.1. Movements of "objects" within and across *nexus of practice* (Adapted from Scollon & Scollon, 2004, p. 3; the arrows were included to indicate physical-digital transitions.)

FRAMING THE "OBJECTS" TO FOLLOW

The "objects" I followed were drawn from two events: the disappearance of Santiago Maldonado in 2017, and the 43 Mexican students in 2014, because they resonated with the historical experiences of the Argentines. First, I examined Ben's Facebook posts on those events. Then, I did online searches with the following keywords: *retratos* (portraits) *y desaparacidos* (the disappeared) and Ben's real name. In the next section, I discussed how Ben navigated across and within *sites of engagement*. I also highlighted the ways in which particular digital literacy practices that he employed challenge monolithic notions of space, his own identities, and those of the Argentines.

FINDINGS AND DISCUSSION

The following section brings together findings across physical and digital spaces.

SITES OF ENGAGEMENT #1 – PHYSICAL → DIGITAL SPACES

For site of engagement #1, Ben navigated linearly, promoting the disappearance of Santiago Maldonado from the physical to digital spaces. To teach people about the Argentine community that he lives with, he posed thought-provoking questions on one space, and re-entextualized the same question in another space. Viewed in the light of critical pedagogy, a question is a call to participate in the pursuit of knowledge. In this case, it is calling viewers to investigate Maldonado's disappearance. Dewhurst (2014) asserts that questioning is "a way of instigating learning with the possibility of transforming how people make sense of the world around them" (p. 69). The questions that Ben posed alongside the portrait that he painted contained particular meanings due to their geosemiotic emplacement, in front of the governmental building of *Casa Rosada*, at *Plaza de Mayo* (see Figure 14.2).

Figure 14.2. Portrait of Santiago Maldonado on the fence of *Casa Rosada* with a slip of note questioning the president at the top left-hand corner.

Posing Thought-Provoking Questions Across Spaces

The *historical bodies* surrounding *Plaza de Mayo* dated back from the years before the military dictatorship of 1976. Recognized as the main square of Buenos Aires, this space has been frequently used for social protests. One of the massive demonstrations that took place on October 17, 1945 involved the release of Juan Domingo Perón, a demagogue, who had been imprisoned. In another instance, during the 2001 economic crisis, people banged pots and pans to protest against devaluation of their savings when the Argentine pesos weakened. When Santiago Maldonado, an indigenous activist disappeared on August 1, 2017, thousands of people demonstrated in front of *Casa Rosada* demanding president Mauricio Macri to "return" him (For details, see https://www.nytimes.com/es/2017/09/06/donde-esta-santiago-maldonado/). For many weeks, this *site of engagement* constituted massive black and white portraits of Santiago Maldonado with the tagline, ¿Dónde está Santiago Maldonado? (Where is Santiago Maldonado?). The appearance of faces of the forcibly disappeared first materialized in 1979 and have since then been incorporated as a central method of protests of disappearances (Longoni, 2010). Daily news reported that Maldonado's disappearance sparked public outrage as it "revived bitter memories of Argentina's 1976-83 military dictatorship" (Goni, 2017).

On the day of Maldonado's disappearance, Ben was one of the sign-creators who contributed to the LL of Buenos Aires:

> I painted his (Santiago Maldonado) portrait the day I heard about his death. I posted it on facebook as a portrait and also presented it as a poster with his name above and the *Presente* (Present), that is characteristic of announcements of victims of state terrorism. The name is said and then *¡Presente!* (Present!). (Interview, 01/01/2017)

Similar to previously held protests, the emplacement of Maldonado's portrait, on the fence of *Casa Rosada,* held a special request from the state who denied culpability for the disappearance. Maldonado's direct *gaze* presented a *demand* for the disappeared to reappear alive (*aparición con vida*). The *demand* could concomitantly be viewed as an invitation to engage with Maldonado and support him in the activist work that led to his disappearance (see Figure 14.1).

***Dónde está?* (Where is he?).** The question, *Dónde está?* (Where is he?), implored through Maldonado's face, provoked further investigations on his whereabouts. His outward *gaze* and the accusatory question of *Dónde está?* by the fence of *Casa Rosada* instigated additional responses, harkening to the dark years during the last dictatorship, to other cases of disappearance after the reestablishment of democracy in 1983 (e.g., Jorge Julio López in 2006, Luciano Arruga in 2009). As Miller (2014) asserts, "meaning is ascribed to a space/place through the dominant historical narratives (in space/places) that are encumbered within specified sociopolitical, educational, cultural and economic policies and laws" (p. 124). Brian's inclusion of another question, *¿Cual es más fácil a descubrir, graffiti o el terrorismo del estado?* (Which is more difficult, to disappear, graffiti or state terrorism?), on the top left-hand corner of the portrait, created possibilities of seeing the everyday issue of graffiti in the capital city through new lenses.

¿Cual es más fácil a descubrir, graffiti o el terrorismo del estado?

(Which is more difficult, to disappear, graffiti, or state terrorism?). This question, as the sign-creator claimed, was added, in response to fleeting graffiti identified as "transgressive signs" (Scollon & Scollon, 2003) or signs that violated the norms, across the city of Buenos Aires.

> at the first march, one month after his disappearance, there was a lot of graffiti, scrawled on government buildings by someone ... purportedly by the unruly demonstrators ... but I never saw anyone doing this. So there was talk about all the destruction (not sure how it occurred in front of many hundreds of police...) but... they had to paint over the graffiti. So I went to the building where they were painting over the graffiti and had a sign that said, "*Es más fácil desaparecer a los seres humanos que desaparecer el graffiti*" (It is easier to disappear human beings than to disappear graffiti). (Interview, 01/01/2017)

Recognizing that the graffiti on this wall was emplaced on an inappropriate space, Ben repositioned his identities as an American, and a sign-creator, to a social activist based in Buenos Aires; he challenged the status quo by transforming the declarative statement, *Es más fácil desaparecer a los seres humanos que desaparecer el graffiti* (It is easier to disappear human beings than to disappear graffiti) on the wall, into a question. This question, which promoted *conscientização* or critical consciousness (Freire, 1970), encouraged viewers to interrogate the commonplace by challenging the unquestioned legitimacy of unequal power relationships between the state, its citizens and those responsible for state terrorism in the previous years. According to Freire (1970), posing and pursuing questions is a means of learning and teaching about social issues. This approach continued and circulated through the digital space that Ben constructed on his Facebook posts as a continuity to the physical space.

Re-entextualization of the Question

A month later, Ben employed re-entextualization where only the question, *Dónde está?* (Where is he?) was "moved" to the digital space (Briggs & Bauman, 1992). He posted his name, current location, and the same question, *Dónde está Santiago Maldonado?* (Where is Santiago Maldonado?) on a solid black background (see Figure 14.3). The simple yet powerful question that formed the *materials in place* had its *historical bodies* circulating across social networks within split seconds; a spontaneous campaign to claim the appearance of Maldonado was initiated using the same form in

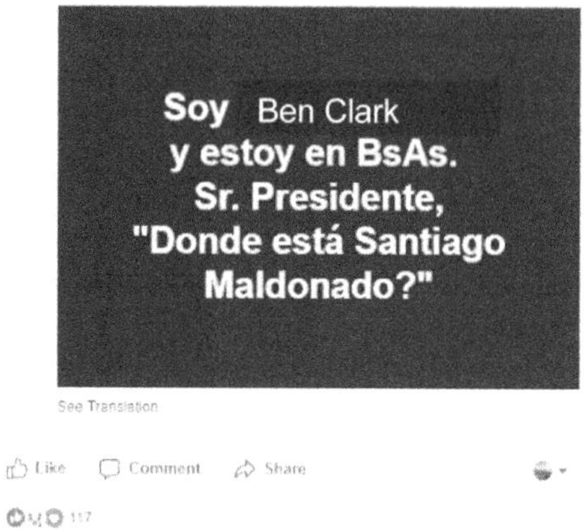

Figure 14.3. A message to all Facebook fans.

all social media (Facebook and twitter) posts. Participants simply mention their names, specify where they are or what they are doing at the time of writing the message, and ask: where is Santiago Maldonado? Argentina's history of political disappearances caused iterations of similar messages to continuously circulate to effect social change. Ben's partcipation could be seen as a form of traversal which Lemke (2001) posited as "catenations of meaningful elements" (p. 86) or extensions of what he did in the physical space, broadening the *sites of engagement* from *Plaza de Mayo* to the digital space on his Facebook. Table 14.1 summarizes the *sites of engagement*, movements of "objects" and the elements that formed the nexus of practice. Further details on sites of engagement #2 will be discussed below.

SITES OF ENGAGEMENT #2 – DIGITAL ↔ PHYSICAL

In *sites of engagement* #2, Ben navigated back and forth, from the digital to physical and vice versa. Drawing parallels with tens of thousands of people who disappeared when Argentina was under the coup (1976–1983), the sign-creator probed into a contemporary problem that happened in another community—the disappearance of 43 Mexican students (For details, see http://www.bbc.com/news/world-latin-america-35539727). Without much knowledge, as he claimed, he turned to the internet, researched the issue, and disseminated the information that he had obtained from the digital space (websites) to his very own Facebook page:

> Unfortunately, I was not aware of what had happened in Mexico until two months after the disappearances. A friend mentioned the Mexican students

Table 14.1.
Summary of Sites of Engagement, Movements and the Elements in Nexus of Practice

Sites of engagement [Event]	**Sites of engagement #1** [The disappearance of Santiago Maldonado]	**Sites of engagement #2** [The disappearance of 43 Ayotzinapa students]
Movement between spaces	Physical → Digital	Digital ↔ Physical
Summary of sites of engagement	• Interaction between sign-creator and sign-viewers	• Interaction between sign-creator and online semiotic resources • Interaction between sign-creator and students • Interaction between students, and "place"
Historical bodies	• *Plaza de Mayo*, a historical, physical space of protests • Ben's Facebook posts, a digital space	• *Plaza de Mayo*, a historical, physical space of protests • Ben's Facebook posts, a digital space • *Cinemplo Nostos*, a cinema in Colombia
Materials in Place	• Portrait of Santiago Maldonado • Facebook post on Santiago Maldonado	• Portraits of 43 missing Ayotzinapa students

> and asked if I was going to paint them. I began reading all I could about what had happened and also began posting the images on Facebook along with links to articles about them. (Interview, 05/01/2017)

Since he was teaching at the time when the disappearance in Ayotzinapa, Mexico, occurred, Ben took the opportunity to conduct lessons that went beyond painting. Integrating the expertise and interest that he had in portraits of *desaparacidos* (the disappeared), the sign-creator provided spaces for his students to engage in the sociopolitical situations to which he is presently residing (Buenos Aires, Argentina) by getting them to paint portraits of a recent case of disappearance involving students in another community as subjects:

> I was teaching painting at the time, and decided to assign the task of painting the portraits to my class as well, asking them to do research, etc ... quite a challenge for beginning painters. They became very engaged with this as the subject was fellow students and, when their paintings were finished they were displayed at the college. (Interview, 05/01/2017)

Each of the photographs given to the students for painting portraits had its own *historical bodies*—What happened to this person? Why did he/she disappear? Who is responsible for this? How is this related to Argentina? To acquaint students with issues surrounding Argentina's past, Ben created opportunities that connected the *materials in place* (portraits of 43 Aytozinapa students) to real-world context. His pedagogical approach in that sense included teaching how to "read the word and the world" (Freire, 1970).

> I brought a student group from Wisconsin to Argentina as well, for a ten day course in Spanish and political art and, of course, taught these kids, most of whom were not art students, about Ayotzinapa and the disappearances.... I took the students to the *Plaza de Mayo*, with the 45 portraits ... they met one of the founders of the *Madres de la Plaza de Mayo* (Mothers of the Plaza de Mayo), we marched with the *Madres* on their weekly *ronda* or rounds about the central structure there, the *Pirámide de Mayo*. (Interview, 30/12/2016) (see Figure 14.3)

The march down *Pirámide de Mayo*, the oldest national monument in Buenos Aires, offered these students a means for learning "with" places wherein Freire's pedagogy of organizing instruction around students' experiences were adopted. By circling around *Pirámide de Mayo*, students gained understanding of Argentina's past and present. These included recognizing key figures who have been campaigning for state-committed crimes against humanity and enforced disappearances (For details, see https://alborada.net/nora-cortinas-argentina-mothers-of-plaza-de-mayo/), and knowing that the main square of *Plaza de Mayo* is both historical and political *sites of engagement*.

Taken as a *nexus of practice*, these experiences provided a basis for praxis or informed actions aimed at eliminating injustices. From a Freirean perspective, the process of "humanization" or becoming more human by taking responsibility for transformation is only possible through *conscientização* or critical consciousness (Freire, 1970). Although this is already happening locally, at the university spaces that Abas and Damico (2018) investigated, the impact would be greater if it is motivated by those from outside of Argentina. Ben's Facebook pages has the potential for eliciting public participation as it raises societal concerns, reaching out to followers who may not be in the country.

CHALLENGING MONOLITHIC NOTIONS OF IDENTITIES, SPACES, AND COMMUNITIES

Apart from raising awareness on past atrocities that haunted the Argentine community, the circulations of signs within and across the nexus of practice (see Figure 14.1) reflected the dynamic LL. They are not merely portraits that were painted, photographed and disseminated to the world. Rather, the existence of such LL espoused particular ways of thinking about identities, spaces, and communities that were made possible with the affordances of technology, or rather, factors that contributed to the types of interactions using technology (e.g., Facebook).

SOCIAL IMAGINARIES OF "SELF" AND "OTHERS"

The LL that Ben cultivated in a temporal space challenged social imaginaries of "self" and "others". Social imaginaries refers to "the way a given people imagine their collective social life" (Taylor, 2000), are often represented by virtue of how individuals typically position themselves in the world. Given the fact that the sign-creator is American, during his social encounters, many questioned the connections between the portraits that he painted and, his personal self:

> One of the first questions I invariably run into at exhibitions or actions from Latin Americans is, "Why are you, a Yankee, making a memorial to Latin Americans? Did you live here? You have relatives here, etc?" I am not Latin American, of course, and I also have no relatives that are or were, and I am only at a preliminary stage of learning Spanish (unfortunately!). So a side benefit of the work is that people in Latin America must question their notions of what "a Yankee", is or thinks or does. And they end up calling me their Yankee friend, or Yankee brother or whatever…with the irony of course that the real meaning is "the single Yankee who is my friend or is my brother, "a fact that amazes them somewhat more than it does me. (Interview, 30/12/2016)

From the *historical bodies* presented earlier in the chapter, Ben is a rare instance. Many of the memorials, works of human rights and activists in Argentina, were championed by natives who either experienced the brutal dictatorship and/or had families and friends who disappeared. The *interaction order* that this American sign-creator had with Argentines and those residing in Buenos Aires in the physical-digital LL, to a certain extent, transformed his initial perceptions of the "others" or community where he is currently living. As he claimed,

> Likewise, any notions I had or may had about "Latin Americans" have been washed away. My ignorance is corrected by interactions, by living with these people, meeting the diverse group with backgrounds from many indigenous peoples and also from Europe, Russia, Asia, etc. "What is an *Argentino* or an Uruguyan?" The only answer that is somewhat accurate is that they are people who live in these countries and have citizenship there. (Interview, 30/12/2016)

By navigating across multiple *sites of engagement* (see Table 14.1), Ben inherently adopted critical pedagogy. In particular, the real-life experiences enable his students to obtain better understanding of the sociopolitical situations attached to the painting of portraits.

A PORTRAIT WITH MANY "LIVES"

Through the physical-digital LL, Ben bore a portrait with many "lives." One possible reason to account for this was the fluidity of transforming each of them into different dimensions and places:

> I enlarged the painting to a poster a meter by a meter and a half and carried this to the Cabildo, to the Ministry of Justice, to the *Casa Rosada*, to *Congresso*, to all three major *encuentros* about Santiago Maldonado held in the *Plaza de Mayo*, and it has been to universities with me and taken by teachers to schools. Photographs of these actions or uses are online and are widely circulated. So, one small painting has a lot of lives, extensions, effect. It is quite amazing to me. (Interview, 30/12/2016)

While typically paintings of portraits remained dormant in the spaces where the sign-creator chose to place them, those painted by Ben circulated within and across *nexuses of practice*. His openness to sharing them resulted in mutiple series of iterations. As Ben explained:

> Students used them as book covers and for assignments, while teachers in *escuela abierto* (public school) reused them as teaching resources. Some people even reproduced them as Facebook profile. I sent images of the 43 portraits to every Mexican human rights group I could access online, to the Ayotzinapa *escuela*, HIJOS Mexico, etc. I have no idea what any of these people did with them. But one image I attach is from a cinematic school that altered my portraits a bit making posters they set up as an installation in a theater, attaching them to the empty seats. (Interview, 30/12/2016)

The same portraits held at the historic space of *Plaza de Mayo* (see Figure 14.2) "travelled" to a another *site of engagement* in Columbia, at *Cinemplo Nostos* (see Figure 14.3). Through its emplacement in a cinema, the significance of the portraits were artistically represented. Each of the faces communicated a *demand* which suggest some form of participation or invitation to take some actions for their disappearance. Positioned at the back of chairs as if they were in a classroom equipped with a screen, the status of the 43 Ayotzinapa students as *desaparacidos* (the disappeared) was magnified. The movements of these "objects" from Argentina to Columbia suggest global concerns. Since the 1970s and 1980s, the problem of forced disappearances were prevalent in Latin American countries under the governance of right-wing military dictatorships ("Latin America's Disappeared," 2014). In Colombia, reconstructing the immediate and remote past is, to this day, an essential practice due to the exponential rise in human rights violations (Villalón, 2016). With the affordances of technology, the production of itinerant space for memorial installation (see Figure 14.5) was made possible. Through Ben's Facebook posts, portraits were transported digitally in the gallery folder, replicated, printed by the Columbians who were involved in the memorial project and pasted onto a fixed, geographical location.

Figure 14.4. Students from America participated in the weekly rounds at Plaza de Mayo, in Argentina, carrying portraits of the 43 Mexican students who disappeared.

Figure 14.5. Portraits of the 43 disappeared Mexicans used by Cinempleo Nostos, in Columbia, to make a memorial installation for a film about the Mexican students. (https://www.facebook.com/cinempleo)

Another affordance of the digital technology as seen in Figure 14.4 and 14.5 is that its use facilitated a collective process of reconstructing historical realities within (e.g., at *Plaza de Mayo*) and outside the contexts of dictatorship (e.g., in Colombia). These historical realities took the form of *materials in place*, or portraits of *desaparacidos* (the disappeared) painted and digitally disseminated. Together with the *interaction order* which involved circling *Plaza de Mayo*, the portraits and the entire *nexus of practice* promote the social act of reimagining histories to raise critical consciousness.

CONNECTING AND (RE)CONNECTING COMMUNITIES

Although major cities in Argentina are replete with visual reminders of atrocities carried out by the dictatorship, traditional boundaries of engaging in past memories traversed digital spaces. The fluidity of movements in the LL resulted in the production of an "imagined community" (Anderson,

1983) where members who may not know one another face-to-face, were connected and for some, (re)connected online based on a shared sense history:

> My Facebook page ... the [online] memorial has connected many people who would not otherwise have met. I have met hundreds of people in person but online, many thousands. At the same time, as we interact, these people are meeting and conversing with each other. many like-minded people, who may have experienced these horrors ... meet one another. It becomes a nexus of hub ... for people who care about it, are related. It is an invitation for conversation and exchange. (Interview, 30/12/2016)

Since the movement primarily happened within a shared digital space (in the form of responses to Facebook posts), the *interaction orders* between the sign-creator and his Facebook followers revolved around postings on contemporary issues and informal discussions. Unlike conducting face-to-face discussions, there is no limit to the response time. The unrestricted participation time could only be afforded in digital spaces.

IMPLICATIONS FOR RESEARCH AND PRACTICE

This chapter outlined selected works of an American sign-creator who has been actively involved in the construction of a LL in Argentina. As aforementioned, I used the term LL to refer to signs that took the form of portraits painted for a geographic place, photographed to be posted onto digital spaces, and/or resemiotized within and/or across spaces. In examining the LL, the *nexus of practice* was seen as a blending of the physical, geographical places and digital spaces. The language which comprised images and/texts in the spaces described above is not arbitrary, "rather, there is a goal to understand the system, the messages it delivers or could deliver, about societies, people, the economy, policy, class, identities" (Shohamy & Gorter, 2009, p. 3). Thus, the question of production (LL by whom?) and of reception (LL for whom?) (Backhaus, 2007) is germane in all LL studies.

Although findings from the study showed a clear delineation of how circulations across spaces function as teaching and learning tools (see Table 14.1), the *interaction order* within and across *sites of engagements* were far more complicated in reality than those summarized in Figure 14.1. While there is a nascent body of scholarship that studied physical-digital spaces employing connective ethnographies (e.g., Leander & Lovvorn, 2006; Warner, 2017), the embedded complexity and dynamic nature of movements across spaces foregrounded a methodological challenge, especially with huge data sets. This could be further complicated in a study where the researcher does not occupy the same geographic location as the participants.

In relation to classroom practice, following the pedagogy employed by the sign-creator involves a paradigm shift from commonplace assumptions of the educator as "a sage on the stage" to a "guide on the side." The merits of this approach is that it creates dialogic spaces for interrogating, questioning and learning about how people think and live. While generally viewed as "teaching resistance" (Hardin, 2001), learners should be taught to participate from a detached standpoint. Given the affordances of technology, both educators and learners could coconstruct knowledge together in a safe, shared digital space. Much like the sign-creator described above, learning should be expanded beyond geographical locations and even within and/or across digital spaces.

ACKNOWLEDGMENT

The author wishes to thank Ben Clark (pseudonym) for participating in the study, sharing the photographs and giving consent to use them.

REFERENCES

Abas, S., & Damico, J. (2018). The language of activism. Representations of social justice in a university space in Argentina. In N. Avineri, L. R. Graham, E. Johnson, R. Riner, & J. Rosa (Eds.), *Language and social justice in practice* (pp. 157–165). United States: Routledge.

Anderson, B. (1983). *Imagined communities: Reflections on the origin and spread of nationalism*. London, England: Verso Books.

Backhaus, P. (2007). *Linguistic landscapes: Comparative study of urban multilingualism in Tokyo*. Clevedon, England: Multilingual Matters.

Briggs, C. L., & R. Bauman. (1992). Genre, intertextuality, and social power. *Journal of Linguistic Anthropology*, *2*(2). 131–172.

Buck, A. (2012). Examining digital literacy practices on social network sites. *Research in the Teaching of English*, *47*(1), 9–38.

Chun, C. W. (2014). Mobilities of a linguistic landscape at Los Angeles City Hall Park. *Journal of Language and Politics, 13*(4), 1569–2159.

Dewhurst, M. (2014). *Social justice art: A framework for activist art pedagogy*. Cambridge, MA: Harvard Education Press.

Freire, P. (1970). *Pedagogy of the oppressed*. New York, NY: Continuum.

Goni, U. (2017, October 21). Argentina—Political storm: The body of missing activist Santiago Maldonado found in icy river. *Dawn News (Argentina)*. Retrieved from https://www.europe-solidaire.org/spip.php?article42291

Hardin, J. M. (2001). *Opening spaces: Critical theory and resistance pedagogy in composition*. Albany, NY: Suny Press.

Hanauer, D. I. (2015). Occupy Baltimore: A linguistic landscape analysis of participatory social contestation in an American city. In R. Rani & S. Ben Selim (Eds.), *Conflict, exclusion and dissent in the linguistic landscape* (pp. 207–222). United States: Palgrave Macmillian.

Kress, G., & van Leeuwen, T. (2006). *Reading images*. London, England: Routledge.

Landry, R., & Bourhis, R. Y. (1997). Linguistic landscape and ethnolinguistic vitality: An empirical study. *Journal of Language and Social Psychology, 1*(16), 23–49.

Lash, S., & Lury, C. (2007). *Global culture industry: The mediation of things*. Cambridge, England: Polity. doi:10.1177/17468477080030030603

Latin America's disappeared. (2014, August 29). *Telesur.* Retrieved from https://www.telesurtv.net/english/analysis/Latin-Americas-Disappeared-20140829-0068.html

Leander, K. M., & Aplin, B. (2014). "After apple picking" and fetal pigs: The multiple social spaces and embodied rhythms of digital literacy practices. In C. Compton-Lilly & E. Halverson (Eds.), *Time and space in literacy research*. United States: Routledge.

Leander, K. M., & Lovvorn, J. F. (2006). Literacy networks: following the circulation of texts, bodies, and objects in the schooling and online gaming of one youth. Cognition and Instruction, *24*(3), 291–340.

Lemke, J. L. (2001). Discursive Technologies and social organization of meaning. *Folia Linguistica, 35*(1–2), 79–96.

Longoni, A. (2010). Photographs and silhouettes: Visual politics in Argentina. *Afterall, 25*, 1–10.

Miller, S. (2014). Spatializing social justice research in English education. In C. Compton-Lilly & E. Halverson (Eds.), *Time and space in literacy research*. United States: Routledge.

Scollon, R., & Scollon, S. W. (2004). *Nexus analysis: Discourse and the emerging Internet.* New York, NY: Routledge.

Shohamy, E., & Gorter, D. (Eds.). (2009). *Linguistic landscape: Expanding the scenery*. New York, NY: Routledge

Silverman, D. (2014). *Interpreting qualitative data.* London, England: SAGE.

Taylor, C. (2000). Modernity and difference. In P. Gilroy, L. Grossberg, & A. McRobbie (Eds.), *Without guarantees: In honor of Stuart Hall*. New York, NY: Verso.

Troyer, R. (2012). English in the Thai linguistic netscape. *World Englishes, 31*(1), 93–112.

Villalón, R. (2016). The complexities of memory, truth and justice processes—Art and cultural resistance. *Latin American Perspectives, 210*(43)5, 3–11.

Warner, J. (2017). *Adolescents new literacies with and through mobile phones*. New York, NY: Peter Lang.

Where is Santiago Maldonado? Argentina searches for missing protester. (2017, August). *BBC News*. Retrieved from http://www.bbc.com/news/world-latin-america-41066685

CHAPTER 15

VIRTUAL CARRELS

(Re)Thinking Space(s) for Professional Development

Beth A. Buchholz
Appalachian State University

Sarah Vander Zanden
University of Northern Iowa

Nicholas E. Husbye
University of Wisconsin—Milwaukee

Christy Wessel Powell
Purdue University

Julie E. Rust
Millsaps College

INTRODUCTION

The use of online resources to support professional development for higher education faculty is an established notion (Sherer, Shea, & Kristensen, 2003), though it is argued emphasis needs to shift from static online content

Negotiating Place and Space Through Digital Literacies: Research and Practice, pp. 275–294

to faculty-generated content (Cohn, Stewart, Theisen, & Comins, 2016) and sustained support systems (Anthony, Lawrence, & Reed, 2017). In this chapter, we move from thinking about online resources to consider the kind of space(s) supporting professional, practice-based learning for faculty members. Geographer Doreen Massey (2013) has argued "space" presents a fundamentally social/political question: "How are we going to live[-work-be] together?" (para. 9), and for us this became an invitation to consider how we might *practice space differently* in order to enact more sustainable material ways of being faculty members at geographically dispersed institutions. We explore how we leveraged digital literacy practices to create "virtual carrels," a digital approximation of the boisterous, generative space shared as graduate students that nurtured scholarly body and soul through camaraderie, reciprocity, critical questioning, and practicality.

CONTEXT(S)

While working on our doctorates, we shared a workspace divided into 16 carrels (cubicles) with horizontal filing cabinets delineating our "offices" from the adjacent hallway. Five-foot tall walls cordoned off each desk, marking the space where each of us worked, vented, planned, talked, wrote, conferred, read, laughed, schemed, cried, and consumed many cups of coffee. The physical/material set-up of the space, with its dizzying array of borders and walls, suggested a very different set of social relations and practices than those enacted by users of the carrels (and producers) of the space. In a testament to Massey's (2005) conceptualization of space as "relations of embedded practices" (p. 10), we actively practiced a very different kind of space, one allowing for the forced negotiation of intersecting trajectories. The carrels may have offered a static location, but the space practiced and produced relied on movement, multiplicities, and relationality.

Formal meetings amongst carrel users were rarely planned; rather, a more typical pattern of interaction was rooted in the continual comings and goings of people and artifacts: "the contemporaneous existence of plurality of trajectories: a simultaneity of stories-so-far" (Massey, 2005, p. 12). Each of us, moving along trajectories and traversing along boundaries, at times together and at times alone, inhabited and produced a space responsive to the needs of individuals as well as the collective—in both personal and professional capacities. In the carrels, space and time were intimately connected: space was not the collection of furniture nor the collective square footage but instead cut through the myriad of stories in which we were all living at any one moment. Movement, not stasis, was the norm; the movement of humans, artifacts, ideas, and emotions. This movement continually reshaped the space over our days, months, and years together, providing a sense of "aliveness" invited and evoked by "good community design" (Wenger, McDermott, & Snyder, 2002, p. 54).

Each of us experienced this *aliveness* in slightly different ways, but it was rooted in a sense that anything could happen at the crossroads that were the carrels. If uninhabited by others, it was a space to rest, reflect, read and think, with office chairs pointing deskward toward solitude, head bent. These same carrels could be a semiprivate conference space with students, or, with a passerby or fellow writer's arrival, they morphed into a collective space, office chairs wheeled outward toward conversation, heads up. The carrels were part of our development as scholars: a place for learning, faltering, questioning, complaining, planning, playing with ideas and trying on new identities. Thus, we sought to resurrect and reshape this space in our current practices.

FRAMING SPACE

We begin by situating how we are thinking about/with *space* in this chapter. Massey (2005) moves us from conceptualizing space as a physical or immaterial *container* of people and artifacts (e.g., a classroom, an online forum, a library) to space as the product of our social relations and connections with each other. In the latter understanding, space is the "product of interrelations" (p. 9), where these relations "are understood as embedded practices" (p. 10). Thus, we produce space rather than exist in space, or, as Massey asserts, we *practice* space. Space is not a flat surface we cross in moving from "here" to "there"—nor is space collapsible or reducible with the emergence of digital technologies, but space is alive, political, and open—a "pincushion of a million stories ... in which we are all living at any moment" (Massey, 2013, p. 2). Whereas "time" is the dimension of succession, Massey's "space" is the dimension of multiplicity and movement. These elements of aliveness, heterogeneity, and relationality are central to the "productiveness of spatiality" (Massey, 2005, p. 94).

As literacy education researchers, we are particularly drawn to scholars whose work has taken up generative views of "space," situating it as something more than a passive, predetermined context for learning (e.g., Leander & Sheehy, 2004; Mills & Comber, 2013; Moje, 2004). If we see space as produced anew in each moment people engage in social relations and literacy practices, a learning space is never static but is iteratively (re)produced across minutes, seconds, and hours. Space is produced when people post and comment on social media, just as space is produced when a teacher and child sit together to read a book. A space, then, "is neither a container for always-ready constituted identities, nor a completed closure of holism.... For the future to be open, space must be open too" (Massey, 2005, p. 12). It is this opening up, this enlivening of learning space(s), that offers possibilities for the emergence of new interrelations, actions, and identities for learners of all ages.

CHANGING SPACE(S): LEARNING TO BE-WRITE-TEACH-RESEARCH "HERE"

Over a series of years we each made the move from our shared graduate institution (and those shared carrels) to five different colleges/universities across the country. This move from students to professors involved geographic as well as complex identity shifts, with each of us working to negotiate the new terrains of our departments, institutions, and fields. We each engaged in the highly emotional process of learning how to work, live, write, research, and teach in a new "community of practice" (Lave & Wenger, 1991). Attributed to Lave and Wenger's work studying learning in "natural" settings (e.g., workplace, cultural groups), the term communities of practice (CoP) is rooted in Scribner and Cole's (1981) "practice account" of literacy where a practice "refers to socially developed and patterned ways of using technology and knowledge to accomplish tasks" (p. 236) based on the interactions and interrelations between community members.

Becoming a full participant in any community necessitates more than acquiring discrete knowledge (e.g., reading a handbook, attending an orientation, following rules); it is about learning and taking up the practices, values, identities, and ways of being accepted by the community. Newcomers develop a "changing understanding of practice over time" (Lave, 1991, p. 68) that leads to assuming the identity of a full participant. We find ourselves having to learn how to be recognized as knowledgeable across communities: classrooms, academic programs, departments, colleges/schools, universities, local communities, and academic fields. Each of these communities practice space in very different ways, offering diverse—and sometimes conflicting—practices, values, and ways of being a scholar 'here' in this space/place. The term "landscape of practice" better captures our movement "interact[ing] in a landscape made up of multiple communities," where the landscape necessarily consists of "boundaries, peripheries, overlaps, connections and encounters" (Wenger, 1998, p. 118; see also Wenger-Trayner et al., 2014). Within this frame, our professional development is not directed toward a singular center of expertise or a stable identity; rather, it is multidirectional: knowledges and identities are created in the boundaries traversed within/across the landscape as we learn to serve, teach, and research at/across our institutions.

METHODS

Participants and Context

We are a group of five self-identified early career literacy education faculty members working at a range of institutions (public regional, public research, and small private liberal arts) geographically dispersed across the United States. Collectively we represent a diverse scope of experiences in academia with group members having from 1–7 years of experience in faculty positions. In late May 2017, we arranged a virtual meeting (via Google Meet) to discuss plans for turning a recent AERA symposium into a coauthored manuscript. We never ended up discussing the symposium or a manuscript. Instead, our conversation focused on a seemingly new "turn" in the literacy research field toward posthuman, poststructural theories and postqualitative methodologies. We animatedly discussed our recent experiences attending sessions focused on research informed by/with these theories and expressed a common curiosity (and crankiness) about what these theories meant for the field as well as our own work. What emerged from this virtual meeting was a shared Google Drive folder ("Cranky Pedagogies") with a single subfolder ("Readings"). Our aim was to read a couple of foundational posthuman, poststructual pieces and to virtually meet again in two weeks to discuss. Subsequent biweekly meetings (60–90 minutes) became a part of our scholarly summer routine.

Our time together generally began with an initial "catching up" conversation, which featured an in-the-moment share of emotional states, personal and professional events, and current stressors or successes. We, then, often moved into discussion of an article we had read, which shunted back and forth between questions, critique, and "What might be useful here?" Dialogue about an evolving writing project often followed and featured reporting out progress, questions from the lead authors of the piece, and a dividing up of sections and future assignments. Though there were no formal leadership roles, Nicholas often took the lead in pulling together loose threads during a meeting, thoughtfully synthesizing our production of knowledge, and always propelling us with, 'How should/can we move forward with this work?' By the fall semester, our shared readings turned to shared data analysis and collaborative writing of a conference proposal, and our Google Drive subfolders multiplied (e.g., "Chapter/Article Calls," "Problems of Practice," "Writing," "Meeting Videos").

The meeting subcomponents described above did not exist in discrete categories. A puppy or child jumping into one of our laps during a virtual meeting, for instance, might shift the trajectory of our conversation. As friends, many of us had already been engaged in texting from time to time, which particularly amped up when we attended conferences. However, one day during the summer, we received a group text from Christy sharing her writing goals. She quickly replied, apologizing that the text had been meant for Nicholas. She explained they tried to keep each other accountable by checking in via text with goals. When the rest of us expressed interest in joining in, she and Nicholas included us in their supportive practice, and group texting became another central aspect of our collaboration. This channel of communication evolved to meet a myriad of functions, from scheduling to problem solving to venting about a stressful day.

Data Collection

Across our time of working together, we have utilized four key digital channels to produce space differently: (1) texting (alphabetic text, "stickers," emojis, GIFs), (2) Google Meet (video), (3) Google Docs (writing, commenting), and (4) Google Drive (file sharing). In terms of data collection, Google Docs and Google Drive offer an artifactual, historical record. With hundreds of documents organized across a range of subfolders, our shared Google Drive folder reflects our varied interests across time. More specifically, Google Docs, with saved "histories" (versions) and "comments," offer additional rich data points. Artifacts from Google Meet include video recordings of some meetings as well as notes recorded on paper and in Google Docs. Finally, we have archived our group text messages, which, at the time of writing this chapter, spanned over 180 pages in a PDF file.

Data Analysis

After 6 months engaging in the collaboration, each group member wrote an analytical memo about the experience of participating in this community across time utilizing the various digital channels. In part, we wrote to attend to the "value" of our emerging community of practice. Wenger and colleagues (2002) argue "a key element of designing for value is to encourage community members to be explicit about the value of the community throughout its lifetime" (p. 60). Though many faculty development organizations/structures attempt to predetermine value at the outset, a more organic process is one where communities "create events, activities, and relationships that help their potential value emerge and enable [the community] to discover new ways to harvest it" (p. 60). Our explicit attempt to articulate the value of our shared practices and space(s) allow us to (re) design for even more aliveness moving forward.

We consider writing analytic memos to be a method of discovery, interpretation, and analysis (Richardson & Lockridge, 2004). Writing individual memos and reading across each other's memos offered a formal opportunity for sense-making (Denzin, 2014). Combing through the data collected over time, we considered frequencies, themes, and patterns in relation to two analytical questions: (1) In what ways did we as scholars leverage digital literacy practices to design a professional, practice-based learning community where space could be practiced differently? (2) What kind(s) of space(s) was/were produced? Ultimately, in explicating the value of the community, we found ourselves engaged in an iterative process of moving between—or entangling—data (artifacts collected across time), lived experiences (embodied, affective), memos, and theory.

DATA AND THEORY: AN ENMESHED SPACE

As literacy education scholars sharing a common academic lineage through our preparation, our philosophies and practices in teaching, and the questions we ask about learning and education in our research, we bring particular lenses to understanding our larger collaboration. As we explore the ways in which Massey asserts space is the projection of embedded practices, our understanding of these practices is grounded in social theories of literacy. Literacy practices conceptualized in this chapter, are best understood "as existing in the relations between people, within groups and communities, rather than as a set of properties residing in individuals" (Barton & Hamilton, 2000, p. 8), echoing Massey with the added caveat of considering the use of written language and how it, in the case of our digital collaborations, facilitated the cocreation of space. Based on this theoretical framing, we refer to "[digital] literacy practices" and "space-making practices" interchangeably throughout the chapter. It is critical to note this framing moved the analysis from a focus on digital channels (e.g., tools, software) to digital practices.

By bringing data and theory into conversation, we identified four digital literacy practices that enabled us to produce—and practice—space differently betwixt and between the various channels: (1) maintaining scholarly-ness, (2) assembling knowledge, (3) maintaining community, and (4) bearing witness. Through these practices, we produced space for new possibilities for collective and individual identities with varied intensities. Table 15.1 offers an overview of the four digital practices (rows) and four channels (columns) identified during the analysis process. It is educative at the outset to holistically see the complexity in how these four key practices and channels produced a multiplicity of routes for and levels of participation in our CoP. The table highlights interactions between/across practices and channels, visually demonstrating practices were not isolated to a single channel. Practices (rows) varied in intensity across channels (columns) as represented by varying shades from light gray indicating less activity, to darker gray indicating more activity.

Table 15.1.
Intensity of Literacy Practices That "Produced Space Differently" Across Digital Channels

Practice 1: Maintaining Scholarly-ness				
Practice 2: Assembling Knowledge				
Practice 3: Maintaining Community				
Practice 4: Bearing Witness				
	Texting	Google Meet/ Video	Google Doc/Writing	Google Drive/File Sharing

Our analytical entanglements and insights are organized as follows: First, we *disentangle* the data by identifying, describing, and theorizing four key space-making digital literacy practices emerging across our practice-based, professional learning community. Then, we *(re)engtangle* the data by offering a vignette of one moment/interaction in our shared history to examine how interconnected, intersecting digital literacy practices (i.e., relations of embedded practices) produced (im)material space(s) for learning new ways of being literacy education scholars. The aim in using this structure is to delineate individual practices, providing some rough borders/edges of separation but then to contextualize and complicate this artificial separation by providing a vignette of these intertwined practices in action. If space is the product of interrelations (Massey, 2005), we must move beyond the labeling of individual practices—and individual digital channels/tools—to consider the relations of these practices and channels, as well as the space(s) produced by these interrelations. As part of this process, we recursively turn to Massey's theories to understand how these practices produced space differently and what effect these new spatial relations had on our daily lives and trajectories as faculty members.

Four Space-Making Digital Literacy Practices

Practice 1: Maintaining Scholarly-ness. Our local spaces greatly impact the ways we enact scholarly identities; for those of us at institutions with higher teaching expectations, the time required to stay abreast on developments in the field is scarce. Furthermore, for those of us at institutions with shrinking faculties or who may not have colleagues who actively share our interests, the ability to engage in collaborative exploration of new work is equally scarce. Essential to our coming together was a curation of common readings about poststructural inquiry. Google Drive assisted in our curation, housing a collection of readings, writings, and notes documenting our collaboration. These readings became the bedrock of our collective work, read individually and discussed via video during biweekly meetings. Google Meet allowed opportunities to talk through new ideas and applications to our work. Text messages played an important role in making sense of the new directions our work was taking, as we encountered elements of shared texts or articles, these were often shared with the group via text message (e.g., "This seems relevant, yes?" with a link to an article uploaded to shared Google Drive folder).

Having a face-to-face community actively, publicly engaged in writing agendas was not common, which made safeguarding time for writing difficult. So, early in the collaboration we moved beyond consumption to production as well. While we had often collaborated in graduate school and, to some extent in our careers afterward, Google Docs provided a way to write together and come to understand *how* we enacted our writerly identities, revealing our individual processes as we sought to establish a literature review or tease out nuance in an existing idea. For example, Figure 15.1 illustrates an instance of cowriting in which Sarah, Julie, and Christy were collaborating on a paper. In the process of copy/pasting the entire paper into a new Google Doc, colleagues' "comments"—in essence, markers of their collaborative thinking—were lost. This loss produced a sense of anxiety and disorientation. In response, Christy painstakingly copy/pasted previous comments into the new document to continue to write with Sarah and Julie. Bringing their comments to the new document maintained the line of thinking and collaborative idea expansion their comments held. In Figure 15.1, the dialogic nature of the practice of scholarly maintenance is highlighted. This work more widely constituted the maintenance and stabilization of our identities as scholars; mediated through digital channels, they opened/created space immediately unlike those physical spaces we routinely inhabited. Graduate school trained us each to be scholars, but it did not train us to be scholars, *and* teachers (with heavy course loads), *and* committee members, *and* grant writers, *and* resources for local schools. Collaborative writing projects produced

Figure 15.1. Collaborative writing and theorizing in a shared Google Doc provided opportunities for the practice of *maintaining scholarly-ness* as well as the (re)construction of particular writerly identities.

a commitment and accountability to maintaining scholarly-ness group members desperately needed amidst long "to-do lists" that often crowded out the space and time necessary to write.

Practice 2: Assembling Knowledge. A pressing need in our various roles is fast, reliable information and resources. The practice of assembling knowledge (Gilster, 1997) foregrounds a temporal component, one that carries the expectation of an answer or useful suggestion. Much like Grice's (1975) maxims for conversation, the relevant response is timely, connected, and matches the quantity and quality of the inquiry. Collectively we used language across several channels, text, Google Docs, comments, and so forth, seeking insights to address individual or community responses around particular questions. We worked within a previously curated 'crowd' so the knowledge generated could be trusted. Examples of assembling knowledge included requests for citations, start-up fund usage, reference materials for tenure proceedings, information about how to best navigate a media interview, and so forth. Importantly, when posing a problem or question (implicitly or explicitly), an action, answer, and/or suggestion from the group was largely expected. For example, when Julie explicitly requested "hints" for engaging fellow faculty members in Twitter chats as a form of professional development, group members provided a range of concrete suggestions almost immediately (see Figure 15.2). Wenger and colleagues (2002) argue communities of practice are more suitable for this kind of "collective knowledge stewardship" compared to other organizational structures (e.g., academic departments, professional development workshops), and as a community grows, the development of a "systematic body of knowledge that can be easily accessed" becomes increasingly important (p. 59). As the group needs shifted and stakes for professional success remained high, turning to an external, trusted group of colleagues

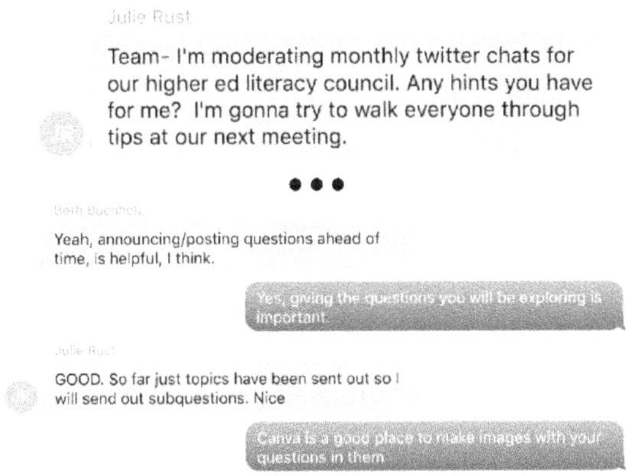

Figure 15.2. The practice of *assembling knowledge* was often initiated through a group member posing a specific question/problem across one or more digital channels with the expectation of an action, answer, and/or suggestion from the group.

offered each of us sounding boards and resource repositories not always found in our respective locations.

Practice 3: Maintaining Community. The glue holding our collaboration together over the busy summer months and the arc of the semester was the practice of community maintenance. Through various channels communication consistently functioned as a way to support one another in meeting individual and collective goals, both scholarly and otherwise. Community maintenance included frequent texts as accountability check-ins (e.g., biweekly Google Meetings structured around shared reading and writing goals; morning texts stating, "What goals are people setting for today?"), opportunities to touch base regularly via friendly pings often laced with humor (e.g. inspirational or funny/relevant GIFs), or as acts of caring (e.g., checking with Beth to be sure she had prioritized lunch in her busy day after skipping the week before, or confirming Julie's commitment to limit advising sessions to 20 minutes). In this way those on the text thread regularly connected, and knew others thought and cared about their well-being. Other examples include weekly shared personal and professional goals on a continuous running Google Doc in which members could bob in and out of when relevant, and the "No Committee" (see vignette below). Over months of meetings and collaborative work, the thrown-togetherness of our place (Massey, 2005) supported engaging with and negotiating how we practiced digital spaces.

Practice 4: Bearing Witness. Over the duration of our collaboration, we have borne witness to one another's experiences and have visibly offered empathy for and acceptance of those experiences through digital channels. From a psychological perspective bearing witness relates to lightening the emotional load an experience or story may hold. Often linked to trauma, bearing witness offers participants, both teller and receiver, validation that something, whatever it may be shared exists-happened-matters. In our almost daily communication, we documented situational administrivia, demands upon our time, teaching strategies, research dilemmas, and deep concern for our profession, usually inextricably interwoven with affect (e.g., annoyance, guilt, humor, worry). One particularly affective example of this was the "#purejoy" text messages exchanged periodically that made 'public' some of the microfrustrations of faculty life (see Figure 15.3).

The practice of bearing witness was most intensely embedded in the text thread (see Table 15.1). Two examples of the ways bearing witness functioned among the group through texting were balancing personal concerns and professional commitments. Given the constraints of our respective institutional locations, untenured, tenured-female, "JR faculty" reaching out prior to decision making facilitated individual and group practice of space in different ways on many occasions. Figure 5.3 shows a sample of "#purejoy" and the opportunities for sharing/validating/hearing/seeing small moments of faculty minutiae that helped to lighten the emotional load. A key component of bearing witness was glimpsing how group members struggled to "negotiate intersecting trajectories" (Massey, 2005, p. 154) in their lives, and, to in some way, participate in the negotiation process itself. This produced a space where the political and the personal were intimately intertwined, and the local context (with localized practices and ways of being) were brought into relief against/within a larger landscape(s) of practice.

DATA AND THEORY: (RE)ENTANGLING PRACTICES, PRODUCING NEW SPACE(S)

Though useful in terms of explicating the value of the community, identifying key literacy practices necessarily imparts artificial dividing lines between "this" practice and "that" practice that do not mirror our lived experiences. We found events/interactions within our community of practice could rarely be labeled by a singular practice. Rather space was constituted by a constellation of interrelated, embedded practices with varying intensities across time and channels, evoking an aliveness critical in good community design. In other words, the space we practiced and produced relied on movement, multiplicities, and relationality; the movement of humans, artifacts, ideas, and emotions via these interconnected and overlapping literacy practices. In this section we offer a vignette highlighting one moment/interaction in our shared history and then explore how this moment/interaction

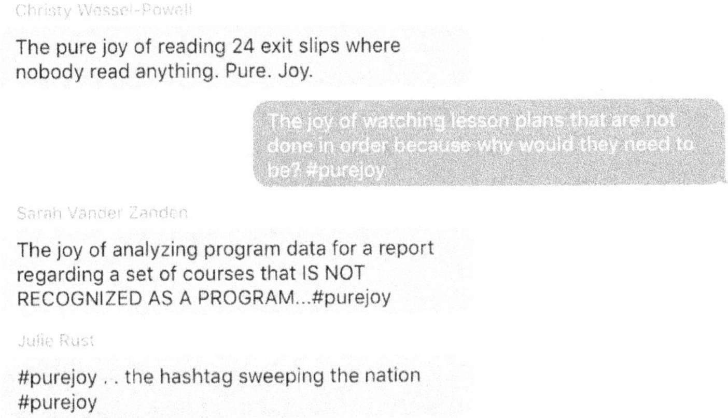

Figure 15.3. The practice of *bearing witness* was intensely embedded across the texting channel.

encompassed the four interconnected, intersecting digital literacy practices (identified above). After fleshing out the practices, we examine how these ways of practicing space produced (im)material space(s) for learning new ways of being literacy education scholars.

A Moment/Interaction: The No-Committee

Fall semester is in full swing. While preparing midtenure review documents one evening, Beth notices the arrival of an e-mail encouraging faculty in the department to attend an important off-campus event later that week regarding the new lab school. In practical terms, attending this event would mean rearranging plans for most of Thursday (a dedicated writing day) and driving 90 miles each way. Glancing at her calendar, Beth has a full week of teaching, meetings, and writing planned, but she worries that many faculty in the department will not attend the event on such short notice. She struggles with the decision, wondering what the 'right' choice is under these circumstances: as a pre-tenure faculty member, she does not want to appear distant or disinterested in a major College of Education initiative, but she also knows that her scholarship is a critical element of her professional life, too.

After wrestling with the decision internally for 24-hours, Beth solicits feedback from the CoP via the texting channel:

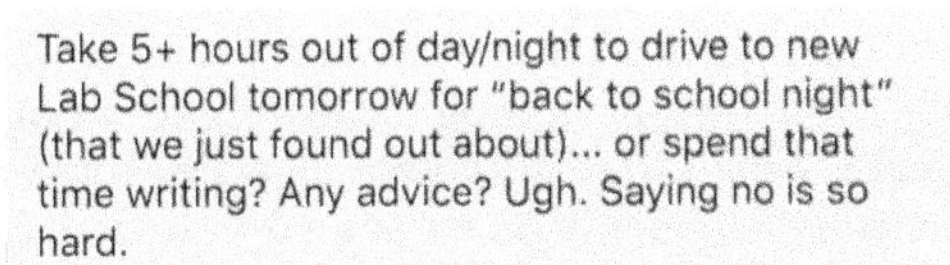

Figure 15.4.

Responses are immediate and decisive:

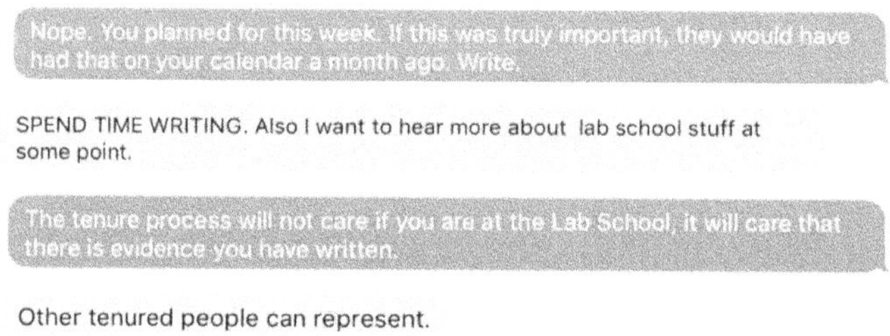

Figure 15.5.

Beth feels relief and a sense of validation. Embedded within these responses is a reminder of the community's commitment to planning for, protecting, and producing scholarly writing: saying "yes" to writing, means sometimes saying "no" to the myriad of requests that vie for our limited time. After this series of texts, Beth sends a quick email to say she will not be able to attend the event and spends Thursday afternoon working on a manuscript.

Analysis of the Intertwined Space-Making Practices

Deceptively simple, this moment/interaction was as typical as it was powerful in producing new ways of doing and being faculty members at our different universities. To understand this particular interaction more clearly, it is important to note two members of the group formally participated in National Center for Faculty Development & Diversity (NCFDD) professional development sessions and often shared insights during our Google Meet sessions. Specifically, the strategy of forming a "No-Committee" (Rockquemore, 2010) was discussed and subsequently taken up heavily within the texting channel. A No-Committee is a trusted group of colleagues who weigh in and filter the "unending stream of requests" (Rockquemore, 2010, para. 3) in faculty life regarding service or administrative tasks.

In relation to the four space-making practices, Beth was seeking to ***maintain scholarly-ness*** by finding time to write, and intentionally reached out to trusted colleagues who supported her inclination to say "no" and clarified writing time as a priority:

> I'm convinced that without this texting conversation, I would have prioritized attending the event over protecting my writing time (and my life outside of work), which is a pattern that I know well across many aspects of my life. As a new-ish faculty member, I am consumed with an ongoing sense of needing to please students and colleagues, and this usually results in me saying "yes" to all things. (Buchholz memo, November, 22, 2017)

Though no formal plan for instituting a No-Committee was created, this group function emerged and gained life in our group message text threads. Group members came to heavily use the texting channel to confirm professional decisions, seek input, and inform others about successful navigation of these kinds of requests (see Table 15.1).

Assembling knowledge in the CoP offered an array of justifications for why sticking to a writing routine was ultimately beneficial and the right choice long-term, and also banished some of the inevitable guilt of saying "no:"

> Beforehand, I dreaded sending the email to my colleague explaining why I wouldn't be at the event, but after our series of text messages, I sent a quick, non-explanatory email and moved on with my writing. That day I worked/wrote until around 6:30 and then cooked dinner at home for one of the first times all week. It was an odd feeling to have said "no" to something and to not feel a lot of guilt about it. (Buchholz memo, November, 22, 2017)

In using digital literacy practices as part of our CoP, a particular kind of space and time was produced in which it became possible for Beth to practice her role(s) as faculty differently, offering opportunities for negotiating the contentious trajectories and boundaries of faculty life collectively and in real time. The practices producing this space and time moved Beth from a fragmented engagement with her own professional development to a more agentic, holistic approach, one where saying "yes" to personal/hidden goals (writing) was as valid as saying "yes" to institutional/visible goals (attending the event). Over time, we have collectively benefited from ***assembling knowledge*** about *how* each of us each makes choices about how to spend our time across the hours, days, weeks, months, and semesters, and how these choices and possibilities are tied to deeper beliefs about our professional "development."

The immediacy and consistency of the group's responses via text actively ***maintained community*** while staring down a professional email request opened up the space for Beth to approach the decision differently: "as a small blip on a never ending timeline of important 'events' " which allowed her to "see/recognize writing as a legitimate event" (Buchholz memo, November 22, 2017). The texting channel is highlighted here, but analyses suggest the embedded and overlapping nature of the digital channels "create[d] points of focus for engaging multiple practices" (Wenger et al., 2014, p. 18). In other words, the spatio-temporal configurations of the digital channels offered a multiplicity of ways to activate, participate in, and maintain the community across time(s). Beth leveraged texting as the most immediate way to energize the community, but biweekly Google Meet gatherings offered extended opportunities to build the deeper structures (e.g., shared goals, empathic listening, collaborative reasoning) necessary for ***maintaining community*** across longer timescales.

In our experiences, universities/colleges largely value face-to-face (and virtual) meetings planned in advance as the main channels for professional development. Our data, alongside spatial and CoP theories, help illuminate that "many of the most valuable community [practices] are the small, everyday interactions" (Wenger et al., 2002, p. 60), such as the text messages exchanged as part of the No-Committee. Daily contact like this allowed our community to maintain its dynamic vitality despite physical distance, settling space among "another set of ideas (heterogeneity; relationality; *coevalness* ... liveliness indeed)" (Massey, 2005, p. 13, emphasis added). Massey's (2005) choice of "coevalness" here, rarely used outside of the field of anthropology, is significant in how its temporal underpinnings frame the production of space as necessitating interactions/practices that are contemporary, simultaneous, and synchronic. It was in texting we experienced the "principle of coexisting heterogeneity" (p. 11), a sense our stories—and development—were necessarily intertwined with others.

Ultimately, ***bearing witness*** undergirded this interaction: the group immediately understood the requirement to spend so much time driving for a last minute back to school night as bordering on absurd. Although we attempt to delineate the four strands of practices, Sarah's response (Figure 15.6) to Beth's query reveals the impossible task of teasing them out as separate:

There is no such thing as balance in this job at this time. We chose imbalance at different times to ensure momentum.

Choose

Figure 15.6.

Sarah's reminder bears witness to the impossible task of truly finding balance as early career faculty. Yet her response also served as a kind of deep knowledge now assembled by the community of practice. Taking to heart the notion we must, at times, "choose imbalance ... to ensure momentum" has the potential to aid in the maintenance of scholarly-ness and our community goals for the moments when multiple deadlines call for late nights. Sarah's text produced, then, a sage human encounter. Through coconstruction of deliberative decision making, the group's scholarly-personal relationship shifted away from a writing support or research conversation group. Insight into decisions and feedback from peers became a valued and integral piece of the CoP.

Analysis of Kind(s) of Space(s) Produced. We argue these interconnected digital literacy practices produced a new "here" allowing each of us to move more adeptly across our own multiple and varied 'heres,' across landscapes of practice from the local to the global, extending the face-to-face shared experiences/space(s) of our graduate school carrels. Importantly, these practices made space for the continued exploration of what it means to be a literacy education scholar. In a higher education culture prioritizing efficiency, rationality, self-promotion, and doing more with less (saying "yes"), this constellation of literacy practices across channels produced space for genuine empathy to emerge. Beth later reflected on the impact of her No-Committee interaction:

> The group's text message responses provided the movement/space/opening for something new to happen; for me to be something new; for me to see a new way of being in the world. In a way, the texting channel helped highlight/recognize my humanness over my knowledgeability (and professional responsibility). (Buchholz memo, Nov. 22, 2017)

Virtual carrels, then, ultimately produce a space for humanness, a humanness full and vivid and multi-dimensional. Virtual carrels do not compartmentalize: friends go in this box; colleagues go in that box; work goes in this box; play goes in that box. Rather, they, like the physical carrels that initially served as the epicenter of our successes and challenges and laughter and tears, make a stunning collage of it all. What is it you need today, professor-researcher-mother-person-friend? A push to get productive? Help wordsmithing a sentence? A reminder you are not alone? Confirmation you do not need to always say "yes" to every request? Or perhaps you just need a good idea for a protocol for observing student teachers in the field? It can all be found here, just a text or Google Meet or Google Doc away.

DISCUSSION

The interweaving of humor, levity, truth-telling, resource sharing, academic engagement, goal setting, compassion, and the sharing of lived realities has made our professional-personal trajectories converge in generative ways. Given the origins of this group, it is not surprising scholarly maintenance was a core set of practices cutting across the various technological channels, though the ways these practices were taken up and what they conveyed about our ideas about who we were as scholars was new for us. These practices were both consumptive as well as productive and worked across a variety of digital platforms. Community maintenance practices afforded group members opportunities for maintaining connections and friendship, and to act and be seen as fully human. They represented our mutual investment in one another, taking time out of the day to respond to one another offering support, advice, humor, and group articulations of reasonable boundaries placed around self and career in different situations. Importantly, the practice of maintaining community invited members to participate in varying levels and modes of participation across the days, weeks, and months (Wenger, McDermott, & Snyder, 2002).

The practice of bearing witness was a call to recognize each other's humanness, forcing members to see each other's "and-ness." Our experiences in life—and our decision making therein—do not fit within simplistic labels based on the physical spaces we traverse across the days and weeks. We are teachers, friends, committee members, crafters, confidants, researchers, caretakers, scholars, parents, writers, *and* on and on, and by bearing witness we learned to see each other (and be) at least some of those things simultaneously. In designing a uniquely *human* space "to realize itself, to become 'alive'" (Wenger et al., 2014), we found bearing witness contributed to the "liveliness, the complexity and openness of the configurational itself" (Massey, 2005, p. 13). As Ehlert and Hollett (2016) suggest, affective life is critical in sustaining "placemaking" and "belonging over time"—and here we argue it was affective life, as part of bearing witness, that was critical in sustaining our efforts to practice space differently.

In impromptu and planned encounters across these channels and enacted through a series of digital literacy practices, we produced a sense of "being [here/there] together" that enabled "something new" to happen (Massey, 2005, p. 94). Crucially, it was in our *movement* between "here" and "there"—and the ease in which digital practices unsettled spatial boundaries—that produced possibilities for "bumping into alterity" (Massey, 2005, p. 94). Punctuated by affective intensities, these brushes with "alterity" opened up space(s) for change, disrupting ingrained patterns of living/doing/being a scholar "here," in *this* place.

IMPLICATIONS

New economies have shifted risk and responsibility for professional development from the shoulders of employers to those of the employees; academia has not been immune to these shifts as colleges and universities respond to fiscal challenges and consumer demands. Local professional development opportunities for the professoriate are often minimal, aligned to institutional goals rather than personal, and are rarely longitudinal. In this chapter, we have delineated the ways in which we, as a group of literacy educators and researchers, have occupied this gap through digital literacy practices, creating a space in which we are able to grow as literacy educators and researchers. This digital space was born out of local necessity and, through participation within this space, we have not only addressed our individual, local needs but also have created collaborative agendas and generative space(s) for intellectual work.

This work, however, has not been solely academic; what has been so powerful throughout this experience is the sense of connection, of aliveness permeating our interactions. This, we believe, is a key component to the perceived successes we have felt as we practice in and produce this digital space. We came together as academic siblings, individuals already invested in the well-being of the others within the group, with understandings of how to engage one another to push ideas and individual competencies forward. It is this mutual investment in one another that amplifies and, to a certain extent, gives meaning to the practices outlined in this chapter. Metaphorically, this investment in one another is the waft and the practices the weft of the fabric of this professional development experience.

AUTHOR NOTE

This work is the product of the distributed intellectual efforts of the whole authorial team; all authors have contributed to the analytical methods used, to the research concept, and to the writing of this piece. Buchholz and Vander Zanden have taken on additional pragmatic responsibilities in relation to the preparation of the manuscript for submission and shepherding the manuscript through development, submission, and revision.

REFERENCES

Anthony, L., Lawrence, H., & Reed, A. (2017, December 15). What are you working on today? *Chronicle of Higher Education*. Retrieved from https://chroniclevitae.com/news/1965-what-are-you-working-on-today

Barton, D., & Hamilton, M. (2000). Literacy practices. In D. Barton, M. Hamilton, & R. Ivanič (Eds.), *Situated literacies: Reading and writing in context*. New York, NY: Routledge.

Cohn, J., Stewart, M. K., Theisen, C. H., & Comins, D. (2016). Creating online community: A response to the needs of 21st century faculty development. *The Journal of Faculty Development, 30*(2), 47–57.

Denzin, N. (2014). Writing and/as analysis or performing the world. In U. Flick (Ed.), *The SAGE handbook of qualitative data* analysis (pp. 569–584). London, England: SAGE.

Ehret, C., & Hollett, T. (2016). Affective dimensions of participatory design research in informal learning environments: Placemaking, belonging, and correspondence. *Cognition and Instruction, 34*(3), 250–258.

Gilster, P. (1997). *Digital literacy*. New York, NY: Wiley.
Grice, H. P. (1975). Logic and conversation. In P. Cole & J. L. Morgan (Eds.), *Syntax and semantics: Speech acts* (Vol. 3, pp. 225–242). New York, NY: Seminar Press.
Lave, J. (1991). Situating learning in communities of practice. In L. B. Resnick, J. M. Levine, S. D. Teasley (Eds.), *Perspectives on socially shared cognition* (pp. 63–82). Washington, DC: American Psychological Association.
Lave, J., & Wenger, E. (1991). *Situated learning: Legitimate peripheral participation*. Cambridge, England: Cambridge University Press.
Leander, K. M., & Sheehy, M. (2004). *Spatializing literacy research and practice*. New York, NY: Peter Lang.
Massey, D. (2005). *For space*. Thousand Oaks, CA: SAGE.
Massey, D. (2013, January). Interview: Doreen Massey on space [blog post]. Retrieved from https://www.socialsciencespace.com/2013/02/podcastdoreen-massey-on-space/
Mills, K. A., & Comber, B. (2013). Space, place and power: The spatial turn in literacy research. In K. Hall, T. Cremin, B. Comber, & L. Moll (Eds.), *International handbook of research in children's literacy, learning and culture* (pp. 412–423). London, England: Wiley-Blackwell.
Moje, E. B. (2004). Powerful spaces: Tracing the out-of-school literacy spaces of Latino/a youth. In K. Leander & M. Sheehy (Eds.), *Spatializing literacy research and practice* (pp. 15–38). New York, NY: Peter Lang.
Richardson, L., & Lockridge, E. (2004). *Travels with Ernest: Crossing the literary/sociological divide*. Walnut, CA: Rowman Altamira.
Rockquemore, K. A. (2010, October 4). The n-word. *Inside Higher Ed*. Retrieved from https://www.insidehighered.com/advice/2010/10/04/n-word
Scribner, S., & Cole, M. (1981). *The psychology of literacy*. Cambridge, MA: Harvard University Press.
Sherer, P. D., Shea, T. P., & Kristensen, E. (2003). Online communities of practice: A catalyst for faculty development. *Innovative Higher Education, 27*(3), 183–194.
Wenger, E. (1998) *Communities of practice: Learning, meaning, and identity*. Cambridge, England: Cambridge University Press.
Wenger, E. C., McDermott, R., & Snyder, W. C. (2002). *Cultivating communities of practice: A guide to managing knowledge*. Cambridge, England: Harvard Business School Press.
Wenger-Trayner E., Fenton-O'Creevy, M., Hutchinson, S., Kuriak, C., & Wenger-Trayner, B. (2014). *Learning in landscapes of practice: Boundaries, identity, and knowledgeability in practice-based learning*. Abingdon, England: Routledge.

ABOUT THE AUTHORS

THE EDITORS

Damiana G. Pyles, PhD, is an Associate Professor at Appalachian State University. Her research interests focus on media production, identity, and media literacy practices in order to understand the intersections of the visual, the spoken, the written, and the performed in digital and print literacies. She created an analytic methodology called *multimodal microanalysis* to understand the media products young people create. She teaches courses for preservice and practicing teachers to learn how to integrate media and technology for teaching and learning. Her current projects include exploring literacy and science learning in kindergarten classrooms, understanding parent and teacher beliefs about preschool literacies, and exploring concepts of space and place around Instagram and local organic farming.

Ryan M. Rish, PhD, is an Assistant Professor at the University at Buffalo (SUNY). His research interests involve the literacy practices of adolescents, especially in regard to how those practices relate to the institutions, social spaces, and geographic places in which they are enacted. This research includes investigations within and across classrooms, online spaces, and communities guided by concerns for learning with participants how to make learning opportunities more equitable for marginalized youth and how to engage students with critical considerations of their social worlds and local communities. Recent projects focus on supporting student inquiry with digital tools that allow for the collection and dissemination of locative data and media.

Julie Warner, EdD, is an Education Research Analyst at the U.S. Department of Education and is also an independent researcher. Her independent research is focused on the digital literacy practices of adolescents, particularly those that happen with and through mobile devices across spaces as explored in her book *Adolescents New Literacies* with and through Mobile Phones (2016) in the series New Literacies and Digital Epistemologies.

THE AUTHORS

Suriati Abas is a PhD candidate in the Department of Literacy, Culture and Language Education at Indiana University. She is currently teaching in the Department of Geography and researching the linguistic landscape of Buenos Aires, Argentina. Her recent coauthored article is on "The Language of Activism: Representations of Social Justice in a University Space in Argentina."

Sandra Schamroth Abrams, PhD, is an associate professor in the Department of Curriculum and Instruction at St. John's University in New York. Her research of digital literacies and videogaming reveals layered meaning making and agentive learning within and across online and offline spaces and practices. She is the author of *Integrating Virtual and Traditional Learning in 6–12 Classrooms: A Layered Literacies Approach to Multimodal Meaning Making* (Routledge), coauthor of *Conducting Qualitative Research of Learning in Online Spaces* (SAGE) and *Managing Educational Technology: School Partnerships and Technology Integration* (Routledge), and coeditor of *Bridging Literacies with Videogames* (Sense). Other publications are featured in *Teachers College Record, Journal of Literacy Research,* and the *Journal of Adolescent & Adult Literacy.*

Nichole M. Barrett, earned her doctorate from the Department of Learning and Instruction from the University at Buffalo in Buffalo, NY. Her dissertation research explored the intersection between digital video composition, identity, and student autonomy in a rural high school film club. Other research interests include finding ways to provide spaces for adolescent students to explore who they are through literacy. More specifically her focuses include digital video composition, rural education, digital literacies, popular culture, and identity. She is currently an adjunct professor at the University at Buffalo specializing in literacy, technology, and foundations of education. She can be reached at nbarrett@buffalo.edu.

David L. Bruce is Associate Professor of English Education in the Department of Learning and Instruction at the University of Buffalo. His research and teaching interests deal with students composing with Digital Video (DV) technology in classroom contexts, incorporating multimodal literacies into teacher education. Together with Sunshine Sullivan, they are Co-PIs with the Writing With Video project. This work centers around the professional learning communities around digital literacies with teachers and students in the rural southern tier of Western New York. He can be reached at dlbruce@buffalo.edu

Rosanne Bruinsma is an archaeologist specializing in heritage theory. She is interested in the relationship between heritage, participation, and social inclusion. In her thesis "Defining Diffusion: A Critical Reappraisal Of Heritage Theory and Practice in the Roman Neighbourhood of Testaccio," she explored the valorization and preservation of Testaccio's diverse heritage in relation to ecomuseological theory, in particular, and critical and recent approaches to heritage conservation, in general. She argued that a re-formulation of the concepts of community and heritage in ecomuseological theory and practice are necessary in order to valorize and preserve heritage in a sustainable and inclusive manner.

Beth A. Buchholz is an Assistant Professor in the Reading Education and Special Education Department at Appalachian State University where she teaches a variety of courses focused on literacy pedagogy and theory as well as qualitative methods. As a researcher, she studies at the intersection of new literacies, play, multimodal composing, and peer culture. She works to extend current sociocultural theories to explore the social, ideological, and critical work of children as they collaboratively compose texts and identities across physical and digital boundaries.

Gert-Jan Burgers has a chair in Mediterranean Archaeology at the Faculty of Humanities of the Vrije Universiteit Amsterdam (VUA). He is also director of CLUE+, the VUA interfaculty research institute for Culture, Cognition, History and Heritage. Over the last few decades, Burgers has developed and directed a series of large scale archaeological field projects in Italy, including others on the famous ancient road of the Via Appia. For the greater part of his academic career to date, Burgers has been concerned with protohistoric and Roman Italy, focusing on urban and rural landscape archaeology and critical heritage studies (conceptual as well as applied).

Sean P. Connors is an associate professor of English education at the University of Arkansas. His scholarship and teaching focuses on multimodality and new literacies, as well as the application of diverse critical perspectives to young adult literature. He has published in a number of scholarly journals and is the editor of *The Politics of Panem: Challenging Genres*, a collection of critical essays about the Hunger Games series.

Erin Daugherty is a doctoral candidate in rhetoric, composition, and literacy studies at the University of Arkansas. Her research focuses on the application of sociospatial and material theories of literacy and how young adults in rural areas can engage in literacy learning by researching and writing about the places they are from.

Mark Diaz is an artist, educator, and arts administrator. As an interdisciplinary artist, he works in various media including video, drawing, and object making to explore issues around migration, memory of place, and natureculture. Related to his arts practice, Mark has taught media literacy, digital arts, and visuals arts courses to inner city youth with several community arts organizations in Chicago. Currently, Mark is the Program Manager at Chicago Arts Partnerships in Education where he manages in-school arts integrated collaborations between teachers and artists.

Charles H. Gonzalez is an assistant professor of Secondary Education in the Department of Educational Leadership and Secondary Education at Alabama A&M University. He has worked with diverse populations of public school students, out-of-school youths, and adult learners and currently teaches literature, pedagogy, and education courses. His research focuses on discovering ways to encourage and support preservice (and in-service) teachers to be culturally relevant and on uncovering ways to develop new culturally sustaining pedagogies. He can be reached at writerchaz@gmail.com.

Nicholas E. Husbye is a teacher educator and literacy education researcher at the University of Wisconsin–Milwaukee, where he is an Associate Professor of Reading Education in the Department of Curriculum and Instruction. A former elementary classroom teacher, his research interests are in literacy teacher preparation, multimodality and learning, and children's literature.

Wayne Steven Jackson is Senior Lecturer in Theatre and Performance at The Arden School of Theatre, UCEN Manchester and a PhD candidate at London South Bank University. He is also a Hull-born performance maker, specializing in contemporary theater and intermedial practices, and a founding member of Escape Theatre. His research focuses on representations of nostalgia and home in the performance of autobiographical memory as a strategy for place making. www.waynestevenjackson.co.uk

Ron Janssen specializes in decision support for environmental and spatial management. His main topics of research are decision analysis, spatial analysis/evaluation, and spatial planning and design. His current topic of interest is the use of geodesign to support interactive land use planning workshops. Examples are the design of a land use plan for the lower Zambezi valley, design of regional adaptation strategies for the Frisian peat meadow areas, locating tidal devices around the Mull of Kintyre and heritage management in Puglia. At present he runs geodesign workshops to support management of road and water infrastructure in the east of the Netherlands.

Chuck Jurich is an Assistant Professor of Language and Literacy in the department of Early Childhood, Elementary, Middle, Literacy, and Special Education at the University of North Carolina Wilmington. His research interests focus on sociocultural and constructivist approaches to both conventional and new literacies practices with particular attention on digital, multimodal, and multi-authored texts. Prior to his work in higher education, Chuck was an elementary classroom teacher for 8 years and program director of a long running after-school video production club for elementary aged children.

Christian Napolitano is a PhD Candidate at VU Vrije Universiteit Amsterdam on Cultural Landscapes of Alto Salento. After obtaining his Master's degree in Archaeology at Università del Salento, he obtained a second level master's, "Geotechnologies for Archaeology," at Università degli Studi di Siena and Scuola di Specializzazione Degree in Classical Archaeology at Scuola di Specializzazione in Archeologia Classica e Medievale "Dinu Adamesteanu." With more than a decade of experience in the archaeological sector, he has worked in several national and international archaeological sites (Turkey, Italy). As a founding member of the Coop. Impact a r. l., he coordinates the management of the Archaeological Park of Muro Tenente, the set-up of museums and archaeological sites and several research projects combining technical, scientific and computer skills with communication and education contribution.

Greg Neal is currently a senior lecturer in the College of Education at Victoria University in Melbourne, Australia. Greg has been involved in a number of research projects over the years with a focus on improving teaching and learning with technology resources. Greg has continued to work with lecturers and teachers in various education settings to explore the ways in which ICT can be in integrated into learning contexts to further engage students and improve learning outcomes. As a course advisor in the Masters of Teaching (Primary) degree at Victoria University, it is Greg's passion to ensure we develop effective teachers prepared for 21st century learners. Greg has a PhD from Melbourne University, an MEd from Ballarat University and a BEd from Deakin University.

Mark Opmeer is a PhD candidate at the Spatial Information Laboratory of the Vrije Universiteit Amsterdam. He received his bachelor's and research master's of philosophy (MPhil) in cultural history where he studied travelers' changing perception of the Dutch cultural landscape in the 19th and 20th century. Currently, he is pursuing his PhD studing the affordances of geospatial technologies (mobile applications and computer games) for teaching ecological thinking in formal and informal learning environments.

Christy Wessel Powell is an Assistant Professor of Literacy and Language Education in the Department of Curriculum & Instruction at Purdue University's College of Education. She is also a former K–2 classroom teacher. Dr. Wessel Powell's research interests include early and elementary literacy (e.g., reading and writing workshops, digital playshops, literacy clinics, and critical literacy); teacher inquiry groups; educational equity and the politics of education; education documentary film; and arts and technology integration.

Erin Preston is an educational researcher and former arts educator who draws upon eight years of teaching visual and digital art. She has worked with the Chicago Humanities Festival, Chicago Arts Partnerships in Education, and Project Zero on program evaluation and research. Her research focuses on tensions of knowing, trust, and values in adult and student collaborative learning in a variety of contexts including professional development settings and arts integrated classrooms. She is particularly interested in the role of tension in learning driven by artistic processes, collaboration, and interdisciplinary inquiry.

Ilaria Ricci is a PhD Candidate in Archeology at Università del Salento and VU Vrije Universiteit Amsterdam focusing on settlement and productive dynamics of the Salento Istmus (Apulia,Italy) from third century BC to first century AD. She received her bachelor and research master in archaeology at Università del Salento (Lecce, Italy). After obtaining her master's degree in 2016, she was involved in Erasmus+ Traineeship for the project "experiencing the diachronic history of Apulia: a Digital Augmented Reality Application" at VU Amsterdam. Since 2016 she has been involved in EVA (Ecomuseo della Via Appia) project coordinated by VU Amsterdam.

Jennifer Rowsell is Professor and a Canada Research Chair in Multiliteracies at Brock University where she directs the Centre for Research in Multiliteracies. Her research interests include: expanding theories of literacy through digital, immersive, and game-based research; conducting longitudinal research in homes; and, applying multimodal, arts-based practices with youth across formal and informal contexts. She is coeditor of *The Routledge Handbook of Literacy Studies* with Dr. Kate Pahl at Manchester Metropolitan University. She is coeditor of the Routledge Expanding Literacies in Education series with Dr. Cynthia Lewis at the University of Minnesota and the Digital Literacy Editor for The Reading Teacher.

Julie E. Rust began her career teaching middle and high school English and then moved on to pursue her PhD in literacy, language, and education at Indiana University Bloomington. She currently works with future teachers as an Assistant Professor of Education at Millsaps College in Jackson, MS. Her research interests include the intersection of new media and ELA classroom spaces, dialogue across difference, and (re)imagining teacher education.

Jane M. Saunders is an Associate Professor of Literacy at Texas State University. She has a keen interest in writing instruction and the ways teachers employ pedagogical and technological innovations to strengthen the literacy learning of students. She is also invested in promoting the professionalism and knowledge of teachers and teacher educators. Dr. Saunders would love to hear from you about this chapter or any interesting new tools you have found that relate to teaching and writing. E-mail her at: janesaunders@txstate.edu

Scott Sikkema is Education Director at CAPE (Chicago Arts Partnerships in Education). At CAPE, he has oversight for programs, partnerships, professional development, and research. He spearheaded the development of research at the organization; in particular, he has focused on research as an aesthetic and pedagogical practice. With the superb CAPE program and research staff, he explores via inquiry site, space, time, process, and other queries, moving away from the immediacy of set answers towards the generative struggle of not knowing.

Louanne Smolin is an urban educator with diverse experiences in technology, arts, teacher education research. Her areas of expertise include curriculum reform through multimedia and arts integration. She currently serves as a researcher on large scale program evaluations for arts organizations serving urban public schools, including working as a principal investigator on studies for U.S. Department of Education funded initiatives Dr. Smolin has experiences with multiple program evaluation approaches. She has published journal articles and book chapters related to program evaluation, multimedia, and teacher professional development. She has presented her work at numerous national and international conferences.

Joseph Spilberg serves as Research Program Manager for Chicago Arts Partnerships in Education (CAPE) managing all after school and family programming. Joseph also manages all research activities across CAPE programs working with external researchers and research organizations to design research, conduct data collection and disseminate locally and nationally

Sunshine R. Sullivan is an associate professor, chair of education, and faculty development coordinator at Houghton College. She teaches literacy and inclusive education courses as well as mentoring student teachers. Together with David Bruce, they are Co-PIs with the Writing With Video project. This work centers around the professional learning communities around digital literacies with teachers and students in the rural southern tier of Western New York. She can be reached at Sunshine.Sullivan@Houghton.edu.

Matthew Thomas-Reid (he/him/his pronouns) is assistant professor of Educational Foundations and affiliate faculty with Gender, Women's and Sexuality Studies. Matthew is faculty advisor for GAPP (Gay and Progressive Pedagogy) and is editor of the South Atlantic Philosophy of Education Society Journal. His areas of research include philosophy of education, social justice education, and queer pedagogy. His current research projects focus on utilizing LGBTQIA histories and narratives with a view toward "queering" pedagogy, praxis, and, most recently, digital literacies.

Mark Vicars is a teaching and research academic in the College of Arts and Education at Victoria University, Melbourne. His main research interests are literacy education, and qualitative research methodologies. An overarching concern of his work is thinking through the connectivities between literacy and identity practices in everyday life. In 2010, he was awarded the Australian Learning and Teaching Council Citation for pedagogical approaches that motivate, inspire and support socially disadvantaged and culturally diverse students to overcome barriers to learning and to experience and attain success. Mark has had his research published in international research journals and edited volumes. He is lead editor of *Qualitative Research Journal.* Mark is a founding member of the International Institute for Critical Pedagogy and Transformative Leadership.

Jordan P. Woodward graduated from the University of Oklahoma in 2017 with her MA in English Composition, Rhetoric, and Literacy, where her research focused on intersections between religious, environmental, and activist rhetorics, community literacy, and digital storytelling. For the 2017–2018 year she was in India as Fulbright-Nehru researcher studying communities' (and especially women's) relationships to water and water bodies through various forms of digital storytelling, ranging from video-making, to soundscaping, and experimental photo essays. She intends to continue research on traditional and alternative forms of storytelling, intersections between religion and environment, activist rhetorics, and local knowledge production.

Sarah Vander Zanden is an Associate Professor at the University of Northern Iowa. She is the Literacy Education Graduate Program Coordinator and Director of the UNI Literacy Clinic. Her areas of interest are critical literacy, multimodal discourse analysis, and literacy teacher education.

www.ingramcontent.com/pod-product-compliance
Lightning Source LLC
LaVergne TN
LVHW020643300926
849161LV00004B/798

List of Abbreviations

AIP	Agreement in Principle
BIT	Bilateral Investment Treaty
CCS	Carbon Capture and Storage
CIL	Customary International Law
CJEU	Court of Justice of the European Union
CO_2	Carbon Dioxide
COP	Conference of the Parties
CPI	Consumer Price Index
CSP	Concentrated Solar Power
EC	European Commission
ECT	Energy Charter Treaty
EU	European Union
FET	Fair and Equitable Treatment
FIP	Feed-in Premium
FIT	Feed-in Tariff
GAL	Global Administrative Law
GHG	Greenhouse Gas
GSE	*Gestore dei Servizi Energetici*
ICCL	International Climate Change Law
ICJ	International Court of Justice
ICSID	International Centre for Settlement of Investment Disputes
IEA	International Energy Agency
IIA	International Investment Agreement

ILC	International Law Commission
IPCC	Intergovernmental Panel on Climate Change
IRR	Internal Return Rate
ISDS	Investor-State Dispute Settlement
ITLS	International Tribunal for the Law of the Sea
LE	Legitimate Expectations
MO	Ministerial Order
MST	Minimum Standard of Treatment
NAFTA	North American Free Trade Agreement
NDC	Nationally Determined Contribution
NZEID	Net Zero Energy Investment Disputes
OECD	Organisation for Economic Co-operation and Development
PCIJ	Permanent Court of International Justice
PV	Photovoltaic
RD	Royal Decrees
RDL	Royal Decree Laws
RE	Renewable Energy
UNCITRAL	United Nations Commission on International Trade Law
UNCTAD	United Nations Conference on Trade and Development
UNFCCC	United Nations Framework Convention on Climate Change
VCLT	Vienna Convention on the Law of Treaties
WTO	World Trade Organisation

Foreword

'This work is about an idea.' This is the first sentence of the present book which is based on a PhD undertaken by Thomas Lehmann, at the School of International Arbitration, Queen Mary University of London. It is quite a daring start, considering that most dissertations in the field of law will normally not start with an idea, but rather with the analysis of a given legal issue with the aim to develop new approaches or new solutions. So, here it's the other way around – top-down instead of bottom-up, to put it slangy – and that makes the reader curious from the start. And to say it right away: The reader will not be disappointed.

So, what is the idea of the book? It is, says the author, that, '*instead of "clashing", international climate change law and international investment law can complement each other*'. The author proposes a novel way to strike a balance between the emergency of adopting policies to mitigate climate change and the foreign investors' interests, by integrating climate change norms in the assessment of the energy investors' legitimate expectations.

As background the author explains in a first chapter how '*climate change threatens the liveability of our planet*' and that States from around the world have agreed to adopt energy producing systems that will reduce global warming and move to net zero carbon emissions. These changes have been agreed in numerous international conventions including the 1992 and 1994 United Nations Framework Conventions on Climate Change (UNFCCC), and the 1998 Kyoto Protocol, the 2015 Paris Agreement and the 2022 Glasgow Climate Pact, all under the UNFCCC. Under these treaties most states around the world have agreed to work to targets to reduce carbon emissions and to implement cleaner/greener systems. The intent is to achieve zero emissions by 2050 – or at least to make major steps by that date.

The author's proposition is based on a careful analysis of scholarly work and of arbitral case law, in particular on 42 publicly available awards rendered before August 2023 in the energy sector concerning the responding states of Spain, Italy, and the Czech Republic. They all concerned cases under the Energy Charter Treaty labelled by the author as 'Legitimate Expectations in Net Zero Energy Investment Disputes'.

The author defines 'Net Zero energy-related investment disputes' as including both, on the one hand treaty-based claims where fossil investors have claimed against alleged unlawful expropriations and abrupt policy changes, and on the other hand, claims by clean energy investors alleging the violation of investment protection when governments withdrew incentives, arguing that withdrawing a financial or commercial incentive frustrates their legitimate expectations.

In a second chapter, the study identifies some contours of the concept of legitimate expectations developed by the relevant case law: a state commitment must be identified, and be legitimate, in the sense of being delivered from a competent authority. In the second stage, the investor must demonstrate its reliance on the state's commitment in its investment decision.

One of the most controversial issues in this context concerns the question whether the regulatory framework as such may be a source of expectations. The author investigates this issue by dividing the relevant awards into 'detrimental reliance' and 'voluntarist-leaning' approaches. Under the voluntarist approach, clear regulatory provisions, emanating from the law or a regulation, intended to induce foreign investment are, like a contract obligation, sufficient to freeze a state's obligation towards the investor. Under the detrimental reliance approach, legitimate expectation may derive from clear regulatory provisions, but they must be balanced with the competing state interests.

The interesting conclusion drawn from this analysis is that, in practice, while arbitral tribunals are split on the correct approach and the concept of legitimate expectations, they align on key factual aspects on the application of legitimate expectations: the time of the investment, the risks assumed by the investor, and the foreseeability of the measures in question.

In a further chapter the author takes the view that climate change regulations are not incompatible with international investment law. While the legal integration of such regulations in the relevant treaty poses a problem, such regulation will, in most cases, act as relevant fact to assess the investor's legitimate expectations.

The author develops this idea further in the fifth chapter. The chapter demonstrates that the legitimacy of fossil fuel investors is impeded over time by the implementation of relevant climate change regulations in this area. Conversely, climate change regulations in the field of clean energy may create a presumption of legitimacy for the expectations of clean energy investors. The author concludes that arbitral tribunals should protect the legitimate expectations of clean energy investors to a higher standard. Conversely, over time, the expectations of fossil fuel investors may become unprotectable. The author concludes that by interpreting legitimate expectations in a balanced way, taking into account all relevant factors affecting the energy sector, arbitral tribunals can further the coordination of international law.

The book's annexes include a very helpful compilation of essential details pertaining to the 42 analysed arbitral awards, with selective quotes from these awards reflecting the tribunal's application of the doctrine of legitimate expectations, the due diligence of the investor, and climate change issues.

The main merit of this impressive study is the successful attempt to bring some intellectual order and structure in this increasingly important field of international investment arbitration. As the analysis of the ECT awards demonstrates, arbitral tribunals are divided in their approach to balance the interests of the investors, on the one hand, and the state, on the other, in the field of climate change. The study shows that despite this division, some key factual features seem to be considered relevant in all these cases. Whether this is sufficient to further harmonise the future case law in this area remains to be seen.

In conclusion, the book's stated aim to develop an idea how to balance international climate change laws and the protection of the investor's legitimate expectations has been successfully achieved. It is so far the first comprehensive study of the existing tension between these two poles. It is not difficult to predict that this book will soon land on the desk of any practitioner in the field.

Prof. Dr Klaus Sachs

Preface

Climate change threatens the liveability of our planet. States agreed at the Paris Agreement to limit global warming to well below 2 °C. This necessitates a transition to net zero carbon emissions by 2050. To meet this ambitious target, states must implement measures that profoundly impact the energy sector. On the one hand, they should incentivise clean investments; on the other hand, they must restrict carbon emissions from fossil fuel production. In both situations, states may create tensions with essential property rights. Phaseouts of coal-fired power plants or prohibitions on oil drilling result in diverging compensation issues. Disputes also arise when regulatory incentives channelling investments into clean energy are modified or revoked. These disputes generate claims under international investment agreements. These claims question the compatibility of international climate change laws with the standard of fair and equitable treatment under IIAs and the protection of energy investors' legitimate expectations.

This monograph examines how international climate change law impacts the legitimate expectations of foreign energy investors. It proposes to integrate climate change norms in the assessment of foreign investors' legitimate expectations. The proposition is based on a careful analysis of relevant case law, which finds that the time of the investment, the risks assumed by the investor and the foreseeability of measures directly affect the scope of investors' expectations. Climate change norms may significantly impact each of these elements and thus affect the protection of energy investors' legitimate expectations. The analysis finds that clean energy investors may expect greater regulatory stability, while fossil fuel investors can expect progressively more stringent legislation affecting their investments.

The study provides the first comprehensive assessment of the effect of international climate change law on the legitimate expectations of foreign investors in the energy sector. It contributes to academic scholarship and offers practical insights for practitioners, arbitrators, investors, and government officials.

Acknowledgements

The present book originates from my doctoral dissertation at the School of International Arbitration, Queen Mary University. As such, it would not have been possible without the inspiring and challenging supervision of Dr Remy Gerbay and Professor Stavros Brekoulakis, to whom I am truly indebted. They entrusted me with the independence to explore a novel topic while providing invaluable critique that transformed mere ideas into well-developed arguments.

I am sincerely thankful to my examiners, Professor Julian Lew and Professor Klaus Sachs, for their extensive engagement with my work, the intellectually stimulating viva, and their thoughtful recommendations for publishing the PhD. I am particularly indebted to Professor Sachs for his masterful and generous foreword.

My gratitude also goes to Eliseo Castineira, whose insights shaped this book's central theme, and to Professors Julien Chaisse, Lukas Rass-Masson, and Hélène Ruiz-Fabri, whose teachings inspired me to undertake a PhD.

Along the way, I had the great privilege of refining my ideas through discussions with brilliant scholars at Queen Mary University, particularly Professor Maxi Scherer, Dr Norah Gallagher, Dr Garry Gabison, and Dr Tibisay Morgandi. I am also deeply grateful for the support of my equally brilliant partner, Miki, my family, and my friends, who generously reviewed earlier drafts, particularly Emmanuel Dercourt, Lilit Nagapetyan, Pierre-Jean Thil, Giovanni Passamonti, and Dr Ilias Ioannou.

Last but not least, I acknowledge the support of Kluwer Law International, with special thanks to Eleanor Taylor for her guidance in bringing this book from proposal to publication.

'So act as if the maxim of your action were to become through your will a universal law of nature
(...) The universality of a law that everyone who believes himself to be in distress could promise whatever occurred to him with the intention of not keeping it would make impossible the promise and the end one might have in making it since no one would believe that anything has been promised him, but rather would laugh about every such utterance as vain pretense.'

Immanuel Kant[1]

1. Immanuel Kant, *Groundwork for the Metaphysics of Moral* (edited and translated by Allen W. Wood, Vail-Ballou Press 2002) 38, 39.

Introduction

This book is about an idea. That, instead of 'clashing', international climate change law and international investment law can complement each other.[2] This research aims to strike a balance between the urgency of adopting policies to mitigate climate change and the value of protecting and compensating private, individual property rights from these measures.[3] It proposes a novel way to attain this balance, namely by integrating climate change norms in the assessment of foreign investors' legitimate expectations.[4] The proposition is based on a careful analysis of relevant case law, which finds that arbitral tribunals assessing legitimate expectations converge on three facts: the time of the investment, the risks assumed by the investor and the foreseeability of measures. Climate change norms may significantly impact each of these elements and affect the protection and compensation of energy investors' legitimate expectations.

Climate change – human-induced emissions of greenhouse gases (GHGs) driving global warming and the resulting large-scale shifts in weather patterns[5] – provokes

2. Bruno Simma and Dirk Pulkowski, 'Of Planets and the Universe: Self-Contained Regimes in International Law' (2006) 17 European Journal of International Law 3 483 https://doi.org/10.1093/ejil/chl015.
3. Jorge Viñuales, *The International Law of Energy* (CUP 2022) Preamble.
4. I pay tribute to the ICC Report led by Wendy Miles KC for pointing out in 2019 the potential impact of climate change law on legitimate expectations and FET claims, *see* ICC, *Arbitration and ADR Commission Report on Resolving Climate Change-related Disputes Through Arbitration and ADR* (Report 2019) 5.63 ('In the international investment treaty context, the Paris Agreement is now expressly referenced in some bilateral investment treaties, including the 2018 Netherlands Model Bilateral Investment Treaty. As a result, arbitral tribunals determining claims made by a private sector investor against a host state under such treaties are obliged to give greater consideration to international climate change obligations bearing on states, specifically the Paris Agreement. Even where there is no reference to the Paris Agreement in the applicable bilateral investment treaty, international obligations are usually interpreted on a progressive basis and it is likely that the Paris Agreement, and NDCs, will inform the investing party's legitimate expectations in determining, for example, a fair and equitable treatment claim').
5. The Framework Convention on Climate Change (UNFCCC) adopted on 9 May 1992 and referred to in the Paris Agreement defines climate change in its Art. 1 as: 'a change of climate which is attributed directly or indirectly to human activity that alters the composition of the global atmosphere and which is in addition to natural climate variability observed over comparable time periods'.

far-reaching environmental,[6] political,[7] ethical,[8] and economic consequences.[9] Climate change is, according to the former UN High Commissioner for Human Rights, 'the greatest threat to human rights in the twenty-first century.'[10] It has a tremendous scope in its effects, increasing the severity of droughts and storms, a social impact on the distribution of food, lodging, and the viability of places to live.[11]

As a response to climate change, states have gradually adopted international agreements aiming at the mitigation of GHG emissions. This international climate change law (ICCL) regime[12] calls upon states to achieve climate neutrality[13] or so-called net zero emissions.[14] Climate neutrality is the goal enshrined in the Paris Agreement[15] and the 2021 Glasgow Climate Pact.[16] A majority of states have since announced policies to achieve net zero within the twenty-first century.[17] Achieving net zero necessitates to transition away from fossil fuels towards clean energy.[18] Attaining net zero means implementing policies that affect the energy sector, which is responsible for about two-thirds of global GHG emissions.[19] Accomplishing net zero requires the support of clean energy investments and the phasing down of fossil fuel energy

6. The Paris Agreement Under the United Nations Framework Convention on Climate Change (adopted 12 December 2015, entered into force 4 November 2016) UN Doc FCCC/CP/2015/L.9/Rev/1 ('Paris Agreement' or 'COP 21') expressly recognises the need to eventually eliminate net emissions to prevent dangerous climate change in its Art. 4.1; 'Climate Impact Explorer' (*Climate Analytics Tool*, 2025) https://climate-impact-explorer.climateanalytics.org accessed 16 February 2025.
7. Thomas Bernauer, 'Climate Change Politics' (2013) 16 Annual Review of Political Science 421 https://doi.org/10.1146/annurev-polisci-062011-154926; Dale Jamieson, 'The Moral and Political Challenges of Climate Change' in Susanne C. Moser and Lisa Dilling, *Creating a Climate for Change: Communicating Climate Change and Facilitating Social Change* (CUP 2007) 482.
8. Stephen M. Gardiner (ed.), *Climate Ethics: Essential Readings* (OUP 2010); Dale Jamieson, *Reason in a Dark Time: Why the Struggle Against Climate Change Failed – and What It Means for Our Future* (OUP 2014).
9. Jarmo Kikstra and others, 'The Social Cost of Carbon Dioxide under Climate-Economy Feedbacks and Temperature Variability' (2021) 16 Environmental Research Letters (9), 5 https://doi.org/10.1088/1748-9326/ac1d0b.
10. Mary Robin Robinson quoted in UNGA 'Report of the Special Rapporteur on the issue of human rights obligations relating to the enjoyment of a safe, clean, healthy and sustainable environment' (1 February 2016) UNHRC 31st Session Agenda Item 3 UN Doc A/HRC/31/52, 7; *see also* Donald Anton and Dinah Shelton, *Environmental Protection and Human Rights* (CUP 2011).
11. Daniel Bodansky, Jutta Brunnée and Lavanya Rajamani, *International Climate Change Law* (OUP 2017), 295.
12. The notion is defined below Introduction.B.1.
13. The balance between the amount of greenhouse gas produced and the amount removed from the atmosphere.
14. The 'net zero' transition refers to a transition towards a low-carbon economy, which would be neutral on the climate based on reduced emissions and capture of remaining ones; *see* Peter Cameron, Xiaoyi Mu and Volker Roeben (eds), *The Global Energy Transition: Law Policy, and Economics for Energy in the 21st Century* (Hart Publishing 2020) 1-2; 11-48.
15. Paris Agreement (n 6), Art. 2.1(a).
16. Glasgow Climate Pact Under the United Nations Framework Convention on Climate Change (adopted 8 March 2022) UN Doc FCCC/PA/CMA/2021/10/Add.1 (Glasgow Pact or COP 26), Arts 15-17.
17. Intergovernmental Panel on Climate Change, *Climate Change 2021: The Physical Science Basis* (IPCC 6th Assessment Report 2021) 8.
18. *See* Chapter 1.B.
19. Cameron et al., *The Global Energy Transition* (n 14) 2 (estimating that the energy sector accounts for more than 70% of global carbon emissions).

production, in particular, coal.[20] While international investment law safeguards both fossil fuel and clean energy investments equally, the International Energy Agency highlights that achieving net zero emissions by 2050 necessitates three crucial steps: (1) a historic surge in clean-energy investment, (2) no further investments in new fossil fuel supply projects, and (3) no final investment decisions for new unabated coal plants.[21] Therefore, in adopting net zero policies, states may generate tensions with the existing legal regime that protects foreign investors under international investment agreements (IIAs).

IIAs promote foreign direct and indirect investments through the legal protection of investors, including energy investors. They protect them not only from expropriation but also from drastic changes in policies and from the frustration of their legitimate expectations.[22] Tensions already arose between the protection offered by investment agreements to energy investors and states' net zero policies. On the one hand, fossil fuel investors have claimed against alleged unlawful expropriations (e.g., a ban on the exploitation of coal[23] or oil without appropriate compensation, a limitation on oil and gas drilling) and abrupt policy changes (e.g., a progressive phasing out of their production capacity).[24] On the other hand, clean energy investors have claimed the violation of investment obligations when governments withdrew incentives,[25] claiming that withdrawing a financial or commercial incentive 'frustrates' their expectation, which may oblige the state to compensate for lost revenue.[26] Thus, IIAs appear both as an impediment to policies affecting fossil fuel investors and as a necessary framework to promote and legally secure large-scale investments in clean energy.[27] Furthermore, there is evidence that disputes under IIAs related to net zero policies are rising. Statistics indicate the prominence of the energy sector in disputes between investors

20. United Nations Environment Programme, *The Closing Window Climate Crisis Calls for Rapid Transformation of Societies* (Emissions Gap Report, 2022) XII.
21. IEA, *Net Zero by 2050* (n 27) 18-21.
22. ICC, *Arbitration and ADR Commission Report on Resolving Climate Change-related disputes Through Arbitration and ADR* (Report 2019) 5.63.
23. For instance, Jack Ballantyne, 'Uniper to Withdraw ECT Claim as Part of German Bailout' Global Arbitration Review (London, 25 July 2022); *see also TC Energy Corporation, TransCanada PipeLines Limited v. The Government of the United States of America*, ICSID Case No. ARB/21/63, Request for Arbitration (22 November 2021) 13.
24. Kyla Tienhaara and others, 'Investor-State Disputes Threaten the Global Green Energy Transition' (2022) 379 Science 701 https://doi.org/10.1126/science.abo4637 (quantifying claims in the fossil fuel sector); Joe Tirado and Alejandro I. Garcia, 'Rise of Renewable Energy Claims' (2015) 16 Renewable Energy Focus 14 https://doi.org/10.1016/s1755-0084(15)30069-7 (offering an overview over cases resulting from the changing regulation of renewable energy investments).
25. *See* the factual background to ECT cases analysed below in Chapter 3.A.
26. At the same time, international investment agreements promote foreign investments in the clean energy sector by securing their expectations of regulatory stability and guaranteeing incentives (i.e., financial and material such as tax breaks or subsidies or permits).
27. International Energy Agency, *Net Zero by 2050: A Roadmap for the Global Energy Sector* (Report, 2021) 81 (estimating the annual amount of clean energy investments required to achieve carbon neutrality by 2050 to rise from currently USD 2 trillion to USD 5 trillion by 2030, and USD 4.5 trillion by 2050); 'How Some International Treaties Threaten the Environment: Investor-State Dispute Settlement Provisions Are Blamed for Impeding Government Action' *The Economist* (London, 5 October 2020) (assessing the stranded fossil fuel assets' valuation at USD 1.8 trillion).

and states.[28] By the end of 2023, 42% of all cases administered by International Centre for Settlement of Investment Disputes (ICSID) occurred in the energy sector.[29] New cases filed in 2023 draw a similar picture (oil, gas, and mining represented 23% and electric power and other energy 12% of newly registered ICSID cases).[30] Observers witness a growing political concern that international investment treaties may impede climate action.[31]

While tensions between international investment law and ICCL appear more evident as claims arise, there is insufficient study on the topic. Foreign investors and states rarely raise arguments related to climate change law in investment disputes.[32] The nexus between ICCL and investment law is often loosely drawn in renewable cases but only as part of the factual background to the disputes.[33] The *substantive* legal relationship between international investment law and ICCL remains largely underexplored.[34] In particular, the protection of legitimate expectations, which is central to the balance between host states' policy freedom and foreign investors' property rights, has received growing attention,[35] but its nexus with ICCL has not yet been subject to a detailed analysis. To address this gap, the research proposes to analyse the scope of energy investors' legitimate expectations under the FET standard in investment disputes related to the net zero transition.[36]

With the concept of legitimate expectations, international investment law secures an investor's predictive expectations about the future, which has been linked to its prudential ability to undertake long-term planning, widely thought to be important to practical agency and autonomy.[37] Under the fair and equitable treatment (FET) provision, the concept of legitimate expectations relates to a situation in which the conduct of the state creates reasonable and legitimate expectations on the part of the investor to invest in reliance on this conduct so that the state's failure to uphold those

28. MSCI, *Global Industry Classification Standard (GICS) Methodology* (Methodology Book, 2020) 5-6, 19 ('The energy sector is a category of stocks that relate to producing or supplying energy. The energy sector or industry includes companies involved in the exploration and development of oil or gas reserves, oil and gas drilling, and refining. The energy industry also includes integrated power utility companies such as renewable energy and coal').
29. World Bank, *The ICSID Caseload: Statistics Issue 2024-1* (Report, 2025) 11.
30. *Ibid.*, 10.
31. *See* below Introduction.B.2.
32. Mala Sharma, 'Integrating, Reconciling, and Prioritising Climate Aspirations in Investor-State Arbitration for a Sustainable Future: The Role of Different Players' (2022) 23 JWIT 5-6 746 https://doi.org/10.1163/22119000-12340269.
33. *See* Annex 1.
34. With recent exceptions, Risteard De Paor, 'Can International Arbitral Tribunals Apply International Climate Change Law and/or Public Policy When Climate Change Issues Arise in Commercial and Investment Arbitration?' (2022) Cahiers de l'Arbitrage 3 809, 815.
35. Moshe Hirsch, 'Between Fair and Equitable Treatment and Stabilization Clause. Stable Legal Environment and Regulatory Change in International Investment Law' (2011) 12 The Journal of World Investment & Trade 783, 783-784, 791 https://doi.org/10.1163/221190011x00300.
36. The World Bank Group and the Energy Charter Secretariat, *Enabling Foreign Direct Investment in the Renewable Energy Sector Reducing Regulatory Risks and Preventing Investor-State Conflicts* (Report 2023) 31 (among sixty energy disputes under the ECT, a breach of FET was found in 83% of cases where the investor prevailed).
37. Nigel Simmonds, *Central Issues in Jurisprudence: Justice, Law and Rights* (4th edn, Sweet and Maxwell 2013) 39.

expectations may result in a failure to provide a FET (legitimate expectations or LE).[38] Legitimate expectations are central to the question of balance between required policy changes and the protection of property rights.[39] The doctrine of LE is, however, not an autonomous obligation under IIAs.[40] Rather it acts as an element to assess the state's duty to treat the investor in a fair and equitable manner.[41]

To align the topic (climate change and international investment law) to the subject (legitimate expectations of energy investors), the research explores the interpretation of legitimate expectations in theory and its application in practice. It then analyses ICCL's impact on the latter.[42] It responds to the following question: To what

38. This definition is loosely based on the Thunderbird tribunal but differs on the wording and on the importance of the harm principle, which is related to the detrimental reliance theory and, although adequate (there is no case in which an investor did not suffer harm), fails to encompass the scope of situations in which legitimate expectations have been upheld; *see International Thunderbird Gaming Corporation v. Mexico*, NAFTA/UNCITRAL, Arbitral Award, 26 January 2006, para. 147 ('Having considered recent investment case law and the good faith principle of international customary law, the concept of "legitimate expectations" relates, within the context of the NAFTA framework, to a situation where a Contracting Party's conduct creates reasonable and justifiable expectations on the part of an investor (or investment) to act in reliance on said conduct, such that a failure by the NAFTA Party to honour those expectations could cause the investor (or investment) to suffer damages').
39. *Renergy S.à r.l. v. Kingdom of Spain*, ICSID Case No. ARB/14/18, Award, 6 May 2022, para. 900 ('At the same time, the Tribunal notes that increasing the use of green energy is likewise of vital public interest, given in particular the positive impact on the environment. Indeed, the Respondent itself committed to pursuing this interest many times, not least in the Preamble of Law 54/1997,1152 and is also under an obligation to do so under EU law, in particular pursuant to EU Directive 2009/28/EC.1153 As it seems difficult to deny that, at least in the short term, the Disputed Measures make investments in green energy projects in Spain less attractive to investors,1154 the Disputes Measures could be seen to run counter to the public interest in saving the environment.'); for a countervailing position *see Matthias Kruck and others v. Kingdom of Spain*, ICSID Case No. ARB/15/23, Partial Dissenting Opinion by Zachary Douglas, 13 September 2022, para. 57.
40. Campbell McLachlan and others, 'Treatment of Investors' in *International Investment Arbitration: Substantive Principles* (2nd edn, OUP 2017) para. 7.179.
41. *Infracapital v. Spain*, ICSID Case No. ARB/16/18, Decision on Jurisdiction, Liability and Directions on Quantum, 13 September 2021, para. 564 ('Before examining the merits of the claim, the Tribunal considers it important to note that the concept of legitimate expectations is not expressly contained as an obligation of host States under Article 10(1) of the ECT. Therefore, it is not an independent obligation. In this regard, the protection of the legitimate and reasonable expectations of investors must be measured against the duty of States to treat investors in a fair and equitable manner'); *Gold Reserve Inc v. Venezuela*, ICSID, Award, 22 September 2014, para. 570; *El Paso Energy International Company v. Argentina*, ICSID Case No. ARB/03/15, Award, 31 October 2011, para. 348.
42. Case concerning the Factory at Chorzow (Claim for indemnity - Jurisdiction) (Dissenting Opinion of Judge Ehrilich) PCIJ Rep Series A No. 9 (1927) 39 ('Interpretation constitutes the process of 'determining the meaning of a rule', while application is the process of 'determining the consequences which the rule attaches to the occurrence of a given fact'); *Industria Nacional de Alimentos SA and Indalsa PerúSA v. Peru*, ICSID Case No. ARB/03/4, Decision on annulment and dissenting opinion of 5 September 2007, (2007) IIC 300, para. 68 ('the Tribunal was called upon to determine what a treaty provision meant, and then to apply it to the circumstances of the case before it'); Anastasios Gourgourinis, 'The Distinction Between Interpretation and Application of Norms in International Adjudication' (2011) 2 JIDS (1) 31, 43-48 https://doi.org/10.1093/jnlids/idq022 ('The PCIJ had the opportunity to further clarify that treaty interpretation refers to the "construction" of the "scope" and "bearing" of a specific provision and its terms' referring to *Tunis and Morocco Nationality Decrees* (Advisory Opinion) PCIJ Rep Series B No 4 (1923) 29-31); *ibid.*, 47-48 (the author distinguishes between interpretation and application

extent does ICCL impact the application of the doctrine of legitimate expectations in energy investment disputes?

The book is analytical. It suggests that international climate change norms should be taken into account as legal facts when tribunals consider what energy investors' legitimate expectations are. Based on an extensive analysis of the case law, the research suggests that ICCL may significantly alter the legitimacy and level of expectations protectable under IIAs. It does so based on a three-level analysis as outlined above.[43] It finds that clean energy investors may expect greater regulatory stability due to the state's net zero commitments, while fossil fuel investors may see their expectations as lacking legitimacy and reasonableness depending on the time of their investment.

The research contributes to alleviating tensions between the regimes of international investment and climate change law.[44] Offering a detailed analysis of the level of protection provided to clean and fossil fuel energy investments,[45] it suggests that, by protecting investors in the clean energy sector *and* recognising greater regulatory freedom in the phasing out of fossil-fuel industries, international investment law could contribute to, rather than impede, both the rule of law and climate change goals.[46]

In the following introductory sections, the notions that underpin the argument are outlined. Section A addresses the definition of investment arbitration, section B defines ICCL. The interconnectedness between the two is elaborated within section C with the creation of a novel typology of investment disputes named 'net zero energy investment disputes' (NZEID). Subsequently, section D explores the gap left so far in the literature.

---

stricto sensu as part of the application lato sensu of an applicable norm. Interpretation is a secondary process which only comes into play when it is impossible to make sense of the plain terms of the treaty, or when they are susceptible of different meanings, while the application *stricto sensu* of norm A, is its application according to the interpretative findings in the specific set of facts, in order to generate specific juridical results.); *see* ICSID Case No. ARB/06/5 *Phoenix Action Ltd v. Czech Republic*, Award, 15 April 2009, (2009) IIC 367, para. 73.

43. These include: the risks assumed by the investor (how risky is the business sector in which it invested?), the time of the investment (could the investor expect regulatory changes at the final investment time?), and the foreseeability of frustrating measures at the time of the investment (was the regulatory framework sustainable and what degree of stability could the investor expect?).
44. Mala Sharma, 'Integrating, Reconciling, and Prioritising Climate Aspirations in Investor-State Arbitration for a Sustainable Future: The Role of Different Players' (2022) 23 JWIT 5-6 746 https://doi.org/10.1163/22119000-12340269.
45. Researchers attempted to converge international regimes such as international investment law and trade law in the past, with inherent limitations. These limitations explain why I propose to see ICCL as a relevant legal fact rather than applicable law. On the limits of convergence *see, e.g.*, Jose Alvarez, 'Epilogue: "Convergence" Is a Many-Splendored Thing' in Szilárd Gáspár-Szilágyi, Daniel Behn and Malcolm Langford (eds), *Adjudicating Trade and Investment Disputes: Convergence or Divergence?* (CUP 2020) 285-287.
46. Bodansky, *Climate Change Law* (n 11) 26 (the authors present the climate change legal regime as a managerial rather than an enforcement model, which has 'tried to encourage and facilitate national action through transparency, peer pressure, and capacity building, rather than to force states to act through legal prescriptions and sanctions').

A INVESTMENT ARBITRATION

'Investment arbitration' is routinely used to designate the procedure for resolving disputes between foreign investors and host states. It pertains to the wider dispute relationship between investors and states, while 'international investment law' is part of public international law governing foreign direct investments and dispute resolution mechanisms peculiar to the protection of investment (*international investment law*).[47] Although referring to investment arbitration as a broader concept of dispute resolution, this book deliberately focuses on the disputes emanating from investment treaties. But much of the reasoning could be applied to purely domestic law, or consent-based arbitrations, where international law is meant to apply to the resolution of the dispute. This explains why I refer to investment arbitration rather than international investment law alone.

Since 1959, international investment law has been mostly shaped by bilateral investment treaties and investment chapters in trade agreements.[48] As of 2023, more than 2,686 IIAs are in force.[49] They aim to protect the investors of the contracting parties.[50] The original purpose of IIAs is for capital-exporting countries to secure a stable and orderly framework for their investors in the host state and for capital-importing countries to further attract investments in their infrastructure, expertise and capital.[51] In the words of the UK Model Bilateral Investment Treaty (BIT), investment agreements are aimed 'to promote greater economic cooperation with respect to investment by nationals and enterprises of one Party in the territory of the other Party'.[52]

1 Substantive Protection Standards in International Investment Agreements

Although differing in wording, IIAs bind the contracting states to provide substantive and procedural treatment standards to investors from the other contracting states. Typically, these standards include an obligation of national treatment,[53] most favoured

47. Rudolf Dolzer and Christoph Schreuer, *Principles of International Investment Law* (2nd edn, CUP 2012) 12.
48. Treaty between the Federal Republic of Germany and Pakistan for the Promotion and Protection of Investments (signed 25 November 1959, entered into force 28 April 1962) 457 UNTS 23.
49. 'International Investment Agreements Navigator' (*UNCTAD*, 2023) https://investmentpolicy.unctad.org/international-investment-agreements accessed 11 October 2023.
50. Roberto Echandi 'Bilateral Investment Treaties and Investment Provisions in preferential Trade Agreements Recent Developments in Investment Rule-Making' in Katia Yannaca-Small (ed.), *Arbitration under International Investment Agreements a Guide to the Key Issues* (OUP 2018) 3, 6-11.
51. Doak Bishop, James Crawford and Michael Reisman (eds), *Foreign Investment Disputes: Cases Materials and Commentary* (2nd edn, Kluwer Law International 2014) 32-34.
52. The United States of America 2012 Model Bilateral Investment Treaty.
53. National treatment is a relative obligation requiring the host State to treat foreign-owned investments at least as well as similarly situated national investments. It protects against both de jure and de facto discrimination; *see* Andrea Bjorklund, 'The National Treatment Obligation' in Yannaca-Small (ed.), *Arbitration Guide* (n 50) 532, 560-561.

nation treatment,[54] expropriation[55] and FET.[56] The last two protection standards, present in most IIAs, are likely to play a significant role in net zero-related investment disputes.

Expropriation provisions protect the foreign investor from unlawful or inadequately compensated investment's outright seizure (direct expropriation) or substantial deprivation (indirect expropriation).[57] A government's taking or revocation of a fossil fuel investor's licence, without *adequate* compensation, would deprive it of the enjoyment of its investment.[58] It may thus be classified as a direct,[59] indirect, or creeping expropriation.[60] Without delving into details, it suffices to say that the case law is divided into two central issues. First, is the effect on the investor solely relevant or is the purpose and measure's proportionality pertinent? Second, is a non-discriminatory measure taken by the host state, in the public interest, and following due process, at all an 'expropriation'? The conflicting views are expressed under the terms of sole effect doctrine, proportionality and police powers.[61] Expropriation

54. Akbar Rasulov, Robin Geiß and Meinhard Hilf, 'Most-Favoured-Nation Clause' in Anne Peters (dir), *Max Planck Encyclopedias of International Law* (OUP 2021) ('A most-favoured-nation ("MFN") clause is a treaty provision whereby one State (the granting State) undertakes the obligation to accord to another State (the beneficiary State), in a designated sphere of economic or other relations, treatment not less favourable than the treatment it extends in the same sphere to any other third State.'); Abby Cohen Smutny, Petr Polásek and Chad Farrell, 'The MFN Clause and Its Evolving Boundaries' in Yannaca-Small (ed.), *Arbitration Guide* (n 50) 594, 624-629.
55. An expropriation clause refers to a commitment not to illegally expropriate investments. The right to expropriate is legal but must be for a public purpose, non-discriminatory, following due process, and upon compensation; *see* Robert Sloane and Michael Reisman, 'Indirect Expropriation and Its Valuation in the BIT Generation' (2004) British Yearbook of International Law 75 115 https://doi.org/10.1093/bybil/74.1.115; Katia Yannaca-Small, 'Indirect Expropriation and the Right to Regulate, Has a Line Been Drawn?' in Yannaca-Small (ed.), *Arbitration Guide* (n 50) 562, 564.
56. *See* Chapter 2.A; *Silver Ridge Power BV v. Italian Republic*, ICSID Case No. ARB/15/37, Award, 16 February 2021, paras 396 ff.
57. Dolzer and Schreuer, *Principles of International Investment Law* (n 47) 148 ('Direct expropriation occurs when an investment is nationalized or otherwise by the host state taken through formal transfer of title or outright physical seizure').
58. *Ibid.*
59. José E. Alvarez, 'The Human Right of Property' (2017) 72 U Miami L Rev 580; Protocol 1 to the European Convention for the Protection of Human Rights and Fundamental Freedoms ETS No. 009 (adopted 20 March 1952, entered into force 18 May 1954) ('Every natural or legal person is entitled to the peaceful enjoyment of his possessions').
60. OECD, '"Indirect Expropriation" and the "Right to Regulate" in International Investment Law' (2004) OECD Working Papers on International Investment 3-4; Christoph Schreuer, 'The Concept of Expropriation under the ECT and Other Investment Protection Treaties' (2005) 2 TDM 3 1, 3-14 ('An indirect expropriation occurs if the host state interferes with the use of the investment or with the enjoyment of its benefits even though the investment has not been seized and the legal title to the investment is not affected.'); Nowadays, the deprivation of an investor's assets is often the consequence of regulations taken by a State to satisfy a public interest rather than the outseizure of property rights of the investor. Where indirect regulations substantially impact the assets of the investor in a way comparable to a direct expropriation, they amount to indirect expropriation. An indirect expropriation is lawful, if it meets the same legal requirements as direct expropriation (public purpose, due process, non-discrimination, and compensation), as the opposite may encourage creeping or disguised expropriations.
61. To justify a fossil fuel phase out measure based on the police powers doctrine would require the demonstration that a climate change measure is *bona fide* and covered by the doctrine under CIL and that the measure complies with the fundamental rules of non-discrimination, good faith,

provisions are key to addressing phasing out policies (e.g., in the coal sector when states shutdown exploitations rendering the initial investment fruitless) but are less relevant when addressing the withdrawal of clean energy incentives. Contrary to expropriation, investment protection under FET is not conditioned on the substantial deprivation of the investor's assets.

FET provisions may offer redress where the threshold of expropriation is not met, but the state behaves in a seriously abusive, discriminatory, or unjust way.[62] FET is generally characterised as a non-contingent substantive standard of investment protection.[63] The scope of the FET provision is intensively debated. However, tribunals agree in principle that a breach may be found when a host state's measure contradicts the 'specific commitment' it accorded to the investor, namely when the state contravenes the 'legitimate expectations' it created and upon which the investor relied to invest capital.[64]

The research focuses on the second standard of FET and one of its most litigated 'elements': legitimate expectations.[65] The doctrine of legitimate expectations has become the cornerstone of the vast majority of NZEIDs.[66] The doctrine of LE, which is a relatively recent addition to investment arbitration,[67] is now widely recognised as an element of the FET standard.[68] Before the development of the notion of LE, tribunals

---

and depending on the arbitral tribunal, underlying treaty and facts, reasonableness or proportionality; *see* Thomas Lehmann, 'Police Powers Doctrine: A Reliable State Defence in Times of Covid-19?' (2021) 18 Brazilian Journal of international Law 2 72, 73 https://doi.org/10.5102/rdi.v18i2.7416; Catharine Titi, 'Police Powers Doctrine and International Investment Law' in Andrea Gattini, Attila Tanzi and Filippo Fontanelli (eds), *General Principles of Law and International Investment Arbitration* (Brill 2018) 323.

62. *See* generally Lucy Reed and Bray Daina, 'Fair and Equitable Treatment: Fairly and Equitably Applied in Lieu of Unlawful Indirect Expropriation?' in Arthur Rovine (ed.), *Contemporary Issues in International Arbitration and Mediation: The Fordham Papers Volume 1* (Brill Nijhoff 2007) 14; *PSEG v. Turkey*, ICSID Case No. ARB/02/5, Award, 17 January 2007, para. 238; *Continental Casualty Co. v. Argentine Republic*, ICSID Case No. ARB/03/9, Award, 5 September 2008, para. 254.
63. *See* Chapter 2.A.
64. Michael Reisman and Mahnoush Arsanjani, 'The Question of Unilateral Governmental Statements as Applicable Law in Investment Disputes' 19 ICSID Review 2 328 https://doi.org/10.1093/icsidreview/19.2.328.
65. It does so because while the expropriation standard is relevant when examining phasing out measures affecting foreign investments, it fails to encompass all claims against policies adopted to meet net zero. Net zero policies may indeed range from time restrictions on exploitation permit to the cancellation of incentives adopted in favour of clean energy providers, which do not generally end up 'expropriating' them (substantially depriving their business.
66. On the notion of net zero investment dispute, *see* below Introduction.C.
67. *Técnicas Medioambientales Tecmed, S.A. v. The United Mexican States,* ICSID Case No. ARB (AF)/00/2, Award, 29 May 2003, para. 154.
68. Michele Potestà, 'Legitimate Expectations in Investment Treaty Law: Understanding the Roots and the Limits of a Controversial Concept' (2013) 28 ICSID Review-Foreign Investment Law Journal 88 https://doi.org/10.1093/icsidreview/sis034; Nitish Monebhurrun, 'Gold Reserve Inc. v the Bolivarian Republic of Venezuela. Enshrining Legitimate Expectations as a General Principle of International Law' (2015) 32 Journal of International Arbitration 551, 551-561 https://doi.org/10.54648/joia2015026; Simon Maynard, 'Legitimate Expectations and the Interpretation of the Legal Stability Obligation' (2016) 1 European Investment Law and Arbitration Review 99 https://doi.org/10.1163/24689017-00101006; Abhijit P.G. Pandya and Andy Moody, 'Legitimate Expectations in Investment Treaty Arbitration: An Unclear Future' (2010) 15 Tilburg Law Review 93, 93-119 https://doi.org/10.1163/22112596-90000007; Trevor Zeyl, 'Charting the

recognised the protection under FET of the detrimental reliance of investors on assurances provided by officials, for instance, in *Metalclad*,[69] *ADF*,[70] and *Wena Hotels*.[71] The tribunal in *Tecmed* then insisted on the investor's '*basic* expectations' – of transparency, consistency and clarity of the state's behaviour.[72] The notion of 'legitimate expectations' – emphasising legitimacy – was thereafter invoked by the Claimant[73] and deliberated by the tribunal in *Thunderbird v. Mexico* in 2006.[74] It has since been widely discussed among arbitral tribunals,[75] mainly as part of the FET provision.[76] Many arbitral tribunals recognised the protection of investors' LE as the 'most important function'[77] of the FET standard. The extensive body of research on FET and legitimate expectations necessitates a clear specification of the adopted theoretical framework for studying these concepts.

Wrong Course: The Doctrine of Legitimate Expectations in Investment Treaty Law' (2011) 49 Alberta Law Review 203 https://doi.org/10.29173/alr131; Felipe Mutis Téllez, 'Conditions and Criteria for the Protection of Legitimate Expectations under International Investment Law' (2012) 27 ICSID Review-Foreign Investment Law Journal 432, 432-342 https://doi.org/10.1093/icsidreview/sis018; Robert Kolb, *Good Faith in the International Law* (Hart Publishing 2017) 243-50; Arwel Davies, 'Investment Treaty Interpretation, Fair and Equitable Treatment and Legitimate Expectations' (2018) 15 Manchester Journal of International Economic Law 314; Srinath Reddy Kethireddy, 'Still the Law of Nations: Legitimate Expectations and the Sovereigntist Turn in International Investment Law' (2019) 44 The Yale Journal of International Law 315.

69. *Metalclad Corp. v. Mexico*, ICSID Case ARB(AF)/97/1, Award, 30 August 2000, paras 88-89.
70. *ADF Group Inc. v. USA*, ICSID Case ARB(AF)/00/1, Award, 9 January 2003, para. 189 ('any expectations that the Investor had with respect to the relevancy or applicability of the case law it cited were not created by any misleading representations made by authorized officials').
71. *Wena Hotels Ltd. v. Egypt*, ICSID Case No. ARB/98/4, Final Award, 8 December 2000, 41.
72. *See* Chapter 2.C.3.
73. *International Thunderbird Gaming Corporation v. The United Mexican State*, Particularised Statement of Claim, 15 August 2003, 111 footnote 161 (citing 'O. Schatcter, International Law in Theory and Practice (Boston: Dordrecht, 1991) at 324 [70]').
74. *International Thunderbird Gaming Corporation v. The United Mexican States* UNCITRAL Award, 26 January 2006, para. 147.
75. Potestà, 'Legitimate Expectations' (n 68) 92; *Gold Reserve v. Venezuela*, ICSID, Award, 22 September 2014, para. 576.
76. *Sevilla Beheer and others v. Spain*, ICSID Case No. ARB/16/27, Decision on Jurisdiction, Liability and the Principles of Quantum, 11 February 2022, para. 712; *Philip Morris Brands SARL, Philip Morris Products SA and Abal Hermanos SA v. Oriental Republic of Uruguay*, ICSID Case No. ARB/10/7, Award 8 July 2016, para. 426; *Rumeli Telekom A.S. and Telsim Mobil Telekomunikasyon Hizmetleri A.S. v. Republic of Kazakhstan*, ICSID Case No. ARB/05/16, Award, 29 July 2008, para. 609; *AWG v. Argentina*, Ad hoc Arbitration, Decision on Liability, 30 July 2010, para. 222; *Vivendi v. Argentina (II)*, ICSID, Decision on Liability, 30 July 2010, para. 222; *Mobil Exploration and Development Argentina Inc. Suc. Argentina and Mobil Argentina Sociedad Anónima v. Argentine Republic*, ICSID Case No. ARB/04/16, Decision on Jurisdiction and Liability, paras 932, 933; *Gold Reserve Inc. v. Venezuela*, ICSID Case No. ARB(AF)/09/1, Award, 22 September 2014, para. 571; *OI European Group B.V. v. Venezuela*, ICSID Case No. ARB/11/25, Award, 10 March 2015, para. 491; *Deutsche Telekom v. India*, PCA, Interim Award, 13 December 2017 336; *Air Canada v. Venezuela* ICSID, Award, 13 September 2021, para. 447; *UAB v. Latvia*, ICSID, Award of the Tribunal, 22 December 2017, para. 834; *Antaris Solar GmbH and Dr Michael Göde v. Czech Republic*, PCA Case No. 2014-01, Award, 2 May 2018, para. 260; *Agility v. Iraq*, ICSID, Final Award, 22 February 2021, para. 162.
77. *FREIF Eurowind Holdings Ltd. v. Kingdom of Spain*, SCC Case No. 2017/060, Final Award of 8 March 2021, para. 534; *Electrabel SA v. Republic of Hungary*, ICSID Case No. ARB/07/19, Decision on Jurisdiction, Applicable Law and Liability, 30 November 2012, para. 7.75; *Saluka Investments B.V. v. Czech Republic*, UNCITRAL, Partial Award, 17 March 2006, para. 302.

2 Public International Law and the Coordination of International Law

Scholars have approached international investment law from different angles, or 'paradigms'.[78] The book adopts a public international law theory.[79] I acknowledge the hybrid nature of international investment law, combining private-inspired procedures with the applicability of public international law rules.[80] However, I do not view international investment law as a purely 'self-contained regime' of law, nor as a public law field.[81] Rather, I conceive it as part of the wider public international law.[82] Analysing investment arbitration as part of this wider field allows the search for the coordination of international law.[83] This forms the basis of the theoretical framework and attempts to integrate ICCL into the resolution of disputes under IIAs.

Furthermore, the research adopts a rule of law theory,[84] which recognises the superiority of law.[85] It suggests that the legalisation and judicialisation of disputes contribute to international peace and security, strengthen the role of law, and oblige states domestically and internationally.[86] The theory posits that states and investors are bound by the legal rules governing their disputes.[87] When appropriate and based on the treaty, it seeks to balance the rights of investors with the ability of states to regulate in the public interest[88] and underscores the significance of legal certainty and predictability while recognising the diversity of standards and the complexity in their application. This nuanced theoretical framework is best suited to reconcile ICCL and international investment law through the doctrine of legitimate expectations.

Having clarified the object of study and the theoretical framework for the research, I now turn to the presentation of ICCL.

78. Anthea Roberts, 'Clash of Paradigms: Actors and Analogies Shaping the Investment Treaty System' (2013) 107 Am JIL 45 https://doi.org/10.5305/amerjintelaw.107.1.0045.
79. *Ibid.*, 83-84; Dolzer and Schreuer, *Principles of International Investment Law* (n 47) 2-5; Bruno Simma, 'Foreign Investment Arbitration: A Place for Human Rights?' (2011) 60 ICLQ 573, 576 https://doi.org/10.1017/s0020589311000224.
80. Jose Alvarez, *The Public International Law Regime Governing International Investment* (The Hague Academy of International Law 2011); Roberts, 'Clash of Paradigms' (n 78) 92; Zachary Douglas, 'The Hybrid Foundations of Investment Treaty Arbitration' (2003) 74 BYBIL 1 152 https://doi.org/10.1093/bybil/74.1.151.
81. Simma and Pulkowski, 'Of Planets and the Universe' (n 2) 484.
82. Jose Enrique Alvarez, 'Is Investor-State Arbitration "Public"?' (2016) 7 Journal of International Dispute Settlement 3 534, 537 https://doi.org/10.1093/jnlids/idw019; José E. Alvarez, '"Beware: Boundary Crossings": A Critical Appraisal of Public Law Approaches to International Investment Law' (2016) 17 JWIT 171 https://doi.org/10.1163/22119000-01702001.
83. Simma and Pulkowski, 'Of Planets and the Universe' (n 2).
84. Hersch Lauterpacht (ed.), *International Law: Collected Papers* (CUP 1970) vol. 1, 25-28.
85. All versions of political liberalism stress the importance of the rule of law. Elements of the idea are at least as old as Pericles' Funeral Oration (431 B.C.). As a modern technical term, 'rule of law' was brought to prominence by A.V. Dicey, *see* Roger Michener and Albert van Dicey, *An Introduction to the Study of the Law of the Constitution* (Liberty Fund 1982) 107-123.
86. Hersch Lauterpacht (ed.), *International Law: Collected Papers* (CUP 1970) vol. 1, 25-28.
87. Joseph Raz, 'The Rule of Law and Its Virtue' in Joseph Raz (ed.), *The Authority of Law: Essays on Law and Morality* (OUP 1979) 210, 211 (For research purposes, I consider the core of the rule of law as the main elements he identifies: the absence of arbitrary power; general non-retrospectivity; the subjection of government to general laws; the independence of the judiciary).
88. Dolzer and Schreuer, *Principles of International Investment Law* (n 47) 20.

B INTERNATIONAL CLIMATE CHANGE LAW

This book addresses climate change law in its various forms and, in particular, its regime on the international plane. This is the reason the research is based on an established concept in environmental studies, namely, 'international climate change law.'[89] ICCL, as defined by its authors, is the legal response to global climate deterioration.[90] It not only consists of the UN climate regime, instruments adopted under the United Nations Framework Convention on Climate Change (UNFCCC) by the Conference of the Parties (COP)[91] but also of 'rules and principles of general international law relevant to climate change,[92] norms developed by other treaty regimes and international bodies;[93] regulations,[94] policies,[95] institutions at the regional, national, and sub-national levels,[96] and judicial decisions of national,[97] regional[98] and international courts'[99,100] The UN climate regime has long lacked enforceable binding norms and thus appeared as a diplomatic endeavour.[101] However, recent private and public law disputes[102] progressively invoke the Paris Agreement. These disputes show that some of the UN climate regime's provisions can be interpreted as legally binding on state parties.[103]

89. *See* Bodansky, *Climate Change Law* (n 11).
90. In its premises, it posits that international law can address the challenges arising from climate change, such as sea-level rise, shifting weather patterns and the resulting migration of people.
91. Bodansky, *Climate Change Law* (n 11) 36; UN instruments adopted under the UNFCCC include the Kyoto Protocol and the Paris Agreement, *see* Chapter 4.A.1.
92. Such as the polluter pays principle which is retrieved in Art. 19(1) of the Energy Charter Treaty ('The Contracting Parties agree that the polluter in the Areas of Contracting Parties, should, in principle, bear the cost of pollution, including transboundary pollution, with due regard to the public interest and without distorting Investment in the Energy Cycle or international trade').
93. Policies specific to climate change include, for instance, the European Union's Directives such as EU FIT for 55 and the directives analysed in Chapter, *see* Chapter 3.A.
94. Regulations are rules that are mandatory and enforceable. Regulations specific to climate change include, for instance, the European Union's Directives such as EU FIT for 55, and the directives analysed in Chapter, *see* Chapter 3.
95. Policies are rules that are made by organisations to achieve their aims and goals. Policies specific to climate change include notably the Nationally Determined Contributions, which are public documents states must publish every five years as part of the Paris Agreement's obligations, *see* Chapter 4.A.6.
96. Norms developed by institutions are usually non-binding. The research does not include these norms as part of the research.
97. Judicial decisions of national courts may have a direct impact on the state's climate change obligations; hence, it can indicate a specific regulatory framework to prospective foreign investors; for an extensive analysis, *see* Chapter 4.A.7.
98. *Ibid.*, regional courts currently seized by questions of climate change obligations include the ECtHR.
99. *Ibid.*, international courts include, *inter alia*, the ITLS and the ICJ.
100. Bodansky, *Climate Change Law* (n 11) 11.
101. *Ibid.*
102. For an overview of ongoing public and private law climate change-related litigation *see* Sabin Center for Climate Change Law and Arnold & Porter, 'U.S. Climate Change Litigation' (*Climate Case Chart*) https://climatecasechart.com/us-climate-change-litigation/ accessed 23 October 2023.
103. *See*, for instance, domestic administrative rulings related to climate change in Chapter 4.A.7.

ICCL increasingly influences the conduct of states, leading to net zero commitments and enactment of climate change policies, or as I propose to call them, 'net zero measures'.[104] Enacting net zero measures may generate a conflict of norms with the protection of investments under international investment law.[105] The conflict would arise, for instance, with a coal phase out decision because the host state is bound simultaneously by investment treaty obligations it owes to foreign investments and its obligations to reduce GHG under ICCL.[106] It may also generate disputes, for instance, when clean energy investors rely on state commitments to develop a certain energy type and the state then frustrates that reliance.[107] This research focuses on ICCL 'relevant' to investment arbitration, including the Kyoto Protocol[108] and the Paris Agreement, which both set binding climate targets. It also analyses the Glasgow Pact (COP 26), which devises the net zero objective and calls for a 'phasedown of unabated coal'.[109] A refined overview of the notion and purpose of ICCL follows.

1 Notion and Purpose

ICCL is an emerging field of international law[110] and is considered part of international environmental law.[111] ICCL originated in the 1980s, with the creation in 1988 of the Intergovernmental Panel on Climate Change (IPCC)[112] by UN General Assembly Resolution 43/53.[113] The General Assembly recognised the need to ensure a healthy environment[114] following the IPCC reports[115] on the effects of climate

104. *See* practical developments in Chapter 1.B.
105. *See* Chapter 4.B.1.
106. *Ibid.*
107. *See* Chapter 3.A, an extensive description of the type of frustrating measures contested by clean energy investors following their investments relying on incentives.
108. Freya Baetens, 'The Kyoto Protocol in Investor-State Arbitration: Reconciling Climate Change and Investment Protection Objectives' in Marie-Claire Cordonnier-Segger, Markus Gehring and Andrew Newcombe (eds), *Sustainable Development in World Investment Law* (Wolters Kluwer 2011) 683.
109. *See* Chapter 4.A.5.
110. Cinnamon Carlarne, Kevin R. Gray and Richard Tarasofsky, 'International Climate Change Law: Mapping an Emerging Field of International Law' in Cinnamon Carlarne, Kevin R. Gray and Richard Tarasofsky (eds), *The Oxford Handbook of International Climate Change Law* (OUP 2016) 3-13.
111. Alan Boyle and Navraj Singh Ghaleigh, 'Climate Change and International Law Beyond the UNFCC' in Carlarne (eds), *Oxford Handbook of International Climate Change Law* (n 110) 31-32; 43-49.
112. Navraj Singh Ghaleigh, 'Science and Climate Change Law: The Role of the IPPC in International Decision-Making' in Cinnamon Carlarne, Kevin R. Gray and Richard Tarasofsky (eds), *The Oxford Handbook of International Climate Change Law* (OUP 2016).
113. UNGA Res 43/53 (6 December 1988) UN Doc A/RES/43/53.
114. UNGA Res 45/94 (14 December 1990) UN Doc A/RES/45/94; UNGA Res 45/212 (21 December 1990) UN Doc A/RES/45/212 (establishing an Intergovernmental Committee to prepare '[a]n effective framework convention on climate change, containing appropriate commitments').
115. *Ibid.*, 133 the IPCC's mission was to scientifically establish the impact of human activities on global climate patterns and their socio-economic consequences.

change.[116] The negotiations led to the adoption of the UNFCCC[117] at the 1992 Rio Earth Summit.[118] The purpose of ICCL is to mitigate GHG emissions globally. This goal has been enshrined with the signature of Article 2 of the 1992 UNFCCC. The article obliges contracting states:

> To achieve, in accordance with the relevant provisions of the Convention, stabilisation of greenhouse gas concentrations in the atmosphere at a level that would prevent dangerous anthropogenic interference with the climate system.[119]

This provision served as a precursor to the Kyoto Protocol,[120] COP 21,[121] and COP 26.[122] Most states are committed to achieving Article 2's objectives.[123] This implementation can create tension with protected property rights under investment protection.

2 Legal and Political Tensions with Investment Protection

The implementation of ICCL generates growing political and legal tensions with investment protection under IIAs. Achieving the objectives of ICCL means adopting net zero policies, which may create tensions with international investment obligations. A number of European states justified their withdrawal from the Energy Charter Treaty (ECT), a major European 1994 investment agreement, based on climate change mitigation arguments.[124] France, Germany, and the Netherlands[125] argued, in essence, that 'the Energy Charter Treaty cannot align with the necessary pace of decarbonization in the energy sector and the level of emissions reduction required by 2030'.[126] The

116. IPCC's mission is threefold. It consists in the preparation of three cyclical reports addressing: (a) a comprehensive review of scientific literature with respect to the science of climate change; (b) a social and economic impact assessment of climate change; and (c) potential response strategies.
117. United Nations Framework Convention on Climate Change (adopted 9 May, entered into force 21 March 1994) U.N. Doc. A/AC.237/18 (Part II)/Add.1 (UNFCC).
118. UNGA Res 47/190 (22 December 1992) UN Doc A/RES/47/190.
119. United Nations Framework Convention on Climate Change (opened for signature 20 June 1992, entered into force 1994) (1992) 31 ILM 848 (UNFCCC) Art. 2.
120. Kyoto Protocol to the United Nations Framework Convention on Climate Change (opened for signature 16 March 1998, entered into force 16 February 2005) (1998) 37 ILM 22 (Kyoto Protocol) Arts 6, 12, 17.
121. Jorge E. Viñuales, 'The Paris Climate Agreement: An Initial Examination' (2015) 6 C-EENRG Working Papers.
122. *See* Chapter 4.A.5.
123. Daniel M. Firger, 'The Potential of International Climate Change Law to Mobilise Low-Carbon Foreign Direct Investment' in Pierre-Marie Dupuy and Jorge Viñuales (eds), *Harnessing Foreign Investment to Promote Environmental Protection. Incentives and Safeguards* (CUP 2013) 189-194.
124. For instance, French High Council on Climate, *Report on the Modernisation of the Energy Charter Treaty* (Report, 2022).
125. 'Governments Should Not Foot the Bill for Stranded Assets: Treaties That Lead to Fossil Fuel Bailouts Need a Rethink' *Financial Times* (London, 21 February 2022).
126. French High Council on Climate, *Modernisation* (n 124) 2 ('The main obstacle posed by the ECT, even in a modernised version, is the *incompatibility* between the timetables for decarbonisation of the energy sector with the safeguards stipulated in the Treaty. (...) Only withdrawal from the ECT combined with cancelling out its "sunset clause" would eliminate the

argument has since divided investment arbitration proponents and opponents.[127] The colossal question that animates academic scholarship is whether ICCL is on a 'collision course' with international investment law.[128]

Scholars and politicians in favour of withdrawing from investment treaties typically argue that measures necessary to achieve climate change objectives are incompatible with the protection of investments in the energy sector. In France, the French *Haut Conseil pour le Climat* (Climate High Council) opined in this sense.[129] The Council's statement prompted France to officially withdraw from the ECT. Such statements and similar ones[130] advanced to justify withdrawal from the ECT may be politically founded but are not always legally sound.[131] As will be demonstrated in the research, there is no direct incompatibility between obligations under international investment law and obligations under ICCL.[132] In reality, international investment law may enforce net zero commitments, as investors in the clean energy sector demand states to uphold subsidies compensating for upfront capital expenses,[133] for instance, in Spain, Italy, Czech Republic,[134] Bulgaria,[135] Ukraine[136] or Japan.[137]

Treaty's *incompatibility* with timetable for decarbonisation by 2030 and restore Member States' sovereignty over their climate and energy policies while limiting the risk of litigation.') (*emphasis added*).

127. OECD, *Investment Treaties and Climate Change: OECD Public Consultation January-March 2022* (Compilation of Submissions, 2022) 75-81, 111-113, 129-132, 137-143.
128. *See* the reform of the ECT in Chapter 5; *see also*, e.g., Carolina Moehlecke, 'The Chilling Effect of International Investment Disputes: Limited Challenges to State Sovereignty' (2020) 64 International Studies Quarterly 1 https://doi.org/10.1093/isq/sqz077, however, from a legal perspective, as demonstrated in Chapter 4, there is no incompatibility between the two regimes of law, and thus no 'clash'; *see* Chapter 4.B.
129. French High Council, *Modernisation of the Energy Charter Treaty* (n 124) 2.
130. UK Climate Change Committee, *Progress in Reducing Emissions 2023 Report to Parliament* (Report, 2023) 52, 66 ('the UK should reconsider its membership of outdated agreements such as the Energy Charter Treaty to ensure it is well placed to keep pace with the growing momentum of the low-carbon transition'), *see also* 69-70.
131. They generally do not address the exact damages potentially incurred by states for their net zero policies, the role of investment treaties in incentivising clean energy investments, nor the 'terminability' of sunset clauses.
132. *See* Chapter 4.B.1.
133. *ESPF Beteiligungs GmbH et al. v. Italian Republic*, ICSID Case No. ARB/16/5, Final Award, 14 September 2020, para. 546 ('The upfront, capital intensive and long-term nature of investments in the PV sector was well known and appears to have been borne in mind in the design of the Conto Energia regime, and in particular the granting of specific tariff rates for a period of 20 years to qualifying PV plants.'); *see also AES Solar and others (PV Investors) v. Spain*, PCA Case No. 2012-14, Final Award, 28 February 2020, paras 227, 307; *Silver Ridge v. Italy* (n 56) para. 463.
134. Discussed at length in Chapter 3.A.
135. *Energo-Pro v. Bulgaria*, ICSID Case No. ARB/15/19; *EVN v. Bulgaria*, ICSID Case No. 13/17.
136. Max Hall, 'Legal Challenge to Ukraine's Retroactive FIT Cuts' (*PV-Magazine*, 5 May 2022) www.pv-magazine.com/2021/05/05/legal-challenge-to-ukraines-retroactive-fit-cuts/ accessed 27 August 2022.
137. King and Wood Mallesons, 'First Japan Investment Treaty Claim Renewable Energy Disputes in Asia' (5 May 2021) https://www.kwm.com/jp/en/insights/latest-thinking/first-japan-investment-treaty-claim-renewable-energy-disputes-in-asia.html accessed 28 August 2022.

In sum, ICCL incentivises the adoption of net zero policies,[138] and these policies may create tension with the substantive standards of expropriation and FET. It may prompt states to withdraw from investment treaties – although their legal reasoning for doing so may be doubtful. Having clarified the notion and role of ICCL in creating tensions with international investment law, it appeared necessary to create a new typology called 'net zero energy investment disputes'.

C NET ZERO ENERGY INVESTMENT DISPUTES

The research requires a new typology to categorise disputes related to net zero transition policies adopted in accordance with climate change agreements. Net zero transition policies pose *political risks* to energy investors. The risks related to the transition arise out of the effective policy implementation, which discriminates coal and fossil fuel investments[139] while incentivising clean energy investments.[140] This discrimination makes the creation of a new typology crucial, as typologies used so far do not adequately reflect the dichotomy.

1 Notion of Net Zero Transition

The 'net zero' energy transition is the term adopted by the Glasgow Climate Pact and is used by states devising their Nationally Determined Contributions (NDCs). 'Net zero' (or climate neutrality) refers to the balance between the amount of GHG[141] produced and the amount removed from the atmosphere.[142] The 'zero-emissions commitment' would set anthropogenic emissions to zero. Attaining net zero GHG emissions requires extensive changes across the economy.[143] Therefore, this is the

138. There are other reasons to implement clean energy measures, such as energy security, environmental and health concerns, but the notion of 'net-zero' originates from a climate change report and the implementation of its recommended measures has a toll on existing assets, economic development, and energy security (phasing out coal also translates into less reliable, non-intermittent sources of energy at disposal).
139. Article 4.20 of the Glasgow Pact, *see* sub-section '5 2021 Glasgow Climate Pact' for a full-fledged analysis.
140. Bodansky, *Climate Change Law* (n 11) 12 ('Policies to reduce emissions include energy efficiency standards, subsidies for renewable energy, a carbon tax, an emission trading system, funding of urban mass transit systems, and technology research and developments').
141. IPCC, *Global Warming of 1.5°C. An IPCC Special Report on the Impacts of Global Warming of 1.5°C Above Pre-industrial Levels* (Report, 2018) 549-551.
142. *Ibid.*, 545 ('*Climate* neutrality is the concept of a state in which human activities result in no net effect on the climate system. Achieving such a state would require the balancing of residual emissions with emission (carbon dioxide) removal as well as accounting for regional or local bio geophysical effects of human activities that, for example, affect surface albedo or local climate.'), *see also* 555 ('Net Zero emissions mean that *greenhouse gas emissions* are balanced by the removal of an equivalent amount of greenhouse gas emissions from the atmosphere. Therefore, this would include methane emissions which are particularly relevant to the oil and gas and agricultural sectors').
143. Climate Change Committee, *2021 Progress Report to Parliament: Progress in Reducing Emissions* (Report, 2021) 8 ('avoiding catastrophic climate change requires a huge shift in the energy base of both the British and global economies'); in France, Law n° 2015-992 passed on 17 August

appropriate terminology to approach ICCL, the phasing down of a specific type of investment and the incentives to 'clean' power generations. The use of the term 'net zero' may have legal consequences on the legitimacy of expectations in the non-renewable sector.[144]

2 Typology of Disputes

Different methods exist to classify environment-related investment disputes. However, the scholarship is legalistic and qualitative,[145] with few quantitative exceptions.[146] In my view, there is, however, a fundamental distinction between disputes comprising an environmental element and disputes arising out of net zero transition measures. Environmental law is virtually always analysed as a state defence, while climate change law can be both a sword and a shield. A sword for foreign investors in the clean energy sector and a shield for states against fossil fuel investors' claims.

One environmental typology by Prof. Jorge Viñuales provides a descriptive category[147] of environment-related investment dispute, which he defines as any dispute related to an environmental component.[148] This descriptive definition presents a breadth of cases, including pro-environmental and anti-environmental measures adopted by states. However, the categorisation handles the 'environment' as a theme rather than an analytical category. The analytical category proposed by Daniel Behn is closer to my endeavour.[149] It allows an analysis of cases where the host state's

---

2015 '*relative à la transition énergétique pour la croissance verte*' establishes the objective to reduce GHG emissions to contribute to the European goal of 40% reduction of emissions by 2030 in comparison with the 1990 reference; in Germany, the '*Erneurbare-Energien-Gesetz*' passed on 1 January 2021 lays down the objectives of the government to achieve net zero by 2050.

144. Notions such as 'zero emissions' or 'zero carbon', which respectively mean that no GHG or CO_2 emissions are produced in the first place, can bear additional legal risks in the non-renewable sector.
145. Cordonnier-Segger, *Sustainable Development* (n 108); *Foreign Investment and the Environment in International Law* (CUP 2012); Dupuy and Viñuales, *Harnessing* (n 123); Kate Miles, *The Origins of International Investment Law: Empire, Environment and the Safeguarding of Capital* (CUP 2013).
146. Daniel Behn and Malcolm Langford, 'Trumping the Environment? An Empirical Perspective on Investment Treaty Arbitration' (2017) 18 JWIT 14, 17 https://doi.org/10.1163/22119000-12340030.
147. *Ibid.*, 3.
148. Jorge Viñuales, 'Foreign Investment and the Environment in International Law: The Current State of Play' (2016) C-EERNG Working Papers 2016-1, 17 ('disputes that arise from the operations of investors (i) in environmental markets (e.g. land-filling, waste treatment, garbage collection, pesticides/chemicals, energy efficiency, emissions reduction, biodiversity compensation, etc.) and (ii) in other activities, where their impact on the environment or certain minorities is part of the dispute (e.g. tourism, extractive industries, pesticides/chemicals, water extraction or distribution) and/or (iii) to disputes where the application of domestic or international environmental law is at stake').
149. Behn and Langford, 'Trumping the Environment?' (n 146) 17 ('an environment-related investment dispute' is 'a treaty-based claim where the Claimant-investor is challenging a domestic measure in the state where the investment is hosted, and that measure is taken and justified by the respondent state, in whole or part, on the grounds of environmental conservation or protection').

environment-related measure is used as a justification, defence, or exception[150] to the alleged breach of the applicable IIA. However, Behn's categorisation is not adequate for this research. First, his typology focuses on environmental cases rather than energy transition disputes. Second, it relies on arguments advanced by the respondent state and thus on that state's capacity to raise the environment as a defence, justification, or exception. However, these arguments may have been left aside for purely strategic questions of the litigation procedure, even if arbitrators have become more receptive to such ideas over time.[151]

In contrast, my proposed analytical typology focuses on the disputed *measures* arising out of a net zero energy transition (which might not have been labelled as such at the time of implementation).[152] For this research, I define net zero energy-related investment dispute as follows:

> Treaty-based claim where the claimant-investor is challenging a domestic measure in the state where the energy investment is hosted, and that measure (i) restricts the net zero energy transition policy the investor relied upon or (ii) is taken and justified by the respondent state, in whole or in part, on the grounds of climate change mitigation.

The typology is limited to energy-related claims and serves an analytical purpose. It includes two types of cases. One type is based on the initial energy transition measure relied upon by the foreign investor (in most instances, this will include clean energy cases). The word 'restrict' pertains to cases in which a foreign investor relied upon incentives and was thereafter frustrated in its expectations by measures 'detrimental to environmental protection' because they hindered or reduced the production of clean energy. The second type is based on the circumstances in which the state justifies its measure, at least partly based on climate change mitigation arguments (in most instances, this will include fossil fuel energy cases). The focus on energy transition measures allows the assessment of 'anti-environmental' (restrictions on incentives to the clean energy sector) and 'pro-environmental' disputes (phasing out of an industry sector or of incentives towards that industry).

The typology was used to compile relevant published and accessible final awards on merits of a FET breach,[153] excluding pending disputes. The focus is on investment

150. Defences are mechanisms that states use to respond to investment claims in arguing that their action was lawful and justified under international law (proportionality, necessity, right to regulate in the public interest). Exceptions are provisions within investment treaties that carve out specific circumstances under which a state's obligation under the treaty does not apply (public health, environment, national security are often mentioned in IIAs as grounds to exclude liability for actions that might otherwise breach an IIA's obligation).

151. Makane Moïse Mbengue and Elena Cima, 'Greening International Investment Arbitration' in Elena Cima and Makane Moïse Mbengue (eds), *A Multifaceted Approach to Trade Liberalisation and Investment Protection in the Energy Sector* (Brill 2021).

152. For instance, early investment claims brought against Canada in relation to its Net Zero energy transition but not analysed in this monograph, *Mesa Power Group, LLC v. Government of Canada*, UNCITRAL, PCA Case No. 2012-17, Award (24 March 2016); *Windstream Energy LLC v. Government of Canada*, PCA Case No. 2013-22, Award (27 September 2016).

153. I thus exclude the significant cases of *Strabag and others v. Germany*, ICSID Case No. ARB/19/29; *Uniper SE, Uniper Benelux Holding B.V. and Uniper Benelux N.V. v. Kingdom of the Netherlands*, ICSID Case No. ARB/21/22; *RWE AG and RWE Eemshaven Holding II BV v.*

treaty-based arbitrations, as non-treaty arbitrations with a respondent state party remain primarily confidential.

The main objective of the typology is to usefully address the literature gap. This gap lies in the insufficient consideration of ICCL's impact on standards of protection under international investment law.

D ICCL's EFFECT ON LEGITIMATE EXPECTATIONS

Given the increasing importance of ambitious decarbonisation efforts, accelerated phase down calls for coal, and the emergence of new business economies in renewables,[154] there has been a growing interest among investment law scholars and practitioners to explore the implications of climate change for investment law.[155] For long, environmental related issues in investment law have attracted the attention of scholars, civil society, and politics,[156] focusing on environmental obligations that contravene investment standards.[157] However, the focus on climate change laws is rather recent.

There is still little research on the impact of ICCL on the application of standards and sub-standards of international investment law. So far, research on the interaction between ICCL and expropriation or FET has been broad. Little research focused on LE

Kingdom of the Netherlands, ICSID Case No. ARB/21/4; *Westmoreland Mining Holdings, LLC v. Canada*, ICSID Case No. UNCT/20/3; *TransCanada Corporation and TransCanada PipeLines Limited v. The United States of America*, ICSID Case No. ARB/16/21; *see* generally regarding recent claims Arman Sarvarian, 'Invoking the Paris Agreement in Investor-State Arbitration' (2023) 38 ICSID Review 2 422 https://doi.org/10.1093/icsidreview/siad006.

154. Rocky Mountain Institute, *How to Retire Early: Making Accelerated Coal Phase out Feasible and Just* (Report, 2020) 6.
155. Sandrine Maljean-Dubois, Hélène Ruiz Fabri and Stephan Schill, 'International Investment Law and Climate Change: Introduction to the Special Issue' (2022) 23 JWIT 5-6 737 https://doi.org/10.1163/22119000-12340268; Anatole Boute, 'Environmental Force Majeure: Relief from Fossil Energy Contracts in the Decarbonisation Era' (2021) 33 Journal of Environmental Law 2 339, 340-342 https://doi.org/10.1093/jel/eqaa034; Cees Verburg and Jaap Waverijn, 'Liberalizing the Global Supply Chain of Renewable Energy Technology: The Role of International Investment Law in Facilitating Flows of Foreign Direct Investment and Trade' (2020) 2 Brill Open Law 101 https://doi.org/10.1163/23527072-00201001; Kyla Tienhaara, 'Regulatory Chill in a Warming World: The Threat to Climate Policy Posed by Investor-State Dispute Settlement' (2018) 7 Transnational Environmental Law 229 https://doi.org/10.1017/s2047102517000309; Jorge Viñuales, 'Foreign Investment and the Environment in International Law: An Ambiguous Relationship' (2009) 80 British Yearbook of International Law 244 https://doi.org/10.1093/bybil/80.1.244.
156. One of the first scholar to methodically explore the question is undoubtedly Kate Miles, 'International Investment Law and Climate Change: Issues in the Transition to a Low Carbon World' (2008) SIEL Working Paper 27/08 1-2; Kate Miles, 'International Investment Law and the Environment: Introduction' in Kates Miles (ed.), *Research Handbook on Environment and Investment Law* (Edward Elgar Publishing 2019) 1-10.
157. *Ibid.*; *see* Lise Johnson, Lisa Sachs and Nathan Lobel, 'Aligning International Investment Agreements with the Sustainable Development Goals' (2019) 58 Columbia Journal of Transnational Law 58, 62-64, 69-79 https://doi.org/10.2139/ssrn.3452070; for an overview of the gap between pledges and fossil fuel production *see* Stockholm Environment Institute and others, *Governments' Planned Fossil Fuel Production Remains Dangerously Out of Sync with Paris Agreement Limits* (Report, 2021) 12-23.

in particular, perhaps because investment lawyers failed to integrate climate change-related arguments into their disputes.[158] Below, I present a brief overview of the literature on the topic so far.

1 Existing Studies on the Relationship Between International Investment Law and Climate Change

There are three main areas of discussion on the relationship between international investment law and climate change. These are briefly summarised below.

The first area in literature is the potential dichotomy in values and objectives between international climate change, environmental objectives and international investment law.[159] In particular, the notion of growth and economic development, which are at the core of international investment law,[160] have been either opposed to the 'green transition' or the notion of 'sustainable development'[161] and the 'green economy'.[162] These concepts provide, however, little guidance in resolving investment disputes nor in resolving normative conflicts.[163] They may signal either a synergy or a divergence of values between human rights and property rights protected under investment treaties.

A second area of research is the increasing role of ICCL in IIAs. This scholarship focuses on 'new generation BITs' and the drafting of new environmental-friendly provisions.[164] Compared to traditional investment agreements, a new generation of

158. Compared to existing studies, I also adopt a legal doctrinal method based on arbitral awards. I decided not to conduct policy or empirical research because it was not suited to analyse arbitral awards in-depth, doctrines and questions of legal compatibility; Sarvarian, 'Invoking the Paris Agreement' (n 153) 430 ('However, in none of these proceedings has the argument been made that mitigation duties under the Kyoto Protocol 1998 shaped the duties of respondents with respect to legitimate expectations under the fair and equitable treatment standard').
159. Fritjof Capra and Ugo Mattei, *The Ecology of Law: Towards a Legal System in Tune with Nature and Community* (BK 2015) 131-146; Lorenzo Cotula, '(Dis)integration in Global Resource Governance: Extractivism, Human Rights, and Investment Treaties' (2020) 23 Journal of International Economic Law 2 431, 435, 442-452 https://doi.org/10.1093/jiel/jgaa003.
160. Kenneth J. Vandevelde, 'Investment Liberalization and Economic Development: The Role of Bilateral Investment Treaties' (1998) 36 Columbia JTL 501, 503, 515.
161. The concept originally stems from International UCN, UNEP and WWF, *World Conservation, Strategy, Living Resource Conservation for Sustainable Development* (Report, 1980).
162. UNEP, *Towards a Green Economy; Pathways to Sustainable Development and Poverty Eradication: A Synthesis for Policy Makers* (Report 2011) 2-3; Daniel Bodansky and Jessica Lawrence, 'Trade and Environment', in Daniel Bethlehem and others (eds), *The Oxford Handbook of International trade Law* (OUP 2009) 505.
163. Among others, Gabčíkovo-Nagyamaros Project (*Hungary v. Slovakia*), ICJ Reports 1997, 7; Iron Rhine (Railway Arbitration (*Belgium v. Netherlands*), RIAAA vol 27 (2005) 25, paras 59-60 ('the mere invocation of [the principle of sustainable development] does not, of course, provide the answers in this arbitration to what may or may not be done, where, by whom and at whose costs').
164. Kezhen Su and Wei Shen, 'Environmental Protection Provisions in International Investment Agreements: Global Trends and Chinese Practices' (2023) 15 Sustainability 8525, 8530 https://doi.org/10.3390/su15118525 (the authors delineate four types of environmental provisions: (1) those preserving the state's right to regulate, e.g., Article 12 of the US Model BIT (2012); (2) provisions recognising environmental protection as a treaty objective (NAFTA,

treaties is starting to contain environmental and climate change-related provisions.[165] It is still unclear how these provisions[166] will affect the resolution of investment disputes, although they affect the objective and purpose of the treaty.[167] It is likely that treaties referring directly to 'climate change' as a legitimate policy objective may help the integration of ICCL norms in the adjudication of disputes.[168]

The third area, and my focus in this research, concerns the interaction between ICCL and international investment law *in resolving investment disputes*.[169] The object is to analyse whether and to what extent ICCL may have an impact on the adjudication of investment disputes.[170] Recent research has emerged on this topic.[171] But there is still a significant gap.[172] In particular, the gap stems from the fact that ICCL's impact on the resolution of investment disputes differs from the impact of other international environmental laws on investment disputes.[173] Environmental law obligations are often analysed as a state defence to fend off investment claims of expropriation or

preamble); (3) provisions prescribing states' continuing duty to impose environmental protection measures; (4) hybrid model comprising both an emphasis on environmental protection as parties' mutual objective and a requirement for high-level environmental protection standards (Dutch Model BIT 2019).

165. Paul Thiessen, 'Reforming the Energy Charter Treaty for sustainability?' (2022) 40 Journal of Energy & Natural Resources Law 4 465, 472-474 https://doi.org/10.1080/02646811.2022.2040214.

166. In particular, scholars have focused on the recent Canada Model 2021 BIT; Canada 2021 Foreign Investment Promotion and Protection Agreement Model.

167. Laura Létourneau Tremblay, 'In Need of a Paradigm Shift: Reimagining *Eco Oro v Colombia* in Light of New Treaty Language' (2022) 23 JWIT 5-6 915 https://doi.org/10.1080/02646811.2022.2040214; Catharine Titi, 'International Investment Law and the European Union: Towards a New Generation of International Investment Agreements' (2015) 26 European Journal of International Law 3 639 https://doi.org/10.1093/ejil/chv040; Marc Bungenberg and Catharine Titi, 'The Evolution of EU Investment Law and the Future of EU-China Investment Relations' in Wenhua Shan and Jinyuan Su (eds), *China and International Investment Law* (Brill Nijhoff 2014) VII.

168. Crina Baltag, Riddhi Joshi, Kabir Duggal, 'Recent Trends in Investment Arbitration on the Right to Regulate, Environment, Health and Corporate Social Responsibility: Too Much or Too Little?' (2023) 38 ICSID Review 2 381, 420-421.

169. OECD, *Investment Treaties and Climate Change* (n 127) 9-15; major works on fragmentation include Simma and Pulkowski, 'Of Planets and the Universe' (n 2) 509; Bruno Simma, 'Universality of International Law from the Perspective of a Practitioner' (2009) 20 European Journal of International Law 2 265, 275-276 https://doi.org/10.1093/ejil/chp028; James Crawford and Penelope Nevill, 'Relations Between International Courts and Tribunals: The "Regime Problem"' in Margaret A. Young (ed.), *Regime Interaction in International Law: Facing Fragmentation* (CUP 2012) 235, 259.

170. Sarvarian, 'Invoking the Paris Agreement' (n 153) 439 (concluding that the Paris Agreement may have the greatest 'impact' on disputes under the ECT).

171. Walid Ben Hamida, 'Droit climatique et du droit des investissements: de la friction à la Coordination' (2021) 18 Revista Brasileira de Arbitragem 71, 84 https://doi.org/10.54648/rba2021031; Ximena Torrijo, 'Climate Change and International Investment Treaties' in *Elgar Encyclopaedia of Environmental Law* (EEP 2016) 309, 319.

172. Among the forty submissions compiled in the OECD Public Consultation on Investment Treaties and Climate Change, FET is mentioned only three times as a critical standard that might hinder climate policies; *see* OECD, *Investment Treaties and Climate Change* (n 127) 119.

173. Behn and Langford, 'Trumping the Environment?' (n 146) 19; Anna Joubin-Bret and others, 'International Investment Law and Development' in Cordonnier-Segger, *Sustainable Development* (n 108) 17-20.

unfair treatment.[174] ICCL, unlike environmental law, may stand both as a state defence against a fossil-fuel company and as a supportive argument for a clean energy investor's claim.[175]

2 Integrating ICCL in the Resolution of Investment Disputes

As mentioned above, there is more research on environmental law's than on ICCL's impact on investment disputes. This obliges us to delve into scholarly works on the role of environmental law in investment disputes. There are three ways scholars have analysed the interaction between environmental and international investment law. First, through a legitimacy discourse on regime conflicts. Second, by referring to sustainable development goals. Third, through a global administrative law (GAL) theory. All three research lenses are insufficient for the concrete resolution of investment disputes in light of ICCL. The three approaches are summarised below.

a) Three Limited Frames Addressing ICCL in Investment Disputes

Below, I present the three aforementioned frames. While providing important background, they are insufficient to address the complex relationship between ICCL and the protection of legitimate expectations.

A significant portion of the scholarly work on the conflict between environmental law and investment law is grounded in the concept of 'legitimacy' rather than 'normative' conflicts.[176] Prof. Jorge Viñuales[177] proposes an analytical approach to the distinction.[178] He suggests that the requirement of states to adopt environmental measures[179] and the 'discipline' imposed by investment agreements create, at least, a

174. Flavia Marisi, *Environmental Interests in Investment Arbitration: Challenges and Directions* (Kluwer Law International 2020) 39 (the author does not address ICCL on the ground that the Paris Agreement has not yet 'created a principle that has been effectively invoked by parties to investment arbitration cases and/or discussed by arbitral tribunals').
175. *See* Chapter 5 on ICCL's three impacts on legitimate expectations.
176. Kate Miles, 'Arbitrating Climate Change: Regulatory Regimes and Investor-State Disputes' (2010) 1 Climate Law 1 63, 92 https://doi.org/10.1163/cl-2010-004 ('While there are indications of more balanced approaches developing, such as those seen in the *Methanex* and *Parkerings* awards and in the drafting of "new generation BITs", the jurisprudential trends discussed in this paper also point to continued problems for environmental matters in investor-state disputes – and this suggests that international investment law may also operate so as to frustrate measures of climate change mitigation in the future').
177. Viñuales, 'Foreign Investment and the Environment in International Law: Current Trends' in Miles, *Handbook* (n 156) 8.
178. Jorge Viñuales, 'Investment Law and Sustainable Development: The Environment Breaks into Investment Disputes in International Investment Law' in Marc Bungenberg, Jörn Griebel, Stephan Hobe and August Reinisch (eds), *International Investment Law: A Handbook* (Nomos/Hart 2015) 1714.
179. Viñuales, 'Foreign Investment and the Environment in International Law: Current Trends' in Miles, *Handbook* (n 156) 18 (according to the author, legitimacy conflicts arise when the norms stem from different legal orders, while normative conflicts arise when they are from the same legal order).

legitimacy conflict.[180] He demonstrates that tribunals increasingly justify their decision from an environmental perspective and integrate environmental norms in the assessment of 'the diligence that can be expected from the investor, the deference that must be accorded to state authorities, the normality and legality of environmental regulatory change over time or environmental justifications for differential treatment'.[181] This type of research is close to my endeavour to investigate whether and how ICCL can integrate the assessment of LE. However, the difficulty with the approach is that it sees the integration of environmental norms as a defence argument for states. On the opposite, I do not focus solely on states' rights, nor on the 'diligence' of the investor, but rather on the objective circumstances of their investment and the legitimacy of their expectations. In my opinion, there is no strict conflict of interest between ICCL and investment protection. In fact, there is even a compatibility in promoting clean energy investments.

A second approach relies on exploiting the concept of 'sustainable development' to decide investment cases.[182] The concept comprehends environmental, social, and economic objectives to deliver fair growth for current and future generations.[183] When examined in relation to international investment law, scholars generally exploit the concept to advocate greater regulatory freedom for host states.[184] They analyse whether recent IIAs' reference to sustainable development goals may impact disputes.[185] Some wish to apply sustainable goals to the conduct of investors,[186] conditioning their rights under investment treaties to their compliance with SDGs.[187] However, from the perspective of treaty interpretation alone, sustainable goals have little concrete meaning in an investment dispute, unless interpreted as a jurisdictional condition of the investment – i.e., as a condition to contribute to the development of the host state.[188] The lack of concrete consequences leads to reform calls for investment

180. *Ibid.*, 27 (according to author, the 'traditional' approach views the tension between investment discipline and the protection of the environment as a 'legitimacy conflict', considering domestic environmental measures as primarily driven by national concerns and economic protectionism. A 'progressive' approach, on the other hand, would consider the tension as a 'normative conflict', where domestic environmental measures are seen as required or justified by international environmental treaties. This perspective aims to place environmental norms on an equal footing with other international norms, including investment treaties. Prof. Viñuales argues that, in practice, investment tribunals seem to adopt a middle ground, incorporating environmental considerations into the interpretation of legal concepts (such as police powers doctrine, reasonableness or definition of 'like circumstances').
181. *Ibid.*, 37.
182. Tarcisio Gazzini, 'Bilateral Investment Treaties and Sustainable Development' (2014) 15 JWIT 5-6 929 https://doi.org/10.1163/22119000-01506008.
183. Manjiao Chi, *Integrating Sustainable Development in International Investment Law: Normative Incompatibility, System Integration and Governance Implications* (Routledge 2017).
184. UNCTAD, *Investment Policy Framework for Sustainable Development* (Report, 2015) 78.
185. UN, *Guiding Principles on Business and Human Rights* (Report, 2011).
186. Chi, *Sustainable* (n 183) 28-30.
187. International Chamber of Commerce, *Business Charter for Sustainable Development* (Charter, 2015).
188. Chi, *Sustainable* (n 183) 34-36.

treaties or the dispute settlement mechanism.[189] The (re)drafting of IIAs remains outside the scope of the research.

The third way to assess international investment law provisions in light of ICCL is by balancing the state's right to regulate with investors' rights. This approach generally relies either on state sovereign prerogatives under public international law or on a public law analysis emphasising proportionality.[190] Proponents of the latter gather under the GAL theory.[191] Under this theory, adjudicating disputes under IIAs would be more than settling individual disputes but be part of a global governance structure.[192] It conceives investment law as 'public law' and advocates for an increased resort to 'proportionality balancing' to respect sovereign policy freedom and predictability.[193] The principle of proportionality could arguably respond to the absence of a balanced system between the rights of the investor and the state.[194] In the GAL view, it is opportune that arbitral tribunals adopt and implement principles of 'global administrative law'[195] to apply systemic values in individual cases, one of these being the principle of proportionality.[196] Under this theory, environmental welfare may amount to a 'global public interest'.[197] Such 'interest' would require employing the proportionality test *stricto sensu*.[198] Accordingly, states would be held to intrusive standards of

189. Joshua Paine and Elizabeth Sheargold, 'A Climate Change Carve-Out for Investment Treaties' (2023) 26 Journal of International Economic Law 2 285, 288-291 https://doi.org/10.1093/jiel/jgad011.
190. Benedict Kingsbury and Stephan Schill, 'Public Law Concepts to Balance Investors' Rights with State Regulatory Actions in the Public Interest: The Concept of Proportionality' (2010) 75 International Investment Law and Comparative Public Law 97 https://doi.org/10.1093/acprof:oso/9780199589104.003.0003.
191. The central thesis of Gus van Harten was to consider international investment agreements and law as instruments of Global Administrative Law. *See* Gus van Harten, *International Treaty Arbitration and Public Law* (OUP 2007) 45 ('Investment treaty arbitration is often viewed as a form of reciprocally consensual adjudication between an investor and a state. The argument of this chapter is that it should be viewed as a mechanism of adjudicative review in public law. That is the case for two reasons: first, the system is established by a sovereign act of the state; second, it is predominantly used to resolve disputes arising from the exercise of sovereign authority (...) As a public law system, investment treaty arbitration engages the regulatory relationship between state and individual, rather than a reciprocal relationship between juridical equals.'); Gus Van Harten and Martin Loughlin, 'Investment Treaty Arbitration as a Species of Global Administrative Law' (2006) 17 European Journal of International Law 121 https://doi.org/10.1093/ejil/chi159; Gus Van Harten and Dayna Scott 'Investment Treaties and the Internal Vetting of Regulatory Proposals: A Case Study from Canada' (2016) 7 Journal of International Dispute Settlement 1 92, 116 https://doi.org/10.1093/jnlids/idv031; Stephan Schill and Djanic Vladislav, 'Wherefore Art Thou? Towards a Public Interest-Based Justification of International Investment Law' (2018) 33 ICSID Review-Foreign Investment Law Journal 1 29 https://doi.org/10.1093/icsidreview/six025.
192. Benedict Kingsbury and Stephan Schill, 'Investor-State Arbitration as Governance' in Albert Jan van den Berg (ed.), *50 Years of the New York Convention: ICCA International Arbitration Conference* (Kluwer Law International 2009) 6.
193. As well as transparency, amicus participation, processes for review of initial arbitral awards, heightened reason-giving.
194. Marisi, *Environmental Interests* (n 174) 165.
195. Kingsbury and Schill, 'Investor-State Arbitration as Governance' (n 192) 7.
196. *Ibid.*, 9-10, 12.
197. Andreas Kulick, *Global Public Interest in International Investment Law* (CUP 2012) 25 ff.
198. *Ibid.*, 188, 266.

review but afforded regulatory space to act in the public interest.[199] This conceptualisation allows the integration of extraneous norms, such as ICCL, into the balancing act when adjudicating international investment disputes. Prof. Stephan Schill proposes a similar view. To him, IIAs allow States to adopt measures pertaining to the mitigation of carbon dioxide (CO_2) emissions, *provided* these climate measures respect the principles of transparency and reasonableness and do not unreasonably change the regulatory framework. To him, the flexibility of the FET standard should allow states to adopt climate measures.[200] The reasoning insufficiently establishes how ICCL may integrate the assessment of LE and could impact the foreseeability and reasonableness of regulatory changes. More generally, the issue with the GAL theory is its universality when investment agreements are bilateral or multilateral but not 'global'.[201] The universal, all-encompassing endeavour is thus difficult to reconcile with the practice of investment arbitration. Investment provisions are necessarily tied to a specific IIA and their interpretation of the Vienna Convention on the Law of Treaties (VCLT).[202] Moreover, there is a growing consensus[203] among practitioners and scholars that investment arbitration is hybrid[204] rather than public or *administrative* law.[205] As a result, the gap lies in the insufficient use of the VCLT and the lack of practical insights on how to resolve conflicts or integrate ICCL elements into the adjudication of an investment dispute.[206]

Having considered the main ways research has so far addressed potential conflicts between ICCL and the FET standard, I turn to the way the gap can be addressed.

b) Taking Climate Change Laws Seriously

Considering the above, the gap remains on whether ICCL may have an impact on the adjudication of investment disputes and, in particular, on the application of certain standards. Some questions are unanswered. Is there an actual conflict between ICCL

199. *Ibid.*, 260-267.
200. Stephan Schill, 'Do Investment Treaties Chill Unilateral State Regulation to Mitigate Climate Change?' (2007) 24 Journal of International Arbitration 5 447; *Ibid.*, (Schill also mentions the role police powers doctrine in relation to the Expropriation provision) *see* Noam Zamir 'The Police Powers Doctrine in International Investment Law' (2017) 14 Manchester JIEL 3 318; Lehmann, 'Police Powers' (n 61) 74.
201. *See* Chapter 2.D.1 for further reasoning on problems arising from a public law approach.
202. *See* Chapter 2.A.
203. Alex Mills, 'The Public-Private Dualities of International Investment Law and Arbitration' in Chester Brown and Kate Miles (eds), *Evolution in Investment Treaty Law and Arbitration* (CUP 2011).
204. *See* for an excellent summary of the distinct positions Jose Enrique Alvarez, 'Is Investor-State Arbitration "Public"?' (2016) 7 Journal of International Dispute Settlement 3 534, 537 https://doi.org/10.1093/jnlids/idw019.
205. *Ibid.*; Niccolò Ridi and Thomas Schultz, 'Empirically Mapping Investment Arbitration Scholarship: Networks, Authorities, and the Research Front' in Katia Fach Gomez (ed.), *Private Actors in International Investment Law* (Springer 2020) 213.
206. *See* the analysis on the compatibility and relevance of ICCL in investment disputes in Chapter 4.B.

and international investment law? Can parties 'invoke' the Paris Agreement in investment disputes?[207] Are climate change norms relevant to the adjudication of investment disputes? If yes, to what extent? These questions are addressed in this book,[208] although the findings are limited to the application of 'legitimate expectations' under the FET standard. To find where climate change and LE meet necessitates delving into the divergences in the interpretation of the LE doctrine, its sources, and theories and whether there are certain convergences. The originality of the book is to demonstrate that there is convergence on factual elements of LE (time of the investment, risks assumed by the investor and foreseeability of the frustrating measure), which allows the factual integration of ICCL as part of energy investors' LE.

3 Doctrinal Analysis

To address the gap, the book provides a doctrinal analysis relying on typical primary and secondary sources. Within the primary sources are international treaties, arbitral awards and non-legal data sources on climate change and energy-related topics (i.e., IPCC, International Energy Agency, Organisation for Economic Co-operation and Development (OECD)). Among the secondary sources are the legal literature on international investment law and ICCL and the literature on the relationship between energy, growth, and climate change. Forty-two awards[209] – rendered before August 2023 and based on the NZEID typology. With due regard to Article 38 of the Statute of the International Court of Justice (ICJ), the research adopts a methodical and hierarchical interpretation of LE, starting with the treaty interpretation, principles of law, ICJ decisions and finally, arbitral awards, which may arguably amount to 'teachings of the most highly qualified publicists'.[210] The research is based on the study of treaties and awards. IIAs[211] constitute a type of international treaty and a source of international law. The book bases most of its findings on one IIA, the ECT, signed in December 1994,

207. Sarvarian, 'Invoking the Paris Agreement' (n 153) 426 ff.
208. *See* Chapter 4.B.
209. An annex compiles all the arbitral awards that form the basis of this doctoral research. It offers an overview of the application of legitimate expectations in NZEID. Each award reproduced in the appendix is structured to render all essential information on the dispute, including the name of the dispute, date of the award, legal instrument, applicable rules, name of arbitrators, disputes' outcomes – including the amount claimed and awarded, cost of arbitration, legal costs – and quotes regarding the tribunal's analysis of the investor's LE, due diligence and any relevant mention of climate change. The experts are limited to fragments of the awards.
210. ICJ Statute, Art. 38(1) ('The Court, whose function is to decide in accordance with international law such disputes as are submitted to it, shall apply: a. international conventions, whether general or particular, establishing rules expressly recognised by the contesting states; b. international custom, as evidence of a general practice accepted as law; c. the general principles of law recognised by civilised nations; d. subject to the provisions of Article 59 [i.e., the decision of the Court has no binding force except between the parties and in respect of that particular case] judicial decisions and the teachings of the most highly qualified publicists of the various nations, as subsidiary means for the determination of rules of law').
211. 'International Investment Agreement' (IIA) describes treaties between two or more states governing the legal protection of investments from nationals or entities of one state (home state) in the jurisdiction of the other (host state). The treaty may only concern investments or be included in a broader International Economic Agreement. The treaty may be bilateral

and *entered* into legal force in April 1998. The ECT is a multilateral treaty containing substantive rules on foreign investment of a sectoral nature. It grew out of the desire of European States to cooperate closely with Russia and the new states in Eastern Europe and Central Asia in exploring and developing the energy sector, which is crucial for political, economic and financial reasons.[212] The substantive standards[213] and dispute resolution mechanism[214] of the ECT resemble other international investment treaties, which form part of the general discussions on FET.[215] Climate change treaties include UN regime treaties adopted under the 1992 Framework Convention on Climate Change. Other relevant climate change norms include potentially binding unilateral statements and domestic court judgments.

In the absence of a system of binding precedent under international law, tribunals enjoy a broad margin of discretion in interpreting international law standards.[216] An arbitral award has *inter partes* effects. Arbitrators are solely requested to rule on the facts and arguments presented before them.[217] This may partly explain the vast differences among tribunals on critical questions of law, notably on the scope of the FET standard. For all these reasons, arbitral decisions do not constitute judicial decisions under Article 38 of the Statute. The study draws upon arbitral awards within the 'NZEID' typology outlined above, along with other pertinent cases that hold significance for specific points of interpretation. It attempts to find points of convergence among tribunals, as a degree of predictability and consistency is desirable in delivering international justice.[218]

The book provides a consistent interpretation of international agreements and arbitral awards. The research follows the principles set out in the VCLT under Article 31 on the General rule of interpretation: It analyses fragmentation issues from the premise of binding norms (both under investment and climate change law).[219] Chapter 3 proposes an in-depth analysis of similar NZEID cases under the Energy Charter Treaty emanating from Italy, the Czech Republic and Spain. The research thus offers an

(Bilateral Investment Treaty) or multilateral (Multilateral Investment Treaties (MITs) or integrated in Preferential Trade Agreements or Free Trade Agreements.

212. Dolzer and Schreuer, *Principles of International Investment Law* (n 47) 15.
213. ECT, Art. 10(1) and (3).
214. *Ibid.*, Art. 26 (allows the investor to bring the claim before ICSID, UNCITRAL arbitration rules, Arbitration Institute of the Stockholm Chamber of Commerce or before the courts or administrative tribunals of the Respondent state).
215. Among others, North American Free Trade Agreement between Canada, The United States and Mexico (NAFTA) 1992, German Model BIT.
216. Jorge Viñuales, 'Sources of International Investment Law: Conceptual Foundations of Unruly Practices' in Samantha Besson and Jean d'Aspremont (eds), *The Oxford Handbook of the Sources of International Law* (OUP 2018) 1080, 1086.
217. Stephan Schill, 'Sources of International Investment Law: Multilateralisation, Arbitral Precedent, Comparativism, Soft Law' in Besson and d'Aspermont (eds), *The Oxford Handbook of the Sources of International Law* (OUP 2018) 1103.
218. Yas Banifatemi, 'Consistency in the Interpretation of Substantive Investment Rules: Is It Achievable?' in Roberto Echandi and Pierre Sauvé (eds), *Prospects in International Investment Law and Policy* (CUP 2013).
219. On fragmentation, the research derives much of the thought-process from the ILC, *see* International Law Commission, 2006 Conclusions of the Work of the ILC Study Group on the Fragmentation of International Law: Difficulties Arising from the Diversification and Expansion of International Law (Conclusions, 2006).

in-depth look into the climate change measures that contributed to disputes and arbitral decisions on FET violations. It proceeds with an extensively analysed factual and legal context of the disputes.[220] This framework allows a better comparison of tribunals' reasoning.[221] The study looks for patterns in reasoning and attempts to draw the line between schools of thought on the interpretation of LE. Beyond the 'arbitral case law', the study investigates judicial decisions by the ICJ on the general principle of good faith and the doctrine of unilateral statements.

The scope and findings of the study are limited. The research's findings are primarily based on the concrete application of legitimate expectations in the highly regulated energy sector and in cases arising from net zero energy measures.[222] The concepts of FET and LE are analysed to a limited extent.[223] Building on past research, the third chapter proposes a divide between voluntary and detrimental reliance theories of legitimate expectations. These are two among many theories to analyse the same concept, meant to serve the search for convergence in the application of LE.[224] I do not assert that it represents an unequivocal classification of cases. I do not claim to make an original contribution to the discourse on legal stability under the FET standard.[225] Similarly, if inferences can be made, I do not specifically address questions of law relating to legitimate expectations in the context of the expropriation standard,[226] damages,[227] and the definition of investment.[228] Other substantive and relative protection standards are excluded from the research. The research does not address issues related to damages, although it expects its findings to have a direct impact on their calculation.

220. Filip Balcerzak, *Renewable Energy Arbitration: Quo vadis? Implications of the Spanish Saga for International Investment Law* (Brill Nijhoff 2023), 443; Deyan Draguiev, 'Investment Treaty Arbitration in the Renewable Energy Sector: Overview of Arbitral Case Law on Legitimate Expectations in the Light of Policy' (2018) 7 TDM.
221. Under international investment law, the legal authority and persuasiveness of a ruling are often established by the references of posterior tribunals to their reasoning; *see* Jeffery P. Commission, 'Precedent in Investment Treaty Arbitration, A Citation Analysis of a Developing Jurisprudence' (2007) 24 Journal of International Arbitration 2 129, 133 https://doi.org/10.54648/joia2007012.
222. Broadening the scope of research on FET to all treaty drafting would be impossible, and in any case methodically weaken the findings of the research in endless debates on FET.
223. The research does not conduct an extensive analysis of LE in municipal systems but builds on existing comparative literature on the topic.
224. *See* Chapter 2.D.
225. *Duke Energy Electroquil Partners & Electroquil S.A. v. Republic of Ecuador*, ICSID Case No. ARB/04/19, Award 28 August 2008, para. 340 ('the investor's expectations must be legitimate and reasonable'); *Electrabel SA v. Republic of Hungary*, ICSID Case No. ARB/07/19, Decision on Jurisdiction, Applicable Law and Liability, 30 November 2012, para. 7.76 'the assessment of legitimate and reasonable expectations').
226. Stephen Fietta, 'Expropriation and the "Fair and Equitable" Standard: The Developing Role of Investor's "Expectations" in International Investment Arbitration' (2006) 23 J Int'l Arb 375 https://doi.org/10.54648/joia2006025.
227. *MTD Equity Sdn. Bhd. and MTD Chile S.A. v. Republic of Chile*, ICSID Case No. ARB/01/7, Award, 25 May 2004, para. 240.
228. Zachary Douglas 'Concepts of Property' in Zachary Douglas, Joost Pauwelyn and Jorge Viñuales (eds), *The Foundations of International Investment Law: Bringing Theory into Practice* (OUP 2014).

4 Chapter Organisation

This book is divided into six chapters.

Chapter 1 clarifies the concept of energy, the nexus between net zero measures and energy investor claims, and the rationale for protecting legitimate expectations. It finds that achieving climate objectives requires not only the phasing down of fossil fuel energy but also the development of clean energy investments and government support, which can be strengthened by IIAs.

Chapters 2 and 3 investigate the concept of LE in theory and practice. They discuss the legal problems the concept poses. Chapter 2 deciphers the contours in the case law and the different interpretations of LE to better understand how ICCL could integrate the assessment of the doctrine. Chapter 3 is based on NZEID cases and tries to elucidate whether arbitral tribunals converge in the *application* of LE. This analysis allows for finding which aspects of LE ICCL can have an impact.

Chapters 4 and 5 review the legal impact of ICCL on LE based on these findings. Chapter 4 assesses the compatibility between ICCL and international investment law in theory and further exhibits that ICCL can act as a determinant *factor* in determining the LE of energy investors at the time of the investment. Chapter 5 focuses on the application of ICCL as a fact in NZEID disputes and provides an analytical framework for its effects on energy investors' expectations.

Chapter 6 presents a novel application of legitimate expectations based on the research findings. This proposal aims to integrate ICCL norms as legal facts when tribunals assess what constitutes legitimate expectations.

CHAPTER 1
Energy Investment Protection in the Net Zero Transition

This chapter addresses the rationale for the protection of energy investments' legitimate expectations in the context of the net zero transition. It adopts a practical perspective based on non-legal literature to demonstrate that energy investments contribute to economic development and that achieving climate objectives requires the phasing down of fossil fuel energy and momentous clean energy foreign direct investments and government support. It finds the protection of clean energy investments' legitimate expectations justified.

The chapter examines the rationale behind international law's protection of *energy* investments and their 'legitimate expectations' (LE) from a primarily non-legal perspective. This examination is essential to understand why the assessment of energy investors' LE should be aligned or reconciled with ICCL and objectives. Studies on energy protection under international law generally focus on the laws and policies that regulate the energy sector,[229] geopolitics, or energy security concerns. They fail to investigate the rationale for energy protection.[230] To remedy this gap, this chapter takes a closer look at what energy *is*, its role in economic development and economic growth and the pervasive risks energy investments face. Against this background, the chapter explores whether the protection offered by international investment law to energy investments aligns with the global goals of mitigating climate change. It finds that climate change objectives necessitate foreign direct investments in the clean energy sector and the phase down of fossil fuel energy. This conclusion opens up questions. The main one is whether international investment law can be harnessed to encourage

229. Raphael J. Heffron, *Energy Law: An Introduction* (Springer 2015); Ma Sai, 'Renewable Energy Law: An International Assessment' (2021) 39 JENRL 2 259 https://doi.org/10.1080/02646811.2020.1810957.
230. Tibisay Morgandi and Jorge Viñuales, 'Energy Security in International Law' in Robin Geiß and Nils Melzer (eds), *The Oxford Handbook of the International Law of Global Security* (OUP 2021).

clean energy investments. The second is whether legal protection of fossil fuel assets is compatible with the achievement of net zero objectives. Both questions constitute the focus of the subsequent doctrinal chapters and justify why integrating ICCL norms into legitimate expectations is of significance.

The chapter aims to (section A) determine *why* energy investment makes up a significant part of international investment-treaty disputes; (section B) establish whether climate change law warrants abandoning legal protection for energy investments; and (section C) question whether achieving the net zero transition justifies protecting clean energy investors' legitimate expectations.

A ENERGY'S ROLE IN THE ECONOMY: A BACKBONE

This section presents what energy is and the accurate reason why it generates more disputes than any other sector.

It is widely agreed that international energy investments are subject to inherent risks.[231] The main ones are economic,[232] commercial (price volatility), financial (interest rate), geological, technical, managerial and natural.[233] Yet, why does the energy sector provide such a high number of disputes with states, including investment disputes?[234] A *common* explanation is that energy is a commodity remarkably vulnerable to political risks.[235] A few reasons explain why energy investments carry a particular 'sensitivity'.[236] First, the energy industry stands as one of the largest economic sectors globally.[237] As such, it requires continuing investments due to growing demand, which proportionally increases the perimeter of potential disputes.[238] Second, the nature of energy investments and projects is characterised by

231. On the notion of risk, *see* Terje Aven and Ortwin Renn 'On Risk Defined as an Event Where the Outcome is Uncertain' (2009) 2 Journal of Risk Research 1, 3-5 https://doi.org/10.1080/13669870802488883 ('Risk refers to uncertainty about and severity of the consequences (or outcomes) of an activity with respect to something that humans value').
232. Stephan Schill, 'Foreign Investment in the Energy Sector: Lessons for International Investment Law' in Eric de Brabandere and Tarcisio Gazzini (eds), *Foreign Investment in the Energy Sector: Balancing Private and Public Interests* (Bril Nijhof 2014) 260; 263.
233. *Ibid.*, 36; Thomas Waelde, 'Investment Arbitration under the Energy Charter Treaty: From Dispute Settlement to treaty Implementation' (1996) 12 Arbitration International 4 429, 431 https://doi.org/10.1093/arbitration/12.4.429.
234. The term 'Energy Investment Law' has been comprehensively defined by Professor Peter Cameron with detailed account of the specific risks energy businesses face, *see* Peter Cameron, *International Energy Investment Law: The Pursuit of Stability* (2nd edn, OUP 2021).
235. Rahmi Kopar, *Stability and Legitimate Expectations in International Energy Investments* (Bloomsbury Publishing 2021) 34.
236. Cameron, *International Energy* (n 234) 3.
237. OECD, *World Energy Investment Outlook 2023* (Report, 2023) 12 ('We estimate that around USD 2.8 trillion will be invested in energy in 2023. More than USD 1.7 trillion is going to clean energy, including renewable power, nuclear, grids, storage, low-emission fuels, efficiency improvements and end-use renewables and electrification. The remainder, slightly over USD 1 trillion, is going to unabated fossil fuel supply and power, of which around 15% is to coal and the rest to oil and gas. For every USD 1 spent on fossil fuels, USD 1.7 is now spent on clean energy. Five years ago, this ratio was 1:1').
238. *Ibid.*, 63-64; 99; 160.

their long duration, large scale, capital intensity and high technology.[239] Their value and long-term business plan make them prone to disputes over time with a state.[240] Third, the most evident explanation is purely political risk over natural resources.[241] As this chapter demonstrates, the reason for disputes over natural resources is probably that energy is the backbone of economic development. As such, it creates 'inherent' tensions over property rights, exploitation, and distribution. Indeed, the backbone of the economy is energy rather than capital or legal persons.[242] The legal protection of energy investments appears more logical once one understands what energy is.

1 Defining Energy

The object of this section is not to discuss energy as an 'investment'.[243] The notion of 'energy investment' has not yet found a clear or consensual definition in the context of international law[244] because of the difficult delineation of the legal framework applicable to 'investments'.[245] Rather, the object of the section is to discuss energy as a resource, a product, a technology and an activity.[246] The section delves into the intricacies of energy sources and types and reminds us that energy is essential to living species. It finds that energy plays a fundamental role in producing goods and services. And that energy is an 'engine' in the construction of the modern economy and of globalisation.

First, 'energy' is a physical concept which responds to specific rules of physics.[247] In physics, 'energy' is defined as 'the capacity to do work'.[248] It exists in two *forms*:

239. UNCTAD, *World Investment Report: Transnational corporations, Extractive Industries and Development* (Report, 2007) 91; Kopar, *Stability* (n 235) 33.
240. *Ibid.*
241. Friedemann Polzin and others, 'Public Policy Influence on Renewable Energy Investments: A Panel Data Study Across OECD Countries' (2015) 80 Energy Policy 98 https://doi.org/10.1016/j.enpol.2015.01.026; Cambridge Economic Policy Associates for the Department of Energy and Climate Change, *Policy Risk in Renewable Energy Investments in Developing Countries* (Report 2014).
242. Bishop, Crawford and Reisman, *Foreign Investment Disputes* (n 51) (1st edn, 2004) 2 ('modern foreign direct investment (FDI) began to take shape in the mid-nineteenth century, stimulated by two independent, but interrelated, trends – the rapidly-increasing rate of technological invention and the growth of corporations and other forms of business association as method of raising, accumulating and deploying capital'). I argue that the invention of the steam engine and use of material resources such as coal were paramount to any technological and corporation innovation.
243. The debate in arbitration regards whether 'investment' found in Art. 25 of the ICSID Convention is defined on an autonomous basis (self-contained approach) or construed by reference to the parties' understanding in a case-by-case analysis (party-defined approach). The latter seems sound, given the negotiating history of the ICSID convention, but flexibility and case-by-case analysis are of the essence when considering the existence of energy investment; Dolzer and Schreuer, *Principles of International Investment Law* (n 47) 74-76.
244. Ozge Varis, 'Redefining Energy in the Post-Pandemic Era' (2020) 2 Global Energy Law and Sustainability 1 164 https://doi.org/10.3366/gels.2020.0021; Kopar, *Stability* (n 235) 32; Schill, 'Foreign Investment' (n 232) 260.
245. Cameron, *International Energy* (n 234) 14.
246. Jorge Viñuales, *The International Law of Energy* (CUP 2022) 10.
247. Robert Jaffe and Washington Taylor, *The Physics of Energy* (CUP 2018) 3.
248. *Ibid.*, 3, 405.

potential and kinetic. Potential energy is stored energy or the energy of position (such as chemical, nuclear, mechanical, and gravitational energy).[249] Kinetic energy is the energy of movement - the motion of electrons, atoms, waves, molecules, substances, and objects (i.e., radiant, thermal, motion, sound, and electrical energy).[250] Any movement, force, or action can be understood as kinetic energy that does work.

Energy *sources* are divided into two main categories: renewable and non-renewable.

Renewable energy (RE) is defined as 'obtained from sources that are essentially inexhaustible, unlike, for example, the fossil fuels, of which there is a finite supply'.[251] The main difference with fossil fuels or solid minerals is that 'during the lifetime of the project, the renewable energy source is being *replenished*'.[252] Primary energy of a renewable energy product includes hydropower, solar, wind, and geothermal heat from inside the earth, tides, waves, and plant biomass.[253] Human and animal muscle, wood, grasses, dung, crops, animal fats, and tallow are also considered renewable energy.[254] Renewable energies are intermittent - they cannot be continuously available due to uncontrollable external factors (wind, sun or water flow). Unlike renewable energy, non-renewable energy, once extracted, can be used without restrictions.[255]

Non-renewable energy is defined as a 'type of energy that cannot be replaced after they have been used'.[256] In other words, non-renewable energy comes from a natural resource that cannot be readily replaced by natural means at a pace quick enough to keep up with consumption.[257] Non-renewable sources rely on existing natural resources, which have accrued over history. They include petroleum, hydrocarbon gas liquids, natural gas, coal, and nuclear energy.[258] They are derived from 'physical' storage that is limited. Non-renewable energy presents exceptional capacities to produce kinetic energy (heat) and thereby action or 'feed' the motion of machines.[259] The fossil fuel category includes upstream oil and gas, mid/downstream oil and gas, coal supply and fossil fuel power.[260]

'Clean energy' is not a physical term. No energy consumed is 'clean' in the sense of free of environmental impact. It is thus a debated term. Nevertheless, it usefully refers to primary energy that creates far lower CO_2 emissions than burning traditional fossil fuels (oil and gas). Energy investment related to the production of renewable energy can be considered 'clean energy' (i.e., solar energy, either photovoltaic (PV) or

---

249. *Ibid.*, 13.
250. *Ibid.*, 12.
251. United Nations Economic and Social Council, 'Specifications for the Application of the United Nations Framework Classification for Fossil Energy and Mineral Reserves and Resources 2009 to Renewable Energy Resources' (30 September 2016) UN ECE/ENERGY/2016/4, 4.
252. *Ibid.*, 5.
253. Robert Jaffe and Washington Taylor, *The Physics of Energy* (CUP 2018) 261ff.
254. *Ibid.*
255. *Ibid.*, 645ff.
256. 'Non-renewable (n)', *Cambridge Business English Dictionary* (CUP 2022).
257. Robert Jaffe and Washington Taylor, *The Physics of Energy* (CUP 2018) 645.
258. Nuclear energy is a fossil fuel and non-renewable energy source. However, it is a low-carbon energy source and thus can be considered clean.
259. Edward A. Wrigley, *Energy and the English Industrial Revolution* (CUP 2010) 272.
260. International Energy Agency, *World Energy Investment Outlook 2022* (Report, 2021).

concentrated solar power (CSP), wind energy production, hydroenergy production, and biomass energy production).[261] It is debated whether nuclear power can be considered 'clean',[262] although it should.[263]

The above classification helps navigate the debates surrounding clean, renewable, and non-renewable energy. It is also crucial to shed light on the role of energy in our society, which is still not fully grasped. Energy is seen as a commodity. It is much more. Energy is the capacity to do work and the backbone of development and economic growth.

2 Role of Energy in Economic Growth

This sub-section assesses why energy investments are, unlike any other investments, vital for economic growth and development.

a) Energy Drives Economic Development

Energy is at the heart of our societies; it determines *how* we heat, produce, build, transport, and work.[264] In this sense, energy *influences* human economic development significantly.[265] Historians of the Industrial Revolution have extensively demonstrated the correlation between the access and exploitation of energy sources (in particular coal) and economic development.

Until the eighteenth century, renewables were the dominant source of energy.[266] Human and animal *muscles* were the main instruments to build and transport. Sun and rivers were the instruments to grow agricultural plants, wood to warm homes, wind to action windmills or drive sails. Biomass energy (trees) has been dominant throughout human history because of its abundance and ease of use on a local scale.[267] By the eighteenth century, the Industrial Revolution triggered a significant energy transition from renewable to non-renewable sources.[268] The Industrial Revolution is associated

261. Daniel Behn and Ole Kristian Fauchald, 'Governments under Cross-Fire: Renewable Energy and International Economic Tribunals' (2015) 12 Manchester Journal of International Economic Law 2 117.
262. International Energy Agency, *World Energy Investment Outlook 2022* (Report, 2021) (the IEA adopts a broad definition of clean energy, which includes nuclear).
263. Eliseo Castineira and Thomas Lehmann, 'After Vattenfall, a Science-Based Proposal to Account for Climate Change and Biodiversity in Energy Arbitrations' (2021) 39 ASA Bulletin 2 286, 297-302 https://doi.org/10.54648/asab2021026.
264. Vaclav Smil, *Energy and Civilization: A History* (MIT Press 2017) 1ff.
265. *Ibid.*
266. Vaclav Smil, *Biomass Energies: Resources, Links, Constraints* (Plenum Press 1983) 1.
267. *Ibid.*, 3.
268. Edward Wrigley, 'The Supply of Raw Materials in the Industrial Revolution' (1962) 15 The Economic History Review 1 1 https://doi.org/10.2307/2593286 (Wrigley claims that the industrial revolution is characterised by the 'substitution of inorganic material and fuels for the previously organic sources of raw material and power' (wood and animal power)); David Landes, *The Unbound Prometheus: Technological Change and Industrial Development in Western Europe from 1750 to the Present* (2003 CUP).

with the invention of the coal-reliant steam engine.[269] The steam engine works by burning coal (chemical energy) creating heat, which actions mechanical energy leading to the motion of an engine. Coal, oil, and gas 'feed' machines, which transform this energy into work. Machines, which 'do work', dominate all the primary and secondary sectors as they replace human labour (human and animal muscle energy).

Most historical scholarship affirms that non-renewable energy sources played a significant role in the English Industrial Revolution and were necessary for economic and industrial growth.[270] They show that the wide access to non-renewable but non-intermittent energy sources has been a condition *sine qua non* of economic growth.[271] At the same time, economic studies show that the Industrial Revolution marked the beginning of a substantial increase in the use of fossil fuels, initially coal, and hence CO_2 emission.[272] This is also why climate policy goals may be formulated in reference to 'pre-industrial' CO_2 levels.[273]

In sum, since the Industrial Revolution, the economy has been running on fossil fuels. Today, oil, coal, and gas represent 84.3% of global energy consumption (including electricity, transport, and heat). Electricity itself represents roughly 20% of global energy final consumption and is still largely produced by fossil fuels. In fact, fossil fuel still produces also about two-thirds of the global electricity (as of 2022, coal produces 36.7% of global electricity, gas 22.4%, nuclear 9.2%, solar and wind around 12%).[274] Dramatic investment levels are thus necessary to reverse the main sources of production of electricity. Only then is the ongoing electrification of transportation and industries foreseeable and manageable. In other words, the task of transitioning towards a clean energy system is gigantic but necessary.

b) Fossil Fuel Consumption Directly Impacts Climate Change

Fossil fuel production and consumption are intricately linked to climate change. The main drawbacks of fossil fuels are the environmental direct (mining, exploitation) and indirect impacts (release of GHG emissions). When burned, coal, gas, and fuels produce CO_2 and other GHGs such as methane. GHG is considered the main factor of human-led climate change, with CO_2 emissions being the most significant and long-lasting harmful

---

269. For instance, *see* Frederic Scherer, 'Invention and Innovation in the Watt-Boulton Steam-Engine Venture' (1965) 6 Technology and Culture 2 165 https://doi.org/10.2307/3101072.
270. Edward Wrigley, *The Path to Sustained Growth: England's Transition from an Organic Economy to an Industrial Revolution* (2016 CUP) 80.
271. Fernand Braudel, *Civilisation, Économie et Capitalisme. XV-XVIII Siècles*, in: Vol.3. Le Temps du Monde (Armand Colin 1980).
272. IPCC, *Annex I: Glossary in: Global Warming of 1.5°C* (Report, 2018) 552.
273. *Ibid.*, 556 (pre-industrial means 'the multi-century period prior to the onset of large-scale industrial activity around 1750. The reference period 1850-1900 is used to approximate pre-industrial global mean surface temperature (GMST)').
274. Hannah Ritchie, Max Roser and Pablo Rosado, 'Energy' (*Our World in Data*, 2022) https://ourworldindata.org/energy accessed 29 April 2023.

gas.[275] According to the International Renewable Energy Agency, the energy sector contributes to more than 60% (about two-thirds, depending on the source) of GHG emissions as GHG includes CO_2 and other gases, all the while its demand increases yearly.[276] In fact, global CO_2 emissions from fossil fuels have risen from 22.5 to 37.2 billion tons between the conference of Rio in 1992 and 2021.[277] Energy demand, and thus the economic development of societies, is largely responsible for this increase.[278] The other characteristic of non-renewable energy sources is that they are extremely convenient, which complicates the transition to other sources. GHG emissions due to human activities have not reached their peak because of the growing, albeit slowing, global energy demand.[279]

In conclusion, it is clear that the energy sector is essential to economic development. Without energy, there are no trucks, no commercial vessels, no planes, no plastic, no construction, and, without fossil fuels and, in hindsight, no modern society. This partly explains why energy has benefited from legal protection beyond that offered to other investments and why it remains one of the most disputed sectors in Investor-State Dispute Settlement (investment arbitration). Since international investment law aims to economically develop state parties, as established in virtually all investment treaty preambles, protecting energy investments, i.e., the backbone of economic development, appears logical.

In this context, should climate change objectives draw a line under energy investment protection? As demonstrated below, ICCL and net zero require drastic reductions of emissions from non-renewable energy sources. A tension thus arises *prima facie* with the investment protection goals. ICCL calls for a halt on new investments in fossil fuels and thus may contradict economic development objectives stated under investment treaties.

B NET ZERO TRANSITION: A TALE OF TWO ENERGY TYPES

We have seen that energy and energy production are essential to economic development and are intricately linked to GHG emissions and climate change. In this section, I turn to the relationship between ICCL and the net zero transition.

275. IPCC, *Climate Change 2014: Synthesis Report. Contribution of Working Groups I, II and III to the Fifth Assessment Report of the Intergovernmental Panel on Climate Change* (Report, IPCC 2015) 151 ('Anthropogenic greenhouse gas emissions have increased since the pre-industrial era, driven largely by economic and population growth, and are now higher than ever').
276. International Renewable Energy Agency, *Renewable Energy: A Key Climate Solution* (Report, 2017) 8.
277. Hannah Ritchie and Max Roser, 'Global CO2 Emissions from Fossil Fuels' (*Our World in Data*, 2020) https://ourworldindata.org/CO2-emissions accessed 4 October 2023.
278. International Energy Agency, *Global Energy Review 2021* (Report, 2021) 6-10.
279. BP, 'BP Energy Outlook 2018' (*Press Release*, 20 February 2018) www.bp.com/en/global/corporate/news-and-insights/press-releases/energy-outlook-2018.html accessed 31 October 2023; World Energy Council, 'World Energy Scenarios 2016' (*World Energy Council*, 2016); Kopar, *Stability* (n 235) 24.

1 ICCL Creates the Framework to Implement the Net Zero Transition

The evidence on the human origin of climate change led to political goodwill to mitigate GHG emissions in the atmosphere under ICCL. And to devise a path towards a global low-carbon economy, named 'net zero transition'.

Evidence shows that to achieve the Paris Agreement's 1.5 degrees by 2100 goals, 80% of all proven fossil fuel reserves would necessarily - arithmetically - 'become stranded resources and investments already made in such resources turn into stranded assets'.[280] Against this background, one question comes to mind. Does ICCL oblige to curb legal protection for energy producers?

From a legal perspective, the answer is not obvious and I deal with the question of conflict in a later chapter.[281] But, to summarise, the phase *post*-Kyoto Protocol is the most relevant to policies in the energy sector.[282] The Protocol's first commitment period ran from 2008 to 2012 to reduce GHGs by an average of 5% compared to 1990 levels.[283] It created a strong impetus, notably in the European Union (EU), to incentivise clean energy investments.[284] The Paris Agreement in turn signalled a consensus, if not unanimity, on the binding objective of the agreement to hold the increase in the global average temperature through energy policies.[285] It obliged states to publish NDCs, which must detail policy plans.[286] The Glasgow Pact nominatively designates fossil fuel and coal investments as impediments to climate action.

It is undeniable that the UN climate regime participated in creating a level playing field, allowing parties to plan energy transitions. In particular, the Glasgow Pact, with its aim to reach climate neutrality, or net zero, showcases the global initiative towards this goal.[287] During the latest Glasgow Climate Pact, 130 governments have taken pledges to reduce the carbon intensity of their economic apparatus by achieving 'net zero'.[288] In this context, net zero-related disputes increase amid regulations adopted by states to meet their objectives.[289]

280. Kyra Bos and Joyeeta Gupta, 'Climate Change: The Risks of Stranded Fossil Fuel Assets and Resources to the Developing World' (2018) 39 Third World Quarterly 3 436 https://doi.org/10.1080/01436597.2017.1387477.
281. *See* Chapter 4.B.1.
282. The fourth phase includes the 2007 Bally action plan, the 2009 Copenhagen Accord, 2011 Durban platform, 2012 Doha amendment which extended the Kyoto Protocol through 2020, the Paris Agreement, and the successive CMAs (Conference of the Parties serving as the meeting of the Parties to the Paris Agreement, i.e., the Glasgow Climate Pact).
283. *Ibid.*, 170-174, however, the parties to the commitment period represented only 12% of global GHG emissions.
284. Bodansky, *Climate Change Law* (n 11) 24.
285. Paris Agreement (n 6) Art. 2.1(a).
286. *See* Chapter 2.D.4 and Chapter 4.A.1.
287. More on the legal aspects of ICCL in Chapter 4.A.
288. Jorge Viñuales and others, 'Climate Policy after the Paris 2015 Climate Conference' (2017) 17 Climate Policy 1 https://doi.org/10.1080/14693062.2016.1242060.
289. Monica Feria-Tinta, 'The Role of International Law and Arbitration in Enforcing the Paris Agreement' (*Kluwer Arbitration Blog*, 31 December 2016) http://kluwerarbitrationblog.com/2016/12/31/the-role-of-international-law-and-arbitration-in-enforcing-the-paris-agreement/ accessed 5 September 2023.

2 Delineating the Implications for Energy Investors

As suggested above, ICCL impacts states' net zero policies. The role of ICCL is crucial in shaping objectives of clean energy generation and setting a level-playing field across the world. Hence, it weighs in on energy investment policies.[290] But what does it concretely mean to pursue a net zero transition, as stated in recent COPs?

We must turn to a more detailed account of the meaning of 'net zero transition'. The Oxford Dictionary defines transition as 'A passing or passage from one condition, action, or (rarely) place, to another; change.'[291] Applied to energy, transition means the process of 'changing' from one energy supply structure to another. In the words of Vaclav Smil, energy transition means 'the change in the composition (structure) of primary energy supply, the gradual shift from a specific pattern of energy provision to a new state of an energy system'.[292] Through a more legal lens, focusing on the policies of the state, 'energy transition' refers specifically to the '*policies* adopted by a State to achieve a particular goal by shifting between sources of energy'.[293] 'Net zero' is a substantiated term, compared to 'Renewable Energy Transition'[294] or 'Green transition',[295] which are unsubstantiated aspirational terms.[296]

Properly understood, net zero transition, in the context of climate change, is the political response to the need to reduce the negative impacts of GHG emissions.[297] It

290. US Department of Energy, 'Investing in American Energy: Significant Impacts of The Inflation Reduction Act and Bipartisan Infrastructure Law on The U.S. Energy Economy and Emissions Reductions' (August 2023).
291. 'Transition' (*OECD Online*, OUP 2023).
292. Vaclav Smil, *Energy Transitions: History, Requirements, Prospects* (Praeger Publishers Inc 2010) In this sense, energy transitions have always existed (i.e., the shift from biomass to non-renewable energy sources during the Industrial Revolution or the phasing out of a certain source of energy for instance nuclear or coal energy); *see* Benjamin Sovacoolab, 'How Long Will It Take? Conceptualizing the Temporal Dynamics of Energy Transitions' (2016) 13 Energy Research and Social Science 202 https://doi.org/10.1016/j.erss.2015.12.020: 'It is natural to shift between energy sources as local resource scarcity, convenience, pollution, technical innovation, cost, energy quality, storage, and other factors come into play, people are not required to keep using a particular source if better options become available.'
293. Debra Davidson, 'Exnovating for a Renewable Energy Transition' (2019) Nature Energy 4 254 https://doi.org/10.1038/s41560-019-0369-3.
294. 'Renewable Energy Transition' is a catchword emphasising the role of renewable energies in transforming the global energy sector, the concept suggests a *replacement of* unsustainable energy sources with renewable energies but does not refer to the climate neutrality targets and thus bears fewer risks to non-renewable investor.
295. Unlike carbon neutrality, it is not solely concerned with CO_2 but also the conservation of biodiversity and the environment. It is an aspirational term that designates a society's evolution towards an economic model that considers planetary boundaries and aims for environmental protection and decarbonisation, The Green Deal refers to the Commission's economic agenda aimed at realising the goal to reach Net Zero emissions target by 2050, constituted of several European Regulations, directives, initiatives, and global strategies. The term is used to translate 'Europe's new growth strategy, which will transform the Union into a modern, resource-efficient and competitive economy.'
296. Additionally, the notions do not clearly include nuclear or hydro energy (they are not 'renewable' and might be considered inadequate to achieve 'green transition' goals because of their impact on land use, protection of biodiversity, or forest and river management).
297. IPCC, *A.3.3 Executive Summary for Policy Makers: Global Warming of 1.5°C* (Executive Summary, 2018) ('future climate-related risks would be reduced by the upscaling and

focuses on mitigation and thus on the reduction of energy-related GHG emissions.[298] This means that net zero and climate change mitigation[299] become, along with adaptation and energy security,[300] primary drivers of regulatory change.[301]

Implementing the net zero transition means keeping fossil fuel reserves largely untouched. With a 50 % probability of keeping global temperature increase below 2 °C, the carbon budget[302] for 2011 to 2050 is around 1,100 gigatons of CO_2. Global fossil fuel reserves hold about three times this amount.[303] This implies that at least 33 % of all oil, 49 % of all gas and 82 % of all coal reserves should remain underground.[304] The vast majority (75 % according to Tienhaara and Cotula) of foreign-owned coal power plants that would need to be 'phased out' to achieve net zero are covered by at least one treaty, which includes investment arbitration.[305] This triggers interrogation about the potential 'regulatory chill' that could result from investment agreements and cause regulatory action to be delayed or scrapped – especially in developing countries where coal power plants are younger.[306]

In sum, implementing the net zero transition means reducing coal and, to a lesser extent, oil and gas production. In clear terms, implementing the 'net zero' transition will financially impact the fossil fuel sector while necessarily needing to incentivise its alternative, i.e., clean energy.

acceleration of far-reaching, multilevel and cross-sectoral *climate mitigation* and by both incremental and transformational adaptation').

298. Castineira and Lehmann, 'After Vattenfall' (n 263) 288-290 ('Any increase in average temperature, however small, may trigger exponential consequences, which include droughts, floods and rising sea levels, mass migration, wars, famine and diseases (e.g., the melting of permafrost which would release various GHGs and ancient viruses and pathogens). Such events would likely be scenarios if global warming exceeded 3 degrees Celsius').
299. IPCC, *Annex I: Glossary in: Global Warming of 1.5°C* (Report, 2018) 554 (the mitigation of climate change means 'a human intervention to reduce emissions or enhance the sinks of greenhouse gases').
300. *Ibid.*, 542 ('In human systems, the process of adjustment to actual or expected climate and its effects, in order to moderate harm or exploit beneficial opportunities. In natural systems, the process of adjustment to actual climate and its effects; human intervention may facilitate adjustment to expected climate and its effects').
301. *Ibid.*, 554 (Mitigation measures are understood as 'technologies, processes or practices that contribute to mitigation, for example, renewable energy (RE) technologies').
302. The carbon budget is the cumulative greenhouse gas (GHG) emissions over a given time frame, which cannot be exceeded if the global average temperature should not rise above a certain threshold. The carbon budget I refer to focuses solely on the increase in the concentration of carbon dioxide from the burning of fossil fuels, which is recognised as the primary cause of global warming.
303. Christophe McGlade and Paul Ekins, 'The Geographical Distribution of Fossil Fuels Unused When Limiting Global Warming to 2 [degrees] C' (2015) 517 Nature 187 https://doi.org/10.1038/nature14016.
304. *Ibid.*
305. Kyla Tienhaara and Lorenzo Cotula, 'Raising the Cost of Climate Action?' (2020) International Institute for Environment and Development, 27 https://doi.org/10.4324/9781849776905-11.
306. *Ibid.*, 32.

3 Net Zero: An Economic Opportunity for Clean Energy Investors

Considering the numbers above, achieving the net zero transition requires supporting clean energy investments. Clean energy is an absolute necessity to achieve climate change goals. States are unlikely to back down from economic development, for reasons spreading from poverty reduction to GDP growth.[307] In this context, producing clean energy appears as the crucial step towards climate neutrality, pursuance of economic development and achievement of sustainable goals.[308]

The net zero energy transition necessitates substantial financial resources, innovation, and sustainable investments to align the needs for energy consumption.[309] Unless done based on a market solution (inflation on all prices),[310] complete de-growth,[311] or by entirely decoupling the economy, a net zero transition implies that two categories of policy measures shall be adopted. The first involves phasing out specific energy sectors considered incompatible with GHG emissions reduction goals.[312] The second consists in creating economic and legal incentives, in the form of tax reductions, subsidies, and a favourable legal environment, to energy sectors considered sustainable and aligned to reduce GHG emissions.[313]

In summary, the clean energy sector is essential to achieving climate objectives. Investments in the non-renewable sector may complicate the path to the net zero goals and face significant regulatory risks. Clean energy sources contribute to both economic development and climate objectives.

C RATIONALE TO PROTECT LEGITIMATE EXPECTATIONS IN THE NET ZERO TRANSITION

Against this background of energy realism, it appears logical that the protection of energy investments becomes a focal point. Most investment treaties reflect an economic endeavour. They prioritise economic development over climate or environmental concerns. Thus, the tensions with net zero have become increasingly palpable. In this context, should energy investments and investors receive international legal protection? I answer in the positive, with due regard to the objectives of ICCL.

307. Brian Ames and others, *Macroeconomic Policy and Poverty Reduction* (IMF & World Bank 2001), 4.
308. IRENA, *Global Energy Transformation: A Roadmap to 2050* (Report, 2019), 69.
309. Carbone 4, *Net Zero Initiative: 2020-2021 Report* (Final Report, July 2021); Antonio Guterres, 'Humanity Is Waging War on Nature. Nature Always Strikes Back: And It Is Already Doing So with Growing Force and Fury' (Columbia University, 2 December 2020).
310. Cameron Hepburn, 'Environmental Policy, Government, and the Market' (2010) 26 Oxford Review of Economic Policy 2, 133 https://doi.org/10.1093/oxrep/grq039.
311. Timothée Parrique and others, 'Decoupling Debunked. Evidence and Arguments Against Green Growth as a Sole Strategy for Sustainability' (Report European Environmental Bureau, 2019), 3.
312. The Conference of the Parties, Decision 'COP26 Glasgow Climate Pact', adopted on 13 November 2021.
313. Legal incentives are elaborated as part of the factual background to NZEID in Chapter 3.A.

1 Investment Agreements Promote and Protect Energy Investments

It is consensually agreed that IIAs contribute to a stable legal environment,[314] even though some contest that they successfully attract foreign investors.[315] Most agree though that the cornerstone of IIAs, compared to customary international law (CIL),[316] is to strengthen the rights of foreign property holders and to afford them the right to sue the host State, whether through investment disputes or other resolution methods.[317] This endeavour appears efficient, as according to the majority of studies, IIAs are beneficial to foreign direct investments, as substantive protections such as FET and expropriation standards can be linked to higher levels of foreign direct investments.[318] More broadly, the conclusion of these IIAs has supported the liberal development of states' diplomatic relations, particularly after the end of the Cold War often on the rationale of promoting investments and securing the rule of law.[319]

The correct question is thus not *whether* energy investment should be protected under IIAs, but if one approaches the question from an environmental perspective, *which* investments should.

2 Clean Energy Investments Condition the Success of the Net Zero Transition

The intervention of states to incentivise investments in clean energy is decisive. According to the International Energy Agency, states' incentives are pivotal for clean energy investments.[320] The global energy supply investments in renewable power have

314. Jeswald W. Salacuse, 'BIT by BIT: The Growth of Bilateral Investment Treaties and Their Impact on Foreign Investment in Developing Countries' (1990) The Intl Lawyer 655-675; from an economic perspective, this claim is debated, *see* for instance Andrew Kerner, 'What Can We Really Know About BITs and FDI?' (2018) 33 ICSID Review 1 1, 12-13 https://doi.org/10.1093/icsidreview/six038; Rod Falvey and Neil Foster-McGregor, 'Heterogeneous Effects of Bilateral Investment Treaties' (2017) 153 Rev World Econ 4 631 https://doi.org/10.1007/s10290-017-0287-z.
315. Bishop, Crawford and Reisman, *Foreign Investment Disputes* (n 51) 21-23.
316. Dolzer and Schreuer, *Principles of International Investment Law* (n 47) 2; Sloane and Reisman, 'Indirect Expropriation and Its Valuation' (n 55) 118.
317. Other common names are Investor-State Dispute Settlement (ISDS) or Investor-State Arbitration (ISA).
318. Peter Egger, Alain Pirotte and Catharine Titi, 'International Investment Agreements and Foreign Direct Investment: A Survey' (2023) The World Economy 1, 33-35, 37 https://doi.org/10.1111/twec.13429.
319. Kenneth Vandevelde, *Bilateral Investment Treaties: History, Policy, and Interpretation* (OUP 2010) Chapter 2.3 ('The decision by virtually the entire communist world to abandon planned economies in favour of free markets delegitimized central planning, leaving liberal economics as seemingly the only effective model for economic growth. The combined effect of these events was the emergence of a consensus in the developing world about the desirability of attracting foreign investment through free market policies').
320. IEA, *Government Energy Spending Tracker* (Flagship Report, 2023) 1 ('Government spending has played a central role in the rapid growth of clean energy investment since 2020, which rose nearly 25% from 2021 to 2023, outpacing growth in fossil fuels in the same period.'); International Energy Agency, *World Energy Investment 2022* (Report, 2022) 198 ('Investors were likely buoyed by governments' sustainable recovery plans emphasising the role of clean

grown steadily since 2015 and were set to reach USD 359 billion in 2020.[321] In 2021, the figure was forecasted to have risen to USD 367 billion after the drawbacks of the COVID-19 pandemic.[322] In 2022, clean energy investment – finally – started to pick up speed and was expected to exceed USD 1.4 trillion in 2022.[323] Nevertheless, this is insufficient. To reach net zero by 2050, Mc Kinsey estimates that:

> In economic terms, spending on physical assets on the course to net-zero would reach about US$275 trillion by 2050, or *US$9.2 trillion per year on average*, an annual increase of US$3.5 trillion. To put it in comparable terms, the US$3.5 trillion increase is equivalent to about half of global corporate profits, one-quarter of total tax revenue, and 7 percent of household spending.[324]

There is a margin between USD 1.4 trillion and the necessary USD 9.2 trillion per year on average. For example, in the EU, more than EUR 90 billion would be required per year by 2025 to stay on the path to achieving net zero objectives in 2050, and 'investment shifts are most drastic for power plants, electricity grids and rail infrastructure'.[325]

If countries fail to provide or support the necessary investments, non-renewable sources will continue to naturally dominate, and successful net zero scenarios become ever less likely.[326] Renewable power thus needs to expand dramatically to meet net zero scenarios by 2030 and 2050.[327]

3 Protecting Legitimate Expectations Is Key to Clean Energy Investments

The legal protection of LE stands on controversial ground in the face of the fast-paced energy transition. The FET standard, and hence LE, are meant to secure the predictability and stability of a legal framework precisely against change or 'transition'. Against this background, the question is whether energy investments should be protected.

Since IIAs generally adopt a broad definition of 'investment', they offer the same levels of protection to all types and do not discriminate.[328] The absence of delineation

---

power. But regulations can also act as a brake, either due to long permitting and environmental processes, or restrictions on windfall profits or caps on allowed returns from grids keeping margins low').

321. Global energy investment is set to rebound by around 10% in 2021, reversing most of the drop caused by the pandemic.
322. International Energy Agency, *World Energy Investment 2021* (Flagship Report, 2021) 7.
323. International Energy Agency, *World Energy Investment 2022* (Flagship Report, 2022) 12.
324. McKinsey, *The Net Zero Transition, What It Would Cost, What It Could Bring* (Report, 2022) VIII, *see also* 79-81.
325. Lena Klaaßen and Bjarne Steffen, 'Meta-Analysis on Necessary Investment Shifts to Reach Net Zero Pathways in Europe' (2023) 13 Nat Clim Change 58, 58, 59-60 https://doi.org/10.1038/s41558-022-01549-5.
326. International Energy Agency, *World Energy Outlook 2022* (Report, 2022) 43.
327. International Energy Agency, *Renewable Power: Tracking progress 2021* (Report, 2021) 1-2.
328. Only a few IIAs cite specific energy sources, mostly without any legal consequences, for instance, Energy Charter Treaty, Art. IV(2)(b).

between fossil fuel and clean energy means that both benefit from similar protection. This approach stands in contrast to ICCL, which discriminates three types of energy investments: coal, fossil fuel and 'clean' energy.[329] The problem is thus rather which source of energy 'deserves' protection. But adherence to the rule of law demands applying the law in the same manner to investments protected under investment treaties.

Nevertheless, when acknowledging the advantages of IIAs and standards of protection such as FET, it becomes clear that investment protection and climate change objectives could align. One way would be to simply exclude the protection of fossil fuel investments. But another more balanced way, and rather than an all-out rejection of international investment law, is to consider aligning or reconciling the regimes of international law. Doing so would not only enhance investment protection in the energy sector but also promote clean energy investments to enhance economic development and contribute to net zero goals. In this perspective, the protection of clean energy inventors' LE is crucial. As the next chapters show, LEs protect clean energy investors that rely upon a clean energy commitment.[330] At the same time, the concept is flexible enough to account for global mitigation efforts, so that fossil fuel investors do not, in practice and depending on the time of their investment, benefit from the same level of protection.

D CONCLUSION

This non-legal chapter is the first building block to answer my research question on ICCL's impact on legitimate expectations. It establishes the nexus between the protection of energy investors' legitimate expectations and net zero transition measures pertaining to the mitigation of GHG emissions.

The chapter presents three key findings.

First, it establishes that the energy sector is predominant in investment disputes because of the particular role energy plays in economic development and growth. From a physical point of view, energy is necessary for all activity. The abundance of energy directly results in economic development – as shown by the Industrial Revolution. Therefore, energy is the backbone of growth and the precondition for the general objective of international investment law, which is to stimulate the flow of private capital and 'maximize effective utilization of economic resources and improve living standards'.[331] However, the centrality of energy to the economy prompts disputes with host states and their net zero transition policies.

Second, there is an apparent discrepancy between the protection of energy investors under international investment law and their discrimination under ICCL. The first offers protection irrespective of the nature of the treaty-covered 'investment'. The broad definition of 'investment' offers the same levels of protection for clean and fossil fuel energy sources. On the contrary, ICCL discriminates between clean, fossil fuel, and

329. IEA, *World Energy Investment 2022: Methodology Annex* (Report, 2022) 19.
330. *See* Chapter 3.A.
331. 2012 United Stated of America Model Bilateral Investment Treaty, preamble.

coal energy in the treaty text. It also justifies a difference in treatment on scientific grounds to maintain global temperatures below 2 °C. Continuous investments in fossil fuel and coal production stand in contradiction to climate neutrality by 2050. This apparent dichotomy does not appear to be irreconcilable. Rather, these issues could be alleviated in practice, for instance, by integrating ICCL when assessing legitimate expectations.

Third, while fossil fuels remain the driver of the economy, the path to net zero implies strong investments in clean sources of energy. Thus, the research finds that states willing to adopt investment agreements can align both economic and climate goals by protecting clean energy investors. Doing so may align the objectives of economic development, climate mitigation, and respect for the rule of law.

Overall, the chapter establishes that energy investments are key to economic development and that clean energy investments contribute to climate mitigation. It suggests that the existence of investment treaties does not constitute an irremediable obstacle to the implementation of the net zero transition. Such a conclusion calls for an alignment of climate change and international investment objectives. One regime does not need to be abandoned for the other.

Before assessing the legal relationship between international investment and climate change law in more detail (Chapters 4 and 5), the research delves into the doctrine of legitimate expectations under the standard of FET in the next two chapters. The legal protection of LE stands in plain contrast to the required fast-paced energy transition since LE is meant to secure the predictability and stability of a legal framework against change. Nevertheless, Chapters 2 and 3 demonstrate that, while very divergent theories exist, the application of LE tends to achieve consensus on factual points. Accordingly, in practice, the level of protection enjoyed by fossil fuels, coal, and clean energy may widely differ and their legal protection align with the host state's climate change objectives. Clean energy may benefit from stronger protection than coal investments. This is because of the foreseeability of regulatory measures and the business risks involved in these respective sectors.

Figure 1.1 summarises the nexus established in Chapter 1.

Figure 1.1 The Relationship Between Energy and Its Protection under International Investment Law, ICCL, and Net Zero Measures

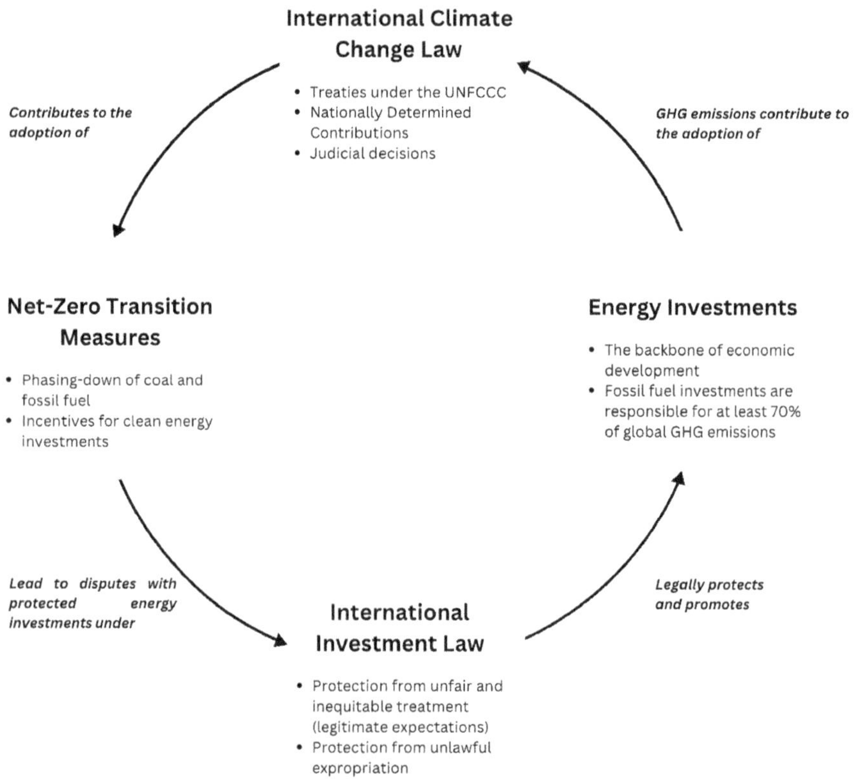

Source: Prepared by the author.

Chapter 2

The Substantive Protection of Legitimate Expectations under the Standard of FET

This chapter offers an overview of the interpretation of legitimate expectations in international investment law. After analysing legitimate expectations' relationship to the FET provision, it turns to the difficulties arising from the interpretation and application of the concept. To best understand the case law, the chapter proposes to divide between voluntary and detrimental reliance theories of legitimate expectations.

As discussed in the previous chapter, energy investments are prone to disputes with states arising from political risks associated with the net zero transition. Standards of FET and expropriation[332] are most likely to ground claims related to net zero measures. Under the FET standard, the investor does not need to establish a substantial or near-total deprivation of its assets to find the state liable, which makes its role more significant in these cases.[333]

This chapter explores the concept on which energy investors have made most of their claims in net zero investment disputes: the central element of the FET standard, the protection of legitimate expectations.[334] The chapter draws the contours of the concept.

After elucidating the doctrine in the context of case law and FET, this chapter tries to ascertain how LE are interpreted and applied. This task is particularly complex for three reasons further explored in the chapter. First, arbitral tribunals and scholars

---

332. Climate Change Counsel, *The Energy Charter Treaty, Climate Change and Clean Energy Transition, A Study of Jurisprudence* (Report, 2022) 7.

333. *Sempra Energy International v. Argentine Republic*, ICSID Case No. ARB/02/16, Award, 28 September 2007, paras 300, 301 ('It would be wrong to believe that fair and equitable treatment is a kind of peripheral requirement. To the contrary, it ensures that even where there is no clear justification for making a finding of expropriation (as in the present case), there is still a standard which serves the purpose of justice and can of itself redress damage that is unlawful and that would otherwise pass unattended').

334. Katia Yannaca-Small, 'Fair and Equitable Treatment Have Its Contour Fully Evolved?' in Yannaca-Small (ed.), *Arbitration Guide* (n 50) 501, 501-502.

disagree about the relationship between LE and the FET provision. Second, the same disagree about the 'roots' and 'justifications' of the *legal concept* of legitimate expectations and its use in investment arbitration.[335] Third, arbitral tribunals and scholars disagree about the interpretation of legitimate expectations – which derives from a theoretical divergence on the role of promise.

The chapter offers a theoretical understanding of the FET standard and the doctrine of LE. Section A justifies the protection of legitimate expectations; section B broadly presents the relationship of LE to the FET standard; section C explores the content of the LE doctrine in investment disputes under the FET provision. It then tries to ascertain why arbitral tribunals disagree about its content by (section D) exploring the sources justifying the use of the doctrine in investment arbitration; and (section E) examining the divide between detrimental reliance and voluntarist theories of legitimate expectations.

A JUSTIFYING THE PROTECTION OF LEGITIMATE EXPECTATIONS

Before delving deeper into the roots and theories of LE, the brief paragraphs below present the rationale for the protection of LE and respond to general criticisms regarding the protection of LE in investment disputes.

Expectations are fundamental to the investment process. When investors contemplate making an investment, they rely on expectations regarding the risks and rewards associated with that investment. These expectations are influenced not only by market factors but also by the conduct,[336] laws, regulations, and general policies[337] of the host state. The concept of investment 'promotion', an objective of most IIAs, intends to create a sense of assurance and expectation of profit in investors' minds. The object is to lead them to commit capital and technology in the host state. Thus, when a state creates specific expectations through its conduct and measures (laws, regulations, or acts), it may be unfair for the state to adopt measures[338] that frustrate those expectations. Nevertheless, the protection of investors' LE is criticised on multiple grounds.[339]

Some argue that, from a policy point of view, the mere existence of the doctrine in international law and its assessment in investment arbitrations would create a regulatory chill, i.e., an inability by the state to regulate according to its discretion and

335. A few scholars argue that LE would itself constitute a general principle of international law, taking inspiration from municipal legal systems. Others find the source in the general principle of estoppel, which tends to flatten the relationship between the state and the investor. Yet others, more convincingly, refer to the general principle of good faith and the doctrine of unilateral statements by states; *see* Chapter 2.D.
336. Acts are understood as unilateral statements or declaration of high officials of a state. These may be inconsistent with their domestic law; *see* Reisman and Arsanjani, 'The Question of Unilateral Governmental Statements as Applicable Law' (n 64) 339.
337. Regulations are enacted at an inferior hierarchical level than laws. Laws are usually adopted by Parliament while Decrees and other Regulations by the Executive Branch of the State. General policies, understood as broad principles of action adopted by a state.
338. Measures are the common denominator for laws, regulations, and general policies.
339. Trevor Zeyl, 'Charting the Wrong Course: The Doctrine of Legitimate Expectations in investment Treaty Law' (2011) 49 Alta L Rev 203, 208 https://doi.org/10.29173/alr131.

sovereign choices.[340] The doctrine would be a speculative right for 'neo-liberal'[341] private interests.[342] This line of criticism is politically oriented and derives from a larger criticism of the legitimacy of the investment arbitration 'regime'.[343] It can be opposed that the protection of expectations cannot hinder regulatory changes, even though it may impact the public money's purse in case compensation for breach is due. Neither can 'legitimate' expectations arise out of a *vacuum* but only from a state's discretionary commitment or conduct that created objective expectations. In other words, mere hopes are not expectations. Moreover, it can be opposed that the concept is not specific to investment arbitration but is widely applied by administrative courts of the highest order, with lesser public condemnation. For instance, when Swedish energy company Vattenfall brought an investment arbitration case against Germany for the phasing out of nuclear energy, it prompted civil society disapproval.[344] However, when the *Bundesverfassungsgericht* (the German Federal Constitutional Court) issued two decisions in December 2016, ruling that the Government's 13th Amendment violated the property rights of the affected nuclear utilities – with 'legitimate expectations' (*Vertrauensschutz*) a main part of the legal basis[345] – and, in September 2020, ruled that a proposed compensation for the utilities in a 2018 draft law was *insufficient*, it did not trigger similar contestation.[346] However criticisable, foreign investments flourish in a stable and predictable legal framework. Thus, the reasonable protection of their foreign investors' property rights and reasonable expectations is vital to attracting them. In principle, the protection of LE can be useful to development goals, as it can substantively protect investors relying on the state's conduct to attract them. Therefore, legitimate expectations should not be considered 'regulatory chills' but 'regulatory facilitators' in the sense that they participate in the country's economic goals based on the state's regulatory promotion in certain sectors. The legal boundary to the protection of LE should lie in a state's ability to adapt policies to fundamentally changing circumstances or to reverse a former government's promises, where these promises were in breach, or in formal contradiction, with the state's international commitments, such as those under climate change agreements.

A more legally founded criticism argues that arbitrators would *interpret* the doctrine of LE expansively to the benefit of investors, thereby again unduly limiting the

340. Tienhaara, 'Regulatory Chill' (n 155) 236, 244-245 https://doi.org/10.1017/s2047102517000309.
341. Muthucumaraswamy Sornarajah, 'The Neo-Liberal Agenda in Investment Arbitration: Its Rise, Retreat and Impact on State Sovereignty' in Wenhua Shan, Penelope Simons and Dalvinder Singh (eds), *Redefining Sovereignty in International Economic Law* (Hart 2008) 199, 206.
342. *Ibid.*
343. *See* BVerfG, Judgment of the First Senate of 6 December 2016 – 1 BvR 2821/11 – paras 1-407; BVerfG, Order of the First Senate of 29 September 2020 – 1 BvR 1550/19 – para. 86; *Vattenfall AB and others v. Federal Republic of Germany*, ICSID Case No. ARB/12/12, Discontinuance Order, 9 November 2021, para. 317.
344. IISD, *The German Nuclear Phase Out Put to the Test in International Investment Arbitration? Background to the New Dispute Vattenfall v. Germany (II)* (Briefing Note, 2012) 7, 10.
345. BVerfG, 2016 (n 343).
346. The German government eventually settled with Vattenfall for an amount of EUR 1,425 million.

state's regulatory freedom.[347] This approach[348] usually points out the narrower interpretation of LE in some domestic jurisdictions.[349] This line of criticism is, however, imperfect. The doctrine of LE is investment law-specific in the sense that is can be narrower or broader than in national jurisdiction, depending on the language of the underlying treaty. States may purposely offer greater protection to foreign investors than to domestic counterparts. In any way, assessing whether LE were breached is operates to establish whether the FET standard was breached. General rules of interpretation bind the interpretation of treaty provisions, including FET clauses. Therefore, arbitrators apply FET provisions in light of the object and purpose of the treaty – which often includes the promotion and protection of foreign investment and, in some treaties, such as the Energy Charter Treaty, the express *stability* of the host state's regulatory framework. Therefore, it is not illogical that the doctrine of LE may, in certain treaties, offer greater protection than domestic counterparts as long as such protection is reasonable.

One ground for criticism remains valid. It questions the value of change against the value of legal stability.[350] It questions the scope of LE against the regulatory rights of states. To put it as a more concrete example: is it justifiable that fossil fuel investments enjoy the same level of legal protection as other investments, considering that reducing CO_2 emissions is critical to the protection of human health?[351] More generally, what is the state's decision margin when altering its regulatory framework? In my opinion, the language of the treaty and the obligations of the state towards the investor and other potentially competing or contradicting international commitments should be paramount in the analysis of LE. In this manner, it is possible to enforce promises when they are legitimate, specific and clear while allowing states to resile from promises that could not be legitimate or clear in the first place because they stood in contradiction with the states' commitments on the international plane.

With this in mind, the next section turns to the scope of FET provisions and whether they allow a plain assessment of investors' LE.

B PROTECTING LEGITIMATE EXPECTATIONS UNDER THE FET STANDARD: GENERAL OVERVIEW OF THE RELATIONSHIP

Most IIAs contain a clause providing for the 'fair and equitable treatment' of foreign investments.[352] The provision constitutes a fundamental element of dispute settlement

347. Emmanuel Laryea, 'Legitimate Expectations in Investment Treaty Law: Concept and Scope of Application' in Julien Chaisse and Leïla Choukroune (eds), *Handbook of International Investment Law and Policy* (Springer 2021) 97, 98.
348. Muthucumaraswamy Sornarajah, 'Power and Justice: Third World Resistance in International Law' (2006) 7 Singapore Yearbook of International Law 36.
349. *See* below Chapter 2.D.1.a).
350. Fergus Green, 'Legal Transitions Without Legitimate Expectations' (2020) 28 The Journal of Political Philosophy 4 397, 397-399 https://doi.org/10.1111/jopp.12231.
351. Viñuales, *The International Law of Energy* (n 246) XIX, 1.
352. Investment Policy Hub, 'Investment Disputes Settlement Navigator' (*UNCTAD*, 2023) https://investmentpolicy.unctad.org/investment-dispute-settlement accessed 24 April 2023, identifies

under IIAs.[353] It is the most frequently[354] and successful 'substantive standard' raised by investors.[355] FET provisions protect investors against arbitrary, discriminatory or abusive conduct by host states.[356] Depending on the underlying treaty, the provision may act as a standard with large substantive content and scope.[357] It is well established that FET constitutes a legal standard that does not equate the power to decide *ex aequo et bono*.[358] Because of its relatively recent origins[359] and the abstract nature of its terms – 'fair' and 'equitable', the FET concept stands among the most debated standards in international law,[360] in particular with regard to its relation to the minimum standard of treatment (MST) under CIL.[361]

2,444 investment treaties out of 2,574 mapped treaties containing a qualified or unqualified FET clause.

353. Alexandra Diehl, *The Core Standard of International Investment Protection: Fair and Equitable Treatment* (Kluwer 2012); Stephan Schill, 'Fair and Equitable Treatment, the Rule of Law, and Comparative Public Law' in Stephan W. Schill (ed.), *International Investment Law and Comparative Public Law* (OUP 2010) 151.
354. Güneş Ünüvar, 'The Vague Meaning of Fair and Equitable Treatment Principle in Investment Arbitration and New Generation Clarifications' (2016) iCourts Working Paper Series 55, 5-6.
355. Dolzer and Schreuer, *Principles of International Investment Law* (n 47) 132; *International Thunderbird Gaming Corporation v. Mexico*, UNCITRAL, Award, 26 January 2006, Separate Opinion Thomas Wälde, para. 37 ('a significant growth in the role and scope of the legitimate expectation principle, from an earlier function as a subsidiary interpretative principle to reinforce a particular interpretative approach chosen, to its current role as a self-standing subcategory and independent basis for a claim under the "fair and equitable standard" as under Art. 1105 of the NAFTA. This is possibly related to the fact that it provides a more supple way of providing a remedy appropriate to the particular situation as compared to the more drastic determination and remedy inherent in concept of regulatory expropriation. It is probably partly for these reasons that "legitimate expectation" has become for tribunals a preferred way of providing protection to claimants in situations where the tests for a "regulatory taking" appear too difficult, complex and too easily assailable for reliance on a measure of subjective judgment').
356. Rudolf Dolzer, 'The Impact of International Investment Treaties on Domestic Administrative Law' (2005) 37 NYU JILP 953, 964.
357. In the same way as expropriation, the FET standard cannot withhold a state from adopting regulatory measures, but they may find the measure to violate the standard and the state to be liable towards the protected investor.
358. Yannaca-Small, 'Contour' (n 334) 510.
359. Jeswald Salacuse, *The Law of Investment Treaties* (3rd edn, OUP 2021) 290; Dolzer and Schreuer, *Principles of International Investment Law* (n 47) 130; Prof. Jeswald Salacuse finds historic provisions based on notions of fairness and equity in international economic agreements from the aftermath of WWII. For instance, in the International Trade Organisation through the Havana Charter for an International Trade Organisation (1948), the Economic Agreement of Bogota (1948), but also in United States commercial (FCN) treaties. In the context of investment treaties, the terms 'fair and equitable treatment' first appeared in the Draft Convention on Investments Abroad (1959), suggested by Hermann Abs and Lord Shawcross in 1959. The clause has since been included in most investment treaties.
360. The United States and Canada have tried to limit the interpretation of FET to CIL. *See* a broader assessment UNCTAD, *World Investment Report 2012: Towards a New Generation of Investment Policies* (Report, 2012) 139.
361. Whether FET reflects the MST under CIL is particularly contentious; *see* Christopher Thomas, 'Reflections on Article 1105 of NAFTA: History, State Practice and the Influence of Commentators' (2002) 17 ICSID Review 1 21 https://doi.org/10.1093/icsidreview/17.1.21; Patrick Dumberry, 'Has the Fair and Equitable Treatment Standard Become a Rule of Customary International Law?' (2017) 8 Journal of International Dispute Settlement 1 155 https://doi.org/10.1093/jnlids/idw002; Patrick Dumberry, 'Fair and Equitable Treatment: Its Interaction with the Minimum Standard and Its Customary Status' (2017) 1 Brill Research Perspectives in

Nevertheless, over time, tribunals dealing with FET claims under different treaties have ensured a material encirclement of the 'standard', which included LE as part of the analysis.[362] This extensive case law[363] is not binding in the absence of *stare decisis* in international investment law but is considered to strongly influence subsequent judgments[364] so that the protection of legitimate expectations is generally considered an element of, at least, the *unqualified* FET provisions.[365]

International Investment Law and Arbitration 2 1 https://doi.org/10.1163/9789004366121_002; there are three views on the question, the strict MST view, the view considering that MST has evolved over time and the view that FET constitute an autonomous standard; The strict MST view holds that FET should be read in light of the 1926 *Neer* case (*Neer v. Mexico* (1926) IV RIAA 60 is widely considered the 'floor' of the minimum standard of international customary law, holding at paras 61-62 that 'the treatment of an alien, in order to constitute an international delinquency should amount to an outrage, to bad faith, to wilful neglect of duty, or to an insufficiency of governmental action so far short of international standards that every reasonable and impartial man would readily recognize its insufficiency'); Martins Paparinskis, *The International Minimum Standard and Fair and Equitable Treatment* (OUP 2013) 160 ff. and 251-256 (considers that FET reflects a customary rule of international law); Stephen Vasciannie, 'The Fair and Equitable Treatment Standard in International Investment Law and practice' (1990) 70 BYBIL 99, 100; 104; 145 https://doi.org/10.1163/9789004366121_002; Prosper Weil, 'The State, the Foreign Investor, and International Law: The No Longer Stormy Relationship of a Ménage à Trois' (2000) 15 ICSID Review-FILJ 401, 415 ('The standard of "fair and equitable treatment" is certainly no less operative than was the standard of "due process of law", and it will be for future practice, jurisprudence and commentary to impart specific content to it.'); Charles Brower, 'Investor-State Disputes under NAFTA: The Empire Strikes Back' (2003) 40 Col JTL 43, 56 https://doi.org/10.1093/icsidreview/15.2.401 (suggesting that fair and equitable treatment constitutes 'an intentionally vague term', designed to give adjudicators a quasi-legislative authority to articulate a variety of rules necessary to achieve the treaty's object and purpose in particular disputes).

362. Stephen Vasciannie, 'The Fair and Equitable Treatment Standard in International Investment Law and practice' (1990) 70 BYBIL 99, 100; 104; 145 https://doi.org/10.1093/bybil/70.1.99; Prosper Weil, 'The State, the Foreign Investor, and International Law: The No Longer Stormy Relationship of a Ménage à Trois' (2000) 15 ICSID Review-FILJ 401, 415 https://doi.org/10.1093/icsidreview/15.2.401 ('The standard of "fair and equitable treatment" is certainly no less operative than was the standard of "due process of law", and it will be for future practice, jurisprudence and commentary to impart specific content to it').
363. Charles Brower, 'Investor-State Disputes under NAFTA: The Empire Strikes Back' (2003) 40 Col JTL 43, 56 (suggesting that fair and equitable treatment constitutes 'an intentionally vague term, designed to give adjudicators a quasi-legislative authority to articulate a variety of rules necessary to achieve the treaty's object and purpose in particular disputes').
364. Gabriele Kaufmann-Kohler, 'Arbitral Precedent: Dream, Necessity or Excuse?' 23 Arb. Int'l 357 (2007) https://doi.org/10.1093/arbitration/23.3.357; Christoph Schreuer and Matthew Weiniger, 'A Doctrine of Precedent?' in Peter Muchlinski, Federico Ortino and Christoph Schreuer (eds), *The Oxford Handbook of International Investment Law* (OUP 2008) 1188; Tai-Heng Cheng, 'Precedent and Control in Investment Treaty Arbitration' (2007) 30 Fordham ILJ 1014.
365. United Nations Conference on Trade and Development, *Fair and Equitable Treatment: UNCTAD Series on Issues in International Investment Agreements II: A Sequel* (Report, 2012) 17-35 (the five main elements emerging under the FET are the following '1. the prohibition of manifest arbitrariness in decision-making, 2. the prohibition of denial of justice and disregard of the fundamental principles of due process; 3. prohibition of targeted discrimination on manifestly wrongful grounds; 4. prohibition of abusive treatment of investors, and 5. protection of the legitimate expectations of investors arising from a government's specific representations or investment-inducing measures, balanced with the host State's right to regulate in the public interest').

1 Unqualified and Qualified FET Provisions

FET provisions are not drafted in identical terms in all treaties. Treaties present it in one of four ways: unqualified; in reference to international law; in reference to the MST; or with an express definition of its content.

The unqualified FET drafting is the most common. This is partly due to the fact that historically, the Draft Convention on Investments Abroad (1959), suggested by Hermann Abs and Lord Shawcross in 1959, proved influential in the drafting of posterior BITs.[366] Embraced by the OECD in the Draft Convention on the Protection of Foreign Property (1967),[367] it provides an unqualified drafting of FET.[368] The Draft Convention was subsequently adopted as a basis for treaty negotiations,[369] indirectly leading to the unqualified FET provision becoming the most common formulation of the provision.[370] Today, unqualified FET provisions are not all drafted in the same way, nor do they have the same context or underlying treaty's purpose,[371] but they are not formally bound to international law or MST, so that arbitrators have a wider margin of interpretation, and can easily include the protection of LE as part of the FET standard, even in the absence of specific treaty text to the effect as explained below.

The unqualified FET's flexibility has been subject to criticism and led states to narrow the FET scope,[372] either by attaching it to MST, international law or by defining its specific content.[373]

366. OECD, *Draft Convention on Investments Abroad* (1959).
367. OECD, *Draft Convention on the Protection of Foreign Property* (1967) ('[e]ach Party shall at all times ensure fair and equitable treatment to the property of the nationals of the other Parties').
368. UNCTAD, *Fair and Equitable Treatment: A Sequel* (n 365) 5 (While the FET was unqualified in the text of the draft article, the notes and comments of the OECD to the article referred directly to CIL as the source of the obligation).
369. OECD, 'Fair and Equitable Treatment Standard in International Investment Law' (2004) OECD Working Papers on International Investment, OECD Publishing, 2004/03, 5.
370. UNCTAD, 'Mapping of IIA Content' (n 352).
371. The research focuses on the 1994 Energy Charter Treaty, which provides under Part III on the 'Investment Promotion and Protection', Art. 10 on 'Promotion, Protection and Treatment of Investments' that: '(1) Each Contracting Party shall, in accordance with the provisions of this Treaty, encourage and create stable, equitable, favourable and transparent conditions for Investors of other Contracting Parties to make Investments in its Area. Such conditions shall include a commitment to accord at all times to Investments of Investors of other Contracting Parties *fair and equitable treatment.*' The FET standard is unqualified, as in most IIAs. However, the ECT emphasises the notion of stability in the first sentence, while other IIAs, such as the German Model BIT 2008 provides a simple unqualified form of FET (stipulates under Art. 2 on 'Admission and protection of investments': '(2) [e]ach contracting State shall in its territory in *every case accord investment by investors of the other contracting State fair and equitable treatment* as well as full protection under this Treaty'.). It can be inferred that the stability of the regulatory framework disserves greater attention under the ECT.
372. Chin Leng Lim, Jean Ho and Martin Paparinskis, *International Investment Law and Arbitration: Commentary, Awards and Other Materials* (CUP 2018) 283-287.
373. Catharine Titi, 'The Evolution of Substantive Investment Protections in Recent Trade and Investment Treaties' (2018) The EU-Singapore IPA provides that fair and equitable treatment is breached if a measure constitutes denial of justice, a fundamental breach of due process, manifestly arbitrary conduct, harassment, coercion, abuse of power, or similar conduct in bad faith. When determining whether there has been a violation of the standard, the adjudicators 'may' consider the investor's legitimate expectations (Art. 2.4, paras 2-3).

Criticism of arbitral tribunals limiting the state's right to regulate prompted new sorts of FET provisions.[374] The EU,[375] European states[376] and Canada[377] stand at the forefront of redefining the FET clause. Instead of tying them to the notion of MST, they define a precise content. The objective is allegedly to limit arbitrators' discretion.[378] It is yet unsettled whether these content-prescribing treaties allow for an assessment of the investor's LE.[379] As for express references to international law, 348 treaties link FET to principles of international law.[380] The relationship between the FET standard and the MST remains subject to debate.[381] Some scholars question the distinction,[382] while some tribunals claim that there is no significant disruption in the level of protection and that CIL has evolved to become indistinguishable from the unqualified FET.[383] It is unsettled whether LE is protected under these types of drafting. The research assumes,

374. Yulia Levashova, *The Right of States to Regulate in International Investment Law: The Search for Balance Between Public Interest and Fair and Equitable Treatment* (Kluwer Law International, 2019) 51.
375. Article 8.10(2) of the Canada–EU CETA (signed on 30 October 2016, not yet entered into force); Art. 9(2) of the Netherlands Model BIT (2019); Art. 2.4(2) of the EU–Singapore Investment Protection Agreement (signed on 15 October 2018, not yet entered into force); Art. 2.5(2) of the EU – Vietnam Investment Protection Agreement (signed on 30 June 2019, not yet entered into force).
376. Article 4(1) of the France – Colombia BIT (signed on 10 July 2014, entered into force on 14 October 2020).
377. Article 8.10(2) of the Canada – EU CETA (signed on 30 October 2016, not yet entered into force). *See also* Art. 9(2) of the Netherlands Model BIT (2019).
378. Ioana Knoll-Tudor, *The Fair and Equitable Treatment Standard in the International Law of Foreign Investment* (OUP 2008) 132.
379. In both cases, it is questionable whether the addition of content remedies the arguable lack of precision of the terms 'fair' and 'equitable'.
380. UNCTAD, 'Mapping of IIA Content' (n 352); *see, inter alia,* Art. 5(1) of the 2012 US Model BIT; Chapter 11, Art. 6(2)(c) of the Agreement Establishing the ASEAN-Australia-New Zealand Free Trade Area (entered into force on 10 January 2010), Art. 91 of the Japan-Philippines Economic Partnership Agreement (entered into force on 12 November 2008). Recent inclusions in Art. 9(1) and (2) of the Pacific Agreement on Closer Economic Relations Plus (entered into force on 13 December 2020); Art. 5(1)(c) of the ASEAN – Hong Kong, China SAR Investment Agreement (signed on 12 November 2017, entered into force on 17 June 2019).
381. Hussein Haeri, 'A Tale of Two Standards: "Fair and Equitable Treatment" and the Minimum Standard in International Law – The Gillis Wetter Prize' (2011) 27 Arbitration International 1 27 https://doi.org/10.1093/arbitration/27.1.27.
382. Nicolas Angelet, 'Fair and Equitable Treatment' in *Max Planck Encyclopaedia of Public International Law* (OUP 2011) 4-5; Dolzer and Schreuer, *Principles of International Investment Law* (n 47) 137-139.
383. *Rusoro Mining Ltd. v. Bolivarian Republic of Venezuela,* ICSID Case No. ARB(AF)/12/5, Award, 22 August 2016, para. 520; *see also Koch Minerals Sarl and Koch Nitrogen International Sarl v. Bolivarian Republic of Venezuela,* ICSID Case No. ARB/11/19, Award, 30 October 2017, paras 8.44, 8.47; *Murphy Exploration and Production Company International v. Republic of Ecuador (II),* PCA Case No. 2012-16, Partial Final Award, 6 May 2016, para. 208 ('The international minimum standard and the treaty standard continue to influence each other, and, in the view of the Tribunal, these standards are increasingly aligned'); for a contrary view *see Infinito Gold Ltd. v. Republic of Costa Rica,* ICSID Case No. ARB/14/5, Award, 3 June 2021, para. 357 (finding that under CIL, absent a denial of justice, judicial decisions interpreting domestic law cannot breach international law) and para. 359 (holding that 'judicial decisions that are arbitrary, unfair or contradict an investor's legitimate expectations may also breach the FET standard even if they do not rise to the level of a denial of justice').

however, that the reasoning for the integration of ICCL in the analysis of LE is applicable to unqualified and qualified FET provisions.

2 Unqualified FET Provisions Protect Legitimate Expectations

We have seen above that states may privilege a wide margin of interpretation through open-ended, unqualified drafting of FET or try limiting the arbitrator's discretion in qualifying by tying the provision to MST, international law, or by defining its content.[384] Below, I assess the relationship of unqualified FET provisions to LE.

As mentioned above, unqualified FET provisions are treaty-specific, their meaning can vary due to the clause drafting.[385] The majority view considers the unqualified FET provision as an autonomous, absolute, and international standard. Although some contemplated FET as an overarching principle embracing or reinforcing the other treatment standards,[386] it is now widely accepted that unqualified FET provisions are 'autonomous'.[387] In other words, the breach of FET is distinct from the violation of another protection standard.[388] Similarly, the unqualified FET is 'absolute' or 'non-contingent' because it is not determined by reference to the treatment accorded by the host state to other, domestic or foreign, investments or investors.[389] In my view, the unqualified FET should be considered an international rule of law in the sense that it is autonomous from the national legal framework of the State.[390] Its content should not be

384. Diehl, *The Core Standard* (n 353) 311 ff.; Notes of Interpretation of Certain Chapter 11 Provisions (NAFTA Free Trade Commission, 31 July 2001) ('2. Minimum Standard of Treatment in Accordance with International Law 2. The concepts of "fair and equitable treatment" and "full protection and security" do not require treatment in addition to or beyond that which is required by the customary international law minimum standard of treatment of aliens').
385. Angelet, 'Fair and Equitable' (n 382) 2; Dolzer and Schreuer, *Principles of International Investment Law* (n 47) 132.
386. *Noble Ventures Inc v. Romania*, ICSID Case No. ARB/01/11, Award, 12 October 2005, para. 182; *Lemire v. Ukraine*, Decision on Jurisdiction and Liability, 14 January 2010, paras 259, 385; *Impreglio v. Argentina*, ICSID Case No. ARB/07/17, Award, 21 June 2011, paras 333-334.
387. Knoll-Tudor, *The Fair and Equitable Treatment Standard* (n 378) 182-202.
388. *Azurix Corp. v. The Argentine Republic*, ICSID Case No. ARB/01/12, Award, 14 July 2006, paras 407-408; *LG&E v. Argentina*, ICSID Case No. ARB/02/1, Decision on Liability, 3 October 2006, paras 162, 163; *Plama v. Bulgaria*, Award, 27 August 2008, paras 161-163, 183-184; since FET is autonomous, its importation through Most-Favoured Nation clause may be questioned, *see* Patrick Dumberry, 'Shopping for a Better Deal: the Use of MFN Clauses to Get "Better" Fair and Equitable Treatment Protection' (2017) 33 Arbitration International 1 16 https://doi.org/10.1093/arbint/aiw036.
389. *SD Myers v. Canada*, UNCITRAL/NAFTA, First Partial Award on the Merits, 13 November 2000, para. 259 (Non-contingent standards provide 'a floor below which treatment of foreign investors must not fall, even if a government were not acting in a discriminatory manner').
390. Rudolf Dolzer, 'Fair and Equitable Treatment: Today's Contours' (2014) 12 SCJIL 7, 12 ('The acceptance of the standard is directly linked to the fundamental moral and legal grounding of the notion of fairness, anchored in a universally accepted sense of justice, but also in classic rules of customary law governing the protection of foreign nationals and companies'); Campbell McLachlan and others, 'Treatment of Investors' in *International Investment Arbitration: Substantive Principles* (2nd edn, OUP 2017) paras 7.15-7.16 ('modern expression of a general principle of due process in its application to the treatment of investors (...). The *standard thus encapsulates the minimum requirements of the rule of law.* [...] The rule of law is properly understood as the principle underlying and animating the concept of fair and

derived from the host state's laws, nor can it be considered a form of national treatment standard.[391] While the words 'fair' and 'equitable' cannot be *easily* elucidated,[392] so the precise limitations on the state's regulatory freedom cannot be precisely drawn in abstract,[393] they should lead to a fact-specific inquiry and allow an interpretation in light of the complete set of circumstances.[394]

The protection of LE appears justified by these considerations, not only because the LE doctrine is 'rooted' in public administrative and public international law and appears as an element of the rule of law in both contexts[395] but also because LE offers the flexibility necessary to consider complex factual circumstances, address regulatory unfairness and redress it. Protecting legitimate expectations is to give full effect to the standard of FET. It allows the investigation of whether a state's treatment was fair and equitable, beyond a due process or arbitrariness assessment, towards an even-handed and *bona fide* analysis of the state's promises.

---

equitable treatment. It does not provide a prescriptive set of rules that may be mechanically applied in the same way in all contexts in which the principle is invoked. [...] The standard is primarily concerned with the decision-making process as it affects the rights of the investor rather than with the protection of substantive rights (the latter being the function of the protection against expropriation and the guarantee of full protection and security')), para. 7.355.

391. Patrick Dumberry, *The Fair and Equitable Treatment Standard: A Guide to NAFTA Case Law on Article 1105* (Kluwer Law International 2013) 27; *Genin v. Estonia*, Award, 25 June 2001, para. 367; *SD Myers v. Canada* (n 389) para. 259; *CME Czech Republic B.V. v. The Czech Republic*, UNCITRAL, Partial Award, 13 September 2001, para. 611; *El Paso v. Argentina* (n 41) para. 337; in other words, the FET standard is 'absolute' in the sense of independence from the treatment accorded to investments from the host state or third-party nationals and domestic law.
392. Schill, 'Fair and Equitable Treatment, The Rule of Law' (n 353) 155.
393. *Ibid.*; For some scholars, this lack of abstract definition may arguably undermine the legitimacy of international investment arbitration because of the uncertain results it produces, *see* Giovanni Dall'Agnola, 'Italy's Spalma-Incentivi Decree and the ECT's FET Obligation: An Assessment of the Legitimacy of the Photovoltaic Incentives Cut' (2021) 3 Diritto del Commercio Internazionale 507, 549.
394. *Waste Management, Inc. v. United Mexican States* ICSID Case No. ARB(AF)/00/3, Award, 30 April 2004, para. 99 ('the standard is to some extent a flexible one which must be adapted to the circumstances of each case'); Angelet, 'Fair and Equitable' (n 382) 2-3; Knoll-Tudor, *The Fair and Equitable Treatment Standard* (n 378) 132.
395. Potestà, 'Legitimate Expectations' (n 68) 88; Nitish Monebhurrun, 'Gold Reserve Inc. v the Bolivarian Republic of Venezuela. Enshrining Legitimate Expectations as a General Principle of International Law' (2015) 32 Journal of International Arbitration 551, 551-561 https://doi.org/10.54648/joia2015026; Simon Maynard, 'Legitimate Expectations and the Interpretation of the Legal Stability Obligation' (2016) 1 European Investment Law and Arbitration Review 99 https://doi.org/10.54648/eila2016007; Abhijit P.G. Pandya and Andy Moody, 'Legitimate Expectations in Investment Treaty Arbitration: An Unclear Future' (2010) 15 Tilburg Law Review 93, 93-119 https://doi.org/10.1163/22112596-90000007; Trevor Zeyl, 'Charting the Wrong Course: The Doctrine of Legitimate Expectations in Investment Treaty Law' (2011) 49 Alberta Law Review 203 https://doi.org/10.29173/alr131; Felipe Mutis Téllez, 'Conditions and Criteria for the Protection of Legitimate Expectations under International Investment Law' (2012) 27 ICSID Review-Foreign Investment Law Journal 432, 432-342 https://doi.org/10.1093/icsidreview/sis018; Robert Kolb, *Good Faith in the International Law* (Hart Publishing 2017) 243-250; Arwel Davies, 'Investment Treaty Interpretation, Fair and Equitable Treatment and Legitimate Expectations' (2018) 15 Manchester Journal of International Economic Law 314; Srinath Reddy Kethireddy, 'Still the Law of Nations: Legitimate Expectations and the Sovereigntist Turn in International Investment Law' (2019) 44 The Yale Journal of International Law 315.

Having briefly presented the FET provision, I now turn to a presentation of the broad contours of LE in the case law.

C CONTOURS OF LEGITIMATE EXPECTATIONS IN THE CASE LAW

As discussed in the introduction,[396] LE is recent in international law,[397] but many arbitral tribunals recognised the protection of investors' LE as the 'most important function'[398] of the FET provision. Notwithstanding its centrality, the doctrine of LE it not to be considered an autonomous obligation.[399] It is part of the FET assessment, not the other way around.

Despite the important scholarship on the subject,[400] the use of the LE doctrine in investment arbitration still raises a number of questions. This section offers a short overview of the doctrine in pivotal cases under the FET standard.

Tribunals agree that expectations do not stem from a vacuum. A state commitment, representation or clear conduct must be identified and be legitimate, at least in the sense of being delivered by or stemming from a competent authority.[401] In the second stage, tribunals require investors to demonstrate a certain reliance on the commitment or representation in their investment decision.[402] Different degrees of evidence of that reliance can be expected from the investor depending on the tribunal's understanding of LE.[403] But tribunals agree that only investors who benefit from the commitment or representation may claim a breach of LE.

The broad contours of the notion are described in the 2012 United Nations Conference on Trade and Development (UNCTAD) report, which enunciates the 'qualifying elements' of the investor's LE as follows:

396. *See* Intorduction.A.1.
397. *Tecmed v. Mexico* (n 67) para. 154.
398. *FREIF v. Spain* (n 77) para. 534; *Electrabel v. Hungary* (n 225) para. 7.75; *Saluka v. Czech Republic* (n 77) para. 302.
399. McLachlan, 'Treatment of Investors' (n 40) para. 7.179.
400. Potestà, 'Legitimate Expectations' (n 68); Levashova, *Right of States to Regulate* (n 374) 316; Niclas Landmann, *Legitimate Expectations and Fair-and-Equitable-Treatment under the Energy Charter Treaty, A comparative Analysis of the Renewable Energy Cases* (Nomos 2022); Kopar, *Stability* (n 235); Yoleth Emilia Lainez Calderon, *Les attentes légitimes en Droit international économique* (Thesis Paris II Panthéon Assas 2021).
401. *Antaris v. Czech Republic* (n 76) para. 360, para. 535 ('a claim based on legitimate expectation must proceed from an identification of the origin of the expectation alleged, so that its scope can be formulated with precision').
402. *Cube Infrastructure Fund SICAV and others v. Kingdom of Spain* ICSID Case No. ARB/15/20, Decision on Jurisdiction, Liability and Partial Decision on Quantum, 19 February 2019, para. 388 ('to the extent that those expectations are objectively reasonable, they give rise to legitimate expectations when investments are in fact made in reliance upon them') Kopar, *Stability* (n 235) 190 ('in order to grant a legitimate expectations protection based on a stability provision under the domestic legislation, tribunals seek additional requirements and elaborate more on the reliance aspect').
403. *See* Chapter 2.E.2.

(a) Legitimate expectations may arise only from a State's specific representations or commitments made to the investor on which the latter has relied;[404]
(b) The investor must be aware of the general regulatory environment in the host country;
(c) Investors' expectations must be balanced against legitimate regulatory activities of host countries.[405]

This is a general statement, and each proposition hides difficulties in practice and can be subject to widely differing opinions.[406] It rightly points out three difficulties: the source of expectations, the responsibility of investors and the balancing act in assessing the legitimacy of expectations. Each is addressed below.

1 The Sources of Expectations

The first difficulty, and not the least, is the source of expectations. Depending on the facts and contexts, arbitral tribunals have judged that three types of situations give rise to LE. *Continental Casualty c. Argentine* famously listed, by the degree of expectations, the diverse sources of commitments or representations that may be issued by the host state and relied on by the investor, on which my analysis relies:

> (i) the specificity of the undertaking allegedly relied upon, considering moreover that political statements have the least legal value, regrettably but notoriously so; ii) general legislative statements engender reduced expectations, especially with competent major international investors in a context where the political risk is high; iii) unilateral modification of contractual undertakings by governments, notably when issued in conformity with a legislative framework and aimed at obtaining financial resources from investors deserve clearly more scrutiny, in the light of the context, reasons, effects, since they generate as a rule legal rights and therefore expectations of compliance; (...)[407]

404. Some tribunals consider that general representations may create legitimate expectations. Similarly, commitments in law or decree addressed to a wide but specified group of investors may create LE; *see* Chapter 3.B.
405. UNCTAD, *Fair and Equitable Treatment: A Sequel* (n 365) 68.
406. For instance, a strict estoppel view on LE finds that the host State can bind itself in the general legislation and does not require due diligence and rejects the theory that states benefit from a margin of change to regulate in the state's public interests; *see* Jack Biggs, 'The Scope of Investors' Legitimate Expectations under the FET Standard in the European Renewable Energy Cases' (2021) 36 ICSID Review 99, 119-128 https://doi.org/10.1093/icsidreview/siaa047 (Biggs advocates the application of the narrowly defined *estoppel*, which would equate to embracing the State as an equal party with the investor, to which I prefer the broader concept of good faith, which, in essence, is more sympathetic to public policy concerns).
407. *Continental Casualty v. Argentine* (n 62) para. 261 ('i) the specificity of the undertaking allegedly relied upon, considering moreover that political statements have the least legal value, regrettably but notoriously so; ii) general legislative statements engender reduced expectations, especially with competent major international investors in a context where the political risk is high; iii) unilateral modification of contractual undertakings by governments, notably when issued in conformity with a legislative framework and aimed at obtaining financial resources from investors deserve clearly more scrutiny, in the light of the context, reasons, effects, since they generate as a rule legal rights and therefore expectations of compliance;

Continental's analysis is widely accepted in the case law. It pinpoints the three general sources of LE and can incidentally apply to ICCL-related representations.[408]

a) *Contractual Agreements: The Highest Degree of Representation*

First, investors may claim LE based on legal rights grounded in contractual arrangements with the states (e.g., a contract entered into with a state agency or state entity,[409] although tribunals have emphasised the difference between LE under a treaty and contractual commitments).[410] LE deriving from contracts have been clearly distinguished from rights deriving from the umbrella clause under IIAs.[411]

b) *Formal and Informal Representations to the Investor*

Second, formal and informal representations made to investors[412] have been recognised as creating expectations. Informal representation must be delivered by a competent authority and have a certain degree of specificity.[413] These representations may

(...)'); Simon Maynard, 'Legitimate Expectations and the Interpretation of the Legal Stability Obligation' (2016) 1 European Investment Law and Arbitration Review 1 104 https://doi.org/10.54648/eila2016007.

408. For the purpose of the research on ICCL and LE, it suffices to say here that net zero commitments and ICCL-related obligations could amount to the first or second source of commitments (political statement or legislative statements), as they are usually not addressed to a single investor and stem from political statements; *see* Chapter 5.
409. *EBO Invest and others v. Latvia* ICSID, Award, 28 February 2020, para. 423, para. 426; *Arif v. Moldova*, ICSID, Award, 8 April 2013; *Glamis Gold, Ltd. v. USA*, UNCITRAL, Award, 8 June 2009, para. 766, para. 813; *Continental Casualty v. Argentine* (n 62) para. 261; *GAMI v. Mexico*, UNCITRAL, Final Award, 15 November 2004, para. 23.
410. *AES Corporation and Tau Power B.V. v. Republic of Kazakhstan*, ICSID Case No. ARB/10/16, Award, 1 November 2013, para. 291; *Impregilo v. Argentina* (I), ICSID, Award, 21 June 2011, para. 292; *Hamester v. Ghana*, ICSID, Award, 18 June 2010, para. 335; *Duke Energy v. Ecuador* (n 225) para. 358; *Parkerings-Compagniet AS v. Republic of Lithuania*, ICSID Case No. ARB/05/8, Award, 11 September 2007, para. 344.
411. It is, at least, consensual that the contract breach must have been substantial to rise to a breach of LE; *see* James Crawford, 'Treaty and Contract in Investment Arbitration' (2008) 24 Arbitration International 351, 374 https://doi.org/10.1093/arbitration/24.3.351.
412. Promises made by a mayor of the host State do not give rise to legitimate expectations when they do not have the authority to make such commitments; *Pawlowski v. Czech Republic* ICSID, Award, 1 November 2021, paras 638-639.
413. *RREEF Infrastructure (G.P.) Limited and RREEF Pan-European Infrastructure Two Lux S.à.r.l. v. Kingdom of Spain*, ICSID Case No. ARB/13/30, Decision on Responsibility and on the Principles of Quantum, 30 November 2018, para. 396; *Charanne B.V., Construction Investments S.A.R.L. v. Kingdom of Spain*, SCC 062/2012, Final Award, 21 January 2016, para. 496; *AES Solar and others (PV Investors) v. Spain*, PCA Case No. 2012-14, Final Award, 28 February 2020, para. 615 considered that advertising campaign by an agency to attract investments, lacks the degree of regulatory power, clarity, and specificity to be a commitment. On the contrary, *Novenergia – Energy & Environment (SCA) (Grand Duchy of Luxembourg), SICAR v. Kingdom of Spain*, SCC Arbitration 2015/063, Final Arbitral Award, 15 February 2018, para. 688; *Watkins Holdings S.à r.l. and others v. Kingdom of Spain* (ICSID Case No. ARB/15/44, Award of 21 January 2020, para. 532, 533 held that the advertising campaign, alongside policy reports, were aimed at incentivising companies to invest – thus constituting a relevant element in the formation of legitimate expectations.

include acts of government officials,[414] repeated assurances by federal officials,[415] public statements,[416] and other publicity-inducing foreign investment.[417] Some tribunals note that such representations must be specific,[418] while others point out that no specific assurances from the state are required to create expectations of protection against unfair changes.[419] In highly regulated sectors such as energy, the threshold to creating expectations has been contested among tribunals.[420]

c) *Regulatory Frameworks: A Valid Source of Legitimate Expectations*

Third, the regulatory framework. There are generally two approaches as to whether the regulatory framework may be a source of legitimate expectations. The distinction is important, as commitments made to clean energy investors are usually made in decrees or laws (the regulatory framework), so one must analyse whether they can engender LE.[421]

One of the most contested issues is whether the general regulatory framework in force in the host state at the time of the investment may create LE.[422] Some

414. *Glencore v. Colombia*, ICSID Case No. ARB/16/6, Award, 27 August 2019, para. 1368; *Venezuela Holdings, B.V., et al. v. Bolivarian Republic of Venezuela*, ICSID Case No. ARB/07/27, Award of the Tribunal, 9 October 2014, para. 256; *Grand River Enterprises Six Nations, Ltd., et al. v. United States of America*, UNCITRAL, Award, 12 January 2011, para. 140, 141; *Total v. Argentina*, ICSID Case No. ARB/04/1, Decision on liability, 27 December 2010, para. 117; *Merrill & Ring v. Canada* ICSID, Award, 31 March 2010, para. 242; *Sempra v. Argentina* ICSID, Award, 28 September 2007, para. 298; *Parkerings v. Lithuania* (n 410) para. 331; *SPP v. Egypt* ICSID, Award, 20 May 1992, para. 82, para. 83.
415. *Kardassopoulos v. Georgia* ICSID, Decision on Jurisdiction, 6 July 2007, para.191, para. 192, para. 194; *Metalclad v. Mexico* ICSID, Award, 30 August 2000, para. 89.
416. *SunReserve Luxco Holdings SRL v. Italy*, SCC Case No. 132/2016, Final Award, 25 March 2020, para. 817; *Border Timbers v. Zimbabwe* ICSID, Award, 28 July 2015, paras 547-551; *MTD v. Chile* (n 227) para. 159.
417. On the role of advertisements, reports, and authoritative statements in assessing legitimate expectations, *see* Landmann, *Legitimate Expectations* (n 400) 208 ff.
418. *Silver Ridge v. Italy* (n 56), Dissenting Opinion of Judge O. Thomas Johnson, 24 February 2021, para. 12; *Tulip Real Estate and Development Netherlands B.V. v. Republic of Turkey*, ICSID Case No. ARB/11/28, Award, 10 March 2014, para. 403; *White Industries v. India*, Ad hoc Arbitration, Final Award, 30 November 2011, para. 10.3.17; *M.C.I. Power Group L.C. and New Turbine, Inc. v. Republic of Ecuador*, ICSID Case No. ARB/03/6, Award, 31 July 2007, para. 278; *Continental Casualty v. Argentine* (n 62) paras 261, 262; *EDF (Services) Limited v. Romania*, ICSID Case No. ARB/05/13, Award, 8 October 2009, para. 217; *Total v. Argentina* (n 414) para. 121; *El Paso v. Argentina* (n 41) para. 375.
419. *Silver Ridge v. Italy* (n 56) paras 410, 421; *Ioan Micula, Viorel Micula and others v. Romania [II]*, ICSID Case No. ARB/14/29, Award, 5 March 2020, para. 362; *Electrabel v. Hungary* (n 225) para. 7.78 ('While specific assurances given by the host State may reinforce the investor's expectations, such an assurance is not always indispensable'); *Saluka v. Czech Republic* (n 77) para. 329 (even though at para. 304 the tribunal stressed that expectations 'must rise to the level of legitimacy and reasonableness in light of the circumstances').
420. *See* Chapter 3.B.1.
421. *Ibid.*
422. *Eco Oro Minerals Corp. v. Republic of Colombia*, ICSID Case No. ARB/16/41, Decision on Jurisdiction, Liability and Directions on Quantum, 9 September 2021, paras 804-805; *Hydro Energy 1 S.à r.l. and Hydroxana Sweden AB v. Spain*, ICSID Case No. ARB/15/42, Decision on Jurisdiction, Liability and Directions on Quantum, 9 March 2020 para. 596; *9REN Holding S.a.r.l v. Kingdom of Spain*, ICSID Case No. ARB/15/15, Award of 31 May 2019, para. 294;

tribunals[423] hold that depending on the clarity of the regulation or law and the intent to induce foreign investments, the regulatory framework may create expectations.[424] Based on past research, I posit that they adopt a voluntary theory of LE.[425] Other tribunals found that laws and regulations cannot, by themselves, form LE due to the dynamic nature of legislation and the state's sovereign prerogatives to respond to changing circumstances.[426] They generally approach LE from a detrimental reliance theory. I explore both strands in more detail below.

i) Two Opposing Approaches to Regulatory Frameworks as Sources of Legitimate Expectations

The first, voluntary theory, considers that states may be under the obligation to respect their promises. In *Micula v. Romania*, the tribunal opined that 'promise, assurance, or representation may have been issued generally or specifically, but it must have created a specific and reasonable expectation in the investor'.[427] In a recent example, *Cube Infrastructure v. Spain* asserted that general legislation could arise to a 'specific commitment' if the representation is sufficiently clear and unequivocal:

> The Tribunal does not consider it necessary that a specific commitment be made to each individual claimant in order for a legitimate expectation to arise. At least in the case of a highly regulated industry, and provided that the representations are sufficiently clear and unequivocal, it is enough that a regulatory regime be established with the overt aim of attracting investments by holding out to potential investors the prospect that the investments will be subject to a set of specific regulatory principles that will, as a matter of deliberate policy, be maintained in force for a finite length of time. Such regimes are plainly intended to create expectations upon which investors will rely; and to the extent that those expectations are objectively reasonable, they give rise to legitimate expectations when investments are in fact made in reliance upon them.[428]

Another example can be found in *Enron v. Argentina*. In this case, the dispute related to legislative incentives introduced by Argentina's Government in the 1990s to

Glencore v. Colombia (n 414) para. 1368; *Pawlowski AG and Project Sever s.r.o. v. Czech Republic*, ICSID Case No. ARB/17/11, Award, 1 November 2021, para. 613; *see also Bilcon of Delaware et al. v. Government of Canada*, PCA Case No. 2009-04, Award on Jurisdiction and Liability, 17 March 2015, para. 474; *National Grid plc v. The Argentine Republic*, UNCITRAL, Award, 3 November 2008, para. 84; *Invesmart v. Czech Republic*, UNCITRAL, Award, 26 June 2009, para. 84, para. 255; *Charanne v. Spain* (n 413), Dissenting Opinion of Guido Santiago Tawil, 21 January 2016, para. 5.

423. *See* Chapter 3.C.1.
424. The next chapter explores this question in-depth on the basis of the case law under the ECT.
425. Teerawat Wongkaew, *Protection of Legitimate Expectations in Investment Treaty Arbitration, A Theory of Detrimental Reliance* (CUP 2019).
426. *Lidercón, S.L. v. Republic of Peru*, ICSID Case No. ARB/17/9, Award, 6 March 2020, para. 206; *PV Investors v. Spain* (n 413) para. 580; *RREEF v. Spain* (n 413) para. 245; *Mobil v. Argentina* (n 76) para. 928; *EDF v. Romania* (n 418) para. 217 ('The idea that legitimate expectations, and therefore FET, imply the stability of the legal and business framework, may not be correct if stated in an overly broad and unqualified formulation').
427. *Ioan Micula, Viorel Micula, S.C. European Food S.A, S.C. Starmill S.R.L. and S.C. Multipack S.R.L. v. Romania*, ICSID Case No. ARB/05/20, Award, 11 December 2013, para. 529 para. 671.
428. *Cube Infrastructure v. Spain* (n 402) para. 388.

encourage foreign investment in natural gas which were withdrawn due to the economic crisis. The tribunal noted that the incentives 'contain[ed] specific guarantees to attract foreign capital to an economy historically unstable and volatile'.[429] The Tribunal held that 'substantial foreign investment' was made in reliance 'on the strength of such guarantees'.[430] In *LG&E,* which related to the same regulatory changes, the Tribunal similarly held that the investor 'relied upon certain key guarantees in the Gas Law'.[431] It further stated that 'an expectation may arise from what are construed as specific guarantees in legislation'.[432] A similar view is proposed by *Novenergia II.* According to the tribunal: '[t]he relevant question is whether the statement or conduct objectively *suffices* to create LE in the recipient (emphasis added)'.[433] Put yet differently by Gary Born:

> [t]he decisive issue is not whether a state's undertaking is 'specific' or 'general', or statutory or contractual, but whether the statements and actions of the state provide a sufficiently clear commitment to give rise under international law to legitimate expectations or legal rights on the part of the investor.[434]

The second approach, which I call detrimental reliance theory, considers, in the words of the tribunal in *Philipp Morris v. Uruguay,* that, as a general rule:

> provisions of general legislation applicable to a plurality of persons or to a category of persons do not create legitimate expectations that there will be no change in the law.[435]

In other words, general legislation may not create LE since it may be changed at the sovereign's discretion. *Philip Morris'* tribunal understands the state's capacity as sovereign compared to a commercial capacity. The tribunal dismisses the possibility that a state may, in its legislation, create binding obligations amounting to a stabilisation clause. In other words, legislation may not be construed as contracts with foreign investors - or unilateral binding commitments.[436] However, a necessary precision is to

---

429. *Enron Corp v. Argentina,* ICSID Case No ARB/01/3, Award, 22 May 2007, para. 264.
430. *Ibid.*
431. *LG&E v. Argentina* (n 388) para. 133.
432. *Antaris v. Czech Republic* (n 76) para. 360 citing *Enron Corp v. Argentina* (n 429) paras 264-266; *LG&E v. Argentina* (n 388) paras 162-163.
433. *Novenergia II v. Spain* (n 413) para. 652.
434. *Jürgen Wirtgen, Stefan Wirtgen, Gisela Wirtgen and JSW Solar (zwei) GmbH & Co. KG v. Czech Republic,* PCA Case No. 2014-03, Dissenting opinion of Gary Born, 11 October 2017, para. 12 ('[t]he decisive issue is not whether a state's undertaking is "specific" or "general", or statutory or contractual, but whether the statements and actions of the state provide a sufficiently clear commitment to give rise under international law to legitimate expectations or legal rights on the part of the investor').
435. *Philip Morris v. Uruguay* (n 76) para. 426.
436. *Matthias Kruck v. Spain,* Partial Dissenting Opinion (n 39) para. 98 ('The problem for legitimate expectations in these cases is that one has to accept a proposition that is patently absurd to get over the first hurdle. That proposition is that RD 661/2007 contained an undertaking of immutability when such an undertaking, if given, would have violated Spanish constitutional and administrative law as well as EU state aid law. The Spanish Government cannot, in a Royal Decree, promise not to amend or repeal that decree if the public interest requires it, nor can it bind the Spanish Parliament not to amend or repeal Law 54/1997, which provides the legislative authority for the Spanish Government to have enacted RD 661/2007 in the first

be added. Further, in *Philipp Morris*, the tribunal explained that there was only one way for the investor to justify LE:

> given the State's regulatory powers, in order to rely on legitimate expectations, the investor should inquire in advance regarding the prospects of a change in the regulatory framework in light of the then prevailing or reasonably to be expected changes in the economic and social conditions of the host State.[437]

Echoing the same reasoning, in *Charanne v. Spain*, the tribunal found that:

> Turning a regulatory provision, due to the limited number of persons that may be subject thereto, into a specific commitment entered into by the State towards each and every one of those persons would be an excessive limitation of the capacity of States to regulate the economy according to the public interest.[438]

Philippe Sands dissented in the *Renergy v. Spain* case, arguing that in the absence of a specific promise or representation made by the State to the investor, 'the latter may not rely on a bilateral investment treaty as a kind of insurance policy against the risk of any changes in the host State's legal and economic framework'.[439] Similarly, according to Levashova, commitments should be specific formal representations, which 'excludes general statements, such as political speeches or general laws; these do not create a specific right on the part of the investor'.[440] Further, she explains that:

> a specific representation can only be one that: (1) is provided by a competent authority with a relevant decision-making power over the investment; (2) is aimed at the express and specific inducement of investment that should be crystallised in an agreement or licence or other assurance in writing and constitutes an explicit right (...) and (3) is directed at the specific investor and is not aimed at a large or even small groups of potential investors.[441]

This detrimental reliance approach justifies the scope restriction by considerations of public interest and necessary amendments to regulatory frameworks. It also relies on the principle of sovereignty. However, does a state uphold the principle of sovereignty when it violates its own unequivocal and clear promises made to a specific group of investors? Is it justified for a state to withdraw its own commitments to clean energy investors in the name of protecting the 'public interest'?

ii) Understanding 'Specificity' and 'Commitments'

From the experts above, we understand that tribunals have different understandings of the words 'specific' and 'commitment'. This observation invites a closer look at the

place') para. 93 ('The general constraints on public power in international law provide a certain measure of stability to foreign investments. They do not guarantee complete stability by creating a strict liability regime that compensates for any change').

437. *Antaris v. Czech Republic* (n 76) para. 360 citing *Philip Morris v. Uruguay* (n 76) paras 426-427.
438. *Charanne v. Spain* (n 413) para. 493.
439. *Renergy S.à r.l. v. Kingdom of Spain*, ICSID Case No. ARB/14/18, Dissent on Liability and Quantum Professor Philippe Sands QC, para. 48.
440. Levashova, *Right of States to Regulate* (n 374) 132.
441. *Ibid.*, 246.

ordinary meaning of the words specific and commitment to better understand where the theoretical divide sits.

The adjective 'specific' is interpreted in two distinctive ways. The detrimental reliance approach privileges an understanding of a 'specific' commitment as an act of the host state *addressed personally* to a single investor.[442] For instance, in a contract or through the registration of the investor with an administrative authority or again through formal administrative acts conveyed to the addressee. A commitment would otherwise miss the legal validity it requires to engage the liability of the State. The voluntary approach understands 'specific' commitment more broadly,[443] as: (1) sufficiently precise in their content, object, and purpose with the aim to induce investments and (2) addressed to a targeted and identifiable group of investors.[444] Accordingly, specific commitments include the legal framework of the host state, general advertisements, reports, and political statements that may be considered specific commitments creating LE.

The noun 'commitment' is interpreted differently as well. The detrimental reliance view considers the form of the commitment first. Accordingly, a state's commitment may only derive from the highest authority possible. This approach affords great deference and weight to the legal, administrative, and judicial framework in which the investor chooses to invest. The difficulty, however, is to find the 'legitimate' commitment – why would a commitment in law, i.e., to 'a reasonable return', be more legitimate than a fixed price adopted by decree when both of these norms are amendable under a state's constitution? The voluntary approach interprets the substance of the state's investment-inducing representation rather than its form. Important is the enforcement of sovereign promises and undertakings. Accordingly, what matters is the letter, substance, or meaning of the law, regulation, or contract. Its authority within the legal framework of the host state is a secondary concern. A more elaborate literal view adds to the assessment of the commitment of an array of facts that are additional evidence of the state's commitment to the foreign investor.

To sum up, 'specific' state commitments are split into two main categories:[445] commitments made directly to the *specific* investor and general commitments addressed to a group of investors *specific* in their language.[446]

These two perspectives are, *prima facie*, irreconcilable. Nevertheless, the case law analysed in the next chapter demonstrates that tribunals are open to considering expectations based on the regulatory framework, at least under the Energy Charter Treaty. Similarly, tribunals tend to converge on certain factors that pose limits to the legitimacy of expectations.

442. UNCTAD, *Fair and Equitable Treatment: A Sequel* (n 365) 69.
443. *Ibid.*
444. For instance, *Mobil v. Argentina* (n 76) para. 957 ('two types of commitments might be considered "specific"; those specific as to their addressee and those specific regarding their object and purpose'); *Silver Ridge v. Italy* (n 56) para. 407.
445. Landmann, *Legitimate Expectations* (n 400) 187-238.
446. *Ibid.*, 205-206.

2 The Legitimacy of Expectations

Beyond the source of expectations, the second and third sources of difficulty in analysing legitimate expectations relate to the notion of 'legitimacy'. While one concerns the level of due diligence that can be expected from investors, the other concerns the balancing act necessary in solving LE claims. Both derive from the fact-intensity of the concept, itself deriving from the ordinary meaning of the concept. The notion of legitimacy is key to integrating ICCL in the analysis of LE. In particular, in the fossil fuel industry, the question of the protection of their LE will likely turn around whether the investors could *legitimately* hold expectations about the stability of the regulatory framework in which they invested.[447]

The ordinary meaning of 'expectation' is a 'feeling or belief that something will or should happen in the future'[448] or, according to the Black Law's Dictionary, 'in general, this is the belief that something will happen based on a series of actions'.[449] The second definition should be preferred, as 'feeling' is too vague. There are two inherent qualities to this definition. First, a belief must stem from a source or action. In legal terms, only actions such as the conduct, promise or representations can create an impression about future events. Second, a belief about future events is necessarily uncertain. Contrary to a debt obligation, a belief is not, in principle, settled in a contract secured by the principles of bindingness. The *degree* of legitimacy of this belief, and hence expectations, is thus central to determining what future events can be expected.[450]

The term 'legitimacy' can encompass several parallel interpretations. According to the Cambridge Dictionary, the term may mean not only 'the fact of being allowed by law or done according to the rules of an organisation or activity' but also the 'state of being fair and honest' or 'the quality of being legal'.[451] A distinction can be made between the understanding of 'legitimate' as 'fair' and its definition as 'legal'. In a strict sense, 'legitimate' means that the source of the state's commitment is lawful, i.e., it can lawfully commit the state towards the investor. Some tribunals have held that the representations must be made by an authority with the power to regulate.[452] Others assessed whether a clear and specific commitment had been made by a state authority.[453] A minority of tribunals required the crystallisation of the investment inducement

447. *See* Chapter 5.B.
448. 'Expectation', *Cambridge English Dictionary* (OUP 2023).
449. 'Expectation', *Black Law's Dictionary* (11th edn, Thomson Reuters 2019).
450. This also explains why legitimate expectations have not the same meaning as estoppel *stricto sensu* or strict liability under contract law, which both underline the immutability of the promise or contractual clause.
451. 'Legitimacy', *Cambridge English Dictionary* (OUP 2023).
452. *Stadtwerke München GmbH and others v. Kingdom of Spain*, ICSID Case No. ARB/15/1, Award, 2 December 2019, para. 286; *Hydro Energy v. Spain* (n 422) para. 663.
453. *Novenergia II v. Spain* (n 413) para. 668; *Infrastructure Services Luxembourg S.à.r.l. and Energia Termosolar B.V. (formerly Antin Infrastructure) v. Kingdom of Spain*, ICSID Case No. ARB/13/31, Award, 15 June 2018, para. 545; *Watkins Holdings v. Spain* (n 413) para. 527; *NextEra v. Spain* (n 638) para. 587.

in a contract.[454] In contrast, a majority of tribunals have accepted the premise that general representations may raise LE – however, often differentiating between laws and decrees. In a broader sense, 'legitimate' resembles 'reasonable' and 'fair', which would require the investor to justify the existence of reasonable expectations in view of the prevailing conditions at the time of his investment. This distinction is relevant when arbitrators assess the legitimacy of expectations regarding: (1) the time of the investment or (2) the level of due diligence required by the foreign investor.

a) Due Diligence: Objective or Subjective?

Investors inherently assume business risks, which is particularly evident in ventures within developing states or under unique circumstances. But one of the most commonly discussed aspects of LE is to what extent investors must demonstrate a certain level of due diligence in making the investment, without which, they would not be able to legitimately rely on the state's promise. Here again, there is a hiatus among arbitral tribunals even if due diligence is a matter recently addressed by virtually all tribunals. The question is whether due diligence obligations should be assessed objectively or subjectively. In other words, at the evidentiary stage, should the investor demonstrate that it adopted a cautious approach, ordering a number of reports pertaining to the regulatory framework or stability of the host state (the subjective approach), or demonstrate that it relied on the state's objective measure, and demonstrate that reliance in the investment decision (the objective approach). As explained below, the first is an approach favoured by the fault-centred detrimental reliance theory, while the second is preferred by the state-centred voluntary theory of LE. The case law shows different approaches to the question.

In *MTD v. Chile* and *Parkerings v. Lithuania*, tribunals underscored that BITs do not serve as insurance against business risks. On the merits of LE, *MTD v. Chile* halved damages by 50% to the investor for breach of LE on the ground of insufficient 'diligence' by the investor and because 'the Claimant should bear the consequences of their own actions as experienced businessmen'.[455] Similarly, in *Parkerings v. Lithuania*, the tribunal opined that the investor, by deciding to invest notwithstanding a possible instability,[456] took the business risk of being faced with changes of laws possibly or even likely to be detrimental to its investment.[457] There is a distinction to draw between the objective conditions in which the investor chose to invest (the

454. *ESPF v. Italy* (n 133) paras 515-517; *Antin v. Spain* (n 453) para. 532; *9REN v. Spain* (n 422) para. 294.
455. *MTD v. Chile* (n 227) para. 178.
456. *Parkerings v. Lithuania* (n 410) paras 332-334, *see* para. 333 ('In principle, an investor has a right to a certain stability and predictability of the legal environment of the investment The investor will have a right of protection of its legitimate expectations provided it exercised due diligence and that its legitimate expectations were reasonable in light of the circumstances. Consequently, an investor must anticipate that the circumstances could change, and thus structure its investment in order to adapt it to the potential changes of legal environment').
457. *Ibid.*, 334 (although the investor 'could (and with hindsight should) have sought to protect its LE by introducing into the investment agreement a stabilisation clause or some other provision protecting it against unexpected and unwelcomed changes').

business risks assumed) and the subjective due diligence it carried out (by requesting reports from specialised law firms, for instance). For some tribunals, subjective due diligence has become one of the conditions assessed to hold LE,[458] while all tribunals consider what legitimate expectations could form objectively at the time of investment. The specificities of the host state, such as its level of development and the context of the investment (a high degree of political volatility,[459] a post-civil war situation), may also affect the legitimacy of expectation.[460] In the case of an investment in a developing state, this may mean expecting a less stable socio-economic and political environment.[461]

Prima facie, ICCL may impact each of these factors. ICCL may: (1) affect the legitimacy of the expectations depending on the timing of the investment and (2) affect the objective conditions in which the investor decided to invest and the risks it assumed, which may not necessarily limit but also support LE.[462]

b) Objective Elements of Legitimacy: The Investment Timing and the Frustrating Measure's Foreseeability

Finally, as part of the legitimacy element of LE, tribunals commonly apply a balancing act in assessing whether a breach of legitimate expectations of investors has occurred. Most tribunals consider that states benefit from a margin of change with regard to the promises they grant. This margin, however small it may be, precisely differentiates

458. *See* Chapter 3.C.1.
459. *Bayindir Insaat Turizm Ticaret Ve Sanayi A.Ş. v. Pakistan*, ICSID Case No. ARB/03/29, Award, 27 August 2009, para. 195.
460. *Duke Energy Electroquil Partners & Electroquil SA v. Ecuador*, ICSID Case No. ARB/04/19, Award, 12 August 2008, para. 340 ('The assessment of the reasonableness or legitimacy [of the investor's expectations] must take into account all circumstances, including not only the facts surrounding the investment, but also the political, socio-economic, cultural and historical conditions prevailing in the host State').
461. *Toto Construzioni Generali S.p.A. v. Lebanon*, ICSID Case No. ARB/07/12, Award, 7 June 2012, para. 245.
462. *Sevilla Beheer and others v. Spain*, ICSID Case No. ARB/16/27, Partial Disssenting Opinion by Peter Cameron, 11 February 2022, para. 63 ('Finally, on this subject, there is much in the record of this case that suggests the relationship between the investor and the host State in a prospective long-term investment in renewable energy development is one that is highly cooperative in character, driven on both sides not solely by commercial goals in which both parties seek to secure advantages for themselves, but also by a common interest in promoting certain kinds of energy that offer or are thought to offer the population of the host State greater benefits than conventional forms of power generation, and more widely a public good in terms of climate change mitigation'); for a countervailing position *see Matthias Kruck v. Spain*, Partial Dissenting Opinion (n 39) para. 57 ('in an era where radical reforms in the energy sector are not only desirable but necessary for the sustainability of human life on Earth, it seems incongruous now to be interpreting the FET standard as requiring States to buy back their right to implement those reforms at the highest price. In this case the investment is in renewable energy. But if the strict liability approach is generalised (and there is no principled basis for limiting it to cases involving renewable energy), then the public interest considerations behind any reform are by definition irrelevant to the determination of liability in damages. The regulatory chill that inevitably accompanies this approach will be no consolation to a warming planet').

legitimate expectations arising from regulatory promises as they are protected under the FET standard from strict contractual obligations or stabilisation clauses that can be found in a private commercial setting.[463] The main point of friction is not so much whether the margin of adaptation exits but the extent to which it exists. One of the related difficulties is to designate the right threshold in assessing a breach of LE: reasonableness or proportionality. Reasonableness and proportionality are both legal concepts that are often used in assessing the legality of government policies or actions in international investment arbitration. Reasonableness refers to whether a policy or action is rational and justified, given the objectives it seeks to achieve. Proportionality, however, involves balancing the benefits of a policy or action against its costs and assessing whether the policy or action is the least restrictive means of achieving its objectives.

In general, the reasonableness approach appears more convincing as part of an objective assessment of the circumstances in which the investor decided to invest and of the representation and its breach. For instance, it allows taking into account legitimacy elements that can be assessed objectively, such as the timing of the investment.

The timing of the investment plays a key role in the legitimacy of expectations, in particular in energy disputes as demonstrated in the next chapter.[464] The primary reason for this is that the investment may not benefit from legitimate expectations because it is finalised after the host state's commitment is terminated.[465] The second reason is that, from an objective and subjective point of view, the investor's expectations may not be legitimate or reasonable when the state announces a policy change prior to the investment time.[466] To prove that expectations are not merely hopes, arbitrators must assess whether, at the time of the investment, it was foreseeable that the incentivising measure could be replaced or that a frustrating policy (phasing out) would be implemented.[467] This is why timing and foreseeability are two interrelated concepts closely related to the assumed business risks. These two factors form the bedrock of the relevance of ICCL in the adjudication of energy disputes, as I show in the next two chapters.

In summary, arbitral tribunals have applied LE to establish liability under the FET standard, although the interpretation of the concept is subject to widely different conceptions. The subsections below explore the reasons for these different conceptions. They turn to the formal sources explored by scholars beyond the FET standard to further justify the use of LE as an element of the FET provision.

463. This difference explains why I reject the notion of 'strict liability', a notion borrowed from private law and which is too broad to designate the voluntary approach to legitimate expectations.
464. *See* Chapter 3.D.1.
465. *CEF Energia BV v. Italian Republic*, SCC Case No. 158/2015, Award, 16 January 2019, paras 234, 289.
466. *Isolux Infrastructure Netherlands B.V. v. Kingdom of Spain*, SCC Case No. V2013/153, Final Award, 17 July 2016, paras 141, 147.
467. *See* Chapter 3.D.1.

D THE ORIGINS OF LEGITIMATE EXPECTATIONS IN INVESTMENT ARBITRATION

As demonstrated above, the specific content of LE remains unsettled.[468] This content is at the heart of the balance between the state's sovereign prerogatives and its obligations towards the investor, and thus at the crossroad between the adoption of net zero measures and the rights of clean and fossil fuel investors.[469] One of the first ways to approach the legal concept is to search for its justification or 'roots'.[470] Given its absence from the vast majority of IIAs, where does the doctrine come from? And does this have an impact on how it is interpreted and applied?

Arbitral tribunals are generally reluctant to clarify the basis for the protection of LE.[471] Arbitral tribunals commonly relied on past arbitral 'case law' to justify their use of the LE doctrine.[472] There is no principle of *stare decisis*[473] or doctrine of precedent in public international law.[474] There is, however, a reliance on earlier judicial decisions, which are listed as 'subsidiary means for the determination of rules of law' in Article 38 of the ICJ Statute.[475] By analogy, this invites the question of whether investor-state awards can be conceived as a subsidiary means of interpretation. The question exceeds

468. *Matthias Kruck v. Spain*, Partial Dissenting Opinion (n 39) para. 2.
469. A minority of scholars have studied the balance from the philosophical perspective of natural and positive law, the practice and decision-making in international investment law reflects an ahistorical debate and eternal polarity between positivist and anti-positivists Diehl, *The Core Standard* (n 353) 313-320; Roland Kläger, *'Fair and Equitable Treatment' in International Investment Law* (CUP 2011) 146ff.; Daniel Behn, *A Theory of Configurative Fairness for Evolving International Legal Orders Linking the Scientific Study of Value Subjectivity to Jurisprudential Thought* (PhD Thesis, University of Dundee 2013) 108.
470. Potestà, 'Legitimate Expectations' (n 68) 89, 92; Florian Dupuy, *La protection de l'attente légitime des parties au contrat: Étude de droit international des investissements à la lumière du droit comparé* (PhD Thesis, Paris Assas University 2007) 396 (the author considers LE as an instrument of interpretation of the FET standard).
471. Wongkaew, *Detrimental Reliance* (n 425) 20.
472. There are public international law arguments to support the constitution of a consistent practice among arbitral tribunals based on VCLT's Art. 38. However, reliance on past arbitration cases should be dealt with caution; Yannick Radi, 'The "Human Nature" of International Investment Law' (2013) 1 TDM, Grotius Centre Working Paper 2013/006-IEL, Leiden Law School Research Paper, 8.
473. 'Stare Decisis', *Black's Law Dictionary* (7th edn, 1999) 1195 (defining precedent as '[a] decided case that furnishes a basis for determining later cases involving similar facts or issues; [s]ec stare decisis'; *ibid.*, 1414, explaining that the doctrine of precedent requires 'a court to follow earlier judicial decisions when the same points arise again in litigation').
474. The absence of *stare decisis* is stated in Art. 59 of the ICJ Statute, which provides that '[the decision of the Court has no binding force except between the parties and in respect of that particular case', wording retrieved in the NAFTA, Statute of the International Court of Justice (26 June 1945) 33 UNTS 993, Art. 59; North America Free Trade Agreement (NAFTA) Art. 1136(1); Jose E. Alvarez, 'The New Dispute Settlers: (Half) Truths and Consequences' (2003) 38 Tex ILJ 405, 406-407; Royal C. Gardner, 'Taking the Principle of Just Compensation Abroad: Private Property Rights, National Sovereignty, and the Cost of Environmental Protection' in (1997) 65 U Cin. LRev 539, 574 (he opines that this language is read as excluding a formal doctrine of precedent).
475. Statute of the International Court of Justice, 26 June 1945, Art. 38(1), 33 U.N.T.S. 993. The Statute codifies international law on this point.

the research scope. It suffices to say that investor-state tribunals are established *ad hoc*, and there are no rules under ICSID or investment treaties expecting or mandating tribunals to follow precedents, which makes the inquiry into the sources of LE relevant.[476]

Below, I find that: (1) considering LE as a general principle of international law is of little usefulness. Then, I explore the (2) concept of estoppel as a justification for LE. Finally, I present why the (3) principle of good faith seems appropriate, drawing an analogy to (4) public international law and the doctrine of unilateral statements.

1 Legitimate Expectations as a General Principle of International Law: A Limited Public-Law Theory

The public law theory of international investment law finds the roots of LE in the municipal law of states.[477] According to, *inter alia*, Professor Zachary Douglas,[478] LE would amount to a 'general principle of international law'.[479] The reasoning adopts a public law theory of international investment law. It considers LE as a general principle through Article 38(1)(c)[480] of the Statute of the International Court of Justice.[481] Although innovative, the public law theory[482] tends to disregard the applicable treaty and principles of treaty interpretations.[483]

476. At the same time, Kaufmann-Kohler is right in pointing to the necessity of consistent and predictable creation of rules, which Fuller calls the 'inner (or internal) morality of law'; Even if arbitrators do not make law, it can be argued that they have a moral obligation to strive for consistency and predictability. LE may be justifiable because past arbitral case law had recourse to the concept, but the divergence in the interpretation of LE is such, that arbitral tribunals should clarify the standards they apply. Any understanding of LE should also be contextualised. There is an umbilical cord between the FET standard provision in the underlying treaty and the doctrine of LE; *see* Gabrielle Kaufman Kohler, 'Arbitral Precedent: Dream, Necessity or Excuse? The 2006 Freshfields Lecture' (2007) 23 Arbitration International 3 357, 374 https://doi.org/10.1093/arbitration/23.3.357; Lon L. Fuller, *The Morality of Law* (rev edn, YUP 1969) 46.
477. Fulvio Maria Palombino, *Fair and Equitable Treatment and the Fabric of General Principles* (T.M.C. Asser Press 2018) 89.
478. *Matthias Kruck v. Spain*, Partial Dissenting Opinion (n 39) para. 33 ('As previously stated, the only bridge between the FET standard and a concept of legitimate expectations is that the latter is a general principle of law').
479. Lainez Calderon, *Les attentes légitimes* (n 400) 7 (Lainez argues that 'the concept [of legitimate expectations] is borrowed from the domestic law of a large majority of states as well as from European law'; the researcher further explains that 'This notion can take the form of a standard or a general principle of law. It is generally accepted that it emerges from a relationship between at least two individuals or when one of them makes representations or assurances, thus creating in the mind of the beneficiary a legitimate expectation of a specific situation').
480. *See* Potestà, 'Legitimate Expectations' (n 68) 92.
481. Tarcisio Gazzini, 'General Principles of Law in the Field of Foreign Investment' (2009) 10 JWIT 103, 112 https://doi.org/10.1163/221190009x00240; *see also* Mclachlan, 'Treatment of Investors' (n 40) 259 (FET is 'expressive of "general principles of law common to civilised nations", following of Article 38(1)(c) of the Statute of the International Court of Justice').
482. Roberts, 'Clash of Paradigms' (n 78) 68.
483. *Ibid.*

a) *The Lack of Uniformity in Domestic Levels of Protection*

Some consider that LE constitute an 'emerging general principle of international law',[484] particularly in its narrow sense because of its presence in municipal laws.[485] However, the generation of a general principle of law is a strict process that requires attention to variations.[486] The ICJ might have discarded this idea, as it expressively noted that '*in general international law [there is no] principle that would give rise to an obligation on the basis of what could be considered a legitimate expectation*'.[487] Nevertheless, the argument is based on various municipal legal systems that confirm the existence of principles similar to the LE doctrine, under which English,[488] German (*Vertrauensschutz*), French (*protection légitime*), European human rights,[489] and EU law.[490] However, the lack of uniformity in municipal laws confuses LE's scope so that no general principle can be easily inferred.[491]

German administrative law provides for the protection of trust (*Vertrauensschutz*) to protect citizens who placed their trust in the validity of an administrative act.[492] In case the administrative act is unlawful but the person relies on it, the public interest in the legality of the administration can be outweighed by that of protecting the trust of the citizen in the representation of the authority.[493] This approach leads to an intense judicial review.[494] However, the principle does not prevent the law from changing but obliges that the revocation of an act, even unlawful, is met with financial compensation on the part of the person relying on it.[495] At the EU level, the protection

484. Potestà, 'Legitimate Expectations' (n 68) 112.
485. Nitish Monebhurun, 'Gold Reserve Inc. v. Bolivarian Republic of Venezuela' (2015) 32 JI Arb 5 551, 562 https://doi.org/10.54648/joia2015026.
486. Giorgio Gaja, 'General Principles of Law' in *Max Planck Encyclopaedia of Public International Law* (CUP 2013) para. 13.
487. *Obligation to Negotiate Access to the Pacific Ocean (Bolivia v. Chile)*, Judgment, ICJ Reports 2018, p. 507, para. 162.
488. *See R. (on the application of Bancoult) v. Secretary of State for Foreign and Commonwealth Affairs*, [2008] UKHL 61, Judgment, 22 October 2008, para. 29.
489. Potestà, 'Legitimate Expectations' (n 68) 95ff.; Lainez Calderon, *Les attentes légitimes* (n 400) 13ff.
490. Cour de Cassation, Chambre Commerciale, Case No. 95-16853, 11 March 1997 [Author's translation: 'as stated by Art. 1134 (3) of the Civil Code, no one can illegitimately contradict himself at the expense of others and offend the legitimate expectation of the other contracting party'].
491. Wongkaew, *Detrimental Reliance* (n 425) 20; *see* more generally Søren Schønberg, *Legitimate Expectations in Administrative Law* (OUP 2000).
492. Christopher F. Forsyth, 'The Provenance and Protection of Legitimate Expectations' (1988) 47 The Cambridge Law Journal 2 238, 243 https://doi.org/10.1017/s000819730011801x.
493. *Bürgerliches Gesetzbuch*, para. 242 ('Leistung nach Treu und Glauben'); The principle of *Vertrauensschutz* is deeply rooted in a natural law understanding of administrative law, deriving directly from the German Constitutional (*Grundgesetz*) and civil law – from the rule of law principle (*Rechtsstaatsprinzip* under Art. 20 Abs. 3 Grundgesetz) of legal certainty, and the civil, natural law, principle of 'faith and belief'.
494. Which can also override statutes, as the idea of parliamentary sovereignty is not embraced under the Basic Law, *see* Georg Nolte, 'General Principles of German and European Administrative Law: A Comparison in Historical Perspective' (1994) 57 Modern Law Review 191, 196 https://doi.org/10.1111/j.1468-2230.1994.tb01932.x.
495. *Ibid.*

of LE[496] is also 'undeniably part of [Union] law'.[497] Similarly, the European Court of Human Rights recognised the existence of an individual's legitimate expectations, albeit with distinctive characteristics due to the Court's jurisdiction.[498] This approach may inspire a few investment tribunals.[499] English administrative law[500] considers LE as part of fairness in public administration.[501] The protection of LE is closely related to considerations of fairness rather than legal certainty.[502] Comparatively, there is no principle of legitimate expectations under French law, only of '*sécurité juridique*'.[503] More broadly, a few scholars find evidence of LE in other sectors of international economic law (in particular, tax law).[504] In summary, LE has different degrees of application depending on the jurisdiction, which complicates the finding of a general principle of international law.

b) The Limited Recognition of Legitimate Expectations as a General Principle of International Law by Tribunals

The purpose of defining LE as a general principle of law is to legitimise its use in international investment law.[505] The issue is that the understanding of LE as a general

496. Eleanor Sharpston, 'European Community Law, and the Doctrine of Legitimate Expectations: How Legitimate and for Whom' (1990) 11 Northwestern JILB 1 87, 87-89; *ISD Polska sp. z.o.o.and others v. European Commission*, CJEU Judgment of the Court (First Chamber), 24 March 2011, C-369/09 P, para. 122; *see* Maja Stanivukovic, 'Legitimate Expectations: A Commentary of Micula v Romania' (2017) 1 TDM 14 1, 7.
497. Advocate General Lenz in CJEU, *Finsider v. Commission of the European Communities*, Judgment of the Court of 19 September 1985, Joined Cases 63 and 147/84, para. B (II)(1)(c).
498. Rimantas Daujotas, 'The Concept of Legitimate Expectation in Investor-State Arbitration and the European Court of Human Rights' (2012) 2 International Commercial Arbitration Review 166, 174.
499. For an instance of moderate public law approach *see Matthias Kruck v. Spain*, Partial Dissenting Opinion (n 39) para. 108 ('If a concept of proportionality were to be applied, international tribunals would, like the EU courts and national courts, have to calibrate the intensity of the review in circumstances where a state authority has had to weigh complex and competing interests to reach a compromise that by definition cannot give full force and effect to the demands of any particular group. They would also have to bear in mind that their judicial mandate is to achieve corrective justice when a State has committed a wrong rather than to indemnify foreign investors against the impact of a fair and transparent redistribution of scarce resources by a State in crisis').
500. Lord Mackenzie Stuart, 'Legitimate Expectations and Estoppel in Community Law and English Administrative Law' (1983) 10 Legal Issues of European Integration 1 53 https://doi.org/10.54648/leie1983007.
501. *R v. Ministry of Agriculture, Fisheries and Food, ex p Hamble (Offshore) Fisheries Ltd* (1995) 2 ALL ER 714, 724.
502. Peter Cane, *Administrative Law* (5th edn, OUP 2011) 165; *Schmidt v. Secretary of State for Home Affairs*, [1969] 2 Ch 149.
503. Jean-Pierre Puissochet and Hubert Legal, 'Le principe de sécurité juridique dans la jurisprudence de la Cour de justice des Communautés européennes' (2001) Cahiers du Conseil Constitutionnel 11; For a contrary view *see* Chester Brown, *The Protection of Legitimate Expectations as a 'General Principle of Law': Some Preliminary Thoughts*, (2009) 6 TDM 1 5.
504. Lainez Calderon, *Les attentes légitimes* (n 400) 399, 463.
505. Gus van Harten and M Loughlin, 'Investment Treaty Arbitration as a Species of Global Administrative Law' (2006) EJIL 121 https://doi.org/10.1093/ejil/chi159; Gus van Harten, *Investment Treaty Arbitration and Public Law* (OUP 2007) 96 ff.

principle may: (1) narrow down the doctrine of LE to its strictest sense because of the diversity of understanding at the domestic level, and (2) disregard the specificity of the underlying treaty.[506] Ultimately, domestic public laws are but a 'point of reference'[507] or 'benchmark'[508] because arbitrators apply the treaty and the FET provision.[509] The scholarship suggests that the doctrine of LE has its roots in domestic jurisdictions. However, applying LE as a general principle would overlook the specificities of each treaty. It would require arbitrators to disregard the nuances in FET provisions or the LE-specific wording, leading to methodological challenges due to the varying interpretations of the concept in domestic laws.

From the perspective of this research on ICCL, even though it does not endorse the idea of a general principle, arbitrators referring to LE as a general principle of international often stress the importance of a proportionality assessment between the state's prerogatives and the investors' rights.[510] Proportionality assessments may include whether, by enacting a phasing out of an energy sector or the withdrawal of incentives, the state acted reasonably, which may involve a balancing of the public interests (including ICCL) at stake.[511]

2 Estoppel: A Horizontal Principle Masking the State's Sovereignty

Another theory finds that LE would derive from the principle of estoppel. Estoppel is consensually recognised as a general principle of international law.[512] The principle is flexible and derives from the Latin maxim *allegans contraria non audiendus est.*[513] A few scholars justify the use of LE in international investment law on this principle.[514] Some tribunals admitted the similarity of LE with estoppel without deriving its authority from it.[515] The major difficulty is that estoppel is a private law doctrine and, as such, presupposes interaction between equal parties.[516]

Originally estoppel is an English domestic law doctrine of equitable origins. Estoppel appeared in the international context in two forms: (1) as an instrument of

506. *PACC Offshore Services Holdings Ltd v. United Mexican States,* ICSID Case No. UNCT/18/5, Concurring and Dissenting Opinion of Professor W Michael Reisman, 11 January 2022, para. 2 (with the risk of 'importing conditions from other treaties under cover of "concerns" couched in grand questions of arbitral policy, which go beyond the BIT and the dispute').
507. *Tecmed v. Mexico* (n 67) para. 121.
508. *Thunderbird v. Mexico* (n 355), Separate Opinion of Mr Thomas Wälde, para. 28.
509. Teerawat Wongkaew, 'The Transplantation of Legitimate Expectations in Investment Treaty Arbitration: A Critique' in Shaheeza Lalani and R Polanco Lazo (eds), *The Role of the State in Investor-State arbitration* (Brill Nijhoff 2015) 69.
510. *Matthias Kruck v. Spain,* Partial Dissenting Opinion (n 39) para. 103.
511. *See* Chapter 6.D.
512. Ian Brownlie, *Principles of Public International Law* (6th edn, OUP 2003) 616.
513. *Ibid.*
514. Wongkaew, *Detrimental Reliance* (n 425) 37-41.
515. *Duke Energy v. Ecuador* (n 225) para. 241; *Marvin Roy Feldman Karpa v. United Mexican States,* ICSID Case No. ARB(AF)/99/1, Award, 16 December 2002, para. 63.
516. Josef Ostřanský, 'An Exercise in Equivocation: A Critique of Legitimate Expectations as a General Principle of Law under the Fair and Equitable Treatment Standard' in Gattini, Tanzi and Fontanelli (eds), *General Principles* (n 61) 352.

prohibition of inconsistent behaviour where it is sufficient to prove an attempt to deny a previous clear, consistent, unconditional and unambiguous statement or representation (broad estoppel, *lato sensu*); (2) in a narrow sense, in which a Claimant must show that the representor's sudden change of position generated a benefit for the same or a detriment for the representee (narrow estoppel, *sensu stricto*). Estoppel helps remedy an abuse of trust deriving from one party's backtrack from its representation. It is a concept which balances the rights and obligations of parties by resorting to corrective justice.[517]

Estoppel appears, however, inadequate to characterise the relationship between the state and the investor. Virtually all recent tribunals stress that the representation of a host state cannot equate to a commitment to freeze the regulatory framework[518] and that changes to the regulatory framework can be generally expected from investors.[519] A state's representation cannot create unfettered rights. It must be sufficiently and objectively legitimate. The individual cannot, in every case, claim that the existence of earlier representations precludes the host state from making decisions which run counter to its 'beliefs'. The public interest *in proper exercise* 'will outweigh the injustice suffered by the individual who has relied on the representation'.[520]

The inadequacy of estoppel to justify the LE lies in the fact that an expectation cannot be treated as a horizontal contract clause; otherwise, it would not be an expectation but an obligation. Nevertheless, traditional, narrow estoppel is relied upon by tribunals adopting the detrimental reliance theory of LE.[521]

3 Good Faith: Connecting Legitimate Expectations to Public International Law[522]

The most convincing source of LE lies perhaps in the principle of good faith.[523] Good faith is employed pursuant to Article 31 of the VCLT for treaty interpretation purposes

517. Piotr Sitnik, *Estoppel in International Investment Law* (PhD Thesis, Maria Curie-Skłodowska University in Lublin 2021) 29.
518. *Matthias Kruck and others v. Kingdom of Spain*, ICSID Case No. ARB/15/23, Decision on Jurisdiction, Liability and Principles of Damages, 14 September 2022, paras 220, 221, 224.
519. *Cube Infrastructure v. Spain* (n 402) para. 509 ('The Tribunal also found that 'non-dramatic' changes in the price support regime were foreseeable'); *RWE Innogy GmbH and RWE Innogy Aersa S.A.U. v. Kingdom of Spain*, ICSID Case No. ARB/14/34, Decision on Jurisdiction, Liability, and Certain Issues of Quantum, 30 December 2019, para. 488; *Silver Ridge v. Italy* (n 56) para. 606.
520. Clive Lewis, 'Fairness, Legitimate Expectations and Estoppel' (1986) 49 The Modern Law Review 2 251, 253.
521. Ian Brownlie, *Principles of Public International Law* (6th edn, OUP 2003) 616 (Ian Brownlie agrees that estoppel rests on the principles of good faith and consistency and that 'it is now reasonably clear that the essence of estoppel is the element of conduct which causes the other party, in reliance on such conduct, detrimentally to change its position or to suffer some prejudice').
522. Emily Sipiorski, *Good Faith in International Investment Arbitration* (OUP 2019) 186.
523. Sipiorski, *Good Faith* (n 522) 4; *see* more generally, *ibid.*, 177-186.

and plays a vital role in the maintenance of justice within the system of international investment law.[524] Good faith is a general principle of law under Article 38(1) of the Statute of the International Court of Justice.[525] Tribunals apply good faith frequently in relation to the FET provision, as it may imply conduct in good faith.[526] Good faith is a flexible principle which would allow the integration of international norms other than international investment law, as long as they are relevant[527] or can act as relevant fact - which is the case of ICCL.[528]

The principle of good faith supports the obligation of states to act fairly in a manner consistent with their international obligations when dealing with foreign investors.[529] It involves upholding commitments, adhering to legal obligations, and maintaining a predictable and stable investment environment. When a state's actions or policies lead investors to reasonably expect certain treatment or benefits, and the state deviates from those expectations, it can be seen as acting in bad faith, potentially giving rise to LE claims. Nevertheless, bad faith is not required to find that a State acted unfairly and inequitably.[530] The emphasis on good faith arises from the overarching duty of states to act fairly and transparently towards foreign investors, particularly under the unqualified FET standard. Prof. Dolzer recognises that LE derive from the international principle of good faith.[531]

The two opposite conceptions of FET both refer to good faith. For the tribunal in *Alex Genin v. Estonia,*[532] a violation of FET would include 'subjective bad faith'.[533] On the contrary, *Tecmed* considered that bad faith was not necessary, but referred to the

524. Roland Kläger, *'Fair and Equitable Treatment' in International Investment Law* (CUP 2011) 130; Rudolf Dozer and Christoph Schreuer, *Principles of International Investment Law* (2nd edn, OUP 2012) 291; Martins Paparinskis, 'Good Faith and Fair and Equitable Treatment in International Investment Law' in Andrew Mitchell, Muthucumaraswamy Sornarajah and Tania Voon (eds), *Good Faith and International Economic Law* (OUP 2015) 144-45.
525. *Total SA v. The Argentina Republic,* ICSID Case No. ARB/04/01, Decision on Liability, 27 December 201, para. 111; Bin Cheng, General Principles of Law as applied by International Courts and Tribunals (CUP 1994) 103; James Crawford, *Brownlie's Principles of Public International Law* (8th edn, OUP 2012) 377; Sipiorski, *Good Faith* (n 522) 2.
526. Sipiorski, *Good Faith* (n 522) 2; Dolzer and Schreuer, *Principles of International Investment Law* (n 47); *inter alia, Frontier Petroleum Services Ltd v. The Czech Republic,* UNCITRAL, final Award, 12 November 2010, para. 301 ('It follows from these authorities that action by the host state that is not in good faith is at variance with the fair and equitable treatment promise. However, not every violation of the standard of fair and equitable treatment requires bad faith').
527. *See* Chapter 4.B.2.
528. *See* Chapter 4.C.
529. Sipiorski, *Good Faith* (n 522) 186.
530. *Mondev International Ltd v. United States of America,* ICSID Case No. ARB(AF) /99/2, Award, 11 October 2002, para. 116.
531. Rudolf Dolzer, 'New Foundations for the Law of Expropriation of Alien Property' (1981) AJIL 75 553, 579 https://doi.org/10.2307/2200686.
532. *Alex Genin, Eastern Credit Limited, Inc. and A.S. Baltoil Genin v. Republic of Estonia,* ICSID Case No. ARB/99/2 Award of 25 June 2001, para. 367.
533. *Genin and Others v. Estonia,* Award (n) para. 367.

principle of good faith.[534] The *Tecmed v. Mexico*[535] tribunal offers a broad approach to protection of LE as part of a 'good faith' assessment. Cited by several tribunals,[536] the relevance of the award has been put into question by the ad hoc Committee in *MTD v. Chile*, which criticised the reasoning of the arbitral tribunal in adopting this standard while not sufficiently reflecting on the treaty's language.[537] At the other end of the spectrum, the tribunal in *Genin v. Estonia* interpreted the qualified FET standard under the US-Estonia 1994 BIT to equate the 1926 'Neer formula'.[538] To the tribunal, the FET standard is breached only if the state's acts amounted to 'wilful neglect of duty, insufficiency of action falling far below international standards and subjective bad faith'.[539] This position is reflective of an MST stance.[540]

In my view, both tribunals are correct in finding the source of LE in good faith but are probably misled. Like the notions of fairness and equitableness, if LE derives from 'good faith', it is difficult to expect an absolute obligation of consistency or an act in bad faith.[541] Good faith helps in understanding the degree to which the state committed.

534. *Tecmed v. Mexico* (n 67) para. 154 ('The Arbitral Tribunal considers that this provision of the Agreement, in light of the good faith principle established by international law, requires the Contracting Parties to provide to international investments treatment that does not affect the basic expectations that were taken into account by the foreign investor to make the investment. The foreign investor expects the host State to act in a consistent manner, free from ambiguity and totally transparently in its relations with the foreign investor (...) The foreign investor also expects the host State to act consistently, i.e., without arbitrarily revoking any pre-existing decisions or permits issued by the State that were relied upon by the investor to assume its commitments as well as to plan and launch its commercial and business activities. The investor also expects the State to use the legal instruments that govern the actions of the investor or the investment in conformity with the function usually assigned to such instruments, and not to deprive the investor of its investment without the required compensation. In fact, failure by the host State to comply with such pattern of conduct with respect to the foreign investor or its investments affects the investor's ability to measure the treatment and protection awarded by the host State and to determine whether the actions of the host State conform to the fair and equitable treatment principle').
535. *Tecmed v. Mexico* (n 67); *SD Myers v. Canada* (n 389) para. 134 ('Article 1105 of the NAFTA requires the Parties to treat investors of another Party in accordance with international law, including fair and equitable treatment. Article 1105 imports into the NAFTA the international law requirements of due process, economic rights, obligations of good faith and natural justice').
536. *LG&E v. Argentina* (n 388) para. 127; *MTD v. Chile* (n 227) para. 114; *Occidental v. Ecuador*, LCIA Case No. UN3467, Final Award, 1 July 2004, para. 185; *CMS Gas Transmission Company v. The Argentine Republic*, ICSID Case No. ARB/01/8, Award, 12 May 2005, para. 279; *Sempra Energy International v. Argentine Republic*, ICSID Case No. ARB/02/16, Award, 28 September 2007, para. 298.
537. *MTD v. Chile*, ICSID Case No. ARB/01/7, Decision on Annulment, 21 March 2007, para. 67.
538. *Alex Genin v. Republic of Estonia* (n 532).
539. *Ibid.*, para. 367.
540. In my opinion, the two cited awards appear similarly too broad and too narrow. One provides a strong case for the protection of expectations while the other only sanction the bad faith of the host State. In any case, 'fairness' and 'equity' cannot be *solely* interpreted from a purely abstract perspective since their ordinary meaning and construction involve balancing legal interests that can only be construed based on case-specific facts.
541. *Sempra Energy International v. Argentine Republic*, ICSID Case No. ARB/02/16, Award, 28 September 2007 para. 297 ('the principle of good faith is thus relied on as the common guiding beacon that will orient the understanding and interpretation of obligations, just as happens under civil codes').

These cannot easily include an absolute freeze of its regulatory framework as the case analysis of ECT cases shows clearly below.[542]

4 Unilateral Declarations by States: The Public International Law Analogy of Legitimate Expectations

As part of the good faith approach to LE, a useful analogy is the doctrine of unilateral statements under international law. Prof. Reisman and Arsanjani propose a comprehensive view of unilateral statements intended to attract foreign capital.[543] According to the theory, unilateral declaration binds the state internationally only if it is made by an authority vested with the power to do so. By virtue of their functions, heads of State, heads of government and ministers for foreign affairs are competent to formulate such declarations.

Some arbitral tribunals explicitly refer to the international doctrine of unilateral declarations to support their reasoning on the protection of LE.[544] In *Waste Management v. Mexico*, the tribunal held that 'it is relevant that the treatment is in breach of representations made by the host state which were reasonably relied on by the Claimant'.[545] In the words of the tribunal in International *Thunderbird v. Mexico*: 'there is a strong case to draw an analogy between LE in investment arbitration and unilateral declarations by states'.[546] The *Cube v. Spain* tribunal adopted the same approach.[547] The concept has also been referred to in *Total v. Argentina*:

> Under international law, unilateral acts, statements and conduct by States may be the source of legal obligations which the intended beneficiaries or addressees, or possibly any member of the international community, can invoke. The legal basis of that binding character appears to be related to the concept of legitimate expectations – being rather akin to the principle of 'estoppel'. Both concepts may lead to the same result, namely, rendering the content of a unilateral declaration binding on the State issuing it.[548]

542. *See* Chapter 3.
543. Reisman and Arsanjani, 'The Question of Unilateral Governmental Statements as Applicable Law' (n 64).
544. To name a few unrelated to the energy transition disputes, *see CMS Gas Transmission Company v. The Argentine Republic*, ICSID Case No. ARB/01/8, Decision on Jurisdiction, 17 July 2003, paras 27, 33; *LG&E v. Argentina* (n 388) para. 133; *Cemex v. Venezuela*, Decision on Jurisdiction, 30 December 2010, paras 80-139.
545. *Waste Management v. Mexico* (n 394) para. 98.
546. *Thunderbird v. Mexico* (n 74) para. 147 (citing among others 'Bin Cheng, *General Principles of Law applied by International Courts and Tribunals* (1987) 123; Joerg Mueller, *Vertrauensss-chutz im Voelkerrecht* (Carl Heymanns Verlag 1971); Elisabeth Zoller, *La bonne foi en droit international public* (Pedone 1977); Orrego Vicuña, *Regulatory Authority and Legitimate Expectations'* (2003) 5 Intl Law Forum 188, 193').
547. *Cube Infrastructure v. Spain* (n 402) para. 275 referring in footnote to the *Nuclear Tests* cases in the International Court of Justice and to the International Law Commission's Guiding Principles applicable to unilateral declarations of States capable of creating legal obligations.
548. *Total v. Argentina* (n 414) para. 131.

These investment tribunals refer to the ICJ, which firmly established the legally binding nature of unilateral commitments made by government officials.[549] Subsequently, the ICJ expanded the potential binding effect of unilateral statements.[550] In the *Case Concerning the Temple of Preah Vihear*, the Court stated that: 'the sole relevant question is whether the language employed in any given declaration does reveal a clear intention',[551] emphasising the role of good faith. In the *Nuclear Tests* cases, the ICJ went further and found that unilateral statements that had been made *erga omnes* could be binding *erga omnes.*[552] In this case, the fact that the highest authority in France, the President of the Republic, had issued an *erga omnes* outside the court declaration was sufficient to find that France had bound itself to cease atmospheric tests.[553] While the Court recognised that the declaration must be interpreted in the context of international security and trust relationships between states, the inferred principle is that addressees may rely on unilateral statements if they are binding upon the state.[554] Since, the ICJ has recognised that unilateral declarations will be binding depending upon the circumstances and wording of the statement.[555] The International Law Commission (ILC) adopted guiding principles applicable to such occurrences.[556]

549. Legal Status of Eastern Greenland (*Denmark v. Norway*), Judgment of 5 April 1933, P.C.I.J., Series A/B, No. 53 (1933) 22. *See also* Case Concerning the Arbitral Award made by the King of Spain on 23 December 1906 (*Honduras v. Nicaragua*), Judgment of 18 November 1960, I.C.J. Reports, 1960, at 192.
550. Reisman and Arsanjani, 'The Question of Unilateral Governmental Statements as Applicable Law in Investment Disputes' (n 64) 331.
551. I.C.J. Reports 1961, p. 32.
552. *Nuclear Tests* (*New Zealand v. France*), ICJ, Judgment, 20 December 1974, I.C.J. Reports 1974, pp. 472-473, para. 49 ('One of the basic principles governing the creation and performance of legal obligations, whatever their source, is the principle of good faith. Trust and confidence are inherent in international cooperation, in particular in an age when this cooperation in many fields is becoming increasingly essential. Just as the very rule of pacta sunt servanda in the law of treaties is based on good faith, so also is the binding character of an international obligation assumed by unilateral declaration. Thus, interested States may take cognizance of unilateral declarations and place confidence in them and are entitled to require that the obligation thus created be respected').
553. *Ibid.*, p. 48.
554. *Nuclear Tests* (*New Zealand v. France*), [1974] ICJ Judgment, 20 December 1974, para. 43 ('It is well recognised that declarations made by unilateral acts, concerning legal or factual situations, may have the effect of creating legal obligations. Declarations of this kind may be, and often are, very specific. When it is the intention of the State to make the declaration that it should become bound according to its terms, that intention confers on the declaration the character of a legal undertaking, the State being thenceforth legally required to follow a course of conduct consistent with the declaration. An undertaking of this kind, if given publicly and with an intent to be bound, even though not made within the context of international negotiations, is binding. In these circumstances, nothing like a quid pro quo nor any subsequent acceptance of the declaration, nor even any reply or reaction from other States, is required for the declaration to take effect since such a requirement would be inconsistent with the strictly unilateral nature of the juridical act by which the pronouncement by the state was made').
555. *Ibid.*, paras 253, 268; Legal Status of Eastern Greenland (*Denmark v. Norway*), 5 April 1933, PCIJ, Series A/B, No. 53, 22, 69.
556. UNGA ILC (58th Session) 'Conclusions of the International Law Commission relating to Unilateral Acts of States' (20 July 2006) UN Doc A/CN.4/L.703 ('1. Declarations publicly made and manifesting the will to be bound may have the effect of creating legal obligations. When the conditions for this are met, the binding character of such declarations is based on good faith;

In conclusion, the good faith source under public international law appears to be the more convincing source to justify the protection of LE under FET provisions. Additionally, due to its flexibility and connection to public international law, it allows the integration of ICCL norms, at least as relevant facts in the assessment of the investor's LE. Similarly, the analogy to unilateral declarations of states is apt to apprehend the situations in which the state may bind itself.

Despite the analysis above, the origins or 'source' of legitimate expectations can only explain parts of the divergences among arbitral tribunals. When analysing the arbitral case law in NZEID, scholars have divided tribunals have proposed two categories, which all differ from one author to another.[557] In purely descriptive terms, when dealing with LE created by the regulatory framework, some tribunals determined a 'complete' or 'full liability' breach of FET and other tribunals identified a violation of the FET standard only to the extent that the new regime fell short of meeting the reasonable rate of return threshold promised by law. Instead of dividing cases between a soft and strict notion of LE as proposed by an eminent author[558] because, according

States concerned may then take them into consideration and rely on them; such States are entitled to require that such obligations be respected. (...) 7. A unilateral declaration entails obligations for the formulating State only if it is stated in clear and specific terms. In the case of doubt as to the scope of the obligations resulting from such a declaration, such obligations must be interpreted in a restrictive manner. In interpreting the content of such obligations, weight shall be given first and foremost to the text of the declaration, together with the context and the circumstances in which it was formulated').

557. For instance, Balcerzak, *Renewable Energy Arbitration* (n 220) 447 (distinguishing between the legal reasoning adopted in two groups of cases: those in which tribunals concluded that a 'full' violation of the FET had occurred and those in which the tribunals found that the FET had been violated only insofar as the new regime failed to meet the RRR threshold.); Federico Ortino, *The Origin and Evolution of Investment Treaty Standards: Stability, Value, and Reasonableness* (OUP 2019) 40 ('he conceptual distinction between a strict and soft notion of legal stability obligation, where the former focuses on the existence of a regulatory change and the latter entails (at least in part) an analysis of the merit (i.e., fairness or reasonableness) of the measure under review. Crudely put, the two key questions are, respectively, whether a change in regulation has occurred or whether the regulatory change was on its merit unreasonable'); *Matthias Kruck v. Spain*, Partial Dissenting Opinion (n 39) para. 11 ('The majority's conception of an action for breach of legitimate expectations is actually indistinguishable from an action for breach of contract. Both rest upon a notion of strict liability: if a promise is made and is then breached, then liability for any losses follows from that breach, and the reasons for the conduct resulting in that breach are irrelevant. The majority thus does not admit of any defence to this action: if the investor has suffered loss as a result of the breach of the commitment or promise, then liability is established. This is strict liability. No public interest or proportionality defence can therefore be raised').

558. Ortino, *The Origin* (n 557) 31-32 ('Based on these various pronouncements, it can be argued that, despite those few early decisions that appeared to easily embrace a strict stability obligation, subsequent arbitral practice has shown more deference vis-à-vis the host State's right to regulate, and supported a softer understanding of a stability obligation under FET. In particular, the focus on (a) the existence of a stabilization commitment or promise; (b) the reasonableness of the host State measure; and/or (c) the need to balance the investor's expectations and the host State's right to regulate represents strong evidence of this softer notion of stability. Under this softer notion, a treaty violation would be established not because of a (substantial) detrimental change in the host State's legal framework applicable to the foreign investment, but because the legal change was judged "unreasonable"').

to his own research, most tribunals have abandoned the 'strict' approach,[559] I propose to rely on the dichotomy presented by Dr Teerawat Wongkaew between voluntary and detrimental reliance theory.[560] This allows scholars to divide the tribunals concerned with the enforcement of the state's promise and others by the proportional correction to the breach of expectations. These two conceptions may resemble traditional estoppel aligned on the detriment of the person relying on the promise (detrimental reliance) and the application of LE as reflective of the state's good faith (voluntary theory). The distinction is important for the integration of ICCL, as I demonstrate that, eventually, both theories converge on key factual elements, which ICCL may influence.[561]

E UNDERSTANDING THE DIVERGENCE: DISTINGUISHING THE VOLUNTARY AND DETRIMENTAL RELIANCE THEORIES OF LEGITIMATE EXPECTATIONS

While the contours of LE can be established as shown above, it appears difficult to pinpoint why the content of LE is so divergent from one case to another. The reason, I posit, lies in the philosophical understanding of sovereignty and promise. Some consider the state to be bound by its own binding promises, others consider the state only liable if it created significant harm. Although the second approach may appeal for its proportionality assessment, it remains that only the first approach is consistent with international law.

With regard to LE, there arguably exists a divide between the voluntarist and detrimental approaches to the promise of states.[562] My working assumption is that this distinction exists and that convergence points exist. In brief, the voluntarist or 'rule of law' theory of promise is concerned with the enforcement of sovereign obligations.[563] And the detrimental reliance theory is concerned with proportional reparation of harm to the individual.[564] Both theories have implications for the adjudication of investment disputes. Voluntarist theory-leaning tribunals are concerned with the substance of the state's promise, the reasonable investor's reliance upon it and its enforcement; detrimental reliance theory-leaning tribunals with proportionality, due diligence of the prudent investor and evidence of substantial harm.

559. *Ibid.*, 33 ('most subsequent investment tribunals seem to have embraced a softer, more deferential reading of the FET provision that would exclude a strict stability obligation').
560. Wongkaew, *Detrimental Reliance* (n 425). Given the complexity of the categories he presents in his PhD turned book, not all nuances of his findigns have been used for the purpose of theis research.
561. *See* Chapter 3.D.
562. Wongkaew, *Detrimental Reliance* (n 425) 53-63.
563. Schønberg, *Legitimate Expectations* (n 491) 9.
564. *Ibid.*, 10 ('A public's authority's freedom to take action in the public interest is limited to the extent that it causes harm to particular individuals. If a public authority has induced a person to rely upon its representations or conduct, realizing that such reliance was a real possibility, it is under a prima facie duty to act in such a way that the reliance will not be detrimental to the representee.').

1 Voluntary Theory of Legitimate Expectations

The voluntary theory is underpinned by moral considerations on the responsibility of the state for wilful commitment and equity towards the individual. It is a state-centric theory seeking a voluntary action, which implies that the representor must act wilfully and deliberately.[565] On the domestic level, this form of LE is often referred to as the 'rule of law' theory.[566] The conception aims at ensuring legal certainty, individual autonomy, and the rule of law.[567]

In essence, based on the voluntarist notion of promise, 'LE means that an investor can legitimately expect an enforcement of the thing promised because it is his or her right granted by the promisor.'[568] In the words of Fuller and Perdue, 'the expectancy created by an enforceable promise should be regarded as a kind of property right, and breach of the promise as an injury to that property'.[569]

If one posits the existence of a voluntary school of interpretation of fairness and equity, then the findings show that a *voluntarist* interpretation of the unqualified FET accords *greater significance* to the obligation of the State to respect its word under the principle of good faith,[570] the legitimacy of the investor's expectations,[571] and the stability and predictability of the regulatory framework.[572] Under the voluntarist

565. Wongkaew, *Detrimental Reliance* (n 425) 66.
566. Schønberg, *Legitimate Expectations* (n 491) 12-24: Vaughan Lowe, 'The Role of Equity in International Law' (1992) 12 Australian Yearbook of International Law 54 https://doi.org/10.1163/26660229-012-01-900000006.
567. *Suez et al. v. Argentina*, ICSID Case No. ARB/03/17, Decision on Liability, 30 July 2010, para. 203 ('reasonable and legitimate expectations are important factors that influence initial investment decisions and afterwards the manner in which the investment is to be managed. The theoretical basis of this approach no doubt is found in the work of the eminent scholar Max Weber, who advanced the idea that one of the main contributions of law to any social system is to make economic life more calculable and also argued that capitalism arose in Europe because European law demonstrated a high degree of "calculability." An investor's expectations, created by law of a host country, are in effect calculations about the future', internal footnote omitted).
568. Wongkaew, *Detrimental Reliance* (n 425) 66.
569. Lon Fuller and William R Perdue, 'The Reliance Interest in Contract Damage (Parts 1 and 2)' (1936-1937) 46 Yale LJ 52 373 https://doi.org/10.2307/791834.
570. Reisman and Arsanjani, 'The Question of Unilateral Governmental Statements as Applicable Law in Investment Disputes' (n 64); Rudolf Dolzer, 'Fair and Equitable Treatment: A Key Standard in Investment Treaties' (2005) 39 The International Lawyer 1 90 https://doi.org/10.1017/cbo9780511974915.004; Biggs, 'The Scope of Investors' (n 406) 120.
571. *Thunderbird v. Mexico*, Separate opinion of Mr Thomas Wälde (n 355) para. 21 ('It is not sufficient that Thunderbird had an "expectation", and that this expectation contributed in a significant way to its readiness to commit risk capital and effort, but the expectation must also have been "legitimate", i.e. it must have been created by government officials in an official way (i.e. attributable to the government of Mexico), they must have been competent (or at least appeared, credibly, to be competent) for the trust-inspiring action. The procedure for issuing the assurance ("comfort") letter must have been legitimate and it must have been "reasonable" for Thunderbird to rely on that letter'; para. 31 ('The greater the formality of an assurance, the greater its ability is to trigger a legitimate expectation').
572. *CMS v. Argentine* (n 536) para. 274 ('The Treaty Preamble makes it clear, however, that one principal objective of the protection envisaged is fair and equitable treatment is desirable "to maintain a stable framework for investments and maximum effective use of economic resources". There can be no doubt, therefore, that a stable legal and business environment is

theory, the protection of LE mainly concerns the enforcement of sovereign promise and the protection of expectation interests.[573]

In other words, the voluntarist school examines a factual situation primarily from the enforceability of the state's undertakings. The school establishes LE by assessing whether: (1) the state intended to attract investments[574] and (2) the state materialised its intent objectively in a clear and unambiguous commitment under a law or regulation.[575] It then examines the investor's conduct in light of what a 'reasonable' investor could expect at the time of the investment. Due diligence does not appear as a precondition to hold LE. Rather, what matters are the objective conditions in which the investor chose to invest and the state created at the time. For instance, Gary Born dissented in the *Antaris v. Czech Republic* case, opining that the legal framework in place at the time of the investment was 'crystal clear'[576] so that prudent investors could expect a determined level of return without producing extensive due diligence.[577] Other tribunals employing the theory are more nuanced and assess, in an objective manner, the level of expectations an investor would be entitled to at the time of the investment while requesting from that investor to demonstrate its reliance.

2 Detrimental Reliance Theory of Legitimate Expectations

The detrimental reliance theory is a form of estoppel in the *strict* sense. The key consideration is the disappointment of an expectation, which may cause considerable harm to the individual who relied upon its fulfilment.[578] It considers that subjective reliance, evidence of due diligence and significant damages must be showcased to engage the state's responsibility. For instance, the tribunal in *Thunderbird v. Mexico* required elements of detrimental reliance and thorough assessment of the subjective

an essential element of fair and equitable treatment'); *see also Occidental Exploration and Production Company v. The Republic of Ecuador*, LCIA Case No. UN3467, Final Award, 1 July 2004, paras 183 and 191.

573. Schønberg, *Legitimate Expectations* (n 491) 10 (strongly opposes the detrimental reliance conception as too narrow. He considers that detriment reliance should not act as precondition to the protection of LE because of considerations of inconsistent conduct, legal uncertainty and absue of power).

574. Reisman and Arsanjani, 'The Question of Unilateral Governmental Statements as Applicable Law in Investment Disputes' (n 64) 342 ('[w]here a host State which seeks foreign investment acts intentionally, so as to create expectations in potential investors with respect to particular treatment or comportment, the host State should, we suggest, be bound by the commitments and the investor is entitled to rely upon them in instances of decision'); this quote was cited in *Total v. Argentina* (n 414) para. 119.

575. *Jürgen Wirtgen v. Czech Republic*, Dissenting opinion (n 434) para. 12.

576. *Antaris v. Czech Republic* (n 76), Dissenting Opinion of Mr Gary Born, para. 12.

577. Biggs, 'The Scope of Investors' (n 406) 124 ('The likelihood of (and nature of) such changes will then influence an investor's legitimate expectations. However, in the European Renewable Energy Cases, the regulatory frameworks (i) already anticipated future changes to the FiT rates and (ii) explicitly provided that existing investments would be shielded from such regulatory changes. As a result, investors' legitimate expectations regarding the FiT rate could not reasonably have been affected by due diligence on that specific issue').

578. Schønberg, *Legitimate Expectations* (n 491) 9-11.

'reasonableness' of expectations and subsequent detrimental situation of the investor proportionally assessed.[579]

The detrimental reliance theory of promise protects reliance-based expectations that are subsequently harmed.[580] 'When the promisor induces the promise to rely on his or her representation and the promise does rely on it to his or her detriment, the promisor will be responsible for rectifying that harm.'[581] In essence, two main elements are required to establish an obligation under this theory of promise: '(1) the fact that the state intended the investor to rely upon it, (2) the fact that the investor has taken detrimental action in the belief that the state will take certain action in the future'.[582] It constitutes a corrective justice mechanism based solely on the host state's representation or conduct inducing reasonably relied-upon expectations, to which the host state has the duty to prevent harm. The failure of which incurs a duty to compensate the investor for his reliance loss.[583]

A good illustration of a balanced detrimental reliance approach is given by the tribunal in *SunReserve v. Italy*:

> While general statements can create legitimate expectations in theory, the general statements made to the public to advertise a particular regulatory regime can only create expectations, if any, that are in line with the regulatory regime itself. These public statements cannot bind the State to commitments above and beyond the legal regime.[584]

This explicit linkage between LE and 'the legal regime' demonstrates that the content of the host state's law is crucial to determining the scope of legitimate expectations, especially when they are based on the regulatory framework. The issue with the detrimental reliance theory, and why it is inconsistent with treaty provisions, is that it moves the question of state liability to the question of private detriment. In other words, what matters is whether and to what extent a prudent investor could have expected to be detrimentally affected by political changes in the host state. This reverses the burden of proof. Instead, one should focus on the state, its commitment, and whether that commitment is legally binding under a unilateral statement doctrine and can be relied upon. This does not mean that all investors affected by any regulations may file a claim against a state but that unreasonable regulations adopted against previously stated positions may incur liability. Similarly, there is no such concept of 'strict' liability. States are able to adopt measures to adapt to changing circumstances. This principle derives from sovereignty rights to regulate (and should not incur liability because of a detriment caused to the investor – the detrimental reliance theory). Rather, where the state clearly and unreasonably reverses previously stated policy, it breaches its commitment and incurs liability.

579. Wongkaew, *Detrimental Reliance* (n 425) 35.
580. *Ibid.*, 134.
581. *Ibid.*
582. *Ibid.*, citing, Neil MacCormick, 'Voluntary Obligation' in Neil MacCormick (ed.), *Legal Right and Social Democracy: Essays in Legal and Political Philosophy* (Oxford, Clarendon Press 1982) 205.
583. Wongkaew, *Detrimental Reliance* (n 425) 139.
584. *SunReserve v. Italy* (n 416) para. 817.

The detrimental reliance approach accords greater significance to the validity and authority of the norm relied upon by the investor, the legitimacy, reasonableness, and detriment of the investor's expectations in light of all circumstances, and the state's right to regulate according to its domestic legal system.[585] In other words, this school accords deference to the state by establishing the domestic legal framework in which the investment was made. It then assesses the legal value of the measure relied upon by the investor and establishes whether it amounts to a specific commitment. Finally, the 'legitimacy' of the investor's expectations is evaluated in light of the objective conditions of investment and subjective due diligence[586] duties expected from a 'prudent' investor at the time of the investment. The approach requires rigorous tests for legal validity.

Prima facie, the detrimental reliance theory allows an easier integration of ICCL norms in the assessment of investors' LE as part of the content of the host state's law and the emphasis on due diligence. However, ICCL can also integrate the analysis under the theory of voluntary LE not only as part of the reasonableness of expectations and good faith but also because the state's obligations or statements under ICCL may amount to binding unilateral declarations.[587] The two theories are further expanded in the next chapter when analysing their practical impact on the resolution of legitimate expectations claims and how they allow ICCL to be taken into account in the assessment of LE claims.

F CONCLUSION

This chapter establishes that the protection of LE is part of the FET standard. It further deciphered the different justifications and conceptions of the doctrine, showing that if arbitral tribunals agree to protect LE, they do not protect the same standard. The chapter constitutes the foundation for understanding ICCL's impact on LE, which is necessarily affected by the conception of LE adopted by arbitral tribunals.

The chapter presents three key findings.

First, the case law generally recognises the protection of LE as part of the unqualified FET provision. Arbitral tribunals protect investors from states withdrawing from their initial commitments in contracts, specific statements, and regulatory frameworks. The scope of states' commitment and the extent of expectations' 'legitimacy' or reasonableness are widely debated. The protection of LE is reasonably justified by the underlying FET clause and the margin of discretion it grants arbitral tribunals. The FET clause, because of its ordinary meaning, cannot be construed as an 'absolute' limitation to the state's right to regulate. It thus remains a balanced and

585. *Cavalum SGPS, S.A. v. Kingdom of Spain*, ICSID Case No. ARB/15/34, Decision on Jurisdiction, Liability and Directions on Quantum, 31 August 2020, para. 427 ('[it would be] inconceivable that a state would make a general commitment never to change its legislation whatever the circumstances, and it would be unreasonable for an investor to rely on such a freeze').

586. Muchlinski P, '"Caveat Investor"? The Relevance of the Conduct of the Investor under the Fair and Equitable Treatment Standard' (2006) 55 International and Comparative Law Quarterly 527 https://doi.org/10.1093/iclq/lei104.

587. *See* Chapter 5.A.

fact-specific standard in which LE can be reasonably protected. It suggests that, based on the case law alone, there are multiple ways for ICCL to integrate the analysis of LE.[588]

Second, the interpretation of LE doctrine is prone to disagreement. Scholars have disagreed on the formal source from which LE takes its origins and justification. The analysis casts doubt on the argument that LE would be a general principle of international law or would derive from estoppel. Rather, it finds that good faith may tie the protection of LE to the underlying FET standard and public international law and so justify its use in investment arbitration. Moreover, it shows that analogies can be drawn with the doctrine of unilateral statements under international law.

Third, the research finds that the formal source is insufficient to explain the divergences between arbitral tribunals. It builds on existing scholarship to propose two conceptions of LE. One is based on detrimental reliance, the other on the voluntarist theory of promise. Under the former, the LE doctrine assesses the reliance of an individual investor on representations issued by the state that, when repelled, cause significant harm. The claimant must prove that it reviewed the risks of its reliance with due diligence. Under the voluntarist theory of promise, LE are assessed as part of the state's obligations to uphold its own commitments, as long as they are legitimate, specific, and clear.

Overall, the chapter offers a high-level study of the key divergences in the protection of legitimate expectations in investment disputes. It is essential to answering my research question, as ICCL can only have an impact on a well-defined and sourced concept of legitimate expectations.

In the next chapter, I investigate arbitral awards by dividing them between detrimental reliance and voluntarist-leaning approaches. This allows me to find where the divergence lies and where points of convergence arise. Finding points of convergence will then help build the case for the impact of ICCL on legitimate expectations.

588. The next chapter looks at whether, despite theoretical differences on the source, interpretation and scope of LE, there are consensus points in the application of LE that allow the consensual integration of ICCL.

CHAPTER 3

Interpretation and Application of Legitimate Expectations in NZEID under the Energy Charter Treaty

This chapter is based on an analysis of forty investment awards in the renewable energy sector under the Energy Charter Treaty. Building on the last chapter, it divides tribunals' reasoning among the voluntarist and detrimental reliance theories of LE. This allows for an analysis of the divergence and convergence points among tribunals. It finds that the vast majority of tribunals recognise the regulatory framework as one of the sources of LE. It further demonstrates that the time of the investment, the foreseeability of the frustrating measure, and the fact-specificity of LE are convergence elements that influence the legitimacy of expectations. These elements are crucial to subsequently analyse the impact of ICCL on investors' legitimate expectations.

The previous chapter linked LE to underlying FET provisions and tried to brush the broad contours of the doctrine in the case law. To better understand the divide and pinpoint convergence allowing the integration of ICCL, it suggested dividing between arbitral tribunals adopting a form of voluntarist theory of promise and those adopting a detrimental reliance theory. This division is exploited in this chapter.

This chapter moves to the review of the protection of renewable energy investors under the Energy Charter Treaty. As I demonstrated in chapter 1, the legal protection of clean energy investors may be necessary to support the momentous amount of foreign direct investments needed to achieve the net zero transition. This chapter tries to ascertain whether energy investors' LE are protected and, if so, to what extent. It also examines whether tribunals sufficiently take into account ICCL in their awards – to spoil the surprise, claimants do, but arbitral tribunals do not sufficiently.[589]

589. All references to climate change and climate change legislation by arbitral tribunals in NZEID is compiled in Annex Legitimate Expectations in Net Zero Energy Investment Disputes:

The chapter is based on forty publicly available NZEID arbitral awards in the renewable sector rendered under the ECT. These were gathered before August 2023 and concern the responding states of Spain, the Czech Republic and Italy.[590] To no surprise, LE are a disputed *leitmotiv* in the selected investment cases, which, because of their similar factual backgrounds, constitute a 'laboratory' for academics.[591] This chapter assesses how tribunals weigh the investor's legitimacy of expectations and their right to compensation against the right of the state to amend its regulations and laws. It finds that, although there is no consensus regarding the source, nature and content of the doctrine, arbitral tribunals converge on factual elements, which are essential to finding expectations legitimate under both theories.

I categorise the arbitral awards under the detrimental reliance and voluntary theories of promise in full knowledge of other relevant distinctions.[592] In particular, Prof. Zachary Douglas proposed an appealing division, which, like my own division, is not always prosperous. Professor Douglas divides between tribunals applying a 'strict liability' approach, which derives from contract law, and those applying a 'fault-based approach', which enshrines proportionality and public law principles.[593] I favour a voluntary/detrimental reliance divide. While it is true that some arbitrators consider state liability from a contractual point of view, it is incorrect to consider that tribunals apply contract law or an analogy of contract law. In fact, not a single tribunal adopting a voluntary theory approach has analysed the binding commitment of Spain as a contractual, 'absolute' obligation – i.e., the frustrating measures still have to be *unreasonable* to breach the FET provision, thus preserving and acknowledging a margin of regulatory freedom for the state. Dividing between 'strict liability' and 'fault-based' falls short of demonstrating why, for instance, the *Silver Ridge v. Italy*

Selected Quotes; it is clear that the Kyoto Protocol and European Directives on emissions targets appear in the vast majority of cases as vague factual 'background'.

590. Since 2000 and the Kyoto Protocol, EU states endeavour to increase the share of renewable energy generation in their energy mix. To achieve this goal, they adopt incentive programmes attracting clean energy investments, in particular, in solar and wind energy. However, the 2008 monetary crisis steered governments into adopting measures scaling down or entirely replacing these incentives. The backpedalling affected energy investors significantly, *see* Daniel Behn and Laura Létourneau-Tremblay, 'Promoting Renewable Energy in the EU: Shifting Trends in Member State Policy Space' (2017) 28 European Business Law Review 2 217, 227 https://doi.org/10.54648/eulr2017015; Remaining renewable cases showcase that disputes over LE will continue to shape the landscape of international investment arbitration for the foreseeable future; World Bank International Center for Settlement of Investment Disputes, accessible at https://icsid.worldbank.org/cases/case-database accessed 24 July 2022.

591. *Eurus Energy v. Spain* award, para. 316. Jonathan Bonnitcha, *Substantive Protection under Investment Treaties: A Legal and Economic Analysis* (CUP 2014) 161-162; Potestà, 'Legitimate Expectations' (n 68) 88 ('[i]f one observes the awards given by investment treaty tribunals in the last few years, one will hardly find any example where the concept of "legitimate expectations" has not been invoked by the Claimant [...]').

592. Landmann, *Legitimate Expectations* (n 400) 145 (dividing cases according to the time when the original investment was made by the investor); I have outlined Filip Balcerzak's, Zachary Douglas' and Federico Ortino's own distinctions above in (n 557).

593. *Matthias Kruck v. Spain*, Partial Dissenting Opinion (n 39) para. 47 ('The touchstone of fault that is generally adopted is proportionality, which is assessed primarily in terms of whether the investment continued to earn a reasonable rate of return after the regime of RD 661/2007 was abolished').

tribunal ruled out the investor's claim, while the *Renergy v. Spain* tribunal upheld it – although both developed a *very* similar reasoning, against the background of similar incentives.[594]

This section seeks to provide an original analysis of key awards.[595] The chapter endeavours to ascertain whether arbitrators reach a consensus regarding the potential of the regulatory framework to create expectations, the legitimacy of expectations concerning the timing of investments, and the foreseeability of measures in relation to their reasonableness. These findings are crucial for the alignment of ICCL's objectives with international investment law. The recognition of the regulatory framework as a source of commitment allows climate change targets and objectives to be taken into account and for investors in clean energy to benefit from the commitments made by states. However, the recognition that there is no LE where the frustrating measure is clearly foreseeable at the time of the investment and is a business risk assumed by the investor may allow states to defend reasonable phasing out of an energy sector without incurring liability for a breach of fossil fuel-related investors' LE.[596]

Section A presents the factual background of selected NZEID under the Energy Charter Treaty and briefly presents the legal difficulties related to the ECT and the main divergence among tribunals in the case law; section B explores the reasoning in 'voluntarist-leaning' arbitral awards; and section C examines the reasoning in awards adopting the 'detrimental reliance-leaning' approach. It then moves to an in-depth analysis of the (section D) convergence of arbitral tribunals on key factual elements, growing consensus on the time of the investment, the risks assumed by the investor and the foreseeability of a frustrating measure.

A FACTUAL BACKGROUND: CLIMATE CHANGE POLICIES AND INVESTMENT DISPUTES

As demonstrated in the first chapter, governments seek to combat climate change by transforming their energy structure and moving to clean energy.[597] To achieve this, they may incentivise energy investors by resorting to subsidies.[598] In this case, investors participate in the construction of clean energy generation in exchange for a financial advantage.[599] Disputes may arise when these advantages, under the form of subsidies or tax breaks, are substantially modified or revoked.

594. Both cases were chaired by Judge Bruno Simma.
595. The case law reveals a puzzling divergence in outcomes despite similarities in factual contexts. This incongruity suggests the presence of distinct 'schools of thought' on LE, as acknowledged by the Masdar tribunal although on wrong premises (it distinguished between tribunals holding the regulatory framework that could create LE and others, while the divide is more granular and concerns notably whether Laws or Decrees have the same weight in creating LE), *see Masdar Solar & Wind Cooperatief U.A. v. Kingdom of Spain*, ICSID Case No. ARB/14/1, Award, 16 May 2018, para. 490.
596. For an extensive analysis *see* Chapter 6.
597. *See* Chapter 1.B.2.
598. *Ibid.*
599. *Sevilla Beheer v. Spain*, Dissenting Opinion (n 462) paras 15 and 82.

Generally, the issue with subsidies in the clean energy sector is that they are time-constrained. Governments can change their priorities too.[600] Governments can turn around on their clean energy policy for many reasons. Governments may review their policy and revert the money invested because other pressing public interests prevail.[601] A state may withdraw its incentives or reduce the amount of financial advantage because, as technology becomes cheaper over time, a project may lose value as the permit process takes time. States may argue that production costs have sunk over time, so incentives become unjustified. Public scrutiny is also high and may endanger permit rights granted by national or local authorities.[602]

Timing is thus key to guarantee the obtainment of subsidies, which reward first investors. To acquire subsidies in time, investors must usually obtain a permit and connect their installation to the national energy grid.[603] The resulting issue is often the creation of delays. These delays are detrimental to the efficiency of the energy generation and the profits of investors. All these risks create a prosperous factual background for investment disputes, as shown below in the context of EU legislation and EU Member States legislation on clean energy.

1 EU's Climate Commitments and Disputed Measures

In the EU, the transition to renewable energy has been first endorsed by individual states following the 1992 Kyoto Protocol.[604] In 2001, the European Council and Parliament adopted directive 2001/77/EC.[605] In 2009, the directive was replaced by directive 2009/28/EC.[606] Both directives refer to international climate change treaties

600. *Ibid.*, 2; 5; 8.
601. *See* European Commission, Report from the Commission to the European Parliament, the Council, the European Economic and Social Committee and the Committee of the Regions: Renewable energy progress report (COM 2013) 175, 5, 9 (criticising Spain's national reforms having a negative impact on the investment climate, despite the general economic crisis).
602. Lawrence Susskind and others, 'Sources of Opposition to Renewable Energy Projects in the United States' (2022) 165 Energy Policy 11292 2 https://doi.org/10.1016/j.enpol.2022.112922 ('Of the projects we studied, 34% faced significant delays and difficulties securing permits, 49% were cancelled permanently, and 26% resumed after being stopped for several months or years.').
603. On the requirement of connection to the grid *ESPF v. Italy* (n 133) para. 105; *Blusun S.A., Jean-Pierre Lecorcier and Michael Stein v. Italian Republic*, ICSID Case No. ARB/14/3, Award, 27 December 2016, para. 374 (in dismissing the Claimants' claim, the tribunal found that the project the Claimants were seeking to establish had never obtained the substantial financing required, had only commenced construction on two of many plants and that no solar panels were ever installed or connected to the grid).
604. Once the European Community ratified the Kyoto Convention, the 'burden-sharing process' was implemented to comply with the allocated limits while allowing extensive policy freedom. *See* Council Decision 2002/358/EC concerning the approval on behalf of the European Community, of the Kyoto Protocol to the United Nations Framework Convention on Climate Change and the joint fulfilment of commitments thereunder, OJ L130/1 (15 May 2002), 84-87.
605. Directive 2001/77/EC on the promotion of electricity produced from renewable energy sources in the internal electricity market.
606. Directive 2009/28/EC of the European Parliament and of the Council of 23 April 2009 on the promotion of the use of energy from renewable sources and amending and subsequently repealing Directives 2001/77/EC and 2003/30/EC.

and aim to implement ICCL commitments to renewable energy quotas to be reached by member countries.[607] The directives provide a goal for the contribution of electricity produced from renewable energy sources to the national gross electricity consumption.[608] To comply with the European Directives and international climate change commitments, European Member States - including Spain, Italy and the Czech Republic - put into place incentives and promotions to attract private investments in renewable energy.[609] Common mechanisms to support and subsidise energy are tax incentives, Feed-in Tariffs (FITs) and Feed-in Premiums (FIPs) above market price.[610] Investment disputes brought against Spain, Italy and the Czech Republic originated from abrogating or replacing such support schemes for renewable energy.[611]

2 Spain's Net Zero Policies and Contested Measures

Spain faced a flood of investment claims after the government's energy reforms affecting renewable energy providers from 2010 to 2013, with a total replacement of the incentive regime in 2013.[612] Foreign investors in the renewable energy sector claimed frustration with their LE in breach of FET due to the overhaul of broad incentives issued by the Spanish government in 2007 to attract foreign investments.[613] The majority of cases have been decided in favour of the investor. However, the State did not incur liability under FET in four cases. Arbitral tribunals showcase significant (prima facie) divergences on LE.

Before delving into the specific policies adopted by Spain, it is important to understand Spain's legal framework and authorities. The Spanish legal hierarchy plays a key role in understanding detrimental reliance-leaning awards. Detrimental reliance-leaning awards clearly distinguish between LE deriving from decrees and LE deriving from the law. The hierarchy of norms in Spain descends as follows: the Constitution sits at the top. Follow 'Laws', 'Royal Decree Laws' (RDL), 'Royal Decrees' (RD), and finally 'Ministerial Orders' (MOs). Laws are enacted by parliament. RDLs are adopted by the government and require the parliament's approval, but they have an immediate effect. RDs are instruments of regulatory power executing laws or approved RDLs. This normative hierarchy influences the assessment of the state's commitment and the investor's objective *LE*.

607. Recital No.1 in the Preamble to Directive 2001/77/EC and Recital No.1 in the Preamble to Directive 2009/28/EC.
608. Leonardo Massai, *European Climate and Clean Energy Law and Policy* (Routledge 2012) 102-108.
609. This was reiterated by all arbitral tribunals in their assessment of relevant facts; *see* for instance *Novenergia II v. Spain* (n 413) para. 665; *Cavalum v. Spain* (n 585) para. 485; *Eskosol v. Italy* (n 658), para. 160.
610. Tomás Restrepo, 'Modification of Renewable Energy Support Schemes under the Energy Charter Treaty: Eiser and Charanne in the Context of Climate Change' (2017) 8 Göttingen Journal of International Law 101, 102.
611. *PV Investors v. Spain* (n 413) para. 597.
612. *Ibid.*, para. 929.
613. *Renergy v. Spain* (n 39) para. 900 (the attraction of renewable foreign investors is of 'vital public interest, given in particular the positive impact on the environment').

In 1997, Spain enacted the Energy Law 54/1997, providing a legal framework that divided electricity production into *Ordinary* and *Special* Regimes.[614] The Ordinary regime covered electricity obtained from fossil energy sources, while the Special Regime concerned electricity produced by renewable sources.[615] To be eligible under the Special Regime, investors had to register their renewable energy plant with the Administration under the Registry for Electrical Power Generating Units (RAIPRE).[616] Law 54/1997 provided that remuneration of electricity producers under the Special Regime would be supplemented by a 'premium' that would be established in subsequent regulations so as to achieve 'reasonable rates of return with regard to the cost of money in the capital market'.[617]

Spain's 1997 energy law was first implemented by two Royal Decrees, RD 2818/1998 and RD 436/2004, which were abrogated and replaced by the incentive-rich RD 661/2007. This Royal Decree 661/2007[618] introduced two subsidies available to renewable energy providers registered under the RAIPRE: FITs or fixed prices.[619] Two salient features of RD 661/2007 were that it established fixed FIT for qualifying PV facilities and priority of access and dispatch to the electricity grid.[620] In addition, the Spanish State launched an advertising campaign, 'The sun can be yours', which pledged a return of up to 15% for solar energy providers.[621] The Royal Decree

614. António Cardoso Marquesa and others, 'Ordinary and Special Regimes of Electricity Generation in Spain: How They Interact with Economic Activity' (2018) 81 Renewable and Sustainable Energy Reviews 1226, 1227 https://doi.org/10.1016/j.rser.2017.09.006.
615. *PV Investors v. Spain* (n 413) para. 182.
616. On the legal value of the RAIPRE, *Charanne v. Spain* (n 413) para. 510 ('Firstly, the Respondent has convincingly demonstrated that, in Spanish law, the registration to the RAIPRE was simply an administrative requirement to be able to sell energy and did not imply that the registered facilities had an acquired right to a determined compensation'); *Eurus v. Spain*, para. 264; *Cube Infrastructure v. Spain* (n 402) followed the *Charanne* analysis, but only when assessing the umbrella clause of Art. 10(1) last sentence, *see* para. 453; on the contrary, in *Novenergia II v. Spain* (n 413) the registration with RAIPRE is considered an assurance, paras 665 and 666 ('The requirements placed on the PV plants to qualify for the Special Regime were limited to registration with the RAIPRE, a requirement which all of the PV Plants had met within the prescribed cut-off date.'); in *OperaFund Eco-Invest SICAV PLC and Schwab Holding AG v. Kingdom of Spain*, ICSID Case No. ARB/15/36, registration with RAIPRE was fundamental to conclude that the investor had legitimate expectations for the regime to remain unchanged, paras 483-484 ('Claimants' investments were made between July 2008 and July 2009, in reliance upon the fact that the PV plants were finally registered in the RAIPRE under RD 661/2007 and granted the RD 661/2007 FIT economic rights. Thus, the formal registration led to the investors' entitlement to receive the benefits under RD 661/2007 (including not being subject to regulatory change)').
617. Law 54/1997, Art. 30.4.
618. RD 661/2007 of 26 May 2007.
619. *See* for greater details *PV Investors v. Spain* (n 413) paras 189-195.
620. *Foresight Luxembourg Solar 1 S.À.R.L., et al. v. Kingdom of Spain*, SCC Case No. 2015/150, Final Award, 14 November 2018, para. 54.
621. IDAE, 'El Sol puede ser suyo', 6 June 2007; *Novenergia II v. Spain* (n 413) paras 112-118; *InfraRed Environmental Infrastructure GP Limited and others v. Kingdom of Spain*, ICSID Case No. ARB/14/12, Award, 2 August 2019, para. 24; *OperaFund v. Spain* (n 638) para. 117; for further details on the legal value of the advertisement campaign *see* Landmann, *Legitimate Expectations* (n 400) 209.

1578/2008 extended limitations on energy production volumes and limited the period of Fixed-in-Tariffs to twenty-five years – reflecting the lifetime of PV plants.[622]

The contested measures arose following the 2008 economic crisis.[623] The incentives provided to the renewable sector deepened a tariff deficit, which rose from EUR 2 billion in 2005 to EUR 28.5 billion at the end of 2013.[624] The ongoing deficit led the government to adopt restrictive measures on the incentive programme in 2009.[625] In particular, RDL 6/2009 obligated operators to register with the Pre-Assignment Registry to benefit from the incentive programme; RD 1003/2010[626] established further limitations for new PV facilities. The additional 2010 Amendments eliminated regulated tariffs from the 26th year of the plant's operation[627] and imposed a limit on annual operation hours covered by premiums.[628]

Following a government change in 2011, the economic incentives for new electricity production were abolished, and the pre-allocation payment was suspended.[629] Subsequently, a hydrocarbon levy on the supply and import of natural gas was reintroduced and created a Tax on the Value of the Production of Electrical Energy (TVPEE).[630] Finally, in 2013 and 2014, several measures eventually replaced the *Special Regime*. RDL 2/2013[631] eliminated the Fixed-price option under RD 661/2007 and left two options to choose from for investors benefiting from the earlier regime: either receive the market price with a lowered Consumer Price Index (CPI) or receive a Fixed-in-tariff that was inferior to the CPI, according to an arbitral tribunal.[632] RDL 9/2013[633] then repealed RD 661/2007 and eliminated the regime of fixed tariffs and

622. Royal Decree 1578/2008, 26 September 2008, on the Payment of the Production of Electricity by Photovoltaic Solar Technology in Facilities established after the Final Date for Payment given by RD 661/2007.
623. *SolEs Badajoz GmbH v. Kingdom of Spain*, ICSID Case No. ARB/15/38, Award, 31 July 2019, para. 434; *PV Investors v. Spain* (n 413) para. 629; *Renergy v. Spain* (n 39) para. 911 ('the Tribunal's view is that a diligent investor in wind and CSP projects would, at the time the Claimant invested, have expected that in case of a global and severe economic crisis and a steep incline of the Tariff Deficit, the Respondent would adopt measures to safeguard the sustainability of the SES').
624. *PV investors v. Spain* (n 413) para. 627.
625. Behn and Létourneau-Tremblay, 'Promoting Renewable Energy' (n 590) 218.
626. Royal Decree 1003/2010, 5 August 2010, on the Liquidation of the Equivalent Premium to the Facilities Producing Electricity from Photovoltaic Technology under the Special regime.
627. Royal Decree 1565/2010, 19 November 2010, on amending Certain Aspects of the Special Regime for Electricity Production.
628. Royal Decree 1614/2010, 7 December 2010, on the Regulation and Modification of Certain Aspects of the Production of Electricity from Solar Thermoelectric and Wind Technologies; Royal Decree Law 14/2010, 23 December 2010, on Urgent Measures to Correct the tariff deficit in the Electricity Sector.
629. Royal Decree Law 1/2012, 27 March 2012, on the Suspension of the Pre-allocation Payment Procedures and the Abolition of the Economic Incentives for New Electricity Production Facilities from Cogeneration, Renewable Energies and Waste.
630. Royal Decree Law 15/2012, 21 April 2012, on Fiscal measures for Energy Sustainability.
631. Royal Decree Law 2/2013, 1 February 2013, on Urgent Measures for the National Electricity and Financial Systems. Reasonable taxes are carved out by the ECT Art. 21(1) so that this tax, while claimed against in investment disputes, was not considered within the jurisdiction of arbitral tribunals; *see, e.g.*, *NextEra*, para. 383; *Eiser*, paras 269-271.
632. *Stadtwerke München v. Spain* (n 452) para. 91.
633. Royal Decree Law 9/2013, 12 July 2013, on the Adoption of Urgent Measures to Guarantee the Financial Stability of the Electric System.

premiums both for new and existing installations. At the last stage of this movement, New energy law 24/2013[634] wholly eliminated the distinction between the *Ordinary* and *Special Regimes* and provided for a revision of the incentive scheme every six years.[635] RD 413/2014[636] established the new regime with new compensation formulas. These were detailed by MO IET/1045/2014, which set the remuneration parameters for renewable facilities. Under Annex III of the MO, the target rate of return for renewable energy producers was set at 7.398% pre-tax. The new scheme applied to already established plants, raising the question as to the retroactivity of the measures.[637]

As of June 2023, twenty-six arbitral awards have been rendered in the Spanish renewable case law. They greatly differ in the interpretation of the measures or acts that were considered commitments of the State. Accordingly, there are two outcomes - in favour of the state or of the claimant - but three distinct lines of reasoning. In fourteen of the twenty-six decisions reviewed, tribunals or majority tribunals adopted a voluntarist theory approach.[638] In nine of the twenty-six decisions, liability was found on the basis that the changes to the regulatory regime were held not to be proportionate by reference to a legitimate expectation of a reasonable rate of return.[639] In three of the

634. Law 24/2013, 26 December 2013, on the Electricity Sector.
635. *PV Investors v. Spain* (n 413) paras 208-211, 803.
636. Royal Decree 413/2014, 6 June 2014, on Electrical Generation by Means of Renewable, Cogeneration and Waste Facilities.
637. For further detail Behn, 'Governments under Cross-fire?' (n 261) 120-122.
638. *9REN v. Spain* (n 422) paras 212, 253, 267, 268, 311; *Cube Infrastructure v. Spain* (n 402) paras 427-428; *Eiser Infrastructure Limited and Energia Solar Luxembourg S.a.r.l. v. Kingdom of Spain*, ICSID Case No. ARB/13/36, Decision on Jurisdiction and Liability of 17 March 2021, paras 393, 398-400; *Foresight v. Spain* (n 620) paras 390, 397-398; *InfraRed v. Spain* (n 621) paras 368-369, 418, 449-451; *Antin v. Spain* (n 453) paras 560, 562-3, 568-570; *Masdar v. Spain* (n 595) paras 520-522; *NextEra Energy Global Holdings B.V. and NextEra Energy Spain Holdings B.V. v. Kingdom of Spain*, ICSID Case No. ARB/14/11, Decision on Jurisdiction, Liability and Quantum Principles, 12 March 2019, para. 590 (however, the tribunal did not base liability on the basis of RD 661/2007 but on specific assurances, which reflects a detrimental reliance approach 'In the view of the Tribunal, statements made in writing by Spanish officials constitute the best evidence of Spanish assurances that could be the basis for legitimate expectations'), paras 596, 598-600; *Novenergia II v. Spain* (n 413) paras 657, 694-695; *OperaFund Eco-Invest SICAV PLC and Schwab Holding AG v. Kingdom of Spain*, ICSID Case No. ARB/15/36, Award, 6 September 2019, paras 485, 488-489; *SolEs Badajoz v. Spain* (n 623) paras 419, 439, 443-444, 458, 461-462; *Watkins Holdings v. Spain* (n 413) paras 569, 597, 601-603.
639. *BayWa r.e. Renewable Energy GmbH and BayWa r.e. Asset Holding GmbH v. Spain*, ICSID Case No. ARB/15/16, Decision on Jurisdiction, Liability and Directions on Quantum, 2 December 2019, paras 463, 471, 477-480, 496, 500; *Cavalum v. Spain* (n 585) paras 619-621, 626, 632, 666; *Eurus Energy Holdings Corporation and Eurus Energy Europe B.V. v. Kingdom of Spain*, ICSID Case No. ARB/16/4, Decision on Jurisdiction and Liability, 17 March 2021, paras 314-319, 358; *Hydro Energy v. Spain* (n 422) para. 676; *Infracapital F1 S.à r.l. and Infracapital Solar B.V. v. Kingdom of Spain*, ICSID Case No. ARB/16/18, Decision on Jurisdiction, Liability and Directions on Quantum, 13 September 2021, paras 528, 529, 531, 601-602, 687, 755); *RREEF v. Spain* (n 413) paras 464-5, 468, 471-472, 550; *RWE v. Spain* (n 519) paras 550, 553-554, 576-578; *PV Investors v. Spain* (n 413) paras 638-639, 648; *Sevilla Beheer v. Spain* (n 76) paras 715, 717, 872; *see also Antaris v. Czech Republic* (n 76) para. 360; *Blusun v. Italy* (n 603) para. 319; *CEF Energia BV v. Italian Republic*, SCC Case No. 158/2015, Award, 16 January 2019, paras 236-243.

twenty-six decisions, liability was not found on the ground that the State was not at fault, either because the measures were proportionate or because the investor could not show sufficient due diligence.[640]

3 Italy's Net Zero Policies and Contested Measures

The withdrawal of certain advantages provided under the Italian incentive scheme led to seven investor-state disputes. Italy's last two decrees were grounds for investors to claim for the violation of the ECT's FET clause. In the Italian cases, tribunals assessed three distinct issues: the time of the investment, the content of the state's commitments, and the hierarchy of norms, i.e., the relevant norm creating a State's specific commitment.

Italy granted incentives to the renewable energy sector through Legislative Decree 387/2003,[641] which implemented the European Directive 2001/77/EC.[642] The support scheme was the foundation for ministerial decrees known as *Conto Energia* (Energy Account).[643] Italy introduced incentives for renewable energy producers in 2005 under the first Conto Energia.[644] Electricity produced by qualified PV solar plants would benefit from green certificates and a monetary value superior to the electricity market price - i.e., through premiums paid in addition to the wholesale electricity price.[645] According to LD 387/2003, the cost of the incentives could not be borne by the State; the *Conto Energia* thus passed the costs to electricity consumers through electricity bills.[646] The AEEG (Authority for Electrical Energy and Gas) collected consumer fees to cover the incentive tariff costs. The *Gestore dei Servizi Energetici* (GSE) was the state-owned company responsible for paying the incentive tariffs to electricity producers under the Conto Energia decrees.[647]

All *Conto Energia* decrees providing for tariff premiums (fees added to the market price) expressly provided that the premiums, once granted, would be paid for twenty

640. *Charanne v. Spain* (n 413) paras 514, 517, 533-536; *FREIF v. Spain* (n 77) paras 525, 531, 571, 589-590; *Stadtwerke München v. Spain* (n 452) paras 317-320, 325 (approach based the investor's due diligence and on the '*reasonableness*' of measures).
641. Law Decree, 29 December 2003, No. 387.
642. Directive 2001/77/EC of the European Parliament and of the Council of 27 September 2001 on the promotion of electricity produced from renewable energy sources in the internal electricity market.
643. Landmann, *Legitimate Expectations* (n 400) 163; Igor Timofeyev, Joseph Profaizer and Adam Weiss, 'Investment Disputes Involving the Renewable Energy Industry under the Energy Charter Treaty', in J William Rowley (ed.), *The Guide to Energy Arbitrations: Fourth Edition* (GAR 2020) 51.
644. Legislative Decree No. 387/03; *see* generally Saverio Massari, 'The Italian Photovoltaic Sector in Two Practical Cases: How to Create an Unfavorable Investment Climate in Renewables' (2015) 12 OGEL 3.
645. *ESPF v. Italy* (n 133) paras 74-76.
646. *CEF v. Italy* (n 639) para. 111.
647. *Greentech Energy Systems A/S, Novenergia II Energy & Environment (SCA) SICAR, and Novenergia II Italian Portfolio SA v. Italian Republic*, SCC Case No. 2015/095, Award, 23 December 2018, para. 110.

years commencing from the date of a PV plant's entry into operation, giving formal conditions were fulfilled. *Conto Energia* 1[648] provided for a twenty-year FIP, set out by private contracts (GES Conventions) confirming the right to a specific rate. An annual cap of 500 Megawatt was implemented.[649] Under Conto Energia 1, the entry into operation was understood as the PV plant's connection to the grid and execution of an agreement with the GSE. In February 2006, *Conto Energia* 1 was amended to eliminate the initial indexation of FIPs on inflation. Subsequent Conto Energia decrees did not provide for an ISTAT inflation adjustment.[650] *Conto Energia* 2[651] removed the formal authorisation phase that existed under *Conto* I, instead offering PV producers access to incentive benefits upon entry into the operation of their facilities.[652] Conto Energia 3[653] specified premiums available to PV plants, reducing these amounts over time.[654]

In 2009, the European Parliament adopted Directive 2009/28/EC, which set mandatory national renewable energy production targets for each EU Member State and a target of 17% of Italy's gross energy consumption by 2020.[655] Italy implemented the European Commission (EC) directive through Legislative Decree 28 of 3 March 2011, referred to as the 'Romani Decree.'[656] However, the Romani Decree negatively affected prospective investments. It shortened the qualifying period for Conto III tariffs, requiring eligible plants to operate by 31 May 2011 instead of 31 December 2013.[657] It excluded plants from the scheme under certain conditions, such as a capacity exceeding 1MW and being built on agricultural land.[658] In connection with the modified qualifying period, the Ministry of Economic Development was to establish revised incentive tariffs for PV plants entering into operation after 31 May 2011, resulting in the fourth CE decree. The Romani Decree also required that future incentive tariff decrees consider cost reductions already achieved for PV technology and the level of incentives being offered in other EU countries.

In 2012, Italy implemented a series of measures diminishing the value of the incentives for new energy producers. It enacted a retroactive policy affecting existing investments under Law Decree No. 145/2013[659] (*Destinazione Italia Decree*) and Law Decree No. 91/2014 of 24 June 2014 (the *Spalma-incentivi Decree*).[660]

Under the *Destinazione Italia Decree*, PV plant owners were given an option: either continue to receive the *Conto Energia* for the twenty-year remainder but foreclose any additional incentive thereafter[661] or accept reductions to their incentives

648. Ministerial Decree No. 18908 of July 2005 of the Ministry of Productive Activities.
649. *Belenergia v. Italy* (n 834) para. 397.
650. Ministerial Decree No. 20998 of February 2006 of the Ministry of Productive Activities.
651. Ministerial Decree of 19 February 2007 from the Ministry of Economic Development.
652. *Greentech v. Italy* (n 647) para. 117.
653. Ministerial Decree of 6 August 2010 from the Ministry of Economic Development.
654. *Greentech v. Italy* (n 647) para. 121.
655. Directive 2009/28/EC.
656. Legislative Decree No. 28/2011.
657. *Ibid.*, Art. 25(9).
658. *Eskosol S.P.A. v. Italy*, ICSID Case No. ARB/15/50, Award, 4 September 2020, para. 157.
659. Legislative Decree No. 145/2013 of 23 December 2013.
660. *Greentech v. Italy* (n 647) para. 11.
661. *Ibid.*, para. 143; *see also Belenergia v. Italy* (n 834) para. 122.

in exchange for their extension for seven years.[662] The *Spalma-incentivi* Decree introduced the reduction in tariff levels to all plants under the five Conto Energia as of 1 January 2015. The legislative Decree became Law[663] and left operators with three options.[664] Article 26 of Law 116/2014 applies a reduction to the tariffs awarded under any Conto Energia to PV plants with a nominal peak power exceeding 200 kW.[665] The law affected all power plant owners, regardless of the rights granted under the GSE agreement.

4 Czech Republic's Net Zero Policies and Contested Measures

The Czech Republic faced a similar pattern of investment claims against renewable energy incentives. The notable difference was the state's development stage and the less significant scale of incentives.

In the Czech Republic, Act 180/2005 provided a support scheme in line with the 2001/77/EC Directive.[666] It offered a fixed FIT that benefited grid operators in renewable energy or a Feed-in-premium ('Green Bonus') paid on top of the regular market price. Power plant operators were initially eligible for fifteen years from commissioning the plants, extended to twenty years by the Czech Energy Regulator.[667] The law provided a 'brake rule' stipulating that the tariff rate set by the Energy Regulator annually could not decrease by more than 5% a year.

In 2010, the Czech Republic lifted the 5% 'brake rule', limited the scheme to small-sized PV plants by 2011, eliminated tax incentives, and applied a solar levy of 26% on FITs and 28% on Green Bonuses in December 2010.[668] In May 2012, the initial support scheme was replaced[669] and later amended in October 2013.[670]

662. *Ibid.*
663. Law No. 116/2014 of 11 August 2014.
664. International Energy Agency, 'Decree on the Cut of Incentives for Photovoltaic Plants (*Spalma Incentivi*)' (*IEA*, 11 December 2014) https://www.iea.org/policies/5653-decree-on-the-cut-of-incentives-for-photovoltaic-plants-spalma-incentivi accessed 28 July 2022.
665. *Ibid.*, ('A) Option A provides for a solution that was already contemplated by the Law-Decree: i.e., a reduction of the tariff by a ratio ranging from 17% to 25% depending on the residual incentivised period compensated by an extension of the incentivised period to 24 years starting from the date of entry into operation of the relevant plant (instead of the current 20 years). B) Option B provides that, without modifying the duration of the incentivised period (i.e., 20 years), during a first part of the remaining incentivised period, the tariff will be reduced and that, during a second part of the remaining incentivised period, the FIT will be increased. The re-modulation ratios will be established by the Italian Ministry for Economic Development. C) Option C provides for a flat reduction of the tariff, for the remaining incentivised period without modifying the duration of the same, equal to 6% for plants with a capacity between 200 and 500 kW, 7% for plants with a capacity between 500 and 900 kW, 8% for plants with a capacity above 900 kW').
666. Act No. 180/2005 Coll. On the Promotion of Electricity Production from Renewable Energy Sources.
667. ERO Regulation No. 346/2007 Coll.; ERO Regulation No. 409/2009 Coll.
668. Respectively amendment Acts No. 137/2010, No. 330/2010, No. 346/2010, No. 401/2010 Coll.
669. Act 165/2012 Coll., on Promotion of Sources of Energy and Amending Certain Acts.
670. Amendments Act No. 310/2013 Coll.

All Czech Republic cases were adjudicated under BITs, which were used as applicable law[671] in combination with the ECT[672] or excluded from the substantive analysis of the merits.[673] All Czech Republic cases have been decided in favour of the State – with dissenting views by Gary Born on the interpretation of the regulatory framework. The Czech Republic refused to consolidate four cases: Europe Nova, Photovoltaic Knopf, I.C.W., and Voltaic Network. However, all four were adjudicated by the same arbitrators[674] and the awards are virtually the same, so all cases are treated as one.

The State's favourable outcomes in the Czech Republic cases were mainly determined by three factors: (1) the reasonable level of amendment of the support scheme, (2) the reasonable remaining profitability of the foreign investor after the amendment measures, (3) the recognition of the sovereign right to regulate 'in the context of the solar boom and its substantial adverse consequences'.[675] The question was whether there was an explicit representation by the Respondent that the value of the investment would not be diminished.

Having presented the factual background, I now turn to a short presentation of the applicable treaty, the underlying unqualified provision of FET, and three main questions of interpretation.

5 FET Provision under the Energy Charter Treaty

To apprehend the Spanish, Italian, and Czech case law, it is crucial to outline Article 10(1) on FET under the Energy Charter Treaty. The 1994 Energy Charter Treaty does not spell out or provide for the protection of the investor's LE. While it is not within the scope of the research to analyse the FET provision under the ECT, I present below the main points of contention.

The first two sentences of Article 10(1) of the ECT read as follows:

> Each Contracting Party shall, in accordance with the provisions of this Treaty, encourage and create stable, equitable, favourable and transparent conditions for Investors of other Contracting Parties to make Investments in its Area. Such conditions shall include a commitment to accord at all times to Investments of Investors of other Contracting Parties fair and equitable treatment.

671. *Jürgen Wirtgen, Stefan Wirtgen, Gisela Wirtgen and JSW Solar (zwei) GmbH & Co. KG v. Czech Republic*, PCA Case No. 2014-03, Final Award, 11 October 2017, para. 274 (Art. 2(1) of the Treaty between the Federal Republic of Germany and the Czech and Slovak Federal Republic on Encouragement and Reciprocal Protection of Investments of 2 October 1990 requires a State 'not to deliberately cause damage to foreign investors; and [t]o protect their legitimate expectations relied on when investing').
672. *Antaris v. Czech Republic* (n 76) para. 262.
673. *Europe Nova v. Czech Republic*, para. 461.
674. Hans van Houtte appointed as President, John Beechey appointed by Claimant, and Toby Landau appointed by Respondent.
675. *Europe Nova v. Czech Republic*, para. 576.

When interpreting the FET standard, tribunals have applied the customary rules of treaty interpretation as reflected in Articles 31 to 33 of the VCLT.[676] Three related issues arose.

The first is whether the entirety of the clause should be read 'in accordance with customary international law', an argument usually advanced by the respondent.[677] This line of reasoning, however, seems a minority view;[678] the majority of tribunals found that ECT's FET standard is unqualified and should be determined autonomously from CIL.[679] There seems nevertheless to be a consensus among tribunals that the ordinary meaning of the words 'fair' and 'equitable' denote that the rights of the investor and state is not absolute.[680]

The second issue is whether the first and second sentences of Article 10(1) should be read as one single concept or as two autonomous standards. Tribunals have disagreed on the obligation of stability deriving from the Preamble and Article 10(1) first sentence. To some, the notion of stability enshrined in ECT's first sentence is a standard by itself.[681] According to *Plama v. Bulgaria,* often cited in the case law, the protection standards 'though related, are separate and autonomous'.[682] Some tribunals held that the standard of FET is likely breached where legal and business stability or the legal framework has been altered in such a way as to frustrate legitimate and reasonable expectations or guarantees of stability.[683] Most considered that the host State's guarantee of stability and transparency of the legal framework is, together with protecting the investor's LE, a vital element of the FET standard.[684] Thus, *ESPF v.*

676. Vienna Convention on the Law of Treaties of 23 May 1969.
677. *Silver Ridge v. Italy* (n 56) para. 401 ('he hermeneutical principle that requires international treaties to be interpreted, if possible, in a manner consistent with general international law').
678. *RWE v. Spain* (n 519) paras 447, 451 (finding that regardless of whether FET is understood autonomously of under CIL that 'FET offers protection from certain forms of fundamental regulatory change').
679. *SunReserve v. Italy* (n 416) paras 671ff.; *Silver Ridge v. Italy* (n 56) para. 401.
680. *SunReserve v. Italy* (n 416) para. 683 ('fairness and/or equitability are not absolute concepts capable of being reduced to universally applicable definitions. Instead, what constitutes fair and/or equitable treatment is a question to be determined by considering all circumstances of a given case').
681. *Sevilla Beheer v Spain,* Dissenting Opinion (n 462) paras 8-17; *Watkins Holdings v. Spain* (n 413) paras 698-699.
682. *Plama Consortium Ltd. v. Republic of Bulgaria,* ICSID Case No. ARB/03/24, Award, 27 August 2008, para. 163.
683. *Eiser,* para. 382 ('Taking account of the context and the ECT's object and purpose, the Tribunal concludes that Article 10(1)'s obligation to accord FET necessarily embraces an obligation to provide fundamental stability in the essential characteristics of the legal regime relied upon by investors in making long-term investments'), cited in approbation by *RREEF v. Spain* (n 413) para. 314; *see also Novenergia II v. Spain* (n 413) para. 646; *AES Summit Generation Limited and AES-Tisza Erömü Kft v. Republic of Hungary,* ICSID Case No. ARB/07/22, Award, 23 September 2010, para. 9.3.29; *see also Tecmed v. Mexico* (n 67) para. 154; *Duke Energy v. Ecuador* (n 225) para. 340; *Bayindir v. Pakistan* (n 459) para. 179; *Electrabel v. Hungary* (n 225) para. 7.74; *Philip Morris v. Uruguay* (n 76) para. 320.
684. Balcerzak, *Renewable Energy Arbitration* (n 220) 317 ('Most of the arbitral tribunals (*Isolux, Eiser, Novenergia, Antin, Foresight, RREEF, BayWa, Stadtwerke, RWE, PV* Investors, *Hydro*) considered that the first sentence does not create a separate obligation to provide regulatory stability, but that this should be read into the FET. Some tribunals failed to adopt a clear position on this question (*NextEra, 9REN, Cube, InfraRed, OperaFund*), whereas the Cavalum tribunal simply observed that there is a "plain overlap" between the two.' For the *Watkins*

Italy[685] and *Silver Ridge*[686] opine that whether there should be one integrated standard including elements or several autonomous protection standards is irrelevant and redundant.

The third issue, related to the provision but mainly to the tribunals' interpretation of LE, is whether laws and regulations create LE in the ambit of an investor and whether this expectation may be reasonable and legitimate. To clarify, the majority of tribunals held that an investor's subjective expectations of profit are not a stand-alone standard against which the conduct of the state should be reviewed.[687] Rather, LE only arise from the state's conduct and the investor's reliance on them. When the state's representations or promises, whether addressed to the investor or general, amount to specific commitments, the investor becomes entitled to expect the state to maintain its commitment. Apart from a minority estoppel *lato sensu* approach,[688] most tribunals held that the state is not strictly bound by the investor's legitimate expectation in exercising its sovereignty and that the investor can expect some level of change.[689] The investor may not 'rely on an investment treaty as a kind of insurance policy' against the risk of any changes in the host state's legal framework,[690] nor can the protection of LE, as a rule, lead to regulatory freezing or *lock-in*.[691] Most tribunals consider that the state retains a 'margin of change'[692] to respond to changing market circumstances or pursue a reasonable, rational policy pursuing a public interest.[693] Nevertheless, even though

---

tribunal (n 413) the first sentence of Art. 10(1) ECT creates a separate obligation to FET. As for the Charanne tribunal, it considered FET to be 'included in the more general obligation to create stable, equitable, favourable and transparent conditions').

685. *ESPF v. Italy* (n 133) paras 443-444.
686. *Silver Ridge v. Italy* (n 56) para. 393.
687. Balcerzak, *Renewable Energy Arbitration* (n 220) 444.
688. Biggs, 'The Scope of Investors' (n 406) 120-126.
689. *Philip Morris v. Uruguay* (n 76) para. 422, citing *Saluka v. Czech Republic* (n 77) 305-306; *Arif v. Republic of Moldova* (n 409) para. 537, Ortino, *The Origin* (n 557) 33 ('subsequent arbitral practice has shown more deference vis-à-vis the host State's right to regulate, and supported a softer understanding of a stability obligation under FET. In particular, the focus on (a) the existence of a stabilization commitment or promise; (b) the reasonableness of the host State measure; and/or (c) the need to balance the investor's expectations and the host State's right to regulate represents strong evidence of this softer notion of stability'.).
690. *EDF v. Romania* (n 418) para. 217; *see also* Yulia S Selivanova, 'Changes in Renewables Support Policy and Investment Protection under the Energy Charter Treaty: Analysis of Jurisprudence and Outlook for the Current Arbitration Cases' (2018) 33 ICSID Review 2 433, 443 https://doi.org/10.1093/icsidreview/siy010.
691. *See*, for instance, *EDF v. Romania* (n 418) para. 217; *Ulysseas, Inc. v. The Republic of Ecuador*, UNCITRAL, Final Award of 12 June 2012, paras 248-249; *Charanne v. Spain* (n 413) paras 499-502; *Teinver S.A., Transportes de Cercanías S.A. and Autobuses Urbanos del Sur S.A. v. the Argentine Republic*, ICSID Case No. ARB/09/1, Award, 21 July 2017, para. 668; *Antaris v. Czech Republic* (n 76) paras 360(6)-(10).
692. *Micula v. Romania* (n 427) para. 529; *Philip Morris v. Uruguay* (n 76) para. 423.
693. *Saluka v. Czech Republic* (n 77) para. 309, approved in *Philip Morris v. Uruguay* (n 76) para. 322; *Sempra Energy International v. Argentina*, ICSID Case No. ARB/02/16, 28 September 2007, para. 318 (not for the tribunal to decide whether measures adopted 'might have been good or bad': there must be some important manifest impropriety); *Plama Consortium Ltd v. Republic of Bulgaria*, Award, 27 August 2008, para. 184; *AES Summit Generation Ltd v. Hungary* (n 683) para. 10.3.7 ('the existence of a rational policy; and the reasonableness of the act of the state in relation to the policy'); *Binder v. Czech Republic*, UNCITRAL, Final Award, 15 July 2011, para. 447; *Micula v. Romania* (n 427) paras 520, 525 ('in the implementation of that

these conditions are interpreted differently, there are signs of relative convergence to consider the regulatory framework as a source of LE.

With these considerations in mind, I now turn to the analysis of arbitral awards and their main divergence point, namely: can the regulatory framework of states amount to specific commitments and to what extent should these expectations be protected? The answer to the question is crucial to the success of the net zero transition and integration of ICCL in the assessment of LE.[694] Below, I assess the arbitral awards.

B VOLUNTARIST-LEANING INTERPRETATION OF LEGITIMATE EXPECTATIONS

The voluntarist approach favoured the enforcement of the state's promise when it was found that the state had committed a certain benefit to a group of investors. Tribunals regarded unilateral statements by states and decrees as having the potential to create LE, even when they are addressed to a group of investors.[695]

The voluntarist approach itself is divided into two strands.[696] The first approach akin to estoppel *lato sensu* considers that clear and unambiguous stabilisation clauses emanating from the law or regulation intended to induce foreign investment are, like a contract obligation, sufficient to freeze a state's obligations towards the investor. The second approach is based on good faith and integrates legitimacy and factual elements. It considers that LE may derive from clear and unambiguous provisions in the regulatory framework, especially when supported by other formal and informal representations; however, the foreseeability of the frustrating measure and competing state interests must be considered in the assessment of the legitimacy of expectations and the level of compensation owed to the investor.[697]

---

policy, the state's acts have been appropriately tailored to the pursuit of that rational policy with due regard for the consequences imposed on investors'); *Electrabel SA v. Hungary*, ICSID Case No. 1RB/07/19, Award, 25 November 2015, para. 155 ('a legitimate policy objective, necessary for that objective, and not excessive considering the relative weight of each interest involved').

694. *Sevilla Beheer v Spain*, Dissenting Opinion (n 462) para. 13 ('In a nutshell, the market alone cannot deliver these investments, so the State steps in to improve the benefits to investors, enhancing their long-term prospects, and simultaneously generating advantages in social welfare and meeting commitments under EU and international climate change law and policy').
695. Nevertheless, in the Spanish cases, two distinct branches exist on whether the 2007 Decree constituted a stabilisation clause or whether it created a legitimate expectation of stability against radical change.
696. *Total v. Argentina* (n 414) para. 117 (The expectation of the investor is undoubtedly 'legitimate' if the host State has explicitly assumed a specific legal obligation for the future, such as by contracts, concessions or stabilisation clauses on which the investor is therefore entitled to rely as a matter of law).
697. *Renergy v. Spain* (n 39) para. 912 ('[T]he Tribunal's view is that a diligent investor in wind and CSP projects would, at the time the Claimant invested, have expected that in case of a global and severe economic crisis and a steep incline of the Tariff Deficit, the Respondent would adopt measures to safeguard the sustainability of the SES. A diligent investor would also have expected that those measures might adversely affect even existing wind and CSP projects, as had previous reforms in Spain').

1 Legitimate Expectations of Absolute Stability

The first strand considers that the state may bind itself through its regulatory framework. Akin to estoppel *lato sensu*,[698] and what Zachary Douglas calls 'strict liability', this line of reasoning considers that a state may bind itself through a stabilisation clause in its regulatory framework that prevents it from changing position thereafter.[699] The line of reasoning is concerned with the enforcement of the state's promise because it found a stabilisation clause and resembles a typical broad estoppel-based reasoning, aimed to prevent the contradiction with previous statements.[700] Accordingly, the Spanish regulatory framework gave rise to the expectation that the FiT scheme would remain unchanged during the projected lifetime of the facilities. The tribunals found that the decree could legitimately bind the state.[701]

The *Masdar Solar v. Spain* award[702] adopted this position, influencing consecutive tribunals. The tribunal found that Spain, through its incentive scheme, had '*guaranteed* the stability of the benefits, if the investors fulfilled a certain number of conditions, both procedural and substantial, during a certain window of time.'[703] Comparatively, *OperaFund v. Spain*[704] found in a clear-cut award that 'it is hard to imagine a more explicit stabilization assurance than the one mentioned in Article 44(3) [of the original incentive scheme]: "revisions [...] shall not affect facilities for which the functioning certificate had been granted."'[705]

In a similar finding, the *STEAG GmbH v. Spain*[706] tribunal held that the investor invested in June 2012 and, by majority,[707] that three LE had been frustrated: the expectation of stability of tariffs, availability of premiums, and fixed upper and lower limits regarding future modifications of the premium option. Nevertheless, the tribunal reflected on STEAG's contribution to its losses (contributory fault) by continuously

698. *See* Chapter 2.D.2.
699. Biggs, 'The Scope of Investors' (n 406) 121 ('If a State makes an explicit representation to a specific group of investors and the investors rely on that representation, it would be inequitable for the State to be able later to go back on that representation without compensating the investor').
700. *Antaris v. Czech Republic* (n 76), Dissenting Opinion of Mr Gary Born, paras 44-45 ('the focus is not on artificial or arbitrary distinctions between "statutory" and "contractual" undertakings or "general legislation" and "specific assurances", but on whether the state's actions and statements have provided undertakings to investors which it would be unfair or in-equitable for the state to dishonor. [...] The decisive question is not the form of a state's representations but whether the content and character of those representations is sufficiently clear to give rise to legitimate investor expectations that the state will abide by its commitments').
701. *Antaris v. Czech Republic* (n 76) para. 489; in *OperaFund, Antin, Masdar, Novenergia,* and *Eiser* rejected Spain's defence based on the 'reasonable return'.
702. *Masdar v. Spain* (n 595). The tribunal was composed of John Beechey, Gary Born, Brigitte Stern.
703. *Ibid.*, para. 513.
704. *OperaFund v. Spain* (n 638). The tribunal was composed of Karl-Heinz Böckstiegel, August Reinisch, Philippe Sands (dissent).
705. *Ibid.*, para. 485.
706. *STEAG GmbH v. Kingdom of Spain*, ICSID Case No. ARB/15/4, Decision on Jurisdiction, Liability and Principles of Quantum, 8 September 2020. The tribunal was composed of Eduardo Zuleta, Guido Santiago Tawil, Pierre-Marie Dupuy.
707. *Ibid.*

making capital injections after contested measures had been adopted (estimated at 25%).[708]

Similarly, albeit considering that the Decree was a guarantee rather than a stabilisation clause, the tribunal in *9Ren Holding S.a.r.l v. Spain*[709] held that 'the clear and specific "guarantee" in RD 661/2007 satisfies the requisite degree of "specificity"'.[710] It added that Spain claims the right to resile from what the Tribunal has concluded was a regulatory guarantee of price stability.[711] In *InfraRed v. Spain,*[712] the tribunal found it reasonable and legitimate for the investor to expect the 'regulated tariff and the pool plus premium (...) would not change for the lifespan of the plants'.[713]

2 Investors Protected from Fundamental Changes: A Good Faith Approach

In a line of reasoning akin to good faith, these tribunals focused on the enforcement of state promises, with the notable difference of not finding the decree as a stabilisation clause, which would prevent any change in regulation. In other words, a margin of reasonable change is deemed acceptable and legitimate given the state's sovereignty. The reasoning is principled and based on international law's principle of good faith or expressively on the doctrine of unilateral statement.

According to the more balanced voluntarist law approach, LE may be created from unilateral statements and the general regulatory framework; however, stabilisation clauses cannot be interpreted lightly. Thus, in the line of cases below, investors could legitimately expect to be protected from *radical changes* to the Special Regime and the measures abrogating and replacing the Special Regime amounted to such radical change.[714] Arbitral tribunals found this to be in line with the fairness of LE and relative stability referred to in Article 10(1) of the ECT.

A more balanced assessment of LE from public international law and voluntarist theory was provided in *Renergy v. Spain.*[715] It was found by a majority that the measures thwarted the Claimant's legitimate expectation of 'relative stability', rejecting the assertion of a stabilisation clause of 'absolute stability'. In a nuanced fashion, examining the *degree* of specific commitment and legitimacy of expectations, the tribunal held that:

708. *STEAG GmbH v. Kingdom of Spain*, ICSID Case No. ARB/15/4, Dissenting Opinion of Pierre-Marie Dupuy, 8 October 2020.
709. *9REN v. Spain* (n 422). The tribunal was composed of Ian Binnie, David Haigh, V.V.Veeder.
710. *Ibid.*, para. 299.
711. *Ibid.*, para. 311.
712. *InfraRed v. Spain* (n 621). The tribunal was composed of Stephen Drymer, William Park, Pierre-Marie Dupuy.
713. *Ibid.*, para. 453.
714. *RWE v. Spain* (n 519) para. 619 ('The Tribunal is looking in this context for total and unreasonable change or subversion').
715. *Renergy v. Spain* (n 39). The tribunal was composed of Bruno Simma, Christoph Schreuer, and Philippe Sands.

> a diligent investor in wind and CSP projects would, at the time the Claimant invested, have expected that in case of a global and severe economic crisis and a steep incline of the Tariff Deficit, the Respondent would adopt measures to safeguard the sustainability of the SES. A diligent investor would also have expected that those measures might adversely affect even existing wind and CSP projects, as had previous reforms in Spain.[716]

However, the majority held that no investor could anticipate the dramatic and abrupt change to the remunerative system that resulted in an adverse disproportionate impact on the Claimant's investment, even in the face of an economic crisis.[717]

Although not found in favour of the investor, the *Silver Ridge v. Italy*[718] tribunal adopted a remarkably similar reasoning to *Renergy v. Spain* discussed above. The legislative framework was not found to contain a freezing commitment but rather would not be subject to fundamental or radical changes.[719] The tribunal further found that the *Spalma incentivi* Decree passed the test of reasonableness, i.e., that Italy acted based on legitimate public policy objectives, notably strengthening the sustainability of the incentive tariff scheme for renewable energy in a situation of economic difficulty.[720] For the tribunal, the *Spalma incentivi* Decree and other measures were sufficiently 'reasonable, foreseeable and proportionate'.[721] FET is not breached in the absence of a freezing commitment or a 'fundamental or radical alteration of the applicable legal framework to the detriment of the investor'. The analysis was thus state-centric rather than focusing on the due diligence and effect of the state's measure on the investor's profitability.

Influential as well, due to the early publication of its award, was *Eiser Infrastructure Ltd v. Spain,*[722] which adopted a combination of LE and relative stability analysis, considering that Article 10(1)'s obligation to accord FET should 'necessarily embrace an obligation to provide fundamental stability in the essential characteristics of the legal regime relied upon by investors in making long-term investments'.[723] Further, 'Article 10(1) of the ECT entitled them to expect that Spain would not drastically and abruptly revise the regime, on which their investment depended, in a way that destroyed its value.'[724] What matters in the tribunal's analysis is the notion of reliance and commitment through unilateral statements of the state.

716. *Ibid.*, para. 912.
717. *Ibid.*
718. *Silver Ridge v. Italy* (n 56). The tribunal was composed of Bruno Simma, Thomas Johnson, Bernardo Cremades.
719. *Ibid.*, para. 437 ('a circumspect and reasonable investor to believe that the incentive tariff regime created by the Respondent would remain intact in its overall structure and its essential elements, i.e., that it would not be subject to fundamental or radical changes to the detriment of the investors').
720. *Ibid.*, para. 452.
721. *Ibid.*, para. 474.
722. *Eiser Infrastructure Limited and Energia Solar Luxembourg S.À.R.I. v. Kingdom of Spain*, ICSID Case No. ARB/13/36, Award (4 May 2017). The tribunal was composed of John Crook, Stanimir Alexandrov, Campbell McLachlan.
723. *Ibid.*, para. 382.
724. *Ibid.*, para. 418.

The tribunal in *Cube Infrastructure v. Spain*[725] agreed with *Eiser* on the fundamental characteristics of the regulatory framework.[726] The tribunal based the source of LE in unilateral declarations of states, citing the ICJ's *Nuclear Test* and *Frontier Dispute* judgments to analogously find that states can give firm undertakings that could be relied upon[727] for the entire lifespan of the plants.[728] The *Cube* tribunal acknowledged the state's right to regulate and change its legislation but considered that Spain committed itself to guarantee the stability of the incentive regime's fundamental characteristics.[729] The tribunal correctly delineated that 'the Respondent had been actively encouraging sufficient investment in renewable energy and had become bound under EU law to increase the proportion of its energy derived from renewable sources. 192 RD 661/2007 was explicitly presented as a part of the Respondent's effort to attract sufficient investment in renewable energy to meet its goals'.[730]

The *Novenergia II v. Spain*[731] is distinguishable by its clearest expression of what constitutes a specific commitment. The tribunal found that the incentive scheme constituted a specific commitment towards a defined group of investors. The tribunal explained: 'The commitment from the Kingdom of Spain could not have been clearer. A considerable number of RE companies also invested in reliance on these statements and assurances.'[732] To the tribunal, the investor had a legitimate expectation that 'there would not be any radical or fundamental changes to the Special Regime as set out in RD 661/2007'.[733]

The tribunal in *Watkins Holdings v. Spain*[734] was less theoretically consistent in its analysis but considered all relevant facts - including EU law - in the assessment of whether LE had been created. The tribunal referred to the reasoning of *Eiser*[735] and *RREEF*,[736] finding the source of LE in the endorsement of the concept by past tribunals.[737] Although it acknowledged the state's right to regulate, it limited its scope to measures that would be 'unfair, inequitable and unreasonable', thereby restating the obvious FET clause. It found that RD 661/2007 amounted to a stabilisation clause. In her dissenting opinion, Professor Hélène Ruiz-Fabri noted that the late stage at which

725. *Cube Infrastructure v. Spain* (n 402). The tribunal was composed of Vaughan Lowe, James Spigelman, Christian Tomuschat.
726. *Ibid.*, para. 354.
727. *Ibid.*, para. 275.
728. *Ibid.*, para. 311 ('claimants were entitled to rely on the maintenance of the relevant tariffs and premiums set out in Article 36 RD 661/2007 throughout the reasonable planned operating life of each power plant'), *see also* para. 390.
729. *Ibid.*, para. 397.
730. *Ibid.*, para. 309.
731. *Novenergia II v. Spain* (n 413). The tribunal was composed of Johan Sidklev, Antonio Crivellaro, Bernardo Spùlveda-Amor.
732. *Ibid.*, para. 667.
733. *Ibid.*, para. 681.
734. *Watkins Holdings v. Spain* (n 413). The tribunal was composed of Cecil Abraham, Michael Pryles, Hélène Ruiz-Fabri (dissent).
735. *Ibid.*, para. 563. The Eiser decision confirms that the Claimants were entitled to an expectation that the Spanish regime in which they invested would not be radically altered in respect of existing investments. The Tribunal adopts the persuasive reasons of the Eiser Tribunal.
736. *Ibid.*, para. 520.
737. *Ibid.*, para. 522.

the investment was made, namely in August 2011, could only result in a weaker degree of expectations from the investor.[738]

The tribunal in *CEF Energia B.V v. Italy*[739] found the State froze its commitment to provide FIP over a twenty-year period in a private contract. Nevertheless, the tribunal correctly opined that two out of three projects were not definite at the time of the contested measures so that the investor could not have derived timely expectations.[740] The tribunal found, nevertheless, that the *Enersol* project, having concluded an agreement with GSE, was entitled to LE[741] and that the frustration of the *Spalma incentivi* Decree constituted a breach of FET with respect to the plant:[742]

> No reading, no matter how indulgent, could lead anyone to consider anything other than a clear promise of twenty years of constant currency incentives under a private law contract. This is not a black letter reading or the Tribunal holding Respondent hostage to blinkered pedantry (which would be unbecoming the dignity of a sovereign state); rather, it is the product of a careful, good faith reading of all of Respondent's unambiguous acts as set out above.[743]

In *ESPF Beteiligungs v. Italy,*[744] the tribunal opined that 'the effect of the *Spalma incentivi* Decree on the Claimants' investments was significant'[745] and that this had 'a sizable impact and cannot be qualified as a *de minimis* effect'.[746] Furthermore, while there was no doubt that a clear and specific commitment is required to create an enforceable legitimate expectation, in the majority's view, there was 'no reason in principle why such a commitment of the requisite clarity and specificity could not have arisen from the regulation itself'.[747] Key for the tribunal is the intent of the state to 'induce investment' through its commitment.[748] In a similar fashion, the majority in *Greentech Energy Systems v. Italy*[749] held that 'while the investor might need to live with some minor adjustments, nothing alerted the Claimants that they would need to accept changes of the magnitude imposed by the *Spalma incentivi* Decree'.[750]

738. *Watkins Holdings S.à r.l. and others v. Kingdom of Spain* (ICSID Case No. ARB/15/44, Dissenting Opinion of Hélène Ruiz Fabri, 9 January 2020, para. 12 ('Even admitting arguendo that there was a stabilization commitment in 2007, can it be considered that the same commitment still existed in 2011, where the stability became so uncertain that a "regulatory risk" became plausible?').
739. *CEF v. Italy* (n 639). The tribunal was composed of Klaus Reichert, Klaus Sachs, Giorgio Sacerdoti.
740. *Ibid.*, paras 188-189.
741. *Ibid.*, para. 217.
742. *Ibid.*, para. 244.
743. *Ibid.*, para. 217.
744. *ESPF v. Italy* (n 133). The tribunal was composed of Henri Alvarez, Micheal Pyres, Laurence Boisson de Chazournes.
745. *Ibid.*, para. 578.
746. *Ibid.*
747. *Ibid.*, para. 512.
748. *Ibid.*
749. *Greentech v. Italy* (n 647). The tribunal was composed of William Park, David Haigh, Giorgio Sacerdoti (dissent).
750. *Ibid.*, para. 448.

In *SolEs Badajoz v. Spain,*[751] the tribunal insisted on the fact-intensive assessment of any FET breach claim, adopting a casuistic analysis.[752] Some tribunals emphasised the stability requirement under the ECT, for instance, the tribunal in *Antin Infrastructure v. Spain.*[753] Similarly, the tribunal in *RWE Innogy GmbH v. Spain*[754] found that the state's measures were disproportionate to the Claimant's investment.[755] The *Foresight v. Spain*[756] tribunal paid more tribute to the role of the investor, holding that 'sophisticated investors like the Claimants should have reasonably expected that [the incentive scheme] could be modified, but within foreseeable limits'.[757] Spain's regulatory amendments went beyond the foreseeable limits.[758]

Somewhat an outlier to my distinction between voluntary and detrimental reliance is the case of *NextEra v. Spain.*[759] The tribunal held that neither the legislation nor the decree created LE, but Spain's letters to the specific investor created expectations. The regulatory framework 'was based on legislation, and legislation can be changed'.[760] As a result, 'Claimants could not have had the expectation that the RD 661/2007 regime was frozen.'[761] For the tribunal, the investor could only expect stability, and that legislation would not fundamentally change,[762] although this assurance was found in the letters to the investor rather than the decree or law itself.

In sum, although each case presents its own factual framework, in this approach, tribunals and individual arbitrators focus on the fairness of the state's measures on the

751. *SolEs Badajoz v. Spain* (n 623). The tribunal was composed of Joan Donoghue, David Williams, Giorgio Sacerdoti.
752. *Ibid.*, paras 443-444 ('the evidence establishes instead that a PV investor in March 2010 had a legitimate expectation that it would receive a FIT that was stable, once assigned to a PV plant, for the 25-year period specified in RD 1578/2008 (save for inflation adjustment). The stable FIT was an essential element of the regulatory regime on which Claimant relied when it made its investment decision, considering the capital intensity, long period of capital recovery and high leverage that is characteristic of investments in PV plants').
753. *Antin v. Spain* (n 453). The tribunal was composed of Eduardo Zuleta, Francisco Orrego Vicuña, Christopher Thomas; *see* para. 532 (Art. 10(1) ECT includes an obligation to afford 'fundamental stability in the essential characteristics of the legal regime relied upon by the investors in making long-term investments'); *see* also para. 572.
754. *RWE v. Spain* (n 519). The tribunal was composed of Samuel Wordsworth, Judd Kessler, Anna Joubin-Bret.
755. *Ibid.*, para. 462 (considered that its main task was to assess whether the change to the tariff regime had been disproportionate and whether Spain had taken into account the impacts on investors in its decision-making process); paras 619-622 (Applying its own test, it did not find that Spain's measures amounted to total and unreasonable changes); para. 600 (finding that some measures adopted were *disproportionate* and that it was 'unfair and inequitable for the adverse impacts (...) to be borne by the Claimants'.).
756. *Foresight v. Spain* (n 620). The tribunal was composed of Michael Moser, Klaus Sachs, Raul Emilio Vinuesa.
757. *Ibid.*, para. 397.
758. *Ibid.*, para. 398.
759. *NextEra v. Spain* (n 638). The tribunal was composed of Donald McRae, Yves Fortier, Laurence Boisson de Chazournes.
760. *Ibid.*, para. 584.
761. *Ibid.*, para. 591.
762. *Ibid.*, para. 600 ('expectations from authorities were not about a reasonable return but about the regulatory certainty *and stability* that *NextEra* could expect. The denial of LE is based on the failure to provide that certainty and security by changing fundamentally the regime under which remuneration was to be calculated').

investment. The approach recognises the possibility of a regulatory framework to create LE. Due diligence is not a precondition for the existence of LE. The revenue loss of the investor is not the centrepiece of analysis. Rather, what matters is the conduct of the state in creating binding obligations and the objective reasonableness of the conditions of the investment.

C DETRIMENTAL RELIANCE-LEANING INTERPRETATION OF LEGITIMATE EXPECTATIONS

Most detrimental reliance-leaning tribunals base their reasoning on the fact that only a direct commitment made to a specific investor may give rise to expectations that can subsequently be harmed. They may admit that the *legislative* framework may give rise to expectations to a certain extent.

The detrimental reliance view on LE offers a restrictive interpretation of what may create LE and expects a greater level of due diligence from foreign investors. It is divided into two approaches. The first approach denies the existence of LE under the FET standard on the basis that the doctrine has no basis in the treaty. This position is found in academic scholarship rather than arbitral case law. Some academics holding the minority view refuse to accept the doctrine - arguing that '[t]he principle of legitimate expectations as part of FET has no treaty basis' - noting that it is generally absent from treaty provisions, represents an innovation introduced by arbitrators, and is not appropriate for assessing a breach of FET. One narrow interpretation holds that LE is operative only upon the cumulative fulfilment of high threshold conditions.[763] The second approach adopts a wider interpretation of LE, even though it limits the potential breach of FET to conduct and representations by competent authorities, creating a reliance. These tribunals usually expect an elevated level of due diligence and generally acknowledge a margin of change to the state. The latter approach relies heavily on the actual harm done to the investor and widely accepts the benchmark of 'reasonable return' as an appropriate remedy compared to the expected return in the voluntary approaches explained above.

1 Regulatory Measures Do Not Give Rise to Legitimate Expectations

At the first end of the spectrum, tribunals consider that regulatory measures targeting a group of investors may, under no circumstances, create LE. This position is different from the usual detrimental reliance theory, as it is a state-centric analysis. For these tribunals, regulatory *incentives* cannot be construed as specific commitments, even less as obligations of the state. The tribunals stress the right of states to regulate and adapt their legislation to changing circumstances, particularly when basic public utilities are at stake.

763. Levashova, *Right of States to Regulate* (n 374) 132.

Charanne v. Spain[764] outlines that the LE of a specific investor cannot arise from the essential features of the legislative framework targeting a group of investors:

> to convert a regulatory standard into a specific commitment of the state, by the limited character of the persons who may be affected, would *constitute an excessive limitation on the power of states to regulate* the economy in accordance with the public interest.[765]

The tribunal found that the regulatory framework could not create LE because it did not issue a specific promise to a single investor. There was no contract nor direct representation to substantiate expectations. The tribunal further stressed the importance of a proportionality assessment based on the stability requirement in the ECT.[766] The tribunal acknowledged that an investor could have LE that regulatory modifications will not be unreasonable, contrary to the public interest, or disproportionate.[767] It emphasised that the proportionality requirement is fulfilled as long as the modifications are not random or unnecessary and do not eliminate the essential features of the regulatory framework in place.[768] Some have objected that the *Charanne* tribunal could have reached another verdict had its jurisdiction not been limited to the changes brought by the 2010 regulations, which excluded Law 24/2013 from their assessment.[769] However, this does not change the fundamental characteristic of proportionality-oriented reasoning that influenced several tribunals thereafter.

A similar reasoning is adopted in *Stadtwerke München v. Spain.*[770] The tribunal refused to interpret the incentive scheme as a stable regime immune to future modifications based on changing market conditions.[771] For investors' expectations to be considered legitimate, justifiable, and reasonable, they should arise from a '*rigorous* due diligence process' conducted by the investor.[772] The tribunal found that: 'a prudent investor, having conducted an appropriate due diligence, would not have reasonably formed an expectation of a legally stable income stream for the life of the [investment]'.[773] The tribunal underscored the 2007 Spanish Supreme Court's judgment on the state's margin of regulation in the energy sector, which was a matter of public record at the time of the investment.[774] It held that a reasonable and prudent investor would have been aware of this decision, comprehended its implications for the

764. *Charanne v. Spain* (n 413). The tribunal was composed of Alexis Mourre, Guido Santiago Tawil, Claus von Webeser.
765. *Charanne v. Spain* (n 413) para. 493. This opinion is expressed and supported to exclude general statements, *see* Levashova, *Right of States to Regulate* (n 374) 132.
766. *Ibid.*, para. 517, 539.
767. *Ibid.*, para. 539.
768. *Ibid.*, para. 514.
769. *Ibid.*, para. 395.
770. *Stadtwerke München v. Spain* (n 452). The tribunal was composed of Jeswald Salacuse, Kaj Hobér, Zachary Douglas QC.
771. *Ibid.*, para. 282.
772. *Ibid.*, para. 126.
773. *Ibid.*, para. 264.
774. Judgment from the Third Chamber of the Supreme Court, of 9 October 2007 (App. 13/2006) (the Court held that owners of facilities under a Special Regime 'are not guaranteed the intangibility of a given benefit or income regime in relation to those obtained in previous years, nor are they guaranteed the indefinite permanence of the formulas used to fix premiums').

contemplated acquisition, and 'adjusted their expectations accordingly'.[775] Neither the regulatory framework nor the FIT scheme could accordingly give rise to expectations of reasonable return or stability.[776] Kaj Hobér issued a dissent, arguing that while the state may adapt its regulatory framework, investors cannot expect 'fundamental and radical changes to the legal and regulatory regime'.[777] In the *Eurus Energy v. Spain* case,[778] the tribunal clearly and expressly applied the detrimental reliance theory and considered all relevant norms that circumvented the expectations but rejected an enforcement model.[779]

The reasoning in *FREIF Eurowind v. Spain* appears less theoretically consistent.[780] The Tribunal said it would step 'into the shoes of FREIF as of October 2011'. Nevertheless, it accepted Spain's reasonable rate of return argument and a benchmark rate of 7%, which came from the legislative framework rather than the advantageous Decree.[781] The tribunal held that given that the Internal Return Rate (IRR) for the wind farms were above the benchmark rate, Spain had not frustrated the expectation of a reasonable return'.[782]

In the case of *Jürgen Wirtgen v. Czech Republic*,[783] the majority decided that 'when subsection 6(1)(b) is read in its entirety, it was clear that the language "amount of revenue stays unchanged" (...) was not an absolute guarantee of revenues to solar PV plants'.[784] In the same way, the tribunal in the four non-consolidated cases estimated that the clause could not be read in isolation and that 'Article 6(1)(b) refers to the FiT and buy-out prices. It does not provide an abstract guarantee of revenues,[785] so that no assurance was ever given by the Respondent that the support system from which the Claimant benefitted would never change'.[786] This interpretation of the

775. *Stadtwerke München v. Spain* (n 452) para. 278, para. 277 (After noting that the amendments did not violate Art. 30 of the 1997 Electricity Law, the Supreme Court dismissed this argument, stating: 'Companies that freely decide to enter a market such as electricity generation under the special regime, knowing that is largely dependent on the setting of economic incentives by public authorities, are or should be aware that they may be modified within legal guidelines, by those same authorities').
776. *Stadtwerke München v. Spain* (n 452) para. 308; *See also OperaFund Eco-Invest SICAV PLC and Schwab Holding AG v. Kingdom of Spain*, ICSID Case No. ARB/15/36, Dissenting Opinion by Philippe Sands on Liability and Quantum, 13 August 2019, para. 44.
777. *Stadtwerke München v. Spain* (n 452), Dissenting opinion by Professor Kaj Hobér, para. 9.
778. *Eurus Energy Holdings Corporation v. Kingdom of Spain*, ICSID Case No. ARB/16/4, Decision on Jurisdiction and Liability (17 March 2021). The tribunal was composed of James Crawford, Oscar Garibaldi, Andrea Giardina.
779. *Ibid.*, para. 319 (It held that no specific commitments 'could be made under a regulatory framework, even though the Claimant had LE that subsidies would be continued in some substantial form, but not that the subsidies regime of RD 661/2007 would be maintained as such for the life of the investment').
780. *FREIF v. Spain* (n 77). The tribunal was composed of Douglas Jones, Kaj Hobér, Thomas Clay.
781. *Ibid.*, para. 544.
782. *Ibid.*, para. 570.
783. *Jürgen Wirtgen v. Czech Republic* (n 434). The tribunal was composed of Gabrielle Kaufmann-Kohler, Gary Born (dissent), Peter Tomka.
784. *Jürgen Wirtgen v. Czech Republic* (n 434) para. 367.
785. *Europe Nova*, para. 549.
786. *Ibid.*, para. 585.

Regulation echoes the findings of the Czech May 2012 Constitutional Court Judgment.[787] Gary Born dissented vigorously. He opined that the majority decision was 'ignoring or rewriting' the Czech legislation[788] and that, read in its 'plain language',[789] the text of section 6 was unequivocal and provided minimum FiT for electricity produced by eligible plants. To him, domestic decisions of the Constitutional Court do not have weight when the tribunal has the independent mandate to apply the treaty under international law.[790]

In sum, these tribunals assert that LE capable of being detrimentally relied upon arises solely from direct commitments made to specific investors, disregarding the efficacy of regulatory measures directed at investor groups. In *Charanne v. Spain* and *Stadtwerke München v. Spain*, the tribunals underscore their reluctance to construe regulatory incentives as specific commitments, emphasising the sovereign right of states to regulate. They underscore the significance of proportionality assessments and advocate for a meticulous due diligence process by investors. Most tribunals adopting the detrimental reliance position considered that the legislative framework can create LE, as shown below.

2 Legislative Frameworks May Give Rise to Reasonable Return Expectations

According to a second, more balanced branch of detrimental reliance, a specific commitment may arise from the legislative framework. However, such commitment does not stem from narrower decrees, oral or written promises but from the hierarchically superior law. Accordingly, tribunals assessed what the original Energy Law 54/1997 promised, namely 'a reasonable return', and not the fixed prices promised under the 2007 Royal Decree. For these tribunals, the contested measures did not frustrate the investor's LE as long as its return remained above the 'reasonable return' rate. These tribunals adopted a fact-minded approach. Pernicious in this factual, detrimental approach is to move the battle of merits to the quantum phase. Deciding quantum is a 'very complex and difficult task'[791] of monetary compensation, especially when based on a concept of 'reasonable return'.[792]

In this tide of awards, the investor was found to be entitled to 'a reasonable return'. Illustrating the detrimental theory, these tribunals held that the Claimant could only legitimately expect the reasonable return rate stipulated by Eenrgy Law 54/1997.[793] Tribunals found that Spain must award damages for any difference

787. May 2012 Constitutional Court Judgment, Ref. No. Pl. ÚS 17/11, para. 68.
788. *Jürgen Wirtgen v. Czech Republic*, Dissenting opinion (n 434) para. 110.
789. *Ibid.*, para. 18.
790. *Ibid.*, para. 64.
791. *Infracapital FI S.a.r.l. and Infracapital Solar B.V. v. Spain*, Award, para. 103.
792. Balcerzak, *Renewable Energy Arbitration* (n 220) 428-436 (for a summary of compensation results in the Spanish case law, finding that DCF is the most common method used to calculate damages), 445.
793. *RREEF v. Spain* (n 413) para. 522; *BayWa r.e. v. Spain* (n 639) paras 589-590; *The PV Investors v. Spain* (n 413) para. 647 ('The guarantee provided by Spain in the 1997 Electricity Law (the

between the reasonable rate of return (7%) and the IRR of the investor. There was, however, dissensus between tribunals considering that the New Regulatory Regime was reasonable and others considering it arbitrary.

This line of reasoning is best reflected in *BayWa r.e. v. Spain*.[794] In a similar holding to the *Blusun v. Italy* case – also chaired by James Crawford, the tribunal held in deference to a state's regulatory margin that:

> The stream cannot rise higher than its source or commit the state to more than the legislative framework allows. A requirement that the remuneration system be such as to allow recipients 'to achieve reasonable profitability rates with reference to the cost of money on capital markets' is general in its terms, but it is perfectly intelligible and imposes some limits on what can be done.[795]

In consequence, 'the only legitimate expectation the Claimants could have had was that of a "reasonable return" in terms of Law 54/1997.[796] Applying the principle of proportionality,[797] it found that the regime of RD 661/2007 did not create LE, also because it (a) was not in force when all the investments were made by the Claimants, (b) was not the subject of a stabilisation regime, and (c) was subordinate to Law 54/1997.[798] Again, here the investment timing was crucial to assess the LE of the investor. To the tribunal, the reasonable rate of return was secured even after the contested measures, but Spain's conduct created an "excessive" burden inconsistent with the principle of stability in Article 10.1 of the ECT'.[799]

The majority in the *PV Investors v. Spain*,[800] presided over by Gabrielle Kaufman-Kohler, proposed the concept of 'reasonable profitability', deriving from the 1997 Law.[801] In the majority's view, the principle of reasonable return serves as the limit of ECT-compliant regulatory changes. If changes cross the '"reasonable return line", that is, if they deprive investors of a reasonable return, the State conduct transgresses the standards contained in Article 10(1) of the ECT',[802] even when the state's New Regulatory Regime offered sufficient justifications deemed reasonable and non-arbitrary.[803] Acknowledging 'the State's concern about the cost of electricity and the

---

"reasonable return" or "reasonable profitability") is economic in nature. This being so, the Tribunal cannot verify whether or not such guarantee was observed without considering the economic impact of the Disputed Measures on the Claimants' investment. Only once it has ascertained such impact will the Tribunal be able to determine whether or not there is a breach of the Treaty.'); *Cavalum v. Spain* (n 585) para. 642; *Hydro Energy v. Spain* (n 422) para. 770.

794. *BayWa r.e. v. Spain* (n 639). The tribunal was composed of James Crawford, Horacio Grigera Naón, Loretta Malintoppi.
795. *Ibid.*, para. 473.
796. *Ibid.*, para. 688.
797. *Ibid.*, para. 493 ('the Tribunal agrees that there was no contractual right or legitimate expectation to an unchanging subsidy, and it agrees that (subject to considerations of proportionality) Article 10.1 did not preclude new regulations from having an immediate effect').
798. *Ibid.*, para. 498.
799. *Ibid.*, para. 496.
800. The *PV Investors v. Spain* (n 413). The tribunal was composed of Gabrielle Kaufmann-Kohler, Charles Brower, Bernardo Sepulveda-Amor.
801. *Ibid.*, para. 638.
802. *Ibid.*
803. *Ibid.*, para. 625.

competitiveness with other means of production of energy',[804] it found that the investors were still detrimentally affected and owed compensation for their loss under the reasonable benchmark. This is a perfect example of detrimental reliance theory. The majority in *Sevilla Beheer B.V. v. Spain*[805] held the same in respect of the conditions set by Law 54/1997.[806] It adopted a similar decision as in *PV Investors*, namely that reasonable profitability has been guaranteed to the investors under Law 54/1997, and the Claimants could legitimately expect to receive a reasonable rate of return.[807]

In a similar fashion, the tribunal in *RREEF v. Spain*[808] held that the Claimants had no legitimate expectation that the regime provided for would remain *unchanged* throughout the term of the investment.[809] However, they decided that the investor had a right to a 'general regime guaranteeing the essential advantages they could reasonably expect when they made their investments'[810] and to get 'a reasonable return on their investments'.[811] The tribunal found that the modifications to the applicable legal regime were neither reasonable nor equitable.[812] Neither did Spain pass the proportionality test, according to the tribunal.[813] The tribunal in *Hydro Energy v. Spain*[814] conducted a balancing exercise like the *RREEF* tribunal. Accordingly, there was no stabilisation clause in the Decree, but the changes to general legislation had exceeded the acceptable 'margin of change in the exercise of the host State's normal regulatory power in pursuance of a public interest'[815] because they breached the investor's expectations to a reasonable rate of return.[816] In *Cavalum SGPS v. Spain*,[817] the tribunal found liability but did not award any damages. For the majority, a reasonable return was the only expectation an investor could legitimately have forged.[818]

In *Infracapital v. Spain*,[819] the majority of the tribunal insisted on the principle of state sovereignty applicable in the bilateral relation between the state and the

804. *Ibid.*, para. 618.
805. *Sevilla Beheer v. Spain* (n 76). The tribunal was composed of Raëd Fathallah, Peter Cameron (dissent), Attila Tanzi.
806. *Ibid.*, para. 876.
807. *Ibid.*, para. 901.
808. *RREEF v. Spain* (n 413). The tribunal was composed of Alain Pellet, Robert Volterra, Pedro Nikken.
809. *Ibid.*, para. 379.
810. *Ibid.*, para. 322.
811. *Ibid.*, para. 399.
812. *Ibid.*
813. *Ibid.*, para. 460.
814. *Hydro Energy v. Spain* (n 422). The tribunal was composed of Collins Mapesbury, Peter Rees, Rolf Knieper.
815. *Ibid.*, para. 676.
816. *Ibid.*, para. 770.
817. *Cavalum v. Spain* (n 585). The tribunal was composed of Lord Lawrence Collins of Mapesbury, David Haigh, Daniel Bethlehem.
818. *Ibid.*, para. 626.
819. *Infracapital F1 S.à r.l. and Infracapital Solar B.V. v. Kingdom of Spain*, ICSID Case No. ARB/16/18, Decision on Jurisdiction, Liability and Directions on Quantum (13 September 2021). The tribunal was composed of Eduardo Siqueiros, Peter Cameron (dissent), Luis González García.

investor.[820] For the tribunal, Respondent breached Article 10(1) only to the extent that the remuneration of each of the plants failed to ensure payment to Claimants of a reasonable rate of return on their investment during the lifetime of Claimants' PV Plants. In *SunReserve Holdings v. Italy*,[821] although the investors acquired the plants prior to confirmation of specific remuneration,[822] the unanimous tribunal found 'an 8% reduction in incentive tariffs [not] to result in an unfair remuneration for any of Claimants' power plants'[823] as well as that 'the remodulation of the incentive tariff regime did not sufficiently harm the investor'.[824]

In other cases, the assessment of legitimate expectations was directly linked to questions of investment timing, foreseeability of regulatory changes and due diligence.

In *Blusun SA v. Italy*,[825] the tribunal noted that LE could not arise before the investment unquestionably existed and relied on specific commitments: 'Circumstances change, and in the absence of specific commitments, the risk of change is for entrepreneurs to assess and assume.'[826] Applying this standard, the tribunal found that Italy had made no such special commitment to the investors concerning the incentive scheme.[827] In the words of the tribunal in *CEF Energia*, the investment in *Blusun* was in the 'preliminary stage of its attempts to invest in the Italian photovoltaic Market'.[828] In sum, the tribunal opined that there was no sufficient causal link between the regulatory acts of the States and the damage of the failed investment project, illustrating a detrimental reliance analysis.

In *Eskosol S.P.A. v. Italy*,[829] Eskosol was established in Puglia in 2010,[830] and the tribunal stated that the investor could not derive LE from the regulatory framework *before* the plants qualified for the support scheme.[831] Indeed, Eskosol's plant had not entered into operation by the time the measures changed.[832] Therefore, 'whether the ECT requires a State, after declaring that it will provide certain "rights" to certain intended beneficiaries upon their fulfilment of certain conditions' was considered

820. *Ibid.*, para. 366 (The tribunal said itself 'mindful of the significant limitation that a "stability" obligation would impose on the host state's sovereign legislative powers' and construed the commitment not as sufficiently specific, i.e., not addressed directly to the investor).
821. *SunReserve v. Italy* (n 416). The tribunal was composed of Albert Jan van den Berg, Klaus Sachs, Andrea Giardina.
822. *Ibid.*, para. 792.
823. *Ibid.*, para. 852 and para. 692.
824. *Ibid.*, para. 867.
825. *Blusun v. Italy* (n 603). The tribunal was composed of James Crawford, Stanimir Alexandrov, Pierre-Marie Dupuy.
826. *Ibid.*, para. 373.
827. *Ibid.*, para. 374, 386 ('[the investment] ran a significant risk of incurring legal or administrative difficulties, even if these could be (and were) overcome. Its success was by no means certain').
828. *CEF v. Italy* (n 639) para. 220.
829. *Eskosol v. Italy* (n 658). The tribunal was composed of Jean Kalicki, Guido Santiago Tawil, Brigitte Stern.
830. *Ibid.*, para. 121.
831. *Ibid.*, para. 449.
832. *Ibid.*, para. 440 ('In this case, however, there is no need for the Tribunal to render an abstract pronouncement on the contours of the legitimate expectations doctrine. That is because, by its terms, Conto Energia III did not purport to promise benefits with respect to any PV power plant unless or until that plant actually entered into operation').

nothing more than a hypothetical question that the tribunal did not need resolve.[833] Failing to invest in time was the decisive factor leading the tribunal to reject the investor's reliance claim. The investor's reliance was void of any legitimacy.

In *Belenergia S.A. v. Italy,*[834] the investments took place from September 2011 to December 2013. The main question of the tribunal was thus whether a 'prudent' investor would believe in the stability of the legal framework when incentives were subject to reductions.[835] They did not find in favour of the investor, pointing out the late stage of investment and several clauses of the GSE conventions which purport to future 'potential changes and updates'.[836] In the non-consolidated cases of *Voltaic Network,*[837] *W.A Europe Nova,*[838] *I.C.W,*[839] and *Photovoltaic Knopf v. Czech Republic,*[840] the tribunals held that the words 'the amount of revenue stays unchanged' could not be read 'in isolation from the remainder of the clause'. The tribunal considered that no stabilisation commitment was made[841] and that it was clear prior to the investment that part of the incentive scheme would be abolished.[842] In *Antaris v. Czech Republic,*[843] the Tribunal held that there is no breach of the FET standard if changes 'do not exceed the exercise of the host State's normal regulatory power in the pursuance of a public interest and do not modify the regulatory framework relied upon by the investor at the time of its investment outside the acceptable margin of change'.[844]

In sum, the second approach considers the hierarchy of norms prior to the detrimental consequences of the frustrating measure on the investor, emphasising the 'reasonable return' promised under legislative frameworks. It is best summarised in Crawford's sentence that 'the stream cannot rise higher than its source or commit the state to more than the legislative framework allows'.[845] Due diligence is also an important factor, as the investor is not considered a 'passive dummy'.[846] These features

833. *Ibid.*, para. 445.
834. *Belenergia S.A v. Italian Republic,* ICSID Case No. ARB/15/40, Award, 6 August 2019. The tribunal was composed of Yves Derains, Beranrd Hanotiau, Jose Carlos Fernandez Rozas.
835. *Ibid.*, paras 594, 595.
836. *Ibid.*, para. 581.
837. *Voltaic Network v. Czech Republic,* PCA Case No. 2014-20, Award, 15 May 2019.
838. *WA Investments-Europa Nova Limited v. Czech Republic,* PCA Case No. 2014-19, Award, 15 May 2019.
839. *I.C.W. Europe Investments Limited v. Czech Republic,* PCA Case No. 2014-22, Award, 15 May 2019.
840. *Photovoltaik Knopf Betriebs-GmbH v. Czech Republic,* PCA Case Np. 2014-21, Award, 15 May 2019.
841. *Ibid.*, para. 486.
842. *Ibid.*, para. 479.
843. *Antaris v. Czech Republic* (n 76). The tribunal was composed of Collins of Mapesbury, Gary Born (dissent), Peter Tomka.
844. *Antaris v. Czech Republic* (n 76) paras 360, 367.
845. *BayWa r.e. v. Spain* (n 639) para. 473.
846. Jeswald Salacuse, *The Law of Investment Treaties* (OUP 2021 Third Edition), 308 ('An evaluation of expectations also requires an examination of the role that the investor played in forming them. A reasonable investor is not a passive dummy. A determination of whether an investor's expectations are reasonable and legitimate requires a tribunal to inquire into the process by which such expectations have been formed. The acquisition by an investor of reasonable and legitimate expectations concerning an investment opportunity require investors to engage in a reasonable due diligence process; that is, a careful investigation of such

indicate a detrimental reliance theory of LE. Under this theory, the investor is equally involved in forming the expectations, while under the former, the state's intent and binding obligations create objective expectations.

Despite these differences, the time of the investment and the foreseeability of the measure bear more weight than theoretical divides. The rejection of claims in *Charanne v. Spain*, *Belenergia v. Italy*, *Blusun v. Italy*, *SolEs v. Spain*, *Antin v. Spain*, *Antaris v. Czech Republic*, *Jürgen Wirtgen v. Czech Republic*, and *Isolux v. Spain*, and partially in *CEF v. Italy* were all based on sets of facts concerning the time of investment and the relative legitimacy of expectations the investor might have. This calls for a further refined analysis of the convergence of arbitral tribunals on the application of LE in the next section.

D RELATIVE CONVERGENCE IN THE APPLICATION OF LEGITIMATE EXPECTATIONS

While questions of theory may be vehemently disputed, in practice, rulings seem more consensus-based than first impressions suggest. This phenomenon primarily arises from the necessity of conducting a fact-specific inquiry, which is inherent to the FET and LE analysis. The major point of convergence among tribunals concerns the 'legitimacy' of expectations, in particular concerning the investment timing and foreseeability of the frustrating measure.

Arbitrators generally agree that not all investments may be compensated for reasonable policy change and that not all statements may amount to a unilateral state commitment. Similarly, most tribunals require the investor to undertake a due diligence analysis.[847] However, such due diligence commonly has no bearing on the finding of liability for breach of LE. Only in one case, in a pure detrimental reliance approach, did the tribunal consider that the lack of due diligence barred the investor from claiming LE.[848] Rather than due diligence, tribunals look at whether a particular investor could have relied on the favourable measure.

---

opportunity that prudent and experienced investor could have undertaken', citing *Stadtwerke München v. Spain* (n 452) para. 264).

847. Only *Eiser*, *9REN*, *BayWa* and *PV Investors* did not address the due diligence of energy investors in the highly regulated sector of Spain's energy, *see* Balcerzak, *Renewable Energy Arbitration* (n 220) 324, 325. ('Thus, in general, the Spanish saga cases recognize the fact of legal due diligence as relevant to forming the content of legitimate expectations. (...) It is closely related to an analysis of whether, when making the investments, investors have relied upon the expectations which they subsequently seek to protect in arbitration. As recently noted in the context of RE cases, "in order to grant a legitimate expectation protection based on a stability provision under the domestic legislation, tribunals seek additional requirements and elaborate more on the reliance aspect".').

848. *Stadtwerke München v. Spain* (n 452) para. 308.

1 Relative Convergence on the Investment's Timing and the Legitimacy of Expectations

The timing of investments has emerged as a crucial factor in the fact-intensive approach adopted by various arbitral tribunals. In eight cases, the arbitral tribunal did not find liability of the state based on a breach of LE because the investor invested at a time when uncertainty prevailed over predictability with little dissent.[849]

The most interesting case on this point is perhaps *Isolux*. In *Isolux Netherlands B.V. v. Spain*,[850] the deciding factor was the time of the investment. The tribunal rejected the claim of LE because, at the time of the investment, the regulatory regime had already been largely modified so that the investor could not be entitled to LE.[851] For the majority,[852] there had been no breach of the FET standard since the investment was made in October 2012,[853] after RDL 1/2012 and Law 15/2012. These laws were considered to introduce substantial changes sufficient for a reasonable investor *not* to expect the stability of the regulatory framework.[854] The tribunal considered the fact that the Spanish Supreme Court had clearly stated in 2009 that there could be no guarantee that the regulatory regime was not going to change in the near future, and therefore drew the conclusion that an informed investor could not ignore this 'wind of change'.[855] To the majority, there had been no breach of the FET standard because the investment was made in October 2012.[856] The legislature passed RDL 1/2012 and Law 15/2012 by that time. In his dissent, Guido Tawil agreed that a late investment would deny LE[857] because investors bear their own business risks. He only disputed the factual time of the investment. He considered that the investment was made on 29 June 2012 - before the laws passed - instead of 29 October 2012. Thus, the dissenting arbitrator agreed that if regulatory changes are predictable at the time of the investment, the claimant would be

849. *Isolux v. Spain* (n 466) paras 792-800.
850. *Isolux v. Spain* (n 466). The tribunal was composed of Yves Derains, Guido Santiago, Claus Von Wobeser.
851. *Ibid.* (Investment in October 2012).
852. President Yves Derains and co-arbitrator Claus von Wobeser.
853. *Isolux v. Spain* (n 466) paras 141, 147.
854. *Ibid.*, paras 784-787.
855. *Cube Infrastructure v. Spain* (n 402) para. 330.
856. *Isolux v. Spain* (n 466) paras 141, 147.
857. *Isolux Infrastructure Netherlands B.V. v. Kingdom of Spain*, SCC Case No. V2013/153, Dissenting opinion of Arbitrators Guido Santiago Tawil, 6 July 2016, para. 5 ('Second, I do not consider that the conclusion reached by the majority vote that the date to be taken as the reference date for determining whether legitimate expectations were created in the present case should be 29 October 2012 is correct. In my view, the relevant date for that purpose was 29 June 2012, i.e., the day on which Claimant entered into (and the Investment Agreement became effective).3 The existence of suspensive conditions in the Investment Agreement or the possibility that Claimant could retract its investment decision without penalty until 29 October 2012 are not compelling reasons for the purpose of determining the point in time from which legitimate expectations could have arisen. The date of 29 October 2012 might be a valid cut-off date in relation to possible shareholder actions or claims, but it is of no similar relevance vis-à-vis the host State of the investment and in respect of whose conduct that date must be assessed in order to determine whether or not legitimate expectations were created' (author's translation, original in Annex No. 2)).

precluded from invoking LE.[858] This finding holds significant importance. It illustrates a convergence of the concepts of foreseeability and LE.

As stated above, in *Eskosol v. Italy*,[859] because the Eskosol facilities did not qualify for the support scheme before it was abrogated,[860] the tribunal found that the investor could not derive LE from the regulatory framework.[861] The same reasoning of timing applied. What is of interest is that arbitrator Guido Tawil *did not* issue a dissenting opinion, demonstrating that the timing can constitute a consensual cut-off condition to hold LE. Indeed, Eskosol's plant had not entered into operation by the time of changing measures.[862] Therefore, the tribunal considered itself faced only with a hypothetical question that does not need to be resolved.[863] The absence of a dissenting opinion suggests a consensus on the timing as a condition of LE.

However, some dissenting viewpoints deviate from the prevailing consensus. They view the relationship between a state and the investor from a commercial, contractual point of view, ultimately dismissing the reliance criteria to only regard the state's intent. For instance, Gary Born in his dissenting opinions considers that the timing of the investment (and incidentally due diligence) are inconsequential concepts. Similarly, the majority in *Watkins* failed to analyse the issue of the date of the investment and its eventual effect on the asserted LE,[864] even though it acknowledged that a reasonable investor should have been more cautious.[865]

2 Relative Convergence on Regulatory Risks and the Foreseeability of the Frustrating Measure

Requiring investors to perform due diligence hides a tricky question of law. Can regulatory changes foreseeable at the investment time breach LE? The foreseeability of the challenged regulatory measures is likely to be an issue in fossil phase out cases in light of state obligations under international climate law.[866]

858. *Ibid.*, para. 6 ('My main disagreement with the majority's decision, however, lies in the way in which the factual circumstances were assessed in order to determine the "foreseeability" of the measures adopted by the Kingdom of Spain. In other words, whether the change of legal regime in Spain after the investment was made was foreseeable for the Claimant, a circumstance which – if so – would prevent it from invoking legitimate expectations as a basis for its claim').
859. *Eskosol v. Italy* (n 658).
860. *Ibid.*, para. 121.
861. *Ibid.*, para. 449.
862. *Ibid.*, para. 440 'In this case, however, there is no need for the Tribunal to render an abstract pronouncement on the contours of the legitimate expectations doctrine. That is because, by its terms, Conto Energia III did not purport to promise benefits with respect to any PV power plant unless or until that plant actually entered into operation.'
863. *Ibid.*, para. 445 ('whether the ECT requires a State, after declaring that it will provide certain "rights" to certain intended beneficiaries upon their fulfilment of certain conditions, to uphold that promise or compensate the qualifying beneficiaries for not doing so, even if the State acted in good faith and not arbitrarily in altering its regulatory regime').
864. *Watkins Holdings S.à r.l. and others v. Kingdom of Spain* (ICSID Case No. ARB/15/44, Dissenting Opinion of Hélène Ruiz Fabri, 9 January 2020, para. 13.
865. *Watkins Holdings v. Spain* (n 413) para. 333.
866. Climate Change Counsel, *The ECT* (n 332) 8.

The question of law is whether an investor has any obligation to demonstrate reasonable acts of due diligence. If acts of due diligence are essential, the second question of law is to what degree the legitimacy of expectations depends on the level of due diligence. In *Sevilla Beheer*, the claimant argued that due diligence 'informs an investor's subjective understanding of the regulatory framework' but 'is not determinative'.[867] Rather, an objective assessment of the reasonability of the investor's understanding should be decisive.[868] On the contrary, the Respondent contended that the tribunal needs to consider the 'subjective circumstances of the investor', particularly its due diligence.[869]

Under the detrimental reliance theory, an investor's due diligence extends beyond standard risk assessments conducted for their own benefit. It has implications for a state's right to regulate in the public interest and a broader notion of business responsibilities. Investors are expected to conduct proper due diligence before investing in a host state. Reasonable efforts to collect information about the rules and regulations that are pertinent to the proposed investment characterise a formal due diligence. In some cases, due diligence extends to an investor's duty to assess the possible risks related to the broader economic situation and socio-political background of a host state.[870] The tribunal in *Charanne v. Spain* indicated that a certain level of care is required in such a 'highly regulated [field] as the energy sector, where a preliminary and comprehensive legal framework applicable to the sector analysis is essential to proceed with the investment'.[871] This stand echoes the *Saluka* decision in which LE was understood as an objective standard autonomous from the subjective expectations of an investor. These expectations, according to the tribunal, 'must rise to the level of legitimacy and reasonableness in the light of circumstances'.[872] The question of due diligence and investment time was particularly important in the Czech cases. To the tribunal in *Europe Nova*, 'even if an assurance had been given by the Respondent, the Tribunal concludes that it was not, or would not have been, relied upon by the Claimant at the relevant time'.[873] For the acquisition of LE, the *Antaris* tribunal required a high level of due diligence[874] as follows: 'given the State's regulatory powers,[875] in order to rely on legitimate expectations, the investor should inquire in advance regarding the prospects of a change in the regulatory framework in light of the then prevailing or reasonably to be expected changes in the economic and social

867. *Sevilla Beheer v. Spain* (n 76) para. 719.
868. *Ibid.*
869. *Ibid.*, para. 722.
870. *Saluka v. Czech Republic* (n 77) para. 306. The tribunal provided that the review of the FET standard requires a 'weighing of the Claimant's legitimate and reasonable expectations on the one hand and the Respondent's legitimate regulatory interests on the other'; *see El Paso v. Argentina* (n 41) para. 358 (the tribunal emphasised that 'legitimate expectations cannot be solely the subjective expectations of the investor [...] investor's legitimate expectations must be grounded in reality, experience and context').
871. *Charanne v. Spain* (n 413) para. 507.
872. *Saluka v. Czech Republic* (n 77) para. 304.
873. *Europe Nova v. Czech Republic*, para. 589.
874. *Antaris v. Czech Republic* (n 76) para. 435.
875. *Ibid.*, para. 444.

conditions of the host State'.[876] In the *Jürgen Wirtgen* decision, the investments took place in late 2009, when, according to the *Jürgen Wirtgen and Antaris and Europe Nova* decisions, fundamental changes were starting to take place.[877] The Claimant may, however, be right in positing that 'a Czech Republic's report of November 2009 still indicated the need of attracting investors to achieve the 8% EU target for 2010'.[878]

Under the voluntarist theory, objective regulatory risks, rather than due diligence,[879] primarily influence the legitimacy of expectations. This distinction is prominently illustrated in the case of *Cube*. Concerning PV investments made prior to 2009, the tribunal interpreted Spanish law to substantiate legitimate expectations specifically related to FITs. However, in the context of the claimant's hydro energy investments made in 2011 and 2012, following the implementation of new legislation and 'climate of change',[880] the tribunal narrowed the scope of legitimate expectations to encompass only stability-related considerations.[881] Considering the regulatory risks assumed by the investor and the foreseeability of frustrating measures, the tribunal held that a 'reasonable' approach would be to reduce the difference between the projected cash flows in the Prevailing Scenario and the But For Scenario by 40%.[882] Similarly, in CEF Energia, the tribunal found that two projects could not claim LE because of the late timing of their investment.[883] The tribunal in *Novenergia* confirmed this need to distinguish based on the date of the investment, referring and indirectly agreeing with the *Isolux* award.[884] Similarly, in the *Foresight* award, the tribunal agreed with *Charanne* in stating that 'After the 3 December 2009 judgment, the Majority of the Tribunal considers that a diligent investor might have been in a position to foresee the possibility of regulatory changes altering RD 661/2007.'[885]

---

876. *Ibid.*, para. 360.
877. *Jürgen Wirtgen v. Czech Republic* (n 434) paras 42-52; *Antaris v. Czech Republic* (n 76) para. 395; *Europe Nova*, paras 555 and 602 ('Further still, and as explained at some length above, the Tribunal finds that already at the relevant times (late August/early September 2009 and April 2010) there had been an accumulation of apparent warning signs that ought to have precluded any such expectation on the part of the Claimant and objectively viewed, did preclude the possibility that the Claimant might be said reasonably to have relied on any such alleged assurances').
878. *Antaris v. Czech Republic* (n 76) para. 287.
879. *Jürgen Wirtgen v. Czech Republic*, Dissenting opinion (n 434) para. 99 ('due diligence is not a condition to protection of an investment under international law, whether under the FET standard or otherwise. What is sometimes referred to as an obligation to conduct due diligence is relevant only where particular inquiries would have led an investor to alter its expectations about national law protections. An investor is under no abstract duty to conduct due diligence').
880. *Cube Infrastructure v. Spain* (n 402) para. 356.
881. Balcerzak, *Renewable Energy Arbitration* (n 220) 319.
882. *Cube Infrastructure v. Spain* (n 402) para. 531.
883. I analyse the award again later in Chapter 5.B.2.
884. *Novenergia II v. Spain* (n 413) para. 165 ('In Isolux, again, as the Claimant rightly points out, the arbitral tribunal was faced with an investor that had made investments in October of 2012, i.e. *at a stage when it must have been clear* to the investor that changes were being made to the Special Regime').
885. *Foresight v. Spain* (n 620) para. 374.

Whether tribunals consider subjective due diligence or not, they always take into account the objective circumstances (incl. the regulatory risks) in which the investment was made. This consideration aligns with the ordinary meaning of FET, which cannot be construed as an absolute guarantee but demands rather a 'matter of degree and balancing'.[886] This finding is crucial to integrate ICCL and find its impact on the protected LE of energy investors.

E CONCLUSION

This chapter established that the interpretation of legitimate expectations selected under the Energy Charter Treaty is subject to the theoretical divergences outlined in chapter 2. Nevertheless, the chapter showed that, in practice, arbitral tribunals align on key factual aspects in the *application* of LE. In particular, arbitral tribunals converge on the significance of the time of the investment, the risks assumed by the investor, and the foreseeability of the frustrating measures.

The chapter presents three key findings.

First, NZEID under the ECT mainly concern renewable energy investors affected by the cancellation of favourable incentives. Their expectations can derive from, *inter alia,* oral statements, direct or indirect promises, advertising materials, decrees, laws, or administrative permits, although not all of these unilateral assurances can produce 'legitimate' expectations. Nevertheless, the majority of arbitral tribunals consider that, under ECT's FET provision, regulatory frameworks can create protected LE and that domestic law's content is crucial to determining the scope of LE.

Second, arbitral tribunals adopt different schools of thought to assess LE in NZEID. Detrimental reliance and voluntarist theories of promise help decipher these differences. The study finds that tribunals are equally split between detrimental reliance and voluntarist conceptions of LE. The main points of disagreement among them pertain to the scope of the state's specific commitments and the due diligence investors must demonstrate to hold LE.

Third, the research shows that investment tribunals take into account the facts of the dispute to assess LE. In this regard, the legitimacy of expectations has become the core development of LE, in particular in the energy sector and under the ECT. Despite the divergences, there is an emerging consensus on the time of the investment, the foreseeability of the measure and the consideration of treaties as relevant facts. Similarly, the majority of the case law acknowledges that the regulatory framework may create LE, even if the investor cannot expect that laws and regulations will freeze absent a stabilisation clause.[887] This consensus is paramount for the consideration of ICCL in international investment disputes.

886. *Silver Ridge v. Italy* (n 56) para. 396.
887. *Hydro Energy v. Spain* (n 422) para. 585; *Watkins Holdings v. Spain* (n 413) para. 543; *Glencore v. Colombia* (n 414) para. 1311; In the early decisions, the obligation to provide a stable regulatory framework for investments has been interpreted broadly, placing strict limits on a state's ability to change its laws, *see CMS v. Argentine* (n 536) para. 274.

Overall, the chapter demonstrated that arbitral tribunals are evenly split on the conception of legitimate expectations but converge on key facts that 'make or break' cases. Arbitral tribunals consensually recognise the prominent level of regulation in the energy sector. They recognise that where the factual context of the investment confers guarantees of stability, the state's regulatory framework can amount to a specific commitment. This finding helps answer the research question, as the UN climate regime and EU climate change-related regulations can confer expectations of stability. It also builds the case for ICCL's impact on the convergence points in the application of LE.

The forthcoming chapter thoroughly examines the interconnection of ICCLs with a focus on their impact on investment disputes and the application of energy investors' LE. This in-depth examination is pivotal for a comprehensive response to the research question, synthesising and applying the wealth of knowledge accumulated thus far on LE.

Chapter 4
The Factual Integration of ICCL in Legitimate Expectations

This chapter investigates whether ICCL, as part of international law, could significantly affect legitimate expectations in investment disputes. First, the chapter details the content of ICCL. It then analyses the compatibility with obligations under international investment law. The chapter then finds that ICCL may act as a significant legal fact in assessing legitimate expectations, which may, in certain circumstances, amount to a state's unilateral commitment.

So far, the book focused on the interpretation and application of the FET standard and LE doctrine in NZEID. It demonstrated that, despite the existence of schools of thought, there is an emerging convergence in the application of LE. This chapter turns to the integration of ICCL norms in the adjudication of investment disputes.[888] It assesses *how* climate change norms and net zero objectives can be taken into account in international investment law and how they specifically interact[889] with the legitimate expectations doctrine.

While some researchers claim there is a 'clash' between ICCL and international investment law,[890] the first section of this chapter examines whether this assertion holds legally. It analyses Member States' obligations under the ICCL regime and finds that this assumed legal incompatibility between ICCL and international investment law should be ruled out. It then moves to the integration of climate change norms into the

888. Ben Hamida, 'Droit climatique' (n 171) 84.
889. The word 'interaction' has a broader meaning than conflict. It is adopted from fragmentation studies referring to 'regime interaction', although I deem difficult to speak of a regime of international investment law due to the increasing diversity of international investment agreements.
890. Anja Ipp, 'Regime Interaction in Investment Arbitration: Climate Law, International Investment Law and Arbitration' (*Kluwer Arbitration Blog*, 12 January 2022) http://arbitrationblog.kluwerarbitration.com/2022/01/12/regime-interaction-in-investment-arbitration-climate-law-international-investment-law-and-arbitration/ accessed 15 March 2022.

resolution of FET claims through VCLT's Article 31(3)(c) and as applicable law, which in both cases is faced with many hurdles. Finally, and based on the previously analysed case law, I assess whether and to what extent ICCL can act as a legal fact and impact standards of protection and LE.

The chapter offers an in-depth understanding of the legal interaction between ICCL and the legitimate expectations of energy investors. Section A searches for binding provisions from ICCL relevant to investment disputes; section B explores whether they conflict or interact with substantive treatment obligations under international investment law; and section C analyses their theoretical impact as facts in the assessment of legitimate expectations.

A RELEVANCE OF ICCL IN THE RESOLUTION OF INVESTMENT DISPUTES

As demonstrated in the preceding chapters, net zero policies lead to investment arbitration disputes.[891] Yet, investors and states rarely raise ICCL arguments in investment disputes.[892] The nexus between ICCL and investment law is often loosely drawn in renewable cases in the factual background to the disputes.[893] Similarly, provisions from the Kyoto Protocol occasionally appear as part of a factual background.[894] This lack of legal consideration is unsatisfactory. In a time when states withdraw from the ECT based on climate change concerns, in-depth research on the legal interaction between international investment law and ICCL becomes critical.[895] Even though ICCL-related arguments will likely grow in fossil fuel-related investment disputes,[896] scholarly work is required to understand how ICCL norms can or cannot be integrated into the resolution of investment disputes.[897] In particular, there are two

891. *See* Chapter 1.C; on resource nationalism leading to disputes *see, e.g.*, Lorenzo Cotula, '(Dis)Integration in Global Resource Governance: Extractivism, Human Rights, and Investment Treaties' (2020) 23 Journal of International Economic Law 2 431, 439 https://doi.org/10.1093/jiel/jgaa003.
892. Mala Sharma, 'Integrating, Reconciling, and Prioritising Climate Aspirations in Investor-State Arbitration for a Sustainable Future: The Role of Different Players' (2022) 23 JWIT 5-6 746 https://doi.org/10.1163/22119000-12340269.
893. *See* Annex 1.
894. *See* Chapter 2(E).
895. IISD, *Energy Charter Treaty Withdrawal Announcements Reflect Reform Outcome is Insufficient for Climate Ambition* (IISD 7 November 2022) accessible at https://www.iisd.org/articles/statement/energy-charter-treaty-withdrawal-announcements accessed 15 November 2022.
896. In *RWE v. The Netherlands* (n 153), Respondent exhaustively presents the role of ICCL in the coal ban measure as part of the Respondent's Counter-Memorial, 5 September 2023.
897. Dr Arman Sarvarian proposes a few ways to integrate the Paris Agreement, *see* Sarvarian, 'Invoking the Paris Agreement' (n 153) 426-442 (displaying the breadth of cases in which Claimants or Respondents could invoke the Paris Agreement (p. 437 'In the absence of an environmental exemption clause and depending upon the applicable law, there could be greater scope for investors to argue beyond standards of arbitrariness towards legitimate expectations of a stable regulatory framework, precluding the imposition of new and stricter environmental standards'), however, contrary to Sarvarian's contention, the Paris Agreement faces many hurdles to act as applicable law; indeed, arbitral tribunals are reluctant, as admitted by the author, to consider laws other than investment law as applicable, in particular under old-generation treaties (p. 427 'This places especial importance on the exact language adopted

theoretical questions to be answered. Are ICCL and international investment law *incompatible*? If not, can ICCL play any role in the adjudication of investment disputes?

The first question of 'incompatibility' questions whether investment treaties and climate change objectives are simply not contradictory. In blunt terms, some consider that IIAs should be terminated to achieve climate change objectives. This issue reflects the broader problem of conflict between legitimate expectations and the urgency of climate legislation.[898] A number of NGOs, some scholars, and a few states have adopted this theory.[899] For example, the IPCC and climate change committees mention investment treaties as 'impediments' to climate action.[900] This type of scholarship and argument is policy-oriented rather than legal doctrinal.[901] From a legal perspective, ICCL and international investment law do not stand in contradiction. According to the traditional definition of 'incompatibility' in international law, a conflict between two norms arises only where a party to two treaties 'cannot simultaneously comply with its obligations under both treaties'.[902] This, I find, is not the case between investment and climate change obligations. This section finds that there is no *incompatibility* between ICCL and international investment law and suggests that standards under international investment law may *contribute to the enforcement* of ICCL.

The second question is likewise little researched.[903] It pertains to the existence of a legal *interaction* between standards of protection, such as FET, and ICCL norms and

---

in reforms to enable disputing parties to invoke the Paris Agreement not as background facts (the experience hitherto) but as applicable law').

898. Fergus Green, 'Legal Transition Without Legitimate Expectations' (2020) 28 The Journal of Political Philosophy 4 397, 397 https://doi.org/10.1111/jopp.12231; The liberal-egalitarian literature on the subject is led by Alexander Brown, 'A Theory of Legitimate Expectations' (2017) 25 Journal of Political Philosophy 435 https://doi.org/10.1111/jopp.12135; *see also* Matt Matravers, 'Legitimate Expectations in Theory, Practice, and Punishment' (2017) 4 Moral Philosophy and Politics 307 https://doi.org/10.1515/mopp-2017-0017; Lukas Meyer and Pranay Sanklecha, 'Individual Expectations and Climate Justice' (2011) 33 Analyse und Kritik 449.

899. OECD, *Investment Treaties and Climate Change* (n 127) (the compilation compiles critical statements from NGOs and scholars).

900. IPCC, *Climate Change 2022 Mitigation of Climate Change* (Report, 2022) Chapter 14 p. 81 ('a great deal of this is still concerned with promoting further development of fossil fuels. One aspect of this is the development of international legal norms. Many bilateral and multilateral agreements, including the 1994 Energy Charter Treaty, include provisions for using a system of investor-state dispute settlement (ISDS) designed to protect the interests of investors in energy projects from national policies that could lead their assets to be stranded', the report restates the literature and referred to the studies of Kate Miles, Tienhaara and Bos and Gupta).

901. Nathan Lobel and Matteo Fermeglia, 'Investment Protection and Unburnable Carbon: Competing Commitments in International Investment and Climate Governance' (2018) 4 Diritto Del Commercio Internazionale 945.

902. Wilfred Jenks, 'The Conflict of Law-Making Treaties' (1953) 30 BYIL 401, 426.

903. As outlined in the introduction, some authors emphasise the legitimacy challenges of investment arbitration and encourage arbitral tribunals to consider wider consequences of their ruling on social and environmental concerns. The approach advocates for greater deference of arbitral tribunals to defence arguments of the Respondent state on the merits – and counterclaims. The intention is to induce environmental or social rationale in the reasoning of arbitrators faced with a dispute involving climate interests. The issue with this approach is twofold. First, arbitral tribunals are not necessarily bound by environmental principles or laws. Second, the net zero energy transition is not a one-way street. A greater regulatory freedom afforded to States does not necessarily favour the achievement of climate change goals. A larger

statements.[904] In other words, do international treaties, other than IIAs, have a role in investment arbitration? To what extent do these treaties apply – as applicable law, legal fact or solely as background to a dispute? The section explores these normative conflicts between ICCL and FET. It rules out a wholly general systemic integration under VCLT's Article 31 (3) (c). Rather, it argues that ICCL can integrate the assessment of FET and LE as a legal fact.

To research these questions, I start by presenting states' obligations under ICCL. I focus primarily on the UN regime because it is common to all state members of the UNFCCC. I then turn to domestic rulings on climate change and NDCs, as they can bind the state to achieve a certain climate target and adopt net zero measures.[905] To clarify, there are three main states' obligations under ICCL: (1) binding provisions under the UNFCCC, (2) the publication of NDCs, and (3) binding interpretations of climate change obligations by domestic courts.[906] They all have the potential to impact the adjudication of NZEID and influence foreign investors' LE.

1 UN Climate Change Regime Anchored in General Rules of International Law

To start with the obvious, let us recall that international climate change treaties under the UNFCCC are firmly anchored in the general rules of international law, such as state sovereignty, treaty-making, interpretation, and state responsibility.[907] Nevertheless, scholars have frequently questioned whether ICCL is binding upon states.[908] The question is not whether the instrument (a treaty) is binding but the substance of the treaty, which can be phrased in such a way that it does not create an enforceable obligation (non-normative statements, aspirations, hortatory language).[909] The reality

regulatory freedom may affect the predictability and stability of norms necessary to induce investments in the clean energy sector. As said above, international investment law can both positively and negatively impact climate change-related goals, depending on which energy sector is targeted.

904. Martin Jarrett, 'Implementing the Energy Transition in the Face of Investment Protection Standards' in Cameron et al., *The Global Energy Transition* (n 14) 217, 226-229; for a novel theory of FET in environmental cases based on a PhD thesis *see* Ying Zhu, 'Fair and Equitable Treatment of Foreign Investors in an Era of Sustainable Development' (2018) 58 Nat Resources J 319, 353-362.
905. I exclude regional legislation (EU regulations, such as EU Fit for 55) as these may widely vary from state to state; the purpose here is to give an overview of norms susceptible to interact with substantive obligations in investment disputes.
906. To answer these questions, one must establish whether treaties adopted under the Framework Convention amount to general commitments, authoritative or political statements. Similarly, the legal value of Nationally Determined Contributions (NDCs), domestic administrative decisions and Net Zero pledges must be determined. The sections below concisely present binding and non-binding provisions under international climate change law and their legal value in the adjudication of NZEID.
907. *Ibid.*, 355.
908. Bodansky, *Climate Change Law* (n 11) 23 (during the Paris Agreement negotiations, a famous political disagreement concerned the use of the imperative and mandatory 'shall' over the hortatory or advisory 'should'. The diplomatic 'should' have won in many instances).
909. *Ibid.*

is that only a few treaty provisions are binding, even though they are critical. Each ICCL provision must thus be analysed to assess whether it is binding or non-binding.[910]

Generally, international agreements on climate change vary in the latitude of commitments they impose on participating parties. A treaty may adopt a top-down approach, setting and enforcing individual obligations, rules, and measures, or a bottom-up approach, which allows each state party to define their commitments towards a consensually agreed goal.[911] The UN climate change regime presents a mixture of top-down and bottom-up obligations. This results from diverging ambitions on key climate goals.[912] Proponents of the top-down approach argue that climate change constitutes a classic collective challenge, which requires collectively negotiated emissions targets for individual states.[913] Advocates of a bottom-up mechanism argue that climate change 'engages virtually every aspect of domestic policies' and thus calls for a facilitative approach whereby international pledges reflect domestic ambitions and policies.[914] In general, bottom-up treaties allow greater participation due to their flexibility, but this comes at the cost of ambition and efficiency.[915] The Kyoto Protocol is an example of a top-down treaty, while the Paris Agreement embodies the success of a bottom-up approach. Relevant[916] climate provisions are mainly situated in the UNFCCC, Kyoto Protocol, Paris Climate Agreement, Paris Rulebook, and the Glasgow Pact.[917] I explore each below.

2 1992 Framework Convention on Climate Change: Crafting the Regime

Negotiated at the Rio Earth Summit in 1992, the UNFCCC came into force on 21 March 1994 and currently has 197 parties.[918] The UNFCCC was the first instrument to devise the critical elements of ICCL: its purpose, means, and legal mechanism. The UNFCCC lies between a framework and a substantive treaty – only some of its provisions have

910. Lavanya Rajamani, 'The Paris Agreement: Interplay Between Hard, Soft and Non-obligations' (2016) 28(2) Journal of Environmental Law 337 https://doi.org/10.1093/jel/eqw015; Jacob Werksman, 'International Legal Character of the Paris Agreement' (Notes for the third 2016 'Environmental Law Brodies Lecture', University of Edinburgh, 9 February 2016).
911. Bodansky, *Climate Change Law* (n 11) 22.
912. It can be argued that top-down commitments have been more difficult to negotiate due to the domestic implications of multilaterally negotiated CO_2 reduction targets.
913. William Hare and others, 'The Architecture of the Global Climate Regime: A Top-Down Perspective' (2010) 10 Climate Policy 6 600 https://doi.org/10.3763/cpol.2010.0161.
914. Bodansky, *Climate Change Law* (n 11) 23.
915. Steve Rayner, 'How to Eat an Elephant: A Bottom-up Approach to Climate Policy' (2010) 10 Climate Policy 6 615 https://doi.org/10.3763/cpol.2010.0138.
916. A provision is deemed relevant when it may be raised as an evidence of a state's policy intent in an investment dispute and thus as an argument to defend or claim against the host State measure.
917. The same articles will serve as foundation for the chapters on the interpretation of FET in renewable and fossil-fuel energy disputes, as a norm does not necessarily need to bear legal effects to create legitimate expectations.
918. 196 States and the EU as a regional economic integration organisation; *see* The United Nations Framework Convention on Climate Change (adopted 9 May 1992, entered into force 21 March 1994) 1771 UNTS 107 (UNFCCC).

a legal character and impose obligations upon specific states. Generally, though, the UNFCCC establishes the governing structure for the international climate change regime and provides the regime's architecture and approach to differentiation.[919] Fundamental principles enumerated in the Convention include the common but differentiated responsibility principle,[920] scientific cooperation, and the formulation of national strategies and measures.

Article 2 of the UNFCCC[921] is the cornerstone of the UN regime on climate change. It encompasses the ambition to reduce GHG emissions in coping with different development levels. The article provides the objective:

> to achieve, in accordance with the relevant provisions of the Convention, stabilisation of greenhouse gas concentrations in the atmosphere at a level that would prevent dangerous anthropogenic interference with the climate system.[922]

Vaguely drafted, the article must be interpreted in relation to IPCC's findings to understand what constitutes a 'dangerous anthropogenic interference'. The article also imposes no timeline, simply specifying that 'such a level should be achieved within a time-frame sufficient to allow ecosystems to adapt naturally to climate change, to ensure that food production is not threatened, and to enable economic development to proceed in a sustainable manner'.[923] In other words, the UNFCCC is diplomatic language at its best. There are no quantifiable targets or compliance mechanisms for Article 4.2 on limiting GHG emissions.[924] The article simply incentivises developed countries (Annex 1 countries in the Framework Convention) to 'take the lead' and obliges them in mandatory language to 'adopt national policies' and 'measures'.[925]

Extraordinarily, little obligations can be inferred from the UNFCC, apart from one crucial fact. The UNFCCC established that the negotiating process for the UN climate

919. *Ibid.*, Arts 1, 2 and 3 set out the regime's basic definitions, principles and objectives. Articles 4 to 6 lay out the four main elements of the regime, mitigation, adaptation, finance, and technology transfer. Articles 7 to 14 create the institutional and procedural mechanisms aimed at implementing the convention. Articles 15 to 26 close the agreement with protocols, Annexs, amendments, ratification, and entry into force of the international treaty.
920. *Ibid.*, Annex I is subject to debates: The principle of Common but differentiated responsibilities is embodied in the differentiation between developed and developing countries. Annex I of the Framework Convention includes developed countries or economies in transition (such as from the former Soviet Bloc), with some notable and controversial exception (such as Israel). Annex II includes the most developed countries, whose economies are not in transition. Not listed in the Annex are considered 'developing' countries.
921. Article 2 of the 1992 United Nations Framework Convention on Climate Change.
922. Firger, 'The Potential of International Climate Change Law' (n 123).
923. UNFCC, Art. 2.
924. *Ibid.*, Art. 1.5 ('"Greenhouse gases" means those gaseous constituents of the atmosphere, both natural and anthropogenic, that absorb and re-emit infrared radiation').
925. *Ibid.*, Art. 4.2 ('The developed country Parties and other Parties included in Annex I commit themselves specifically as provided for in the following: (a) Each of these Parties shall adopt national policies and take corresponding measures on the mitigation of climate change, by limiting its anthropogenic emissions of greenhouse gases and protecting and enhancing its greenhouse gas sinks and reservoirs. These policies and measures will demonstrate that developed countries are taking the lead in modifying longer-term trends in anthropogenic emissions consistent with the objective of the Convention, recognizing that the return by the end of the present decade to earlier levels of anthropogenic emissions of carbon dioxide and other greenhouse gases (...)').

change regime would be consensus,[926] by general agreement,[927] at the 'Conference of the Parties.'[928] Since the UNFCC, there have been only four examples of explicit objections to such general consensus.[929] This showcases the broad consent of states in adopting *progressively more stringent provisions towards decarbonisation and mitigation policies*. Since the landmark adoption of the UNFCCC, the Kyoto Protocol,[930] and the Paris Agreement[931] have indeed propelled the major economies towards mitigation and 'greener' energy policies.[932]

3 1997 Kyoto Protocol: Binding States to Mitigate

The Kyoto Protocol[933] was adopted on 13 December 1997 under the framework of the UNFCCC convention.[934] The Protocol was the first legally binding treaty containing pledges by participating industrialised nations to reduce their total emissions of six GHGs.[935] The Protocol's first commitment period ran from 2008 to 2012 to reduce GHGs by an average of 5% compared to 1990 levels. However, its parties represented only 12% of GHG emissions.[936] The Protocol also introduced emissions trading, a clean development mechanism, and opened the fulfilment of commitments to joint implementation.[937] The Protocol came into force on 16 February 2005[938] but was only legally

926. UNEP, *Multilateral Environmental Agreement: Negotiators Handbook* (Report Second Edition, UNEP 2007) 3-12; Consensus is distinct from unanimity: only an explicit objection may break consensus.
927. Antto Vihma, 'Climate of Consensus: Managing Decision-Making in the UN Climate Change Negotiations' (2015) 24 Review of European, Comparative and International Environmental Law 1 58, 62 https://doi.org/10.1111/reel.12093.
928. Bodansky, *Climate Change Law* (n 11) 77; This is due to complex, multifaceted negotiations between states with diverging priorities and perspectives. The negotiating procedure has, at times, been a battleground for substantive disagreement among states, as process may have been used to block, delay, or limit substantive progress.
929. At COP 2 in Geneva in 1996, COP 15 in Copenhagen in 2009, COP 16 in Cancun (2010), and COP 18 in Doha (2012); *see* Duncan French and Lavanya Rajamani, 'Climate Change and International Environmental Law: Musing on a Journey to Somewhere' (2013) 25 Journal of Environmental Law 3 437, 448 https://doi.org/10.1093/jel/eqt022.
930. Kyoto Protocol (n 120), Arts 6, 12, 17.
931. Jorge E Viñuales, 'The Paris Climate Agreement: An Initial Examination' (2015) 6 C-EENRG Working Papers.
932. Monica Feria-Tinta, 'The Role of International Law and Arbitration in Enforcing the Paris Agreement' (*Kluwer Arbitration Blog*, 31 December 2016) https://arbitrationblog.kluwerarbitration.com/2016/12/31/the-role-of-international-law-and-arbitration-in-enforcing-the-paris-agreement/ accessed 1 November 2023.
933. Daniel Bodansky, 'The United Nations Framework Convention on Climate Change: A Commentary' (1993) 18 Yale Journal of International Law 451 https://doi.org/10.1515/9783110874815-048; Joanna Depledge, 'Tracing the Origins of the Kyoto Protocol: An Article-by-Article Textual History' (25 November 2000) UNFCCC Technical Paper, FCCC/TP/2000/2.
934. The Kyoto Protocol became a legal agreement when ratified in Bonn on 23 July 2001.
935. The six Greenhouse gas emissions were CO_2, methane, nitrous oxide, hydrofluorocarbons, perfluorocarbons, and sulphur hexafluoride.
936. Bodansky, 170-174.
937. Kyoto Protocol (n 120) Art. 17 (emissions trading), Art. 12 (clean development mechanism) and 3 and 4 (joint implementation).
938. Thanks to the ratification of Russia, which met the prerequisite for the entry into force of the Protocol.

binding in December 2007 after the ratification of Australia.[939] Developing countries were excluded from the Protocol based on the differentiated responsibilities.[940] The US signed but pulled out from the treaty in 2005.[941]

The Kyoto Protocol set out legally binding emissions targets for thirty-seven industrialised countries, including the fifteen members of the European Community.[942] Article 3 and Annex B provide for quantified emissions-reduction commitments. The treaty adopts an imperative language and provides a compliance mechanism, which makes its constituent provisions binding. In the first period of the Protocol (2008-12), participating countries committed to reducing their emissions by an average of 5% below 1990 levels.[943] This means that parties accepting the legally binding emissions targets were bound under the principle of state responsibility to achieve these goals. In the EU, the target reduction was 8%. The EU divided the target into legally binding national targets limiting or reducing GHG emissions.[944] These national targets were tailored to the relative wealth of EU Member States as a form of 'burden sharing'.[945] The binding character of the Kyoto Protocol makes it prone to relevance in investment disputes. In the NZEID cases analysed above, the Kyoto Protocol, together with the European Directive, have been further exploited to showcase the expectation of regulatory stability from clean energy investors, as they directly contribute to reaching mitigation objectives.[946]

The Doha Amendment (COP 18), adopted on 8 December 2012, established the second-period commitment of the Kyoto Protocol (2013-2020), albeit with less success.[947] The Amendment set a goal of reducing GHG emissions by 18% compared to 1990 levels for participating countries. Because of its ambitious emission reduction target, the amendment came into force at an extremely late stage, on 31 December

939. Which met the threshold of global GHG emissions to make the treaty binding.
940. Kyoto Protocol, Art. 3.1.
941. Bodansky, *Climate Change Law* (n 11) 161.
942. EU-15, Bulgaria, Czech Republic, Estonia, Latvia, Liechtenstein, Lithuania, Monaco, Romania, Slovakia, Slovenia, Switzerland, Hungary, Japan, Poland, Croatia, New Zealand, Russian Federation, Ukraine, Norway, Australia, Iceland, Canada (On 15 December 2011, the Depositary received written notification of Canada's withdrawal from the Kyoto Protocol. This action became effective for Canada on 15 December 2012).
943. The allowed emissions are divided into assigned units. The Kyoto Protocol introduces Emissions Trading in Art. 17, which allows countries to sell this excess emission units to countries that are over their targets.
944. Table of quantified emission limitation or reduction commitments for the purpose of determining the respective emission levels allocated to the European Community and its Member States in accordance with the Art. 4 of the Kyoto Protocol [2002] Annex 2 OJ L 130/19.
945. Council Decision 2002/358/EC of 25 April 2002 concerning the approval, on behalf of the European Community, of the Kyoto Protocol to the United Nations Framework Convention on Climate Change and the joint fulfilment of commitments thereunder [2002] OJ L 130/1; Council Decision of 14 December 2006 determining the respective emission levels allocated to the Community and each of its Member States under the Kyoto Protocol pursuant to Council Decision 2002/358/EC [2006] OJ L 358/87.
946. *See* Chapter 5.C.1.
947. The following parties notified the Secretariat on their agreement to fulfil their commitments for the second commitment period: Austria, Belgium, Bulgaria, Croatia, Cyprus, Czech Republic, Denmark, Estonia, European Union, Finland, France, Germany, Greece, Hungary, Iceland, Ireland, Italy, Latvia, Lithuania, Luxembourg, Malta, Netherlands, Poland, Portugal, Romania, Slovakia, Slovenia, Spain, Sweden, United Kingdom of Great Britain and Northern Ireland.

2020. Nevertheless, since Kyoto, COPs witnessed an increase in signs of progressive collective action towards global mitigation.[948]

4 2015 Paris Agreement: Setting the Climate Target

The 2015 Paris Agreement is likely to be the world's 'greatest diplomatic success'.[949] It generated a long-term, balanced, and quasi-universal agreement reshaping the state's relationship to GHG emissions and, eventually, energy supply. The Paris Agreement adopts a hybrid architecture of bottom-up and top-down provisions. Its greatest success is the creation of National Determined Contributions, which now constitute the cornerstone of the bottom-up climate change regime.[950] The 2015 Paris Agreement is ratified by 194 states and the EU.[951] Due to geopolitical tensions amid US elections,[952] the treaty entered into force earlier than expected, on 4 November 2016.[953] There are three vital considerations to keep in mind when analysing the Paris Agreement.

First, the Paris Agreement is an international treaty according to Article 2.1 of the VCLT (1961 VCLT). It was not adopted under Article 17 of the UNFCCC, which governs the adoption of 'protocols'.[954] The Agreement is rather fully implemented under the UNFCC,[955] using its institutions and referring to its objective.

Second, the Agreement's focus is on mitigation.[956] Provisions on technology, adaptation, capacity-building, and loss and damage are accessory and either advisory or aspirational. This means that the Parties' primary legal obligation under the

948. The COP adopted the 2007 Bali Action Plan, which set out a new negotiation procedure to tackle climate change based on four elements – mitigation, adaptation, technology, and financing. The 2010 Cancun Agreements then called for the creation of a Green Climate Fund with the aim of collecting USD 100 billion per annum to tackle climate change – objective not yet met; *see also* the unadopted Copenhagen Rapport, UNFCCC, 'Report of the Conference of the Parties on its fifteenth session, held in Copenhagen from 7 to 19 December 2009, Addendum Part Two: Action taken by the Conference of the Parties at its fifteenth session', (18 December 2009) FCCC/CP/2009/11/Add.1 Decision-/ 2/CP.15, Art. 2.
949. Fiona Harvey, 'Paris Climate Change Agreement: The World's Greatest Diplomatic Success' *The Guardian* (London, 14 December 2015).
950. Paris Agreement (n 6) Art. 4.2 and 4.3; today, 193 states are parties to the Paris Agreement, meaning that virtually all states have adopted nationally determined contributions. Bottom-up approaches allow greater discretion and autonomy to states, which in turn can be less effective but more compatible with national circumstances, development goals and political constraints.
951. As of September 2023.
952. Bodansky, *Climate Change Law* (n 11) 247.
953. Its entry into force was conditioned upon Art. 21, which provided a specific emissions threshold for entry into force.
954. Bodansky, *Climate Change Law* (n 11) 212.
955. UNFCCC, 'Decision 1/CP.21 Adoption of the Paris Agreement' (29 January 2016) FCCC/CP/2015/10/Add.1, 2, para. 1.
956. The Durban Platform made clear that the US and Australia wished to see the mitigation challenge as the core issue negotiated at the Paris COP. On the contrary, China and India insisted on other components and particularly the sustainable development and intellectual property rights. *See* Embassy of India in Beijing, 'Joint Statement Issued at the Conclusion of the 13th BASIC Ministerial Meeting on Climate Change Beijing, China 19-20 November 2012' (Embassy of India in Beijing, 21 November 2012); UNFCCC, China's submission on the Work of the Ad Hoc Working Group on Durban Platform for Enhanced Action (30 April 2012) FCCC/ADP/2012/MISC.3.

Agreement is to submit NDC addressing mitigation following Article 4.2. Sustainable development and human rights goals are present in the preamble of the Agreement. However, the treaty fails to accredit them binding force upon the Parties in relation to climate goals. According to Article 4.1, the global mitigation goals are to be achieved within the '*context*' of sustainable development and poverty eradication. This formulation separates the protection of *human rights* and pursuance of sustainable development goals from mitigation or climate change policies.[957]

Third, obligations on mitigation are differentiated. The principle of common but differentiated responsibilities plays an essential role in the Paris Agreement. It is present in the Agreement's preamble,[958] the provision relating to the purpose of the agreement,[959] progression,[960] and long-term low GHG development strategies.[961] Many provisions are accompanied by the wording 'in light of the national circumstances', signalling flexibility, notably in establishing whether a State is in a developed or developing state.[962] Only one mitigation provision is undifferentiated: Article 4.5, which states that support shall be provided to developing countries. Concretely, this means that expectations to adopt mitigation measures are higher in developed countries than in developing ones. While all Parties shall prepare, communicate, and maintain successive NDCs clearly and transparently, update them every five years and account for them, Article 4.4 of the Agreement nuances this obligation in placing differentiation as an element of the obligation.[963]

The adoption of the treaty by 191 parties signalled a consensus, if not unanimity, on the binding objective of the agreement: 'holding the increase in the global average temperature to well below 2°C above pre-industrial levels and pursuing efforts to limit the temperature increase to 1.5°C above pre-industrial levels'.[964] Particularly, it is to 'achieve a balance between anthropogenic emissions by sources and removals by sinks of GHGs emissions in the second half of the century'.[965] In general, Parties refer to GHG emissions and not only to CO_2 emissions. This indicates greater ambition, as measures adopted to reduce GHG emissions are more far-reaching than CO_2 emissions measures.

957. In practice, this means that a defence argument based on the State climate change measure must be differentiated from a human rights or sustainable development goals defence. The regulatory freedom required to achieve climate goals is therefore not necessarily tied to the regulatory freedom necessary to achieve human rights goals.
958. Paris Agreement (n 6) Preambular Recital 3.
959. *Ibid.*, Article 2.2.
960. *Ibid.*, Art. 4.3.
961. *Ibid.*, Art. 4.19.
962. Bodansky, *Climate Change Law* (n 11) 223; Regarding the INDCs, the Warsaw decision prior to the Paris Agreement invited the Parties to 'self-determine' 'the scope, form, rigor, and information of their contributions'.
963. Paris Agreement (n 6) Art. 4.4. reads ('Developed country Parties *should* continue taking the lead by undertaking economy-wide absolute emission reduction targets. Developing country Parties *should* continue enhancing their mitigation efforts and are encouraged to move over time towards economy-wide emission reduction or limitation targets in the light of different national circumstances' (emphasis added)). The use of the advisory term 'should' need to be noted, as this article cannot constitute the basis of legitimate expectations due to its non-binding character.
964. Paris Agreement (n 6) Art. 2.1(a).
965. *Ibid.*, Art. 4.1.

Successful top-down provisions[966] include the five-year cycles of global stocktake to assess collective progress towards long-term goals, obligation to publish NDCs,[967] transparency framework[968] and a facilitative compliance system.

Critical to energy investment decisions is the obligation to publish NDCs under Article 4.1, which reads:

> Each party shall prepare, communicate, and maintain successive nationally determined contributions that it intends to achieve. Parties shall pursue domestic measures with the aim of achieving the objectives of such contributions.

The provision applies to all parties since it refers to 'each party' and thus creates *individual* obligations. The imperative 'shall' reflects the binding language of the provision. Preparing, communicating, and maintaining NDCs are binding obligations in the same way as pursuing 'domestic measures'. The article creates an obligation of conduct rather than result. With the terms 'intends to achieve' and 'with the aim of achieving the objectives of their contribution', the Agreement places an *expectation* of good faith on the Parties. NDCs that are written in precise terms may serve to specify a state's intent and conduct. There is also a good faith expectation that parties will aim to achieve the objectives of their contributions.[969] As of 21 March 2022,[970] 194 countries have put forward NDCs. These NDCs are critical as political statements, as they generally include statements regarding domestic energy sector.

In addition to the Paris Agreement, the Paris Rulebook is a body of decisions and annexes adopted by Parties to it (CMA).[971] The Rulebook aims at operationalising the Paris Agreement. It details how the parties intend to achieve the goal of holding the increase in the global average temperature to 'well below 2°C above pre-industrial levels'.[972] The Paris Rulebook provides few legally binding obligations.[973] In a nutshell, it obliges state parties to account in detail on how they intend to achieve their NDCs.[974] This constitutes a concrete legal obligation.[975] It shapes and forms NDC submissions.[976] From the perspective of international investment law, the Paris Rulebook obliges states to detail their NDCs, so that these could eventually be interpreted as unilateral commitments.

966. *Ibid.*, Art. 15.
967. *Ibid.*, Art. 14.
968. *Ibid.*, Art. 13.
969. Bodansky, *Climate Change Law* (n 11) 231.
970. World Resources Institute, 'Climate Watch Data Explorer' (*Climate* Watch) https://www.climatewatchdata.org/ accessed 1 November 2023.
971. The CMA is distinct from the COP as it only comprises States having ratified the Paris Agreement. Today, 196 Parties are Party to the Paris Agreement. The difference made sense when the USA stepped out of the Paris Agreement. Eritrea, Libya and Yemen have also not ratified the agreement. Iraq ratified the agreement on 1 November 2021.
972. Petra Minnerop, 'The Legal Effect of the Paris Rulebook under the Doctrine of Treaty Interpretation' in Cameron et al., *The Global Energy Transition* (n 14) 131.
973. *Ibid.*, 101.
974. 4/CMA. 1 Annex II para. 1 (c).
975. Minnerop, 'Legal Effect' (n 972) 132.
976. *Ibid.*, 133.

5 2021 Glasgow Climate Pact: Devising Net Zero

The 'Glasgow Climate Pact'[977] is where the net zero carbon emission target became the global ambition, with each country invited to provide a set date to reach the objective.[978] It also directly mentioned the need to phase down coal and incentivise clean energy investments. The Glasgow COP further marked the return of the US to the CMA. The Pact achieved several procedural outcomes operationalising the Paris Agreement.[979]

On top of these procedural achievements, 130 governments pledged to reduce their economy's carbon intensity; most used the 'net zero' notion as a standard,[980] which derived from a 2018 IPCC report'.[981] The report clearly showed that to achieve 1.5°C, the global economy would need to reach zero carbon emissions by about 2050 and then achieve negative carbon emissions for the other half of the century.[982] A number of countries committed to net zero by 2050,[983] China by 2060 and India by 2070.[984] The consensus reached in the Pact is reflected in numerous national policies aiming to decarbonise their economy.[985]

Among the most notable provisions of the Glasgow Agreement, Article 4.20 definitely attracted the most attention because it calls parties to phase down coal while deploying clean energy. Article 4.20 of the Glasgow Climate Pact is non-binding. But it is vital to assess the legitimacy and reasonableness of mitigation measures affecting foreign investors' rights. The article reads:

977. It adopted decision 'COP26 of the Glasgow Climate Pact', on 13 November 2021.
978. The Climate Change Commission, *COP26: Key Outcomes and Next Steps for the UK* (Report, CCC 2021) 3 ('global ambition has increased, particularly for the long-term, with Net Zero adopted as the standard goal for emissions across the world').
979. The parties adopted a mechanism to trade emission reductions to reach their NDCs without double counting (Art. 6); an enhanced transparency framework (Art. 13) obliging Parties to report their GHG emissions in detail; the requirement to raise their ambitions from 2022 if their NDC is not in line with the Paris Agreement; the creation of an annual summary report of the parties' annual contributions.
980. Jorge Viñuales and others, 'Climate Policy after the Paris 2015 Climate Conference' (2017) 17 Climate Policy 1 15 https://doi.org/10.1080/14693062.2016.1242060.
981. IPCC, *Global Warming of 1.5° C* (Report, 2018) 5.
982. Meinhard Doelle, 'The Paris Agreement: Historic Breakthrough or High Stakes Experiment?', (2016) 6 Climate Law Special Issue 1-2 1 https://doi.org/10.1163/18786561-00601001; Daniel Klein and others (eds), *The Paris Climate Agreement: Analysis and Commentary* (OUP 2017); Sebastian Oberthür and Ralph Bolde, 'Legal Form and Nature of the Paris Outcome' (2016) 6 Climate Law Special Issue 1-2 40 https://doi.org/10.1163/18786561-00601003.
983. Net Zero Tracker, 'Data Explorer' (*Net Zero Tracker*, 2023) https://zerotracker.net accessed 21 December 2022. Among the countries to have pledged to achieve Net Zero carbon emissions by 2050 are the EU, Canada, Chile, Bhutan, Costa Rica, Fiji, Iceland, Japan, New Zealand, Norway, Sweden, Singapore, Slovakia, South Africa, South Korea, the UK, USA, and Uruguay.
984. Climate Action Tracker, 'Glasgow's 2030 Credibility Gap: Net Zero's Lip Service to Climate Action' (Report, Climate Action Tracker 2021), 4; Nan Luo, 'The Net Zero Transition in China: Progress Has Been Made, But Challenges Remain' (*United Nations Principles for Responsible Investment*, 20 June 2022); regarding India's ambitions *see* Maura McGrath Kristoff, 'New Coal-fired Power Plants in India: Reality or Just Numbers? New Coal Capacity Additions Face Major Stranded Asset Risk' (2021) Institute for Energy Economics and Financial Analysis.
985. *See* Chapter 3 (UK climate change committee 'Avoiding catastrophic climate change requires a huge shift in the energy base of both the British and global economies').

> (The Conference of the Calls) upon Parties to accelerate the development, deployment and dissemination of technologies, and the adoption of policies, to transition towards low-emission energy systems, including *by rapidly scaling up the deployment of clean power generation* and energy efficiency measures, including *accelerating efforts towards the phasedown of unabated coal power and phase-out of inefficient fossil fuel subsidies*, while providing targeted support to the poorest and most vulnerable in line with national circumstances and recognising the need for support towards a just transition.

As a word of caution, a number of points must be outlined. Looking at the ordinary meaning first. State parties do not 'commit' to 'scaling up' or 'phasedown' but are 'called upon' to do so. They are under no obligation to achieve this goal. Thus, the article is *hortatory* and lacks legal bindingness. Regarding clean power energy, the Pact does not define the interpretation of the adjective 'rapidly' nor the verb 'scale up'. If stated without a different timeline or interpretative tools, these two elements cannot be deemed to create obligations on state parties. The word 'deployment' is subject to ambiguity, resembling an obligation of means rather than result. 'Deployment' here implies that state parties would put effort into bringing resources into effective action. But again, without a timeline, the wording does not create binding obligations. Generally, the wording of the article is ambiguous due to the choice of vague language, leaving margins of interpretation in considering national circumstances.

Second, the concepts regarding coal are vague. The word 'phasedown' is a consensus-oriented term, meaning 'to remove or stop using something gradually or in stages'.[986] It was adopted in place of the term 'phase-out', which fell due to China and India's oppositions and would have set a clearer direction with: (1) no prospect of regulatory stability for new investments and (2) clear regulatory risks to existing investments, which would be less gradual than with the term 'phasedown'. The use of adjective 'unabated' to qualify the coal plants arguably means that the article refers to coal power plants without CC(U)S technology equipment.[987] The word 'abated' is a common term used to describe regulations related to the technological level of a carbon power plant as used by the G21.[988] 'Unabated' is defined by the Cambridge Dictionary as 'without becoming weaker in strength or force'.[989] This seemingly restricts the perimeter of coal-fired power generation affected by the provision to those not exploiting effective Carbon Capture and Storage (CCS) Technology. No indication is given as to how the implementation of the CCS technology should be controlled, allowing individual states the discretion to set such standards. However, we could induce from the definition above that coal would qualify as 'abated' only if CCS is effectively working.

---

986. 'Phase st Down', *Cambridge English Dictionary* (OUP 2023).
987. The 2021 G7 Leaders' meeting press release stated that 'Unabated coal power generation refers to the use of coal that isn't mitigated with technologies to reduce the CO2 emissions, such as Carbon Capture Utilisation and Storage (CCUS).'
988. Prime Minister's Office, 'G7 Leaders Commit To Protect Planet and Turbocharge Global Green Growth' (*Press release*, 12 June 2021) https://gov.uk/government/news/g7-leaders-commit-to-protect-planet-and-turbocharge-global-green-growth accessed 2 November 2023.
989. 'Unabated', Cambridge English Dictionary (OUP 2023).

Third, the object and purpose of the article are unclear. The Pact remains relatively broad regarding fossil fuels, targeting solely the 'subsidies' that fossil fuel industries may receive. There is no universal definition of what constitutes a subsidy, leaving state parties with great discretion in defining their policies. Second, there are two main types of subsidies: those given to consumers[990] and those given to producers.[991] The amount of fossil subsidies combined is considered a significant barrier to the energy transition with, according to some calculations, half a trillion dollars being invested into artificially lowering the price of fossil fuels – triple what renewable energies receive, according to numbers by the International Energy Agency and the OECD.[992] There again, with no agreed measurement method, it seems complicated to expect the implementation of an ambiguous provision. The other difficulty in the legal phrasing of 'fossil fuel subsidy' is using the adjective 'inefficient'. With no agreement on what constitutes inefficiency (whether in energy terms or economic terms), it can with difficulty be expected to create obligations on state parties.

Despite the textual analysis above, the inclusion of 'coal', 'fossil fuel', and 'clean power generation' in Article 4.20 is a significant step towards net zero's implementation. Article 4.20 of the Glasgow Climate Pact effectively discriminates two segments of the energy industry – fossil fuels and coal, and 'clean' energy. There is thus an acute need to understand the scientific distinction between these energy sources.[993] The inclusion of energy types creates expectations on the part of investors. As further demonstrated below, the article influences LE. Especially when a state party develops its interpretation of the provision, replicates it in its domestic legislation, or details its energy commitment in an NDC. Finally, as I demonstrate below, 'net zero' Glasgow-inspired policies directly affect clean and fossil fuel energy investments.

In summary, the ICCL regime adopts a managerial model rather than an enforcement one.[994] Nonetheless, it heavily contributes to the translation of climate change objectives into net zero transition policies. In particular, the Kyoto Protocol

---

990. Jocelyn Timperley, 'Explainer: The Challenge of Defining Fossil Fuel Subsidies' (*CarbonBrief*, 6 December 2017) https://carbonbrief.org/explainer-the-challenge-of-defining-fossil-fuel-subsidies/ accessed on 21 March 2022 ('Consumption (or consumer) subsidies are those which reduce the price of energy to consumers, for example, through government controls on the cost of petrol or power').
991. *Ibid.* ('Production subsidies are those which make it less costly for producers to develop resources in the first place. They can include things such as tax breaks for capital investment, requiring a lower share of profits to be given as tax from developing a resource, public finance specifically given to fossil fuel production, and, in some analysis, investment by state-owned enterprises (SOEs)').
992. Jocelyn Timperley, 'Why Fossil Fuel Subsidies Are So Hard to Kill' (2021) 598 (7881) Nature 403 https://doi.org/10.1038/d41586-021-02847-2.
993. *See* James Friedman, 'The Scientist as Expert Witness: Why Lawyers and Scientists Can't Talk to Each Other' (1977) 18 Jurimetrics Journal 2 99 (If the relationship between lawyers and scientists is notoriously thin, it is not a reason for the legal community to discard the importance of science when interpretating a fact-based dispute).
994. Bodansky, *Climate Change Law* (n 11) 26 (the climate change regime tries 'to encourage and facilitate national action through transparency, peer pressure, and capacity building, rather than to force states to act through legal prescriptions and sanctions').

directly influenced European legislation on carbon reduction and electricity production – the same policies that led to disputes in renewable energy in Spain, the Czech Republic and Italy.[995] ICCL provisions are increasingly influential in judicial decisions concerning climate change.[996] The binding obligation to publish NDCs creates authoritative roadmaps.[997] These indicate a country's general policy on climate change mitigation.[998] A general policy may amount to unilateral commitments if it is sufficiently clear and addressed to a specific group of persons. Eventually, as demonstrated below, ICCL should form part of an energy investor's LE.[999]

6 NDCs: Non-binding but Authoritative

NDCs are 'measures determined and intended to be applied by the country to face climate change in terms of adaptation and mitigation'. Under the Paris Agreement, each state party must establish a report stating its national contribution towards climate change mitigation and update it every five years.[1000] The Glasgow Pact urged parties to revisit and strengthen their NDCs in 2022.[1001] There is a good faith expectation of 'progression' of the parties' commitment with every updated NDC.[1002] As of 16 March 2022, 194 Parties submitted their first NDCs and 13 their second NDCs.[1003] Generally, the government, most likely the relevant ministries, oversees the creation, publication and submission of NDCs to the United Nations Registry.[1004]

It is possible to interpret NDC reports as political statements. NDCs enshrine states' commitments or pledges on mitigation and, for some, on finance, adaptation and technology strategies.[1005] The format of NDC report has evolved from discretionary to specific, so that states must now clearly spell out the measures they intend to implement to mitigate climate change.[1006] Today, NDCs must detail ways in which the

995. *See* Chapter 3.A.1.
996. Bodansky, *Climate Change Law* (n 11) 289 (mentioning ICSID as one of the forums in which cases 'tangentially relate to climate change, involving the issuance of permits for coal fired plants. Claims might also be possible challenging subsidies for renewable energy').
997. The publication of Nationally Determined Contributions (NDCs), which, becoming more detailed with every COP, becomes an important instrument when forming expectations on the behaviour of the Host State.
998. *Ibid.*; UNFCCC, 'Nationally Determined Contributions Registry' (*UNFCCC*, n.d.) unfccc.int/NDCREG accessed 2 November 2023.
999. Bodansky, *Climate Change Law* (n 11) 283-290.
1000. Paris Agreement (n 6) Art. 4 para. 9.
1001. Glasgow Climate Pact, Art. 7.
1002. Paris Agreement (n 6) Art. 4 para. 11; *see* Bodansky, *Climate Change Law* (n 11) 231; 233-34.
1003. UNFCCC, 'Nationally Determined Contributions Registry' https://unfccc.int/NDCREG accessed 2 November 2023.
1004. The authority issuing NDC may vary from country to country.
1005. Paris Agreement (n 6) Art. 4 para. 14 whereby the treaty *invites* Parties to 'take into account existing methods' to account for anthropogenic emissions and removals.
1006. Decision 4/CMA.1 Further guidance in relation to the mitigation section of decision 1/CP.21, paras 6-10; *see* more generally Pieter Pauw and Richard Klein, 'Beyond Ambition: Increasing the Transparency, Coherence and Implementability of Nationally Determined Contributions' (2020) 20 Climate Policy 4 405; 407-408 https://doi.org/10.1080/14693062.2020.1722607.

state intends to achieve its emission target.[1007] This is vital with regard to the legal obligations under international law that may arise from unilateral commitments under NDCs. The more specific the NDC language, the more likely it may constitute a unilateral declaration that creates legal obligations for the state.[1008]

7 National Administrative Courts' Rulings: Binding on the State

National administrative rulings also impact the host state's obligations and investors' LE. In the Spanish cases, a court's ruling on the withdrawal of incentives proved crucial in the assessment of the reasonableness of the expectations.[1009] The same reasoning may be applied to domestic court decisions on ICCL. As administrative law exploits the Paris Agreement to condemn states or imply obligations over specific industry sectors, host state's obligations on mitigation become more defined. I illustrate this type of ruling with five recent examples from major economies below:

- *Example 1:* In France, on 1 July 2021, the French Conseil d'Etat issued the Commune Grande-Synthe ruling.[1010] It gave the government nine months to adopt all necessary measures to curb GHG emissions on the national territory to ensure it complies with the national climate targets under the Paris Agreement.[1011]
- *Example 2:* In Germany, on 24 March 2021,[1012] the Federal Constitutional Court of Germany ruled that Germany's 2019 Federal Climate Act was incompatible with fundamental human rights because it left much of the burden to reduce emissions after 2030.[1013] Invoking human rights, it ruled that 'practically every freedom is potentially affected [by these future emission reduction obligations] because today almost all areas of human life are bound

1007. *Ibid.*
1008. Benoit Mayer, 'International Law Obligations Arising in Relation to Nationally Determined Contributions' (2018) 7 Transnational Environmental Law 251 https://doi.org/10.1017/s2047102518000110.
1009. For instance, *PV Investors v. Spain* (n 413) para. 611 ('In sum, prior to the Claimants' investment and thereafter, the Spanish courts had consistently held that tariffs and related incentives were not "immutable" and investors had no vested right to specific subsidy for the future; that RD 436/2004 did not freeze the remuneration system in spite of Article 40.3; that the State had the power to change the regulatory system, and that the law guaranteed operators that they would achieve a reasonable rate of return on investments').
1010. ECLI:FR:CECHR:2021:427301.20210701.
1011. *Ibid.*, para. 12 ('Si les stipulations de la CCNUCC et de l'accord de Paris citées au point 9 requièrent l'intervention d'actes complémentaires pour produire des effets à l'égard des particuliers et sont, par suite, dépourvues d'effet direct, elles doivent néanmoins être prises en considération dans l'interprétation des dispositions de droit national, notamment celles citées au point 11, qui, se référant aux objectifs qu'elles fixent, ont précisément pour objet de les mettre en œuvre').
1012. Heiner Adamski, 'Klimaschutz und Grundrechtsschutz. Das Bundesverfassungsgericht verkündet eine fast revolutionäre und historische Entscheidung–und folgt damit jungen Beschwerdeführern' (2021) 70 GWP–Gesellschaft. Wirtschaft. Politik 4 33.
1013. BVerfG, Beschluss des Ersten Senats vom 24 März 2021 – 1 BvR 2656/18.

up with greenhouse gas emissions [...] and could therefore be threatened by drastic constraints after 2030'.[1014]

- *Example 3:* In the Netherlands, the 2019 *Urgenda Foundation v. Netherlands* case also concerned the Dutch government's reduction of GHG emissions. An initial ruling ordered the Government to reduce emissions by at least 25% by the end of 2020, compared to 1990. The judgment was upheld by the Dutch Supreme Court, which affirmed that the government had breached its duty of care under Articles 2 and 8 of the European Convention on Human Rights.[1015]
- *Example 4:* In the *VZW Klimaatzaak v. Kingdom of Belgium & Others* case, the Court of Appeal of Brussels decided on 30 November 2023 and ordered the competent Belgian public authorities (the Federal State, Flemish Region, and the Brussels-Capital Region) to reduce their GHG emissions of 55% compared to the 1990 level by 2030. The grounds of this decision are based on the breach of human rights (Articles 2 and 8 of the ECHR) and civil liability rules.[1016]
  Climate change-related administrative cases pursued against the US and UK governments have been less successful.
- *Example 4:* In the *Juliana v. USA*[1017] case, Claimants argued that the US government violated constitutional rights by continuing to use a national energy system powered by fossil fuels. The Ninth Circuit Court of Appeals rejected the request, dismissing its jurisdiction over complex policy decisions that are the executive and legislative government's responsibility.[1018]
- *Example 5:* The *UK Supreme Court case R (Friends of the Earth Ltd and others) v. Heathrow Airport Ltd* (2020)[1019] concerned the expansion of Heathrow Airport. Claimants argued that the development was inconsistent with government climate targets under the Paris Agreement. The Supreme Court ruled out the reasoning. The mere announcement of emissions targets did not constitute 'government policy'.[1020]

To summarise, the UN regime provides few binding provisions and indicates a progression in stringency on the net zero path. NDCs, when specific and written in a language capable of binding the state, may constitute one of the bases of a foreign investor's LE. Domestic rulings may inform a state's binding climate and energy policy obligations.

1014. *Ibid.*, para. 117; the ruling is founded on Art. 20(a) of the German Constitution (*Grundgesetz*), which requires the government to act for the protection of 'future generations', and indirectly refers to Germany's obligations under the Paris Agreement. Finally, the court ordered the Federal government to introduce provisions by 2022 that detail how it intends to meet its targets and how reductions in emissions are to be adjusted after 2030.
1015. ECLI:NL:HR:2019:2006.
1016. *VZW Klimaatzaak v. Kingdom of Belgium & Others* (2023) Court of Appeal of Brussels, Rn 2022/AR/891.
1017. 947 F.3d 1159 (9th Cir. 2020).
1018. *Ibid.*
1019. *R v. Heathrow Airport Ltd* [2020] UKSC 52.
1020. *Ibid.*, para. 192.

B COMPATIBILITY OF ICCL AND INTERNATIONAL INVESTMENT LAW

Against this background, I examine whether the assumed incompatibility between ICCL and international investment law exists. As a reminder, the legal interaction between international norms from different orders before arbitral tribunals is particular. The majority of authors consider that there is no formal hierarchy of international law.[1021] This reasoning would apply to ICCL. But I demonstrate below that there can be no conflict between a binding command (i.e., an international investment treaty) and non-binding or insufficiently relevant binding commands (i.e., unrelated climate provisions, UN clauses mandating mitigation objectives without specific mechanisms or recommendations to incentivise renewable energies).

1 Absence of Conflict *Stricto Sensu*

The question of conflict between ICCL and international investment law raises much-discussed questions of 'fragmentation'. The literature conventionally talks of fragmentation. But that assumes conflict. Which there is not in the strict sense (*stricto sensu*), and only in the broad sense (*lato sensu*). The 'fragmentation of international law'[1022] studies how conflicts may arise between special and general international law and between different branches of international law and provides legal techniques to avoid or resolve them.[1023] To establish whether there is fragmentation, some sort of conflict must exist between the obligations deriving from climate change law and investment protection law.[1024]

a) Definitions of Conflict

'Conflict' has received two main definitions. One definition is narrow and classical (*stricto sensu*), the other broad and concerned with the consistency of public international law as a legal order (*lato sensu*).[1025]

1021. Władysław Czapliriski and Gennadiĭ Danilenko, 'Conflicts of Norms in International Law' in *NetherlandsYearbook of International Law* (CUP 1990) 7 ('The rejection of a hierarchy of sources means that all international norms have equal force, irrespective of their source, and that conflicts between them must be decided according to conflict rules other than those inspired by the concept of *lex superior*').
1022. *Ibid.*
1023. Harro van Asselt, 'Managing the Fragmentation of International Environmental Law: Forests at the Intersection of the Climate and Biodiversity Regimes' (2010) International Law and Politics 44 1205, 1208 https://doi.org/10.1007/978-94-007-5440-9_13.
1024. Crina Baltag, Riddhi Joshi and Kabir Duggal, 'Recent Trends in Investment Arbitration on the Right to Regulate, Environment, Health and Corporate Social Responsibility: Too Much or Too Little?' (2023) 38 ICSID Review 2 381, 421 https://doi.org/10.1093/icsidreview/siac031 ('While dealing with the fragmentation of public international law, one must also deal with the integration of environmental, human rights and CSR obligations within the framework of international investment law and ISDS, as an expression of the rule of law. This will allow States and investors equally to take advantage of and be held accountable for their respective obligations').
1025. Herve Ascensio 'Article 31 of the VCLT's and International Investment Law' (2016) 31 ICSID Review 2 366, 383 https://doi.org/10.1093/icsidreview/siw008.

In the classic approach, 'conflict in the strict sense of direct incompatibility arises only where a party to the two treaties cannot simultaneously comply with its obligations under both treaties'.[1026]

In the broader approach proposed in the ILC Report, conflict is defined 'as a situation where two rules or principles *suggest* different ways of dealing with a problem (emphasis added)'.[1027] This larger approach resonates with Pauwelyn's research[1028] on the concept of 'conflict of norms'. To him, conflicts of legally binding norms - which can consist of obligations and rights - may trigger four situations of conflict.[1029]

b) *Absence of Conflict* **Stricto Sensu**

Under the classic definition, I find no conflicts between ICCL and international investment law. Three considerations induce this conclusion.

First, there is no conflict *stricto sensu* between investment protection and the Paris Agreement and the Glasgow Pact. The Paris Agreement obliges states to 'hold the increase in the global average temperature to well below 2°C above pre-industrial levels and pursue efforts to limit the temperature increase to 1.5°C above pre-industrial levels'.[1030] This requires in good faith Parties to the Paris Agreement to enact mitigation measures. These may or may not include the phasing-out of fossil fuel investments, especially coal. No ratifying member has the obligation to *enact* specific policy measures in the energy sector. One state's mitigation objective could be *theoretically* achieved through complete energy efficiency or 'degrowth'. The Paris Agreement supplies no enforcement system either. In the strict sense, the binding obligations under the Paris Agreement[1031] regard the implementation of NDCs. NDCs are themselves non-binding goals unless they create unilateral commitments. In the Glasgow Agreement, COP parties were diplomatically called upon to 'transition towards low-emission energy systems'. No binding obligation is inferred from the use of diplomatic language.[1032] In the meaning of the classic definition, the Paris Agreement and the Glasgow Pact do not provide directly incompatible obligations with investment

1026. Wilfred Jenks, 'The Conflict of Law-Making Treaties' (1953) 30 British Yearbook of International Law 401, 426; Gabrielle Marceau, 'Conflicts of Norms and Conflicts of Jurisdictions: The Relationship Between the WTO Agreement and MEAs and Other Treaties' (2001) 35 Journal of World Trade 1081 https://doi.org/10.54648/384808; Władysław Czapliriski and Gennadiĭ Danilenko, 'Conflicts of Norms in International Law' in *Netherlands Yearbook of International Law* (CUP 1990) 13 ('In our opinion, the conflicts arise at the stage of application of the agreements when the later treaty in a particular situation violates the rights of any other party to the earlier treaty, or when the provision of the later treaty seriously infringes provisions of the earlier treaty which are indispensable for the effective implementation of the object or aim of that treaty.').
1027. ILC, *Fragmentation of International Law: Difficulties Arising* (n 219) para. 25.
1028. Joost Pauwelyn, *Conflict of Norms in Public International Law. How WTO Law Relates to Other Rules of International Law* (Cambridge: Cambridge Univ. Press 2003) 5-8.
1029. Joost Pauwelyn, *Conflicts of Norms in Public International Law How WTO Law Relates to Other Rules of International Law* (CUP 2003), 179.
1030. Article 2.1(a) of the Paris Agreement (n 6).
1031. They are characterised by the imperative verb 'shall', instead of the diplomatic 'should'.
1032. For the full extent analysis *see* Chapter 5.

protection. The obligation to publish a NDC is consistent with the foreign investor's protection against expropriation. There is no direct incompatibility between affording foreign investor protection and respecting the obligation to reach a global CO_2 reduction target by 2100.

Second, regarding the Kyoto Protocol and EU law provisions on climate change, there is no conflict *stricto sensu* either. The Protocol imposes binding emission reduction targets on its Parties. The difficulty lies in the host state's choice of regulatory action to implement its goals. A State may argue that phasing out a specific energy sector is not necessary to meet its emissions target. For instance, the EU's 'Fit for 55' package sets a binding target of achieving climate neutrality by 2050.[1033] But it provides no strict obligations to phase out an industry sector, even less in a way that would be unproportionate, unlawful or without adequate compensation.[1034]

Third, in practice, incompatibility is a high threshold. Many of the cases discussed above were intra-EU disputes. They commonly discussed the relevance of EU law. Host states referred to EU law to argue for the regimes' incompatibility at the jurisdictional level.[1035] They also argued for the legal impact of EU state aid law on admissibility and FET. The tribunal in *Green Power and SCE v. Spain*[1036] barred jurisdiction because of EU law and Court of Justice of the European Union (CJEU) rulings. It contended that an ECT dispute arising between an investor from a Member State and a host state that is also an EU Member State is incompatible with EU law.[1037] The rationale is that only the EU and the European Court of Justice would have jurisdiction over these disputes.[1038] Most tribunals refused this defence argument with various degrees of strictness.[1039] To be considered 'incompatible' in practice, tribunals found that only a 'material inconsistency' between two treaties could amount to incompatibility and bar jurisdiction.[1040] Most other tribunals found no material inconsistency.[1041] Some tribunals found such inconsistency but applied ECT's Article 16 to

1033. European Commission, 'Communication on "Fit for 55": Delivering the EU's 2030 Climate Target on the Way to Climate Neutrality' COM (2021) 550.
1034. David Khachvani D., 'Non-compensable Regulation Versus Regulatory Expropriation: Are Climate Change Regulation Compensable?' (2020) 35 ICSID Review 154 https://doi.org/10.1093/icsidreview/siaa009.
1035. *See Achmea Judgment, Slovak Republic v. Achmea BV*, Case C-2084/16, Judgment of the Court of Justice of the European Union (Grand Chamber) (6 March 2018) in some cases, among others, *9REN v. Spain* (n 422) and *Foresight v. Spain* (n 620). *See also* Republic of *Moldova v. Komstroy LLC*, Case C-741/19, Judgment of the Court of Justice of the European Union (Grand Chamber) (2 September 2021).
1036. *Green Power K/S and SCE Solar Don Benito APS v. Kingdom of Spain*, SCC Case No. V2016/135.
1037. Federico Ortino and Petros Mavroidis, 'Intra-EU Investment Disputes and the Monopoly over the Interpretation of EU Law' (2023) 33 The American Review of International Arbitration 4 12-13 https://doi.org/10.2139/ssrn.4769352.
1038. *Green Power and SCE v. Spain*, para. 469 finding that EU law in the relations between Denmark and Spain is a matter of lex superior.
1039. *Ibid.*, paras 437-38; comparing the position of the tribunal to the rejection of the intra-EU disputes argument in *Masdar v. Spain* (n 595) and *Vattenfall v. Germany.*
1040. *RREEF v. Spain* (n 413) Decision on Jurisdiction, 6 June 2016, paras 75, 87; *Vattenfall v. Germany* (II), Decision on the Achmea Issue, para. 229; *FREIF v. Spain* (n 77) para. 325.
1041. *Ibid. Electrabel v. Hungary* (n 225) paras 4.175-176 and 4.189 finding otherwise that EU would prevail otherwise.

find that EU law could not prevail.[1042] In sum, in practice, only a material, clear and material inconsistency between investment law provisions and other rules from international law may bar jurisdiction. ECT tribunals have only considered the TFEU as a relevant treaty in their rulings. Investment treaties do not prohibit states from 'phasing-out' coal; they prohibit unlawful expropriation. Thus, there is no material inconsistency between phasing out an investor's assets for mitigation purposes and doing so lawfully, fairly, and equitably.

The substantive content of ICCL and investment agreements cannot be said to be *directly* contradictory.

c) Conflict **Lato Sensu** *Limited to the Fossil Fuel Sector*

Regarding the broad definition of 'conflict', I find that such conflict may exist but is limited to the fossil fuel sector.

First, ICCL *suggests* that energy producers in the coal and fossil fuel industries may be discriminated against under international law. It thus justifies the state's actions in climate measures pertaining to the phase down of coal generation and the withdrawal of subsidies for fossil fuel generation. On the contrary, investment agreements generally do not discriminate between investments, protecting the investment irrespective of its nature. Second, that conflict stems from the divergence in objectives. IIAs promote foreign investment by creating a predictable legal environment that provides for fair and non-discriminatory treatment of foreign investors. At the same time, ICCL suggests that parties must change their national laws to favour more sustainable and cleaner investments. The goals' divergence can thus amount to a conflict *lato sensu*. This conflict does not extend to clean energy investments, which are promoted both under ICCL and investment agreements.

In sum, despite the common assumption that ICCL and international investment law are incompatible,[1043] I find no normative conflict *stricto sensu*. In other words, there is no legal incompatibility between ICCL, climate change goals and the protection of foreign investments, irrespective of the nature of the investment. However, there is a conflict under the broad definition of 'conflict' proposed by the ILC in its Report on Fragmentation.[1044] I must now turn to considering ICCL as either applicable law or fact. To do so requires first an in-depth review of the standing practice of investment tribunals in relation to treaties of international law. Second, I assess whether systemic integration via VCLT's Article 31(3)(c) is possible. Third, I will look at ICCL as a fact in the *application* of investment provisions such as FET.

1042. *Ibid.*
1043. Haut Conseil pour le Climat, *Avis sur la modernisation du traité sur la Charte de l'énergie* (19 October 2022).
1044. ILC, *Fragmentation of International Law: Difficulties Arising* (n 219) 25.

2 ICCL as 'Relevant' International Law Impacting Investment Disputes

Now that I have established no direct legal incompatibility between the two regimes, I must turn to whether ICCL can impact the adjudication of investment disputes and LE claims. In theory, yes. Investment tribunals consider that international law rules, other than investment law, may be relevant to resolving an investment dispute. International law may be part of the factual background of a dispute, an applicable law, or a relevant norm in the interpretation of a provision. Finally, it may, as I find below, act as a relevant fact in the application of an investment standard.

Investment tribunals have a standing practice of considering *relevant* international treaties to assess investors' and states' rights under an IIA. The reason is that they are bound by the general rules of interpretation of the VCLT. They must apply, if relevant, international law to interpreting IIA provisions. Article 42 of the ICSID Convention, dealing with the applicable law, refers to 'such rules of international law as may be applicable', which is to be read as including principles of law.[1045] Also, in those instances where an applicable law clause is included in a BIT, the treaty usually adopts a formulation referring to 'international law' (typically in combination with domestic law).[1046] It is commonly recognised that rules of international law may play a role in adjudicating investment disputes.[1047] In the words of the tribunal in *SolEs Badajoz v. Spain* on the Energy Charter Treaty:

> [W]hen the ECT is interpreted and applied pursuant to the VCLT, treaties other than the ECT could also play a role as applicable law in a variety of ways, e.g., as agreements relevant to the interpretation of the ECT (pursuant to Article 31 of the VCLT) or as agreements that modify the ECT (pursuant to VCLT Article 40). Thus, under both the ECT and the law of treaties, there are circumstances in which the provisions of a treaty other than the ECT could have an impact on the law to be applied in a dispute in which a breach of Part III of the ECT is alleged and thus can play a role as applicable law.[1048]

International investment law is permeable because it does not stem from a vacuum. It is part of broader public international law, and its provisions must be interpreted according to the customary rules reflected in the VCLT.[1049] The VCLT, established in 1969, plays a vital role in resolving conflicts arising from the application of international treaties. The role of the VCLT in international investment law is

1045. Christoph Schreuer and others, *The ICSID Convention: A Commentary* (CUP 2009), 607-610; *See also* ICSID, *ICSID Convention, Regulations and Rules* (ICSID 2006) 46.
1046. Tarcisio Gazzini, 'General Principles of Law in the Field of Foreign Investment' (2009) 10 The Journal of World Investment & Trade 103, 112 https://doi.org/10.1163/221190009x00240 (providing examples of applicable law clauses in BITs).
1047. A majority of the awards reviewed mentioned an international agreement other than the ECT – most frequently the VCLT – but it is only in relation to EU law that arbitrators engaged in substantive inquiry.
1048. *SolEs Badajoz v. Spain* (n 623) para. 162.
1049. Martins Paparinskis, 'The Interpretation of Treaties and Investment Arbitration: Introductory Reflections' in Esme Shirlow and Kiran N. Gore (eds), *The Vienna Convention on the Law of Treaties in Investor-State Disputes: History, Evolution and Future* (Kluwer Law International 2022) 26.

consensual among practitioners and scholars.[1050] Arbitrators interpret agreements drafted and ratified by sovereign states; thus, general rules of interpretation apply to their interpretation.[1051] Nevertheless, investment arbitration is not purely a form of dispute resolution under public international law. It is rather best characterised as a hybrid, specialised form of dispute resolution, combining elements of private and public international law.[1052] Concretely, it means that arbitrators consider the scope of jurisdiction of an investment tribunal limited by the underlying investment agreement.[1053] This hybridity, limits in jurisdiction's scope, and natural limits of international law and the VCLT explain why few tribunals have integrated other rules of international law than the VCLT in resolving investment disputes.[1054] Since ICCL is part of international law, the question becomes whether it is relevant to investment claims as applicable law or fact. To assess the relevance, one should first assess potential conflicts before turning to more specific interactions.

3 Obstacles to Incorporating ICCL under Articles 31 and 32 of the VCLT

The Convention provides helpful solutions to the *lato sensu* conflict of norms. Article 31 of the VCLT outlines the primary principles of interpretation, allowing the interpreter to refer to relevant agreements between the State parties,[1055] subsequent State

1050. Esme Shirlow and Kiran N. Gore, 'Chapter 1: An Introduction to the VCLT and Its Role in ISDS: Looking Back, Looking Forward', in Shirlow and Gore, *Vienna* (n 1049) 5.
1051. Ashwita Ambast and Dirk Pulkowski, 'The VCLT as a Unifying Force in Treaty Design: How Special Is Investment Law?' in Shirlow and Gore, *Vienna* (n 1049) 440-441.
1052. *See* for an excellent summary Alvarez Jose Enrique Alvarez, 'Is Investor-State Arbitration "Public"?' (2016) 7 Journal of International Dispute Settlement 3 534, 537 https://doi.org/10.1093/jnlids/idw019; Niccolò Ridi and Thomas Schultz, 'Empirically Mapping Investment Arbitration Scholarship: Networks, Authorities, and the Research Front' in Katia Fach Gomez (ed.), *Private Actors in International Investment Law* (Springer 2020) 209, 213.
1053. For instance, Art. 16 of the ECT.
1054. The proposals to integrate other regimes of law in international investment law have not been scarce. However, I agree with the cautiousness of José Alvarez, *Boundaries of Investment Arbitration: The Use of Trade and European Human Rights Law in Investor-State Disputes* (Juris Net LCC 2018). I believe that reliance on ECHR law, WTO law, and ICCL in ISDS may be useful to fill in potential gaps and address specific criticisms of investment law. However, their use shall be carried out with caution and due regard to the text of applicable instruments. To read prominent proposals on the interaction between international investment law and other internal law regimes, *see* Bruno Simma and Theodore Kill, 'Harmonizing Investment Protection and International Human Rights: First Steps Towards a Methodology' in Christina Binder and others (eds), *International Investment Law of the 21st Century: Essays in Honour of Christoph Schreuer* (2009) 678; Silvia Steininger, 'What's Human Rights Got to Do With It? An Empirical Analysis of Human Rights References in Investment Arbitration' (2018) 31 LJIL 33 https://doi.org/10.1017/s0922156517000528; Adam Bradlow, 'Human Rights Impact Litigation in ISDS: A Proposal for Enabling Private Parties to Bring Human Rights Claims Through Investor-State Dispute Settlement Mechanisms' (2018) 43 Yale Journal of International Law 2 355; Karsten Nowrot, 'How to Include Environmental Protection, Human Rights and Sustainability in International Investment Law?' (2014) 15 The Journal of World Investment & Trade 3-4 612 https://doi.org/10.1163/22119000-01504013.
1055. Article 31(3)(a).

practice in the application of the treaty[1056] or 'other relevant rules of international law applicable in the relations between the parties'.[1057] Other interpretative rules include Article 32 referring to supplementary means of interpretations such as 'preparatory work of the treaty and the circumstances of its conclusion'.[1058] Other principles include the primacy of more specific treaties (*lex specialis*) or later treaties (*lex posteriori*).

Although Articles 31 and 32 of the VCLT offer valuable insights into treaty interpretation, there are certain constraints that must be recognised. One primary limitation is the requirement of relevance. These provisions apply specifically to treaties closely related to the treaty under consideration.[1059] In particular, Article 31(2) and (3)(a) and (b) apply only to subsequent agreements and practices between the original State parties in the application of the treaty, making it difficult to extend their application to unrelated treaties. Similarly, the *lex specialis* and *posteriori* principles are restricted to provisions directly linked to the specific clauses of the IIA. But ICCL is, as demonstrated above, neither a subsequent treaty on the same subject as IIAs, nor *lex specialis*. Therefore, these interpretation rules do not apply to incorporate ICCL in investment treaty interpretation. Indeed, ICCL

This leaves as a guideline Article 31(3)(c), studied below.

4 Limited Integration of ICCL Through Article 31(3)(c) VCLT

Are climate change and ICCL relevant to adjudicating energy transition-related investment disputes as part of the systematic integration under Article 31(3)(c)?[1060] The answer depends on the treaty at stake. ICCL may not be relevant in interpreting FET or expropriation provisions when a treaty does not refer to the environment or climate mitigation in a treaty provision. Article 31(3)(c) is, however, useful to interpret climate or environment-related clauses.

1056. Article 31(3)(b).
1057. Article 31(3)(c).
1058. Article 32 VCLT.
1059. My argument regarding 'closely related treaties' refers to the tremendous difficulties in theory to define the 'subjet matter of a treaty' referred to in Art. 31 of the VCLT, *see* ILC, *Fragmentation of International Law: Difficulties Arising* (n 219) paras 21-24; E.W. Vierdag, 'The Time of the "Conclusion" of a Multilateral Treaty: Article 30 of the Vienna Convention on the Law of Treaties and Related Provisions' (1988) 59 British Year Book of International Law 75, 100 https://doi.org/10.1093/bybil/59.1.75 ('[t]he requirement that the instruments must relate to the same subject-matter seems to raise extremely difficult problems in theory, but may turn out not to be so very difficult in practice. If an attempted simultaneous application of two rules to one set of facts or actions leads to incompatible results, it can safely be assumed that the test of sameness is satisfied').
1060. The idea has been supported in relation to the inclusion of human rights, environmental protection and sustainable development, Roland Kläger, 'Revising Treatment Standards: Fair and Equitable Treatment in Light of Sustainable Development' in Steffen Hindelang and Markus Krajewski (eds), *Shifting Paradigms in International Investment Law* (OUP 2016) 65, 70; McLachlan, 'Treatment of Investors' (n 40) 67, 222-223.

Article 31(3)(c) is part of the mandatory part of the interpretation process; however, it can be referred to when the 'meaning of the treaty terms is ambiguous, obscure, absurd or unreasonable'.[1061] The article sets out three conditions.

First, in terms of applicability, the applicable rule must be identified at a time to be decided. The article does not specify whether it concerns the treaty's parties or the dispute. Similarly, it does not indicate temporal provision. It is unclear whether the applicable rule is to be determined at the conclusion of the treaty or when the dispute arose. This may constitute an important hurdle because, for instance, the Kyoto Protocol came into force after the ECT's conclusion, and the Paris Agreement was signed after.

Second, the article refers to the 'rules of international law'. On the one hand, for interpretation purposes, the reference must be rules and not broader principles or considerations that cannot be firmly established as rules, such as the concept of 'sustainable development'. On the other hand, rules of international law include general principles, customs and, where applicable, other treaties with binding provisions. The issue here is the legal quality of provisions under the Paris and Glasgow Pact, which may default the quality of rules.

Third, the rules must be relevant to the interpretation of the treaty. The relevancy hurdle explains why arbitrators prefer general principles of international law and customary rules rather than other treaties which would over-extend their jurisdiction.[1062]

In practice, the integration of provisions of international law under VCLT's Article 31(3)(c) is therefore faced with many hurdles. The tribunal in *Philip Morris* offers an interesting illustration. In this case, the Uruguayan government adopted a regulation to disincentive tobacco consumption. The tribunal found that the regulation was 'adopted in fulfilment of Uruguay's national and *international legal obligations* for the protection of public health'.[1063] However, the international health treaty justifying the regulation was not exploited under Article 31(3)(c). Instead, it was used as a legal fact. As such, it justified the reasonableness of the measures. It also warranted the integration of the customary doctrine of police powers in the interpretation of the expropriation standard.[1064] Similarly, in assessing the FET claim, the tribunal integrated international health law provisions as legal facts rather than under Article 31(3)(c).[1065]

Nevertheless, systemic integration is possible in specific situations. For instance, the Paris Agreement and the Glasgow Pact may inform the interpretation of specific treaty provisions pertaining to the right to regulate climate mitigation purposes.[1066] In

1061. On this aspect, the interpretation of the Fair and Equitable Treatment could qualify, given the recurrent criticism as to its lack of clarity; on this principle *see* ILC, *Fragmentation*, para. 425; and *WTO Panel in European Communities: Measures Affecting the Approval and Marketing of Biotech Products*, para. 7.69.

1062. Herve Ascensio 'Article 31 of the VCLT's and International Investment Law' (2016) 31 ICSID Review 2 366, 383 https://doi.org/10.1093/icsidreview/siw008.

1063. *Philip Morris v. Uruguay* (n 76) para. 302.

1064. *Ibid.*, paras 290-301.

1065. *Ibid.*, para. 430.

1066. Sarvarian, 'Invoking the Paris Agreement' (n 153) 427-428, 431.

other words, where a treaty specifically refers to the right to regulate climate change purposes, arbitrators may turn to ICCL through Article 31(3)(c) for a better understanding of what this means. To draw a parallel, in the *World Trade Organisation (WTO) United States-Shrimp* case,[1067] the appellate body opined that the terms 'natural resources' and 'exhaustible' in Article XX (g) were 'by definition evolutionary'.[1068] The appellate body thus referred to Article 56 of the United Nations Convention on the Law of the Sea in support of the proposition that natural resources could include both living and non-living resources. The Tribunal expressly relied on Article 31(3)(c) and said its task was 'to interpret the language of the chapeau, seeking additional interpretative guidance, as appropriate, from the general principles of international law'.[1069] The same reasoning could apply to investment disputes, whereby arbitrators turn to the UN regime to interpret a climate change provision. The analysis stops here because of the numerous possibilities of treaty clauses that must be first interpreted through concentric circles, each providing assistance in interpreting the treaty.[1070] In the words of the ILC: 'the question of the normative weight to be given to particular rights and obligations at the moment when they appear to clash with other rights and obligations can only be argued on a case-by-case basis'.[1071]

International treaties may be considered the applicable law in interpreting an investment provision pertaining to the right to regulate for environmental purposes or climate mitigation exceptions, following Article 31(3)(c). However, the hurdle for its integration into investment treaties without referring to the environment is particularly high. Given this quasi-impossibility of using the principles of general public law interpretation to integrate ICCL in assessing energy disputes, ICCL can act as fact or applicable law. International treaties may be regarded as facts, amount to business risks for energy providers, and thus affect the existence or legitimacy of their expectations.

5 Limited Integration of ICCL as Applicable Law

Certain investment agreements contain rules regarding the applicable law to the disputes. For instance, the Energy Charter Treaty provides under Article 26(6) that arbitral tribunals may apply 'applicable rules and principles of international law' with respect to liability and quantum. Thus, the question is whether the Claimant or

1067. *United States – Import Prohibition of Certain Shrimp and Shrimp Products*, WTO Appellate Body Report (12 October 1998) WT/DS58/AB/R, paras 126-134.
1068. *Ibid.*, para. 130.
1069. *Ibid.*, para. 158.
1070. Annuaire de l'Institut de droit international, vol. 44-I (Session of Sienna), pp. 200-201 (Max Huber, 'Il faut donc chercher la volonté des parties dans le texte conventionnel, d'abord dans les clauses relatives à la contestation, ensuite dans l'ensemble de la convention, ensuite dans le droit international général, et enfin dans les principes généraux de droit reconnus par les nations civilisées. C'est par cet encerclement concentrique que le juge arrivera dans beaucoup de cas à établir la volonté presumptive des parties "conformément aux exigences fondamentales de la plénitude du droit et de la justice internationale", ainsi que le rapporteur formule admirablement la tâche du juge').
1071. ILC, *Fragmentation of International Law: Difficulties Arising* (n 219) para. 474.

Respondent could 'invoke' the Paris Agreement or Glasgow Pact as applicable law to the dispute. For instance, a claimant or respondent could put forth the argument that the respondent's obligation to mitigate GHG emissions, as outlined in Article 4 of the Paris Agreement, constitutes a 'relevant rule of international law'. This rule could be instrumental in determining whether a breach of investor rights (e.g., legitimate expectations) concerning a specific energy-related investment occurred under Article 10(1) of the ECT, considering its role in the NDCs of that State.[1072]

In the case of a fossil fuel investment, the state could also contend, for quantum purposes, that even if the respondent's conduct in regulating the specific investment breached its substantive obligations towards the investor, the duty under the Paris Agreement to mitigate GHG emissions could diminish the damages owed to the investor.[1073] Excessive emissions from the investment impacting the host state's NDCs under the Paris Agreement may help define the content of the applicable law.

The difficulty here is that arbitral tribunals are reluctant to introduce even mandatory rules as part of the applicable law of the dispute. For instance, the NZEID case law under the ECT proves that there is no consensus to apply (mandatory) EU state aid law as part of the applicable law. Even when they do integrate EU law as part of applicable law, it is only in case of 'incompatibility' or 'unlawfulness' that the latter becomes relevant, as demonstrated below.

Several tribunals found that EU law should be part of the applicable law. In this particular case, the arbitral tribunals regarded EU law as an integral component of the domestic legal framework governing the investment. The tribunal in *Photovoltaik v. Czech Republic* treated EU law as applicable domestic law to assess whether the state's revisions to the incentive scheme for solar energy had breached the FET standard.[1074] It found that since the EC had not approved the incentive scheme at the time of the investment, the foreign investor could not reasonably expect that the scheme would remain unchanged.[1075] Similarly, the tribunal in *BayWare v. Spain* considered that EU state aid law is part of the applicable law of the state and hence crucial to assess legitimate expectations when these are based on unlawful commitments.[1076] Professor Vinuesa agrees with the BayWare assessment and proposes in his dissenting opinion to appropriately integrate EU state aid law as part of the applicable law. Nevertheless, he, like *BayWare and Photovoltaik*, emphasised that such integration is only relevant when an incompatibility or unlawfulness arises:

1072. Sarvarian, 'Invoking the Paris Agreement' (n 153) 426-427.
1073. *Ibid.*, 127-128.
1074. *Photovoltaik v. Czech Republic* (n 840) paras 514-533.
1075. *Ibid.*, paras 514, 522 ('Consequently, the relevant question is whether, at the time the investment was made, the EC had, upon due notification, positively decided that the solar support regime was compatible with EU law. In the absence of due notification and any such decision, the investor – as in the present case – was not entitled to hold any legitimate expectations that the un-notified support system would not be changed').
1076. *BayWare v. Spain* (n 639), para. 569 ('[i]n principle, an investor cannot have a legitimate expectation of treatment which is unlawful under the law of the host State, provided that the host State law itself is not inconsistent with the treaty under which the tribunal exercises its jurisdiction').

> In case of *incompatibilities,* the very content of the rules in conflict would determine the criteria to be followed in order to decide which law must be applied to the particular situation.[1077]

Other tribunals refused to integrate EU state aid law as part of the applicable law. They rather found that it was part of the factual context. For instance, the tribunal in *Cube* stated in a statement (relied by other tribunals) that:

> This Tribunal does not have to apply, or take a decision on any question of, Spanish law or EU law. Under the provisions concerning the applicable law that are binding on this Tribunal, Spanish law and EU law are relevant only as facts in the light of which the rights and duties of the Parties under the ECT and international law are to be determined. Thus, for example, the provisions on EU law concerning State aid are not applied by this Tribunal, nor does the Tribunal make any decision on their interpretation. They are relevant only as part of the factual matrix, and in this case particularly as part of the factual basis for determinations of how the Claimants could expect to be treated in respect of their power plants in Spain.[1078]

Considering the above, besides the fact that some tribunals refuse to apply international law other than the underlying treaty, there are two main difficulties in integrating ICCL norms as applicable law in a dispute relying on a treaty integrating international rules to the applicable law.

First, the arbitral tribunal must find that ICCL is a 'relevant' international law. This is not straightforward, as demonstrated above.[1079] The reasoning for EU state aid law is difficult to apply to ICCL, as climate change norms usually do not target a specific sector, request specific state's measures or set binding rules on one set of production.[1080] In other words, they qualify with difficulty as applicable domestic law to the investment and hardly as applicable law on the host state in relation to a particular sector, but this can change as ICCL norms and states' obligations develop in their own jurisdiction.

Second, the arbitral tribunal must establish whether: (a) the state's specific commitment is unlawful considering its international obligation (by analogy to EU state aid law), or (b) whether the obligation under the investment treaty is incompatible with the respect of international obligations of the state. It is difficult to respond to both questions in the abstract. Regarding the first question, it appears difficult to answer in the affirmative, as only mandatory legislation or judicial decisions could

---

1077. *Foresight v. Spain* (n 620), Partial Dissenting opinion Co-arbitator Raùl E. Vinuesa, para. 15 (finding that EU law (on state aid) is part of the applicable law to the dispute and should be applied to the merits of the case).

1078. *Cube Infrastructure v. Spain* (n 402) para. 158, approved in *FREIF v. Spain* (n 77) at para. 531 and 532; on the contrary, *BayWa r.e. v. Spain* (n 639) considered EU State Aid Law to be part of the applicable law at paras 553-572.

1079. *See* Chapter 4.B.2.

1080. But the progressive elaboration of the UN regime can disprove this statement, *see* Attracta Mooney, Aime Williams and Simeon Kerr, 'Countries Reach "Historic" COP28 Deal to Transition from Fossil Fuels' *Financial Times* (London, 13 December 2023).

render the state's measure 'unlawful' with respect to its climate commitments. Regarding incompatibility, there is more room for argument. Are new fossil fuel permits incompatible with states' own binding net zero goals (that may be enshrined in law) or with compliance with the Paris Agreement? Potentially, it will depend on the state's international commitments and its own obligations (potentially adjudicated by its own judicial apparatus). The Respondent would have to prove that it is obliged under international law to curb its emissions and that the advantage or permit it offered to the investor was incompatible with its climate change commitments. Finding an incompatibility may mean that the state could not have issued a specific commitment in the first place. In this case, no LE could be claimed.

To summarise this section, there is no normative conflict *stricto sensu* between international investment law and ICCL. Investment and climate treaties address different subjects. The latter aims at reducing GHG emissions, and the former aims at ensuring the lawfulness of a state's measures affecting foreign private property. There is nevertheless a normative conflict in the broad understanding. When states phase down the production and use of non-renewable sources of energy to implement ICCL, they may breach obligations under international investment law. This broad conflict is unlikely to affect investment disputes. Rather, ICCL appears as a relevant legal fact in the adjudication of an NZEID. It may affect the investor's LE and the reasonableness of the state's measure. Under Article 31(3)(c), binding ICCL provisions may help interpret clauses directly referring to climate change in IIAs. If the underlying treaty considers relevant international treaties as part of the applicable law, one must prove that ICCL is 'relevant' and that the state's measures are incompatible, in which case no specific commitment could have been issued and no expectation protected.

C ICCL AS A RELEVANT FACT TO ASSESS LEGITIMATE EXPECTATIONS

The broadest port of entry of ICCL into resolving investment disputes is as a fact. As fact, it helps examine a climate policy's arbitrariness, reasonableness, and proportionality. Through ICCL, states publicly provide information regarding future measures, which should be considered by the investor when planning their investment. This research suggests that ICCL can inform foreign investors' LE and the foreseeability of frustrating measures, altering the level of protection to which they are entitled.[1081]

Below, I address the role of legal facts in the resolution of investment disputes, and LE claims in general before delving into the specificity of ICCL as a fact.

1081. ICC, *Resolving Climate Change-Related Disputes* (n 22) paras 5.60-5.63 (preferring the word 'informing' in relation to legitimate expectations' assessments, 'Even where there is no reference to the Paris Agreement in the applicable bilateral investment treaty, international obligations are usually interpreted on a progressive basis and it is likely that the Paris Agreement, and NDCs, will inform the investing party's legitimate expectations in determining, for example, a fair and equitable treatment claim').

1 Role of Legal Facts in the Application of Legitimate Expectations

To find whether ICCL can act as a relevant fact, one must turn again to the ECT cases. These show that investment tribunals apply international law as relevant facts, regardless of the voluntary or detrimental reliance theory of LE applied by the tribunal.

A first finding in the study on NZEID is that arbitral tribunals consensually recognise international treaties as relevant facts in assessing their own jurisdiction. On jurisdiction, ECT tribunals have considered the TFEU as a relevant treaty in their rulings.[1082] One tribunal found that EU law prevails over the ECT in intra-EU disputes, but all others reached opposite conclusions.[1083]

A second finding is that international law, as a fact, influenced two main questions on the merit phase and in the assessment of legitimate expectations. On the latter, it helped find whether the investor was entitled to LE for regulatory stability and whether the regulatory frustrating measure was reasonable and proportional. Additionally, international law can be a decisive factor in assessing a frustrating measure's foreseeability.

International treaties have been found to be relevant in other past cases. In the *Methanex v. United States* case, the tribunal dismissed all the claims of the Canadian investor, a producer of an additive prohibited in California. In the absence of specific commitment from the State and because California had adopted a constant observance of an environmental protection policy, the tribunal dismissed the claims.[1084] The principle deriving from this case was a 'presumption of awareness of the general regulatory environment'[1085] by the foreign investor prior to the investment date. The tribunal stressed the need for the investor to be aware of the regulatory environment in which it was operating as a condition for applying the LE. To the tribunal, Methanex should have been aware that it had entered a political economy:

> in which it was widely known, if not notorious, that governmental environmental and health protection institutions at the federal and state level [...] continuously monitored the use and impact of chemical compounds and commonly prohibited or restricted the use of some of those compounds for environmental and/or health reasons.[1086]

Second, the *Philip Morris* tribunal considered international law at length in its decision related to human health. Adopting a detrimental reliance approach and emphasising regulatory rights,[1087] the tribunal set an important milestone on the foreseeability of regulatory changes. In a finding bearing significance for climate

1082. Climate Change Counsel, *The ECT* (n 332) 6; *see* for an extensive summary of the case law in its interaction with the Achmea decision, Balcerzak, *Renewable Energy Arbitration* (n 220) in particular 79ff., 143 (finding that 'Regardless of whether the tribunals in the Spanish saga cases issued their jurisdiction decisions before or after the Achmea judgment was handed down, they were unanimous in dismissing the intra-EU objection').
1083. *Ibid.*
1084. *Methanex Corporation v. United States of America*, UNCITRAL, Final Award, 3 August 2005.
1085. UNCTAD, *Fair and Equitable Treatment: A Sequel* (n 365) 71.
1086. *Methanex v. United States* (n 1084) pt IV, Chapter D, para. 10.
1087. *Philip Morris v. Uruguay* (n 76) para. 427.

change-related disputes, the arbitral tribunal concluded that 'in light of widely accepted articulations of international concern for the harmful effect of tobacco, the expectation *could only have been of progressively more stringent* regulation of the sale and use of tobacco products' (emphasis added).[1088] Analogically, in light of the widely accepted articulation of international concern for the harmful effect of climate change, the expectation can only be progressively more stringent regulation of the production and consumption of carbon-intense energy types.

Third, regarding reasonableness, the *AES Summit v. Hungary's* tribunal noted the potential importance of EU law as fact in the assessment of the reasonable nature of a state's measure:

> Rather, the dispute is about the conformity or non-conformity of Hungary's acts and measures with the ECT. Therefore, it is the behaviour of the state (the introduction by Hungary of the Price Decrees) which must be analysed in light of the ECT, to determine whether the measures, or the manner in which they were introduced, violated the [Energy Charter] Treaty. The question of whether Hungary was, may have been, or may have felt obliged under [EU] law to act as it did, is only an element to be considered by this Tribunal when determining the 'rationality,' 'reasonableness,' 'arbitrariness' and 'transparency' of the reintroduction of administrative pricing and the Price Decrees.[1089]

In summary, arbitral tribunals have recognised that international law provisions may have consequences on foreign investors' LE. International law may affect the foreseeability of regulatory changes at the time of the investment and the reasonableness assessment of the state's measure.

2 ICCL May Be Exploited as a Relevant Fact by Energy Investors and States in Net Zero Investment Disputes

On the merits of international investment disputes, ICCL appears relevant, as a fact, to assess the investors' expectations.

On the merits and LE, there are examples of tribunals considering ICCL as a fact to either alleviate or devalue expectations. In the NZEID cases, the vast majority of tribunals recognised that the host country was bound under EU law to achieve certain emission reductions. Could this not be part of the expectations of the investor? Most of the tribunals have simply mentioned the Kyoto Protocol and the EU directive as a 'broader context' to the dispute.[1090] A few arbitrators mentioned the importance of the cases to environmental regulation but did not fully achieve their reasoning to back the claim that ICCL may constitute or form part of the LE of a clean energy investor. However, some tribunals explicitly and correctly linked the international objective of the development of RE energy to meet GHG emissions targets to the expectations of the

1088. *Ibid.*, para. 430.
1089. *Aes Summit Generation Limited Aes-Tisza Erömü Kft v. The Republic of Hungary*, ICSID Case No. ARB/07/22, Award (23 September 2010), para. 7.6.9.
1090. *See* Appendix n°2.

investor.[1091] There are few but significant examples to support the finding. The tribunal in *PV investors*, adopting a detrimental reliance approach, correctly considered climate change as an important fact in the assessment of LE.[1092] Similarly, Charles Brower, although dissenting from the majority in the same case, referred to the *Novenergia* case, which established a clear nexus between the factual relevance of ICCL and the legitimate expectations of the investors:

> The Tribunal considers that Law 54/1997 and RD 661/2007 were clearly enacted with the objective of ensuring that the Kingdom of Spain achieved its emissions and RE targets. In order to achieve that objective, the Kingdom of Spain created a very favourable investment climate for RE investors, and the nucleus of such investment climate was the Special Regime.[1093]

The tribunal in *Watkins Holding v. Spain*'s award considered EU law and international commitments on climate change as significant facts in assessing whether the investor was entitled to legitimate and reasonable expectations.[1094] The tribunal explained that the investor's expectations were legitimate and that the investor was reasonable to rely on Spain's incentive scheme partly because it 'was part of a wider international and domestic policy to develop RE power generation infrastructure and to specifically encourage and attract the necessary investments'.[1095] In other words, Spain's incentive scheme was part of an international energy policy. This wider factual complex is a factor in determining that the investors could legitimately rely on the scheme.

Adopting a good faith approach of LE, the tribunal in *Renergy* also correctly found that Spain committed to pursuing the 'vital interest' of increasing RE production to

1091. *Watkins Holdings v. Spain* (n 413) para. 527 ('The Tribunal finds that the Claimants' expectations on the continued application of the economic regime to the Project Companies were legitimate and reasonable [for reasons including] (...) the economic regime (...) was part of a wider international and domestic policy to develop RE power generation infrastructure and to specifically encourage and attract the necessary investments.'); *PV investors v. Spain* (n 413) para. 591 (the tribunal correctly considers as part of LE that: 'Following the 1997 Electricity Law, Spain enacted a number of regulations which sought to specify the general parameters set out in the Law. These regulations were passed in the context of global, regional and national efforts to address climate change, aimed at the reduction of emissions of carbon dioxide. Against the background of the 1992 UN Framework Convention on Climate Change (UNFCCC) and the 1997 Kyoto Protocol to the UNFCCC, the European Union had also adopted rules committing Member States, including Spain, to reduce greenhouse gas emissions. These rules included measures to encourage the use of renewable and other environment-friendly technologies').

1092. *PV Investors v. Spain* (n 413) para. 591 ('Following the 1997 Electricity Law, Spain enacted a number of regulations which sought to specify the general parameters set out in the Law. These regulations were passed in the context of global, regional and national efforts to address climate change, aimed at the reduction of emissions of carbon dioxide. Against the background of the 1992 UN Framework Convention on Climate Change (UNFCCC) and the 1997 Kyoto Protocol to the UNFCCC, the European Union had also adopted rules committing Member States, including Spain, to reduce greenhouse gas emissions. These rules included measures to encourage the use of renewable and other environment-friendly technologies').

1093. *PV Investors v. Spain* (n 413), Concurring and Dissenting Opinion of Charles N. Brower, para. 14 citing *Novenergia II v. Spain* (n 413) para. 665.

1094. *Watkins Holdings v. Spain* (n 413) para. 527.

1095. *Ibid.*, paras 527-529.

meet emission targets.[1096] Similarly, reverting to a good faith approach combined with the unilateral statements doctrine, the *Cube Infrastructure v. Spain* tribunal considered EU law as a fact in assessing whether the investor was entitled to LE that Spain's incentive scheme for renewable energy investments would not be significantly altered. The tribunal explained that the investor's expectations were legitimate and reasonable in part because of EU law. In other words, the fact that Spain's incentive scheme was part of an international energy policy entitled the investors to rely on the scheme:

> For several years, the Respondent had been actively encouraging sufficient investment in renewable energy and had become bound under EU law to increase the proportion of its energy derived from renewable sources.192 RD 661/2007 was explicitly presented as a part of the Respondent's effort to attract sufficient investment in renewable energy to meet its goals.[1097]

The tribunals show that international law, other than investment law, may have a significant impact on a party's LE. On this basis, one could expect tribunals to take into consideration the line of commitments from Spain under its domestic and international framework. Therefore, tribunals should apply the notions of equity from the subject of law to the sovereign rather than the contrary. This means that when assessing whether a regulation created LE, one should not start from the perspective of the hierarchy of norms but from the content of the commitment. LE is conceived as a state-centric concept that allows investors to inspect the state's measures *from* the investor's angle to ensure equity.

Given the arbitral tribunal's consideration of relevant facts, I find that ICCL and NDCs can be considered: (1) *facts* in the interpretation of the expectations of investors and their legitimacy, (2) *facts* in the interpretation of the regulatory freedom of states to regulate in specific energy sectors, and (3) binding *provisions* to be considered in the interpretation of the regulatory stability of the host state and the consecutive LE of the investor.

Each of these points is demonstrated in the next chapter, which proposes more in-depth research into the effect of ICCL on the LE of energy investors.

D CONCLUSION

This chapter aimed to decipher the ways ICCL can integrate the resolution of investment disputes. Assessing the binding force of international climate change treaties and the relevance of NDCs and domestic judicial proceedings, it found no conflict *stricto*

1096. *Renergy v. Spain* (n 39) para. 900 ('At the same time, the Tribunal notes that increasing the use of green energy is likewise of vital public interest, given in particular the positive impact on the environment. Indeed, the Respondent itself committed to pursuing this interest many times, not least in the Preamble of Law 54/1997,1152 and is also under an obligation to do so under EU law, in particular pursuant to EU Directive 2009/28/EC.1153 As it seems difficult to deny that, at least in the short term, the Disputed Measures make investments in green energy projects in Spain less attractive to investors,1154 the Disputes Measures could be seen to run counter to the public interest in saving the environment').

1097. *Cube Infrastructure v. Spain* (n 402) para. 309.

sensu with international investment law but found ICCL, at least, to be a relevant fact in assessing legitimate expectations.

The chapter presents three findings.

First, the study establishes that not all ICCLs are created equal. Some ICCL treaties include binding norms, while it is difficult to see more than merely diplomatic language in some provisions. Nevertheless, the study identified three main sources of ICCL: treaties, legal domestic decisions, and scientific writings. Whenever ICCL is used as fact, it can be useful to assess the foreseeability and reasonableness of a measure. In this way, it is established that norms from the Paris Agreement and calls from the Glasgow Climate Pact are the most significant facts. They influence, alongside domestic legal decisions, certain economic and investment decisions as they announce 'winds of change'.

Second, I demonstrated that ICCL does not conflict *stricto sensu* with international investment law but conflicts *lato sensu*. In other words, ICCL does not inherently 'clash'[1098] with international investment law. The provisions emanating from both regimes are not sufficiently incompatible to pass the relevancy hurdle under the systemic integration rule of Article 31(3)(c) VCLT. To be precise, the integration through 31(3)(c) is particularly difficult when the underlying treaty fails to incorporate or reference other norms of international law. Similarly, if the treaty does not include 'relevant' international law as part of the applicable law to apply, it becomes challenging to argue that extraneous climate change norms apply to the specific circumstances of the dispute. If, conversely, the treaty opens the applicable law to relevant international law, one could argue that ICCL may apply as part of the substantive law. In this case, the tribunal will have to assess whether the commitment by the state contradicted its obligations under the applicable law, in which case no LE could be claimed.

Third, I have shown that, in most cases, ICCL will act as a relevant fact, capable of significantly influencing the assessment of an investor's LE. I illustrated this by drawing parallels with how other international treaties have been interpreted as relevant facts in the past. The analysis draws on examples from past cases, highlighting how ICCL influences the foreseeability of regulatory changes, the reasonableness of state measures, and the overall expectations of investors. I underscored the importance of considering ICCL as a factual element in interpreting investor expectations and evaluating the regulatory landscape. The conclusion suggests further exploration of ICCL's impact on energy investors' legitimate expectations.

Based on previous research and my own data set, it has been shown that investment tribunals tend to adopt a circumscribed understanding of their jurisdiction and applicable law. This can be explained by the limitations of the underlying treaties, which may privilege the protection of the investor over other potentially applicable norms. Therefore, I suggest that rather than as an applicable law, which depends

1098. Anja Ipp, 'Regime Interaction in Investment Arbitration: Climate Law, International Investment Law and Arbitration' (*Kluwer Arbitration Blog*, 12 January 2022) http://arbitrationblog.kluwerarbitration.com/2022/01/12/regime-interaction-in-investment-arbitration-climate-law-international-investment-law-and-arbitration/ accessed 15 March 2022.

largely on the underlying treaty and circumstances, ICCL can in all energy-related cases be exploited as a relevant fact. As a fact, a climate change provision may inform on the foreseeability of a measure as well as its reasonableness.

CHAPTER 5

Factoring ICCL into Energy Investors' Legitimate Expectations

This chapter examines the practical effects of factoring ICCL in the assessment of legitimate expectations. The chapter outlines the three impacts of ICCL: creating expectations, supporting or denying the legitimacy of expectations, and influencing the foreseeability of measures affecting clean and fossil fuel energy investments.

The previous chapter assessed whether ICCL could be taken into account in the resolution of investment disputes and how it could integrate the assessment of energy investors' legitimate expectations. I used an analogy to other treaties that have been found relevant in past case law or NZEID to find that ICCL may most likely act as a relevant legal fact which may directly impact the investor's LE.

This chapter turns to the factual value of ICCL and its effect on the assessment of LE. It assesses whether ICCL may amount to a specific commitment, whether it may bar a state's conduct from creating legitimate expectations, and assesses the impact of ICCL concretely based on the convergence points arising from the application of the voluntary and detrimental reliance theories of LE.

First, the chapter deciphers whether ICCL and related declarations, such as NDCs, can become binding on any given host state. Second, it explores the regulatory risks associated with ICCL and finds that ICCL norms may affect: (1) the level of specificity and clarity of the state's representation required to create LE and (2) the level of legitimacy of these expectations, even when a specific representation induces the investment. Third, it finds that ICCL can inform the foreseeability of net zero measures. In all these aspects, the timing of the investment is key. As seen above, a late investment made at a time when a frustrating reform is in full swing or changes to the regulatory framework are clearly foreseeable can withhold the creation of LE. It finds that fossil fuel energy investors may lack legitimacy in claiming for LE, while clean energy investors can count on increasing regulatory stability.

A ICCL MAY CREATE LEGITIMATE EXPECTATIONS

ICCL can amount to a specific commitment. This is evident not only in the context of domestic regulations that offer incentives, as demonstrated in case law, but also extends to broader state obligations under the UN climate regime. State's NDCs may, at the very least, amount to representations and political statements, which have been found in past arbitration cases to possibly qualify as specific commitments.[1099] Indeed, NDCs are content wherein countries formally commit to specific obligations under the framework of the Paris Agreement. These commitments are articulated through detailed reports that delineate a Member State's intended actions, encompassing targets for GHG emissions reduction and strategies on adaptation and mitigation.[1100] According to Sharaban Tahura Zaman, in an article from 2015, 'It is a unilateral declaration of the state, without the "intention" of being bound by its terms.' Consequently, NDCs are substantive content that clarifies a country's proposed measures in addressing climate change.[1101]

In a similar way to political statements, the policy announced by the host state to mitigate climate change may be clear in its scope and addressed to a specific group of investors, so that it may constitute, by itself, a commitment. Naturally, this type of commitment is considered the 'weakest', as it is neither addressed to a single investor nor does it generally have the binding force of law. In the future, parties could have recourse to the argument, as there are elements in NDCs similar to political statements that may induce clean energy investments.

To begin with, NDCs are non-binding. They constitute general reports on the state's policy. An NDC can be considered a reflection of the general regulatory environment of the state on its climate policy. But it may also contain a state's specific representations or commitments towards a particular sector of the economy. NDCs are public, known *erga omnes*, and generally issued by a competent governmental authority. As such, they should fill the condition of legitimacy in the sense of released by a competent authority. On mitigation, NDCs usually reflect the national and regional policies implementing ICCLs and goals but can also announce broad policies and GHG targets. For example, the EU's December 2020 NDC[1102] states 'EU fossil fuel production

1099. *SunReserve v. Italy* (n 416) para. 817; *Border Timbers v. Zimbabwe*, ICSID, Award, 28 July 2015, para. 547, para. 548, para. 549, para. 550, para. 551; *MTD v. Chile* (n 227) para. 159.
1100. Sharaban Tahura Zaman, 'Exploring the Legal Nature of Nationally Determined Contributions (NDCs) under International Law' (2015) 26 Yearbook of International Environmental Law 98, 107 https://doi.org/10.1093/yiel/yvx006 ('As a compromise, the Paris Agreement anchored NDCs as an "obligation of conduct" rather than as an "obligation of result", wherein parties have a "duty to implement" as opposed to a "duty to achieve"').
1101. *Ibid.*, 124.
1102. UNFCCC, 'Nationally Determined Contributions Registry' (*UNFCCC*, n.d.) unfccc.int/NDCREG accessed 2 November 2023.

and consumption will continue to decrease, resulting in fewer fugitive non-CO2 emissions.'[1103] NDCs may also contain a review of the main policies adopted by the state to achieve the energy transition by reducing CO_2 emissions. The latest NDCs synthesis report demonstrates the factual value and potential to become binding commitments of many NDCs.[1104] For the sake of the argument, the report's finding is reproduced in full below:

> in the most recent synthesis report on NDCs, the priority area of energy supply, energy generation, transmission and storage was by far the most frequently identified sub-area for domestic mitigation measures. Some Parties communicated measures for reducing emissions from fossil fuel exploration, production, transport and distribution, and a few identified measures in the cross-cutting sub-area. (...) The mitigation options indicated by Parties in this area include renewable energy generation (e.g., solar, wind, biomass, hydropower, geothermal); nuclear energy generation; reducing primary energy from coal, energy storage; grid improvement; shifting to low- or zero-carbon fuels; energy efficiency improvement; carbon dioxide capture and storage; electrification; and reducing or utilising fugitive emissions.[1105]

Thus, NDCs are likely to contain political statements regarding the energy sector. As such, they may create or at least inform expectations on the regulatory framework and inform on the foreseeability of frustrating measures. When sufficiently clear, authoritative, and addressed to a specific group of investors, they may even induce energy investors to commit capital.

One could argue that, following the doctrine of unilateral statements and in an analogous manner to the *France v. New Zealand* case, a Tribunal may deduce from the authority, clarity and publicity of NDCs that they equal an engagement with binding legal effect on the state.[1106] They would effectively, along with ICCL obligations, bind the state with legal effect.[1107] However, given the opposition of states during the Paris Agreement to the legally binding nature of NDCs, this is unlikely.[1108]

Alternatively, it is more likely that they form part of a more comprehensive array of political statements alongside the regulatory framework. Arbitral tribunals may assess political statements made by the host state, such as NDCs and other declarations on climate change commitments, together with other representations on the energy sector, and assess whether the investor relied on such statements to invest. As such,

1103. *Ibid.*, p 22.
1104. UNCC, *2022 NDC Synthesis Report* (Report, 2022).
1105. *Ibid.*
1106. *Ibid.*, para. 51 'It was bound to assume that other States might take note of these statements and rely on their being effective. The validity of these statements and their legal consequences must be considered within the general frame-work of the security of international intercourse, and the confidence and trust which are so essential in the relations among States. It is from the actual substance of these statements, and from the circumstances attending their making, that the legal implications of the unilateral act must be deduced. The objects of these statements are clear, and they were addressed to the international community as a whole, and the Court holds that they constitute an undertaking possessing legal effect.'
1107. *See* the reasoning in Chapter 2.D.4.
1108. Sharaban Tahura Zaman, 'Exploring the Legal Nature of Nationally Determined Contributions', 107.

NDCs would contribute to finding a binding legal commitment or, at the very least, authoritatively indicate the host state's policy direction and thus the regulatory risks an enterprise would accept to face if it were to invest in the country. Subject to their clarity, NDCs may constitute a relevant representation that creates investors' expectations. For instance, a renewable energy investor could be induced to invest in a specific country because of general regulations *and* political statements under an NDC.

The same reasoning may apply to UN obligations agreed by the host state and accompanying declarations made during the conferences and in the domestic settings. UN conventions do not generally target a specific energy sector, but one could argue that the Glasgow Pact's 'call' to scale up RE[1109] may be part of the host state's ensemble of official statements on RE targets and the expectations it creates in investors. The same reasoning can be applied to judicial proceedings, which would oblige the state to comply with specific targets in the energy sector.

Tribunals with a voluntarist inclination may contend that norms related to ICCL could constitute factors imposing obligations on the state to enforce them. On the other hand, tribunals addressing detrimental reliance are likely to scrutinise whether ICCL played a crucial role in influencing the investment and whether the investor exercised due diligence, recognising that ICCL does not inherently bind the host state.

In sum, NDCs may be read as a unilateral commitment or form part of such analysis together with the regulatory framework at the time of the investment. Due to their authority, NDCs, depending on their specificity regarding the energy sector and mitigation targets, may range from a political statement on the state's general policy on climate change to a unilateral declaration binding the state under international law.[1110] ICCL, in fact, may amount to a political declaration and, perhaps, depending on the clarity and specificity of the state's declaration, could bind the state under the doctrine of unilateral statements. Below, I assess how ICCL affects the legitimacy of expectations based on other sources of commitments.

B ICCL IMPACTS THE 'LEGITIMACY' OF EXPECTATIONS DEPENDING ON THE TIME OF INVESTMENT

As stated in the introduction, LE has been linked to individuals' prudential ability to undertake long-term planning.[1111] However, faced with unprecedented and global challenges, such as climate change, one may ask what the value of private and

1109. *See* Chapter 4.A.5.

1110. Benoit Mayer, 'International Law Obligations', 273 ('unilateral declarations such as (I)NDCs are not directed towards any particular state. They are made to the international community as a whole (erga omnes), which includes, but is not necessarily limited to, states. Therefore, unilateral declarations can be invoked by states not parties to the relevant treaty. They may also create obligations owed towards non-state actors more readily than treaties do. Individuals, groups and societies within a state and abroad have a stronger basis for calling on states to comply with such obligations because they arguably are intended to benefit all').

1111. Nigel Simmonds, *Central Issues in Jurisprudence: Justice, Law and Rights* (4th edn, Sweet and Maxwell 2013) 39.

individual expectations are in relation to global and existential crises.[1112] This 'value' can be retrieved in the concept of 'legitimacy' of expectations.[1113]

The concept of 'legitimacy' can have a profound impact on the investor's LE. Legitimacy, akin to reasonableness, is a multifaceted concept influenced by various factors, as demonstrated above including: (1) the timing of the investment; (2) the foreseeability of the frustrating measure; and (3) the regulatory risks assumed by the investor. As stated above, it is essential to distinguish requirements of 'due diligence', which are subjective endeavours from the investor to ensure that his expectations are correct, and of 'legitimacy', which embraces an objective perspective on the reasonableness of holding LE. Many but not all tribunals are likely to request higher degrees of subjective due diligence from fossil fuel investors, while all are likely to adopt a stricter approach to what reasonable investors can *objectively* expect when investing in a highly regulated and highly uncertain business sector (e.g., coal).

In light of this nuanced understanding of legitimacy, ICCL can exert a significant influence on the LE held by investors in both the fossil fuel and clean energy sectors. This influence results from ICCL's impact on the three elements of convergence in the case law, which I assess below.

1 Business Risks Associated with Net Zero Measures

I suggest that, since the ratification of the Kyoto Protocol, three key risks have emerged for energy investors in host states parties to the treaty. These business and regulatory risks are likely to be taken into account by tribunals when assessing what the investor can legitimately expect.

First, fossil fuel investors are faced with increasing long-term economic uncertainty. Climate treaties introduced measures aimed at reducing GHG emissions and transitioning towards cleaner energy sources. For investors in the fossil fuel industry, this implies an exposure to long-term economic uncertainty. The uncertainty is due to three phenomena. First, as demonstrated in the first chapter, CO_2 emissions are tied to the level of physical production and economic growth in a particular country. Reducing or limiting GHG emissions equates to limiting the economic production relying on fossil fuel energy.[1114] This could result in a peak demand for fossil fuels. Peak demand poses a significant challenge for fossil fuel investors.[1115] As renewable energy sources become more efficient and cost-effective, coupled with increasing efforts to improve energy efficiency, the demand for traditional fossil fuels may plateau and subsequently decline. This peak demand scenario presents a considerable risk for investors in the fossil fuel industry, as their assets could depreciate in value, and future returns may be compromised. As the demand for fossil fuels may decline over time, investments in this

1112. Viñuales, *The International Law of Energy* (n 246) Preamble.
1113. *See* our analysis Chapter 2.C.2.
1114. International Energy Agency, *World Investment 2023* (Report, 2023) 64.
1115. Sini Matikainen, 'What Are Stranded Assets' (LSE Grantham Research Institute on Climate Change, 27 July 2022) https://www.lse.ac.uk/granthaminstitute/explainers/what-are-stranded-assets/ accessed on 18 December 2023.

sector could become less profitable or even stranded.[1116] This risk cannot be covered by the investment treaty or FET standard.

Second, as demonstrated above, fossil fuel energy is largely responsible for the global level of CO_2 emissions. Implementing the Kyoto Protocol effectively means enacting a shift in policy to energy transition and prioritising low-carbon, clean investments. In other words, fossil fuels come into competition with other means of energy production at the cost of their economic long-term return. Additionally, significant market instability may come from the system of market-based emissions trading.[1117] For example, in Europe, such a market was created in 2005 to partly comply with the objectives of the Kyoto Protocol and monitor the decrease in CO_2 emissions on a market basis. The underlying uncertainty in this type of market is the price of CO_2 emission. The higher the price, the less economic return can be expected from the investor. A high CO_2 price could render an investment unprofitable, and state intervention is not a factor in mitigating this risk. The state's measure is thus not responsible for the economic instability, but the market is.

Third, socio-political uncertainty poses long-term risks to fossil fuel investments.[1118] As governments increasingly prioritise environmental policies, regulations may be implemented that restrict or discourage fossil fuel-related activities. Investors face the risk of their investments being negatively impacted by such measures in the host state.[1119] For instance, domestic rulings may have two effects on energy investments.[1120] Either they create a binding legal effect and address the state's GHG emissions or a specific sector's obligation to reduce emissions. In this case, they may eviscerate the possibility of having LE in a carbon-intensive energy sector if the investment is made after the judicial ruling. If the investment is made prior to the ruling, the decision still creates a presumption that the state's frustrating measure is reasonable and not simply a protectionism in disguise.

The Kyoto Protocol raises expectations for investors in the fossil fuel industry to demonstrate a higher level of due diligence. This means that arbitrators will expect investors to consider the foreseeable measures and policies related to the mitigation of climate change when making investment decisions. They might also expect investors

---

1116. *Saluka v. Czech Republic* (n 77) para. 304 (the legitimate expectations doctrine does not just protect the subjective expectations of an investor; they 'must rise to the level of legitimacy and reasonableness in the light of circumstances').
1117. OECD, *Financial Markets and Climate Transition: Opportunities, Challenges and Implications* (Report, 2021) 33 ('While fossil fuel generation technologies are well established, fossil fuel investment can be associated with risks across the supply chain, including exploration and transportation of the fuel, which can be observed through historically volatile prices. 30 On the other hand renewable energy assets have an inherent low risk and show greater resilience to fossil fuel and climate related vulnerabilities and volatilities (Bachner, Mayer, Steininger, 2019). In addition, policies that support the transition by further penalising fossil fuel usage and carbon emissions (i.e., through carbon pricing, taxes or the removal of fossil fuel subsidies where they exist)').
1118. International Energy Agency, *World Investment 2023* (Report, 2023) 107.
1119. *Duke Energy v. Ecuador* (n 225) para. 340.
1120. *See* above Chapter 4.A.7, examples 1 to 4, domestic judicial decisions ordering states to curb their emissions by a certain amount can have direct consequences on the sectors of the economy that are mainly responsible for the GHG or CO_2 emissions as a reminder that the energy sector represents two-third of global emissions.

to ensure unilateral declarations by states are substantiated. Failing to account for these factors could lead to an absence of objectiveness and legitimacy.[1121]

Conversely, it may be argued that investors in the clean energy sector will face fewer business and regulatory risks. They could benefit from the increasing demand for sustainable and eco-friendly alternatives; as governments and businesses commit to reducing their carbon footprint, clean energy investments offer the potential for long-term growth and stability. Not to underestimate, however, is the potential for environmental norms, for instance, on mining or biodiversity preservation to create regulatory risks for these investors.

2 Risks Associated with the Timing of the Investment

My findings suggest that the timing will be crucial in assessing the risks assumed by the investor and hence, the reasonableness of its legitimate expectations. To remind, the tribunal in *CEF Energia B.V v. Italy*[1122] unanimously held that the State froze its commitment to provide FIP over a twenty-year period in a private contract but that the investors could not hold LE regarding two plants, considering the stage of these investments.[1123] Its test to assess legitimate expectations did not extensively involve the assessment of due diligence but rather of 'the origin and scope, precisely, of the legitimate expectation',[1124] drawing on the summary of LE proposed in the *Antaris* award.[1125] The tribunal opined that two out of three projects were not definite at the time of the contested measures, so the investor could not have derived timely expectations.[1126]

The expectation of regulatory stability in the *fossil fuel* industry is contingent upon the timing of investment. The later the investment in fossil fuel, the less legitimate the expectation of regulatory stability. This is due to the progressive stringency of ICCLs, regulations, and policies. International and domestic laws and judicial decisions are regulatory risks that undermine the legitimate stability expected

1121. Yulia Levashova, 'Fair and Equitable Treatment and Investor's Due Diligence under International Investment Law' (2020) 67 Netherlands International Law Review 233, 250 https://doi.org/10.1007/s40802-020-00170-7.

1122. *CEF v. Italy* (n 639). The tribunal was composed of Klaus Reichert, Klaus Sachs, Giorgio Sacerdoti.

1123. *Ibid.*, para. 186.

1124. *Ibid.*, para. 191; also, the tribunal finds that Claimant did reasonably rely on expectations based on its due diligence reports at para. 225.

1125. *Ibid.*, para. 185.

1126. *Ibid.*, para. 188 ('Claimant, in reality, at the time of the making of both the Megasol and Phenix investments still had a number of steps to take before it knew for certain that the hoped-for incentives were actually awarded to it. It enjoyed no guarantee of success at the time of investment, and nothing in any of Respondent's Contos could infer that a party in Claimant's position as of such dates was inevitably going to be awarded the incentives. The fact that Claimant did indeed, at a later time, succeed in all respects for both Megasol and Phenix does not assist it as of the dates upon which it made those investments. What is decisive is that as of those dates the protection of Claimant's investment rights had not yet crystallised').

by fossil fuel investors.[1127] Finally, it is expected that investors will be requested to consider the risks and opportunities associated with climate change in their investment decisions.[1128]

In contrast, the timing of investments in the clean energy sector is less likely to be a decisive factor in determining the reasonableness of expectations, as the overarching trend favours these investments. Against the background of multiple international commitments to clean energy, from a good faith perspective, claiming that 'no regulations can create legitimate expectations' would be fundamentally flawed. Even if one considers that judicial proceedings indicate a possible retroactivity of the law, they cannot override climate change obligations, nor the legitimate expectations formed based on these commitments by the investor. In my opinion, the question is not whether the domestic regulation may create LE. Rather, the question is to what *degree*[1129] regulations may foster expectations and what legitimacy such expectations would have.[1130]

3 Risks Associated with the Foreseeability of Frustrating Measures

The findings suggest, finally, that the foreseeability of frustrating measures will play a crucial role in assessing fossil fuel investment's LE.

Arbitral awards have relied on the principle of foreseeability to allow for increases in environmental protections. The findings on convergence have been demonstrated above in Chapter 3, but I can only reiterate that in *Isolux*, the factual context in which the investor invests was crucial to establishing LE.[1131] Due diligence was strictly separated from the objective conditions prevailing at the time of the investment. And, most importantly, the dissenting arbitrator Prof. Tawil agreed that the time of the investment and foreseeability of the frustrating measure could act as a cut-off condition to hold LE. Professor Tawil contested what could be considered the

1127. *See* example of judicial proceedings in Chapter 4.A.7.

1128. This last line of reasoning can be debated since the foreign investor is not subject to international climate change law, which only governs the conduct of the State. The conflict may arise because two differing norms bind the host State under international law,. i.e., the discipline it owes to foreign investments in general and the role in achieving its own nationally determined contributions (NDCs).

1129. *Ibid.*, para. 396 ('the general nature of the words "fair" and "equitable" suggests that the protection of the investors' position is not absolute and unqualified, but rather a matter of degree and balancing').

1130. In the Spanish cases, the law gave the authority to the government to adopt support schemes to benefit renewable investors, which was in line with international commitments.

1131. *Isolux v. Spain* (n 466) para. 781 ('The Arbitral Tribunal accepts that an investor cannot be required to conduct extensive legal research. What is important in determining whether the expectations alleged by the investor are reasonable is what any prudent investor needs to know about the regulatory framework before investing and the actual information of the investor invoking specific expectations. In particular, an investor *cannot have legitimate expectations generated by the regulatory framework when his personal information enabled him to foresee and anticipate the unfavourable evolution of this regulatory framework before investing*. In order to breach the investor's legitimate expectations, the new regulatory measures must not have been foreseeable, either by a prudent investor or by an investor who, because of his personal situation, had specific information to foresee them').

proper time of the investment and whether the Supreme Court judgment could have created that foreseeability and opined that only legislative changes could indicate foreseeable frustrating measures.[1132] In the case of fossil fuel investment, legislative changes are not only foreseeable but in full swing. Of course, a tribunal would need to assess the content of the host state's law to assess the foreseeability. Depending on the interpretation of LE adopted, the tribunal would need to assess, at least, previous legislative changes (prior to the investment – the 'Guido Tawil' approach), judicial proceedings and general representations (the good faith approach and detrimental reliance approach) and perhaps on the general *direction* of the host state's legislation (the *Charanne* approach). In all cases, there is room to argue that ICCL has already affected the foreseeability of stability that can be expected, especially by fossil fuel investors.

There is further proof that the foreseeability of frustrating measures is a consensual fact assessed by tribunals, whether they adopt a voluntarist or detrimental leaning interpretation. While the *Philipp Morris* tribunal emphasised the state's right to adapt its legal system to changing circumstances[1133] and a standard of prudent diligence,[1134] the tribunal in *Tecmed v. Mexico*, considered to have adopted a 'strict liability' approach, also took into consideration whether the investor could foresee a ban on its product.[1135] In this case, a substantial part of the investment was made *before* political and social circumstances arose, indicating that a depriving measure would be adopted by the state.

1132. *Isolux v. Spain*, Dissenting Opinion of Tawil (n 857) para. 6 ('My main disagreement with the majority's decision, however, *lies in the way in which the factual circumstances* were assessed in order to determine the "foreseeability" of the measures adopted by the Kingdom of Spain. In other words, whether the change of legal regime in Spain after the investment was made was foreseeable for the Claimant, *a circumstance which – if so – would prevent it from invoking legitimate expectations as a basis for its claim*').

1133. *Philip Morris v. Uruguay* (n 76) para. 422 ('[i]t is common ground in the decisions of more recent investment tribunals that the requirements of legitimate expectations and legal stability ... do not affect the State's rights to exercise its sovereign authority to legislate and to adapt its legal system to changing circumstances').

1134. *Ibid.*, paras 427 and 430. ('to rely on legitimate expectations, the investor should inquire in advance regarding the prospects of a change in the regulatory framework in light of the then prevailing or reasonably expected changes in the economic and social conditions of the host State').

1135. *Tecmed v. Mexico* (n 67) paras 149-150 ('The Arbitral Tribunal does not agree with the Respondent's position denying that upon making its investment, the Claimant had legitimate reasons to believe that the operation of the Landfill would extend over the long term. The political and social circumstances referred to above, which conclusively conditioned the issuance of the Resolution, were shown with all their magnitude after a substantial part of the investment had been made and could not have reasonably been foreseen by the Claimant with the scope, effects and consequences that those circumstances had. [...] This shows that even before the Claimant made its investment, it was widely known that the investor expected its investments in the Landfill to last for a long term and that it took this into account to estimate the time and business required to recover such investment and obtain the expected return upon making its tender offer for the acquisition of the assets related to the Landfill. To evaluate if the actions attributable to the Respondent – as well as the Resolution – violate the Agreement, such expectations should be considered legitimate and should be evaluated in light of the Agreement and of international law').

Foreseeability is therefore critical. An investor may not expect the stability of the regulatory framework if, at the time of its investment, the regulatory framework is changing or will foreseeably change. If one understands LE from the perspective of a reasonable investor, then one ought to consider all the circumstances a reasonable investor should objectively foresee. Therefore, the argument that energy is a highly regulated sector requiring substantial due diligence is perfectly relevant. It is likely that ICCL will be integrated under the detrimental reliance theory because of obligations of due diligence as part of the reliance condition, and of the 'detriment' condition, and the emphasis by tribunals on the proportionality of the state's measures. In turn, ICCL will be integrated under the voluntarist theory of promise because of its impact on the state's representations (for instance, a representation from a government official cannot override the ratification of the Paris Agreement); the risks assumed by the investor at the time of the investment, and the reasonable foreseeability of regulatory changes.

In the context of investing in fossil fuels, once the Kyoto Protocol becomes effective in the host country, it becomes evident that not only do the political and social conditions not support the belief in a stable regulatory framework, but also that the trend in climate policy becomes irreversible due to the UNFCCC obligations. Consequently, a foreseeable ban on fossil fuel investments is possible. Conversely, the existence of incentives under the ICCL regime bolsters the expectations of investors in clean energy generation. The more defined unilateral declarations and incentives in clean energy, the more legitimate the expectations of regulatory stability. This implies that investments in this sector are more likely to result in protected returns, even when the business risks are the investor's sole responsibility.

Based on the analysis of the relevant energy investment case law, I find that ICCL creates four effects and risks: long-term economic uncertainty, long-term socio-political risks, foreseeable frustrating measures, and the expectation of higher due diligence. On the flip side, ICCL may also create opportunities, for instance, when NDCs transform into binding state commitments, creating LE.

C FORESEEABILITY OF NET ZERO TRANSITION MEASURES IN PRACTICE

The development of ICCL constitutes mounting political risks and opportunities for energy investors.[1136] The implementation of the net zero transition is likely to create legal disputes between foreign investors and states.[1137] I highlight the main elements of foreseeability chronologically below.

1136. International Energy Agency, *World Energy Outlook 2021* (Report, 2021), 4 ('As always with the energy sector, investment is critical. The IEA has been warning for years that current investment levels in the global energy sector are inadequate – both to meet near-term energy needs and long-term transition goals. It is hard to understate the dangers inherent in today's shortfall in spending on clean energy transitions, compared with the levels required. If we do not correct it soon, the risks of destabilizing volatility will only grow as we move forward').
1137. Sarvarian, 'Invoking the Paris Agreement' (n 153) 429.

In the following, I place the analysis at the time when the Kyoto Protocol entered into force on 16 February 2005. It is also important to note that investors are considered reasonable from the outset under Investment law. According to the tribunal in *Parkerings*: 'any businessman or investor knows that laws will evolve. What is prohibited, however, is for a State to act unfairly, unreasonably, or inequitably in the exercise of its legislative power'.[1138] Below, I scrutinise how these risks materialise after each major treaty and national or regional climate laws.

1 Expectations of Fossil Fuel Investors since the Kyoto Protocol

The paragraph below presents the factual background against which fossil fuel investors choose to invest. It provides details about the economic and political risks. It demonstrates that the investors must establish a clear commitment by the state to claim to have LE. Indeed, as ample evidence shows, fossil fuel investors, and in particular coal investors, have been exposed to increasingly frustrating regulatory measures since the Kyoto Protocol.

Inherent long-term economic instability in the fossil fuel industry has significant consequences on the level of expectations the foreign investor can base on the stability of the regulatory framework. If states are required to maintain a certain degree of stability and predictability in their regulatory framework, as this is relied upon by investors when making investments,[1139] I argue that the threshold to breach this requirement is higher if the inherent economic risk of the investment operation is high. In other words, where the economic sector is uncertain, the expectation of regulatory stability requires a high threshold to be considered legitimate.

Regarding political risks, coal was much longer targeted than fossil fuels in general by climate policy risks. Even prior to the entry into force of the Kyoto Protocol, the uncertain future of coal was underscored in 2000[1140] by the then Director of the International Energy Agency in these terms:

> However, future coal use now faces major challenges. The liberalisation of the electricity generating sector, the major customer of coal, and the gas market, coal's main competitor as an input fuel for power generation, is introducing new uncertainties into the coal market. At the same time, the environmental commitments of governments are increasing significantly, especially with the signature of the Kyoto Protocol. The mechanisms to be adopted to meet these environmental objectives are still being elaborated, but it is inevitable that coal, with its relatively high carbon content, faces an increasingly uncertain future.[1141]

1138. *Parkerings v. Lithuania* (n 410) para. 387.
1139. Roland Kläger, *'Fair and Equitable Treatment' in International Investment Law* (CUP 2011) 164; Kenneth Vandevelde, 'A Unified Theory of Fair and Equitable Treatment' (2010) 43 NY Univ J Int Law Policy 1 43, 66.
1140. International Energy Agency, *The future role of coal: Markets, Supply and the Environment* (Report, 2000).
1141. *Ibid.*, 1.

In an OECD report on 'Clean Coal Technologies Accelerating Commercial and Policy Drivers for Deployment' from March 2008,[1142] Executive Director Nobuo Tanaka indicated in a foreword that: 'Strong environmental policies could see substantially lower coal use – it is, after all, the most carbon-intensive fuel.'[1143] In Europe, following the Stern Report, it became clear that a political impetus based on the findings of the IPCC and the commitments under the Kyoto Protocol was taking shape.[1144]

On the request of the G8, the International Energy Agency also stated cautious warnings in 2010,[1145] on the prospect of coal energy investments.[1146] In 2012, it added that 'Coal is also particularly affected by the global climate change agenda – which has been recently marked by disappointing inaction (…) The result is that, without serious constraints on coal consumption by climate change policies in most places, demand and CO2 will continue to grow.'[1147] While regulatory changes affecting drastically fossil fuel investment could not be foreseen to happen in 2005, it was clear from the first and second-period commitment of the Kyoto Protocol that obligations could only become progressively more stringent.

The Kyoto Protocol and following climate treaties have significant long-term implications for investors in the fossil fuel industry. The *Uniper* and *RWE v. Netherlands* cases illustrate this point, as both claimed against the Netherlands' Coal Ban. To meet climate objectives, the Netherlands passed a Law Prohibiting the Use of Coal in the Production of Electricity,[1148] effectively banning Coal production on its territory by 2030, which triggered two investment claims,[1149] of which one was dropped after a

1142. International Energy Agency, *Clean Coal Technologies* (Report, 2008).
1143. *Ibid.*, 5 ('However, given coal's abundance, there will be pressure to exploit this resource for energy security and economic reasons. Improving coal's environmental performance is key to coal's future role in the energy mix.'); *see* p. 9 ('In particular, a group of technologies, known as carbon dioxide capture and storage (CCS), offers the potential to balance the sometimes competing goals of energy security, economic development and environmental sustainability').
1144. *Ibid.*, 12 ('These [IPCC and Stern] reports are having a significant impact on policy thinking, particularly in Europe. (…) Clearly, there is a growing scientific and political consensus to seek real reductions in total global GHG emissions in the next three to four decades, rather than delaying further. The reconciliation of the drive to consume coal for economic activity and the commitment to reduce GHG emissions in this time frame requires that an enormous technological effort be made in the next two decades').
1145. International Energy Agency, *Power Generation from Coal: Measuring and Reporting Efficiency Performance and CO2 Emissions* (Report, 2010) 13.
1146. *Ibid.* ('Coal-fired power plants, also known as power stations, provide over 42% of global electricity supply. At the same time, these plants account for over 28% of global carbon dioxide (CO2) emissions').
1147. International Energy Agency, *Medium-Term Coal Market Report 2012* (Report, 2012) 3 (the quote continues 'Yet without progress in CCS, coal is at risk to a potential climate policy backlash and rising concerns over emissions').
1148. Law Staatsblad 2019/493, adopted on 11 December 2019, accessible at https://www.eerstekamer.nl/9370000/1/j9vvkfvj6b325az/vl4kf9h8kewd/f=y.pdf accessed 7 September 2022.
1149. Ji Ma, 'Bridging Multinational Corporations' Investment – Climate Gap: Prospects for the Direct Claims Approach' (2023) 32 Review of European, Comparative & International Environmental Law 348, 354.

bailout.[1150] Prior to the investment, COP 23 already gave birth to the 'Power Past Coal Alliance', which did not commit parties to any particular phase out date but called to 'restrict the financing of unabated coal power stations'.[1151] The Coal Ban is a typical example of a long-planned net zero restructure of a country's energy system.

In conclusion, since the implementation of the Kyoto Protocol, all investors in the fossil fuel industry may not expect the same level of stability, primarily for economic reasons. Under the Kyoto Protocol, states are free to adopt the measures they deem necessary and proportionate to achieve their specific emission reduction targets. Even though it is impossible to prove that any decarbonisation measure is required to achieve an emission target, the fact that the Kyoto Protocol was adopted on 11 December 1997 and entered into force on 16 February 2005 ensures significant foreseeability on public policies in the energy sector. Arbitrators can assume that an investor should anticipate changes to the regulatory framework.

To adopt a famous sentence by the *Charanne* tribunal, fossil fuel investors would have known that the legal system of members of the Kyoto Protocol was 'open to the possibility' that the system applicable to fossil fuel generation could be modified.[1152] The result would be the same if the tribunal adopts a relative stability and voluntarist approach, for the tribunal in *Renergy* correctly stated that 'legislative change only violates the notion of relative stability if it exceeds the margin of change that a diligent investor – who, by definition, conducted sufficient due diligence – could have foreseen'.[1153] An adequate indicator for future changes can be the fact that the regulatory framework has been changed or modified prior to the investment.[1154] Similarly, case law issued prior to the investment can confirm the state's right to amend the regulatory framework.[1155] In case the regulatory changes can be foreseen, the expectations amount to speculative hope rather than protected expectations under the FET standard.

1150. Jack Ballantyne, 'Uniper to Withdraw ECT Claim as Part of German Bailout' *GAR* (London, 25 July 2022).
1151. Powering Past Coal Alliance: Declaration (16 November 2017).
1152. *Charanne v. Spain* (n 413) para. 505 ('in the present case, the Arbitration Tribunal considers that the Claimants could have easily foreseen the possibility that the regulatory framework was going to be modified [...]. Indeed, the Spanish Law left wide open the possibility of modifying the remuneration scheme applicable to photovoltaic energy. [...]') approved by the majority in *Foresight v. Spain* (n 620) para. 376; *Isolux v. Spain* (n 466) para. 818, (translation by the author 'A party who decides to invest in a country which, according to it, lacks legal certainty, cannot later complain that it was not provided such certainty').
1153. *Renergy v. Spain* (n 39) para. 707; *see also Silver Ridge v. Italy* (n 56) para. 457 ('In this regard, the Tribunal agrees with the submission of the Respondent (Resp. Counter-Memorial, paras 394-395) that a prudent investor acting in a highly regulated market such as the electricity market must, in the course of its risk assessment, analyze and take into consideration the whole range of potential advantages and disadvantages associated with the dynamics of the market which might also call for policy adjustments on the part of the host State. Having said that, this does not mean that every turn of policy must be anticipated. In particular, even the reasonable and circumspect investor must not anticipate radical change, which takes the Tribunal to the third step of its analysis').
1154. *Isolux v. Spain* (n 466) para. 787; *9REN v. Spain* (n 422) para. 298 mentioned that the amendment of the Special Regime contemplated further revision and made changes foreseeable; *see also Belenergia v. Italy* (n 834) para. 591.
1155. *Isolux v. Spain* (n 466) paras 789-792.

Considering the evidence above, the margin of legislative change foreseeable by the coal industry sector in states having ratified the Kyoto Protocol can be fundamental and amount to a complete ban. In other words, a ban on coal would draw on a reasonable public policy purpose, should be expected by the Claimant, i.e., foreseeable, and would not exceed what is necessary, i.e., proportionate,[1156] where specific mechanisms are adopted to compensate the investor, whether by allowing a reasonable time period between the decision and the ban or by reasonably compensating the investor financially.

2 Expectations of Fossil Fuel Investors since the Paris Agreement

While expressing international objectives – to hold the increase in the global average temperature to well below 2°C above pre-industrial levels – the Paris Agreement imposes no obligation upon Member States to implement the objective in any particular way. It expresses global objectives and aspirations regarding national contributions to meet those objectives through NDCs. Nevertheless, with regard to decarbonisation efforts, the Paris Agreement makes a clear case for progressive efforts. In particular, the Paris Agreement and the IPCC Special Report on the Pathway to 1.5°C warn investors to significantly reduce the climate risk associated with their energy investments.[1157]

Because of this economic uncertainty, the assumption on the part of the investor that the general regulatory framework relied upon at the time of the investment will remain stable is significantly altered. The long-term risk makes it less likely that the state will issue a specific representation regarding its investment. If the state does issue a representation, despite the economic risk the investment is naturally exposed to, then this representation shall be of the highest standing to create legitimate expectations. In other words, relying on political statements, the general regulatory framework absent the stabilisation clause, and the treaty obligation of relative stability may not be sufficient to support the claim that the investor could not have foreseen fundamental changes at the time of the investment.

Tribunals following the Charanne interpretation of LE might argue that, given the 'changing' legal environment since the Paris Agreement, fossil fuel investors should have known that the legal systems of states party to the Kyoto Protocol were 'open to

1156. *Silver Ridge*, para. 419 ('There is even, to a certain degree at least, common ground between the Parties as regards the relevant factors in assessing whether a fundamental or radical change has occurred. While those factors are interrelated and partly overlapping, the pertinent submissions of the Parties (*see* paras 338-339, 342, 351, 358-361) can be classified in three groups, namely as to whether or not the modifications brought about by the *Spalma-incentivi* Decree (1) could draw on a public policy purpose, i.e., were reasonable, (2) should have been expected by the Claimant, i.e., were foreseeable, and (3) did not exceed what was necessary, i.e. were proportionate').

1157. Grantham Research Institute on Climate Change and the Environment, *Climate Change and the Just Transition: A Guide for Investor Action* (Guide, 2018) 8-9; *see also* the useful panorama of climate law at Grantham Research Institute, 'Climate Change Laws of The World' (GRICCE, n.d.) https://climate-laws.org accessed 18 October 2021.

the possibility' of modifications to the framework governing fossil fuel generation. Under this general idea of possible changes in environmental policy towards a general direction, there can be no breach of legitimate expectations, unless the state committed to a stabilisation clause specifically towards the investors. A more balanced assessment would however assess the degree of commitment and compare it to the foreseeability of regulatory changes at the time of the investment.

As ICCL provisions progress, this balancing act between the degree of commitment and the circumstances and content of the host State's laws at the time of the investment can only become more stringent on the investor, in particular, since the Glasgow Pact. The consensus reached by the Glasgow Climate Pact to achieve net zero is reflected in national policies aiming to decarbonise their economy and adopting the net zero benchmark. Article 4.20 of the Glasgow Climate Pact applies to all COP parties and effectively discriminates two segments of the energy industry – non-renewables and 'clean' energy.[1158] Under the Paris Agreement, NDCs must provide emissions-cut goals, and many States have presented mitigation strategies by 2030 and, since Glasgow, long-term net zero carbon goals.[1159]

Notoriously, the EU is advanced on questions of net zero measures so that fossil fuel investments in Europe are at particular risk of not having their LE protected. For instance, climate action is central to the European Green Deal[1160] a package of policy measures to achieve Net Zero ambitions. The European Climate Law,[1161] passed in June 2021, enshrines the goal of Net Zero by 2050. The EC's adoption of 'Fit for 55'[1162] forges the EU's legislative path to cutting carbon emissions by 55% by 2030. Globally, there is evidence that climate litigation is ramping up in national administrative courts against the state[1163] and specific companies,[1164] which may affect the LE depending on the host State in which the investor decides to invest.

All these considerations are warning signals of a climate of change for coal, fossil fuels, and renewable energy. They announce significant political risks, which must form part not only of a reasonable investor's due diligence but also of an assessment of the frustration of any expectations the state may have created.

1158. If the relationship between lawyers and scientists is notoriously thin, it is not a reason for the legal community to discard the importance of science when interpretating a fact-based dispute. *See* James Friedman, 'The Scientist as Expert Witness: Why Lawyers and Scientists Can't Talk to Each Other' (1977) 18 Jurimetrics Journal 2 99.

1159. United Nations Climate Change, 'Nationally Determined Contributions Registry' (*UNCC*, 2023) https://unfccc.int/NDCREG accessed 29 April 2023.

1160. European Commission, Communication on The European Green Deal, COM/2019/640, 11 December 2019.

1161. Regulation (EU) 2021/1119 of the European Parliament and of the Council of 30 June 2021 establishing the framework for achieving climate neutrality and amending Regulations (EC) No. 401/2009 and (EU) 2018/1999 ('European Climate Law') [2021] OJ L 243/1.

1162. European Commission, Communication on 'Fit for 55': delivering the EU's 2030 Climate Target on the way to climate neutrality, COM/2021/550, 14 July 2021.

1163. Sabin Center, 'US Climate Change' (n 102).

1164. German Federal Constitutional Court, Order of the First Senate from 24 March 2021 – 1 BvR 2656/ 18, 1 BvR 288/20, 1 BvR 96/20, 1 BvR 78/20 – Rn. (1-270).

D FORESEEABILITY OF REGULATORY STABILITY IN THE CLEAN ENERGY SECTOR

To restate Chapter 1's findings, the role of clean energy is crucial in the global energy transformation.[1165] The energy sector constitutes an estimated two-thirds of global GHG emissions,[1166] meaning clean energy must step up to meet reductions in emissions. Conversely to expectations of fossil fuel energy investors, clean energy investors may rely on binding commitments of states domestically and internationally as well as public statements to base their claims of LE. There are three main sources of legitimacy for clean investors.

First is the domestic legal framework on which net zero transition-related incentives are based. Second, clean energy investors may base the legitimacy of their expectations on ICCL and the state's commitment to binding provisions. Third, public statements, judicial decisions, and other relevant facts can render expectations legitimate. Moreover, within each of these categories, the commitment of the state can be divided among the commitments that are binding, diplomatic, and soft law. The latter two can only serve as benchmarks to assess the legitimacy of expectations rather than their source.

In other words, ICCL may contribute to giving rise to objective expectations on the part of the investor. In general, ICCL may help find that the state specifically committed to the foreign investor, the expectations were objective and reasonable,[1167] the threshold to meet the requirements of due diligence was lower,[1168] and the frustration of the expectations was unexpected.[1169]

1 Expectations of Clean Energy Investors since the Kyoto Protocol

The commitments made under ICCL can be seen as a means to reinforce the regulatory stability expected by investors. When governments demonstrate a strong commitment to addressing climate change through comprehensive legislation and regulations, it creates a stable and predictable environment for investors that can transform into enforceable rights.

The bulk of investment disputes reviewed in this study were triggered by measures adopted to meet the Kyoto targets in emission reductions.[1170] In the Spanish

1165. Dolf Gielen and Francisco Boshell (eds), 'The Role of Renewable Energy in the Global Energy Transformation' (2019) 24 Energy Strategy Reviews 38.
1166. In 2021, global energy-related CO_2 emissions approached the 33.0 CO_2 Gt emissions of the estimated total of 50Gt. According to some of the most authoritative research, emissions need to fall to 9.7Gt in 2050 for an emissions pathway compatible with the 2°C target of the Paris Agreement.
1167. *Watkins Holdings v. Spain* (n 413), para. 527; *Renergy v. Spain* (n 39) para. 900.
1168. *Renergy v. Spain* (n 39) para. 707.
1169. *Charanne v. Spain* (n 413) para. 517; *Antin v. Spain* (n 453) para. 532 ('stripped of its essential features'); *Novenergia II v. Spain* (n 413) para. 656 ('radically altered the essential characteristics') and *Micula v. Romania* (n 427) para. 684 ('stripped [the previous legal framework] of most of its practical content and reduced almost to nothing its advantages').
1170. *Cavalum v. Spain* (n 585) para. 495.

disputes, the regulatory framework at the source of disputes stems from the EC directive 2001/77/EC on the Promotion of Electricity Produced from Renewable Energy Sources in the Internal Electricity Market, which obliged all EU Member States (a) to 'take appropriate steps to encourage greater consumption of electricity produced from renewable energy sources' in order to 'meet Kyoto targets more quickly', (b) 'to set national indicative targets for the consumption of electricity produced from renewable sources', and (c) to report regularly to the EU on their progress in meeting those targets.[1171]

2 Expectations of Clean Energy Investors since the Paris Agreement

The Paris Agreement creates a legally binding obligation to publish NDCs. Arbitral tribunals should assess the binding force of these public statements, as they may be issued by different governmental powers and with different binding forces. In any case, these NDCs can serve to show the intention of a state to attract foreign investors and provide a regulatory framework incentivising these investments.[1172]

The implementation of NDCs can attract climate finance and investment by signalling longer-term investment potential through sectoral targets and policies. NDCs also provide assurance to businesses that their investments are in a climate-friendly framework and their services will be profitable. There is evidence that states specifically target and encourage clean energy investments in their NDCS. Of the 109 Parties that have defined targets for renewables in the power sector in their NDCs, 49 presented them in the form of additions – mostly in the form of capacity (GW) and a few in terms of output (GWh).[1173] Of the 60 Parties with targets defined as a share of the power mix, 14 committed to achieving less than 24% share of renewable energy, 22 committed to shares between 25% and 59%, 13 committed to shares between 60% and 89%, and 11 Parties committed to shares between 90% to 100%.[1174] According to a report from 2020, targets set in NDCs still need to be aligned with national energy plans and renewable energy targets. In '178 out of the 196 countries analysed (91%), a mismatch exists between renewable energy targets in NDCs and those featuring in national laws and official strategies and plans.'[1175] In this sense, ICCL, by enforcing clean investor's rights based on the implementation of net zero transition policies may improve the level of implementation rather than hinder it.

In summary, I find that, in light of widely accepted articulations of international concern for the harmful effects of GHG, expectations can only be of progressively more stringent regulation of the production and sale of fossil fuel products and progressively more favourable to clean energy production.

1171. *Ibid.*, Art. 3, Recitals (1) and (5).
1172. IRENA, *NDCs and Renewable Energy Targets in 2021: Are We on the Right Path to a Climate-Safe Future?* (Report, 2022) 7.
1173. *Ibid.*, 24.
1174. *Ibid.*
1175. *Ibid.*, 7.

E CONCLUSION

The chapter determined *how* ICCL may be relevant to the resolution of net zero investment disputes. It builds on the previous findings on the consensual facts affecting LE's application. This chapter completes the demonstration that ICCL can have a significant impact on the assessment of energy investors' LE in investment disputes.[1176]

The chapter presents three key findings.

First, the study identifies three sources of binding ICCL: treaties, unilateral statements such as clear NDCs, and legal domestic decisions. It suggests that norms from the Paris Agreement, NDCs, and the Glasgow Climate Pact, along with domestic legal decisions, may clearly affect the resolution of investment disputes. It finds no direct conflict between international investment law and ICCL norms. It suggests that a potential conflict *lato sensu* may arise when IIAs protect investments in sectors that climate change law seeks to phase down (i.e., coal).

Second, it demonstrates that ICCL can be exploited as a relevant fact in the resolution of investment disputes. ICCL may have multiple impacts on legitimate expectations, ranging from creating legitimate expectations of energy investors and supporting their expectations of regulatory stability to informing the foreseeability and reasonableness of a frustrating net zero measure. The chapter demonstrates that the legitimacy of fossil fuel investors is impeded over time by the implementation of ICCL. Conversely, the legitimate expectations of clean energy investors can be supported by the host State's climate change commitments. These findings apply whether the arbitral tribunal adopts a voluntarist-leaning or detrimental-reliance-leaning approach to LE considering the convergence points found in the last chapter.

Third, this chapter bridges the findings on the convergence of the application of LE with the findings on ICCL. Applying ICCL to LE may render the expectations of clean-energy investors more legitimate. The findings have practical implications for investors. It demonstrates that international investment law may be used to enforce climate change commitments. Conversely, it demonstrates that, over time and depending on the level of commitments, the *expectations* of fossil fuel investors may become unprotectable.

Overall, the chapter concludes the research on the relationship between international norms pertaining to the protection of energy investments and those pertaining to the mitigation of GHG emissions. It finds that energy investors' LE can be significantly impacted by the host State's climate change commitments.

In the next chapter, I propose to build a novel interpretation and application of LE in light of these findings and to illuminate their relationship.

1176. The findings are, at least, applicable to investment disputes under the Energy Charter Treaty similar to the cases analysed in chapter three.

CHAPTER 6

Reconciling International Investment Law with ICCL

This chapter proposes an interpretation and application of legitimate expectations that align with the rule of law and a voluntarist-leaning approach and illuminates the relationship between legitimate expectations and ICCL.

As explained in the introduction, the investment policy debate on climate change has resulted in two distinct camps. One advocate for investment treaty protection as a key component of promoting clean investment. The other favours drastic regulations based on energy efficiency and conservation, which would arguably require abandoning investment protection. This debate impacts state policies. While European countries file notices of withdrawal to the ECT based on climate change concerns,[1177] IIAs continue to be signed around the world. African states are also contemplating joining the Energy Charter Treaty.[1178]

Do climate change commitments force states to withdraw from investment protection treaties? Should the law retreat before the urgency of climate change regulations? From a rule of law perspective, the answer is negative. The legal protection of foreign investors does not stand in direct contradiction with climate change goals. There is no incompatibility of norms, as demonstrated in the last chapter. In fact, the legal protection of clean energy investments may align with the enforcement of ICCL. This chapter draws from the totality of the research and proposes a novel way to assess the expectations of energy investors in light of ICCL.

1177. World Bank Energy Charter, *Enabling* (n 36).
1178. *See* Energy Charter Secretariat, *Decision of the Energy Charter Conference CCDEC 2021 26 WPR* (Decision, 2021) 14 ('Responding to enquiries about ratification of the ECT by countries already invited by the Conference to accede (Pakistan, Mauritania, Eswatini, Burundi), or to countries which have officially requested an invitation to accede (i.e., Uganda)').

A A VOLUNTARY INTERPRETATION OF LEGITIMATE EXPECTATIONS

Based on the research conducted and in the context of an unqualified FET provision, I propose to determine and apply a voluntary theory of legitimate expectations with due consideration to ICCL.

To determine the LE of an investor, the first step is to start with the treaty. Any interpretation of LE only derives from a meticulous examination of the FET clause and treaty drafting. It has been demonstrated that the FET clause is necessarily unique.

The VCLT should help decipher the meaning of FET provisions as a single concept[1179] despite some tribunals calling the exercise 'worthless'.[1180] The tribunal in *Joseph Charles Lemire v. Ukraine* stated that 'any effort to decipher the ordinary meaning of the words used only leads to analogous terms of almost equal vagueness'.[1181] The reasoning does not stand well. The exercise of interpreting the ordinary meaning of 'fair' and 'equitable' cannot be dismissed. First, treatment can be understood as the 'conduct, behaviour; action or behaviour towards a person'.[1182] Second, 'fair' and 'equitable' have been correctly deciphered by the tribunal in *National Grid v. Argentina* as follows:

> In their ordinary meaning, the term 'fair' means 'just,' 'even-handed,' 'unbiased,' 'legitimate,' 'reasonable.' Equitable is defined as 'fair' and 'just,' 'just', fair, and right, in consideration of the facts and circumstances of the individual case.[1183]

This ordinary meaning emphasises the significance of facts and circumstances of the individual case and the question of degree in assessing rights.[1184] I agree with the tribunal in *Silver Ridge v. Italy*,[1185] for which the ordinary meaning of the provision indicates that the acts of the state and its conduct towards an investor cannot be unrestricted. The FET provision is a clear indication that the host State is not *free* to act or behave vis-à-vis protected investors 'ad libitum or to interfere with their rights and assets at its whim'.[1186] At the same time, the general nature of the words 'fair' and 'equitable' suggests that the protection of the investors is not absolute, but rather a matter of degree and balancing.'[1187] Assessing whether a measure is reasonable requires such balancing. The general nature of FET also indicates that all conduct

1179. Yannick Radi, *Rules and Practices of International Investment Law and Arbitration* (CUP 2020) 82.
1180. *Antin v. Spain* (n 453) para. 518 (the tribunal fell short of concluding any normative value from the ordinary meaning and turned immediately to the 'context, object and purpose of the treaty').
1181. *Joseph Charles Lemire v. Ukraine*, ICSID Case No. ARB/06/18, Decision on Liability, 14 January 2010, para. 258.
1182. 'Treatment', *The Oxford English Dictionary* (2nd edn, Clarendon Press 1989) vol 1, 602.
1183. *National Grid v. Argentina*, UNCITRAL, Award 3 November 2008, para. 168.
1184. Katia Yannaca-Small, 'Fair and Equitable Treatment Standard in International Investment Law', (2004) OECD Working Papers on International Investment, Number 3, 3 ff.
1185. *Silver Ridge v. Italy* (n 56) paras 392-396.
1186. *Ibid.*
1187. *Ibid.*, para. 396.

attributable to the state may constitute the basis for an FET claim.[1188] As suggested, the ordinary meaning of an unqualified FET clause warrants the protection of reasonable LE,[1189] even though the state retains a degree of regulatory freedom.[1190] In my opinion, this ordinary meaning of 'fair'[1191] and 'equitable'[1192] warrants the protection of *legitimate* and *reasonable* expectations in consideration of the facts and circumstances of the case.[1193] This is particularly important for the eventual integration of ICCL as a factual circumstance of the case and an important legal consideration.[1194]

1188. *Saluka v. Czech Republic* (n 77) para. 459 (the term 'measures' covers any action or omission of the host State referring to the ICJ's decision in the *Fisheries Jurisdiction Case (Spain v. Canada)* where the ICJ found that the term is ('wide enough to cover any act, step or proceeding'); on the term 'treatment' in the MFN context, *see* UNCTAD, *Most-Favoured-Nation Treatment: A Sequel* (Report, 2010) 15-17.
1189. *CMS v. Argentine* (n 536) para. 273; *Sempra v. Argentina*, Award, 28 September 2007, para. 296; *Rumeli v. Kazakhstan* (n 76) para. 610; *Suez v. Argentina* (n 567) paras 196ff.; *Total S.A. v. The Argentine Republic*, ICSID Case No. ARB/04/01, Decision on Liability, 27 December 2010, paras 106-9; Barnali Choudhury, 'Evolution or Devolution? Defining Fair and Equitable Treatment in International Investment Law' (2005) 6 Journal of World Investment and Trade 297-320 https://doi.org/10.1163/221190005x00091; Patrick Juillard, 'L'évolution des sources du droit des investissements' (1994) 250 *Recueil des cours* 9 133.
1190. *Devas v. India*, Decision on Jurisdiction and Liability (2016), para. 464 ('FET is an objective concept; it is the result of interests and rights of both the investor and the State, and the result of such balancing may vary with the circumstances').
1191. Rudolf Dolzer, 'Fair and Equitable Treatment: Today's Contours' (2014) 12 SCJIL 7, 12 ('The acceptance of the standard is directly linked to the fundamental moral and legal grounding of the notion of fairness, anchored in a universally accepted sense of justice, but also in classic rules of customary law governing the protection of foreign nationals and companies').
1192. Most scholars have also identified FET as one single concept, not dissociating the two terms; Roland Kläger, *'Fair and Equitable Treatment' in International Investment Law* (CUP 2011) 41; Jeswald Salacuse, *The Law of Investment Treaties* (2nd edn, OUP 2010) 221ff. ('Two considerations support this view. First, the consistency with which states have linked the two terms in the verbal formula of "fair and equitable treatment" supports the view that states believe there is a single standard ... Second, if states intended "fair and equitable" to refer to two separate standards, they would have made that meaning explicit in the treaty texts. No state has chosen to do so. They could, for example, set out the fairness standard in one treaty provision, and the equity standard in another. The fact that they have not done so indicates that the contracting states intended the phrase "fair and equitable treatment" to connote a single standard.'); for a countervailing position *see* Thomas Wälde, 'Energy Charter Treaty-based Investment Arbitration: Controversial Issues' (2004) 5 Journal of World Investment & Trade 373, 385 (it is plausible that 'fairness' refers to concepts of 'good governance', and 'equity' relates to the international law and civil law concepts of 'good faith', 'Treu und Glauben', 'abus de droit' and *'venire contra factum proprium'*, which are reminiscent of LE's origins).
1193. Dolzer and Schreuer, *Principles of International Investment Law* (n 47) 133.
1194. OECD, *Fair and Equitable Treatment Standard in International Investment Law Working Papers on International Investment 2004/03* (Command Paper, 2004) 2 (The OECD suggested in 2004 that unqualified FET treaty provision was drafted in broad terms 'to give arbitrators the possibility to articulate the range of principles necessary to achieve the treaty's purpose in particular disputes'); for a contra position *see* Muthucumaraswamy Sornarajah, 'The Fair and Equitable Standard of Treatment: Whose Fairness? Whose Equity?' in Federico Ortino and others (eds), *Investment Treaty Law: Current Issues Volume II, Nationality and Investment Treaty Claims, Fair and Equitable Treatment in Investment Treaty Law* (BIICL 2007), 168 (dismissing the idea as improbable adding that 'in a document that contains a limitation on their sovereignty, the state parties agreed [that] a casually appointed arbitrator should have the capricious discretion as to how their sovereignty should be limited in the future').

Last, the treaties' context and purpose may alter the degree of LE's protection. Most investment agreements promote stable investment environments and the peaceful resolution of disputes.[1195] Beyond this objective, one of the purposes present in the preamble of a wide array of IIAs generally relates to, in the words of the UK Model BIT, 'promote greater economic cooperation with respect to investment by nationals and enterprises of one Party in the territory of the other Party'.[1196] In other words, IIAs generally aim to secure a stable and orderly framework for their investors and for importing countries to further attract infrastructure, expertise and capital.[1197] One could thus argue that protecting investors' LE reflect this obligation of legal certainty, favouring a higher level of substantive protection.[1198] Where, however, states tie FET to the CIL standard, they may intend to restrict their scope of liability and potentially exclude recourse to the concept of LE.[1199]

B BALANCING THE REPRESENTATION AND THE EXPECTATION'S LEGITIMACY

Once the FET provision has been interpreted, one must turn to analyse the promise or representation made by the state to the investor. This analysis should consider whether the promise made by the state includes a stabilisation clause in the law or contract. The interpretation of the stabilisation clause should be done in good faith. In the absence of a stabilisation clause, the tribunal may consider the state's regulatory framework, public written and oral statements at the time the promise was made, as well as the circumstances surrounding the potential commitment.

The arbitral tribunal should assess in good faith whether statements deriving from a state's authority[1200] may have created a clear and specific commitment towards the investor or a group of investors. According to the analogy to the doctrine of unilateral statements, those unilateral representations or declarations made by states that concern legal or factual situations may create legal obligations when: (i) the state intended to bind itself to a legal or factual situation; (ii) the declaration is given publicly and repeatedly; and (iii) those to whom the statements were directed could reasonably

1195. UNCTAD, *Fair and Equitable Treatment* (Report, 1999) 5.
1196. The United States of America 2012 Model Bilateral Investment Treaty.
1197. Bishop, Crawford and Reisman, *Foreign Investment Disputes* (n 51) 32.
1198. Rudolf Dolzer, 'Fair and Equitable Treatment: Today's Contours' (2014) 12 SCJIL 7, 12 ('The acceptance of the standard is directly linked to the fundamental moral and legal grounding of the notion of fairness, anchored in a universally accepted sense of justice, but also in classic rules of customary law governing the protection of foreign nationals and companies').
1199. Notes of Interpretation of Certain Chapter 11 Provisions (NAFTA Free Trade Commission, 31 July 2001) '2. Minimum Standard of Treatment in Accordance with International Law 2. The concepts of "fair and equitable treatment" and "full protection and security" do not require treatment in addition to or beyond that which is required by the customary international law minimum standard of treatment of aliens.'
1200. International Law Commission, *Draft Articles on Responsibility of States for Internationally Wrongful Acts* (ILC A/56/10, 2001) Art. 7 ('The conduct of an organ of a State or of a person or entity empowered to exercise elements of the governmental authority shall be considered an act of the State under international law if the organ, person or entity acts in that capacity, even if it exceeds its authority or contravenes instructions').

rely upon them.[1201] The representation will be reinforced if the state making the declaration expects to receive clear benefits from it, as it constitutes a reliable indicator that the state had every intention of creating expectations in its intended audience and that it intended to bind itself. Based on the research conducted, I suggest that the regulatory framework may create LE when the state's clear and specific representation and its intention to attract their investment can be deciphered from it. Similarly, even in the absence of specific commitments to the investor, the unqualified FET standard may protect foreign investors from fundamental or radical modifications to the legal framework when the state's conduct stands in contradistinction from its previous legitimate, specific and clear representations to a delimited economic sector.[1202]

The second step is to analyse the context in which such a promise was made. The tribunal must consider whether there are contextual elements that could undermine interpreting a representation as a commitment made by the state. The context in which the promise is made includes the foreseeability of adverse measures, such as net zero policy measures affecting energy sectors at the time of the investment, in particular when the state committed to obligations on the international plane.

The third step is to analyse whether the investor relied on the commitment. To do so requires an *objective* assessment of not only the regulatory incentive but also the risks assumed by the investor in his business sector. Investing in a high-risk sector may widely influence the extent to which an investor holds LE. There are three types of risks that the tribunal should consider. The first type is regulatory risks, which arise from changes in the legal and regulatory framework. The second type is business risks, which arise from changes in market conditions, technology, and other factors that affect the profitability of the investment. The third type is global regulatory risks, which arise from the host State's commitment under international law and its domestic policy obligations, such as those related to climate change.[1203] Evidence of subjective due diligence may support the investor's reliance on the state's conduct but should not constitute a requirement for determining whether a state breached LE. This contrasts with the detrimental reliance theory of LE, in which subjective due diligence of the investor in the specific host State is crucial.[1204]

Fourth, it is widely agreed that IIAs cannot serve as an insurance policy. This has the concrete consequence that if the investor decides to invest capital in a business that is objectively at eminent risk, it cannot reasonably hold LE. Business risks are widely recognised as an exception to the protection of LE.[1205] Where the investor invests while the regulatory framework is structurally changing, it may not hold the same LE as an investor who invested at a time when that regulatory framework was stable.

Fifth, the investor does not hold expectations of 'reasonable return' per se. It only matters whether the state created a promise of a legitimate, specific and clear return,

1201. *See* analysis in Chapter 2.D.4.
1202. *Silver Ridge v. Italy* (n 56) para. 410.
1203. *See* Chapter 5.B.1.
1204. *See* Chapter 3.C.1, especially *Stadtwerke München v. Spain* (n 452) para. 278.
1205. *See* Chapter 3.D.2.

which, if found to be reasonably relied upon at the time of the investment, should be enforced. Investor's hope for a 'reasonable return' where there is no representation should be dismissed.

In summary, in analysing the LE of an investor, the tribunal must consider the treaty language, the content of the promise made by the state, the context in which the promise was made, and the risks involved in the business at the time of the investment. By taking these factors into account, the tribunal can arrive at a fair assessment of the state's commitment and legitimacy of expectations.

C ALIGNING THE TIME OF THE INVESTMENT TO THE EXPECTATIONS' LEGITIMACY

The investment's timing is crucial in assessing LE. Many tribunals stressed that the timing of the investment decision is the condition for expectations to exist. But timing also influences the foreseeability of general regulatory risks assumed by the investor. According to the tribunal in *Enron v. Argentina*, 'What seems to be essential ... is that these expectations derived from the conditions that were offered by the State to the investor at the time of the investment and that such conditions were relied upon by the investor when deciding to invest.'[1206] This is largely concurred in the Spanish case law.[1207]

It is established that LE can only arise at the time the investment is made.[1208] To opine otherwise, namely, to think that an investment that predates a state's representation has LE, would run contrary to the meaning of 'expectations' itself. Where no representations are made, the state may have to uphold a certain degree of stability, but it cannot be held accountable for representations or expectations that have not been made in the first place. The difficulty remains that tribunals recognise an investment as a process rather than a single transaction so that the investment timing can be difficult to pinpoint.[1209] The tribunal in *Novenergia II* is right to point out that:

> the Tribunal is of the view that the relevant time for making the assessment of the Claimant's legitimate expectations is at the time when the investment was made. The more difficult issue is to determine in an actual case when such investment was in fact made. It is of course not unusual in larger projects that the investment phase transcends through various stages; negotiations, due diligence, internal corporate decisions, external contractual commitments, financing, acquisition,

1206. *Enron Corp v. Argentina* (n 429) para. 262; *Tecmed v. Mexico* (n 67) para. 154; *LG&E v. Argentina* (n 388) para. 130; *BG Group v. Argentina*, UNCITRAL, Final Award, 24 December 2007, para. 298.
1207. Among others, *Antin v. Spain* (n 453) para. 537.
1208. *Bayindir v. Pakistan* (n 459) para. 190 ('Several awards have stressed that the expectations to be taken into account are those existing at the time when the investor made the decision to invest'); *Frontier Petroleum v. Czech Republic* (n 526) para. 287; *Mamidoil Jetoil Greek Petroleum Products Societe S.A. v. Republic of Albania*, ICSID Case No. ARB/11/24, Award, 30 March 2015, para. 695.
1209. Christoph Schreuer and Ursula Kriebaum, 'At What Time Must Legitimate Expectations Exist?' in Christoph Schreuer (ed.), *A Liber Amicorum: Thomas Wälde* (CMP Pub Ltd 2009) 265.

> construction, registration, start-up and the first generation of revenues. In addition, the investment is sometimes structured to be executed in consecutive stages even if there are binding commitments predating such subsequent stages. The Tribunal is of the view that the timing of the investor's decision to invest sets a backstop date for the evaluation of legitimate expectations.[1210]

Where it is impossible to pinpoint a specific date of investment, tribunals must find the timing of the investor's final decision to invest, which is inherently factual. Accordingly, 'tribunals must attempt to place themselves into the time of the investment, consider the information and conditions available at such time, and refrain from appraising the investor's expectations with the benefit of hindsight'.[1211] In other words, the tribunal must try to place itself in the shoes of the investor when the investment is made. This might have significant repercussions on the level of expectations that may be legitimately expected – for instance, if a major policy change is made before the finalisation of the investment.[1212]

Although the date of the investment can be factually assessed, once it is established, it must take due consideration of the regulatory risks. I personally agree with the *Foresight* tribunal, which itself agreed in principle with the *Charanne* tribunal on the concept of foreseeability, adapting the degree of legitimacy of expectations to the conduct of the state at the time of the investment.[1213] The solution in *Cube v. Spain* should also be held as a correct assessment. The decision considered that there was a 'climate of change' with unambiguous signals that regulatory change would approach and the level of expectations changes.[1214] *Cube* tribunal's analysis is right in its assessment of the regulatory framework, balancing the intensity of expectations based on the legal framework in place. Similarly, the tribunal in *Isolux v. Spain* refuted the claim of LE because, at the time of the investment, in October 2012, regulatory changes, such as Law No. 15/2012 of 6 June 2012, were in full swing.[1215] The tribunal in *Novenergia II* agreed with such an assessment.[1216]

1210. *Novenergia II v. Spain* (n 413) paras 538-539.
1211. *Antin v. Spain* (n 453) para. 537.
1212. Michal Krzykowski et al., 'Principle of Reasonable and Legitimate Expectations in International Law as a Premise for Investments in the Energy Sector' (2021) 21 Int Environ Agreements 75 https://doi.org/10.1007/s10784-020-09471-x.
1213. *Foresight v. Spain* (n 620) para. 374 citing *Charanne*, para. 508 ('Although decisions of the Spanish courts are not binding on the Arbitral Tribunal, they remain relevant as factual elements to verify that an investor could not, at the time of the disputed investment, have the reasonable expectation that in the absence of a specific commitment the regulation would not be modified throughout the life of the plants').
1214. *Cube Infrastructure v. Spain* (n 402) para. 330 ('The regulatory regime was largely the same as that applicable when the PV investments were made, but with the important difference that the 2010-2011 regulatory changes had by that time been adopted and with retroactive effect. The laws of 2010 and 2011 had demonstrated that the respondent would at least adjust the periods for which price incentives were payable and the levels of price incentives if it considered this necessary in order to address the tariff deficit. (...) 333. In these circumstances, the Tribunal considers that any reasonable investor would have taken a much more cautious view of the extent to which the continuation of the existing legal regime could be relied on but would not have had reason to expect the complete abandonment of the Special Regime').
1215. *Isolux v. Spain* (n 466) paras 792-800.
1216. *Novenergia II v. Spain* (n 413) para. 686.

Therefore, and as demonstrated in this book, from a voluntarist-leaning perspective, the time of the investment remains crucial to determining the legitimacy of expectations. It sets a backdrop to ascertain the conduct of the state, the risks assumed by the investor, and the foreseeability of frustrating measures.

D ASSESSING THE PROPORTIONALITY OF THE STATE'S FRUSTRATING MEASURE

A final aspect to address is whether the purpose of the frustrating measure should play a role in the assessment of liability. As indicated above, the reasonableness of the frustrating measure can be established *ex ante*, i.e., at the time of the investment. This means that an investment in the coal industry in a country that agreed to ICCL should expect to meet reasonable frustrating measures. In this sense, the later the investment, the less legitimate the expectations, and the more reasonable the frustrating measure, *a priori*.

The use of international treaties to assess the frustration is warranted, whether the tribunal chooses the benchmark of reasonableness or proportionality.[1217] For the sake of the argument, the following paragraphs explore whether an abstract state's net zero measure might pass the demanding proportionality standard.

1 Appropriateness: Causality Between Net Zero Policies and Mitigation Objectives

On this basis, the investor may claim that the state is not required to adopt a specific energy measure to meet its obligations under a climate agreement. Indeed, agreements under the UNFCCC usually do not address conflicts between their provisions and other instruments of international law. As demonstrated above, no conflict *stricto sensu* exists. The state must thus demonstrate the relationship between its measure and international commitment factually.

To achieve the targets set out in the Paris Agreement, 80% of fossil fuel reserves should stay in the ground. An important number of fossil fuel investments may become redundant, in other words, 'stranded assets'.[1218] The most significant risk is posed to developing countries, whose reliance on fossil fuels is acute to meet economic and political agendas. To meet the Paris Agreement, these countries might phase out certain energy sectors[1219] to comply with ICCL and their own NDCs. To illustrate the amount of GHG emissions allowed by countries to meet the Paris Agreement, research institutes created the 'carbon budget'. The carbon budget calculates the cumulative GHG emissions over a specific time that cannot be exceeded should global temperature not rise over 2°C.[1220]

1217. *See* the analysis Chapter 4.C.
1218. Bos and Gupta, 'Climate Change: The Risks of Stranded Fossil Fuel Assets' (n 280).
1219. *Ibid.*
1220. Carbon Tracker, *Unburnable Carbon 2013: Wasted Capital and Stranded Assets* (Report, 2013).

To keep the rise below 2°C (with a probability of 50%), 'the carbon budget for 2011 to 2050 is around 1,100 gigatons of carbon dioxide (Gt CO_2). The issue is that global fossil fuel reserves have a potential of Gt CO_2 three times higher than this amount'.[1221] Concretely, this means that 33% of the current and known resources in oil, 49% in gas and 82% in coal should be left unused. To be more certain of achieving the 2°C goals (with an 80% probability), the world should not produce more than 565 Gt CO_2 (for 2010-2050). This would infer that 20% of fossil fuel reserves can be extracted. Achieving the 1.5°C target would prove even more speculative, as it would translate into a carbon budget of 365 Gt CO_2 over 2011-2100; and this scenario would only have a 50% probability of meeting the 1.5°C target. This seems rather complicated when in 2020 alone, 38 Gt CO_2 have been emitted by the energy sector, of which 14, 8 Gt CO_2 from coal only.[1222]

The findings of the IPCC which led to the adoption of constraining norms for the reduction of GHG emissions can be exploited to demonstrate the appropriateness of measures.[1223] It is specified that a drastic reduction of CO_2 levels may, from a scientific point of view, drastically reduce the level of climate change and its impact on our societies and the planet.[1224] IPCC reports *can* become instrumental in international investment arbitration. They may serve as a guide for expertise in NZEID.

2 Necessity: Reaching Net Zero and Renewable Targets

Achieving ICCL's objectives and the specific obligations laid out in NDCs requires energy reforms.[1225] These may have an impact on the regulatory framework of States in the energy sector and the expectations of foreign investors. The question is whether a net zero policy targeting the energy sector is 'necessary'. Most of the answers can be found in non-legal discussions.[1226] Evidence shows that the vast majority (potentially up to 75%) of foreign-owned coal power plants that would need to be 'phased out' according to the Glasgow Agreement are covered by at least one treaty with investment arbitration.[1227] On the flip side, reaching net zero targets requires state incentives, as demonstrated in Chapter 1, so the frustration of such measure is difficult to argue.

1221. Cristopher McGlade and Paul Ekins, 'The Geographical Distribution of Fossil Fuels Unused When Limiting Global Warming to 2 Degree C' (2015) 517 Nature 187 https://doi.org/10.1038/nature14016.
1222. IEA, *Energy 2021* (n 278).
1223. IPCC, *Climate Change 2021: The Physical Science Basis. Contribution of Working Group I to the Sixth Assessment Report of the Intergovernmental Panel on Climate Change* (Report, 2021) 1 ('it is unequivocal that human influence has warmed the atmosphere, ocean, and land (...) Widespread and rapid changes in the atmosphere, ocean, cryosphere and biosphere have occurred').
1224. *Ibid.*
1225. On the economic analysis on the necessity of CO_2 reductions to achieve net zero, *see* Thomas Schöb and others, 'Die Notwendigkeit negativer Emissionen für ein treibhausgasneutrales Deutschland-eine modellgestützte Analyse' (2021) 12 Internationale Energiewirtschaftstagung TU Wien.
1226. ICC, *Resolving Climate Change-Related Disputes* (n 22) 5.63.
1227. Tienhaara and Cotula, 'Raising the Cost' (n 305) 27.

3 Temporal Quality of the Measure and Effect on the Investment

The balancing act of proportionality *stricto sensu* is a result-oriented test. This last test of proportionality distinctly delineates the approach taken by the German Constitutional Court from that of other legal systems. Notably, English Courts abstain from applying this test to prevent encroachment upon the legislative domain, conscientiously refraining from assuming the role of legislating judges. According to it, to justify a limitation on a constitutional right, a proper relationship should exist between the benefits gained by fulfilling the purpose and the harm caused to the constitutional right by obtaining that purpose. The proportionality *stricto sensu* test is a result-oriented test.

Is the withdrawal of licences to meet climate change targets reasonable? The answer depends on the temporal quality of the expectations. In general, cutting energy-related emissions is considered the most efficient way to cut down CO_2 emissions, as recognised in the Glasgow Pact, although in diplomatic language. However, it is difficult to consider that a stringent measure to close fossil fuel production instantly would not breach LE nor incur compensation and damages.

On the other hand, the withdrawal of 'clean' incentives to meet financial objectives is reasonable only where national circumstances reasonably justify such a measure. While arbitrators cannot proceed with a thorough standard of review, it is up to the state to justify how international commitments it undertook publicly under climate change treaties could be reasonably withdrawn.

E REFORMING TO RECONCILE?

This research may not conclude without addressing the possibility of reconciling international investment law and ICCL through proposed reforms. The Energy Charter Treaty has been at the centre of the discussion to reconcile investment arbitration with climate change action. Although the EU's reform proposal has not been successful and failed to convince, the modernisation of the ECT has since been adopted on 3 December 2024 and may indicate a way forward for the net zero energy transition.[1228]

Before addressing the reform proposal and its effect on legitimate expectations (2), I address below a few elements of general misperception about the ECT (1). Finally, I issue a word of caution against withdrawing entirely from investment treaties (3).

1 The ECT and Its Misconceptions

Reforming a treaty protecting investments necessitates taking distance from the political sphere and delving into the complexity of arbitral awards – an attempt of the

1228. Energy Charter Secretariat, *Agreement in Principle on the Modernisation of the Energy Charter Treaty* (24 June 2022) (AIP) www.bilaterals.org/IMG/pdf/reformed_ect_text.pdf accessed 17 October 2023.

current study. This complexity has been largely overlooked in the EU reform proposal, which, in my view, has been construed on a number of misconceptions.

The general misconception about the ECT mainly concerns the share of clean and fossil fuel investors making use of the treaty[1229] and the damages awarded by arbitral tribunals.[1230] Hard statistics challenge the common misperceptions around the ECT being averse to the net zero energy transition.

So far, only two cases brought under the ECT countervail climate mitigation measures. In other words, two cases fall into the typology defined above as 'anti-environmental' cases, i.e., cases in which the state's measure '(ii) is taken and justified by the respondent state, in whole or in part, on the grounds of climate change mitigation'.[1231] These include the claims brought against the coal-phaseouts in *RWE v. Netherlands*[1232] and *UNIPER v. The Netherlands*,[1233] both of which have been discontinued.

Critics of the ECT often rely on a 23 August 2022 award in *Rockhopper v. Italy*[1234] to demonstrate that the ECT would contravene climate action or the net zero transition.[1235] However, that case concerned environmental concerns of the local population related to offshore oil exploitation and its impact on the seashore. The climate policy dimension was an aspect left unaddressed by the Respondent and therefore by the Tribunal as well.[1236] More generally, statistics show the divide between political metaphors and reality.

First, as of 1 May 2023, 158 cases had been filed under the ECT. Out of these known cases, 58% were related to the renewable industry, 34% to the fossil fuels

1229. *See* European Parliament, 'MEPs Consent to the EU Withdrawing from the Energy Charter Treaty' (April 2024) (announcing that 'The recommendation from the Industry, Research, Energy, and Interntional Trade committees was adopted with 560 votes to 43, with 27 abstentions'; and citing Rapporteur for the Trade Committee Anna Cavazzini (Greens/EFA, DE): 'Today's vote is a major step in the right direction. The EU is finally withdrawing from the climate-hostile Energy Charter Treaty. In view of the climate crisis, the EU must become a climate-neutral continent as quickly as possible. Finally the fossil dinosaur treaty is no longer standing in the way of consistent climate protection, as we no longer have to fear corporate lawsuits demanding billions of euro in compensation brought before private arbitration tribunals.').

1230. *Ibid.* (Rapporteur for the Industry, Research and Energy Committee Marc Botenga (The Left, BE): 'The Energy Charter Treaty allows fossil fuel multinationals to sue states and the European Union if climate policies affect their profits. In the midst of a climate crisis, this is a contradiction, in addition to being very costly for taxpayers. Alongside civil society, a significant movement has been built to exit from this treaty and I am happy to see this is bearing fruit today. It is now necessary to speed up the rate of public investments in renewables.').

1231. *See* Introduction.C.2.

1232. *RWE v. The Netherlands* (n 153).

1233. Uniper SE, *Uniper Benelux Holding B.V. and Uniper Benelux N.V. v. Kingdom of the Netherlands*, ICSID Case No. ARB/21/22.

1234. *Rockhopper Italia S.p.A., Rockhopper Mediterranean Ltd, and Rockhopper Exploration Plc v. Italian Republic*, ICSID Case No. ARB/17/14.

1235. Paolo Mazzotti, 'Rockhopper v. Italy and the Tension Between ISDS and Climate Policy: A Missed Moment of Truth?' (Völkerrechtsblog, 21 December 2022).

1236. *Rockhopper Italia S.p.A., Rockhopper Mediterranean Ltd, and Rockhopper Exploration Plc v. Italian Republic*, ICSID Case No. ARB/17/14, Final Award, 23 August 20221.

industry, 3 % to nuclear and 4 % to other sources of energy production.[1237] Out of these cases, renewable investors claimed for damages totalling EUR 23 billion. So far, among the ones decided, they have been awarded approx. EUR 1.25 billion. At the same time, fossil fuel investors, the Yukos exception notwithstanding, claimed for damages totalling EUR 13 billion and, so far, received a total of approximately EUR 1 billion EUR (in the *Yukos* case, EUR approx. 87 million were claimed and EUR 40 billion were awarded).[1238]

Second, another misconception is that only large companies are users of the treaty. Statistics debunk this claim. Out of the 158 cases referred to above, SMEs represent 55 % of all claimants (387), holdings 32 % (223), individual investors 8 % (60), as for banks (6) and large corporations (10) only 1 %. Investment funds (21) represent 3 % of investors.

Third, out of the 87 final awards, 40 claims were outrightly rejected. Forty decisions found a breach and awarded damages to the investor, 4 settled and 3 remain unknown in their outcome.

Despite these statistics, the widespread misunderstanding is that the ECT exclusively benefits fossil fuel investments, impeding the net zero energy transition. Such claims have prompted the EU commission to propose reform that exaggeratedly circumscribes the potential for investors, especially clean energy investors, to defend their treaty rights.

2 The EU Reform Proposal Was of No Support to the Net Zero Energy Transition

The EU Commission's ECT reform proposal included a wide array of changes regarding climate change and investment governance. It added additional wording in the preamble and throughout the treaty on the contracting parties' right to regulate in the interest of legitimate policy objectives and a stand-alone article on the right to regulate in the interest of legitimate policy objectives, including climate change mitigation and adaptation. In the reform proposal, the treaty *reaffirmed* the respective rights and obligations of the contracting parties under multilateral environmental agreements, such as the UNFCCC and the Paris Agreement, and the contracting parties' commitment to net zero energy transition, promotion of low-carbon technologies in energy trade and investment, and cooperation in implementing climate change-related policies.[1239] At the same time, it

1237. Secretariat of the Energy Charter Treaty, 'Renewable Energy Investors Continue to Rely on Treaty Protection: Updated Statistics on Investment Cases under the ECT' (*ECT*, 2023).

1238. *Ibid.*, a few caveats should be stated regarding this statistic: fifty-three cases are still pending; the damages claimed, and damages awarded exclude tax gross-up and interest on damages claimed and awarded; in some of the cases, there is no publicly available information on the exact amounts claimed and/or awarded; one case involves more than one form of energy sources; in six cases, it has not been possible to identify particular energy sources.

1239. Johannes Tropper and Kilian Wagner, 'The European Union Proposal for the Modernisation of the Energy Charter Treaty: A Model for Climate-Friendly Investment Treaties?' (2022) 23 JWIT 5-6 813 https://doi.org/10.1163/22119000-12340271.

widely circumscribed the scope of disputes, affecting primarily clean energy investors from bringing a claim.

In particular, the EU reform proposal suggested clarification and circumscription of the FET standard under Article 10 as follows:

> (1) Each Contracting Party shall accord to Investments in its Area of Investors of other Contracting Parties, and their related activities and to Investors of other Contracting Parties with respect to such Investments fair and equitable treatment and the most constant protection and security in accordance with sub-paragraphs (i) to (iv).
>
> (i) A Contracting Party breaches the obligation of fair and equitable treatment referenced above through measures or series or measures that constitute: (a) denial of justice in criminal, civil or administrative proceedings; or (b) fundamental breach of due process, including a fundamental breach of transparency in judicial and administrative proceedings; or (c) manifest arbitrariness; or (d) targeted discrimination on manifestly wrongful grounds, such as gender, race or religious belief; or (e) abusive treatment such as harassment, duress or coercion.
>
> (ii) When applying the above fair and equitable treatment obligation, *a tribunal may take into account* whether a Contracting Party made *a specific representation to an investor to induce a covered investment,* that *created a legitimate expectation, upon which the investor relied* in deciding to make or maintain the covered investment, but that the Contracting Party subsequently *frustrated.*
>
> (iii) For greater certainty, 'most constant protection and security' refers to the Contracting Party's obligations relating to ensure the physical security of investors and investments.
>
> (iv) For greater certainty, a breach of another provision of this Treaty, or of any other international agreement, does not constitute a breach of this paragraph.[1240] *(emphasis added).*

Three preliminary remarks are necessary on this FET reform proposal before moving to the interpretation of legitimate expectations under the second sub-paragraph. First, the EU proposed a closed list of potential breaches of the FET standard. While meant to provide guidance to investors and states, this formulation denies the inherent flexibility of the ordinary meaning of the words 'fair' and 'equitable', which may address situations not falling in specific situations – situations that are qualified with the adjectives 'fundamental', 'manifest' suggesting that a high threshold must be met. Second, the EU reformed proposal dismisses the word 'stability', which has been at the centre of several tribunals and arbitrators' reasoning under the ECT. It aims hereby to accentuate the right of the state to regulate to adapt to changing circumstances. Third, the proposal specifically includes a provision stating that the 'breach of any other international agreement, does not constitute a breach of this paragraph'. This last paragraph would render clean energy investor's claim based

1240. European Commission, 'Text Proposal for the Modernisation of the Energy Charter Treaty' (May 2020) https://ccsi.columbia.edu/sites/default/files/content/docs/tradoc_158754%20(1)_0.pdf accessed 4 February 2025; *see also* Bagdat G Kuzhatov, 'The Energy Charter Treaty Reform: Why and How to Reach a Consensus on Fair and Equitable Treatment?' (2022) 163 Energy Policy 112769 https://doi.org/10.1016/j.enpol.2021.112769.

on climate change treaties more difficult – although climate treaties can still be considered as facts, as demonstrated above.[1241] In general, this FET standard appears as an impediment to investors in the clean energy sector, relying on stability and other treaties to bring their claims. As rightly noted by Johannes Tropper and Kilian Wagner, '[i]n contrast, an ambitious climate-friendly investment treaty would harness the potential of investors acting as incidental enforcers of climate protection through investor-State arbitration and even explicitly stipulate that legitimate expectations may emerge in relation to a State's commitments undertaken in MEAs [Multilateral Environmental Agreements]'.[1242]

Regarding legitimate expectations specifically, the EU reform proposal: (1) denies the quality of LE's as a stand-alone element under the FET standard by excluding it from the closed list and referring only to the possibility of taking it into account in assessing other breaches; (2) adds complexity to an already complex concept and (3) adds qualifiers akin to a restrictive interpretation of legitimate expectations along the lines of the strictest detrimental reliance theory. Indeed, the proposal lists five requirements for the legitimate expectation to be 'taken into account':

First, there must be a state's 'specific representation' to 'an investor' (singular). It is likely that the reform proposal aims to circumvent the use of LE by investors that are part of a targeted and incentivised group. With the use of the words 'specific' and 'investor' the EU proposal meant that a protected investor shall be a 'direct addressee'. Nevertheless, as explained before, 'representation' remains a broader term than 'commitment'.

Second, the specific representation shall 'create a legitimate expectation'. This consists in a clarification of the concept of LE, which denies investors' reliance on mere hopes. Instead of an investor 'having' legitimate expectations [e.g., of regulatory stability], the EU reform proposal insists that only the state's specific representation may create expectations, emphasising the 'legitimacy' element of such creation.

Third, specific representation shall 'induce' a 'covered investment'. It is unclear why 'covered' investment is emphasised twice in this paragraph, as only covered investments are susceptible to receiving compensation for a breach of the FET standard in any case. It can only indicate lower quality drafting intended to emphasise that only 'specifc adressees' may benefit from superficial LE. As for the word 'induce', it appears as another attempt to circumscribe the number of investors able to rely on the concept of LE. Inducing means more than causing.[1243] It is closer to persuading, while the proposal could have chosen broader words such as 'promoting' or 'encouraging'.

Fourth, the investor must 'rely' upon the expectation in 'deciding to make or maintain' its covered investment. The concept of reliance is fully endorsed by the EU reform proposal, advocating overall a strict detrimental reliance theory. With regard to the formulation 'deciding to', the EU's proposal again circumscribes the scope of LE by

1241. *See* above Chapter 4.C.

1242. Johannes Tropper and Kilian Wagner, 'The European Union Proposal for the Modernisation of the Energy Charter Treaty: A Model for Climate-Friendly Investment Treaties?' (2022) 23 JWIT 5-6 813, 840 https://doi.org/10.1163/22119000-12340271.

1243. 'Inducement', *Black's Law Dictionary* (8th edn, 2009) ('[t]he act or process of enticing or persuading another person to take a certain course of action').

adding a subjective condition (the decision-making of the investor) as part of the legal test to consider LE.

Fifth, the state must 'frustrate' the legitimate expectation or the specific representation, the choice between the two being unclear due to the sentence's deliberate complexity – although it was clear to the drafter that only expectations could be frustrated. In contrast to other conditions, 'frustration' does not appear to pose a high threshold.

To put it differently, if interpreted strictly, this sub-paragraph on legitimate expectations would have no *effet utile*. Not only do the qualifiers confer to the strictest detrimental reliance theory, but more importantly, this second sub-paragraph on LE would only be taken into account as a fact to assess the breach of other obligations under the FET standard. Clearly, this version of LE would not advantage clean energy investors compared to the current one. If the intent of the EU was indeed to fight climate change, the carve-out of the most polluting industries (i.e., coal) from investment protection would appear more convincing. If, however, the intent is to circumscribe all types of claims under LE, whether from clean energy or fossil fuel investors, then such a deliberately complex formulation appears appropriate.

The chief critic that may be issued against this reformed FET proposal is that it protects larger, established and profitable companies better than SME, which rely on state's policies and incentives to achieve profitability. In other words, by emphasising that only individual recipient of a state's representation may rely on legitimate expectations, the treaty favours those enterprises that may negotiate with a state or have enough bargaining power to receive a specific 'representation'. More often than not, these would be fossil fuel companies, not scale ups in clean energy production. A better reform proposal would have suggested that 'clear' or 'clear and unequivocal' representations may create expectations. Adding that these expectations must be 'legitimate' *and* 'reasonable' would have, in contrast, emphasised the importance of foreseeability, timing of investment and assumed risks – favouring clean energy investments over politically risk-sensitive fossil fuel investments.

In the end, the EU reform proposal was abandoned, and the EU withdrew from the treaty as a whole. The AIP reached on 24 June 2022[1244] and the modernisation adopted on 3rd December 2024 appear more in line with the preferred formulation described above, notably by blessing LE as a stand-alone element of FET.[1245] The AIP adopted a language more favourable to the protection of clean energy investors' LE:

> *frustration* of an Investor's legitimate expectations where these *were central to its Investment,* and arose from a *clear and specific representation or commitment* by that Contracting Party upon which the Investor *reasonably* relied in deciding to make or maintain the Investment.[1246] *(emphasis added).*

1244. Agreement in Principle on the Modernisation of the Energy Charter Treaty (24 June 2022) www.bilaterals.org/IMG/pdf/reformed_ect_text.pdf accessed 17 October 2023.
1245. *Ibid.*
1246. Johannes Tropper and Kilian Wagner, 'The European Union Proposal for the Modernisation of the Energy Charter Treaty: A Model for Climate-Friendly Investment Treaties?' (2022) 23 JWIT 5-6 813 https://doi.org/10.1163/22119000-12340271, footnote 140.

Moreover, the amendment to the ECT is consistent in its promotion of clean energy as it proposed a novel 'flexibility mechanism' allowing contracting parties to exclude investment protection for fossil fuels in their territories, which may resonate with net zero energy transition aspiration despite the related risks described in the sub-section below.[1247]

To conclude, the EU's reform proposal on the FET standard defeats the sense of 'fair' and 'equitable'. By infusing complexity instead of the inherent flexibility of the standard, the EU reform proposal does not appear to protect investors from unfair and inequitable behaviours by states. On the contrary, the modernisation adopted in 2024 proposes a revised but not significantly restricted circumscription of LE claims. What matters to succeed in advancing the energy transition is to provide legal security, which is essential to long-term investments. Reform proposals that pursue greater protection of *bona fide* investments relying on state policies can contribute to the enforcement of climate goals rather than impeding them. It appears that the adopted reform pursues the latter effort, attempting to combine investment protection, energy transition and the expressed need for certain countries to exclude fossil fuels from treaty protection.

3 The Risks of 'Contractualising' Investment Disputes in the Wake of Treaty Withdrawals

In face of the difficulties states faced in reforming the ECT, a number of states have decided to withdraw entirely from it.[1248] These withdrawals come into effect despite the willingness of certain African parties to join the ECT[1249] because of primary energy poverty[1250] and the ultimate reform efforts of the parties.

A word of caution should be issued against withdrawals and general carve-outs. States withdrawing from investment treaties should be warry of the legal consequences

1247. Energy Charter Secretariat, *Decision on the Energy Charter Conference* (24 June 2022) CCDEC 2022 10 GEN, 3; *see also* Claude Turmes, 'Energy Charter Treaty Modernization Process: Definition of Economic Activities to Terminate Investment Protection in Fossil Fuels' (Letter to the European Commission, 5 February 2021).

1248. *See* generally Secretariat of the Energy Charter Treaty, 'Written Notification of Withdrawal from the Energy Charter Treaty' (*ECT*, 2024). It is highly likely that the misconceptions stated above prompted the withdrawal of a number of countries, including France (effective on 8 December 2023); Germany (effective on 20 December 2023); Poland (effective on 29 December 2023); the Grand-Duchy of Luxembourg (effective on 17 June 2024); Slovenia (effective on 14 October 2024); Kingdom of Spain (effective on 17 April 2025); and the United Kingdom (effective on 27 April 2025).

1249. Secretariat of the Energy Charter Treaty, 'Members and Observers to the Energy Charter Conference' (*ECT*, 2024), African signatories but non-members of the Energy Charter Treaty include: Chad, Burundi, Morocco, Mauritanie, Niger, Uganda, Syria, Niger (1991). In recent years, Benin, Burkina Faso, East African Community, Economic Community of Central African States, G5 Sahel, Gambia, Kenya, Mali, Nigeria, Rwanda, Senegal, Tanzania, Eswatini (2015).

1250. The ten most climate vulnerable countries globally are all in Africa; *see* Mo Ibrahim Foundation, 'The Road to COP27: Making Africa's Case in the Global Climate Debate' (Report 2022) 40 ('only 55.7 per cent of Africa's 1.3 billion people have reliable access to electricity'); The World Bank Group and the Energy Charter Secretariat, Enabling Foreign Direct Investment in the Renewable Energy Sector Reducing Regulatory Risks and Preventing Investor-State Conflicts (Report 2023) 9.

for individual investments. Withdrawing from investment treaties, or excluding certain energy types for that matter, may prompt investors *and* states to turn to contractual protections when energy sources become necessary.[1251]

Investors may 'contractualise' their relationships with governments, notably by including stabilisation, confidentiality, and arbitration provisions in their contracts. Such contracts are not always beneficial for the country's development and may have worse effects on the state's protection of public interest and right to regulate compared to investment arbitration under investment treaties.[1252]

The contractualisation of investment disputes is not a theoretical risk, it is already taking place. For instance, the Natural Resource Governance Institute conducted a 2021 review of thirty-four publicly available petroleum contracts signed between majors (Total, BP, ExxonMobil) and eleven developing countries with oil resources, since the 2015 Paris Agreement. The study found that all reviewed contracts contained stabilisation clauses, with almost all providing stabilisation clauses for the duration of the contract, thereby protecting the company's investment against legal changes for two or three decades. The majority restricted the state's application of tax and climate regulations to the investment. Fewer than half excluded changes in environmental laws from the scope of the stabilisation clause. And, most importantly for the future of investment arbitration, twenty-seven of these contracts contained a commercial arbitration clause.[1253]

Even though the contractualisation of investment disputes may face legal hurdles in the EU,[1254] it is a reason for concern that the protection of investments moves away from an international regime in which states may draft treaties in accordance with their priorities[1255] towards one in which they negotiate single-handedly with investors in

1251. For example, a case of necessity could arise during a war or energy sanctions, when a country loses access to a vital energy source, requiring the activation of alternative sources such as coal, gas, or nuclear energy. *See* Josephine Fokuhl and Todd Gillespie, 'Germany Revives Coal as Energy Security Trumps Climate Goals' *Bloomberg* (London, 22 December 2022).
1252. *See also* Karl P. Sauvant, 'Importance of Negotiating Good Contracts' (2017) 201 Columbia FDI perspectives.
1253. Natural Resource Governance Institute, 'Tying Their Hands: How Petroleum Contract Terms May Limit Governments Climate Flexibility' (Report 2021).
1254. Within the EU, however, arbitration contracts between intra-EU investors and EU states may be considered invalid. After the *Achmea* case of 2018 (which has put an end to the intra-EU BIT-based arbitration) and the *Komstroy* case of 2021 (having prohibited the ECT-based, EU-seated and EU law-related arbitration), PL Holdings comes to round out the trilogy by barring the states from entering into intra-EU implicit ad hoc arbitration agreements, which are identical to BIT arbitration clauses. In the *PL Holdings* case, an arbitration procedure has been brought against them by an investor; Member States must challenge, before the arbitration body or before the court having jurisdiction, the validity of the arbitration clause or that of the ad hoc arbitration agreement. In case an arbitral award is issued on the basis of an arbitration clause contained in a BIT, the Member States must request the competent national courts to set aside, annul or challenge the recognition and enforcement of the arbitral award, pursuant to Art. 7(b) of the Agreement for the termination of Bilateral Investment Treaties between the Member States of the European Union. As for the national courts, they shall uphold any application that seeks the setting aside of an arbitration award made on the basis of an arbitration agreement infringing EU law.
1255. Leal-Arcas R, 'The Contribution of Free Trade Agreements and Bilateral Investment Treaties to a Sustainable Future' (2020) 23 Zeitschrift für Europarechtliche Studien–ZEuS 3.

contractual terms, thereby privileging strict liability – and regulatory stabilisation – over reasonable investment protection.

F CONCLUSION

Stability and predictability are core elements of the rule of law. Their absence can cause citizens to face undue challenges in managing their affairs effectively.[1256] LE appears as a doctrine that allows to appropriately measure the fairness and equity of the measure adopted by the state and its effect on the investor. By adopting a balanced understanding of LE, the arbitrator may respect the ordinary meaning of FET and adapt the level of protection to the context, purpose of the treaty and factual situation at hand.

Regardless of this position, the research shows a consensus on the importance of the time of the investment, regulatory risks assumed by the investor, and the accurate assessment of the foreseeability of measures to identify the level of commitment of the state and the level of legitimacy of the investor's expectations. ICCL affects all three factors, calling for an acute analysis of its relevant provisions as relevant facts in future NZEID.

The chapter suggested that a correct interpretation and application of LE is primarily based on the underlying treaty and facts of the case. Crucial facts include the state's commitment, the foreseeability of the climate change frustrating measure and the risks assumed by the investor at the time of the investment. Breaking up the international investment system would not do climate change goals justice. International investment law is not just a creation of the twentieth century. The rights of aliens date back to customary diplomatic protection. Instead, international investment law should be harnessed to pave the way for the required investments for adaptation and mitigation, including by promoting the transformation of the energy sector.[1257] The gigantic task of 'transitioning' towards clean energy will require ambitious and flexible policies and massive private investments. ECT modernisation can benefit such a move by providing a predictable legal infrastructure to renewable energy investors while enlarging the states' right to regulate. However, an overly strict reform proposal, such as the EU's ECT reform proposal, would contravene the clean energy transition's ambitions and constitute a hurdle to investment protection rather than facilitating the clean energy transition.

1256. William Eskridge and Philip Frickey, 'The Making of Legal Process' (1994) 8 Harvard Law Review 107 https://doi.org/10.2307/1341767.
1257. World Bank Energy Charter, *Enabling* (n 36) 6.

General Conclusion

Since 1992, the IPCC's successive alarming reports highlight the risks of climate change, advocating for progressively stringent GHG emission targets. The International Energy Agency stresses that achieving net zero requires an immediate reduction in fossil fuel investments and a scaling up of clean energy investments. These developments have significant consequences for the protection of international investments in the energy sector, which the book aimed to decipher.

This monograph attempted to determine the impact of ICCL on the resolution of energy investment disputes arising from the alleged breach of FET, in particular, the energy investors' legitimate expectations. The book addressed the intricate interplay between these three concepts in the context of net zero energy investment disputes. Each chapter backed distinct insights on the relationship, relying on a novel typology of investment disputes.

The first chapter laid the foundation by establishing the crucial need for investments in clean energy production, and the need to provide stability for 'clean' energy investors to achieve 'net-zero' and GHG emissions targets. It suggested that international investment law and the protection of clean energy investors' expectations could be leveraged to achieve these net zero transition objectives.

Chapter 2 explored the theoretical foundations of legitimate expectations in investment disputes. It highlighted the divergence among arbitral tribunals in justifying and conceptualising LE as part of the FET standard. The chapter highlighted how the interpretation of the LE doctrine sparked disagreements on its origins, sources and justifications, and questioned claims of finding LE to be a general principle of international law, preferring a good faith origin. To further explain arbitral divergences, the chapter uncovered an opposition between detrimental reliance and voluntarist theories of LE. It considers the former to focus on investor reliance, requiring sovereign commitments and subjective due diligence, while the latter views LE as originating in the state's representation, emphasising specificity and clarity of commitments.

Chapter 3 examined NZEID under the Energy Charter Treaty primarily involving renewable energy investors facing incentive cancellations. It found that tribunals acknowledged that the state's regulatory framework could constitute a specific commitment when providing guarantees of stability. Arbitral tribunals recognised that regulatory frameworks could create legitimate expectations, but they exhibited differing approaches to assessing LE, with a split between detrimental reliance and voluntarist theories. Despite conceptual divergences, the book identifies an emerging consensus on key factual elements shaping the legitimacy of expectations, including the time of investment, risks assumed by the investor, and the foreseeability of frustrating measures. The chapter further demonstrated a growing consensus on the materiality of facts, such as the investment timing. These insights set the stage for understanding the potential impact of ICCLs on the application of LE.

Chapter 4 examined how ICCL could impact the legitimate expectations of energy investors. It identified three theoretically binding sources of ICCL – treaties, nationally determined contributions, and domestic court decisions. No direct conflict between ICCL and international investment law was found, but *lato sensu* conflicts could be identified, in particular concerning the fossil fuel energy sector. It further found that the integration of ICCL through Articles 31 and 32 faced significant hurdles, even though less hurdles would prevent application through Article 31(3)(c) of the VCLT. It found that ICCL could be part of the substantive law applicable to the dispute, depending on the underlying treaty and the circumstances of the investment. It established that, in any case, ICCL could be exploited as a significant *fact* in resolving investment disputes, directly impacting the application of legitimate expectations.

Chapter 5 assessed the impact of ICCL on legitimate expectations of energy investors in practice. It found that ICCL could, by itself create legitimate expectations and induce investments, in particular under the unilateral statement doctrine. Moving to the influence of ICCL as a fact, it found that it could affect the foreseeability of frustrating measures and the assessment of the expectations at the investment timing. Furthermore, it found that the legitimacy of fossil fuel investors' expectations may diminish over time due to ICCL. Conversely, ICCL should strengthen the legitimate expectation claims of clean-energy investors'. The chapter established that international investment law can be used to enforce climate change commitments, with fossil fuel investors' expectations potentially becoming unprotectable.

The last chapter offered an innovative interpretation of legitimate expectations, proposing a 'voluntarist-leaning' approach based on good faith. It advocated for an alignment of expectations with the time of investment, the level of commitment by the state, and the foreseeability of frustrating measures. This novel framework considers the practical implications of ICCL, presenting a balanced understanding that could guide arbitrators in navigating future net zero investment disputes.

The present study provides the first comprehensive assessment of the effect of ICCL on the legitimate expectations of foreign investors in the energy sector. The insights gained from the study may assist practitioners, arbitrators, government officials, and treaty drafters faced with net zero disputes or willing to further the scholarship on the theoretical and practical relationship between climate change and investment arbitration. The book invited a nuanced and balanced approach, promoting the convergence of international law. It proposed original approaches to the nexus between international investment and climate change law. It endeavoured to provide a few solutions and contributes to adapting investment arbitration to the twenty-first century and its main challenge, climate change.

In conclusion, any monograph, including the present, could not exhaust the discussions on ICCL and international investment arbitration. Remaining gaps of research include the arbitral authority to incorporate ICCL under the expropriation provisions. Additionally, research is required on the quantification of climate damage and use of scientific evidence by arbitral tribunals. It is hoped that this book will serve as a starting point for future investigations into these complex and evolving issues at the intersection of investment arbitration and climate change.

ANNEX

Legitimate Expectations in Net Zero Energy Investment Disputes: Selected Quotes

The following annex comprises a compilation of arbitral awards that serve as the primary source for this doctoral research. Each section below provides essential details pertaining to the respective investment dispute, encompassing information such as the award details, legal instrument, arbitrators' names, dispute outcome (including claimed and awarded amounts, arbitration costs, and legal costs, where available), and notable quotes reflecting the tribunal's analysis of the doctrine of legitimate expectations, due diligence of the investor, and climate change.

Disclaimer: It is imperative to note that the selection of quotes presented herein is intended to support the research and is not exhaustive. Given the diverse application of the protection of legitimate expectations by arbitral tribunals, the excerpts provided are confined to fragments of awards. The inclusion of specific quotes is for illustrative purposes, and readers are encouraged to refer to the complete awards for a comprehensive understanding of the tribunals' analyses and reasoning.

'Clean Energy' Awards

Spanish Cases

<table>
<tr><td colspan="3">Charanne B.V. and Construction Investments S.A.R.L. v Spain, SCC Case No. 062/2012, Final Award, 21 January 2016</td></tr>
<tr><td>Treaty</td><td colspan="2">ECT (1994)</td></tr>
<tr><td>Applicable Rules</td><td colspan="2">SCC Rules of Arbitration</td></tr>
<tr><td>Arbitrators</td><td colspan="2">President (P): Alexis Mourre - Claimant (C): Guido Santiago Tawil - Respondent (R): Claus von Wobeser</td></tr>
<tr><td>Outcome</td><td>In favour of the state
Amount claimed: EUR 17.831 million
Amount awarded: ZERO</td><td>Costs of arbitration: EUR 269,208.29 and USD 10,310
Award legal costs: Respondent was awarded EUR 1,176,181.31
Award costs of arbitration: Parties share costs equally</td></tr>
<tr><td>Main Facts</td><td colspan="2">143 'the Claimants claim to have an investment in Spain through the T-Solar company, which is dedicated to generation and sale of electricity produced by means of photovoltaic solar power plants. Charanne and Construction acquired stakes in T-Solar in February 2009 and December 2009, respectively.'
395 'the Claimants have limited the subject of this dispute to the alleged unlawful nature of RD 1565/2010 and RDL 14/2010 ("the 2010 norms") and decided to exclude from their claims RD 9/2013 and subsequent legislation. Thus, the claims have been limited to the consequences of the 2010 norms (...)'</td></tr>
<tr><td>Legitimate expectations of the investor</td><td colspan="2">486 'a State cannot induce an investor to make an investment (thus giving rise to legitimate expectations) and then disregard the commitments arising out of those expectations'.
490 'In the present case, there are no specific commitments entered into by Spain towards the Claimants. This kind of commitment could have been entered into on the basis of a stabilization clause, or through any kind of declaration made by the State to the investors, stating that the existing regulatory framework would not change. The Claimants were not the addressees of any such declaration.'
493 'Even if RD 661/2007 and 1578/2008 were addressed to a limited group of investors, that does not turn them into commitments specifically addressed to each of those investors. Having a specific scope does not mean that the disputed provisions lose the general nature that characterizes any legislative or regulatory measure. Turning a regulatory provision, due to the limited number of persons that may be subject thereto, into a</td></tr>
</table>

	specific commitment entered into by the State towards each and every one of those persons would be an excessive limitation of the capacity of States to regulate the economy according to the public interest.' 510 'The tribunal found that RD 1565/2010 and RD 14/2010 did not violate the FET standard because the claimants could not have had a legitimate expectation that the regulatory framework "is not to be modified at any time to adapt to the needs of the market and to the public interest."' 514 'A]n investor has the legitimate expectation that, when modifying the regulation under which it made the investment, the State will not act unreasonably, contrary to the public interest, or in a disproportionate manner.'
Due diligence of the investor	The tribunal held that legitimate expectations can only be formed after a due diligence analysis of the relevant regulatory framework. 499 '[I]n the absence of a specific commitment an investor cannot have the legitimate expectation that the regulation in place is going to remain unchanged.' 505 '[I]n order for regulatory measures to be in violation of the investor's legitimate expectations, these regulatory measures must not have been reasonably foreseeable at the time of the investment.' 506 'For instance, the Spanish Supreme Court had considered in December 2005 that: "There is no legal obstacle for the Government, in the exercise of the regulatory powers entrusted thereto as well as its broad powers in a heavily regulated area such as electricity, to modify a specific remuneration scheme, provided that it remains in compliance with the framework provided by the LSE." Likewise, in October 2006, the Supreme Court decided that: "the owners of electricity production facilities under the special regime do not have an 'unmodifiable right' to have the feed-in remuneration scheme remain unchanged."' 547 'The Tribunal has already determined in previous sections of this award that, in Spanish law, the registration with the RAIPRE was simply an administrative requirement to sell energy and that it did not imply that the registered facilities had a acquired right to a certain remuneration.'
Climate change mention	503 'In this case, the Claimants could not have the legitimate expectation that the regulatory framework laid down by RD 661/2007 and RD 1578/2008 would remain unchanged during the entire lifespan of their plants. Accepting such an expectation would, in fact, amount to freezing the regulatory framework applicable to eligible plants, even though the circumstances may change. Any modification to the tariff amount or any limitation in the number of eligible hours would thus constitute a violation of

<table>
<tr><td></td><td>International Law. In practice, the situation would be equivalent to that resulting from the signing by a State of a stabilisation agreement, or of a commitment to never modify the regulatory framework. The Arbitral Tribunal cannot accept such a conclusion. In fact, the Claimants themselves have clearly stated that they could not reasonably expect that the regulatory framework would remain unchanged.'

507 'The Tribunal does not agree with the Claimants that said decisions [of the Spanish Supreme Court] are irrelevant or out of context. Although they refer to different rules, those judgments clearly lay down the principle that domestic law can modify, in compliance with the LSE, an economic regime, such as the one provided in RD 661/2007 and RD 1578/2008, aimed at fostering renewable energy production. To the Tribunal's understanding, at the time of making the investment in 2009 the Claimants could have carried out an analysis of their investment's legal framework in Spanish law and understood that the regulations enacted in 2007 and 2008 could be modified. At least that is the degree of diligence that could be expected from a foreign investor in a heavily regulated sector like the energy industry. In such a sector, thorough prior analysis of the legal framework applicable thereto is essential to make an investment.'</td></tr>
</table>

<table>
<tr><td colspan="3">Isolux Infrastructure Netherlands B.V. v Kingdom of Spain, SCC Case No. V2013/153, Award, 12 July 2016</td></tr>
<tr><td>Treaty</td><td colspan="2">ECT (1994)</td></tr>
<tr><td>Applicable Rules</td><td colspan="2">SCC Rules of Arbitration</td></tr>
<tr><td>Arbitrators</td><td colspan="2">P: Yves Derains - C: Prof. Dr. Guido Santiago Tawil - R: Claus Von Wobeser</td></tr>
<tr><td>Outcome</td><td>In favour of the state

Amount claimed: EUR 68,900,000

Amount awarded: ZERO</td><td>Costs of arbitration: EUR 565,220.58

Award legal costs: Respondent bears 30% of the claimant's costs (EUR 1,368,606), whereas the claimant bears 70% of the respondent's costs (EUR 785,690)

Award costs of arbitration: Claimant bears 70% of the costs</td></tr>
<tr><td>Main Facts</td><td colspan="2">141. El 29 de junio de 2012 se firmó un Acuerdo de Inversión entre, por un lado, los accionistas de la sociedad brasileña Isolux Infrastructure, S.A. ('Isolux Infrastructure'), es decir las sociedades españolas Grupo Isolux Corsan Concesiones, S.L. ('GIC Concesiones' o 'GICC'), y Grupo Isolux Corsan, S.A. ('GIC') (conjuntamente designadas también como 'ISOLUX'), y por otro lado las sociedades canadienses inversores Public Sector Pension</td></tr>
</table>

	Investment Board ('PSP' o 'PSP Investments') y su filial Infra-PSP Canada 61 Inc. ('Infra-PSP') (el 'Acuerdo de Inversión'). 147. La operación de inversión de PSP tenía que concretizarse tras la realización, en particular, de ciertas condiciones suspensivas, el 1 de octubre de 2012, de acuerdo con los Artículos 6.1 y 6.2 del Acuerdo de Inversión.
Legitimate expectations of the investor	*See paras 775 ff* The tribunal ruled that an investor may derive legitimate expectations from rules that are not specifically addressed to a particular investor but which are put in place with a specific aim to induce foreign investments and on which the foreign investor relied in making its investment, with reference to an UNCTAD study. The tribunal also found no breach of the FET standard, albeit on the basis that by the time the claimants made their investment, the regulatory regime had already been modified. Because it had been changed once, the tribunal held, no reasonable investor could have had the expectation that the framework would not be modified again in the future. 787 'Sin embargo, el 29 de junio de 2012, cuando la Demandante decidió invertir en España, el marco regulatorio de las energías renovables, ya había sido modificado y estaba siendo objeto de varios estudios que hacían su revisión inevitable. En consecuencia, ningún inversor razonable podía tener la expectativa de que éste marco no sería modificado en el futuro y quedaría inmutable. La Demandante lo acepta, pero sostiene que "Ningún inversor realizando su inversión en octubre de 2012 hubiera llegado a la conclusión de que su única expectativa básica sería la de obtener una rentabilidad razonable". El Tribunal Arbitral no comparte esta observación y, además, considera que la Demandante tenía conocimientos especiales que no le permitían tener la expectativa legítima de que el sistema de FIT a largo plazo consagrado en los RRDD 661/2007 y 1565/2008 duraría durante la vida de las plantas. La única expectativa legítima de la Demandante era la de una rentabilidad razonable de su inversión.' *Opiniòn disidente del Árbitro Prof. Dr. Guido Santiago Tawil* 6 'Mi principal discrepancia con la decisión de la mayoría radica, sin embargo, en el modo en que se valoraron las circunstancias de hecho para determinar la "*previsibilidad*" de las medidas adoptadas por el Reino de España. En otras palabras, si el cambio de régimen jurídico producido en España luego de haberse realizado la inversión era previsible para la Demandante, circunstancia que –en caso afirmativo– le impediría invocar expectativas legítimas como fundamento de su reclamo.'

Due diligence of the investor	781 'El Tribunal Arbitral acepta que no se puede exigir de un inversor que haga una investigación jurídica extensiva. Lo importante para determinar si las expectativas alegadas por el inversor son razonables es lo que todo inversor prudente tiene que saber del marco regulatorio antes de invertir y la información efectiva del inversor que invoca expectativas específicas. En particular, un inversor no puede tener expectativas legitimas generadas por el marco regulatorio cuando su información personal le permitía prever y anticipar la evolución desfavorable de este marco regulatorio antes de invertir. Para vulnerar las expectativas legitimas del inversor, las medidas regulatorias nuevas no deben haber sido previsibles, sea de parte de un inversor prudente, sea de parte de un inversor que, en razón de su situación personal, disponía de elementos específicos para preverlas.'
Climate change mention	No direct mention.

***Eiser Infrastructure Limited and Energía Solar Luxembourg S.à r.l. v Kingdom of Spain*, ICSID Case No. ARB/13/36, Award, 4 May 2017**		
Treaty	ECT (1994)	
Applicable Rules	ICSID Arbitration Rules (2006)	
Arbitrators	P: Prof. John R. Crook – C: Dr. Stanimir A. Alexandrov – R: Prof. Campbell McLachlan QC	
Outcome	In favour of the investor Amount claimed: EUR 298 million Amount awarded: BUT 128 million	The Award of May 4, 2017 (ICSID Case No. ARB/13/36) is annulled in its entirety (11 June 2020).
Main Facts	119 'Eiser's contemporaneous documents show that those responsible for Claimants' initial decision to invest in Spain were keenly aware of the features of the RD 661/2007 regime, and that their assessment of the feasibility of the investment, and that of the banks that loaned money to finance it, were all based on that regime. Both the ASTE project and its financing were structured in expectation of the stable cash flows provided by RD 661/2007. The evidence shows that Claimants recognized that there could be changes in regulatory regimes; indeed, the initial briefing paper prepared for Eiser's Investment Committee in June 2007 identified as a possible risk "regulatory risk: change of position of government"'. However, that same paper indicated Claimants' reasons for expecting continuity of government policy, listing as a risk mitigation factor that 'Spain is a world leader in solar	

	technology. The Spanish Government is promising the development of solar energy, the solar industry and promising the solar companies development help both in Spain and abroad.' 229 'Further, the Investment here involved a substantial duration. Claimants began their involvement in this process in early summer of 2007; the plants did not become operational until 2012; and Claimants continue to own minority interests in them (albeit, alleged to have little or no value to them).'
Legitimate expectations of the investor	382 'Article 10(1)'s obligation to accord fair and equitable treatment necessarily embraces an obligation to provide fundamental stability in the essential characteristics of the legal regime relied upon by investors in making long-term investments.' 418 '[Spain's amendments to the regime] deprived Claimants of essentially all of the value of their investment' and that 'doing so violated Respondent's obligation to accord fair and equitable treatment.'
Due diligence of the investor	387 'Claimants could not reasonably expect that there would be no change whatsoever in the RD 661/2007 regime over three or four decades. As with any regulated investment, some changes had to be expected over time. However, Article 10(1) of the ECT entitled them to expect that Spain would not drastically and abruptly revise the regime, on which their investment depended, in a way that destroyed its value. But this was the result of RDL 9/2013, Law 24/2013, RD 413/2014, and implementation of the new regime through Ministry implementing Order IET/1045/2014. As it was put in Parkerings: "any businessman or investor knows that laws will evolve over time. What is prohibited however is for a State to act unfairly, unreasonably or inequitably in the exercise of its legislative power."'
Climate change mention	100 'The ECT's emphasis on developing secure long-term energy cooperation is coupled with provisions addressing the environmental aspects of energy development.'

***Novenergia II – Energy & Environment (SCA) (Grand Duchy of Luxembourg), SICAR v The Kingdom of Spain*, SCC Case No. 2015/063, Final Award, 15 February 2018**	
Treaty	ECT (1994)
Applicable Rules	SCC Rules of Arbitration
Arbitrators	P: Mr. Johan Sidklev – C: Prof. Antonio Crivellaro – R: Judge Bernardo Spùlveda-Amor

Outcome	In favour of the investor Amount claimed: EUR 61.3 million Amount awarded: EUR 53.3 million	Valuation method: income-based approach (discounted cash flow) Interest rate: host State's sovereign bonds (10-year) Costs of arbitration: EUR 562,920.96 + SEK 6,867 Award legal costs: Claimant was awarded EUR 2.6 million (including full costs of arbitration) Award costs of arbitration: Costs follow the award
Main Facts	2 'The investment in the eight photovoltaic ("PV") plants (the "PV Plants") was structured through Novenergia II Energy & Environment España, S.L. ("Novenergia Spain"). The Claimant acquired its interest in Novenergia Spain on 3 July 2007. At this time, Novenergia Spain was wholly- and directly-owned by the Claimant.' 156 'RD 661/2007 could not have been clearer. To PV plants that registered with the RAIPRE by 28 September 2008, it guaranteed: the right to incorporate all energy production into the grid; a fixed FIT for the lifespan of the PV plants; and that there would be no changes to the FIT except for updates in accordance with the CPI.'	
Legitimate expectations of the investor	*Novenergia v Spain* found that the incentive scheme constituted a specific commitment towards a defined group of investors. 667 'The commitment from the Kingdom of Spain could not have been clearer. A considerable number of RE companies also invested in reliance on these statements and assurances.' 674 'a "reasonable rate of return" would be limited to 7%, that stability and predictability could not be expected in the SES, [or] that the Special Regime could be abolished.'	
Due diligence of the investor	681 'Claimant had a legitimate and reasonable expectation that there would not be any radical or fundamental changes to the Special Regime as set out in RD 661/2007. The tribunal does not address the notion directly in its findings although Respondent built an important case on this issue.'	
Climate change mention	85 'RD 2818/1998 was adopted for the purpose of reducing greenhouse gas emissions. The goal was that, by 2010, 12% of the total energy demand in Spain would be covered by renewable energy sources.8 It developed and gave substance to the Special Regime outlined in Law 54/1997. RD 2818/1998 targeted certain types of facilities with a power capacity not exceeding 50 MW, including "facilities that solely employ solar energy as primary energy."'	

	665 'The Tribunal considers that Law 54/1997 and RD 661/2007 were clearly enacted with the objective of ensuring that the Kingdom of Spain achieved its emissions and RE targets.507 In order to achieve that objective the Kingdom of Spain created a very favourable investment climate for RE investors, and the nucleus of such investment climate was the Special Regime. The requirements placed on the PV plants to qualify for the Special Regime were limited to registration with the RAIPRE, a requirement which all the PV Plants had met within the prescribed cut-off date.'

<table>
<tr><td colspan="3">Masdar Solar & Wind Cooperatief U.A. v Kingdom of Spain, ICSID Case No. ARB/14/1, Award, 16 May 2018</td></tr>
<tr><td>Treaty</td><td colspan="2">ECT (1994)</td></tr>
<tr><td>Applicable Rules</td><td colspan="2">ICSID Arbitration Rules (2006)</td></tr>
<tr><td>Arbitrators</td><td colspan="2">P: Mr John Beechey - C: CBE Gary Born - R: Prof Brigitte Stern</td></tr>
<tr><td>Outcome</td><td>In favour of the investor
Amount claimed: EUR 260 million
Amount awarded: EUR 64.5 million</td><td>Valuation method: income-based approach (discounted cash flow)
Interest rate: host State's sovereign bonds (3-year for pre-award; 10-year for post-award)
Costs of arbitration: USD 1,151,994.59
Award legal costs: Each party bears its legal and other expenses
Award costs of arbitration: Parties share costs equally</td></tr>
<tr><td>Main Facts</td><td colspan="2">5 'Claimant's claims arise out of investments made by Claimant in November 2008 and July 2009 in three CSP Plants, Gemasolar (in 2008) and Arcosol and Termesol (both in 2009).'
513 'One of the elements of this procedure was the registration first in the Pre-Allocation Registry, then with the RAIPRE ("Registro Administrativo de Instalaciones de Producción en Régimen Especial"). The three Plants were duly registered with RAIPRE on 29 April 2011 (Gemasolar) and 22 December 2011 (Arcosol and Termesol) – that is to say, within the prescribed "window."'</td></tr>
<tr><td>Legitimate expectations of the investor</td><td colspan="2">513 '[Through its incentive scheme, Spain] guaranteed the stability of the benefits, if the investors fulfilled a certain number of conditions, both procedural and substantial, during a certain window of time.'</td></tr>
</table>

	520 'It would be difficult to conceive of a more specific commitment than a Resolution issued by Spain addressed specifically to each of the Operating Companies, confirming that each of the Plants qualified under the [incentive scheme] for their "operational lifetime".'
Due diligence of the investor	494 'If the general legislation is to be regarded as a source of an investor's legitimate expectations, the investor must demonstrate that it has exercised appropriate due diligence and that it has familiarised itself with the existing laws.' The tribunal found that the investors in the case had undertaken sufficient due diligence, including by commissioning external reports, conducting discussions with Spanish banks that put up 80% of the capital, and consulted two law firms in respect of regulatory issues.
Climate change mention	112 'In 2005, the Spanish Government published its PER. Particular attention was devoted to CSP installations for which Spain was ideally suited. (...) Specifically, it recorded that renewables would contribute: (i) decisively to guaranteeing the long-term supply of energy through independent and inexhaustible energy sources; (ii) to job creation (particularly in rural areas) and improved industrial competitiveness and accordingly they should be encouraged in order to secure long-term economic growth; (iii) to the increased use of renewables to provide electricity in cities, which would reduce emissions from fossil fuels; and (iv) to the development of renewables in Spain, which would help to achieve binding EU carbon emission goals.'

***Infrastructure Services Luxembourg S.à.r.l. and Energia Termosolar B.V. (formerly Antin Infrastructure Services Luxembourg S.à.r.l. and Antin Energia Termosolar B.V.) v Kingdom of Spain,* ICSID Case No. ARB/13/31, Award, 15 June 2018**		
Treaty	ECT (1994)	
Applicable Rules	ICSID Arbitration Rules (2006)	
Arbitrators	P: Eduardo Zuleta – C: Prof. Francisco Orrego Vicuña – R: Christopher Thomas	
Outcome	In favour of the investor Amount claimed: EUR 238 million Amount awarded: EUR 112 million	Valuation method: income-based approach (discounted cash flow) Interest rate: host State's sovereign bonds (10-year) Costs of arbitration: N/A

<table>
<tr><td></td><td></td><td>Award legal costs: Claimant was awarded GBP 2,447,008.61 (60% of legal costs)

Award costs of arbitration: Respondent bears 60% of the costs</td></tr>
<tr><td>Main Facts</td><td colspan="2">70 'The investments made by the Claimants (...) consisted of the acquisition of shareholding participations in Andasol-1 Plant and Andasol-2 Plant, two operational concentrated solar power ("CSP") plants located in Granada, southern Spain (together, the "Andasol Plants") in 2011.'

110 'Construction of the Andasol Plants, located in the province of Granada, southern Spain, were finished in 2008 and 2009. The Andasol-1 Plant received its final commissioning certificate on 25 November 2008 and registered with the RAIPRE on 24 April 2009, while the Andasol-2 Plant received its commissioning certificate on 5 June 2009 and registered with the RAIPRE on 22 December 2009. (...) Spain does not dispute that, as a consequence, both Andasol Plants were qualified to receive Special Regime benefits under RD 661/2007 and RD 1614/2010.'</td></tr>
<tr><td>Legitimate expectations of the investor</td><td colspan="2">532 '[Article 10(1) ECT includes an obligation to afford] fundamental stability in the essential characteristics of the legal regime relied upon by the investors in making long-term investments (...) "a regulatory regime specifically created to induce investments in the energy sector cannot be radically altered - i.e., stripped of its key features - as applied to existing investments[.]"' Here, as in the awards requiring a specific commitment of stability, the tribunal focused on the fact that Spain had actively sought to attract the investments.

538 'Third, the expectations of the investor need to originate from some affirmative action of the State, either in the form of specific commitments made by the host State to the investor - as several international investment tribunals have recognized - or in the form of representations made by the host State, for example, with respect to certain features of a regulation aimed at encouraging investments in a specific sector. In other words, legitimate expectations cannot arise from subjective considerations of the investor absent an affirmative action of the State which, objectively determined, evidences that the State intended to describe a particular treatment or regime on which the investor could rely when making its investment.'

572 'Under these circumstances, the Tribunal cannot agree that the Tariff Deficit justified the elimination of the key features of the RD 661/2007 regime and its replacement by a wholly new regime, not based on any identifiable criteria.'</td></tr>
</table>

Due diligence of the investor	536 'First, the expectations of the investor cannot be analysed in the abstract nor can they be based on the investor's subjective beliefs. On the contrary, the finding that there has been a violation of the investor's legitimate expectations must be based on an objective standard, which must be assessed on a case-by-case basis.' 537 'Second, the *investor's expectations must be assessed at the time of the investment's making.* Accordingly, the Tribunal must consider when the investment was made, what the circumstances were at that time and the information that the investor had or should reasonably have had, had it acted with the requisite degree of diligence (considering its expertise). In carrying out this assessment, tribunals must attempt to place themselves at the time of the investment and consider the information and conditions available at such time, and to refrain from appraising the investor's expectations with the benefit of hindsight.'
Climate change mention	83 'It further required EU Member States to take appropriate measures to meet targets on the reduction of emission of greenhouse gasses, as well as to increase the proportion of electricity produced using renewable resources and to set national indicative targets consistent with the global indicative target of 12% of gross domestic energy consumption from renewable sources by 2010.' 427 'Spain subsequently reduced the charges, one of the elements of the regulated system revenues, in breach of Law 24/2013 and contributing to broadening the Tariff Deficit.584 The contribution of CSP to the Tariff Deficit is very limited, and there were other available measures that were less harmful for the Claimants' investments, such as introducing a tax on CO2 emissions or raising electricity tariffs.' 480 'This regulation was introduced at a time when the implementation of solar thermal technology facilities was beginning, and their promotion and development advised promoting the use of this technology in optimum conditions.682 However, in 2012, in light of the need of a comprehensive reform to the energy sector, the CNE pointed out the problem of incentivizing the production of energy from fossil fuels under the protection of renewable energies, when the ultimate purpose was promoting energy supply security, reducing dependence from fossil fuels and guaranteeing the protection of the environment.683 This purpose was enshrined in the preamble of Law 15/2012 and is consistent with EU guidelines on the issue, under which only the electricity produced from RE sources shall be taken into account for calculating the RE implementation targets created by EU law. The Claimants could not have any expectations to the contrary.'

<table>
<tr><td colspan="3">Foresight Luxembourg Solar 1 S.À.R.L., et al. v the Kingdom of Spain, SCC Case No. 2015/150, Final Award, 14 November 2018</td></tr>
<tr><td>Treaty</td><td colspan="2">ECT (1994)</td></tr>
<tr><td>Applicable Rules</td><td colspan="2">SCC Rules of Arbitration</td></tr>
<tr><td>Arbitrators</td><td colspan="2">P: Dr. Michael Moser – C: Prof. Dr. Klaus Michael Sachs – R: Dr. Raúl Emilio Vinuesa</td></tr>
<tr><td>Outcome</td><td>In favour of the investor
Amount claimed: EUR 50 million
Amount awarded: EUR 39 million</td><td>Valuation method: hybrid approach (income-based approach (discounted cash flow) for the 'but-for' scenario + market-based approach (completed or imminent arm's length transactions) for the 'actual' scenario)
Interest rate: host State's sovereign bonds (5-year) for pre-award; claimants' cost of borrowing for post-award
Costs of arbitration: EUR 404,953.21 + USD 18,359.83
Award legal costs: Claimants were awarded EUR 3,900,374.73 + USD 2,9997,596.33 (including full costs of arbitration)</td></tr>
<tr><td>Main Facts</td><td colspan="2">94 'The Claimants' investments were comprised of three PV plants: (i) Madridejos, an 8 MW PV plant, acquired by Foresight 1 in May 2009; (ii) La Castilleja, a 9.8 MW PV plant, in which Foresight 2 and GMW II jointly invested in March 2010; and (iii) Fotocampillos, a 1.8 MW PV project comprised of eighteen 100 kW plants, in which GWM II invested in May 2010.'
97 'On 28 August 2008, Madridejos received its registration under RD 661/2007.'
102 'On 25 September 2008, La Castilleja received its RAIPRE registration under RD 661/2007.'
107 On 20 May 2008, the Fotocampillos PV project received their RAIPRE registrations.</td></tr>
<tr><td>Legitimate expectations of the investor</td><td colspan="2">The tribunal found that Spain's regulatory amendments went beyond the foreseeable limits and constituted a 'wholly different regulatory approach, based on wholly different premises'. In the tribunal's view, such a 'fundamental change to the legal and regulatory framework crossed the line from a non-compensable regulatory measure to a compensable breach of the FET standard in the ECT'.</td></tr>
</table>

	388 As explained above, the Tribunal considers that the Claimants had a legitimate expectation that the regulatory framework would not be fundamentally and abruptly altered so as to deprive investors of a significant part of their projected revenues. The Claimants did not, however, have a legitimate expectation that there would be no regulatory changes to RD 661/2007 at all. In the Tribunal's view, none of the changes enacted by RD 1565/2010, RDL 14/2010 or RD 2/2013 meet the threshold requirement of a fundamental change to the regulatory framework. Accordingly, the Tribunal finds that neither RD 1565/2010, RDL 14/2010 nor RD 2/2013 breached the FET standard. 397 '[S]ophisticated investors like the Claimants should have reasonably expected that [the incentive scheme] could be modified, "but within foreseeable limits."' 398 'The Majority of the Tribunal concludes that the Respondent's enactment of the New Regulatory Regime constituted a fundamental change to the legal and regulatory framework that crossed the line from a non-compensable regulatory measure to a compensable breach of the FET standard in the ECT.'
Due diligence of the investor	380 '[T]he Majority of the Tribunal considers that it is reasonable for an investor to assume that its legal advisors would have raised a red flag had they detected any risk of fundamental change to the regulatory regime.' *Partial Dissenting Opinion Co-Arbitrator Raül E. Vinuesa* 49 'Spanish Supreme Court has confirmed that, "Companies that freely decide to enter a market such as electricity generation under the special regime, knowing that it is largely dependent on the setting of economic incentives by public authorities, are or should be aware that they may be modified within legal guidelines by those same authorities. One of the 'regulatory risks' to which they submit and which they must take into account is precisely the variations of parameters for premium or incentives, something which, the electricity sector limits, as previously discussed, but does not preclude."' 50 'Whereas, the constant jurisprudence of Spanish Courts has clearly determined the general legal framework of electricity generation under special regime, there is no reasonable justification for Claimants' negligent behaviour. As the *Blusun* tribunal has confirmed: "... investors like anyone else have access to independent advise. If it avoids outright misrepresentation, the Government does not offer warranties in that regard."'
Climate change mention	53 'The broader context of the EU's and Spain's measures was the international effort to reduce greenhouse gas emissions, most notably in the Kyoto Protocol 1997, pursuant to which signatories, including the EU and Spain, accepted ambitious targets for emissions reductions.'

<table>
<tr><td colspan="3">RREEF Infrastructure (G.P.) Limited and RREEF Pan-European Infrastructure Two Lux S.à r.l. v Kingdom of Spain, ICSID Case No. ARB/13/30, Decision on Responsibility and on the Principles of Quantum, 30 November 2018</td></tr>
<tr><td>Treaty</td><td colspan="2">ECT (1994)</td></tr>
<tr><td>Applicable Rules</td><td colspan="2">ICSID Arbitration Rules (2006)</td></tr>
<tr><td>Arbitrators</td><td colspan="2">P: Prof. Alain Pellet - C: Prof. Robert Volterra - R: Prof. Pedro Nikken</td></tr>
<tr><td>Outcome</td><td>In favour of the investor
Amount claimed: EUR 441 million
Amount awarded: EUR 59.6 million</td><td>Valuation method: income-based approach (discounted cash flow)
Interest rate: host State's sovereign bonds (10-year)
Costs of arbitration: N/A
Award legal costs: Each party bears its own legal costs
Award costs of arbitration: Parties share costs equally</td></tr>
<tr><td>Main Facts</td><td colspan="2">142 'RREEF first invested in Spain in February 2011, in a project known as the "Dédalo Project" by indirectly acquiring an equity interest in three project companies with activities in the wind power sector. Subsequently, in July 2011, RREEF indirectly invested in a project for the development of a 49.9 MW CSP Plant, in Andalucía, known as the "Arenales Plant." Also in June 2011, RREEF indirectly invested in two other CSP plants, also in the south of Spain. The plants, referred to by the Claimants as the "Andasol Plants" were already operational at the time of the investment.'
160 'On 11 December 2009, before RREEF's investment in this project and before the parks' construction work was finalized, the Dédalo wind parks got registered in the Pre-Assignment Register. The Dédalo wind parks achieved final registration with the RAIPRE on 28 December 2010.'
169. 'On 25 September 2013, the Arenales Plant obtained definitive registration with RAIPRE. It became operational in October 2013.'
175 'The Andasol Plants were duly registered with RAIPRE by December 2009, before the Claimants' investment in the project.'</td></tr>
<tr><td>Legitimate expectations of the investor</td><td colspan="2">379 'The Tribunal has already ruled that the Claimants had no legitimate expectation that the regime provided for in [the incentive scheme] would remain unchanged throughout the term of the investment.'
399 But the tribunal found that the investors were nonetheless entitled to 'a legitimate expectation to get a reasonable return on their investments'.</td></tr>
</table>

	This included an expectation that any modifications to the applicable legal regime would be reasonable and equitable, which, in consideration of all the circumstances, the tribunal found that they were not (para 399). In making that determination, the tribunal emphasized that the modified regulatory framework did not allow the investors a 'reasonable rate of return' on their investment. 399 '[T]he Claimants had, when they made their investments, a legitimate expectation to get a reasonable return on their investments. Such expectation did not include a guarantee to have the legal regime in place unchanged until the end of the operation of the plants, but it did include to have any modifications reasonable and equitable. Whether such a legitimate expectation was violated can only be assessed by way of a global view of the situation that resulted from the modifications introduced by the Respondent after the date of the investment. It is only in case the answer to this question is in the affirmative that compensation is due to the Claimants under this head of claim.'
Due diligence of the investor	Tribunal starts with assessment of 'Stability and Predictability' then moves to Claimant's alleged legitimate expectations. 398 'The Claimants' diligence might have been due. However, due or not, the Claimants were made aware that the Respondent's legal regime was subject to possible changes in the future. This is evidence of the fact that any expectation of the Claimants that the applicable legal regime was never subject to any change whatsoever was not legitimate.'
Climate change mention	87 'In 1992, Spain signed the United Nations Framework Convention on Climate Change ("UNFCCC"). In 1998 the European Union and Spain, as a Member State, signed the 1997 Kyoto Protocol, an international instrument negotiated to implement the UNFCCC. Under this international framework, Spain, with many other nations, committed to a reduction of greenhouse emissions, through among others, the allocation of important resources to that effect.' 440 'The Claimants submits that other less harmful measures could have been adopted, including: (a) raising electricity prices; (b) introducing a fuel tax; (c) adopting a tax on CO2 emissions; (d) profiling of FITs.'

***Cube Infrastructure Fund SICAV and others v Kingdom of Spain*, ICSID Case No. ARB/15/20, Decision on Jurisdiction, Liability, and Partial Decision on Quantum, 19 February 2019**	
Treaty	ECT (1994)
Applicable Rules	ICSID Arbitration Rules (2006)

<table>
<tr><td>Arbitrators</td><td colspan="2">P: Prof Vaughan Lowe – C: James Jacob Spigelman – R: Prof Christian Tomuschat</td></tr>
<tr><td>Outcome</td><td>In favour of the investor
Amount claimed: EUR 74.1 million
Amount awarded: EUR 33.7 million</td><td>Valuation method: income-based approach (discounted cash flow)
Interest rate: EURIBOR (6-month)
Costs of arbitration: USD 764,114.02
Award legal costs: Claimants were awarded EUR 1,545,501.8 (50% of legal costs)
Award costs of arbitration: Respondent bears its own share of costs of arbitration and 50% of the claimants' share</td></tr>
<tr><td>Main Facts</td><td colspan="2">327 'It was in 2011 that the Claimants acquired rights to 10 hydro facilities in Spain. They acquired rights to six others in June 2012.'
238 'The Claimants assert that they "decided to invest in the PV sector" in April-June 2008. By the end of 2010, Cube had "decided not to make further investments in PV facilities in Spain." The Claimants say that "[a]fter more than a year of considering the more stable hydro sector," they invested in that sector in 2011-2012. Cube and Demeter invested in ten RPI plants in Spain "in reliance on the guarantees in RD 661" in June 2011, and invested in a further six (the "Blue Rain") projects, in which Spanish government entities also held an interest, in June 2012.'</td></tr>
<tr><td>Legitimate expectations of the investor</td><td colspan="2">Whereas it agreed that states have the right to regulate and change their legislation, it also noted that Spain committed itself to guarantee the stability of the incentive's regime. Consequently, it decided by majority that the claimants correctly relied upon the representations made by Spain in RD 661/2007 and the accompanying press release.
158 'This Tribunal does not have to apply, or take a decision on any question of, Spanish law or EU law. Under the provisions concerning the applicable law that are binding on this Tribunal, Spanish law and EU law are relevant only as facts in the light of which the rights and duties of the Parties under the ECT and international law are to be determined. Thus, for example, the provisions on EU law concerning State aid are not applied by this Tribunal, nor does the Tribunal make any decision on their interpretation. They are relevant only as part of the factual matrix, and in this case particularly as part of the factual basis for determinations of how the Claimants could expect to be treated in respect of their power plants in Spain.'
311 'Claimants were entitled to rely on the maintenance of the relevant tariffs and premiums set out in Article 36 RD 661/2007</td></tr>
</table>

	throughout the reasonable planned operating life of each power plant.' 388 'The Tribunal does not consider it necessary that a specific commitment be made to each individual claimant in order for a legitimate expectation to arise.' The tribunal explained that in highly regulated industries, incentive schemes established with the overt aim of attracting investments 'are plainly intended to create expectations upon which investors will rely; and to the extent that those expectations are objectively reasonable, they give rise to legitimate expectations when investments are in fact made in reliance upon them'. 397 'We emphasise that no investor is entitled to assume that the regulatory regime in place at the time that its investment is made will continue to remain in force. States have the sovereign right to amend their legislation. But States also have the right, and the legal power, to make representations as to the future treatment of investments in such a manner as to create expectations that cannot be defeated without violating a duty of Fair and Equitable Treatment. In this case, the Respondent held out the assurance of the stability of specific regulatory provisions as an inducement to invest in the renewable energy sector, and was not free to walk away from that assurance at will. Investors were entitled to rely upon that assurance of stability as a firm commitment.'
Due diligence of the investor	396 '[T]he right to rely upon the representations made in this case do[es] not depend on there being evidence of any particular form or scale of legal due diligence by external advisors.' The investors were entitled to rely on representations made by Spain even in the absence of evidence that they had conducted detailed or formal legal due diligence to affirm that the regulatory framework would not be significantly changed retroactively. In the tribunal's view, it was sufficient that the investors had considered the question of regulatory stability, sought expert advice, and reached an understanding of the significance of the representations made by Spain.
Climate change mention	241 'Prior to 2008, Spain had been attempting to increase greatly the proportion of its energy that is obtained from renewable sources. Among the factors driving this policy were global concern with climate change and the effects of fossil fuels, and the evolving EU policy of fixing targets for Member States relating to the share of energy coming from renewable sources.' 318 'Among the premises on which Directive 2009/28/EC was constructed was the following proposition: "that a framework that includes mandatory targets should provide the business community with the long-term stability it needs to make rational, sustainable investments in the renewable energy sector which are capable of reducing dependence on imported fossil fuels and boosting the use of new energy technologies."'

<table>
<tr><td colspan="3">NextEra Energy Holdings B.V. v Kingdom of Spain, ICSID Case No. ARB/14/11, Award, 31 May 2019</td></tr>
<tr><td>Treaty</td><td colspan="2">ECT (1994)</td></tr>
<tr><td>Applicable Rules</td><td colspan="2">ICSID Arbitration Rules (2006)</td></tr>
<tr><td>Arbitrators</td><td colspan="2">P: Prof. Donald McRae, C.C. – C: Honourable L. Yves Fortier, P.C., C.C., Q.C. – R: Prof. Laurence Boisson de Chazournes</td></tr>
<tr><td>Outcome</td><td>In favour of the investor
Amount claimed: EUR 393.6 million
Amount awarded: EUR 290.6 million</td><td>Valuation method: hybrid (return on the capitalised costs of assets on the basis of weighted average cost of capital + 200bps)
Interest rate: host State's sovereign bonds (5 year)
Costs of arbitration: USD 835,234.15
Award legal costs: Claimants were awarded USD 4,147,031 and EUR 1,042,135.3 (1/3 of legal costs)
Award costs of arbitration: Respondent bears 2/3 of the costs</td></tr>
<tr><td>Main Facts</td><td colspan="2">168 'The involvement of the NextEra companies with solar energy in Spain began with the agreements entered into in 2007, by a subsidiary of NextEra, relating to land easements, water rights and the development of up to four 49.9 MW CSP plants in Extremadura. In 2008, the Claimants were incorporated. Between 2008 and 2009, the Claimants devoted their efforts to development activities.'
178 'On 29 May 2013, the Termosol 1 Plant obtained final registration into the RAIPRE; and on 7 June 2013, the same was granted to the Termosol 2 Plant.'</td></tr>
<tr><td>Legitimate expectations of the investor</td><td colspan="2">584 'The [Regulatory] Framework was based on legislation and legislation can be changed.'
585. 'Equally, the Tribunal does not consider that registration in the Pre-Assignment Registry or in the RAIPRE, while a necessary part of the process for obtaining the benefits of the regulatory regime, did of itself grant any right to the economic regime set out in RD 661/2007.'
591 'Claimants could not have had the expectation that the RD 661/2007 regime was frozen and could not be changed.'
Yet, NextEra relied on specific assurances given to the investor, which confirmed that the Spanish Government had no intention to change the incentives regime as contained in RD 661/2007. (para592 ff).</td></tr>
</table>

	597 'The changes made to the economic regime under Regulatory Framework III were substantial. They included that, the Termosol Plants were now to be paid on the basis of capacity, not on the basis of the amount of electricity produced.' 600 'Respondent argues that the Claimant could expect a reasonable return. The tribunal "expectations from authorities were not about a reasonable return; they were about the regulatory certainty and stability that NextEra could expect. the denial of legitimate expectations is based on the failure to provide that certainty and security by changing fundamentally the regime under which remuneration was to be calculated."'
Due diligence of the investor	595 'Respondent argues that "lack of due diligence prevents the expectations [...] from being considered to be real and objective" and that Claimants did not do proper due diligence. However, the Tribunal is not convinced that a lack of due diligence has been established. Claimants had the Poyry consultant reports and Claimants refer to legal opinions they received on Spanish law. The fact that Claimants refused to waive their privilege in respect those legal opinions should not lead to any adverse inferences. Non-disclosure means that Respondent and the Tribunal have not had access to the content of those opinions, but the fact that Claimants received legal advice is not really contested. In short, the Tribunal does not consider that the assertion that there was a lack of due diligence on the part of Claimants has been established.'
Climate change mention	100 'Within the context of the 1992 United Nations Framework Convention on Climate Change (UNFCC), on 11 December 1997 a number of nations adopted the Kyoto Protocol, an international agreement committing its Parties by setting internationally binding greenhouse emission reduction targets. The protocol was signed by Spain on 29 April 1998 and ratified on 31 May 2002. It entered into force on 16 February 2005. 101 On 14 May 1997 the European Commission issued Communication COM (97) 196, setting a target to reduce greenhouse gas emissions by 15% by year 2010, vis-a-vis the levels existing in year 1990. C-026, Communication from the European Commission: The Energy Dimension of Climate Change, COM(97) 196 Final, 14 May 1997.'

***9REN Holding S.a.r.l v Kingdom of Spain*, ICSID Case No. ARB/15/15, Award, 31 May 2019**	
Treaty	ECT (1994)
Applicable Rules	ICSID Arbitration Rules (2006)
Arbitrators	P: Honourable Ian Binnie, C.C., Q.C. – C: Mr. David Haigh, Q.C. – R: Mr. V. V. Veeder, Q.C.

<table>
<tr><td rowspan="1">Outcome</td><td>In favour of the investor
Amount claimed: EUR 52.2 million
Amount awarded: EUR 41.76 million</td><td>Valuation method: income-based approach (discounted cash flow) for the investment the claimants continued to own + hybrid approach for the investments the claimants sold (income-based approach (discounted cash flow) for the 'but-for' scenario + market-based approach (completed arm's length transaction) for the 'actual' scenario)
Interest rate: host State's sovereign bonds (5-year)
Costs of arbitration: USD 599,816.33
Award legal costs: Claimant was awarded USD 4,814,570 and EUR 562,458 (80% of legal costs)
Award costs of arbitration: Costs follow the award</td></tr>
<tr><td>Main Facts</td><td colspan="2">103 'As mentioned earlier, the cut-off date for registration under RD 661/2007 was 29 September 2008. The evidence establishes that the Claimant and its Spanish subsidiaries, Solaica Power S.L.U. ("Solaica") and 9REN España, constructed, commissioned and registered with the RAIPRE seven PV projects before that date.'
127 'On 23 April 2008, according to the Claimant, its investment of €211 million in Spanish renewable energy projects assets was complete, as explained by one of its directors (...).'</td></tr>
<tr><td>Legitimate expectations of the investor</td><td colspan="2">The 9REN tribunal decided that RD 661/2007 constitutes a clear and specific commitment. Referring to Masdar, it concluded that the specific letters the investor in Masdar had received 'simply confirmed' the content of RD 661/2007.
293 'The relative absence of direct government to investor communications is a factor of some weight although, as the Claimant points out, the specific "in person" communications in Masdar and some of the other cases did little more than repeat what was already plain on the face of RD 661/2007, and in any case post-dated rather that pre-dated the investment.'
294 Tribunal accepts as correct the observation of UNCTAD (2012) that legitimate expectations may arise from 'rules not specifically addressed to a particular investor, but which are put in place with a specific arm to induce foreign investments and on which the foreign investor relied on making his investment'. To similar effect, the El Paso tribunal distinguished between 'two types of commitments ... those specific as to their addressee and those specific regarding their object and purpose'.</td></tr>
</table>

	299 'The Tribunal notes the helpful legal analysis in Masdar which identifies a spectrum of situations where a claimant relies only on a bare regulatory measure addressed to the entire world, which lies at the weaker end of the spectrum, to clear and specific undertakings to a particular investor, which lies at the strongest end. In Masdar, the claimant had (as this Claimant does not) specific letters of commitment from the government. However, as earlier noted, those letters simply confirmed what was already in RD 661/2007 and were issued after not before the claimant in that case made its investment. In the Tribunal's view, the clear and specific "guarantee" in RD 661/2007 satisfies the requisite degree of "specificity".'
Due diligence of the investor	No mention of the due diligence obligation by the arbitrators, despite lengthy arguments on it by Spain. 311 'The financial vulnerability of renewable energy projects is the heavy up-front capital costs. Once money is "sunk" in the PV facilities, the funds of the developer (and its bankers) are locked into the FIT contracts with their investments effectively (as the Claimant put it) long-term hostages. If energy prices rise, the benefit accrues to Spain not the operators who, in Spain's view, will recover only what Spain unilaterally declares to be a reasonable return by reference to the bond market. On the other hand, if energy prices fall, Spain claims the right to resile from what the Tribunal has concluded was a regulatory guarantee of price stability. Spain's position is that it alone should benefit from rising prices, but the burden of falling prices is to be off-loaded onto investors. As a matter of Spanish domestic law, such treatment of local investors has been held to be constitutional, but in the Tribunal's view, such one-sided treatment is neither fair nor equitable. Under the ECT, the Claimant, as a foreign investor, was entitled to fair and equitable treatment and in this case did not receive it.'
Climate change mention	212 'The fundamental controversy between the parties is whether under international law Spain did indeed owe, as the Claimant contends but Spain denies, an irrevocable obligation to the Claimant to pay the feed-in tariff established by RD 661/2007 for 25 years and thereafter at 80% of the original base rate for the life of the facility.' 216 'The Claimant argues that Spain's "clear commitments in its legislative and regulatory framework", the "well-known purposes and motivations" of its RD 661/2007 and RD 1578/2008 regimes, the manner in which those regimes "specifically addressed the concerns of PV investors (based on the significant upfront costs of PV installations)", Spain's need to aggressively promote PV and other renewable energy investments to meet its EU commitments and domestic policy goals, and the "clear, repeated statements and conduct" of Spanish officials concerning the "total legal certainty"

	and other features of RD 661/2007 and RD 1578/2008 all gave rise to legitimate expectations …' 218 'Spain needed significant renewable energy investments to ensure that it would meet binding EU targets for renewable energy, as well as to reduce its dependence on non-renewable and foreign energy sources …'

***SolEs Badajoz GmbH v Kingdom of Spain*, ICSID Case No. ARB/15/38, Award, 31 July 2019**		
Treaty	ECT (1994)	
Applicable Rules	ICSID Arbitration Rules (2006)	
Arbitrators	P: Judge Joan Donoghue – C: Sir David Williams, Stanimir Alexandrov (replaced) – R: Prof. Giorgio Sacerdoti, Anna Joubin-Bret (replaced)	
Outcome	In favour of the investor Amount claimed: EUR 81.8 million Amount awarded: EUR 40.98 million	Valuation method: income-based approach (discounted cash flow) Interest rate: host State's sovereign bonds (10-year) Costs of arbitration: USD 714,012.15 Award legal costs: Each party bears its own legal costs Award costs of arbitration: Costs follow the award
Main Facts	135 'The resolution registering Badajoz I was issued on 10 December 2009 and the resolution registering Badajoz II was issued in February 2010. These dates determined the FIT applicable to each plant.' 137 'Construction of Badajoz I was completed on 12 July 2010 and construction of Badajoz II was completed on 14 January 2011.87 Claimant states that Badajoz I began producing and selling energy "by the end of August 2010 at the latest" and that Badajoz II began producing and selling energy "by 8 February 2011 at the latest."' 138 'On 25.03.2010, the claimant acquired a Spanish company which owned 2 PV plants.'	
Legitimate expectations of the investor	334 'Even when cases arise under the same treaty (the ECT) and involve the same regulatory regime, the awards reveal variations in critical evidence, including the date of investment, the type of renewable energy, and the evidence given by witnesses and experts. These distinctions mean that the conclusion in any one case is highly specific to that case.' 430 'The Tribunal approaches with caution the evidence regarding Judgments of the Supreme Court. The Supreme Court is applying	

	Spanish law, not the ECT. Because each Judgment addresses specific facts and provisions of law and regulation, the Parties' selective quotations from various Judgments are of limited assistance to the Tribunal.' 444 'The evidence establishes instead that a PV investor in March 2010 had a legitimate expectation that it would receive a FIT that was stable, once assigned to a PV plant, for the 25-year period specified in RD 1578/2008 (save for inflation adjustment). The stable FIT was an essential element of the regulatory regime on which Claimant relied when it made its investment decision, taking into account the capital-intensity, long period of capital recovery and high leverage that is characteristic of investments in PV plants.'
Due diligence of the investor	331 'The Tribunal considers that a formal due diligence process is not a precondition to a successful claim of legitimate expectations. However, an investor cannot benefit from gaps in its subjective knowledge of the regulatory environment because, under an objective standard, the investor's legitimate expectations are measured with reference to the knowledge that a hypothetical prudent investor is deemed to have had as of the date of the investment. The extent of inquiry that is incumbent on a prudent investor depends on the particular circumstances of the case.' 427 'Respondent's defence has emphasized the case law of the Supreme Court "as a decisive factual element to configure the legitimate expectation of any investor".'
Climate change mention	364 'Claimant states that there were alternatives to the Disputed Measures that Respondent could have employed to address the tariff deficit, including (i) raising regulated tariffs; (ii) eliminating the regulated tariffs for electricity generation; (iii) imposing a tax on all CO2 emissions; (iv) imposing a broad levy on fuel consumption; and (v) temporarily changing the profile of FITs for concentrated solar power.' 415 'PV plants cannot compete with conventional forms of energy production without substantial public subsidy or other form of incentive. They are capital-intensive, meaning that most of an investor's costs are incurred prior to operation (90%, according to Claimant's expert). They face a long period for capital recovery. Investments in PV plants are usually heavily leveraged (in the range of 55-80% leverage).'

***InfraRed Environmental Infrastructure GP Limited and others v Kingdom of Spain*, ICSID Case No. ARB/14/12, Award, 2 August 2019**	
Treaty	ECT (1994)
Applicable Rules	ICSID Arbitration Rules (2006)

<table>
<tr><td>Arbitrators</td><td colspan="2">P: Mr. Stephen Drymer - C: Prof. William Park - R: Prof. Pierre-Marie Dupuy</td></tr>
<tr><td>Outcome</td><td>In favour of the investor
Amount claimed: EUR 75.7 million
Amount awarded: EUR 28.2 million</td><td>Valuation method: income-based approach (discounted cash flow)
Interest rate: host State's sovereign bonds (10-year)
Costs of arbitration: USD 1,285,515.4
Award legal costs: Claimants were awarded 66.66% of their legal costs
Award costs of arbitration: Costs follow the award</td></tr>
<tr><td>Main Facts</td><td colspan="2">57 'On 23 June 2011, Claimants' investment committee approved an investment of up to €31 million in the Morón and Olivenza 1 Plants. Claimants subsequently invested in the Plants on 28 July 2011. As discussed above, this was some 19 months after the Plants' registration on the Pre-Allocation Registry (on 11 December 2009), and some 16 months before their final registration on the RAIPRE (on 31 May 2012 for Morón, and on 18 December 2012 for Olivenza 1).'</td></tr>
<tr><td>Legitimate expectations of the investor</td><td colspan="2">366 '[A] legitimate expectation of stability ... can only arise in the presence of a specific commitment tendered directly to the investor or industry sector at issue.'
The Tribunal found that Spain's representations toward the renewable energy investors amounted to such a commitment, albeit of a limited scope (at 449-450).
449. 'Scope of Respondent's Specific Commitment - In the light of the above, the Tribunal finds that, by 2010, Respondent had in fact made a specific commitment to the CSP sector that CSP plants registered in the Pre-allocation Register would be shielded from subsequent regulatory changes at least as regards certain elements of the Original Regulatory Framework.'
450. 'It remains to consider which particular elements of the Original Framework were subject to Respondent's specific commitment; and whether their modification or abrogation by the Measures at Issue violated Claimants' legitimate expectation?'
453 'Finally, the Tribunal is of the view that the abrogation of the regulated tariff and the pool premium and their replacement with a system based on a remuneration per unit of installed capacity calculated according to an "efficient" standard plant of the type at issue frustrated Claimants' legitimate expectation. First, the uncontradicted evidence produced in the record and administered at the Hearing shows that Claimants relied on the values of the regulated tariff and of the pool plus premium (colloquially dubbed the "FiT" by Claimants' witnesses at the Hearing). It is clear that Claimants forecasted that these values would not change for the</td></tr>
</table>

	lifespan of the plants. For the reasons mentioned above, the Tribunal finds this expectation reasonable and legitimate.' 454 'Second, it is clear that the change enacted by the Measures at Issue is significant. The abrogation of the feed-in remuneration system and its replacement with the "specific remuneration" under the EPA 2013 caused Claimants significant losses of up to €38 million (slightly higher than the value of Claimants' investment).' 455 'For these reasons, the Tribunal is of the view that Respondent breached its FET obligation under Article 10(1) by frustrating a legitimate expectation held by Claimants that future regulatory changes would not affect the CSP producers' right to receive the pool price premium set out at RD 661/2007 and reiterated by RD 1614/2010.'
Due diligence of the investor	435 'This means that as of the date of the issuance of the December Resolutions (i.e., 29 December 2010), being less than six (6) months before investing, Claimants could reasonably expect that the CSP plants at issue would benefit from the "tariffs, premiums and lower and upper limits" established by RD 661/2007 for their entire operational lifetime.' 436 'The Tribunal finds this expectation reasonable and legitimate. The Tribunal finds no evidence dated between 29 December 2010 and 23 June 2011 that could controvert the reasonability or legitimacy of Claimants' expectation in this regard.'
Climate change mention	3 'This policy furthered Spain's international commitments and obligations set out, among others, in the directives of the European Union and the Kyoto Protocol.' 442 'The Tribunal is of the view that even a perfect analysis of such jurisprudence could not have led the Claimants to foresee that Respondent might abrogate the very tenets of the Original Regulatory Framework (i.e., the premium and the lower and upper limits) that it undertook to maintain unchanged for the CSP sector.'

***OperaFund Eco-Invest SICAV PLC and Schwab Holding AG v Kingdom of Spain*, ICSID Case No. ARB/15/36, Award, 6 September 2019**		
Treaty	ECT (1994)	
Applicable Rules	ICSID Arbitration Rules (2006)	
Arbitrators	P: Prof. Dr. Karl-Heinz Böckstiegel – C: Prof. Dr August Reinisch – R: Prof. Philippe Sands, K.C. (dissent)	
Outcome	In favour of the investor Amount claimed: EUR 42 million Amount awarded: USD 29.3 million	Valuation method: income-based approach (discounted cash flow) Interest rate: host State's sovereign bonds (10-year)

		Costs of arbitration: USD 1,042,994.37 Award legal costs: Claimants were awarded USD 2,206,586.56 (75% of legal costs) Award costs of arbitration: Respondent bears 75% of the costs
Main Facts	173 'The Parties agree that Claimants invested between July 2008 and July 2009. Claimant OperaFund's investment began in July 2008, and Schwab's in April 2009.' 181 'Claimants state that all their facilities were registered in RAIPRE by 29 September 2008.'	
Legitimate expectations of the investor	485 '[I]t is hard to imagine a more explicit stabilization assurance than the one mentioned in Article 44(3) [of the original incentive scheme]: "revisions [...] shall not affect facilities for which the functioning certificate had been granted."' 489 'Further, the Tribunal is aware and shares the view of the Tribunals in Antin, Masdar, Novenergia, and Eiser which also rejected Spain's defence based on the "reasonable return" argument. Antin and Eiser rejected Spain's defense based on the Tariff Deficit.'	
Due diligence of the investor	487 'However, the Tribunal does not see a lack of due diligence by the Claimants. Both Claimants did what could be expected under the circumstances and at the time of their investments by a prudent investor. Claimants' reliance on a Legal Opinion by Cuatrecasas was also sufficient at least in confirming their expectations.' It also agrees with the reasoning of the *Antaris* tribunal, namely that the absence of 'real due diligence' on the part of the investors would vitiate a legitimate expectations claim. 486 'It also agrees with the assessment of the tribunal in Antin which held that it "[...] must consider when the investment was made, what the circumstances were at that time and the information that the investor had or should reasonably have had, had it acted with the requisite degree of diligence (considering its expertise). In carrying out this assessment, tribunals must attempt to place themselves at the time of the investment and consider the information and conditions available at such time, and to refrain from appraising the investor's expectations with the benefit of hindsight."' 679 'The Tribunal agrees with the decision in Novenergia, accepting the requirement of "an adequate due diligence prior to making its investment", was met when it held that the investor did, in fact, "carry out a reasonable analysis of the Spanish regulatory framework prior to its investment."'	

<table>
<tr><td>Climate change mention</td><td>169 ‘On 23 January 2008, there was a Communication from the EC to the European Parliament, the Council, the European Economic and Social Committee and the Committee of the Regions entitled “20 20 by 2020 Europe’s Climate Change Opportunity,” which adopted the EU’s 2006 recommendations for increasing RE consumption to 20% by 2020.’

[Dissent 5] ‘Against the background of the 1992 UN Framework Convention on Climate Change (UNFCCC) and the 1997 Kyoto Protocol to the UNFCCC, the European Union adopted legislation committing Member States, including Spain, to reduce greenhouse gas emissions.’</td></tr>
</table>

<table>
<tr><td colspan="3">Stadtwerke München GmbH and others v Kingdom of Spain, ICSID Case No. ARB/15/1, Award, 2 December 2019</td></tr>
<tr><td>Treaty</td><td colspan="2">ECT (1994)</td></tr>
<tr><td>Applicable Rules</td><td colspan="2">ICSID Arbitration Rules (2006)</td></tr>
<tr><td>Arbitrators</td><td colspan="2">P: Prof. Jeswald W. Salacuse – C: Prof. Kaj Hobér – R: Prof. Zachary Douglas, Q.C.</td></tr>
<tr><td>Outcome</td><td>In favour of the state

Amount claimed: EUR 423 million

Amount awarded: ZERO</td><td>Costs of arbitration: USD 869,404.53

Award legal costs: Respondent was awarded EUR 2,396,728.88 (83.33% of legal costs)

Award costs of arbitration: Claimants bear their own share of costs of arbitration and 83.33% of the respondent’s share</td></tr>
<tr><td>Main Facts</td><td colspan="2">79 ‘The Claimants in this case built and operated the Andasol 3 Plant, an electrical generation facility located in Aldeire, in the Spanish province of Granada in Andalusia, southern Spain, an area offering some of the highest and prolonged levels of solar irradiation in the EU. Commissioned in November 2011, the Andasol 3 Plant has the capacity to generate 182 million kWh of electricity a year, which according to the Claimants would supply the needs of approximately half a million people and save some 150,000 tonnes of CO2 when compared to a coal-fired power plant.’

383 ‘The Tribunal has further concluded that the registration of the Andasol 3 Plant in the RAIPRE did not create any rights besides those granted – to all qualifying installations – by the RD 661/2007.’</td></tr>
<tr><td>Legitimate expectations of the investor</td><td colspan="2">282 ‘[I]t would have been unreasonable for the Claimants to have interpreted [the incentive scheme] as constituting a stabilized regime for the calculation of the premium that would be impervious to any future modification regardless of a change in the market conditions.’</td></tr>
</table>

Due diligence of the investor	264 'The FET standard in the ECT does not, however, protect the investor from any and all changes that a government can introduce into its legislation. As concluded in the previous section, it does not protect it against the changes introduced to safeguard the public interest to address a change of circumstances, nor does it protect the investor who unreasonably and unjustifiably expects that the host government will introduce no amendments will to the legislation governing the investment. In the absence of a specific commitment contractually assumed by a State to freeze its legislation in favor of an investor, when an investor argues - as is the case here - that such expectation is rooted, among others, in the host State's legislation, the Tribunal is required to conduct an objective examination of the legislation and the facts surrounding the making of the investment to assess whether a prudent and experienced investor could have reasonably formed a legitimate and justifiable expectation of the immutability of such legislation. *For such an expectation to be reasonable, it must also arise from a rigorous due diligence process carried out by the investor.*' 278 'This Supreme Court Judgment was a matter of public record at the time that the Claimants invested in Spain. A reasonable and prudent investor would have known of this decision, understood it implications for a contemplated investment, and adjusted expectations accordingly.' 308 '[The Tribunal] finds that a prudent investor, having conducted an appropriate due diligence, would not have reasonably formed an expectation of a legally stable income stream for the life of the [investment].'
Climate change mention	50 'This dispute has its distant origins in the efforts by Spain, both as a sovereign state and as a member of the EU, to increase its generation of energy from renewable sources, notably the sun among others, and to reduce its dependence on fossil fuels for the production of electricity. It was hoped that the pursuit of such a fundamental change would have at least three positive social and economic effects: a) a reduction in green-house gases in the atmosphere and thereby a diminished impact on climate change; b) a reduced dependence by Spain on the importation of fossil fuels; and c) a stimulus to investment, employment and regional development.'

***BayWa r.e. Renewable Energy GmbH and BayWa r.e. Asset Holding GmbH v Kingdom of Spain*, ICSID Case No. ARB/15/16, Decision on Jurisdiction, Liability and Directions on Quantum, 2 December 2019**	
Treaty	ECT (1994)
Applicable Rules	ICSID Arbitration Rules (2006)

<table>
<tr><td>Arbitrators</td><td colspan="2">P: Judge James R. Crawford
C: Dr. Horacio A. Grigera Naón
R: Ms. Loretta Malintoppi</td></tr>
<tr><td>Outcome</td><td>In favour of the investor
Amount claimed: EUR 61.931.524
Amount awarded: EUR 22.006 million</td><td>Valuation method: income-based approach (see Award, para. 27: present value of the future payments the claimants were deprived of as a result of the breach calculated by reference to the disputed regulatory measures)
Interest rate: EURIBOR (6-month)
Costs of arbitration: USD 1,355,697.23
Award legal costs: Each party bears its costs
Award costs of arbitration: Each party carries its own legal representation costs, while the ICSID costs are to be shared equally between the Parties.</td></tr>
<tr><td>Main Facts</td><td colspan="2">66 'On 28 December 2001, the main participants to the Projects at the time entered into a financing agreement ("Framework Agreement for the investment in the WindFarms").15 The Wind Farms were to be financed with a ratio of approximately 25% capital and 75% debt. The capital was provided by the participants / investors using a combination of equity and subordinated loans. A syndicate of banks provided the bank financing.'
67 'On 25 November 2002, the installations were commissioned.16 The Diputación General de Aragón attested their Final Registration at the RAIPRE, with effect as of 22 November 2002, through Certificates issued on 26 March 2003.17 Around the same dates the Wind Farms started commercial operation.'</td></tr>
<tr><td>Legitimate expectations of the investor</td><td colspan="2">The tribunal essentially adopts the same reasoning as in the Blusun case (the acting president is the same).
515 'The Tribunal therefore decides that the Respondent has not breached its obligation to ensure a reasonable return for the future.'
569 '[i]n principle, an investor cannot have a legitimate expectation of treatment which is unlawful under the law of the host State, provided that the host State law itself is not inconsistent with the treaty under which the tribunal exercises its jurisdiction.'
591 '[I]n the circumstances, the clawing back by Spain, in and after 2013, of subsidies earlier paid at levels in excess of the amounts that would have been payable under the Disputed Measures, had they been in force in previous years, was in breach of the obligation</td></tr>
</table>

	of stability under Article 10.1, first and second sentences of the ECT.'
Due diligence of the investor	473 'The stream cannot rise higher than its source or commit the state to more than the legislative framework allows. A requirement that the remuneration system be such as to allow recipients "to achieve reasonable profitability rates with reference to the cost of money on capital markets" is general in its terms, but it is perfectly intelligible and imposes some limits on what can be done.'
Climate change mention	86 'The promotion of renewable energy production was one of the objectives of the new legal framework which included specific renewable energy targets. This was in line with international commitments adopted by Spain at the time (and later) to reduce greenhouse gas emissions and increase the share of renewable energy sources. These included the Kyoto Protocol and multiple EU directives.'

<table>
<tr><th colspan="3">RWE Innogy GmbH and RWE Innogy Aersa S.A.U. v Kingdom of Spain, ICSID Case No. ARB/14/34, Decision on Jurisdiction, Liability, and Certain Issues of Quantum, 30 December 2019</th></tr>
<tr><td>Treaty</td><td colspan="2">ECT (1994)</td></tr>
<tr><td>Applicable Rules</td><td colspan="2">ICSID Arbitration Rules (2006)</td></tr>
<tr><td>Arbitrators</td><td colspan="2">P: Mr. Samuel Wordsworth, Q.C. - C: Mr. Judd Kessler - R: Ms. Anna Joubin-Bret</td></tr>
<tr><td>Outcome</td><td>In favour of the investor
Amount claimed: EUR 273 million
Amount awarded: EUR 28,080,000</td><td>Valuation method: income-based approach
Interest rate: host State's sovereign bonds (10-year)
Costs of arbitration: USD 1,431,480.72
Award legal costs: Claimants were awarded EUR 2,373,909.24 (50% of legal costs for jurisdiction and liability phase)
Award costs of arbitration: Costs follow the award</td></tr>
<tr><td>Main Facts</td><td colspan="2">191 'As follows from the details below, the investments were acquired in three broad tranches: first, in a series of transactions in 2001 to early 2004 totalling in excess of EUR 45 million, in particular with respect to the acquisition of 100% of the share capital of Agrupació Energías Renovables, S.A.U. (Aersa) (the "Aersa Acquisition"); second, on 6 June 2008, the Claimants acquired a 100% interest in Urvasco Energía, S.A. (Urvasco) for EUR 363.5 million (the "Urvasco Acquisition"); third, in a series of</td></tr>
</table>

	transactions from December 2008 up until December 2012, the Claimants increased their shareholding interests in the various plants in which they already had an interest through their prior acquisitions.'
Legitimate expectations of the investor	451 '[E]ven absent a showing of specific commitments that the regulatory regime would not change, a breach of Article 10(1) may be established if there has been some form of total and unreasonable change to, or subversion of, the legal regime.' 462 The tribunal explained that its task was to assess whether the change to the tariff regime had been disproportionate, and whether Spain had taken into account the impacts on investors in its decision-making process. Applying this test, the tribunal found that certain of the measures adopted by Spain were disproportionate. 600 '[The Tribunal] finds that is unfair and inequitable for the adverse impacts to these specific plants to be borne by the Claimants.'
Due diligence of the investor	510 'In the Tribunal's view, there was however ample reason for a diligent investor to carry out specific regulatory due diligence at the time of the Urvasco acquisition in June 2008, as well to keep this up to date in respect of the regulatory developments that were taking place, and the Tribunal rejects the view that it could reasonably be left to the Claimants' lawyers to advise without their being tasked with a specific regulatory due diligence exercise. The Urvasco acquisition was a very substantial Investment indeed. Moreover, it was the first Investment by the Claimants under the new regime established by RD 661/2007, which had been formulated in the context of considerable industry controversy and complaint as to the instability of the regime. Yet no external legal advice was sought on the regulatory regime (cf. the level of legal due diligence as to the regulatory regime noted by the tribunal in the Antin case).' 513 'It follows from the above that, given the scale of the acquisitions being made and the fact that there was some plainly visible regulatory instability given RDL 7/2006 and then the controversial repeal and replacement of RD 436/2004 by RD 661/2007, it must be regarded as having been incumbent on the Claimants – in the context of the application of the FET standard under Article 10(1) – to have performed some discrete due diligence exercise on the applicable law and regulations, and they failed to do this.' 514 'It does not automatically follow that the Claimants' could not reasonably base their Investments on RDL 661/2007 and/or RD 1614/2010 or rely on stability in the Special Regime. However, the Tribunal must bring into account any statements, reports or legal decisions that would have been considered in a due diligence exercise, in particular the decisions of the Spanish Supreme Court on which the Respondent has placed great weight, while the

	absence of due diligence is consistent with the evidence in sub-section (b) above which shows that the Claimants' key Investments were not made by reference to a specific understanding of and reliance on individual provisions of RD 661/2007.'
Climate change mention	174 'The adoption of RD 661/2007 was accompanied by a press release from Spain's Ministry of Industry, Tourism and Commerce entitled "The Government prioritises profitability and stability in the new Royal Decree on renewable energy and combined heat and power." (...) This guarantees legal certainty for the electricity producer and stability for the sector, favouring development. The new legislation will not be retroactive. Facilities functioning by 1 January 2008 may keep to the previous legislation in the fixed tariff option during their entire lifespan. When they participate in the market, they may keep to their regulation prior to 31 December 2012. The emission of 6.3 million tonnes of C02 per year will be avoided by achieving the objectives set out for combined heat and power for 2010.' 557 'The CNE proposed a number of possible "urgent and necessary" short and medium term measures, some of which were radical in nature i.e. financing the cost of the special regime through CO2 auctions and a tax on the sale of petrol and gas, some of which envisaged relatively minor reductions to the remuneration to RE generators (such as reductions to the annual increase in accordance with the CPI, reductions impacting solar thermoelectric plants pre-registered but not yet finally registered in the RAIPRE, and restrictions on use of fossil fuels in generation of renewable energy to 5%), some of which envisaged an increase in access tolls The CNE did not propose the replacement of the Special Regime fixed tariff / premium put in place by RD 661/2007 but the Tribunal sees its report as strong evidence that it was necessary to act in some way to address the Tariff Deficit.'

***Watkins Holdings S.à r.l. and others v Kingdom of Spain,* ICSID Case No. ARB/15/44, Award, 21 January 2020**		
Treaty	ECT (1994)	
Applicable Rules	ICSID Arbitration Rules (2006)	
Arbitrators	P: Tan Sri Dato' Cecil W.M. Abraham - C: Dr. Michael C. Pryles - R: Prof. Dr. Hélène Ruiz-Fabri (dissenting)	
Outcome	In favour of the investor Amount claimed: EUR 123.9 million Amount awarded: EUR 77 million	Valuation method: income-based approach (discounted cash flow) Interest rate: host State's sovereign bonds (10-year for pre-award; 10-year + 1% for post-award)

<table>
<tr><td></td><td></td><td>Costs of arbitration: USD 680,255.62

Award legal costs: Claimants were awarded 75% of their legal costs

Award costs of arbitration: Respondent bears its own share of costs of arbitration and 75% of the claimants' share</td></tr>
<tr><td>Main Facts</td><td colspan="2">134 'According to the Claimants, in 2011, Watkins Spain, Redpier and Northsea "acquired the entire share capital" of the Marmellar SL and La Boga SL. Marmellar SL holds the wind farm known as Parque Eólico Marmellar (49.5 MW) ("Parque Marmellar") and La Boga SL holds the following seven wind farms.'</td></tr>
<tr><td>Legitimate expectations of the investor</td><td colspan="2">529 'The Tribunal finds that Spain by enacting RD 1614/2010 which applied to qualifying wind installations confirm that they would not be affected by any review of the FIT under RD 661/2007. This was consistent with the commitments of Spain pursuant to Article 44(3) of RD 661/2007 and furthermore, RD 1614/2010 also broadened the scope of protection under Article 44(3) to include premiums.'

531 'The Tribunal therefore holds that the July 2010 Agreement which is a contemporaneous document of Spain, amounts to a representation to the Claimants especially in view of the fact that Spain referred to the July 2010 Agreement in the following terms: "This agreement furthermore assumes the reinforcement of the visibility and stability of the regulation of these technologies in the future, guaranteeing the current incentives and rates of RD 661/2007 for the facilities in operation (and for those included in the pre-registration) starting in 2013 ..."'

532 'Spain made various representations which included the promotion of advertising materials such as the English Language documents, presentation in foreign countries designed to attract foreign investment for the RE projects. The Tribunal finds that the Claimants are entitled to rely on these expectations which were reasonable.'

563 'The Eiser decision confirms that the Claimants were entitled to an expectation that the Spanish regime in which they invested, would not be radically altered in respect of existing investments. The Tribunal adopts the persuasive reasons of the Eiser Tribunal.'</td></tr>
<tr><td>Due diligence of the investor</td><td colspan="2">588 'The Tribunal having considered the due diligence conducted by the Claimants in respect of (a) the A&O Memorandum, (b) the information memorandum, and (c) the BCG Report, is of the view that the due diligence exercised by the Claimants, is on the basis that the Claimants believed they had a legitimate expectation that the laws would not be modified especially as the above documents included a stabilisation clause. Furthermore, the Tribunal is of the</td></tr>
</table>

	view that the Claimants did undertake an appropriate fact-finding mission in Spain with a view to their investments in RE.' 589 'The Tribunal believes that there is no basis for Spain to contend that the Claimants have not exercised proper due diligence with regards to their proposed investment in the RE sector in Spain.'
Climate change mention	The tribunal in *Watkins Holding v Spain* considered EU law as a fact in assessing whether the investor was entitled to legitimate expectations that Spain's incentive scheme for renewable energy investments would not be significantly altered. The tribunal explained that the investor's expectations were legitimate and reasonable. 527 'The Tribunal finds that the Claimants' expectations on the continued application of the economic regime to the Project Companies were legitimate and reasonable [for reasons including] ... the economic regime ... was part of a wider international and domestic policy to develop RE power generation infrastructure and to specifically encourage and attract the necessary investments.'

***AES Solar and others (PV Investors) v Spain*, PCA Case No. 2012-14, Final Award, 28 February 2020**		
Treaty	ECT (1994)	
Applicable Rules	UNCITRAL Arbitration Rules (1976)	
Arbitrators	P: Prof. Gabrielle Kaufmann-Kohler - C: Honourable Charles Brower - R: Judge Bernardo Sepulveda-Amor	
Outcome	In favour of the investor Amount claimed: EUR 1.16 billion Amount awarded: EUR 91.1 million	Valuation method: income-based approach (discounted cash flow) Interest rate: host State's sovereign bonds (10-year) Costs of arbitration: EUR 442,152.22 (jurisdiction) and EUR 2,467,847.78 (pre-jurisdiction and merits) Award legal costs: Each party bears its own legal costs Award costs of arbitration: Parties share costs equally
Main Facts	195 'The Claimants began investing in the Spanish PV sector under RD 661/2007 and, on their case, relying on the alleged "immutability" of the incentives contained in such decree.' 196 'The 85% threshold set for the PV sector was achieved in and around August 2007. As a result, pursuant to Article 22 of RD 661/2007, Spain announced on 27 September 2007 that the time	

	limit for RAIPRE registrations would expire on 29 September 2008.61 All of the Claimants' PV installations were registered with RAIPRE within this deadline and accordingly fell within the purview of the benefits available under RD 661/2007.'
Legitimate expectations of the investor	638 'For all of these reasons, the Primary Claim cannot be upheld. In summary, the Tribunal reaches the conclusion that from the start of the Special Regime for RE with the 1997 Electricity Law, the Spanish legislature provided that investors would be entitled to "reasonable profitability" of their investments. The reasonable return on investments was also a key element of the regime established by RD 661/2007. *In the Tribunal's view, the principle of reasonable return serves as the limit of ECT-compliant regulatory changes. If changes cross the "reasonable return" line, that is if they deprive investors of a reasonable return, the State conduct transgresses the standards contained in Article 10(1) of the ECT.*' 639 'In other words, the Claimants are only entitled to compensation under Article 10(1) of the ECT if they establish that the new regime violates the guarantee of reasonable rate of return. This approach strikes the right balance between, on the one hand, the protection of investors who have committed substantial resources in a sector which continues to provide Spain with the environmental benefits of clean solar power, and, on the other hand, Spain's right to regulate and adapt its framework to changed circumstances, provided that right is exercised in a manner that is proportionate, reasonable, and non-arbitrary manner.' 640 'The Tribunal must now examine whether the regime substituting RD 661/2007 deprived the Claimants of a reasonable return.'
Due diligence of the investor	613 '[W]hether the Claimants engaged in diligence or not and whether that diligence was "due" or not, cannot alter the fact that on the basis of the law and the jurisprudence the Claimants knew or should have known that changes to the regulatory framework could happen. As a consequence, expectations that they would not happen cannot be deemed legitimate.'
Climate change mention	591 'Following the 1997 Electricity Law, Spain enacted a number of regulations which sought to specify the general parameters set out in the Law. These regulations were passed in the context of global, regional and national efforts to address climate change, aimed at the reduction of emissions of carbon dioxide. Against the background of the 1992 UN Framework Convention on Climate Change (UNFCCC) and the 1997 Kyoto Protocol to the UNFCCC, the European Union had also adopted rules committing Member States, including Spain, to reduce greenhouse gas emissions. These rules included measures to encourage the use of renewable and other environment-friendly technologies.'

<table>
<tr><td colspan="3">Hydro Energy 1 S.à.r.l. and Hydroxana Sweden AB v Kingdom of Spain, ICSID Case No. ARB/15/42, Decision on Jurisdiction, Liability and Directions on Quantum, 9 March 2020</td></tr>
<tr><td>Treaty</td><td colspan="2">ECT (1994)</td></tr>
<tr><td>Applicable Rules</td><td colspan="2">ICSID Arbitration Rules (2006)</td></tr>
<tr><td>Arbitrators</td><td colspan="2">P: Lord Collins Mapesbury, LL.D., F.B.A. - C: Mr. Peter Rees, Q.C. - R: Prof. Rolf Knieper, Q.C.</td></tr>
<tr><td rowspan="3">Outcome</td><td>In favour of the investor</td><td>Costs of arbitration: USD 893,685.74</td></tr>
<tr><td>Amount claimed: EUR 132.1 million</td><td>Award legal costs: Each party bears its own legal costs</td></tr>
<tr><td>Amount awarded: EUR 30.9 million</td><td>Award costs of arbitration: Parties share costs equally</td></tr>
<tr><td>Main Facts</td><td colspan="2">64 ‘The Claimants paid EUR 26.3 million for a 100% equity interest in Hidro Xana S.L.U. (“Hidro Xana”).’

68 ‘The Claimants paid EUR 46.0 million for a 100% equity interest in Hidrodata. As part of the Claimants’ acquisition of Hidrodata, Hydroxana made a debt investment in Hidrodata of EUR 7.8 million in the form of a mezzanine loan in January 2012. The mezzanine loan was transferred from Hydroxana to Hydro Energy, i.e. within the Claimants, on 30 December 2012.’

435 ‘Each of the Claimants’ plants was certified as meeting the criteria necessary to qualify for the RD 661/2007 regime by the relevant Spanish authorities (including through registration in the RAIPRE).’</td></tr>
<tr><td>Legitimate expectations of the investor</td><td colspan="2">590 ‘[C]hanges to general legislation (at least in the absence of a stabilization clause) are not prevented by the FET standard if they do not exceed the acceptable margin of change in the exercise of the host State’s normal regulatory power in pursuance of a public interest.’

In determining whether the regulatory amendments had exceeded the acceptable margin of change, the tribunal in Hydro Energy conducted a balancing exercise similar to the RREEF tribunal, eventually concluding that the modifications went beyond the margin of change if they did not afford the investor a reasonable rate of return. (para 770)

770 ‘For the reasons set out above: (1) the Tribunal declares that it has jurisdiction over the Claimants’ claims in the present arbitration; (2) the Tribunal dismisses the Claimants’ claim under ECT, Article 13(1); (3) the Tribunal declares that the Respondent might (or would) be in breach of ECT, Article 10(1), if and to the extent that the remuneration of each of the plants in the Ondina and Xana portfolios failed to accord with a reasonable post-tax rate of return in the small-hydro market in Spain on the basis of WACC plus 1%, with the risk-free rate being the Spanish 10 year bond rate</td></tr>
</table>

	of 4.398%; (4) the Tribunal accordingly directs the Parties to endeavour to agree on the bases in Section VIII B hereof (i) an agreed post-tax reasonable rate of return calculated using the WACC as at June 2013; and (ii) agreed post-tax holding IRRs for each of the plants; (5) the Tribunal directs the Parties to report to the Tribunal within 60 days hereof whether agreement has been reached, and if not, on the principal areas of disagreement; (6) the Tribunal will give such further directions as may be necessary; (7) the Tribunal reserves all consequential matters, including interest (if any) and costs, to a further Decision or final Award.'
Due diligence of the investor	600 '[G]iven the State's regulatory powers, in order to rely on legitimate expectations, the investor should inquire in advance regarding the prospects of a change in the regulatory framework in light of the then prevailing or reasonably to be expected changes in the economic and social conditions of the host State.' 604 '[I]n considering whether there was … a commitment and whether it was reasonable to rely on it, it is necessary to look at it in the context of … the advice which an investor took or should have taken on the nature of the commitment if any.'
Climate change mention	79 'The Electricity Act 54/1997 was implemented by a series of Royal Decrees, following Spain's signature in April 1998 of the Kyoto Protocol to the United Nations Framework Convention on Climate Change, which required the contracting parties to reduce greenhouse gas emissions and set binding emission targets to achieve reduction.'

***Cavalum SGPS, S.A. v Kingdom of Spain*, ICSID Case No. ARB/15/34, Decision on Jurisdiction, Liability and Directions on Quantum, 31 August 2020 31 August 2020**		
Treaty	ECT (1994)	
Applicable Rules	ICSID Arbitration Rules (2006)	
Arbitrators	P: Lord Lawrence Collins of Mapesbury – C: Mr. David Haigh, Q.C. – R: Sir Daniel Bethlehem, Q.C.	
Outcome	In favour of the investor Amount claimed: EUR 59.2 million Amount awarded: The Tribunal, by majority, declares that by enacting and applying the New Regulatory Regime, Spain has undermined the Claimant's legitimate expectations implicit in the	Costs of arbitration: N/A Award legal costs: N/A Award costs of arbitration: N/A

	FET obligation in Article 10(1) to the extent (if any) that the return on its investments in the plants falls short of a reasonable return by reference to the cost of money in the capital markets and, to that extent also, breached the obligation of stability in Article 10(1) ECT.	
Main Facts	*91* 'Spain enrolled Calzadilla into the RD 1578/2008 pre-allocation registry in 2011, but Cavalum and Valsolar sold that facility in April 2012. The Claimant states that the three other projects were never developed, because they did not secure a spot in the RAIPRE registration before the enactment of Royal Decree - Law 1/2012 (the "Abandoned Projects").'	
Legitimate expectations of the investor	470 'In determining an investor's legitimate expectations at the time of investment, the legal and commercial environment has to be considered in the light of the due diligence which an investor can be expected to undertake.' 471 'A foreign investor will not itself normally have a detailed knowledge of the legal system, the laws governing the investment or the history of government policy statements. But it will plainly know the essential commercial characteristics of the law governing the incentives for its investment, and will take a commercial view on the likely future stability of the system.' 472 'The detailed knowledge, on the other hand, will reside in its legal, commercial and financial advisers and that is why the extent and quality of the due diligence undertaken by the investor is so important in determining its legitimate expectations. Since legal due diligence, in the light of the surrounding circumstances, is the most directly relevant in determining legitimate expectations, it is appropriate to start with (a) the state of the legislation at the time of investment, and (b) the relevant decisions of the Spanish Supreme Court.' 626 'In the view of the majority of the Tribunal, a reasonable rate of return (but not one which is unilaterally determined by Spain) is the only legally protected expectation that the Claimant could legitimately have had.' 642 'The overall effect of the findings of the majority of the Tribunal is that, by enacting and applying the New Regulatory Regime, Spain has undermined the Claimant's legitimate expectations implicit in the FET obligation in Article 10(1) to the extent (if any) that the return on its investments in the plants falls	

	short of a reasonable return by reference to the cost of money in the capital markets and, to that extent also, breached the obligation of stability in Article 10(1) ECT.'
Due diligence of the investor	176 'Spain argues that the Electricity Law 54/1997 guaranteed renewable energy generators enrolled in the Special Regime a reasonable rate of return calculated by reference to the cost of money in the capital market (Article 30.4). Nothing else was promised, much less guaranteed.' 538 'What they may reasonably be entitled to expect, in reliance on appropriate due diligence to this effect, is that the legal and regulatory regime into which they were investing would not change radically and fundamentally without notice.' 549 '[T]hrough its advisers, the Claimant must be taken to have been on notice that the regulatory conditions could be altered to adapt to changed circumstances, or, alternatively, that if the Claimant was not so advised, this was a shortcoming in its due diligence such that it could not rely on the advice that it received to properly found a claim of legitimate expectations.' 556 '[I]nformed industry observers would have known that the Government, any government, would implicitly have reserved the right to make changes in the public interest, and that these statements were being made in the context of changes which had had some resistance.' 610 'In the view of the majority of the Tribunal these are not answers to the basic point that, as confirmed by later judicial and legislative developments, the basis of the enabling legislation was the reasonable rate of return principle.'
Climate change mention	485 'EU Directive 2001/77/EC: In 2001, the EU adopted Directive 2001/77/EC331 on the Promotion of Electricity Produced from Renewable Energy Sources in the Internal Electricity Market, in order to comply with the Kyoto Protocol.' 486 'The Directive provided that support schemes for renewable energy sources would be set by the Member States subject to the European Union state aid rules.332 It obliged all EU Member States (a) to "take appropriate steps to encourage greater consumption of electricity produced from renewable energy sources" in order to "meet Kyoto targets more quickly", (b) "to set national indicative targets for the consumption of electricity produced from renewable sources", and (c) to report regularly to the EU on their progress in meeting those targets. Spain's indicative target was to draw 24.9% of its electricity from renewable sources by 2010. The Directive required Spain to enact implementing legislation by October 27, 2003.'

***STAEG GmbH v Kingdom of Spain*, ICSID Case No. ARB/15/4, Decision on Jurisdiction, Liability and Principles of Quantum, 8 September 2020**		
Treaty	ECT (1994)	
Applicable Rules	ICSID Arbitration Rules (2006)	
Arbitrators	P: Eduardo Zuleta Jaramillo – C: Guido Santiago Tawil – R: Pierre-Marie Dupuy	
Outcome	In favour of investor Amount claimed: EUR 79 million Amount awarded: EUR 27.70 million	Costs of arbitration: Award legal costs: Award costs of arbitration:
Main Facts	144 'Steag es una compañía alemana especializada en la planificación, construcción y explotación de centrales eléctricas que utilizan combustibles fósiles y fuentes de energía renovables a través de varias filiales. Al momento de la presentación de la reclamación, Steag era propietaria de la totalidad de las acciones de Steag 1 Beteiligungs-GmbH ("Steag 1"), también constituida en Alemania que. a su vez, según se explica a continuación, para ese momento era titular del 26,01% de las acciones de Arenales Solar PS S.L., propietaria de la planta CSP Arenales, con una potencia teórica de 49,9MW.' 145 'A finales de 2011 Steag conoció sobre la posibilidad de adquirir la participación de Solar Millenium AG ("SMAG") en Arenales Solar a través del propio SMAG68. El 21 de diciembre de 2011, SMAG se declaró en estado de insolvencia.' 146 'Arenales Solar PS es una sociedad española domiciliada en Madrid, inicialmente constituida por la sociedad Fotowatio, S.L. para la promoción y construcción de una planta de energía solar termoeléctrica en el municipio de Morón de la Frontera. El 8 de abril de 2011, Fotowatio, S.L. vendió el 100% de sus participaciones a las sociedades OHLI y SMAG. Con posterioridad, RREEF adquiriría de OHLI y SMAG un 49% de las participaciones en Arenales Solar.'	
Legitimate expectations of the investor	639 'Específicamente, la expectativa se vio vulnerada por tres medidas: (i) el cambio en la manera como se ajustaba la tarifa regulada, que dejó de ajustarse con referencia al IPC, para ser ajustada en adelante con referencia al IPC subyacente (que excluye los precios de productos energéticos y alimentos no procesados); (ii) la reducción a cero de la prima de la opción pool + prima, que supuso el paso a una tarifa fija; y, finalmente, (iii) la sustitución del régimen remuneratorio preexistente por un nuevo régimen remuneratorio, que determina la rentabilidad con base en la hipótesis de una "instalación tipo".'	

	640 'En cambio, no se encontró una reclamación suficientemente determinada y clara respecto de la supuesta frustración de una expectativa legítima de Steag a través de la eliminación de la posibilidad de vender la electricidad producida con gas bajo la tarifa regulada. Por otra parte, como se señaló anteriormente, el Tribunal no tiene jurisdicción para decidir sobre la supuesta violación del artículo 10(1) del TCE a través de la introducción del IVPEE.' 641 'La Demandante argumenta que el artículo 10(1) del TCE, aunque no constituye una cláusula estabilizadora, protege al inversionista frente a un "cambio total e irrazonable del marco regulatorio". Para Steag, hay una garantía de "estabilidad fundamental" respecto de las "características esenciales" del marco jurídico vigente al momento de la inversión.'
Due diligence of the investor	523 'Relevancia de la conducta de Steag y del due diligence realizado con anterioridad a la fecha de la inversión para la determinación de la existencia y alcance de las expectativas legítimas.' 532 'Estos elementos fueron fundamentales para la decisión de Steag de acometer una inversión en el proyecto Arenales Solar. En efecto, la Demandante ha explicado que los informes fueron puestos a consideración de los análisis internos presentados a los órganos de Steag. El Sr. Voswinkel insistió en el registro de pre-asignación como uno de los puntos fuertes de su proceso de inversión. Haciendo referencia al propósito del "due diligence" legal que se llevó a cabo, el Sr. Voswinkel explicó: "Según nuestra manera de ver las cosas lo que analizamos fue la base para el sistema de tarifa regulada de los feed in tariff; si ha habido cambios, sí o no, y cuál fue la situación en el momento en que ı́bamos a entrar y cómo iba a desarrollarse en el futuro. Y esta evolución es de la mayor importancia, porque muestra si el proyecto es factible a través del tiempo o no".'
Climate change mention	111 'La Ley 54/1997 trazó una distinción entre un "Régimen Ordinario", aplicable a las fuentes de producción de energía convencionales (tales como las centrales de carbón), y un "Régimen Especial", destinado a favorecer la generación de electricidad a partir de fuentes de energía renovables por distintos medios y aplicable a las instalaciones de producción de electricidad de menos de 50MW que generaban electricidad a partir de fuentes de energías renovables no consumibles.'

***FREIF Eurowind Holdings Ltd v Kingdom of Spain*, SCC Case No. 2017/060, Award, 8 March 2021**	
Treaty	ECT (1994)
Applicable Rules	SCC Rules of Arbitration

<table>
<tr><td>Arbitrators</td><td colspan="2">P: Doug Jones – C: Mark Baker, Kaj Hobér (replaced) – R: Thomas Clay</td></tr>
<tr><td>Outcome</td><td>In favour of the investor
Amount claimed: EUR 124 million (including tax gross-up) Amount awarded: ZERO</td><td>Costs of arbitration: EUR 608,608 and USD 9,451.14
Award legal costs: Respondent was awarded EUR 2,730,536.62 (100% of legal costs)
Award costs of arbitration: Costs follow the award</td></tr>
<tr><td>Main Facts</td><td colspan="2">252 (...) 2008.03.07 – Two other of the wind projects that Claimant would later acquire, Casa del Aire I and Casa del Aire II, receive their RAIPRE registrations. (...) 2008.05.09 – Three other of the wind projects that Claimant would later acquire, La Muñeca, Alconada, and Cuesta Mañera, receive their RAIPRE registrations.
288 FREIF submits that in reliance on the legal framework that had developed, and the Spanish government's sustained assurances as to the stability of that regime, it entered into the joint venture with Spanish company, Renovalia. FREIF and Renovalia created a Spanish company called Renovalia Reserve S.L and invested in the wind farms the subject of this Arbitration in December 2011. FREIF owns 50% minus one share of the equity of the joint venture, although its equity is a preferred class that is entitled to higher equity distributions up to 2021.</td></tr>
<tr><td>Legitimate expectations of the investor</td><td colspan="2">553 'Royal Decrees enacted subsequent to Law 54/1997 are subordinate to it. A diligent investor would be aware that Royal Decrees can be enacted by the Government and be replaced with other Royal Decrees as a regulatory tool while remaining in the parameters of Law 54/1997. The advice provided by Linklaters regarding the Supreme Court's position on this matter confirms as much. Likewise, it was stated by the Isolux majority that "[w]ithout requiring a reasonable investor to perform an extensive legal investigation at the time of investing, knowledge of important decisions from the highest authority regarding the regulatory framework for investment may be assumed".'
571 'The Tribunal concludes that the only guarantee made by Spain was to ensure a reasonable rate of return. Its level of due diligence, including the Linklaters Memorandum, does not establish that FREIF was guaranteed anything other than a reasonable return. FREIF took the risk in making its investment that there could be a re-adjustment in the tariff regime. It may have lost the opportunity to earn higher profits, but it did not lose the expectation of a reasonable return.'</td></tr>
<tr><td>Due diligence of the investor</td><td colspan="2">549 The Tribunal considers that even if FREIF's 'impression' was that any changes would be minor, this impression was not reasonable in the light of the Supreme Court's position and, in any</td></tr>
</table>

<table>
<tr><td></td><td>event, establishes that some degree of regime change was contemplated by FREIF. Spain argues convincingly that FREIF should not have an expectation contrary to Spanish or EU law. As the Spanish Supreme Court is the highest interpreter of Spanish law, and its position on this issue was clearly presented to FREIF in the Linklaters Memorandum, FREIF ought not have had expectations contrary to the Supreme Court's rulings.</td></tr>
<tr><td>Climate change mention</td><td>156 The present dispute concerns investments made by FREIF in the Spanish renewable energy sector. In the mid-2000s, Spain, alongside other European countries, implemented a series of policies aimed at reducing CO2 emissions. The policies were enacted in response to an EU directive, which required Member States to reduce their carbon emissions in line with obligations committed to under the Kyoto Protocol. The relevant policy mechanism employed to affect these reductions sought to promote investments in the renewable energy sector.</td></tr>
</table>

<table>
<tr><td colspan="3">Infracapital F1 S.à.r.l. and Infracapital Solar B.V. v Kingdom of Spain, ICSID Case No. ARB/16/18, Decision on Jurisdiction, Liability and Directions on Quantum, 13 September 2021</td></tr>
<tr><td>Treaty</td><td colspan="2">ECT (1994)</td></tr>
<tr><td>Applicable Rules</td><td colspan="2">ICSID Arbitration Rules (2006)</td></tr>
<tr><td>Arbitrators</td><td colspan="2">P: Mr. Eduardo Siqueiros T. – C: Prof. Peter D. Cameron – R: Mr. Luis González García</td></tr>
<tr><td>Outcome</td><td>In favour of the investor
Amount claimed: N/A
Amount awarded: EUR 28,200,000 (Source: IA Reporter)</td><td>Costs of arbitration: N/A
Award costs of arbitration: Respondent bears the costs and to pay Claimants the costs of the arbitration incurred by Claimants in a total amount of US$642,757.7, as well as an amount equivalent to 66.66 % of the legal costs.</td></tr>
<tr><td>Main Facts</td><td colspan="2">174 According to Claimants, they 'began looking at investment opportunities in Spain in 2009.'112 On 2 June 2010, Claimants signed three share purchase agreements ('SPAs') for the following [3] PV facilities (...)
178 'The purchase of the above-listed plants (the "First Investment Plants") was conditional upon certain regulatory conditions. Specifically, (i) "a new regulation on the FIT of the First Investment Plants being enacted without any retroactivity of the FIT;" and (ii) no new regulation that could affect the First Investment Plants' value negatively by more than 0.75% (the "Regulatory Conditions"). (...)'</td></tr>
</table>

	179 'Between June and October 2011, Claimants invested in two additional groups of PV facilities.' 182 'Claimants finalized their investments in the Fontanellas Plants and the Lasesa Plants on 22 June 2011 and 18 October 2011, respectively (the "Second Investment Plants").' 183 'On 13 October 2016, Claimants sold their interest in the six PV plants.'
Legitimate expectations of the investor	366 'The Tribunal does, however, accept and agree with Respondent's position to the effect that a legitimate expectation of stability (i.e. immutability) can only arise in the presence of a specific commitment tendered directly to the investor or industry sector at issue. This finding is in keeping with the recent decisions in ECT cases concerning the changes enacted by Spain to the remuneration of renewable energy producers, as well as with other arbitral decisions that assessed the issue of a legitimate expectation of stability, be it in application of Article 10(1) of the ECT or of similar investor protection clauses contained in other treaties. This finding is also in keeping with the principle of state sovereignty – enshrined in the ECT and considered by tribunals as part of the balancing exercise carried out when assessing an investor's bilateral relation with the state. The Tribunal is mindful of the significant limitation that a "stability" obligation would impose on the host state's sovereign legislative powers. The Tribunal cannot give effect to such a significant limitation of state sovereignty in the absence of a specific expression of consent by the host state.'
Due diligence of the investor	436. This means that as of the date of the issuance of the December Resolutions (i.e., 29 December 2010), being less than six (6) months before investing, Claimants could reasonably expect that the CSP plants at issue would benefit from the 'tariffs, premiums and lower and upper limits' established by RD 661/2007 for their entire operational lifetime. The Tribunal finds this expectation reasonable and legitimate. The Tribunal finds no evidence dated between 29 December 2010 and 23 June 2011 that could controvert the reasonability or legitimacy of Claimants' expectation in this regard. 442. The Tribunal is of the view that even a perfect analysis of such jurisprudence could not have led the Claimants to foresee that Respondent might abrogate the very tenets of the Original Regulatory Framework (i.e. the premium and the lower and upper limits) that it undertook to maintain unchanged for the CSP sector.
Climate change mention	113 'The development of renewable energy ("RE") in Spain dates back to the 1992 United Nations Framework Convention on Climate Change ("UNFCCC"). The European Union ("EU") and Spain signed the 1997 Kyoto Protocol, which was negotiated to implement the UNFCCC. The Protocol was signed by Spain on 29 April 1998 and ratified on 31 May 2002. It entered into force on 16 February 2005.'

<table>
<tr><td colspan="3">JGC Holdings Corporation (formerly JGC Corporation) v Kingdom of Spain, ICSID Case No. ARB/15/27, Award, 9 November 2021</td></tr>
<tr><td>Treaty</td><td colspan="2">ECT (1994)</td></tr>
<tr><td>Applicable Rules</td><td colspan="2">ICSID Arbitration Rules (2006)</td></tr>
<tr><td>Arbitrators</td><td colspan="2">P: Prof. Hi-Taek Shin – C: Prof. Dr. August Reinisch, Prof. Rudolf Dozer (replaced) – R: Prof. Dr. Mónica Pinto</td></tr>
<tr><td>Outcome</td><td>In favour of the investor
Amount claimed: EUR 161 million
Amount awarded: EUR 23.5 million</td><td>Valuation method: income-based approach (discounted cash flow) Interest rate: pre-award – 2.75%; post-award – 1.6% Costs of arbitration: N/A
Award legal costs: Claimant was awarded 40% of legal costs
Award costs of arbitration: Respondent bears 75% of the costs</td></tr>
<tr><td>Main Facts</td><td colspan="2">278 'The Claimant is one of Japan's biggest global engineering companies and specializes in the design and construction of large energy infrastructure projects around the world. Traditionally, JGC's business has been strongly focused on the hydrocarbons sector.'
279 'In 2010 the Claimant invested in two of the Spanish special purpose vehicle companies which own and operate CSP plants in Andalusia, Spain. The Claimant acquired 26% interests each in Solacor Electricidad Uno, S.A. which owns Solacor 1 plant, and Solacor Electricidad Dos, S.A. which owns Solacor 2 plant (Solacor Electricidad Uno, S.A and Solacor Electricidad Dos, S.A. will collectively referred to as "Solacor SPVs". The Solacor 1 and Solacor 2 plants, as previously indicated, will be collectively referred to as the "Solacor Plants" or "Solacor Projects", as appropriate). As of the closure of this arbitral proceedings, the Claimant has 13% interests each in Solacor SPVs.'</td></tr>
<tr><td>Legitimate expectations of the investor</td><td colspan="2">832 'The Tribunal considers that the stability promises in the domestic law and regulations such as Royal Decrees of the Respondent, as well as other official and informal assurances and representations made to attract investment could be the basis of establishing or reinforcing the Claimant's legitimate expectations on the stability of the regulatory regime relied on by the Claimant to be protected under international law. Previous tribunals took similar views, in particular when such stability promises were made to attract foreign investment.'
848 'None of the tribunals in Spanish renewable cases has considered that the existence of legitimate expectations would have the effect to freeze the legal order of the host State in relation to the investor; changes and adaptations of a limited magnitude would</td></tr>
</table>

	have to be made over time in response to changing circumstances, and an investor should not thereby be surprised.'
	854 'if specific commitments, promises or assurances have been made by the host State, the form, content, clarity and specificity of the commitment, promise or assurance determines the degree to which such a limitation applies to the host State's exercise of its sovereign right to amend or modify the regulatory framework relied on by the investors and that specific commitments are not just those addressed to a particular investor or group of investors, but also those which are "specific regarding their object and purpose".'
	855 'However, this Tribunal considers that an investor who knew, or should have known, at the time of his or her investment, that the host State would not be able or willing to respect the legal stability should not under all circumstances act on the assumption that the law would not change. The investor who made an investment in such circumstances could not have a legitimate expectation that the law or regulatory framework would not change. This maxim has been recognized by tribunals in the context of the change of Spanish legislation after 2010.'
	856 'This Tribunal considers, however, that the scope of application of this principle is significantly narrowed down by the recognition that, as a rule, an investor is entitled to believe that a State is able and willing to accept the previous expressions of its will and to honour its commitments.'
	1022 'The Tribunal does not find any evidence on the record of this proceeding that such changes were predictable and that the Claimant knew or should have known such changes in the future at the time of its investment.'
	1024 'The majority of the Tribunal considers that the reduction of the amount of the premium to a value in the pool plus premium option to zero was in breach of the specific commitment the Respondent made in Article 4 of RD 1614/2010 which included "premium" in the scope of the grandfathering clause. In the Tribunal's view, it was in effect an elimination of the option to choose the FiP given to the Special Regime producers, which was one of the essential characteristics of the remuneration regime relied on by the Claimant.'
	1025 'The majority of the Tribunal considers that the use of back-up fuel up to certain percentage of the total production and the annual updating mechanism for the values of the tariffs, premiums, supplements and the lower and upper limits using CPI as an index were essential elements of the remuneration regime under the RD 661/2007 and RD 1614/2010 relied on by the Claimant, irrespective of whether each of them could be deemed as a right under Spanish domestic law.'

Due diligence of the investor	870 'The Tribunal is of the view that the assessment of an investor's legitimate expectation should consider the totality of the regulatory framework relied on by the investor taking into account the stability commitments built in the laws and regulations, duly interpreted, and representations and assurances made by the host State to attract the investment from the international law perspective.' 973 'Having reviewed the Parties' respective submissions and the evidence on the record of this proceeding, the Tribunal considers that the Claimant conducted an *appropriate level of due diligence* expected of investors in similar circumstances.'
Climate change mention	894 'In the Tribunal's view, the 2005-2010 Energy Plan1156 approved in 2005 clearly illustrated the Respondent's continuing desire to promote renewable energies to fulfil the target of 29.4% set for Spain in the 2001 EU Renewable Directive. This plan indicated the Respondent's realization that the solar energy development was notably below its objective. The need for subsidies to promote investment in initial projects and the uncertainty regarding the institutions that could be sources of financing were identified as the economic barriers in the use of solar resources.' 427 'With respect to the Claimant's contention that the TVPEE sought to achieve a purpose entirely unrelated both to their stated environmental aim and to the aim of raising general revenue for the Respondent, this Tribunal does not find any credible basis to discredit the Respondent's submission that the revenue corresponding to the TVPEE is public revenue that is included in the Spanish General Budgets369, which, together with the other State revenue, contributes to form the State's resources with which public expenditures are financed.'

***Sevilla Beheer B.V. and others v Kingdom of Spain*, ICSID Case No. ARB/16/27, Decision on Jurisdiction, Liability And The Principles Of Quantum, 11 February 2022**		
Treaty	Energy Charter Treaty (1994)	
Applicable Rules	ICSID Arbitration Rules (2006)	
Arbitrators	P: Dr. Raëd Fathallah – R: Prof. Attila Tanzi – C: Prof. Peter D. Cameron (dissent)	
Outcome	In favour of the investor Amount claimed EUR 37.2 million	Costs of arbitration: Award legal costs: Award costs of arbitration: Parties share costs

	Amount awarded: EUR 6.76 million	equally, except for costs incurred from Respondent's Second Request for Reconsideration amounting to USD 15,000 to be borne by the Respondent.
Main Facts	110 'The Claimants are controlled by a Dutch national, Mr. Reinier Bouman, who is the majority owner of the Claimant entities and a CEO of Sevilla Beheer.' 113 'through Ra Solar, Cross Retail and the Spanish Project Companies Mr. Bouman acquired interests in the following five PV plants between 2007 and 2010: Mahora PV, Villar de Cañas PV, Ronda PV, Matapozuelos PV, and Fuentes de Año PV (the "PV Plants"), which had a total installed capacity of approximately 8.8 megawatts ("MW")'. 135 'The Respondent does not contest the facts related to the making and development of the Claimants' investments in Spain (other than the reasonableness of the Claimants' alleged investment costs (...). The Respondent however argues that the Claimants' decision to invest in the first PV Plant was not taken under the legal regime created by RD 661/2007 (...), but under the previous legal regime put in place by RD 439/2004 (...).'	
Legitimate expectations of the investor	*846* 'In the Tribunal's view, by majority, RD 661/2007 cannot be read as altering the conclusions reached earlier regarding RD 436/2004, namely that these Royal Decrees did not guarantee that the subsidy scheme would remain unmodified: the hierarchical position of these Royal Decrees as well as the relevant provisions of Law 54/1997 remained unchanged.' 875 'For these reasons, the Tribunal, by majority, concludes that the Claimants' primary claim based on the non-alteration of the FiT regime under RD 661/2007 and RD 1578/2008 cannot be upheld. Rather, the Tribunal considers that Spanish law contained indicators such as, for example, the 2005 Supreme Court Decision ...' 876 'In that sense, the replacement of the FiT scheme with the New Regime based on a different methodology was not prohibited under Spanish law. To the contrary, Spanish law explicitly allowed for the modification of a specific system of remuneration, subject to respecting the conditions set by Law 54/1997, namely the guarantee of a reasonable rate of return. Thus, the replacement of the FiT regime does not per se qualify as a modification so "drastic" or "unexpected" so as to constitute a violation of the FET obligation under the ECT and the stability obligation it subsumes.' 877 'At the same time, considering that reasonable profitability has indeed been guaranteed to the investors under Law 54/1997, the Claimants could legitimately expect to receive a reasonable rate of return.'	

	901 'In view of the Tribunal's earlier findings, by majority, that the only expectation that the Claimants could have legitimately had was the expectation of a reasonable return (see paragraphs 816-874 above), the Tribunal is therefore called to determine whether such a return was maintained for the Claimants' PV Plants despite the changes in the remuneration scheme introduced by the New Regime. In this regard, the Tribunal finds pertinent the following conclusion from the *PV Investors v Spain*: [...] the principle of reasonable return serves as the limit of ECT-compliant regulatory changes. If changes cross the "reasonable return" line, that is if they deprive investors of a reasonable return, the State conduct transgresses the standards contained in Article 10(1) of the ECT.'
Due diligence of the investor	*894* 'Based on the above, the Tribunal, by majority, finds it difficult to support the Claimants' position regarding the alleged sufficiency of their due diligence. Rather, the Tribunal, by majority, considers that the investors' conduct was not deterred by the signs of risk of potentially unfavourable regulatory changes that were apparent between 2005 and 2006, when Mr. Bouman started considering to invest in the Spanish market.'
Climate change mention	169 'Spain's initiatives to promote RE were undertaken in a broader context of intergovernmental efforts to tackle climate change that resulted in the adoption of the 1992 United Nations Framework Convention on Climate Change and the 1997 Kyoto Protocol. The EU was also receptive to the environmental concerns and adopted in 1997 a White Paper for a Community Strategy and Action Plan entitled "Energy for the future: renewable sources of energy."' 401(Context) Law 2/2011 also set out the principles of energy policy: Article 77. Principles of the energy policy. 1. The energy policy shall be oriented towards guaranteeing supply, economic efficiency and environmental sustainability. In particular, the model of energy consumption, generation and distribution should be compatible with EU regulations and targets, and with international efforts in the struggle against climate change. 860 'In addition, the Claimants argue that the legitimate character of their expectations is underlined by the fact that the Special Regime was part of a wider international and domestic policy of promoting renewable energy.' 861 'The Tribunal is generally sympathetic to this argument but finds it unpersuasive in the instant case. The Tribunal agrees with the reasoning expressed in *Allard v. Barbados*, according to which "consideration of a host State's international [environmental] obligations may well be relevant in the application of [a] standard to particular circumstances." This is in line with the general consideration that obligations stemming from a treaty with investment provisions, such as the ECT, "has to be construed in harmony with other rules of international law of which it forms part".'

	862 'However, the fact that a State is bound by international obligations in the field of environmental law and participates in the international debate concerning renewable energy sources does not as such give rise to a "State representation." A fortiori, such a participation can hardly be construed as creating an expectation that FiTs granted under a host State's legal framework at a given time could not be modified or replaced by another subsidy system in the future. At best, such a participation could be said to reinforce an expectation that any adjustment measures taken by a host State remain within the realm of reasonableness.'

<table>
<tr><th colspan="3">RENERGY S.à.r.l. v Kingdom of Spain, ICSID Case No. ARB/14/18, Award, 6 May 2022</th></tr>
<tr><td>Treaty</td><td colspan="2">ECT (1994)</td></tr>
<tr><td>Applicable Rules</td><td colspan="2">ICSID Arbitration Rules (2006)</td></tr>
<tr><td>Arbitrators</td><td colspan="2">Chair: Judge Bruno Simma – C: Prof. Christoph Schreuer – R: Prof. Philippe Sands, Q.C.</td></tr>
<tr><td>Outcome</td><td>In favour of the investor
Amount claimed: EUR 141 million
Amount awarded: EUR 32,896,240</td><td>Valuation method: income-based approach (discounted cash flow)
Interest rate: host State's sovereign bonds (10-year)
Costs of arbitration: USD 1,801,865.44
Award legal costs: Each party bears its own legal costs
Award costs of arbitration: Parties share costs equally</td></tr>
<tr><td>Main Facts</td><td colspan="2">118 'For the purpose of holding investments of Mr. Gerardo David Gómez-Sáinz García ("Mr. Gómez") in the renewable energy sector in Spain, the Spanish limited liability company Inversiones Dagosa S.L.U. ("Dagosa") was incorporated in 1997. In 1999, Mr. Gómez and a partner decided to start promoting wind farms at the Spanish communities of Hedroso-Aciberos (…).'
121 On 6 November 2007, the Claimant acquired from Mr Gómez 100% shareholding interest in Condeu for a price of EUR 72 million.
122 On 10 September 2009, the Claimant acquired from Condeu as a dividend in kind 100% of interest in Dagosa, valued at approximately EUR 5.43 million.
126 'On 21 November 2007, the Claimant purchased from Dagosa a 33.33% shareholding interest in Iberéolica Solar S.L. ("Iberéolica Solar"), a limited liability company incorporated under Spanish law, for an amount of EUR 1 million.'</td></tr>
</table>

Legitimate expectations of the investor	912 '[T]he Tribunal's view is that a diligent investor in wind and CSP projects would, at the time the Claimant invested, have expected that in case of a global and severe economic crisis and a steep incline of the Tariff Deficit, the Respondent would adopt measures to safeguard the sustainability of the SES. A diligent investor would also have expected that those measures might adversely affect even existing wind and CSP projects, as had previous reforms in Spain. The Tribunal finds, however, that no diligent investor would have expected measures with such far-reaching effects on investments as the Disputed Measures. Specifically, no investor could have anticipated that the Respondent would change the level of remuneration and the entire remunerative system as dramatically and as abruptly as it did, resulting in an adverse impact on the Claimant's investment that, taking into account all circumstances, the Tribunal considers to be dispropriate even in the face of the economic crisis prevailing at the time. Therefore, the Tribunal finds that the Disputed Measures were a radical departure from RF1 and thus violated the ECT's FET standard by thwarting the Claimant's legitimate expectation of Relative Stability.'
Due diligence of the investor	707 'The Tribunal agrees with the Respondent that, based on the record, the Claimant's legal due diligence in preparation of its investment was very limited, to say the least. However, *the Tribunal does not consider that a lack of legal due diligence is an indication of the Claimant not having relied on the expectation of Relative Stability. Rather, if at all, a lack of legal due diligence could raise the question of whether such reliance was misplaced, i.e., whether the expectation relied upon was not legitimate.* In this regard, however, the Tribunal wishes to stress that legislative change only violates the notion of Relative Stability if it exceeds the margin of change that a diligent investor – who, by definition, conducted sufficient due diligence – could have foreseen. Accordingly, legal due diligence on the part of the investor would not lead the investor to expect anything else than Relative Stability. In other words, even if one considered that the ECT imposed a duty of a formal due diligence on investors and even if the Claimant breached such duty, there would be no causal link between this breach and the legitimacy of the expectation of Relative Stability. Under these circumstances, the Tribunal finds that any lack of due diligence is not an obstacle to the Claimant relying on the Relative Stability of the regulatory framework under which it invested.' 708 'This being so, the Tribunal does not find it necessary to make a finding on whether the Claimant's legal due diligence did in fact meet the standards required of a diligent investor. Irrespective of whether this was the case, the Claimant placed reliance on the legitimate expectation of Relative Stability.'

<table>
<tr><td>Climate change mention</td><td>899 'While the Claimant may be correct that there would have been different ways in which the Respondent could have tackled the Tariff Deficit, e.g. through network access tolls or by levying a CO2 tax, it is not for the Tribunal to pass judgment on what would have been the best policy decision for the Respondent to take.'

Dissent on Liability and Quantum of Professor Phillippe Sands QC

1 '[A]s it faced a grave financial crisis and sought to balance the competing interests of protecting the environment (by encouraging the use of renewable energy sources), safeguarding the legitimate interests of investors, and preventing the collapse of the public purse.'

46 'In short, the Claimant was not deprived of their investments, although the income generated was reduced. In my view, the reduction fell within "the acceptable margin of change"; against the background of the economic and environmental challenges urgently faced by Spain, and the generous rates of return offered by RD 661/2007, which created a bubble of significant profitability for investors, Spain opted instead for a balanced approach. It did so supported by decisions of its own Supreme Court, some of which were known to the Claimant before it made its investment.'</td></tr>
</table>

<table>
<tr><td colspan="3">Matthias Kruck and others v Kingdom of Spain, ICSID Case No ARB/15/23, Decision on Jurisdiction, Liability and Principles of Quantum, 14 September 2022</td></tr>
<tr><td>Treaty</td><td colspan="2">ECT (1994)</td></tr>
<tr><td>Applicable Rules</td><td colspan="2">ICSID Arbitration Rules (2006)</td></tr>
<tr><td>Arbitrators</td><td colspan="2">P: Prof. Vaughan Lowe, K.C. – C: Dr. Michael Pryles A.O., P.B.M., Gary Born (replaced) – R: Prof. Zachary Douglas, K.C.</td></tr>
<tr><td>Outcome</td><td>In favour of the investor

Amount claimed: EUR 67.481 million

Amount awarded: EUR 15,019,540</td><td>Costs of arbitration: US$ 1,083,839.10

Award legal costs and award costs of arbitration: Respondent should pay its own costs and contribution to the costs of the Tribunal and pay to the Claimants three-fifths of the Claimants' costs (including the Claimants' contribution to the costs of the Tribunal), i.e., EUR 2,885,356.85 plus US$ 340,151.73.</td></tr>
<tr><td>Main Facts</td><td colspan="2">45 'In the light of the success of RD 661/2007, further legislation was adopted in 2008. RD 1578/2008 was adopted on 26 September 2008. By that time, each of the companies who are Claimants 1-20 (referring to the list at paragraph 5, above) had, on 28 February 2008, purchased the assets of one of the Project Alcolea PV plants</td></tr>
</table>

	through the Claimant company's wholly-owned Spanish subsidiary.42 Similarly, Claimants 21-35 had, on 21 August 2008, each purchased the assets of one of the Project Calasparra PV plants; and each of Claimants 36-65, also on 21 August 2008, had purchased the assets of one of the Project Tordesillas PV plants, and again in each case through the Claimant company's wholly-owned Spanish subsidiary.43 The position of Claimant 66 (DSG Deutsche Solargesellschaft mbH), Claimant 67 (DSG Spanien Verwaltungs GmbH), Claimant 68 (Mr. Mathias Kruck), Claimant 69 (Mr. Joachim Kruck), Claimant 70 (Mr. Peter Flachsmann), Claimant 71 (Mr. Ralf Hofman), Claimant 72 (Mr. Rolf Schumm), and Claimant 73 (Mr. Frank Schumm) is more complicated; but, anticipating conclusions reached below,44 it can be said that for practical purposes all of their investments that are material and in principle compensable in the present case were made under the regulatory regime established by RD 661/2007.'
Legitimate expectations of the investor	193 'No-one questions that Spain had the legal capacity to change the regulatory regime. The question is whether it was fair and equitable to do so in a manner that caused harm to certain investors who had relied on representations that Spain would not exercise that undoubted power in relation to their investments.' 202 'The Tribunal accepts the main thrust of that argument, subject to the qualification that modifications to the regime that did not affect its fundamental characteristics could be adopted by Spain without breaching the legitimate expectations of those who had invested on the basis of RD 661/2007. Those fundamental characteristics, in the view of the Tribunal, included the predetermined tariffs, independent of the actual amounts invested in constructing and operating each PV facility and independent of past profits derived from the facility, fixed for a definite period of time which approximated to the useful life of a PV facility, and with no minimum or maximum limit on the returns for each plant Spain's commitment was that those fundamentals would not be abrogated.' 204 'It is obvious that no investment made before the adoption of RD 661/2007 could be said to have been made in reliance upon it, and that Spain cannot incur liability based on the doctrine of legitimate expectations in relation to such an investment. While some investors, including some or all of the Claimants, may have been following the evolution of Spain's compensation framework for renewable energy for many months before the adoption of RD 661/2007 on 25 May 2007, investments made before its final adoption were necessarily speculative, and made in the hope that what became RD 661/2007 would indeed be enacted in such a form as to provide favourable and secure terms for investors.'

	Partial Dissenting Opinion by Prof. Zachary Douglas KC 5 'In summary: the concept of legitimate expectations has no textual embodiment in the ECT and in investment treaties more generally. Unless it is accepted that arbitrators have the power to legislate for new grounds for liability under investment treaties (i.e. the power just to make it up), then the only path to a doctrine of legitimate expectations through the FET standard is by interpretation. The terms "fair and equitable" cannot be interpreted to mean the arbitrators' subjective notions of what is fair and equitable on any given day. But the FET standard can conceivably be interpreted as encompassing general grounds for liability in damages against public authorities as recognised by the major legal systems of the world (or by "*civilised nations*" if the more archaic language of Article 38 of the ICJ's Statute is to be preferred). No legal system imposes strict liability in damages for a breach of legitimate expectations; it is always based on fault. There is no reason in principle for international investment law to take a radically different approach.' 6 'The failure to incorporate an element of fault into the assessment of legitimate expectations in many decisions has led to the creation of a unique no-fault compensation scheme for foreign investors disappointed with the profitability of their projects. There is no evidence to suggest that state parties to investment treaties ever envisaged such a possibility and there is no legal or moral justification for tribunals to redistribute public funds on this basis.' 113 'In my preferred approach, the concept of a reasonable rate of return would play an important role in the proportionality assessment. In determining whether the disputed measure placed a disproportionate burden on the investor, it would be highly relevant to assess whether the investor continued to earn a reasonable rate of return after the disputed measure came into force. This again would breathe life into the voluminous exchanges between the quantum experts in this case as to what the "target" rate of return was for PV investments under RD 661/2007, what the average rate of return is for such investments on a comparative basis, and what rate of return the Claimants' projects are now earning under the new regime.'
Due diligence of the investor	191 'The Tribunal has reached this conclusion on the basis of its reading of RD 661/2007, and other materials relating to that Decree. It does, however, consider that investors must undertake appropriate due diligence before relying on assurances and commitments of this kind. This need not involve detailed analysis by national or international experts in the relevant field.'

Climate change mention	29 'Spain had set its national energy policy in a series of National Energy Plans, beginning in 1975, with the Plan for the years 1991-2000 ("*PEN 1991*") including provisions regarding the development of renewable energy production.8 The need for such development was brought into sharper focus by the work associated with the 1992 United Nations Framework Convention on Climate Change, and in particular by the 1997 Kyoto Protocol on greenhouse gases. In 2001, EU Directive 2001/77/EC set targets for the proportion of its energy that each Member State was to derive from renewable sources. Spain, which in 1997 derived around 19.9% of its energy from renewable sources, was given a target of 29.4%, to be achieved by 2020.9 That target sat alongside Spain's obligations under EU Law, which limit the grant of State Aid.' *Partial Dissenting Opinion by Prof. Zachary Douglas KC* 57 'Third, in an era where radical reforms in the energy sector are not only desirable but necessary for the sustainability of human life on Earth, it seems incongruous now to be interpreting the FET standard as requiring States to buy back their right to implement those reforms at the highest price. In this case the investment is in renewable energy. But if the strict liability approach is generalised (and there is no principled basis for limiting it to cases involving renewable energy), then the public interest considerations behind any reform are by definition irrelevant to the determination of liability in damages. The regulatory chill that inevitably accompanies this approach will be no consolation to a warming planet.'

Italian Cases

Blusun S.A., *Jean-Pierre Lecorcier and Michael Stein v Italian Republic*, ICSID Case No. ARB/14/3, Award (27 December 2016)		
Treaty	ECT (1994)	
Applicable Rules	ICSID Arbitration Rules (2006)	
Arbitrators	P: Judge James Crawford, A.C. – C: Dr. Stanimir Alexandrov – R: Prof. Pierre-Marie Dupuy	
Outcome	In favour of the state Amount claimed: EUR 187.8 million Amount awarded: ZERO	Costs of arbitration: USD 608,821.38 Award legal costs: Each party bears its own legal costs Award costs of arbitration: Parties share costs equally

Main Facts	83 'Blusun completed the acquisition of the 12 local companies through Eskosol between 18 May and 23 July 2010, as Eskosol signed the relevant final share purchase agreements. Prior to the constitution of Blusun, SIB and Eskosol, the 12 local development companies had obtained land rights through land sale and purchase agreements and through a series of long-term lease agreements with land owners.'
Legitimate expectations of the investor	373 '[A] reasonable market expectation as to some state of affairs, justified or not, is not a basis for shifting risks to the public sector, i.e. the state budget. Circumstances change and in the absence of specific commitments, the risk of change is for entrepreneurs to assess and assume.' Applying this standard, the tribunal found that Italy had made no such special commitment to the investors with respect to the incentive scheme. (374.) 374 'To conclude, the Respondent made no special commitment to the Claimants with respect to the extension and operation of FITs, nor did it specifically undertake that relevant Italian laws would remain unchanged. For these reasons the Claimants have not established a breach of Article 10(1), second sentence, of the ECT.' 386 '[T]he [investor's] Project ran a significant risk of incurring legal or administrative difficulties, even if these could be (and in the event largely were) overcome. Its success was by no means certain.'
Due diligence of the investor	319 '[The question is whether the Disputed Measures operated] in a manner which is not disproportionate to the aim of the legislative amendment and should have due regard to the reasonable reliance interests of recipients who may have committed substantial resources on the basis of the earlier regime.' (*Blusun v Italy* (Award), para. 372, RL-0105, endorsed in *RREEF v Spain* (Decision on Responsibility), para. 516, CL-0239.) 372 'In the absence of a specific commitment, the state has no obligation to grant subsidies such as feed-in tariffs, or to maintain them unchanged once granted. But if they are lawfully granted, and if it becomes necessary to modify them, this should be done in a manner which is not disproportionate to the aim of the legislative amendment, and should have due regard to the reasonable reliance interests of recipients who may have committed substantial resources on the basis of the earlier regime. These considerations apply even more strongly when the context is subsidies or the payment of special benefits for particular economic sectors.'
Climate change mention	No direct mention.

<table>
<tr><td colspan="3">Greentech Energy Systems A/S; NovEnergia II Energy & Environment (S.C.A.) SICAR; NovEnergia II Italian Portfolio S.A. v Italy, SSC Case No. 2015/095, Award, 5 December 2018</td></tr>
<tr><td>Treaty</td><td colspan="2">ECT (1994)</td></tr>
<tr><td>Applicable Rules</td><td colspan="2">SCC Rules of Arbitration</td></tr>
<tr><td>Arbitrators</td><td colspan="2">P: Prof. William Park – C: Mr. David Haigh, Q.C. – R: Prof. Giorgio Sacerdoti (dissent)</td></tr>
<tr><td>Outcome</td><td>In favour of the investor

Amount claimed: EUR 25.06 million

Amount awarded: EUR 11.9 million</td><td>Valuation method: income-based approach (discounted cash flow)

Interest rate: LIBOR (annual) + 2%

Costs of arbitration: EUR 490,479 + USD 2,325

Award legal costs: Claimants were awarded EUR 1,408,268 (50% of legal costs)

Award costs of arbitration: Costs follow the award</td></tr>
<tr><td>Main Facts</td><td colspan="2">See paras 132 to 136 In late 2008, NovEnergia and NIP began developing PV projects in Italy. From 2010 to 2013, they invested in fifty-two PV projects, held as of 1 January 2015. (...)

134 'Each of the PV facilities acquired by HFV was either already receiving incentive tariffs or was eligible to receive them under the Conto Energia decrees.66 Some of those facilities also benefitted from minimum guaranteed prices under the off-take regime. HFV acquired those facilities over the course of 2010, 2011, 2012, and 2013. In addition to the fifty PV projects held through HFV, NovEnergia and NIP invested directly in two PV projects, which were eligible to receive incentives under Conto IV and minimum guaranteed prices under the off-take regime.'

136 'The total combined capacity of those plants exceeded 90 MW. In acquiring and developing those fifty-two plants, NovEnergia and NIP invested more than EUR 175 million.'</td></tr>
<tr><td>Legitimate expectations of the investor</td><td colspan="2">448 'Respondent has not provided any persuasive reason to conclude that despite entitlement to the incentive tariffs, an investor, when making the investment, should not expect the tariffs to remain constant. While the investor might need to live with some minor adjustments, nothing alerted the Claimants that they would need to accept changes of the magnitude imposed by the Spalma-incentivi Decree.'

449 'When Claimants invested in the PV facilities, they received assurances which were not subject to any reservation of a discretion to change the rate of return as effected by the Spalma-incentivi Decree.'</td></tr>
</table>

	450 'While Italy submitted that its "right to regulate" must be balanced against the need to protect investors' legitimate expectations, such arguments appear to miss the point in this context. The repeated and precise assurances to specific investors amounted to guarantees that the tariffs would remain fixed for two decades. Italy effectively waived its right to reduce the value of the tariffs.' 451 'The better view must be that Italy's assurances constituted non-waivable guarantees. Italy thus crossed a threshold such that the reduction of the incentive tariffs by the Spalma-incentivi Decree defeated Claimants' legitimate expectations.'
Due diligence of the investor	No direct mention of due diligence obligations by the investor.
Climate change mention	105 'In 1998, Italy signed the Kyoto Protocol to the United Nations Framework Convention on Climate Change and committed to reduce carbon dioxide emissions by 8% by the end of 2012.' 106 'On 27 September 2001, the European Parliament and Council enacted Directive 2001/77/EC, requiring Member States to "take appropriate steps to encourage greater consumption of electricity produced from renewable energy sources ...." The Directive listed reference values by which the Member States were supposed to adopt "national indicative targets" for the consumption of renewable energy to be achieved by 2010. The reference values for the European Community and Italy were 22% and 25%, respectively.' 665 'The Tribunal considers that Law 54/1997 and RD 661/2007 were clearly enacted with the objective of ensuring that the Kingdom of Spain achieved its emissions and RE targets. In order to achieve that objective, the Kingdom of Spain created a very favourable investment climate for RE investors, and the nucleus of such investment climate was the Special Regime. The requirements placed on the PV plants to qualify for the Special Regime were limited to registration with the RAIPRE, a requirement which all of the PV Plants had met within the prescribed cut-off date.'

***CEF Energia BV v Italian Republic*, SCC Case No. 158/2015, Award, 16 January 2019**	
Treaty	ECT (1994)
Applicable Rules	SCC Rules of Arbitration
Arbitrators	P: Mr. Klaus Reichert - C: Prof. Dr. Klaus Sachs v R: Prof. Giorgio Sacerdoti

<table>
<tr><td rowspan="1">Outcome</td><td>In favour of the investor
Amount claimed: EUR 10.3 million (with respect to the Enersol PV plant only)
Amount awarded: EUR 9.6 million (with respect to the Enersol, the Tribunal having excluded compensation for the Megasol and Phenix plants, see para 268).</td><td>Valuation method: income-based approach (discounted cash flow)
Interest rate: LIBOR (annual) + 2%
Costs of arbitration: EUR 589 276.07
Award legal costs: Claimant was awarded EUR 900,000
Award costs of arbitration: Respondent bears its own share of costs of arbitration and EUR 100,000 of the claimant's share</td></tr>
<tr><td>Main Facts</td><td colspan="2">151 'In January 2010, Claimant acquired Sunholding S.r.l. ("Sunholding"). Sunholding owned Megasol S.r.l., a company that held all project rights to a photovoltaic plant of approximately 13 MW located in Montalto di Castro in the Lazio region ("Megasol"). The Megasol photovoltaic plant was connected to the grid in May 2011 and under Conto II, as i 1: received an incentive tariff of confirmed by a GSE Agreement dated 2 November 2011. Claimant's acquisition of Sunholding, therefore, pre-dated the relevant GSE Agreement.'
156 'In December 2010, Claimant acquired a 70% controlling stake in Phenix S.r.l. ("Phenix"), a company that held all project rights to a photovoltaic plant of approximately 24 MW located in Canino in the Lazio region ("Sugarella"). The Sugarella photovoltaic plant was connected to the grid in April 2011 and was entitled to an incentive under Conto III, as confirmed by a GSE Agreement dated 23 November 2011. Claimant's acquisition of that 70% controlling stake in Phenix, therefore, pre-dated the relevant GSE Agreement.'
161 'On 30 March 20122, Claimant acquired Enersol S.r.L, a company that held all project rights to a multi-section photovoltaic plant of approximately 48 MW located in Canaro in the Veneto region ("Enersol"). The Enersol photovoltaic plant was partitioned in seven sections. Section 1 of the plant was connected to the grid in April 2011, and was entitled to an incentive tariff of (redacted) under Conto III, as confirmed by a GSE Agreement dated 2 November 2011.'</td></tr>
<tr><td>Legitimate expectations of the investor</td><td colspan="2">217. Claimant's expectation was based on 'a clear promise of twenty years of constant currency incentives pursuant to a private law contract'.
220 'It is also important to differentiate the situation of Claimant as on 30 March 2012 in respect of Enersol with that of the claimant in Blusun. That claimant was, unlike Claimant and its investment in Enersol, still at a preliminary stage of its attempts to invest in the Italian photovoltaic market. That led to it falling at the first legal hurdle for causation as a matter of Article 10(1) of the ECT before</td></tr>
</table>

	that tribunal which found (para. 386) that: [T]o conclude, in the Tribunal's view, the Project ran a significant risk of incurring legal or administrative difficulties, even if these could be (and in the event largely were) overcome. Its success was by no means certain.' 243 'It is readily apparent to the Tribunal that the greater the level of engagement as between a sovereign and an investor, such as here through Respondent's undertaking to maintain a specific incentivized tariff for 20 years, ultimately resulting in legitimate expectations which are clear in both scope and origin, the more rigorous the scrutiny must be of acts which, even if reasonable, cut across those legitimate expectations.'
Due diligence of the investor	209 'As on 30 March 2012, when Claimant bought Enersol, what can be objectively identified as unquestionably in place and explicitly known to it?' 225 'The Tribunal readily, therefore, sees that Claimant relied on the circumstances of Enersol (described above) when deciding whether or not to invest. All of the matters set out in both the Legal Due Diligence Report and the Serenissima presentation carefully record the circumstances of Enersol and, therefore, reliance can well be understood to have been reasonable.'
Climate change mention	Mentions in factual background targets of 25% total electricity consumption by Italy from renewable sources by 2010. 123 'In line with Respondent's goal of making photovoltaic investments more competitive until the technology matured and their costs decreased, Conto II stated that the Ministry of Economic Development would issue a subsequent decree revising the incentive tariffs for photovoltaic plants connected to the grid after 2010, taking into account energy products and component price trends as well as technological monitoring from the ENEA. In practice, through the Salva Alcoa decree (Law Decree 8 July 2010, n. 105), Respondent later extended the Conto II incentive tariffs to plants entering into operation after 2010.'

***SunReserve Luxco Holdings SRL v Italy*, SCC Case No. 132/2016, Final Award, 25 March 2020**	
Treaty	ECT (1994)
Applicable Rules	SCC Rules of Arbitration
Arbitrators	P: Prof. Dr. Albert Jan van den Berg – C: Prof. Dr. Klaus Sachs – R: Prof. Andrea Giardina

<table>
<tr><td>Outcome</td><td>In favour of the state
Amount claimed: EUR 40.89 million
Amount awarded: ZERO</td><td>Costs of arbitration: EUR 393,169.44
Award legal costs: Respondent was awarded EUR 990,000 (75% of legal costs)
Award costs of arbitration: Costs follow the award</td></tr>
<tr><td>Main Facts</td><td colspan="2">189 'Between 2010 and 2011, the First Claimant, i.e., SunReserve Luxco Holdings S.À.R.L, acquired a total of seven photovoltaic plants in Italy, which constituted a portfolio of 27.7 MW. In this process, according to Claimants, the First Claimant invested more than EUR 61 million.'</td></tr>
<tr><td>Legitimate expectations of the investor</td><td colspan="2">683 'First, the Tribunal considers that fairness and/or equitability are not absolute concepts that are capable of being reduced to universally applicable definitions. Instead, what constitutes fair and/or equitable treatment is a question to be determined by taking into account all circumstances of a given case.'
684 'Second, stability and transparency in the legal framework are important ingredients of the host State's FET obligation. This is evidenced not only from the above discussed context and object and purpose of the ECT, but is also unanimously accepted in investment arbitration case law.'
685 'Third, keeping in mind that the FET obligation requires all relevant circumstances to be considered in a case (see 683 above), the objectives of creating a stable, transparent and favourable legal framework for investments are required to be balanced against the host State's right to regulate.'
725 'Therefore, the Tribunal concludes that the precise timing of the investor's decision to make (or expand) the investment(s) remains the focal point in time to examine the existence and scope of any legitimate expectations created by the host State and relied upon by the investor, regardless of whether the investment(s) were made as one-stop transactions or multi-step processes.'
817 'While that general statements can create legitimate expectations in theory (see 699-703 above), the general statements made to the public in order to advertise a particular regulatory regime can only create expectations, if any, that are in line with the regulatory regime itself. These public statements cannot bind the State to commitments above and beyond the legal regime in existence.'</td></tr>
<tr><td>Due diligence of the investor</td><td colspan="2">714 'This placement of the burden of proof is in line with investment arbitration case law. The standard of due diligence that investors are expected to adhere to should meet the threshold of what a "prudent investor" would "reasonably" do to know about regulatory framework in question. This standard of reasonable due diligence, as opposed to "extensive legal investigation", has found</td></tr>
</table>

	the endorsement of many tribunals, including the tribunal in Electrabel v Hungary (quoted in 708 above) and several others in more recent cases. A more specific articulation of this standard, with which the Tribunal agrees, can be found in the Antaris v Czech Republic award, in the following passage: "Given the State's regulatory powers, in order to rely on legitimate expectations the investor should inquire in advance regarding the prospects of a change in the regulatory framework in light of the then prevailing or reasonably to be expected changes in the economic and social conditions of the host State."'
Climate change mention	99 'In February 1998, the EC prepared a report in relation to this EC Directive 96/92/EC, specifically concerning renewable energy and the EU's targets under the Kyoto Protocol, which had been adopted in December 1997. In this connection, the EC's report, inter alia, stated that pursuant to "the 'Third Conference of the Parties to the United Nations framework on Climate Change' ... held in Kyoto in December 1997 ... the [EC] agreed to a commitment of an 8% reduction of greenhouse gas emissions for the period 2008 to 2012 compared to 1990." This would require "major energy policy decisions, focusing on reducing energy and carbon intensity", and "accelerating the penetration of renewable energy sources in the production of electricity".' 100 'Italy signed the Kyoto Protocol in 1998.30 Shortly thereafter, in April 1999, Italy's National Agency for New Technologies, Energy and Sustainable Economic Development issued a White Paper for the development of renewable energy sources.31 The White Paper considered numerous principle and strategy matters relating to the growth of renewable energy in Italy, while recognizing the EU's targets as well.' 101 'Pertinently, the White Paper laid out a target of "additional contribution of renewables of approximately 8.6 Mtoe running from 11.7 Mtoe to 20.3 Mtoe for 2008-2012 in terms of substituted conventional fuel."' Further, in respect of photovoltaic solar energy, while recognizing that significant research is required in this field, which was still in its 'young' stage, the White Paper, inter alia, stated the following:

***Silver Ridge Power B.V. v* Italy, ICSID Case No. ARB/15/37, Award, 26 February 2021**	
Treaty	ECT (1994)
Applicable Rules	ICSID Arbitration Rules (2006)
Arbitrators	P: Judge Bruno Simma - C: Judge Thomas Johnson - R: Prof. Bernardo Cremades

Outcome	In favour of the state Amount claimed: N/A Amount awarded: ZERO	Costs of arbitration: USD 1,120,871.78 Award legal costs: Each party bears its own legal costs Award costs of arbitration: Parties share costs equally
Main Facts	*See paras 107-109* Silver Ridge Power BV, a Dutch private limited company, indirectly owned Silver Ridge Power Italia s.r.l., which controlled ten local development companies operating 25 PV plants in Italy. These plants became operational between September 2010 and May 2012. Each plant entered into 'GSE conventions' with Gestore dei Servizi Energetici S.p.A. (GSE). All the plants benefited from feed-in tariffs under the Second, Third, Fourth, and Fifth Energy Accounts. Additionally, most plants participated in the off-take regime, with some qualifying for minimum guaranteed prices.	
Legitimate expectations of the investor	396 'Applying the aforementioned regime of treaty interpretation to Article 10(1), second sentence, of the ECT, the ordinary meaning of the term "fair and equitable treatment" contains a clear indication that the host State is not free to act vis-à-vis investors protected under the ECT *ad libitum* or to interfere with their rights and assets at its whim. At the same time, the general nature of the words "fair" and "equitable" suggests that the protection of the investors' position is not absolute and unqualified, but rather a matter of degree and balancing.' 452 'Against this background, the Tribunal is satisfied that the Respondent, when adopting the Spalma-incentivi Decree, could plausibly claim to have acted on the basis of legitimate public policy objectives, notably strengthening the sustainability of the incentive tariff scheme for renewable energy in a situation of economic difficulty. In that sense, the measures taken by the Respondent in response to these challenges, in particular the Spalma-incentivi Decree, can claim to be reasonable.' 457 'In this regard, the Tribunal agrees with the submission of the Respondent (Resp. Counter-Memorial, paras 394-395) that a prudent investor acting in a highly regulated market such as the electricity market must, in the course of its risk assessment, analyze and take into consideration the whole range of potential advantages and disadvantages associated with the dynamics of the market which might also call for policy adjustments on the part of the host State. Having said that, this does not mean that every turn of policy must be anticipated. In particular, even the reasonable and circumspect investor must not anticipate radical change, which takes the Tribunal to the third step of its analysis.'	

	474 'Against this background, the Tribunal concludes that the changes brought about by the Respondent's adoption of the *Spalma-incentivi* Decree (notably the 8 % FIT reduction applied to the Claimant's PV plants from 1 January 2015 on) were, considering all relevant elements of the case, reasonable, foreseeable and proportionate and did therefore not constitute a fundamental or radical alteration of the applicable legal framework to the detriment of the investor. Thus, the corresponding legitimate expectation of the Claimant was not frustrated and the fair and equitable treatment claim based on the *Spalma-incentivi* Decree must be rejected.'
Due diligence of the investor	437 'a circumspect and reasonable investor to believe that the incentive tariff regime created by the Respondent would remain intact in its overall structure and its essential elements, i.e., that it would not be subject to fundamental or radical changes to the detriment of the investors'. 443 'In the Tribunal's view, in spite of certain contentions on the part of the Respondent to the contrary (see para. 353), the quality of the Claimant's due diligence efforts does not raise any concerns regarding the reasonableness of the Claimant's reliance on the Respondent's commitment to protect the Claimant from fundamental or radical modifications of the legal framework applicable to it.'
Climate change mention	113 'On 27 September 2001, the European Parliament and the Council adopted Directive 2001/77/EC, the "First Renewables Directive", in order to reduce greenhouse gas emissions and to meet the international targets set by the Kyoto Protocol.'

***ESPF Beteiligungs GmbH, ESPF Nr. 2 Austria Beteiligungs GmbH, and InfraClass Energie 5 GmbH & Co. KG v Italian Republic*, ICSID Case No. ARB/16/5, Award, 14 September 2021**		
Treaty	ECT (1994)	
Applicable Rules	ICSID Arbitration Rules (2006)	
Arbitrators	P: Mr. Henri Alvarez, Q.C. – C: Dr. Micheal Pyres – R: Prof. Laurence Boisson de Chazournes	
Outcome	In favour of the investor Amount claimed: EUR 28.6 million Amount awarded: EUR 16 million	Valuation method: income-based approach (discounted cash flow) Interest rate: annual EURIBOR + 4% Costs of arbitration: USD 913,142.58 Award legal costs: Claimants were awarded EUR 1,758,577 (60% of legal costs)

<table>
<tr><td></td><td></td><td>Award costs of arbitration: Costs follow the award</td></tr>
<tr><td>Main Facts</td><td colspan="2">143 ‘In 2010-2012, ICE 5 invested in three projects owning 102 PV plants. The first project, consisting of 100 plants, was known as Carlino 2 and was acquired on 20 December 2010. It entered into operation in April 2011. Twenty-five plants qualified for an incentive tariff of €0.3460/kWh for 20 years under Conto II, while the other 75 plants obtained a tariff of €0.3210/kWh for 20 years under Conto III; all of which was confirmed by DLA Piper in its due diligence report.’

144 ‘ICE 5 also acquired the 10-section Torina plant, which entered into operation in April 2011 and obtained an incentive tariff of €0.3460/kWh for 20 years under Conto II.’

145 ‘In September 2012, ICE 5 acquired a PV plant called Ginosa, which had entered into operation in October 2011, and qualified for a tariff of €0.2120/kWh for 20 years under Conto IV.’

146 ‘The GSE Letters and subsequent GSE Agreements confirmed the applicable incentive tariff rate and duration for each facility.166 147. By the end of 2012, ICE 5 had invested €110.9 million in 102 plants, with an overall capacity of 22 MW.’</td></tr>
<tr><td>Legitimate expectations of the investor</td><td colspan="2">444 ‘The Tribunal finds that the FET standard includes multiple sub-standards, including the protection of legitimate expectations, consistency and transparency, and good faith.’

465 ‘As a result, the Tribunal concludes that the incentive tariff scheme implemented by the Legislative Decrees and the Conto Energia Decrees was an ex-ante regime which provided for specific fixed tariff rates for a period of 20 years for qualifying investors.’

508 ‘For the reasons set out below, the majority of the Tribunal has concluded that it was unfair or inequitable for the Respondent to have reduced the FIT rates set out in the relevant Conto Energia Decrees and said to be constant for twenty years after the Claimants’ investments had qualified for those tariffs. The majority of the Tribunal finds that, at the time they invested, the Claimants had the legitimate expectation that the PV plants in which they invested would benefit from the specific tariff set out in the relevant Conto Energia Decrees and then reflected in the GSE Letters and GSE Agreements for a period of 20 years.’

512 ‘In the Tribunal’s view, there is no doubt that a clear and specific commitment is required in order to create an enforceable legitimate expectation. However, in the majority’s view, there is no reason in principle why such a commitment of the requisite clarity and specificity cannot be made in the regulation itself where (as here) such a commitment is made for the purpose of inducing investment, which succeeded in attracting the Claimants’ investments and, once made, resulted in losses to the Claimants.’</td></tr>
</table>

Due diligence of the investor	513 'Legitimate expectations are based on the investor's objective understanding of the legal framework within which the investor has made its investment or, in other words, what a reasonable investor at the time would have expected.' 540 'In the majority's view, in light of the clear language of the Conto Energia Decrees, the GSE Letters and GSE Agreements, the statements in the investment memorandum do not reflect a failure in the Claimants' due diligence or a relevant risk which should have affected the Claimants' expectations or decision to invest in Italy.' 537 'None of the due diligence reports indicates that the tariff rates are subject to modification. As noted above, the Respondent maintains that if the due diligence had involved an assessment of the risks of the modification of the Conto Energia Decrees, conducted by Italian lawyers, they would have disclosed that long-term regulatory schemes are subject to modification under Italian law. In this regard, it referred to the 2017 Constitutional Court Decision. On that basis, the Respondent suggested that the due diligence undertaken by the Claimants was inadequate.' 538 'The majority of the Tribunal is not persuaded by this argument.'
Climate change mention	73 '[In 1998] Italy signed the Kyoto Protocol, which aimed to reduce carbon dioxide emissions by eight percent before the end of 2012.'

Czech Republic Cases

***Antaris Solar GmbH and Dr Michael Göde v The Czech Republic*, PCA Case No. 2014-01, Award, 2 May 2018**		
Treaty	Czech and Slovak Federal Republic (Czech Republic and Slovak Republic) - Germany BIT (1990), Energy Charter Treaty (1994)	
Applicable Rules	UNCITRAL Arbitration Rules (1976)	
Arbitrators	P: Lord Collins of Mapesbury - C: Mr. Gary Born - R: HE Judge Peter Tomka	
Outcome	In favour of State Amount claimed: CZK 306,500,000 Amount awarded: ZERO	Costs of arbitration: Redacted Award legal costs: Respondent was awarded USD 1.75 million Award costs of arbitration: Claimants bear 2/3 of the costs
Main Facts	401 'It is important to have in mind the dates when the plants were built and commissioned. The Holýšov plant was commissioned on December 18, 2008. It was not affected by the Solar Levy or the	

	repeal of the tax incentives. But the Claimants maintain a claim in respect of the plant on the basis that the Respondent's measures increased uncertainty in the solar energy investment environment, which indirectly caused a negative impact on the Holýšov SPV's enterprise value.' *See paras 402 to 409* with redacted details about the dates of investment and contracts.
Legitimate expectations of the investor	10 'The Claimants submit that the Respondent breached its obligations under the ECT and the BIT by repealing incentive arrangements to attract investors in photovoltaic power generation contrary to its guarantees.' 11 '[T]he Respondent submits that the measures did not violate either the ECT or the BIT on the grounds that "(a) the Czech Republic never made [a] stabilization commitment to the Claimants, (b) the Czech Republic did not otherwise violate any legitimate expectations, and (c) the measures were reasonably tailored to achieve appropriate and rational state objectives."' 367 'The documents which establish this have already been referred to, and it is only necessary to mention that the Czech Ministry of Industry and Trade, when submitting the bill to Parliament, stated that one of the main objectives of the Act on Promotion was to establish a secure, stable and predictable regime; the 2003 Explanatory Report on the Act on Promotion stated that the support system was based "on providing a guarantee to investors"; the former Minister of Environment stated that the most important principle of the law was the guarantee of a stable FiT for a 15 year period; the Respondent in the 2005 UN Report described the purpose of Section 6(1)(b)(2) as: "providing guarantees to the investors and owners … that … revenue … will be maintained for a period of 15 years …"; and the ERO described the Act on Promotion as "bringing a guarantee of long-term and stable promotion …" including a "guarantee of revenues … for a period of 15 years".' 437 'Investors know that the legislative framework may change and evolve in the light of circumstances and of political developments. It is not every change which gives rise to a claim based on breach of legitimate expectation.'
Due diligence of the investor	360 '[G]iven the State's regulatory powers, in order to rely on legitimate expectations, the investor should inquire in advance regarding the prospects of a change in the regulatory framework in light of the then prevailing or reasonably to be expected changes in the economic and social conditions of the host State.'
Climate change mention	81 'In 1992, following the conclusion of the 1992 United Nations Framework Convention on Climate Change, the Czech Republic implemented two tax incentives through Act 586/1992 (the "Act on Income Tax". Section 19(1)(d) provided an exemption from income tax for the year in which solar facilities were put into operation and

	the following five calendar years (the "Income Tax Exemption"). Section 30, with Annex I, provided an accelerated depreciation period (between 5 to 10 years) for specific categories of electrical equipment and components for photovoltaic installations, such as solar panels, inverters, switchboards, fuse boxes, cut-out boxes and security camera systems (the "Shortened Depreciation Period").' 115 'In the 2005 Fourth National Communication of the Czech Republic on the UN Framework Convention on Climate Change (the "2005 UN Report"), the Czech Republic described the purpose of Section 6(1)(b)(2) of the Act on Promotion as: providing guarantees to the investors and owners of installations, producing electricity from renewable sources who are subject to support pursuant to the Act, that the amount of revenue per unit of produced electricity from renewable sources acquired by the producers from the support will be maintained for a period of 15 years from bringing the installation into operation (or for a period of 15 years for installations that were brought into operation prior to the date of effect of the Act).'

***Mr. Jürgen Wirtgen, Mr Stefan Wirtgen, and JSW Solar (zwei) GmbH & Co.KG v Czech Republic*, PCA Case No. 2014-03, Final Award, 11 October 2017**		
Treaty	Czech Republic - Germany BIT (1990)	
Applicable Rules	Ad hoc arbitration	
Arbitrators	P: Prof. Gabrielle Kaufmann-Kohler - C: Mr. Gary Born - R: Judge Peter Tomka	
Outcome	In favour of the state Amount claimed: CZK 500 million Amount awarded: ZERO	Costs of arbitration: not disclosed Award legal costs: not disclosed Award costs of arbitration: not disclosed
Main Facts	*See paras 29-41*: In 2009, Mr. T, managing director of a company focused on PV projects, introduced the Claimants to investment opportunities in the Czech solar sector, leading to their investment in three solar PV plants: Struhařov, Světlá, and Verneřov. The Struhařov plant received its construction permit on 27 November 2009, an electricity generation license on 14 December 2009 and was connected to the grid on 16 December 2009. The Světlá plant obtained its construction permit on 18 May 2010, an electricity generation license on 22 September 2010 and was connected to the grid on 13 October 2010. The Verneřov plant secured its construction permit on 20 September 2010, an electricity generation license on 11 October 2010, and was connected to the grid on 17 December 2010.	

Legitimate expectations of the investor	367 'In the Tribunal's view, when subsection 6(1)(b) is read in its entirety, it is clear that the language "amount of revenue stays unchanged" in section 6(1)(b)(2) was not an absolute guarantee of revenues to solar PV plants.' 374 'The Claimants' own returns were in excess of 7% per year, both before and after the contested measures.' 416 '[T]he Claimants continue to receive a level of revenue through the FIT system that ensures a 15-year payback of capital expenses and a return on investment of at least 7% per year over a period of 15 (later 20) years. In the circumstances, as the guarantees given by the Czech Republic continue to be complied with in respect of the Claimants, there can be no breach of the Claimants' legitimate expectations.' *Dissenting Opinion of Arbitrator Gary Born* 17 '[T]he only question in this arbitration, and the only question that divides the Tribunal, is what these statutory guarantees provided.' 18 '[T]he plain language and obvious purposes of Section 6(1) of the Act leave no serious doubt that the Claimants were guaranteed a minimum level of FiTs over a specified statutory period (first 15, later, 20 years) for electricity produced by the renewable energy sources that they constructed in the Czech Republic.'
Due diligence of the investor	331 'The Respondent stresses that the Claimants had no prior experience in the solar PV sector. Had they acquired a proper understanding of the legal framework or given due regard to the circumstances at the time, they would not have formed the expectation that they would continue to benefit from excessive profits without any regulation limiting these profits.' 439 'The Tribunal cannot agree with the Claimants. While it is, of course, true that the FET standard may be breached if a state's conduct is not "substantively proper" - to use the words of the Micula tribunal - the Tribunal sees no impropriety here. The circumstances of this case are not those contemplated by the tribunal in Waste Management v Mexico, when it observed that a "deliberate act" by a state to "set out to destroy or frustrate" an investment by "improper means" could constitute a violation of the fair and equitable treatment standard under the North American Free Trade Agreement. Neither are the circumstances here comparable with those in Vivendi II, where the Tribunal concluded that the respondent "improperly and without justification" pursued an "illegitimate campaign" against the investment. The circumstances here are quite different.'
Climate change mention	306 'Further and in any event, the 8% target had already been superseded by a new target for 2020, and "it is hardly plausible that the Czech Republic would have intentionally committed electricity

	consumers and taxpayers to pay enormous subsidies for a period as long as 20 years simply to achieve a non-binding target."' 382 'The resulting solar energy production vastly exceeded original expectations; it was 40 times higher than envisioned when enacting Act 180. Instead of the expected 15 GWh production, the actual production in 2010 was 616 GWh and the actual production in 2011 was 2,182 GWh, more than three and a half times higher than the 2010 figure.225 Similarly, while in September 2008 installed capacity was predicted to be 10 MW by the end of 2010, the real figure turned out to be almost 200 times higher, at 1,960 MW.'

***WA Investments-Europa Nova Limited v The Czech Republic*, PCA Case No. 2014-19, Award, 15 May 2019**		
Treaty	ECT (1994) and Cyprus-Czech Republic BIT (2001)	
Applicable Rules	UNCITRAL Arbitration Rules (1976)	
Arbitrators	P: Prof. Dr. Hans van Houtte – C: Mr. John Beechey, CBE, Mr. Gary Born (replaced) – R: Mr. Toby Landau, Q.C., Doak Bishop (replaced)	
Outcome	In favour of State Amount claimed: CZK 76.6 million Amount awarded: ZERO	Costs of arbitration: N/A Award legal costs: Each party bears its own legal costs Award costs of arbitration: Claimant bears 75% of the costs
Main Facts	152 'The Claimant was incorporated in Cyprus at the beginning of 2007. It was founded and owned at all times by Czech nationals.' 153 'On 29 October 2008, the Claimant decided to invest in the Czech solar business through the acquisition of, and equity contributions in, a Czech limited liability company, Lambreti Estates s.r.o., which was renamed SolarOne s.r.o. ("SolarOne") upon its acquisition. (…)'	
Legitimate expectations of the investor	585 'First, having carefully considered all materials and submissions before it, the Tribunal accepts that no assurance was ever given by the Respondent that the support system from which the Claimant benefitted would never change. 589. Second, even if an assurance had been given by the Respondent, the Tribunal concludes that it was not, or would not have been, relied upon by the Claimant at the relevant time.' 599 'Third, even if the Claimant relied on some alleged "stabilization" assurances from the Czech Authorities – quod non – any such reliance would not have been reasonable.' 605 'The Tribunal observes additionally that the law of the European Union on State Aid precluded, in any event, any	

	legitimate expectation that plants which entered into operation in 2009-2010 would necessarily maintain the benefit of the support system as it then existed, as long as this support system was not duly notified.' 623 'In summary, when the investments were made, the Incentive Regime, although State aid, had not been notified to, and approved by, the EC. Under EU law, it therefore follows that as at that time, there could not have been any legitimate expectations as alleged by the Claimant.'
Due diligence of the investor	523 'In this regard, the Claimant emphasizes that, in the solar sector, investors are usually small businesses and that accordingly it is unreasonable to expect them to conduct extensive legal due diligence.' 574 'Moreover, the Tribunal observes that the Solar Levy did not, in fact, repeal the fundamental features of the Incentive Scheme, as described earlier. The Claimant still received a stable FiT. The Solar Levy had either to be paid quarterly by the energy producer or it could be withheld by the energy distributor.' 575 'Further, and in any event, the Tribunal points out that the Tax Statute did not contain a reference to stability or to the maintenance of the Income Tax Exemption and the Shortened Depreciation Period.' 576 'The Tribunal finds that the changes introduced by the Respondent to the Incentive Regime were part of the exercise of the Respondent's sovereign right to regulate tariffs - in particular in the context of the solar boom and its substantial adverse consequences as described earlier. They did not violate the Respondent's obligation to provide a stable and predictable legal framework for foreign investment.' 577 'The Tribunal is confirmed in this conclusion by the fact that, even after the Solar Levy reduced excessive profits, PV investors still secured a more than reasonable return. Without the legislative amendments, the reference plant would have received a full payback in 7.8 years. Following the amendments, the payback could still be achieved in 9.9 years, and was therefore well below the promised 15 years. (...) In other words, despite the amendment measures, PV investments were as profitable - and in fact more profitable - than envisaged when the support system was created.'
Climate change mention	136 'On 31 March 2005, the Czech Republic adopted the Act on Promotion, which entered into force on 1 August 2005.31 Section 1(2) of the Act on Promotion defined its objectives as follows: Section 1: Subject Matter of Regulation [...] (2) The aim of this Act is to, in the interest of climate protection and environmental protection,

	a) promote the exploitation of renewable energy sources ("Renewable Sources"), b) ensure that the share of Renewable Sources in the consumption of primary energy sources continually increases, c) contribute to conservation in the exploitation of natural resources and to the sustainable development of society, d) put in place the conditions for achieving the indicative target so that the share of electricity produced from Renewable Sources accounts for 8% of gross electricity consumption in the Czech Republic in 2010 and to put in place the conditions for further increasing such share after 2010.' 142 'In the same year in which the Act on Promotion entered into force, various governmental officials and entities of the Czech Republic promoted the Incentive Regime for RES producers and emphasised the importance of the guaranteed electricity purchase price on several occasions.' *Footnote 37* 'The State will support renewable energy, 23 February 2005 (Ex. C-25); Fourth National Communication of the Czech Republic on the UN Framework Convention on Climate Change of 2005 (Ex. C-68).'

***Photovoltaik Knopf Betriebs-GmbH v The Czech Republic*, PCA Case No. 2014-21, Award, 15 May 2019**		
Treaty	ECT (1994) Czech Republic - Germany BIT (1990)	
Applicable Rules	UNCITRAL	
Arbitrators	P: Prof. Dr. Hans van Houtte - C: Mr. John Beechey, CBE, Mr. Gary Born (replaced) - R: Mr. Toby Landau, Q.C., Doak Bishop (replaced)	
Outcome	In favour of the state Amount claimed: CZK 61.3 million Amount awarded: ZERO	Costs of arbitration: N/A Award legal costs: Each party bears its own legal costs Award costs of arbitration: Claimant bears 75% of the costs
Main Facts	*See paras 150-154* Photovoltaik Knopf Betriebs-GmbH, owned by Knopf Privatstiftung, invested in the Czech solar sector on 10 August 2010 by acquiring FVE Kněžmost s.r.o. and a plot of land. The licensing process included applying for grid connection, obtaining a binding statement and a grid connection agreement, applying for an energy production license, and signing a power purchase agreement. The solar plant's construction and licensing were completed by the end of 2010, with grid connection achieved	

	on 23 December 2010 and operations starting on 12 January 2011. The power purchase agreement was executed on 20 January 2011.
Legitimate expectations of the investor	486 'In the Tribunal's considered view, signal an undertaking by the Respondent, much less a specific undertaking to this Claimant, that there would be no changes whatsoever to the legal framework created by the Act on Promotion - in particular in the event of radically changed circumstances (such as the solar boom in 2009-2010, which fundamentally changed the financial soundness of the support regime). On any view, this would have been a far-reaching undertaking, with potentially extreme consequences for the Respondent and its citizens. No such agreement can be inferred from the few words or other matters relied upon by the Claimant.' 493 'The state has a right to regulate, and investors must expect that the legislation will change, absent a stabilization clause or other specific assurance giving rise to a legitimate expectation of stability.' 486 'The Tribunal disagrees with the Claimant's argument that the fact that the Incentive Regime was intended to attract foreign investment, in and of itself, meant that it also offered a commitment of stability and predictability to foreign investors. To support its argument, the Claimant points not only to the Act on Promotion, but also to the Explanatory Report and the implementing regulations. While the Tribunal acknowledges that the Explanatory Report in particular used terms such as "stable" and "maintain", the Tribunal considers that such language, in the absence of an express stabilization commitment, is insufficient to ground the obligation for which the Claimant contends. In particular, the use of such words in the context in which they appear did not, in the Tribunal's considered view, signal an undertaking by the Respondent, much less a specific undertaking to this Claimant, that there would be no changes whatsoever to the legal framework created by the Act on Promotion - in particular in the event of radically changed circumstances (such as the solar boom in 2009-2010, which fundamentally changed the financial soundness of the support regime). On any view, this would have been a far-reaching undertaking, with potentially extreme consequences for the Respondent and its citizens. No such agreement can be inferred from the few words or other matters relied upon by the Claimant.'
Due diligence of the investor	Same reasoning as in *Europe Nova* case
Climate change mention	*Photovoltaik v Czech Republic* also treated EU law as a fact in its analysis of whether the state's revisions to its incentive scheme for solar energy had breached the FET standard. (para 522) The tribunal found that because the incentive scheme constituted state

	aid under EU law, and because it had not been approved by the EC at the time of the investment, the foreign investor could not reasonably expect that the scheme would remain unchanged. 522 'Consequently, the relevant question is whether, at the time the investment was made, the EC had, upon due notification, positively decided that the solar support regime was compatible with EU law. In the absence of due notification and any such decision, the investor - as in the present case - was not entitled to hold any legitimate expectations that the un-notified support system would not be changed. The Tribunal is aware that the Czech Republic had stated in the Explanatory Report of November 2003 that the future Act on Promotion would be "compatible with the public aid law of the European Union". The Republic repeated that view in a few instances up to 2009. However, statements from domestic authorities cannot give rise to legitimate expectations when they are counter to mandatory EU law. In its 2016 Decision, the EC formally confirmed that the Incentive Regime, as applicable to installations commissioned between 1 January 2006 and 31 December 2012, constituted State aid. Statements from domestic authorities cannot alter this. Given that it is not for a Member State to declare its own aid schemes compatible with EU law, any such declaration cannot be a basis for a legitimate expectation.'

***Voltaic Network GmbH v The Czech Republic*, PCA Case No. 2014-20, Award, 15 May 2019**		
Treaty	Czech Republic - Germany BIT (1990) and ECT (1994)	
Applicable Rules	UNCITRAL Arbitration Rules (1976)	
Arbitrators	P: Prof. Dr. Hans van Houtte - C: Mr. John Beechey, CBE, Mr. Gary Born (replaced) - R: Mr. Toby Landau, Q.C., Doak Bishop (replaced)	
Outcome	In favour of the state Amount claimed: CZK 320.07 million Amount awarded: ZERO	Costs of arbitration: N/A Award legal costs: Each party bears its own legal costs Award costs of arbitration: Claimant bears 75% of the costs - In favour of State
Main Facts	*See paras 150-156* Voltaic was established on 23 March 2010, controlled by Mr. Schulte, Mr. Peter Bassmann, and Mr. Udo Ley through various companies. The decision to invest in a solar plant in the Czech Republic was made on 8 May 2010, and on 14 May 2010, Voltaic acquired Solarpark Rybníček s.r.o., which already had the necessary licenses to build a photovoltaic plant. The investment was considered 'sunk' when the acquisition and an Engineering,	

	Procurement, and Construction contract were concluded on 14 May 2010. The total investment amounted to EUR 17,475,378, funded through loans. Key licensing steps included a grid connection agreement on 15 March 2010, an energy production license on 14 October 2010, and a Power Purchase Agreement on 7 December 2010.
Legitimate expectations of the investor	Same reasoning as in *Europe Nova* case
Due diligence of the investor	Same reasoning as in *Europe Nova* case
Climate change mention	231 '[A]n increase of the Solar Levy rate from 26% to 50% was discussed so as to avoid the imposition of a tax on emission allowances, the question of a direct reduction of the FiT was not in issue.'

<table>
<tr><th colspan="3">I.C.W. Europe Investments Limited v The Czech Republic, PCA Case No. 2014-22, Award, 15 May 2019</th></tr>
<tr><td>Treaty</td><td colspan="2">Czech-Republic - United Kingdom BIT (1990) ECT (1994)</td></tr>
<tr><td>Applicable Rules</td><td colspan="2">UNCITRAL Arbitration Rules (1976)</td></tr>
<tr><td>Arbitrators</td><td colspan="2">P: Prof. Dr. Hans van Houtte – C: Mr. John Beechey, CBE – R: Mr. Toby Landau, Q.C.</td></tr>
<tr><td>Outcome</td><td>In favour of the state
Amount claimed: CZK 62.1 million
Amount awarded: ZERO</td><td>Costs of arbitration: N/A
Award legal costs: Each party bears its own legal costs
Award costs of arbitration: Claimant bears 75% of the costs</td></tr>
<tr><td>Main Facts</td><td colspan="2">151 'On 19 July 2010, the Claimant acquired from Enkory a.s. 51% of the shares of Hutira FVE-Omice a.s. ("Hutira" or "SPV") for CZK 1,020,000, which by that time had already entered into a grid connection agreement. According to the Claimant the investment is "sunk" when the SPV is acquired and when the Engineering, Procurement and Construction ("EPC") contract is concluded "so that the Claimant puts the money in the project". Hutira entered into the EPC contract on 2 August 2010.'
152 'On 13 September 2010, the Claimant increased its shareholding in the SPV to 76%, acquiring a further 25% share in it from Hutira Omice s.r.o. for CZK 5,000,000. The investment was made with a view to constructing a solar plant in Omice, South Moravia, with a capacity of MW 1.052.'</td></tr>
</table>

Legitimate expectations of the investor	Same reasoning as in *Europe Nova* case
Due diligence of the investor	Same reasoning as in *Europe Nova* case
Climate change mention	Same reasoning as in *Europe Nova* case

Fossil Fuel Awards

<table>
<tr><td colspan="3">Rockhopper Exploration Plc, Rockhopper Italia S.p.A. and Rockhopper Mediterranean Ltd v Italian Republic, ICSID Case No. ARB/17/14, Award, 23 August 2022</td></tr>
<tr><td>Treaty</td><td colspan="2">ECT (1994)</td></tr>
<tr><td>Applicable Rules</td><td colspan="2">ICSID Arbitration Rules (2006)</td></tr>
<tr><td>Arbitrators</td><td colspan="2">P: Mr. Klaus Reichert - C: Dr. Charles Poncet - R: Prof. Pierre-Mary Dupuy</td></tr>
<tr><td>Outcome</td><td>In favour of the investor
Amount claimed: EUR 275.00 million
Amount awarded: EUR 184.000 million (pre-tax) and EUR 6,675,391 for decommissioning costs</td><td>Costs of arbitration: USD 679,445.85
Award legal costs: Respondent to pay Claimants GBP 3,500,000.00
Award costs of arbitration: Respondent to pay the Claimant 80% of the expended portion of the Claimants' advances to ICSID, i.e. USD 301,284.18</td></tr>
<tr><td>Main Facts</td><td colspan="2">95 'The Tribunal draws the factual conclusion that the relevant date of the investment for the purposes of the arbitration is August 2014 as this appears to be common to both sides. This also is confirmed by Fact No. 37. Further, as confirmed by Fact No. 36, the third Claimants announced in May 2014 a recommended share and cash offer to acquire MOG and subsequently paid approximately EUR 36,000,000.00.'
92 'Put another way, the rejection by the Respondent in January 2016 of the Claimants' production permit application is the key moment through which to see the overall and relevant factual background to this arbitration. Once one sets out what finally happened, the task then is to analyse the "how" (and to a certain</td></tr>
</table>

	extent, the "why" though that is more by way of ensuring the full facts are duly taken into account) it happened.'
	122 'As a matter of fact, therefore, at the time the investment was made in August 2014, there was: (1) a pending application for a production concession; (2) the relevant law in force prohibited exploration within 12 miles of the Italian coastline but provided for an exception for pending applications (i.e. there was a carve-out saver for applications such as that of the Claimants pending since 2008); (3) the outcome of administrative litigation concerning a requirement to file an Integrated Environmental Authorisation as a prerequisite to the relevant Ministry signing off on the Environmental Impact Assessment had recently emerged. That litigation outcome was to the effect that the Claimants were going to have to file such an Integrated Environmental Authorisation or an "AIA" (which in fact was submitted on 13 May 2014 (C-113)); and (4) the Claimants understood that "additional technical and engineering work, combined with some patience and funds available to support an appraisal of the discovery, its value can be significantly increased over time."'
Legitimate expectations of the investor	No statement from the tribunal on FET.
Due diligence of the investor	No statement from the tribunal on FET.
Climate change mention	6 The Ombrina Mare oil and gas field did not proceed to production, and as is clear from the record of this case and the discussion later on in this Award, this came about because Italy decided to pass a law in late 2015 which banned offshore production within a certain distance of Italian shores. That was a sovereign decision made by Italy and the Tribunal indicates at the very outset that it should not be taken in any way to either criticize or deprecate that decision from either a political or environmental standpoint. Italy's sovereign choice to proscribe such offshore production, based on its own inherent authority and dignity, was its to make. However, that sovereign choice or act or decision (the label is not important) of Italy may carry with it a concomitant consequence to pay certain compensation pursuant to internationally-binding promises it made to foreign investors arising from its being a party to the ECT at the material time. 10 The Tribunal appreciates and is acutely sensitive to the fact that there are strongly-held environmental, civic and political views about offshore production in Ombrina Mare. However, the

	outcome of this case passes no judgment whatsoever on the legitimacy or validity of those views. In particular, the Tribunal is at pains to point out that this award is not a 'victory' for one side or the other in that environmental debate, which is of a civic or political character, but rather addresses the legal issue at hand, namely, whether compensation is due to a foreign investor in respect of its investment, based on specific international criteria as contained in a treaty to which Italy was, at the material time, a contracting party. As is discussed and analysed later in this Award, the material factual circumstances which have led to the final result of this arbitration are both specific and discrete from the environmental considerations which have been argued before the Tribunal. 198 As already discussed above, the Tribunal has found that the environmental concerns most likely engaged the precautionary principle *before* the Decree of 7 August 2015; *but* once that Decree emanated from the Respondent the wish to engage the same principle again, on the same basis, is irreconcilable with a 'positive opinion on the environmental compatibility assessment regarding the implementation of the "Cultivation project of Ombrina Mare hydrocarbons in the scope of the d30 B.C-MD concession"' (the express language of that Decree). The more likely reason for the position taken by the Respondent culminating in the letter of 29 January 2016 is the political and civic engagements as discussed earlier in this Award.

***Westmoreland Mining Holdings, LLC v Government of Canada*, ICSID Case No. UNCT/20/3, Award, 31 January 2022**	
Treaty	NAFTA (1992)
Applicable Rules	UNCITRAL Arbitration Rules (1976)
Arbitrators	P: Ms. Juliet Blanch – C: James Hosking – R: Professor Zachary Douglas QC
Outcome	Dismissed on jurisdiction
Main Facts	74 'In 2007, Alberta imposed emission performance standards and a carbon pricing system on large industrial facilities pursuant to its Specified Gas Emitters Regulation ("SGER"). The SGER was originally scheduled to expire in September 2014 but the Government of Alberta extended it to June 2015 whilst it engaged in consultations with the various stakeholders. Meanwhile in 2012, Canada enacted the Reduction of Carbon Dioxide Emissions from Coal-fired Generation of Electricity Regulations (the "Federal Regulations")5 pursuant to the Canadian Environmental Protection Act 1999. These regulations addressed greenhouse gas emissions, committing to phasing out and eventually closing all coal-fired power stations within a fifty-year period.'

	75 'Westmoreland Coal Company ("WCC") is incorporated in Delaware, United States of America. In April 2014, WCC acquired the coal assets of Sherritt International ("Sherritt"), a Canadian company, paying in excess of US$ 320 million and assuming liabilities in excess of US$ 420 million. Sherritt's assets included Prairie which owned a number of mine-mouth coal mines, including three in Alberta: the Genesee, Sheerness and Paintearth Mines (the "Mines"). Mine-mouth operations are those where the coalmine is developed adjacent to and in conjunction with a power plant enabling economic delivery of the coal to the power plant. The Mines are dependent on the mine-mouth operations as the adjacent coal-burning units are the only viable market for the coal produced from the Mines. At the time of this acquisition, Canadian Federal Regulations contained a comprehensive scheme to address greenhouse gas emissions from coal-burning power plants, ensuring that all such facilities would be phased out over a period of fifty years from the date of commissioning. Five of the mine-mouth coal-burning units fed by coal produced from the Mines qualified for this full fifty year useful life under these Regulations.'
Legitimate expectations of the investor	Dismissed on jurisdiction
Due diligence of the investor	Dismissed on jurisdiction
Climate change mention	5 This dispute arises out of the Claimant's ownership of various coalmines in Alberta, Canada, and Alberta's subsequent actions to phase out coal-fired power plants by 2030. 73 Given the increasing awareness of the negative environmental and human health impacts of coal combustion to produce electricity, governments around the world have increasingly been committed to reducing emissions from coal-fired electricity generation.

Glossary

Clean Energy

Low-carbon-emitting energy sources such as solar, photovoltaic (PV) or concentrated solar power (CSP), wind, hydro, bio-mass and nuclear.

Coal

Includes both primary coal (including lignite, coking and steam coal) and derived fuels (including patent fuel, brown-coal briquettes, coke-oven coke, gas coke, gas-works gas, coke-oven gas, blast-furnace gas, and oxygen steel furnace gas). Peat is also included.

CO_2

Carbon Dioxide: a naturally occurring gas and also a by-product of burning fossil fuels from fossil carbon deposits, such as oil, gas, and coal; burning biomass; land use changes; and other industrial processes. It is the principal anthropogenic greenhouse gas that affects the Earth's radiative balance.

COP

Conference of the Parties: the main decision-making body of the United Nations Framework Convention on Climate Change (UNFCCC). It currently meets once a year to review the UNFCCC's progress.

ECT

Energy Charter Treaty: multilateral agreement for the promotion and protection of foreign energy investments Adopted on 17 December 1994 and entered into force on 24 April 1998, it provides for the resolution of disputes between investors and states through arbitration.

Fossil Fuel

Carbon-based fuels from fossil hydrocarbon deposits, including coal, peat, oil, and natural gas.

GHG

Greenhouse Gas Emissions: gaseous constituents of the atmosphere, both natural and anthropogenic, that absorb and emit radiation at specific wavelengths within the spectrum of thermal infrared radiation emitted by the Earth's surface, the atmosphere itself, and by clouds.

ICCL

International Climate Change Law: includes not only the UN climate regime but also rules and principles of general international law relevant to climate change, norms developed by other treaty regimes and international bodies; regulations, policies, and institutions at the regional, national, and sub-national levels; and judicial decisions of national, regional, and international courts

Mitigation

An anthropogenic intervention to reduce the anthropogenic forcing of the climate system includes strategies to reduce greenhouse gas sources and emissions and enhance greenhouse gas sinks.

NDC

Nationally Determined Contribution: Submissions by countries that have ratified the Paris Agreement to present their national efforts to reach the Paris Agreement's long-term temperature goal of limiting warming to well below 2°C. New or updated NDCs are to be submitted in 2020 and every five years thereafter. NDCs thus represent a country's current ambition or target for reducing emissions nationally.

Net Zero

The balance between the amount of greenhouse gas (GHG) produced and the amount removed from the atmosphere.

NZEID

Net Zero Energy Investment Disputes: Treaty-based claim where the claimant-investor is challenging a domestic measure in the state where the energy investment is hosted and that measure: (i) restricts the net zero energy transition policy the investor relied upon or (ii) is taken and justified by the respondent state, in whole or in part, on the grounds of climate change mitigation.

Renewable Energy

Energy obtained from sources that are essentially inexhaustible, unlike, for example, fossil fuels, of which there is a finite supply.[1258]

1258. United Nations Economic and Social Council, 'Specifications for the Application of the United Nations Framework Classification for Fossil Energy and Mineral Reserves and Resources 2009 to Renewable Energy Resources' (UN ECE/ENERGY/2016/4, 19.07.2016) 4.

Bibliography

Books

Alvarez JE, Boundaries of Investment Arbitration: *The Use* of *Trade and European Human Rights Law in Investor-State Disputes* (Juris Publishing 2018).

Alvarez JE, *The Public International Law Regime Governing International Investment* (The Hague Academy of International Law 2011).

Ames B and others, *Macroeconomic Policy and Poverty Reduction* (IMF & World Bank 2001).

Angelet N, *'Fair and Equitable Treatment'* in *Max Planck Encyclopaedia of Public International Law* (OUP 2011).

Anton D and Shelton D, *Environmental Protection and Human Rights* (CUP 2011).

Balcerzak F, *Renewable Energy Arbitration: Quo Vadis? Implications of the Spanish Saga for International Investment Law* (Brill Nijhoff 2023).

Behn D, *A Theory of Configurative Fairness for Evolving International Legal Orders Linking the Scientific Study of Value Subjectivity to Jurisprudential Thought* (PhD Thesis, University of Dundee 2013).

Bishop D, Crawford J and Reisman M (eds), *Foreign Investment Disputes: Cases Materials and Commentary* (2nd edn, Kluwer Law International 2014).

Bodansky D, Brunnée J and Rajamani L, *International Climate Change Law* (OUP 2017).

Bodansky D, *The Art and Craft of International Environmental Law* (HUP 2010).

Bonnitcha J, *Substantive Protection under Investment Treaties: A Legal and Economic Analysis* (CUP 2014).

Braudel F, *Civilisation, Économie et Capitalisme. XV-XVIII Siècles* (Le Temps du Monde 2nd edn, Armand Colin 1980).

Brownlie I, *Principles of Public International Law* (6th edn, OUP 2003).

Bücheler G, *Proportionality in Investor-State Arbitration* (OUP 2015).

Cameron P, *International Energy Investment Law: The Pursuit of Stability* (2nd edn, OUP 2021).

Cane P, *Administrative Law* (5th edn, OUP 2011).

Capra F and Mattei U, *The Ecology of Law: Towards a Legal System in Tune with Nature and Community* (Berrett-Koehler Publishers 2015).

Caron D and others, *Practising Virtue: Inside International Arbitration* (OUP 2015).

Cheng B, *General Principles of Law as Applied by International Courts and Tribunals* (CUP 1994).

Chi M, *Integrating Sustainable Development in International Investment Law: Normative Incompatibility, System Integration and Governance Implications* (Routledge 2017).

Cordonnier-Segger MC, Gehring M and Newcombe A (eds), *Sustainable Development in World Investment Law* (Wolters Kluwer 2011).

Crawford J, *Brownlie's Principles of Public International Law* (8th edn, OUP 2012).

Crawford J, *Chance, Order, Change: The Course of International Law, General Course on Public International Law* (Martinus Nijhoff Publishers 2014).

de Vattel E, *The Law of Nations or Principles of the Law of Nature Applied to the Conduct and Affairs of the Nations and Sovereigns* (5th edn, 1839).

Di Benedetto S, *International Investment Law and the Environment* (Edward Elgar Publishing 2013).

Dicey AV, *An Introduction to the Study of the Law of the Constitution* (Roger Michener ed., Liberty Fund 1982).

Diehl A, *The Core Standard of International Investment Protection: Fair and Equitable Treatment* (Kluwer Law International 2012).

Dolzer R and Schreuer C, *Principles of International Investment Law* (OUP 2012).

Dolzer R and Stevens M, *Bilateral Investment Treaties* (Martinus Nijhoff Publishers 1995).

Dumberry P, *The Fair and Equitable Treatment Standard: A Guide to NAFTA Case Law on Article 1105* (Kluwer Law International 2013).

Dupuy F, *La protection de l'attente légitime des parties au contrat: Étude de droit international des investissements à la lumière du droit comparé* (PhD Thesis, Paris Assas University 2007).

Fuller LL, *The Morality of Law* (rev edn, YUP 1969).

Gardiner SM (ed.), *Climate Ethics: Essential Readings* (OUP 2010).

Heffron RJ, *Energy Law: An Introduction* (Springer 2015).

Jaffe R and Taylor W, *The Physics of Energy* (CUP 2018).

Kläger R, *'Fair and Equitable Treatment' in International Investment Law* (CUP 2011).

Klein D and others (eds), *The Paris Climate Agreement: Analysis and Commentary* (OUP 2017).

Knoll-Tudor I, *The Fair and Equitable Treatment Standard in the International Law of Foreign Investment* (OUP 2008).

Kolb R, *Good Faith in the International Law* (Hart Publishing 2017).

Kopar R, *Stability and Legitimate Expectations in International Energy Investments* (Hart Publishing 2021).

Kulick A, *Global Public Interest in International Investment Law* (CUP 2012).

Landes D, *The Unbound Prometheus: Technological Change and Industrial Development in Western Europe from 1750 to the Present* (CUP 2003).

Landmann N, *Legitimate Expectations and Fair-and-Equitable-Treatment under the Energy Charter Treaty: A Comparative Analysis of the Renewable Energy Cases* (Nomos Verlagsgesellschaft 2022).

Lauterpacht H (ed.), *International Law: Collected Papers* (CUP 1970).

Levashova Y, *The Right of States to Regulate in International Investment Law: The Search for Balance Between Public Interest and Fair and Equitable Treatment* (Kluwer Law International 2019).

Lim CL, Ho J and Paparinskis M, *International Investment Law and Arbitration: Commentary, Awards and Other Materials* (CUP 2018).

Marisi F, *Environmental Interests in Investment Arbitration: Challenges and Directions* (Kluwer Law International 2020).

Massai L, *European Climate and Clean Energy Law and Policy* (Routledge 2012).

McLachlan C, Shore L and Weininger M, *International Investment Arbitration: Substantive Principles* (2nd edn, OUP 2017).

Miles K, *The Origins of International Investment Law: Empire, Environment and the Safeguarding of Capital* (CUP 2013).

Newcombe A and Paradell L, *Law and Practice of Investment Treaties: Standards of Treatment* (Kluwer Law International 2009).

Palombino FM, *Fair and Equitable Treatment and the Fabric of General Principles* (T.M.C. Asser Press 2018).

Paparinskis M, *The International Minimum Standard and Fair and Equitable Treatment* (OUP 2013).

Pauwelyn J, *Conflict of Norms in Public International Law: How WTO Law Relates to Other Rules of International Law* (CUP 2003).

Radi Y, *Rules and Practices of International Investment Law and Arbitration* (CUP 2020).

Reinisch A and Schreuer C, *International Protection of Investments: The Substantive Standards* (CUP 2020).

Rubins N and Kinsella S, *International Investment, Political Risk and Dispute Resolution: A Practitioner's Guide* (OUP 2005).

Ortino F, *The Origin and Evolution of Investment Treaty Standards: Stability, Value, and Reasonableness* (OUP 2019).

Salacuse J, *The Law of Investment Treaties* (3rd edn, OUP 2021).

Schill S (ed.), *International Investment Law and Comparative Public Law* (OUP 2011).

Schønberg S, *Legitimate Expectations in Administrative Law* (OUP 2000).

Schreuer C and others, *The ICSID Convention: A Commentary* (CUP 2009).

Shue H, *Climate Justice: Vulnerability and Protection* (OUP 2014).

Simmonds NE, *Central Issues in Jurisprudence: Justice, Law and Rights* (4th edn, Sweet and Maxwell 2013).

Sipiorski E, *Good Faith in International Investment Arbitration* (OUP 2019).

Sitnik P, *Estoppel in International Investment Law* (PhD Thesis, Maria Curie-Skłodowska University Lublin 2021).

Smil V, *Biomass Energies: Resources, Links, Constraints* (Plenum Press 1983).

Smil V, *Energy and Civilization: A History* (MIT Press 2017).

Smil V, *Energy Transitions: History, Requirements, Prospects* (Praeger Publishers Inc 2010).

Sornarajah M, *Resistance and Change in the International Law on Foreign Investment* (CUP 2015).

Sornarajah M, *The International Law on Foreign Investment* (CUP 2021).

Subedi SP, *International Investment Law: Reconciling Policy and Principle* (4th edn, Hart Publishing 2020).

Titi C, *The Right to Regulate in International Investment Law* (Hart Publishing 2014).

Tudor I, *The Fair and Equitable Treatment Standard in International Investment Law of Foreign Investment* (OUP 2008).

Van Harten G, *International Treaty Arbitration and Public Law* (OUP 2007).

Van Harten G, *Sovereign Choices and Sovereign Constraints: Judicial Restraint in Investment Treaty Arbitration* (OUP 2013).

Vandevelde KJ, *Bilateral Investment Treaties: History, Policy, and Interpretation* (OUP 2010).

Viñuales J, *Foreign Investment and the Environment in International Law* (CUP 2012).

Viñuales JE and Dupuy PM (eds), *Harnessing Foreign Investment to Promote Environmental Protection: Incentives and Safeguards* (CUP 2013).

Wongkaew T, *Protection of Legitimate Expectations in Investment Treaty Arbitration, A Theory of Detrimental Reliance* (CUP 2019).

Wrigley E, *Energy and the English Industrial Revolution* (CUP 2010).

Wrigley E, *The Path to Sustained Growth: England's Transition from an Organic Economy to an Industrial Revolution* (CUP 2016).

Yannaca-Small K (ed.), *Arbitration under International Investment Agreements: A Guide to the Key Issues* (2nd edn, OUP 2018).

Yoleth Emilia Lainez Calderon, *Les attentes légitimes en Droit international économique* (Thesis Paris II Panthéon Assas 2021).

Chapters in Edited Books

Alex M, 'The Public-Private Dualities of International Investment Law and Arbitration' in C Brown and K Miles (eds), *Evolution in Investment Treaty Law and Arbitration* (CUP 2011).

Alvarez J, 'Epilogue: "Convergence" Is a Many-Splendored Thing' in S Gáspár-Szilágyi, D Behn and M Langford (eds), *Adjudicating Trade and Investment Disputes: Convergence or Divergence?* (CUP 2020).

Ambast A and Pulkowski D, 'The VCLT as a Unifying Force in Treaty Design: How Special Is Investment Law?' in E Shirlow and KN Gore (eds), *The Vienna Convention on the Law of Treaties in Investor-State Disputes: History, Evolution and Future* (Kluwer Law International 2022).

Baetens F, 'The Kyoto Protocol in Investor-State Arbitration: Reconciling Climate Change and Investment Protection Objectives' in MC Cordonnier-Segger, M Gehring and A Newcombe (eds), *Sustainable Development in World Investment Law* (Wolters Kluwer 2011).

Baetens F, 'Combating Climate Change Through the Promotion of Green Investment: From Kyoto to Paris Without Regime-Specific Dispute Settlement' in K Miles (ed.), *Research Handbook on Environment and Investment Law* (Edward Elgar Publishing 2019).

Banifatemi Y, 'Consistency in the Interpretation of Substantive Investment Rules: Is It Achievable?' in Roberto Echandi and Pierre Sauvé (eds), *Prospects in International Investment Law and Policy* (CUP 2013).

Bjorklund A, 'The National Treatment Obligation' in K Yannaca-Small (ed.), *Arbitration under International Investment Agreements: A Guide to the Key Issues* (2nd edn, OUP 2018).

Bodansky D and Lawrence J, 'Trade and Environment', in D Bethlehem and others (eds), *The Oxford Handbook of International trade Law* (OUP 2009).

Boyle A and Ghaleigh NS, 'Climate Change and International Law Beyond the UNFCC' in C Carlarne, KR Gray and R Tarasofsky (eds), *The Oxford Handbook of International Climate Change Law* (OUP 2016).

Bungenberg M and Titi C, 'The Evolution of EU Investment Law and the Future of EU-China Investment Relations' in W Shan and J Su (eds), *China and International Investment Law* (Brill Nijhoff 2014).

Carlarne C, Gray KR and Tarasofsky R (eds), 'International Climate Change Law: Mapping an Emerging Field of International Law' in *The Oxford Handbook of International Climate Change Law* (OUP 2016).

Chaisse J and Marisi F, 'Investor-State Dispute Settlement and Environment' in *Elgar Encyclopaedia of Environmental Law* (Edward Elgar Publishing Limited 2021).

Crawford J and Nevill P, 'Relations Between International Courts and Tribunals: The "Regime Problem"' in MA Young (ed.), *Regime Interaction in International Law: Facing Fragmentation* (CUP 2012).

Douglas Z, 'Concepts of Property' in Z Douglas, J Pauwelyn and J Viñuales (eds), *The Foundations of International Investment Law: Bringing Theory into Practice* (OUP 2014).

Douglas Z, 'The Enforcement of Environmental Norms in Investment Treaty Arbitration' in Jorge Viñuales (ed.), *Harnessing Foreign Investment to Promote Environmental Protection* (CUP 2013).

Echandi R, 'Bilateral Investment Treaties and Investment Provisions in preferential Trade Agreements Recent Developments in Investment Rule-Making' in K Yannaca-Small (ed.), *Arbitration under International Investment Agreements A Guide to the Key Issues* (2nd edn, OUP 2018).

Firger DM, 'The Potential of International Climate Change Law to Mobilise Low-Carbon Foreign Direct Investment' in JE Viñuales and PM Dupuy (eds), *Harnessing Foreign Investment to Promote Environmental Protection: Incentives and Safeguards* (CUP 2013).

Focarelli C, 'Denial of Justice', *Max Planck Encyclopaedia of Public International Law* (OUP 2013).

Gaja G, 'General Principles of Law', *Max Planck Encyclopaedia of Public International Law* (OUP 2013).

Gallus N, 'The "Fair and Equitable Treatment" Standard and the Circumstances of the Host State' in C Brown and K Miles (eds), *Evolution in Investment Treaty Law and Arbitration* (CUP 2011).

Ghaleigh NS, 'Science and Climate Change Law: The Role of the IPPC in International Decision-Making' in C Carlarne, KR Gray and R Tarasofsky (eds), *The Oxford Handbook of International Climate Change Law* (OUP 2016).

Henckels C, 'Legitimate Expectations and the Rule of Law in International Investment Law' in A Reinisch and S Schill (eds), *Investment Protection Standards and the Rule of Law* (OUP 2023).

Henly K, 'Rule of Law' in CB Gray (ed.), *The Philosophy of Law, an Encyclopaedia* (Garland Publishing 1999).

Joubin-Bret A and others, 'International Investment Law and Development' in M Cordonnier-Segger, M Gehring and A Newcome (eds), *Sustainable Development in World Investment Law* (Kluwer Law International, 2011).

Kingsbury B and Schill SW, 'Public Law Concepts to Balance Investors' Rights with State Regulatory Actions in the Public Interest–the Concept of Proportionality', in *International Investment Law and Comparative Public Law* (OUP 2010).

Kingsbury B and Schill S, 'Investor-State Arbitration as Governance: Fair and Equitable Treatment, Proportionality and the Emerging Global Administrative Law' in Albert Jan van den Berg (ed.), *50 Years of the New York Convention: ICCA International Arbitration Conference* (Kluwer 2009).

Kläger R, 'Revising Treatment Standards: Fair and Equitable Treatment in Light of Sustainable Development' in S Hindeland and M Krajewski (eds), *Shifting Paradigms in International Investment Law* (OUP 2016).

Laryea ET, 'Legitimate Expectations in Investment Treaty Law: Concept and Scope of Application' in J Chaisse, L Choukroune and S Jusoh (eds), *Handbook of International Investment Law and Policy* (Springer 2020).

MacCormick N, 'Voluntary Obligation' in N MacCormick (ed.), *Legal Right and Social Democracy: Essays in Legal and Political Philosophy* (Oxford Clarendon Press 1982).

Jarrett M, 'Implementing the Energy Transition in the Face of Investment Protection Standards' in P Cameron, X Mu and V Roeben (eds), *The Global Energy Transition: Law Policy, and Economics for Energy in the 21st Century* (Hart Publishing 2020).

McLachlan C and others, 'Treatment of Investors' in C McLachlan, L Shore, M Weiniger (eds), *International Investment Arbitration: Substantive Principles* (2nd edn, OUP 2017).

Miles K, 'International Investment Law and the Environment: Introduction' in K Miles (ed.), *Research Handbook on Environment and Investment Law* (Edward Elgar Publishing 2019).

Minnerop P, 'The Legal Effect of the Paris Rulebook under the Doctrine of Treaty Interpretation' in P Cameron, X Mu and V Roeben (eds), *The Global Energy Transition: Law, Policy and Economics for Energy in the 21st Century* (Hart Publishing 2020).

Morgandi T and Viñuales JE, 'Legal Aspects of Energy Policy' in M Ozawa and others (eds), *In Search of Good Energy Policy* (1st edn, CUP 2019).

Niccolò Ridi and Schultz T, 'Empirically Mapping Investment Arbitration Scholarship: Networks, Authorities, and the Research Front' in KF Gomez (ed.), *Private Actors in International Investment Law* (Springer 2020).

Ostřanský J, 'An Exercise in Equivocation: A Critique of Legitimate Expectations as a General Principle of Law under the Fair and Equitable Treatment Standard' in A Gattini, A Tanzi and F Fontanelli (eds), *General Principles of law and International Investment Arbitration* (Brill Nijhoff 2018).

Paparinskis M, 'Good Faith and Fair and Equitable Treatment in International Investment Law' in A Mitchell, M Sornarajah and T Voon (eds), *Good Faith and International Economic Law* (OUP 2015).

Paparinskis M, 'The Interpretation of Treaties and Investment Arbitration: Introductory Reflections' in E Shirlow and KN Gore (eds), *The Vienna Convention on the Law of Treaties in Investor-State Disputes: History, Evolution and Future* (Kluwer Law International 2022).

Reed L and Daina B, 'Fair and Equitable Treatment: Fairly and Equitably Applied in Lieu of Unlawful Indirect Expropriation?' in A Rovine (ed.), *Contemporary Issues in International Arbitration and Mediation: The Fordham Papers* (Brill Nijhoff 2007).

Schill SW (ed.), 'Fair and Equitable Treatment, the Rule of Law, and Comparative Public Law', in *International Investment Law and Comparative Public Law* (OUP 2010).

Schill SW (ed.), 'Foreign Investment in the Energy Sector: Lessons for International Investment Law' in E de Brabandere and T Gazzini (eds), *Foreign Investment in the Energy Sector: Balancing Private and Public Interests* (Bril Nijhof 2014).

Schill SW (ed.), 'Sources of International Investment Law: Multilateralisation, Arbitral Precedent, Comparativism, Soft Law' in S Besson and J d'Aspermont (eds), *The Oxford Handbook of the Sources of International Law* (OUP 2018).

Schreuer C and Kriebaum U, 'At What Time Must Legitimate Expectations Exist?' in C Schreuer (ed.), *A Liber Amicorum: Thomas Wälde* (CMP Pub Ltd 2009).

Schreuer C and Weiniger M, 'A Doctrine of Precedent?' in P Muchlinski, F Ortino and C Schreuer (eds), *The Oxford Handbook of International Investment Law* (OUP 2008).

Shirlow E and Gore KN (eds), 'Chapter 1: An Introduction to the VCLT and Its Role in ISDS: Looking Back, Looking Forward' in *The Vienna Convention on the Law of Treaties in Investor-State Disputes: History, Evolution and Future* (Kluwer Law International 2022).

Simma B and Kill T, 'Harmonizing Investment Protection and International Human Rights: First Steps Towards a Methodology' in C Binder and others (eds), *International Investment Law of the 21st Century: Essays in Honour of Christoph Schreuer* (OUP 2009).

Smutny AC, Polásek P and Farrell C, 'The MFN Clause and Its Evolving Boundaries' in K Yannaca-Small (ed.), *Arbitration under International Investment Agreements: A Guide to the Key Issues* (2nd edn, OUP 2018).

Sornarajah M, 'The Fair and Equitable Standard of Treatment: Whose Fairness? Whose Equity?' in F Ortino and others (eds), *Investment Treaty Law: Current Issues*

Volume II, Nationality and Investment Treaty Claims, Fair and Equitable Treatment in Investment Treaty Law (BIICL 2007).

Sornarajah M, 'The Neo-Liberal Agenda in Investment Arbitration: Its Rise, Retreat and Impact on State Sovereignty' in W Shan, P Simons and D Singh (eds), *Redefining Sovereignty in International Economic Law* (Hart Publishing 2008).

Morgandi T and Viñuales J, 'Energy Security in International Law' in Robin Geiß and Nils Melzer (eds), *The Oxford Handbook of the International Law of Global Security* (OUP 2021).

Timofeyev I, Profaizer J and Weiss A, 'Investment Disputes Involving the Renewable Energy Industry under the Energy Charter Treaty' in J William Rowley (ed.), *The Guide to Energy Arbitrations: Fourth Edition* (GAR 2020).

Titi C, 'Police Powers Doctrine and International Investment Law' in A Gattini, A Tanzi and F Fontanelli (eds), *General Principles of Law and International Investment Arbitration* (Brill 2018).

Torrijo X, 'Climate Change and International Investment Treaties' in *Elgar Encyclopaedia of Environmental Law* (EEP 2016).

Viñuales J, 'Investment Law and Sustainable Development: The Environment Breaks into Investment Disputes in International Investment Law' in M Bungenberg and others (eds), *International Investment Law: A Handbook* (Hart Publishing 2015).

Viñuales J, 'Foreign Investment and the Environment in International Law: The Current State of Play' in K Miles (ed.), *Research Handbook on Environment and Investment Law* (Edward Elgar 2016).

Viñuales J, 'Sources of International Investment Law: Conceptual Foundations of Unruly Practices' in S Besson and J d'Aspermont (eds), *The Oxford Handbook of the Sources of International Law* (OUP 2018).

Wongkaew T, 'The Transplantation of Legitimate Expectations in Investment Treaty Arbitration: A Critique' in S Lalalni and RP Lazo (eds), *The Role of the State in Investor-State Arbitration* (Brill Nijhoff 2015).

Yannaca-Small K (ed.), 'Fair and Equitable Treatment Have Its Contour Fully Evolved?' in *Arbitration under International Investment Agreements A Guide to the Key Issues* (OUP 2018).

Yannaca-Small K (ed.), 'Indirect Expropriation and the Right to Regulate, Has a Line Been Drawn?' in *Arbitration under International Investment Agreements A Guide to the Key Issues* (OUP 2018).

Journal Articles

Adamski H, 'Klimaschutz und Grundrechtsschutz. Das Bundesverfassungsgericht verkündet eine fast revolutionäre und historische Entscheidung–und folgt damit jungen Beschwerdeführern' (2021) 70 GWP–Gesellschaft. Wirtschaft. Politik 4 33.

Alvarez JE, 'The New Dispute Settlers: (Half) Truths and Consequences' (2003) 38 Tex ILJ 405.

Alvarez JE, 'A Bit on Custom Symposium: 14th Annual Herbert Rubin and Justice Rose Luttan Rubin International Law Symposium: A Special Tribute to Andreas

Lowenfeld' (2009) 42 New York University Journal of International Law and Politics 17.
Alvarez JE, 'Is Investor-State Arbitration 'Public'?' (2016) 7 Journal of International Dispute Settlement 3.
Alvarez JE, 'The Human Right of Property' (2017) 72 University of Miami Law Review 580.
Ascensio H, 'Article 31 of the VCLT's and International Investment Law' (2016) 31 ICSID Review 2 366.
Aven T and Renn O, 'On Risk Defined as an Event Where the Outcome Is Uncertain' (2009) 2 Journal of Risk Research 1.
Baltag C, Joshi R and Duggal K, 'Recent Trends in Investment Arbitration on the Right to Regulate, Environment, Health and Corporate Social Responsibility: Too Much or Too Little?' (2023) 38 ICSID Review 2 381.
Baumstark L and others, 'Cost–Benefit Assessment of Public Investments in France: The Use of Counter-Experts' (2021) 12 Journal of Benefit-Cost Analysis 152.
Behn D and Fauchald OK, 'Governments under Cross-Fire: Renewable Energy and International Economic Tribunals' (2015) 12 Manchester Journal of International Economic Law 2.
Behn D and Langford M, 'Trumping the Environment? An Empirical Perspective on Investment Treaty Arbitration' (2017) 18 JWIT 14.
Behn D and Létourneau-Tremblay L, 'Promoting Renewable Energy in the EU: Shifting Trends in Member State Policy Space' (2017) 28 European Business Law Review 217.
Bernauer T, 'Climate Change Politics' (2013) 16 Annual Review of Political Science 421.
Biggs J, 'The Scope of Investors' Legitimate Expectations under the FET Standard in the European Renewable Energy Cases' (2021) 36 ICSID Review 99.
Bodansky D, 'The United Nations Framework Convention on Climate Change: A Commentary' (1993) 18 Yale Journal of International Law 451.
Bos K and Gupta J, 'Climate Change: The Risks of Stranded Fossil Fuel Assets and Resources to the Developing World' (2018) 39 Third World Quarterly 436.
Boute A, 'Combating Climate Change Through Investment Arbitration' 35 Fordham International Law Journal 613.
Boute A, 'Environmental Force Majeure: Relief from Fossil Energy Contracts in the Decarbonisation Era' (2021) 33 Journal of Environmental Law 2 339.
Bradlow A, 'Human Rights Impact Litigation in ISDS: A Proposal for Enabling Private Parties to Bring Human Rights Claims Through Investor-State Dispute Settlement Mechanisms' (2018) 43 Yale Journal of International Law 2 355.
Brewer TL and Young S, 'Investment Issues at the WTO: The Architecture of Rules and the Settlement of Disputes' (1998) 1 Journal of International Economic Law 457.
Brower C, 'Investor-State Disputes under NAFTA: The Empire Strikes Back' (2003) 40 Col JTL 43.
Brown A, 'A Theory of Legitimate Expectations' (2017) 25 Journal of Political Philosophy 435.

Brown C, 'The Protection of Legitimate Expectations as a "General Principle of Law": Some Preliminary Thoughts' (2009) 6 TDM 2.

Campbell C, 'House of Cards: The Relevance of Legitimate Expectations under Fair and Equitable Treatment Provisions in Investment Treaty Law' (2013) 30 Journal of International Arbitration 361.

Castineira E and Lehmann T, 'After Vattenfall, a Science-Based Proposal to Account for Climate Change and Biodiversity in Energy Arbitrations' (2021) 39 ASA Bulletin 2.

Chaisse J, 'Exploring the Confines of International Investment and Domestic Health Protections: Is a General Exceptions Clause a Forced Perspective?' (2013) 39 American Journal of Law and Medicine 332.

Chaisse J, 'Investor-State Arbitration in International Tax Dispute Resolution: A Cut above Dedicated Tax Dispute Resolution' (2015) 35 Va Tax Rev 149.

Cheng TH, 'Precedent and Control in Investment Treaty Arbitration' (2007) 30 Fordham ILJ 1014.

Chriki D, 'Is the Washington Consensus Really Dead: An Empirical Analysis of FET Claims in Investment Arbitration' (2018) 41 Suffolk Transnat'l L Rev 291.

Commission JP, 'Precedent in Investment Treaty Arbitration, A Citation Analysis of a Developing Jurisprudence' (2007) 24 Journal of International Arbitration 2.

Cotula L, '(Dis)integration in Global Resource Governance: Extractivism, Human Rights, and Investment Treaties' (2020) 23 Journal of International Economic Law 2.

Dall'Agnola G, 'Italy's Spalma-Incentivi Decree and the ECT's FET Obligation: An Assessment of the Legitimacy of the Photovoltaic Incentives Cut' (2021) 3 Diritto del Commercio Internazionale 507.

Daujotas R, 'The Concept of Legitimate Expectation in Investor-State Arbitration and the European Court of Human Rights' (2012) 2 International Commercial Arbitration Review 166.

Davidson DJ, 'Exnovating for a Renewable Energy Transition' (2019) 4 Nature Energy 254.

Davies A, 'Investment Treaty Interpretation, Fair and Equitable Treatment and Legitimate Expectations' (2018) 15 Manchester Journal of International Economic Law 314.

De Paor R, 'Can International Arbitral Tribunals Apply International Climate Change Law and/or Public Policy When Climate Change Issues Arise in Commercial and Investment Arbitration?' (2022) Cahiers de l'Arbitrage 3.

Doelle M, 'The Paris Agreement: Historic Breakthrough or High Stakes Experiment?', (2016) 6 Climate Law 1.

Dolzer R, 'New Foundations for the Law of Expropriation of Alien Property' (1981) AJIL 75.

Dolzer R, 'Fair and Equitable Treatment: A Key Standard in Investment Treaties' (2005) 39 The International Lawyer 1.

Dolzer R, 'The Impact of International Investment Treaties on Domestic Administrative Law' (2005) 37 NYU JILP 953.

Douglas Z, 'The Hybrid Foundations of Investment Treaty Arbitration' (2003) 74 BYBIL 1 152.

Douglas Z, 'Nothing If Not Critical for Investment Treaty Arbitration: Occidental, Eureko and Methanex' (2006) 22 Arb Int'l 27.

Draguiev D, 'Investment Treaty Arbitration in the Renewable Energy Sector: Overview of Arbitral Case Law on Legitimate Expectations in the Light of Policy' (2018) 7 TDM.

Dumberry P, 'The Protection of Investors' Legitimate Expectations and the Fair and Equitable Treatment Standard under NAFTA Article 1105' (2014) 31 Journal of International Arbitration 47.

Dumberry P, 'Shopping for a Better Deal: The Use of MFN Clauses to Get "Better" Fair and Equitable Treatment Protection' (2017) 33/1 Arbitration International 1.

Dumberry P, 'Fair and Equitable Treatment: Its Interaction with the Minimum Standard and Its Customary Status' (2017) 1 Brill Research Perspectives in International Investment Law and Arbitration 2.

Dumberry P, 'Has the Fair and Equitable Treatment Standard Become a Rule of Customary International Law?' (2017) 8 Journal of International Dispute Settlement 1 155.

Echeverri J, 'Some Philosophical Questions to Understand the Role of Arbitrators Through the Notion of Fair and Equitable Treatment' (2022) 24 Estudios Socio-Jurídicos.

Egger P, Pirotte A and Titi C, 'International Investment Agreements and Foreign Direct Investment: A Survey' (2023) 00 The World Economy 1.

Eskridge WM and Frickey PP, 'The Making of "The Legal Process"' (1994) 107 Harvard Law Review 2031.

Falvey R and Foster-McGregor N, 'Heterogeneous Effects of Bilateral Investment Treaties' (2017) 153 Rev World Econ 4.

Fietta S, 'Expropriation and the "Fair and Equitable" Standard: The Developing Role of Investor's "Expectations" in International Investment Arbitration' (2006) 23 J Int'l Arb 375.

Forsyth CF, 'The Provenance and Protection of Legitimate Expectations' (1988) 47 The Cambridge Law Journal 238.

Franklin A, 'Legitimate Expectations: Lessons from Recent Energy Arbitration Cases on Renewable Energy Relationship of Fair and Equitable Treatment Standard to Indirect Expropriation' (2018) SSRN Electronic Journal www.ssrn.com/abstract =3167034 accessed 8 January 2023.

French D and Rajamani L, 'Climate Change and International Environmental Law: Musing on a Journey to Somewhere' (2013) 25 Journal of Environmental Law 3 437.

Friedman J, 'The Scientist as Expert Witness: Why Lawyers and Scientists Can't Talk to Each Other' (1977) 18 Jurimetrics Journal 2 99.

Fuller L and Perdue WR, 'The Reliance Interest in Contract Damage (Parts 1 and 2)' (1937) 46 (52) Yale LJ 373.

Gardner RC, 'Taking the Principle of Just Compensation Abroad: Private Property Rights, National Sovereignty, and the Cost of Environmental Protection' (1997) 65 U Cin. LRev 539.

Gazzini T, 'General Principles of Law in the Field of Foreign Investment' (2009) 10 The Journal of World Investment & Trade 103.

Gazzini T, 'Bilateral Investment Treaties and Sustainable Development' (2014) 15 The Journal of World Investment & Trade 929.

Gielen D and others, 'The Role of Renewable Energy in the Global Energy Transformation' (2019) 24 Energy Strategy Reviews 38.

Gourgourinis A, 'Delineating the Normativity of Equity in International Law' (2009) 11 International Community Law Review 327.

Green F, 'Legal Transitions Without Legitimate Expectations' (2020) 28 The Journal of Political Philosophy 4.

Gupta J and Arts K, 'Achieving the 1.5 °C Objective: Just Implementation Through a Right to (Sustainable) Development Approach' (2018) 18 International Environmental Agreements: Politics, Law and Economics 11.

Haeri H, 'A Tale of Two Standards: 'Fair and Equitable Treatment' and the Minimum Standard in International Law: The Gillis Wetter Prize' (2011) 27(1) Arbitration International 27.

Hamida WB, 'Droit Climatique et Du Droit Des Investissements: De La Friction à La Coordination' (2021) Revista Brasileira de Arbitragem 84.

Hare W and others, 'The Architecture of the Global Climate Regime: A Top-Down Perspective' (2010) 10 Climate Policy 600.

Hepburn C, 'Environmental Policy, Government, and the Market' (2010) 26 Oxford Review of Economic Policy 2.

Hirsch M, 'Between Fair and Equitable Treatment and Stabilization Clause. Stable Legal Environment and Regulatory Change in International Investment Law' (2011) 12 The Journal of World Investment & Trade 783.

Howse R, 'The Appellate Body Rulings in the Shrimp/Turtle Case: A New Legal Baseline for the Trade and Environment Debate' (2002) 27 Columbia Journal of Environmental Law 491.

Huber M and Tereposky G, 'The WTO Appellate Body: Viability as a Model for an Investor-State Dispute Appellate Mechanism' (2017) 32 ICSID Review 545.

Jenks W, 'The Conflict of Law-Making Treaties' (1953) 30 BYIL 401.

Johnson L, Sachs L and Lobel N, 'Aligning International Investment Agreements with the Sustainable Development Goals' (2019) 58 Columbia Journal of Transnational Law 58.

Juillard P, 'L'évolution des sources du droit des investissements' (1994) 250(9) Recueil des cours 133.

Kaufmann-Kohler G, 'Arbitral Precedent: Dream, Necessity or Excuse?' (2007) 23 Arb. Int'l 357.

Kerner A, 'What Can We Really Know About BITs and FDI?' (2018) 33 ICSID Review 1.

Kethireddy SR, 'Still the Law of Nations: Legitimate Expectations and the Sovereigntist Turn in International Investment Law' (2019) 44 The Yale Journal of International Law 315.

Khachvani D, 'Non-compensable Regulation Versus Regulatory Expropriation: Are Climate Change Regulation Compensable?' (2020) 35 ICSID Review 154.
Kikstra JS and others, 'The Social Cost of Carbon Dioxide under Climate-Economy Feedbacks and Temperature Variability' (2021) 16 Environmental Research Letters 094037.
Klaaßen L and Steffen B, 'Meta-analysis on Necessary Investment Shifts to Reach Net Zero Pathways in Europe' (2023) 13 Nat Clim Change 58.
Kläger R, 'Fair and Equitable Treatment: A Look at the Theoretical Underpinnings of Legitimacy and Fairness' (2010) The Journal of World Investment & Trade 435.
Krzykowski M, Mariański M and Zięty J, 'Principle of Reasonable and Legitimate Expectations in International Law as a Premise for Investments in the Energy Sector' (2021) 21 Int Environ Agreements 75.
Kuzhatov BC, 'The Energy Charter Treaty Reform: Why and How to Reach a Consensus on Fair and Equitable Treatment?' (2022) 163 Energy Policy 112769.
Leal-Arcas R, 'The Contribution of Free Trade Agreements and Bilateral Investment Treaties to a Sustainable Future' (2020) 23 Zeitschrift für Europarechtliche Studien–ZEuS 3.
Lehmann T, 'Police Powers Doctrine: A Reliable State Defence in Times of Covid-19?' (2021) 18 Brazilian Journal of international Law 72.
Levashova Y, 'Fair and Equitable Treatment and Investor's Due Diligence under International Investment Law' (2020) 67 Netherlands International Law Review 233.
Lewis C, 'Fairness, Legitimate Expectations and Estoppel' (1986) 49 The Modern Law Review 2.
Lobel N and Fermeglia M, 'Investment Protection and Unburnable Carbon: Competing Commitments in International Investment and Climate Governance' (2018) 4 Diritto Del Commercio Internazionale 945.
Lowe V, 'The Role of Equity in International Law' (1992) 12 Australian Yearbook of International Law 54.
Ma J, 'Bridging Multinational Corporations' Investment–Climate Gap: Prospects for the Direct Claims Approach' (2023) 32 Review of European, Comparative & International Environmental Law 348.
Maljean-Dubois S, Fabri HR and Schill S, 'International Investment Law and Climate Change: Introduction to the Special Issue' (2022) 23 JWIT 5-6 737.
Marquesa AC and others, 'Ordinary and Special Regimes of Electricity Generation in Spain: How They Interact with Economic Activity' (2018) 81 Renewable and Sustainable Energy Reviews 1226.
Massari S, 'The Italian Photovoltaic Sector in Two Practical Cases: How to Create an Unfavorable Investment Climate in Renewables' (2015) 12 OGEL 3.
Matravers M, 'Legitimate Expectations in Theory, Practice, and Punishment' (2017) 4 Moral Philosophy and Politics 307.
Mayer B, 'International Law Obligations Arising in Relation to Nationally Determined Contributions' (2018) 7 Transnational Environmental Law 251.
Maynard S, 'Legitimate Expectations and the Interpretation of the Legal Stability Obligation' (2016) 1 European Investment Law and Arbitration Review 99.

McGlade C and Ekins P, 'The Geographical Distribution of Fossil Fuels Unused When Limiting Global Warming to 2 [degrees] C' (2015) 517(7533) Nature 187.

Meyer L and Sanklecha P, 'Individual Expectations and Climate Justice' (2011) 33 Analyse und Kritik 449.

Miles K, 'International Investment Law and Climate Change: Issues in the Transition to a Low Carbon World' (2008) SIEL Working Paper 27/08 1-2.

Miles K, 'Arbitrating Climate Change: Regulatory Regimes and Investor-State Disputes' (2010) 1 Climate Law 1 63.

Moehlecke C, 'The Chilling Effect of International Investment Disputes: Limited Challenges to State Sovereignty' (2020) 64 International Studies Quarterly 1.

Monebhurrun N, 'Gold Reserve Inc. v the Bolivarian Republic of Venezuela. Enshrining Legitimate Expectations as a General Principle of International Law' (2015) 32 Journal of International Arbitration 551.

Muchlinski P, '"Caveat Investor"? The Relevance of the Conduct of the Investor under the Fair and Equitable Treatment Standard' (2006) 55 International and Comparative Law Quarterly 527.

Nolte G, 'General principles of German and European Administrative Law: A Comparison in Historical Perspective' (1994) 57 Modern Law Review 191.

Nowrot K, 'How to Include Environmental Protection, Human Rights and Sustainability in International Investment Law?' (2014) 15 The Journal of World Investment & Trade 3-4 612.

Oberthür S and Bolde R, 'Legal Form and Nature of the Paris Outcome' (2016) 6 Climate Law Special Issue 1-2 40.

OECD, 'Fair and Equitable Treatment Standard in International Investment Law' (2004) OECD Working Papers on International Investment 2004/03.

Ortino F and Mavroidis P, 'Intra-EU Investment Disputes and the Monopoly over the Interpretation of EU Law' (2023) 33 The American Review of International Arbitration 4 12-13.

Paine J and Sheargold E, 'A Climate Change Carve-Out for Investment Treaties' (2023) 26 Journal of International Economic Law 2 285.

Pandya APG and Moody A, 'Legitimate Expectations in Investment Treaty Arbitration: An Unclear Future' (2010), 15 Tilburg Law Review 93.

Pauw P and Klein R, 'Beyond Ambition: Increasing the Transparency, Coherence and Implementability of Nationally Determined Contributions' (2020) 20 Climate Policy 4 405.

Polzin F and others, 'Public Policy Influence on Renewable Energy Investments: A panel Data Study Across OECD Countries' (2015) 80 Energy Policy 98.

Potestà M, 'Legitimate Expectations in Investment Treaty Law: Understanding the Roots and Limits of a Controversial Concept' (2013) 28 ICSID Rev–FILJ 88.

Puissochet JP and Legal H, 'Le principe de sécurité juridique dans la jurisprudence de la Cour de justice des Communautés européennes' (2001) Cahiers du Conseil Constitutionnel 11.

Radi Y, 'The "Human Nature" of International Investment Law' (2013) 10 TDM, Grotius Centre Working Paper 2013/006-IEL.

Rajamani L, 'The Paris Agreement: Interplay Between Hard, Soft and Non-obligations' (2016) 28(2) Journal of Environmental Law 337.
Rayner S, 'How to Eat an Elephant: A Bottom-up Approach to Climate Policy' (2010) 10 Climate Policy 6 615.
Reisman M and Arsanjani M, 'The Question of Unilateral Governmental Statements as Applicable Law in Investment Disputes' 19 ICSID Review 2.
Restrepo T, 'Modification of Renewable Energy Support Schemes under the Energy Charter Treaty: Eiser and Charanne in the Context of Climate Change' (2017) 8 Göttingen Journal of International Law 101.
Roberts A, 'Clash of Paradigms: Actors and Analogies Shaping the Investment Treaty System' (2013) 107 Am J Int'l L 45.
Dolzer R, 'Fair and Equitable Treatment: Today's Contours' (2014) 12 SCJIL 7.
Sai M, 'Renewable Energy Law: An International Assessment' (2021) 39 JENRL 2.
Salacuse J, 'BIT by BIT: The Growth of Bilateral Investment Treaties and Their Impact on Foreign Investment in Developing Countries' (1990) 24 The Intl Lawyer 655.
Sarvarian A, 'Invoking the Paris Agreement in Investor-State Arbitration' (2023) 38 ICSID Review 422.
Scherer F, 'Invention and Innovation in the Watt-Boulton Steam-Engine Venture' (1965) 6 Technology and Culture 2.
Schill SW, 'Do Investment Treaties Chill Unilateral State Regulation to Mitigate Climate Change' (2007) Journal of International Arbitration 469.
Schill SW and Vladislav D, 'Wherefore Art Thou? Towards a Public Interest-Based Justification of International Investment Law' (2018) 33 ICSID Review-Foreign Investment Law Journal 1 29.
Schöb T and others, 'Die Notwendigkeit negativer Emissionen für ein treibhausgas-neutrales Deutschland–eine modellgestützte Analyse' (2021) 12 Internationale Energiewirtschaftstagung TU Wien.
Schreuer C, 'The Concept of Expropriation under the ECT and Other Investment Protection Treaties' (2005) 2 TDM 3 1.
Schreuer C, 'Full Protection and Security' (2010) 1 Journal of International Dispute Settlement 2 353.
Selivanova YS, 'Changes in Renewables Support Policy and Investment Protection under the Energy Charter Treaty: Analysis of Jurisprudence and Outlook for the Current Arbitration Cases' (2018) 33 ICSID Review 2.
Sharma M, 'Integrating, Reconciling, and Prioritising Climate Aspirations in Investor-State Arbitration for a Sustainable Future: The Role of Different Players' (2022) 23 JWIT 5-6.
Sharpston E, 'European Community Law, and the Doctrine of Legitimate Expectations: How Legitimate and for Whom' (1990) 11 Northwestern JILB 1.
Simma B and Pulkowski D, 'Of Planets and the Universe: Self-Contained Regimes in International Law' (2006) 17 European Journal of International Law 3 483.
Simma B, 'Universality of International Law from the Perspective of a Practitioner' (2009) 20 European Journal of International Law 2 265.
Simões FD, 'Blusun S.A. and Others v Italy: Legal (In)stability and Renewable Energy Investments' (2017) 26 RECIEL 3 298.

Sloane R.D. and Reisman W.M. 'Indirect Expropriation and Its Valuation in the BIT Generation' (2004) 74 The British Yearbook of International Law 115.

Sornarajah M, 'Power and Justice: Third World Resistance in International Law' (2006) 7 Singapore Yearbook of International Law 36.

Sovacool BK, 'How Long Will It Take? Conceptualizing the Temporal Dynamics of Energy Transitions' (2016) 13 Energy Research & Social Science 202.

Stanivukovic M, 'Legitimate Expectations: A Commentary of Micula v Romania' (2017) 1 TDM 14.

Steininger S, 'What's Human Rights Got to Do With It? An Empirical Analysis of Human Rights References in Investment Arbitration' (2018) 31 Leiden Journal of International Law 33.

Stuart LM, 'Legitimate Expectations and Estoppel in Community law and English Administrative Law' (1983) 10 Legal Issues of European Integration 1.

Susskind L and others, 'Sources of Opposition to Renewable Energy Projects in the United States' (2022) 165 Energy Policy 11292.

Téllez FM, 'Conditions and Criteria for the Protection of Legitimate Expectations under International Investment Law' (2012) 27 ICSID Review-Foreign Investment Law Journal 432.

Thiessen PV, 'Reforming the Energy Charter Treaty for Sustainability?' (2022) 40 Journal of Energy & Natural Resources Law 465.

Thomas JC, 'Reflections on Article 1105 of NAFTA: History, State Practice and the Influence of Commentators' (2002) 17 ICSID Review – Foreign Investment Law Journal 21.

Tienhaara K and others, 'Investor-State Disputes Threaten the Global Green Energy Transition' (2022) 379 Science 701.

Tienhaara K, 'Regulatory Chill in a Warming World: The Threat to Climate Policy Posed by Investor-State Dispute Settlement' (2018) 7 Transnational environmental law 229.

Timperley J, 'Why Fossil Fuel Subsidies Are so Hard to Kill' (2021) 598(7881) Nature 403.

Tirado J and Garcia AI, 'Rise of Renewable Energy Claims' (2015) 16 Renewable Energy Focus 14.

Titi C, 'International Investment Law and the European Union: Towards a New Generation of International Investment Agreements' (2015) 26 EJIL 639.

Tremblay LL, 'In Need of a Paradigm Shift: Reimagining *Eco Oro v Colombia* in Light of New Treaty Language' (2022) 23 JWIT 5-6.

Tropper J and Wagner K, 'The European Union Proposal for the Modernisation of the Energy Charter Treaty: A Model for Climate-Friendly Investment Treaties?' (2022) 23 JWIT 5-6 813.

Ünüvar G, 'The Vague Meaning of Fair and Equitable Treatment Principle in Investment Arbitration and New Generation Clarifications' (2016) iCourts Working Paper Series 55.

Vadi V, 'Beyond Known Worlds: Climate Change Governance by Arbitral Tribunals' (2015) 48 Vand. J. Transnat'l L. 1285.

Van Asselt H, 'Managing the Fragmentation of International Environmental Law: Forests at the Intersection of the Climate and Biodiversity Regimes' (2010) 44 International Law and Politics 1205.

Van Harten G and Loughlin M, 'Investment Treaty Arbitration as a Species of Global Administrative Law' (2006) 17 European Journal of International Law 121.

Van Harten G and Scott D, 'Investment Treaties and the Internal Vetting of Regulatory proposals: A Case Study from Canada' (2016) 7 Journal of International Dispute Settlement 1 92.

Vandevelde KJ, 'Investment Liberalization and Economic Development: The Role of Bilateral Investment Treaties' (1998) 36 Columbia JTL 501.

Vandevelde KJ, 'A Unified Theory of Fair and Equitable Treatment' (2013) 43 New York University Journal of International Law and Politics 43.

Varis O, 'Redefining Energy in the Post-Pandemic Era' (2020) 2 Global Energy Law and Sustainability 1.

Vasciannie S, 'The Fair and Equitable Treatment Standard in International Investment Law and Practice' (2000) 70 British Yearbook of International Law 99.

Verburg C and Waverijn J, 'Liberalizing the Global Supply Chain of Renewable Energy Technology: The Role of International Investment Law in Facilitating Flows of Foreign Direct Investment and Trade' (2020) 2 Brill Open Law 101.

Vicuña FO, 'Regulatory Authority and Legitimate Expectations' (2003) 5 Intl Law Forum 188.

Vihma A, 'Climate of Consensus: Managing Decision-Making in the UN Climate Change Negotiations' (2015) 24 Review of European, Comparative and International Environmental Law 1 58.

Viñuales J and others, 'Climate Policy after the Paris 2015 Climate Conference' (2017) 17 Climate Policy 1.

Viñuales J, 'Foreign Investment and the Environment in International Law: An Ambiguous Relationship' (2009) 80 British Yearbook of International Law 244.

Viñuales J, 'Foreign Investment and the Environment in International Law: The Current State of Play' (2016) C-EERNG Working Papers 2016-1.

Wälde T, 'Investment Arbitration under the Energy Charter Treaty: From Dispute Settlement to Treaty Implementation' (1996) 12 Arbitration International 4.

Wälde T, 'Energy Charter Treaty-based Investment Arbitration: Controversial Issues' (2004) 5 Journal of World Investment & Trade 373.

Weil P, 'The State, the Foreign Investor, and International Law: The No Longer Stormy Relationship of a Ménage à Trois' (2000) 15 ICSID Review-FILJ 401.

Wrigley E, 'The Supply of Raw Materials in the Industrial Revolution' (1962) 15 The Economic History Review 1.

Zamir N, 'The Police Powers Doctrine in International Investment Law' (2017) 14 Manchester Journal of International Law 318.

Zeyl T, 'Charting the Wrong Course: The Doctrine of Legitimate Expectations in Investment Treaty Law' (2011) 49 Alta L Rev 203.

Zhu Y, 'Fair and Equitable Treatment of Foreign Investors in an Era of Sustainable Development' (2018) 58 Nat Resources J 319.

Reports

British Petroleum, 'BP Energy Outlook 2018' (2018) www.bp.com/content/dam/bp/business-sites/en/global/corporate/pdfs/energy-economics/energy-outlook/bp-energy-outlook-2018.pdf accessed 4 December 2021.

Cambridge Economic Policy Associates and DECC, *Policy Risk in Renewable Energy Investments in Developing Countries* (Report 2014).

Carbon Tracker, *Unburnable Carbon: Are the World' Financial Markets Carrying a Carbon Bubble?* (Report 2011).

Carbon Tracker, *Unburnable Carbon 2013: Wasted Capital and Stranded Assets* (Report 2013).

Carbone 4, *Net Zero Initiative: 2020-2021 Report* (Report 2021).

Clifford Chance, 'Delivering a Climate Trade Agenda: Summary of Recommendations' (White Papers, September 2021).

Climate Action Tracker, *Glasgow's 2030 Credibility Gap: Net Zero's Lip Service to Climate Action* (Report 2021).

Climate Change Committee, *2021 Progress Report to Parliament: Progress in Reducing Emissions* (Report 2021).

Climate Change Counsel, *The Energy Charter Treaty, Climate Change and Clean Energy Transition, A Study of Jurisprudence* (Report 2022).

French High Council on Climate, *Report on the Modernisation of the Energy Charter Treaty* (Report 2022).

Grantham Research Institute on Climate Change and the Environment, *Climate Change and the Just Transition: A Guide for Investor Action* (Policy Guide 2018).

Haut Conseil pour le Climat, *Avis sur la modernisation du traité sur la Charte de l'énergie* (Report 2022).

International Chamber of Commerce, *Business Charter for Sustainable Development* (Charter, 2015).

International Chamber of Commerce, *Arbitration and ADR Commission Report on Resolving Climate Change-related disputes through arbitration and ADR* (Report 2019).

IISD, *The German Nuclear Phase Out Put to the Test in International Investment Arbitration? Background to the new dispute Vattenfall v. Germany (II)* (Briefing Note, 2012).

Intergovernmental Panel on Climate Change, *Climate Change 2014: Mitigation of Climate Change. Contribution of Working Group III to the Fifth Assessment Report of the Intergovernmental Panel on Climate Change* [Edenhofer O and others (eds)] (CUP 2014).

Intergovernmental Panel on Climate Change, *Climate Change 2014: Synthesis Report. Contribution of Working Groups I, II and III to the Fifth Assessment Report of the Intergovernmental Panel on Climate Change* (Report 2015).

Intergovernmental Panel on Climate Change, 'IPCC, 2018: Annexe I: Glossary' [Robin Matthews (ed.)] in V Masson-Delmotte, P Zhai and others (eds), *Global Warming of 1.5 °C* (Report 2018).

Intergovernmental Panel on Climate Change, Global Warming of 1.5°C. An IPCC Special Report on the Impacts of Global Warming of 1.5°C above Pre-industrial Levels and Related Global Greenhouse Gas Emission Pathways, in the Context of Strengthening the Global Response to the Threat of Climate Change, Sustainable Development, and Efforts to Eradicate Poverty (Masson-Delmotte, V and others (eds), IPCC, 2018).

Intergovernmental Panel on Climate Change, *Climate Change 2021: The Physical Science Basis. Contribution of Working Group I to the Sixth Assessment Report of the Intergovernmental Panel on Climate Change* (Report 2021).

Intergovernmental Panel on Climate Change, *Climate Change 2022 Mitigation of Climate Change* (Report 2022).

International Energy Agency, *The future role of coal: Markets, Supply and the Environment* (Report 2000).

International Energy Agency, *Clean Coal Technologies* (Report 2008).

International Energy Agency, *Power Generation from Coal: Measuring and Reporting Efficiency Performance and CO2 Emissions* (Report 2010).

International Energy Agency, *Medium-Term Coal Market Report 2012* (Report 2012).

International Energy Agency, *Net Zero by 2050: A Roadmap for the Global Energy Sector* (Report 2021).

International Energy Agency, *Global Energy Review 2021* (Report 2021).

International Energy Agency, *Renewable Power: Tracking progress 2021* (Report 2021).

International Energy Agency, *World Energy Outlook 2021* (Report 2021).

International Energy Agency, *World Energy Investment 2021* (Report 2021).

International Energy Agency, *World Energy Investment Outlook 2022* (Report 2021).

International Energy Agency, *World Energy Investment 2022* (Report 2022).

International Energy Agency, *World Energy Investment 2022: Methodology Annex* (Report 2022).

International Energy Agency, *World Investment 2023* (Report 2023).

International Energy Agency, *Government Energy Spending Tracker* (Flagship Report 2023).

International Renewable Energy Agency, *Renewable Energy: A Key Climate Solution* (Report 2017).

International Renewable Energy Agency, *Global Energy Transformation: A Roadmap to 2050* (Report 2019).

International Renewable Energy Agency, *World Energy Transitions Outlook: 1.5°C Pathway* (IRENA, 2021).

International Renewable Energy Agency, *NDCs and Renewable Energy Targets in 2021: Are We on the Right Path to a Climate-Safe Future?* (Report 2022).

International UCN, UNEP and WWF, *World Conservation, Strategy, Living Resource Conservation for Sustainable Development* (Report 1980).

Kristoff MM, 'New Coal-fired Power Plants in India: Reality or Just Numbers? New Coal Capacity Additions Face Major Stranded Asset Risk' (Institute for Energy Economics and Financial Analysis Report 2021).

Malik M, 'The Full Protection and Security Standard Comes of Age: Yet Another Challenge for States in Investment Treaty Arbitration?' (2011) IISD Best Practices Series.

Mallet B, 'Total Énergies table sur un pic de demande de pétrole avant 2030' Challenges (Paris, 27 Septembre 2021).

McKinsey & Company, *The Net Zero Transition: What It Would Cost, What It Could Bring* (Report 2022).

Mo Ibrahim Foundation, *The Road to COP27: Making Africa's Case in the Global Climate Debate* (Report 2022).

MSCI, *Global Industry Classification Standard (GICS) Methodology* (Methodology Reference 2020).

Natural Resource Governance Institute, *Tying Their Hands: How Petroleum Contract Terms May Limit Governments Climate Flexibility* (Report 2021).

OECD, *'Indirect Expropriation' and the 'Right to Regulate' in International Investment Law* (OECD Working Papers on International Investment 2004).

OECD, *Fair and Equitable Treatment Standard in International Investment Law Working Papers on International Investment* (Command Paper, 2004).

OECD, *Investment Treaties and Climate Change: OECD Public Consultation January-March 2022* (Compilation of Submissions 2022).

OECD, *World Energy Investment Outlook 2023* (Report 2023).

Parrique T and others, *Decoupling Debunked. Evidence and Arguments Against Green Growth as a Sole Strategy for Sustainability* (European Environmental Bureau Report 2019).

Queen Mary University of London, '2020 QMUL-CCIAG Survey: Investors' Perceptions of ISDS' (Survey Report 2020).

Rocky Mountain Institute, *How to Retire Early: Making Accelerated Coal Phase out Feasible and Just* (Report 2020).

S&P Global, 'Climate Change Litigation: The Case For Better Disclosure And Targets' (S&P Global Ratings, 6 October 2021).

Stockholm Environment Institute and others, *Governments' Planned Fossil Fuel Production Remains Dangerously Out of Sync with Paris Agreement Limits* (Report 2021).

The Climate Change Commission, *COP26: Key Outcomes and Next Steps for the UK* (Report 2021).

The World Bank Group and the Energy Charter Secretariat, *Enabling Foreign Direct Investment in the Renewable Energy Sector Reducing Regulatory Risks and Preventing Investor-State Conflicts* (Report 2023).

Tienhaara K and Cotula L, *Raising the Cost of Climate Action?* (International Institute for Environment and Development Report 2020).

Titi C, 'The Evolution of Substantive Investment Protections in Recent Trade and Investment Treaties' (IDB & ICTSD Think Piece, Report 2018).

UK Climate Change Committee, *Progress in Reducing emissions 2023 Report to Parliament* (Report 2023).

UN, *Guiding Principles on Business and Human Rights* (Report 2011).

UNCC, *2022 NDC Synthesis Report* (Report 2022).

UNCTAD, *Fair and Equitable Treatment* (Report 1999).
UNCTAD, *World Investment Report: Transnational corporations, Extractive Industries and Development* (Report 2007).
UNCTAD, *World Investment Report 2012: Towards a New Generation of Investment Policies* (Report 2012).
UNCTAD, *Fair and Equitable Treatment: UNCTAD Series on Issues in International Investment Agreements II: A Sequel* (Report 2012).
UNCTAD, *Investment Policy Framework for Sustainable Development* (Report 2015).
UNEP, *Multilateral Environmental Agreement: Negotiators Handbook* (2nd edn, Report 2007).
UNEP, *Towards a Green Economy; Pathways to Sustainable Development and Poverty Eradication: A Synthesis for Policy Makers* (Report 2011).
UNEP, *The Closing Window Climate Crisis Calls for Rapid Transformation of Societies* (Report 2022).
UNHRC, 'Issue of Human Rights Obligations Relating to the Enjoyment of a Safe, Clean, Healthy and Sustainable Environment: Report of the Special Rapporteur' (8 January 2019) UN Doc A/HRC/40/55.
US Department of Energy, *Significant Impacts of the Inflation Reduction Act and Bipartisan Infrastructure Law on the U.S. Energy Economy and Emissions Reductions* (Office of Policy Report 2023).
World Bank, *The ICSID Caseload: Statistics Issue 2024-1* (Report 2025).
World Energy Council, *World Energy Scenarios 2016* (Report 2016).

Documents

Abs H and Shawcross L, 'The Proposed Convention to Protect Foreign Investment: A Round Table: Comment on the Draft Convention by its Authors' (1960) 9 Journal of Public Law 119.
Depledge J, 'Tracing the Origins of the Kyoto Protocol: An Article-by-Article Textual History' (2000) UNFCCC Technical Paper FCCC/TP/2000/2.
Energy Charter Secretariat, Decision on the Energy Charter Conference (24 June 2022) CCDEC 2022 10 GEN.
Energy Charter Secretariat, Agreement in Principle on the Modernisation of the Energy Charter Treaty (24 June 2022) www.bilaterals.org/IMG/pdf/reformed_ect_text.pdf accessed 17 October 2023.
European Commission, 'Report from the Commission to the European Parliament, the Council, the European Economic and Social Committee and the Committee of the Regions: Renewable energy progress report' COM (2013) 175.
European Commission, 'Communication on the European Green Deal' COM (2019) 640.
European Commission, 'Communication on "Fit for 55": Delivering the EU's 2030 Climate Target on the Way to Climate Neutrality' COM (2021) 550.
ILC, 'Draft Articles on Responsibility of States for Internationally Wrongful Acts' (2001) UN Doc A/56/10.
ILC, 'Conclusions of the International Law Commission relating to Unilateral Acts of States' (20 July 2006) UN Doc A/CN.4/L.703.

ILC, 'Conclusions of the Work of the ILC Study Group on the Fragmentation of International Law: Difficulties Arising from the Diversification and Expansion of International Law' (2006) UN Doc A/61/10.

ILC, 'Guiding Principles Applicable to Unilateral Declarations of States Capable of Creating Legal Obligations, with Commentaries Thereto' (2006) UN Doc A/CN.4/L.703.

Knox J, 'Report of the Special Rapporteur on the Issue of Human Rights Obligations Relating to the Enjoyment of a Safe, Clean, Healthy and Sustainable Environment' (1 February 2016) UN Doc A/HRC/31/52.

UNFCCC, 'Report of the Conference of the Parties on Its Fifteenth Session, Held in Copenhagen from 7 to 19 December 2009, Addendum Part Two: Action taken by the Conference of the Parties at its fifteenth session' (2009) FCCC/CP/2009/11/Add.1 Decision-/ 2/CP.15.

UNFCCC, 'China's Submission on the Work of the Ad Hoc Working Group on Durban Platform for Enhanced Action' (2012) FCCC/ADP/2012/MISC.3.

UNFCCC, 'Decision 1/CP.21 Adoption of the Paris Agreement' (29 January 2016) FCCC/CP/2015/10/Add.1.

United Nations Economic and Social Council, 'Specifications for the Application of the United Nations Framework Classification for Fossil Energy and Mineral Reserves and Resources 2009 to Renewable Energy Resources' (2016) UN ECE/ENERGY/2016/4.

Others

Ballantyne J, 'Uniper to Withdraw ECT Claim as Part of German Bailout' *GAR* (London, 25 July 2022).

Claude Turmes, 'Energy Charter Treaty Modernization Process: Definition of Economic Activities to Terminate Investment Protection in Fossil Fuels' (Letter to the European Commission, 5 February 2021).

Climate Analytics, 'Climate impact explorer' (Climate Analytics Tool, n.d.) https://climate-impact-explorer.climateanalytics.org/ accessed 16 February 2025.

Editorial, 'Governments Should Not Foot the Bill for Stranded Assets: Treaties That Lead to Fossil Fuel Bailouts Need a Rethink' *Financial Times* (London, 21 February 2022).

Editorial, 'How Some International Treaties Threaten the Environment: Investor-State Dispute Settlement Provisions Are Blamed for Impeding Government Action' *The Economist* (London, 5 October 2020).

Embassy of India in Beijing, 'Joint Statement Issued at the Conclusion of the 13th BASIC Ministerial Meeting on Climate Change Beijing, China 19-20 November 2012' (Embassy of India in Beijing, 21 November 2012).

European Commission, 'Text Proposal for the Modernisation of the Energy Charter Treaty' (May 2020) https://ccsi.columbia.edu/sites/default/files/content/docs/tradoc_158754%20(1)_0.pdf accessed 4 February 2025.

European Parliament, 'MEPs Consent to the EU Withdrawing from the Energy Charter Treaty' (April 2024) https://www.europarl.europa.eu/news/en/press-room/20

240419IPR20549/meps-consent-to-the-eu-withdrawing-from-the-energy-charter-treaty.

Fokuhl J and Gillespie T, 'Germany Revives Coal as Energy Security Trumps Climate Goals' *Bloomberg* (London, 22 December 2022).

Grantham Research Institute, 'Climate Change Laws of The World' (*GRICCE*, n.d.) https://climate-laws.org accessed 18 October 2021.

Greenwood C, 'Is the Age of Arbitration in International Law Drawing to a Close' (The 11th Kaplan Lecture at The Hong Kong Club, 21 November 2018).

Guterres A, 'Humanity Is Waging War on Nature. Nature Always Strikes Back: And It Is Already Doing so with Growing Force and Fury' (Lecture Columbia University, 2 December 2020).

Hall M, 'Legal Challenge to Ukraine's Retroactive FIT Cuts' (*PV-Magazine*, 5 May 2022) www.pv-magazine.com/2021/05/05/legal-challenge-to-ukraines-retroactive-fit-cuts/ accessed 27 August 2022.

Harvey F, 'Paris Climate Change Agreement: The World's Greatest Diplomatic Success' *The Guardian* (London, 14 December 2015).

IISD, Energy Charter Treaty Withdrawal Announcements Reflect Reform Outcome is Insufficient for Climate Ambition (*IISD*, 7 November 2022) accessible at https://www.iisd.org/articles/statement/energy-charter-treaty-withdrawal-announcements accessed 15 November 2022.

International Energy Agency, 'Decree on the Cut of Incentives for Photovoltaic Plants (*Spalma Incentivi*)' (*IEA*, 11 December 2014) www.iea.org/policies/5653-decree-on-the-cut-of-incentives-for-photovoltaic-plants-spalma-incentivi accessed 28 July 2022.

Investment Policy Hub, 'Investment Disputes Settlement Navigator' (*UNCTAD*, 2023) investmentpolicy.unctad.org/investment-dispute-settlement accessed 24 April 2023.

Ipp A, 'Regime Interaction in Investment Arbitration: Climate Law, International Investment Law and Arbitration' (*Kluwer Arbitration Blog*, 12 January 2022) arbitrationblog.kluwerarbitration.com/2022/01/12/regime-interaction-in-investment-arbitration-climate-law-international-investment-law-and-arbitration/ accessed 15 March 2022.

Kwan E and others, 'First Japan Investment Treaty Claim Renewable Energy Disputes in Asia' (*King & Wood Mallesons*, 5 May 2021) www.kwm.com/jp/en/insights/latest-thinking/first-japan-investment-treaty-claim-renewable-energy-disputes-in-asia.html accessed 28 August 2022.

Luo N, 'The Net Zero Transition in China: Progress Has Been Made, But Challenges Remain' (*United Nations Principles for Responsible Investment*, 20 June 2022) https://unpri.org/pri-blog/the-net-zero-transition-in-china-progress-has-been-made-but-challenges-remain/10132.article accessed 2 November 2023.

Mazzotti P, '*Rockhopper v. Italy* and the Tension Between ISDS and Climate Policy: A Missed Moment of Truth?' (Völkerrechtsblog, 21 December 2022).

Meagher D, 'Broken promises: Legal recourse for retroactive FIT' (*PV-Magazine*, 23 January 2020) www.pv-magazine.com/magazine-archive/broken-promises-legal-recourse-for-retroactive-fit-cuts/ accessed 27 August 2022.

Monica Feria-Tinta, 'The Role of International Law and Arbitration in Enforcing the Paris Agreement' (*Kluwer Arbitration Blog*, 31 December 2016) https://arbitrationblog.kluwerarbitration.com/2016/12/31/the-role-of-international-law-and-arbitration-in-enforcing-the-paris-agreement/ accessed 1 November 2023.

Net Zero Tracker, 'Data Explorer' (*Net Zero Tracker*, 2023) zerotracker.net accessed 21 December 2022.

Prime Minister's Office, 'G7 Leaders Commit To Protect Planet and Turbocharge Global Green Growth' (Press release, 12 June 2021) gov.uk/government/news/g7-leaders-commit-to-protect-planet-and-turbocharge-global-green-growth accessed 2 November 2023.

Ritchie H and Roser M, 'Global CO2 Emissions from Fossil Fuels' (*Our World in Data*, 2020) ourworldindata.org/co2-emissions accessed 4 October 2023.

Ritchie H, Roser M and Rosado P, 'Energy' (*Our World in Data*, 2022) ourworldindata.org/energy accessed 29 April 2023.

Sabin Center for Climate Change Law and Arnold & Porter, 'U.S. Climate Change Litigation' (*Climate Case Chart*) https://climatecasechart.com/us-climate-change-litigation/ accessed 23 October 2023.

Sauvant K P, 'Importance of Negotiating Good Contracts' (2017) 201 Columbia FDI perspectives.

Secretariat of the Energy Charter Treaty, 'List of Cases' (*ECT*, 2023) www.energychartertreaty.org/cases/list-of-cases/ accessed 30 September 2022.

Sini Matikainen, 'What Are Stranded Assets' (LSE Grantham Research Institute on Climate Change, 27 July 2022) https://www.lse.ac.uk/granthaminstitute/explainers/what-are-stranded-assets/ accessed on18 December 2023.

The European Commission, 'European Green Deal: Commission Proposes Transformation of EU Economy and Society to Meet Climate Ambitions' (Press release, 14 July 2021) www.ec.europa.eu/commission/presscorner/detail/en/ip_21_3541 accessed 5 November 2021.

Timperley J, 'Explainer: The Challenge of Defining Fossil Fuel Subsidies' (*CarbonBrief*, 6 December 2017) https://carbonbrief.org/explainer-the-challenge-of-defining-fossil-fuel-subsidies/ accessed on 21 March 2022.

UNCTAD, 'International Investment Agreements Navigator' (*Investment Policy Hub*) https://investmentpolicy.unctad.org/international-investment-agreements/iia-mapping accessed 4 February 2025.

UNFCCC, 'Nationally Determined Contributions Registry' (*UNFCCC*, n.d.) unfccc.int/NDCREG accessed 2 November 2023.

Werksman J, 'International Legal Character of the Paris Agreement' (Notes for the third 2016 'Environmental Law Brodies Lecture', University of Edinburgh, 9 February 2016).

World Resources Institute, 'Climate Watch Data Explorer' (*Climate Watch*, n.d.) www.climatewatchdata.org accessed 1 November 2023.

Dictionary entries

'Expectation', *Cambridge English Dictionary* (OUP 2023).
'Induce', *Black's Law Dictionary* (7th edn, 1999).
'Legitimacy', *Cambridge English Dictionary* (OUP 2023).
'Phase st down', *Cambridge English Dictionary* (OUP 2023).
'Stare Decisis', *Black's Law Dictionary* (7th edn, 1999).
'Transition, n' (OECD Online, OUP 2023).
Treatment', *The Oxford English Dictionary* (2nd edn, Clarendon Press 1989).
'Unabated', *Cambridge English Dictionary* (OUP 2023).

Table of Cases

Table of Treaties and Legislation

Treaties

Legislation

UN Resolutions

1. Moshe Hirsch, *The Arbitration Mechanism of the International Center for the Settlement of Investment Disputes,* 1993 (ISBN 07-923-1993-1).
2. Aida B. Avanessian, *Iran-United States Claims Tribunal in Action,* 1993 (ISBN 18-533-3902-4).
3. Isaak I. Dore, *The UNCITRAL Framework for Arbitration in Contemporary Perspective,* 1993 (ISBN 18-533-3573-8).
4. Vesna Lazić, *Insolvency Proceedings and Commercial Arbitration,* 1998 (ISBN 90-411-1115-8).
5. Joachim Frick, *Arbitration in Complex International Contracts,* 2001 (ISBN 90-411-1662-1).
6. Katherine Lynch, *The Forces of Economic Globalization: Challenges to the Regime of International Commercial Arbitration,* 2003 (ISBN 90-411-1994-9).
7. Christoph Liebscher, *The Healthy Award: Challenge in International Commercial Arbitration,* 2003 (ISBN 90-411-2011-4).
8. Hamid G. Gharavi, *The International Effectiveness of the Annulment of an Arbitral Award,* 2003 (ISBN 90-411-1717-2).
9. Abdulhay Sayed, *Corruption in International Trade and Commercial Arbitration,* 2004 (ISBN 90-411-2236-2).
10. Gabrielle Kaufmann-Kohler & Thomas Schultz, *Online Dispute Resolution: Challenges for Contemporary Justice,* 2004 (ISBN 90-411-2318-0).
11. Christopher R. Drahozal & Richard W. Naimark (eds), *Towards a Science of International Arbitration: Collected Empirical Research,* 2005 (ISBN 90-411-2322-9).
12. Ali Yeşilirmak, *Provisional Measures in International Commercial Arbitration,* 2005 (ISBN 90-411-2353-9).
13. Christian Bühring-Uhle, *Arbitration and Mediation in International Business,* second revised edition, 2006 (ISBN 978-9-041-12256-8).
14. Bernard Hanotiau, *Complex Arbitrations: Multi-party, Multi-contract and Multi-issue – A Comparative Study*, Second Edition, 2020 (ISBN 978-94-035-1261-7).
15. Loukas A. Mistelis & Julian D.M. Lew (eds), *Pervasive Problems in International Arbitration,* 2006 (ISBN 978-9-041-12450-0).
16. Julian D.M. Lew & Loukas A. Mistelis (eds), *Arbitration Insights – Twenty Years of the Annual Lecture of the School of International Arbitration, Sponsored by Freshfields Bruckhaus Deringer,* 2006 (ISBN 978-9-041-12606-1).
17. Mark Kantor, *Valuation for Arbitration: Compensation Standards, Valuation Methods and Expert Evidence,* 2008 (ISBN 978-9-041-12735-8).
18. Christoph Brunner, *Force Majeure and Hardship under General Contract Principles: Exemption for Non-Performance in International Arbitration,* 2009 (ISBN 978-90-411-2792-1).

19. Loukas A. Mistelis & Stavros L. Brekoulakis (eds), *Arbitrability: International & Comparative Perspectives,* 2009 (ISBN 978-90-411-2730-3).
20. Sam Luttrell, *Bias Challenges in International Commercial Arbitration: The Need for a 'Real Danger' Test,* 2009 (ISBN 978-90-411-3191-1).
21. Monique Sasson, *Substantive Law in Investment Treaty Arbitration: The Unsettled Relationship Between International Law and Municipal Law,* Second Edition, 2017 (ISBN 978-90-411-6103-1).
22. Ileana M. Smeureanu, *Confidentiality in International Commercial Arbitration,* 2011 (ISBN 978-90-411-3226-0).
23. Won Kidane, *China-Africa Dispute Settlement: The Law, Economics and Culture of Arbitration,* 2011 (ISBN 978-90-411-3674-9).
24. Karel Daele, *Challenge and Disqualification of Arbitrators in International Arbitration,* 2012 (ISBN 978-90-411-3799-9).
25. Crina Baltag, *The Energy Charter Treaty: The Notion of Investor,* 2012 (ISBN 978-90-411-3428-8).
26. Alexandra Diehl, *The Core Standard of International Investment Protection: Fair and Equitable Treatment,* 2012 (ISBN 978-90-411-3869-9).
27. Manuel Indlekofer, *International Arbitration and the Permanent Court of Arbitration,* 2013 (ISBN 978-90-411-4766-0).
28. Günther J. Horvath & Stephan Wilske (eds), *Guerrilla Tactics in International Arbitration,* 2013 (ISBN 978-90-411-4002-9).
29. Albert Badia, *Piercing the Veil of State Enterprises in International Arbitration,* 2014 (ISBN 978-90-411-5162-9).
30. Nadja Erk, *Parallel Proceedings in International Arbitration: A Comparative European Perspective,* 2014 (ISBN 978-90-411-5264-0).
31. Simon Vorburger, *International Arbitration and Cross-Border Insolvency: Comparative Perspectives,* 2014 (ISBN 978-90-411-5419-4).
32. Ahmad Ali Ghouri, *Interaction and Conflict of Treaties in Investment Arbitration,* 2015 (ISBN 978-90-411-5417-0).
33. Reto Marghitola, *Document Production in International Arbitration,* 2015 (ISBN 978-90-411-5159-9).
34. Alfonso Gómez-Acebo, *Party-Appointed Arbitrators in International Commercial Arbitration,* 2016 (ISBN 978-90-411-6671-5).
35. Jonas von Goeler, *Third-Party Funding in International Arbitration and Its Impact on Procedure,* 2016 (ISBN 978-90-411-5015-8).
36. Dean Lewis, *The Interpretation and Uniformity of the UNCITRAL Model Law on International Commercial Arbitration: Focusing on Australia, Hong Kong and Singapore,* 2016 (ISBN 978-90-411-6700-2).
37. Stavros Brekoulakis, Julian D.M. Lew & Loukas Mistelis (eds), *The Evolution and Future of International Arbitration,* 2016 (ISBN 978-90-411-7004-0).
38. Rémy Gerbay, *The Functions of Arbitral Institutions,* 2016 (ISBN 978-90-411-6217-5).

39. Maximilian Clasmeier, *Arbitral Awards as Investments: Treaty Interpretation and the Dynamics of International Investment Law*, 2017 (ISBN 978-90-411-8357-6).
40. Tony Cole (ed.), *The Roles of Psychology in International Arbitration*, 2017 (ISBN 978-90-411-5921-2).
41. Pietro Ferrario, *The Adaptation of Long-Term Gas Sale Agreements by Arbitrators*, 2017 (ISBN 978-90-411-8232-6).
42. Jacob B. van de Velden, *Finality in Litigation: The Law and Practice of Preclusion – Res Judicata (Merger and Estoppel), Abuse of Process and Recognition of Foreign Judgments*, 2017 (ISBN 978-90-411-8342-2).
43. Dolores Bentolila, *Arbitrators as Lawmakers*, 2017 (ISBN 978-90-411-8354-5).
44. Giacomo Marchisio, *The Notion of Award in International Commercial Arbitration: A Comparative Analysis of French Law, English Law, and the UNCITRAL Model Law*, 2017 (ISBN 978-90-411-8391-0).
45. Csaba Kovács, *Attribution in International Investment Law*, 2018 (ISBN 978-90-411-9675-0).
46. Mary Mitsi, *The Decision-Making Process of Investor-State Arbitration Tribunals*, 2019 (ISBN 978-90-411-9600-2).
47. Ahmet Cemil Yıldırım, *Interpretation of Contracts in Comparative and Uniform Law*, 2019 (ISBN 978-94-035-1130-6).
48. Beata Gessel-Kalinowska vel Kalisz, *The Legal, Real and Converged Interest in Declaratory Relief*, 2019 (ISBN 978-94-035-1244-0).
49. Maximilian Pika, *Third-Party Effects of Arbitral Awards: Res Judicata Against Privies, Non-mutual Preclusion and Factual Effects*, 2019 (ISBN 978-94-035-1273-0).
50. Yulia Levashova, *The Right of States to Regulate in International Investment Law: The Search for Balance Between Public Interest and Fair and Equitable Treatment*, 2019 (ISBN 978-94-035-0931-0).
51. Flavia Marisi, *Environmental Interests in Investment Arbitration: Challenges and Directions*, 2020 (ISBN 978-94-035-1723-0).
52. Martina Magnarelli, *Privity of Contract in International Investment Arbitration: Original Sin or Useful Tool?*, 2020 (ISBN 978-94-035-2020-9).
53. Xu Qian, *Water Services Disputes in International Arbitration: Reconsidering the Nexus of Investment Protection, Environment, and Human Rights*, 2020 (ISBN 978-94-035-2203-6).
54. Nobumichi Teramura, Ex Aequo et Bono *as a Response to the 'Over-Judicialisation' of International Commercial Arbitration*, 2020 (ISBN 978-94-035-2073-5).
55. Bruno Guandalini, *Economic Analysis of the Arbitrator's Function*, 2020 (ISBN 978-94-035-2265-4).
56. Zena Prodromou, *The Public Order Exception in International Trade, Investment, Human Rights and Commercial Disputes*, 2020 (ISBN 978-94-035-2031-5).

57. Jürg Künzle, *Multiple Contracts and Coordination in International Construction Projects: A Swiss Law Analysis*, 2020 (ISBN 978-94-035-2024-7).
58. Cornel Marian, *The State's Power to Tax in the Investment Arbitration of Energy Disputes: Outer Limits and the Energy Charter Treaty*, 2020 (ISBN 978-94-035-1752-0).
59. Luke Nottage, Shahla Ali, Bruno Jetin & Nobumichi Teramura (eds.), *New Frontiers in Asia-Pacific International Arbitration and Dispute Resolution*, 2021 (ISBN 978-94-035-2855-7).
60. Eva Litina, *Theory, Law and Practice of Maritime Arbitration: The Case of International Contracts for the Carriage of Goods by Sea*, 2021 (ISBN 978-94-035-3035-2).
61. Franco Ferrari & Friedrich Rosenfeld (eds), *Autonomous Versus Domestic Concepts under the New York Convention*, 2021 (ISBN 978-94-035-3173-1).
62. Doğan Gültutan, *Moral Damages under International Investment Law: The Path Towards Convergence*, 2022 (ISBN 978-94-035-4025-2).
63. Simon Foote QC, *The Bona Fide Investor: Corporate Nationality and Treaty Shopping in Investment Treaty Law*, 2022 (ISBN 978-94-035-4185-3).
64. George A. Bermann, *Twilight Issues in International Arbitration: Latent Choice of Law Challenges*, 2023 (ISBN 978-94-035-1746-9).
65. Emmanuel Obiora Igbokwe, *Dealing with Bribery and Corruption in International Commercial Arbitration: To Probe or Not to Probe*, 2023 (ISBN 978-94-035-2066-7).
66. Peter Sester, *Contract Law in International Commercial Arbitration*, 2023 (ISBN 978-94-035-1036-1).
67. Julian Bickmann, *Fact-Finding in International Arbitration: The Emergence of a Transnational* Lex Evidentiae, 2023 (ISBN 978-94-035-1886-2).
68. Giovanna E. Gismondi, *International Environmental Law and International Human Rights Law in Investment Treaty Arbitration: The Contribution of Host States' Argumentation in Re-Shaping International Investment Law*, 2023 (ISBN 978-94-035-3047-5).
69. Fabricio Fortese, *Early Determination of Jurisdiction*, 2024 (ISBN 978-94-035-0268-7).
70. Sabrina Pearson-Wenger, *Good Faith in International Commercial Arbitration: Its Application by Arbitral Tribunals to the Parties' Contract and the Arbitration Agreement*, 2024 (ISBN 978-94-035-0738-5).
71. Charalampos Tagaroulias, *International Investment Law and the Law of the European Union: How Regionalism and Interregionalism Have Shaped the Relationship in the Post-Lisbon Era*, 2024 (ISBN 978-94-035-0708-8).
72. Dan Xie, *Transnational Due Process and Article V(1)(b) of the New York Convention: Grounding Interpretation and Application of the Due Process Defence in the Public International Law Framework for Treaty Interpretation*, 2024 (ISBN 978-94-035-2437-5).
73. Thomas Lehmann, *Investment Arbitration and International Climate Change Law: Revaluing Legitimate Expectations*, 2025 (ISBN 978-94-035-2799-4).

www.ingramcontent.com/pod-product-compliance
Lightning Source LLC
LaVergne TN
LVHW020644300926
849161LV00004B/803